ALSO BY GARY M. POMERANTZ

The Devil's Tickets

WILT, 1962

Nine Minutes, Twenty Seconds

Where Peachtree Meets Sweet Auburn

THEIR LIFE'S WORK

The Brotherhood of the
1970s Pittsburgh Steelers, Then and Now

Gary M. Pomerantz

Simon & Schuster

New York   London   Toronto   Sydney   New Delhi

Simon & Schuster
1230 Avenue of the Americas
New York, NY 10020

Interior design by Joy O'Meara
Jacket design by Dan Rembert
Jacket photograph by Anthony Neste/Getty Images

Manufactured in the United States of America

10 9 8 7 6 5 4 3 2 1

Library of Congress Cataloging-in-Publication Data

Pomerantz, Gary M.
    Their life's work : the brotherhood of the 1970s Pittsburgh Steelers / Gary M. Pomerantz.
        pages   cm
    1. Pittsburgh Steelers (Football team)—History.   I. Title.
    GV956.P57P66 2013
    796.332'640974886—dc23   2013007393

ISBN 978-1-4516-9162-7
ISBN 978-1-4516-9164-1 (ebook)

For Glenn & Greg,
big brothers,
consummate teammates

CONTENTS

I. INTRODUCTION

Reverie & Reality   3

II. WHEN THE CHIEF WAS YOUNG

1. The Chief at the Racetracks, 1937   23

III. ASSEMBLING THE PIECES

2. The Rooneys   35

3. The Man from the *Courier*   47

4. Noll & Mean Joe   58

5. The Rock & the Frenchman   75

6. Immaculate   83

IV. AN EMPIRE BORN, 1974

7. In the Film Room   105

8. The 1974 Draft   109

9. Quarterback Controversy: Brad, Rat, or Joe Gillie?   119

10. The Steel Curtain   138

11. Stall & Webby   150

12. 1974 AFC Title Game   159

13. Super Bowl IX   171

V. STEEL EMPIRE
14. Days of Empire: 1975–1981   187

VI. THEIR LIFE'S WORK
15. Bar Scene at Pro Bowl, 1982   231

16. Mean Joe   234

17. Brad   252

18. Franco   270

19. Stall   287

20. Webby   300

21. The Rooneys   325

VII. EMPIRE IN TWILIGHT
22. It's Still Their Town   343

23. The Legacy Haunted   353

24. Noll & the Ambassador   370

25. The Sauna, Once More   377

POSTSCRIPT
Mortal Immortals   381

Acknowledgments   385

Notes   389

Bibliography   443

Index   449

THEIR LIFE'S WORK

What has the game given me? It's given me my teammates. . . .
You want to talk about what the game takes away from you?
It takes away your teammates.

—John Banaszak, Pittsburgh Steelers (1975–1981)

I

INTRODUCTION

REVERIE & REALITY

BECAUSE WE SEE SPORTS DYNASTIES through the prism of stopped time, the players never grow old. We forever see the 1970s Pittsburgh Steelers in their days of empire—Bradshaw airing it out, Mean Joe enraged, Lambert toothless, stamping his feet before the snap, the long, elegant strides of Stallworth, Franco, still immaculate. But time does not stop, not for us, not for the Steelers of the 1970s.

Have a cigar, m'boy! Sitting in his living room near Dallas, wearing slippers, Mean Joe Greene remembers Art Rooney Sr. He hears the old man's voice with its smoker's rasp. He shared conversations with the Chief at the Rooney home on Pittsburgh's North Side at 940 North Lincoln Avenue. They sat in the den beside the fireplace. Through the front windows, they saw moonlight play on Three Rivers Stadium. The Chief sat in his favorite black leather recliner (it vibrated), a brass spittoon at his feet, his TV turned to local news or an old Western (the volume too loud); on a nearby table he kept his rosary beads.

Such a compelling pair, the Chief and Mean Joe: the Pittsburgh Steelers' founding owner was an old horse player with a map-of-Ireland face and thick white hair combed back, as much a part of Pittsburgh as the waters of the Allegheny, Monongahela, and Ohio Rivers. The massive defensive tackle was an African American born in segregated Temple, Texas; dark and handsome, he played football with an anger that even he did not understand. Mean Joe knew the outline of the Chief's story, that he might've become a priest, but became a gambler instead, and that he played a semipro football game against Jim Thorpe, and might've won an Olympic gold medal in boxing in 1920, and that he was pals with the old fighter Billy Conn and with Tip O'Neill, Speaker of the US House of Representatives. He knew that when the old man took his night strolls through his neighborhood, the thugs didn't rob him, they protected him.

Mean Joe called him Mr. Rooney, as everyone did, never the Chief. That was an endearing nickname given by the youngest of his five sons, the twins, Pat and John, for his resemblance to the actor who played editor in chief Perry White on the television show *Superman*. Among all Steelers players dating to the team's founding in 1933, Mean Joe was the Chief's favorite. The old man was a tough guy, too. At a 1975 practice, Terry Bradshaw completed a pass to rookie running back Mike Collier, who turned to the sideline and ran over the Chief. He knocked him flat, snapped his cigar in half. Collier froze as the trainer and the Chief's driver rushed to his aid. But the Chief, at seventy-four, stood, brushed himself off, and eased Collier's fears: "Thanks, Mike. I needed that."

Mean Joe's appreciation for those Bances Aristocrat cigars grew with his appreciation for the Chief. Now, Mean Joe is a grandfather, his toddler granddaughter calls him Gumpa, his beard is flecked with gray, and he is nearly the same age as the Chief was in 1969 when they first met. Whereas once he threw his body around on the field like a desperado, now he moves slower, creakier. Mean Joe's emotions never were far from the surface, and now he turns sentimental. He has filed away postcards the Chief wrote to him and his wife, Agnes, usually hellos from racetracks or Catholic shrines. He even kept one of those unsmoked cigars long after the Chief's death as a memento of a defining friendship in his life. He remembers the Chief's handshake, the way he put his small hand in his and held it there, a little longer than most men would.

Franco Harris returns to Pittsburgh International Airport late at night from another business trip. His frame is fuller, his hairline receding, yet he remains, unmistakably, Franco. As he approaches the lobby escalators, nearing the Immaculate Reception statue, he'll see recognition spread across a bystander's face: the eyes wide, the mouth agape, and then . . . the request: "Franco, would you, uhm, mind?" The bystander wants to take a cell-phone photograph of Harris standing next to his famous likeness.

Harris knows that if he poses for one, he'll be asked to pose for five more. He consents, nearly always. This is his way. This is his town. Mean Joe calls him *Mister Pittsburgh*.

The statue of Harris is colorful and life-sized, the running back in black and gold bending forward on the run to make the shin-high catch that stunned the Oakland Raiders in a 1972 playoff game at Three Rivers Stadium, named by NFL Films the most controversial play in league history. Along the edge of Pittsburgh's north shore, there are statues of television's Mister Rogers and Bill Mazeroski, and by PNC Park, of Roberto Clemente, Pops Stargell, Honus Wagner, and several Negro Leaguers, including Josh Gibson and Satchel Paige. In this city that reveres them, only two of the 1970s Steelers are so honored, Harris, and the Chief, seated in bronze at Heinz Field.

Phil Villapiano was the Raiders' linebacker covering Harris on the play that, to him, remains a great American tragedy. "I'm gonna tackle that fuckin' airport statue one of these days," Villapiano tells me, half in jest. "Franco can tell the police, 'I know who did it!' "

Baseball has the New York Yankees of the 1920s, basketball the Boston Celtics of the 1960s, and football the 1970s Steelers.

The rise of sports empires is a matter of talent and timing. Baseball in the '20s had moved beyond the Black Sox scandal into the live-ball era, and basketball in the '60s flourished with an end to the whites-only game. In the '70s, as television became an American phenomenon, football became its most popular show, and the Super Bowl virtually a national holiday. And no team celebrated more often than these Steelers. "It was," tight end Randy Grossman would say of being a Steeler during that time, "almost like living in a wonderland."

The Steelers rose like the sun over a landscape that once belonged to Lombardi's Packers, the defining dynasty of the league's first half century, and the team that fired the American imagination during the 1960s, when football first moved past baseball as the nation's preferred pastime. Pittsburgh won four Super Bowls in six seasons between 1974 and 1979, its feat unmatched in the postmerger modern era. Its record during that span was 80-22-1. The Steelers won Super Bowls against Minnesota, Dallas (twice), and the Los Angeles Rams, and their intraconference blood rivalry with Oakland brought suffering to both sides. The 1970s Steelers sent a dozen men to the Pro Football Hall of Fame in Canton, Ohio: nine players, head coach Chuck Noll, Art Rooney Sr., and his son, Dan, who emerged as the Steelers' day-to-day chief executive and later became within the NFL much like John Quincy Adams to his father's John Adams, a founding family's second generation risen to power. The Steelers' likenesses are cast in bronze: Mel Blount's shaved head reflecting in a spotlight, Mike Webster's neck thick and muscular, and the bearded Jack Ham, half smiling, as if he knows the next play is coming at him.

The story line in 1974 was too good to be missed by the sports press. Everyone wanted the Chief, football's lovable loser for forty years, to win his first NFL championship, and that wish extended far beyond a derelict steel town. Art Rooney Sr. was an American archetype, up from the streets, a *Daily Racing Form* in one hand, his leather-bound prayer book in the other. By habit, he dashed off thousands of postcards—each only a couple sentences, always handwritten—to family, friends, and acquaintances, including one to me after I interviewed him in 1985 for a story about sports in Pittsburgh. His language was quaint and dated, still stuck in the 1920s. He used terms like *yeggs, greasy bums,* and *Hey Rube* (a free-for-all fight), expressions that passed from the language when carnivals stopped coming to town. It wasn't that the Chief needed to win a Super Bowl. His life, and his achievements, already had been certified. He had been a big winner with the Thoroughbreds. But the NFL publicity machine dreamed that the old man might one day hoist a Lombardi Trophy, for he was as likable as anyone the league had known; his Steelers' players felt the same way, and figured he might have one last chance.

On both sides of the ball, the 1970s Steelers were methodically destructive. But it is the Steelers' defense that still thunders across our imagination. The unit played the game at high speed, with blunt force and malice. Its nickname, the Steel Curtain, sprang from a local radio contest, a twist on Winston Churchill's "Iron Curtain" description for the postwar divide that fell across Europe. Greene became a folk hero, and by the 1974 playoffs opposing teams were measuring their rushing gains against the Steelers' defense not in yards per carry but in *feet* per carry. In 1976, eight of the Steelers' eleven defensive starters made the Pro Bowl.

That same season, the team began with a 1-4 record and then reeled off nine consecutive victories, the defense producing five shutouts and allowing only twenty-eight points. And that was a season in which Pittsburgh did *not* win the Super Bowl.

There was so much that went unseen, like Lambert's telegram to his rival and buddy, Kansas City center Jack Rudnay, days before a game against the Chiefs. "If you hold me," Lambert wrote, "I will kick you in your teeny-weeny balls." And Rudnay, in a return note delivered to the Steelers' hotel: "I would love to have a chance to hold you, you toothless bastard, but you are always hiding behind Joe's big ass."

The Steelers' defensive huddle often became bedlam, voices demanding to be heard. Years later, Ronnie Lott, a Hall of Fame defensive back who began his career with San Francisco in 1981, would let his imagination run: "Can you imagine if you could create a virtual huddle and you were standing in a virtual huddle *with those guys*?" Lott's eyes grew wide. "Man, it would've been great to line up with them!"

Here is the sound track of that huddle: Safety Edwards, the so-called Chobee Kid from Florida, unleashing his anger on the front four after the defense gave up a few too many yards on the ground. Edwards's teammates would say they could not understand what he said in the best of circumstances—his words seemed to come from the depth of a swamp, thick and jumbled. As Blount, a southerner himself, said, "Glen had—it wasn't a speech impediment—it was this southern, long drawn-out—he just couldn't talk." But now Edwards gets his point across by cursing a blue streak at the front four. In the huddle Blount asks teammates to hold hands as a show of unity and brotherhood, but Lambert won't do it. Lambert will not hold hands with any man. As his roommate on road trips, Ham learned plenty about Lambert's personality. In their hotel room the night before games, Lambert studied his defensive checklists, drank Michelob beer in bottles (never cans, always bottles), and smoked his cigarettes, a combination that made him snore all night; he awoke snarly. Two years, they were roommates on the road, but Ham quantified that, saying, "Two years with Jack is like 'dog years'—fourteen years is what it felt like." Now, in the huddle, Ham tries to talk strategy with Andy Russell, left linebacker to right linebacker, but Russell can't hear him because of Edwards, and because of Dwight White, who after complaining to referees about the spot of the ball, orates in the huddle about his plans for his opponent: "HE'S GONNA HAVE A BAD DAY! HE CAN TAKE HIS ASS-WHIPPING ANY WAY . . . BUT HE WILL TAKE IT!!!"

Greenwood, an easygoing Mississippian, laughs at the chaos. *Heh-heh-heh.* This fit cornerback J. T. Thomas's theory that the left side of the Steelers' defense was the quiet, steady side—Greenwood, Ham, Wagner, and Thomas. *Everybody's cool. Ain't no big deal. Nobody goes to the league office for fighting.* But, Thomas theorized, once you moved one player over to the middle of the defense, to Greene and Lambert, "a metamorphosis takes place." If a fight broke out, Mean Joe was in it, perhaps the cause of it, and, Thomas said, "And Lambert: oh, my God! You've got a psycho. If you go down an alley and you're in a fight, take Lambert with you. You'll come out with him, no doubt about it." Then there was the Chobee Kid who, though just 180 pounds, hammered wide receivers, plus Holmes and White—the rogue side of the defense. In the huddle, Lambert makes the defensive call. Eleven Steelers prepare to break—no, wait! There are only ten players. Holmes stands at the line of scrimmage, over the ball, pointing a finger at the guard opposing him, interrupting whatever is being said in the offensive huddle. Greene shouts for Holmes to come back to the huddle. Too late. Lambert, sneering, says, "Just leave him out there!" The defensive signal called doesn't matter to Holmes because he will run his own stunt anyway. Holmes hollers to the offensive guard what the Steelers' defensive line will do on the next play. "Don't check off," Holmes warns. "I'm coming right over your ass! YO' MAMA GONNA SEE YOU!!"

The 1970s Steelers' roster was filled with players who had spent their boyhoods during the Eisenhower '50s and came of age during the turbulence of the '60s. They hailed from the working or middle class, from small towns and rural outposts in the South and Midwest, military and coal towns in the Northeast, from the big-city West; from football power-houses such as Penn State and Southern Cal, and from historically black universities such as Southern, Tennessee State, and Arkansas Agricultural Mechanical & Normal. As teammates, these Steelers had their differences. Some had never had teammates of a different race. In 1974, Joe Gilliam, the league's only starting black quarterback, received racist mail. "We saw you go home," one letter began. "WE KNOW WHERE YOU LIVE!" Gilliam stored the letters in a cardboard box in his closet.

It was the truest meritocracy the NFL had yet known. The earlier dynasties, the Cleveland Browns of the '50s and the Green Bay Packers of the early '60s, had comparatively few black players. (In 1960, the four black Packers joked that they made up four-fifths of Green Bay's total black population, the shoe-shine man at the Hotel Northland being the fifth.) The civil rights movement brought change. A photograph of the Steelers at Super Bowl IX in January 1975 showed a roster with twenty-five white players, twenty-one blacks, and the biracial Harris. When the NFL named its seventy-fifth-anniversary all-time team in 1994, five players hailed from the 1970s Steelers, more than from any other dynasty; the Browns of the '50s and Packers of the '60s placed five players on the team *combined.* With free agency and the salary cap, we'll never see another NFL team like these Steelers. Keeping together such a collection of stars would cost a king's (and queen's) ransom. With so much talent gathered on one roster, Dwight White would say, "I liken it to the Big Bang theory, something that happens once in time . . . something that happens once in a zillion years."

At a charity event in Northern California in 2003, Gordon Gravelle, a tackle on the Steelers' first two Super Bowl–winning teams, introduced himself to Bill Walsh. "I remember you," said Walsh, the retired San Francisco 49ers coach. Then he thumped Gravelle's chest and said of those 1970s Steelers, "Best team ever!" Walsh's 49ers won four Super Bowls across nine years during the 1980s.

"Even better than your 49ers?" Gravelle asked.

Walsh thought for a moment. "We might have given you a run for your money," he said. Walsh's eyes twinkled. "But you were the best team ever."

What wouldn't any of us give for recognition like that?

Once, in San Francisco's Candlestick Park, grouped with other sportswriters in the corner of the end zone in the final seconds of the 1981 NFC title game, I saw 49ers quarterback Joe Montana throw a touchdown pass to receiver Dwight Clark to beat Dallas, and I'll never forget that thunderous roar from the home crowd—pure euphoria. I've never experienced anything else like it. This was the glory of the NFL as a national sensation.

But later I gave up on pro football. As a sportswriter for the *Washington Post* during the early and mid-1980s, I saw the game from the inside, and though I admired the athletic artistry and grace, and genuinely liked the men who played, the violence disturbed me. For two years I covered the Washington Redskins as a daily beat reporter; I later reported on the NFL at large, traveling to the biggest game each week, to owners' meetings in Maui, and to the courthouse in Manhattan's Foley Square for the US Football League trial against the NFL. I stood on the sidelines during practices and games, amazed by the physical power of the players. Once, at the end of a Redskins' practice, a few players lured me onto the field and playfully surrounded me. From behind, Joe Jacoby, six-foot-seven, nearly three hundred pounds, an all-pro tackle, put his arm under my neck and pulled back slightly. It was all in fun, done for only a second, but my neck hurt for a month. Jacoby was that strong.

I saw and heard the violent collisions, the injured players carted off. Steroid use was rampant in the NFL then. One team doctor told me a new generation of injuries was emerging: muscles tearing and bones breaking, he said, in new and surprising ways. The night the New York Giants' linebacker Lawrence Taylor snapped Redskins quarterback Joe Theismann's leg, I sat in the press box at RFK Stadium. So gruesome was the injury, even Taylor winced. I followed the ambulance carrying Theismann to a local hospital, and filed a story from there. A few years later, over dinner with the Redskins' retired special teams ace Pete Cronan and his wife, Debbie, I heard how several times a month she was awakened in the night by her husband's pained wails from his shoulder separating in his sleep. She knew the proper maneuver: she pushed up on his elbow and in on his shoulder. "It just goes 'Click,' " Cronan explained, and they went back to sleep.

This was the game's dark underside: the players were physical marvels, and yet week after week their bodies broke down. I blamed it on the physics of the game—head-on collisions between behemoths—and, in some cases, steroids. I thought, *What will life be like for these guys when they are sixty years old?*

In the summer of 1981 I visited the Steelers' training camp in Latrobe, Pennsylvania. The team had failed to make the playoffs the previous season for the first time in nine years. My assignment: find out if the dynasty was done. Most of the Steelers' stars from the seventies were still there. Thousands of Steeler Nation fans crowded behind fences, waved Terrible Towels, and called out the names of their heroes. As a young sportswriter, I was struck by the team's personalities. Nearly all savvy interview subjects, they carried themselves with swagger. Terry Bradshaw took me to his dorm room; as he spoke his eyes were alight with playful mischief. Lynn Swann, handsome, aloof, self-important, reminded me of a movie star. Harris carefully considered my questions before answering. "What is old? Chronologically we are old. But physically we are fine. I wouldn't call this an old team," Harris said. "It is a seasoned team, a vintage team." Mean Joe wore shorts in the sweltering heat. He sat beside me on a bench. I noticed that his right bicep was as big as my thigh. He was philosophical. "I don't mean to brag but we've been on top for eight or nine years," he told me. "You can't say that because we had one bad year that we are done. That's crazy. Just look at the graph of anything, the weather, our economy, our political power. There is a shifting of balance. It is not constant. Well, we've been on the top of the bell on the graph for a long time. Last year was just our dip in the bell. It happens to everybody." A nice, well-conceived answer, but I wanted more specifics. "But *why* did it happen, Joe?" I asked. He turned cross. *"Why?"* he said, his voice a rumble. "I just told you *why!*" I shifted to a new question.

On the practice field, Coach Noll, his arms folded, said, "People want us beaten. Our team has become a cliché, a truism. We are always there. We have always won." Thomas told me, "We're just like the Ringling Brothers Circus. They lost four elephants, a giraffe, and a gorilla, but the show went on. The same thing will happen here." Thomas spoke the Steelers' party line—"Everyone is replaceable"—but time proved that a lie. Some talents are so exquisite they are not replaceable.

Though I didn't realize it at the time, my work on this book began on that August day.

✦ ✦ ✦

Here is Walt Whitman on the 1863 Civil War battle of Chancellors-ville: "Who know the conflict, hand-to-hand—many conflicts in the dark, those shadowy-tangled, flashing moonbeam'd woods—the writhing groups and squads—the cries, the din, the cracking guns and pistols—the distant cannon—the cheers and calls and threats and awful music of the oaths—the indescribable mix—the officers' orders, persuasions, encour-agements—the devils fully rous'd in human hearts—the strong shout, *Charge, men, charge*—the flash of the naked sword, and rolling flame and smoke?"

A century and more later, Whitman might have been writing about the magnificent physical strife and sensory overload of football. *Awful music of the oaths?* From the line of scrimmage, the louder half of the Steel Curtain—White and Holmes—yowled at the opposition. That *cracking* sound came from helmets colliding, safety Donnie Shell, in *the indescrib-able mix*, launching himself into Houston running back Earl Campbell's ribs, or the safety Edwards sending a two-forearm shiver into the chin-strap of Vikings receiver John Gilliam in Super Bowl IX. *The devils fully rous'd in human hearts*—Lambert body-slamming Cliff Harris onto his hip pad in Super Bowl X, or cornerback Blount, Superman to teammates, beating smaller receivers into the earth. Steeler running back Reggie Harrison once was asked which defensive tackle hit harder, Greene or Holmes. Harrison answered sincerely: "It all depends on what you prefer: Excedrin or Motrin. If you can find the rest of your body after they hit you, that's good."

In those days, concussions were of little concern. Smelling salts did the trick. In 1976, Gary Dunn, a rookie defensive lineman, practiced head butts with the Steel Curtain front four before games. "You're going to set the head-butt record today," defensive coach George Perles told him. Perles said the record was fifty: "And you are going to do sixty." And Dunn did, each time picking a spot on the opposing man's helmet, and then firing off the ball and striking him at that spot with his own helmet. Dunn estimated that he executed thousands of head butts in his career in drills alone. In short order, Dunn began wearing a neck collar on the field because the back of his neck bled from his helmet jerking backward.

The violence ratcheted up in the 1970s as players grew bigger and faster. The point wasn't to kill your opponent but to render him less functional. In those *shadowy-tangled, flashing moonbeam'd woods*, the 1970s Steelers doled out suffering. They absorbed their share, too, and more than once from the Chiefs' Willie Lanier. A fearless linebacker, Lanier sometimes slammed into ballcarriers with his face mask. The Steelers' running back John "Frenchy" Fuqua broke through the line of scrimmage once only to be struck down by *the flash of the naked sword*—Lanier. As their face masks merged, Fuqua saw Lanier's eyes, his nose, his intensity. And then, literally, he saw a flash. The force of the helmet-to-helmet collision registered in Fuqua's brain, a lightning bolt of trauma between his eyes. Down went the Frenchman, knocked out momentarily, unsure even if the ball remained in his hands. What came back to him first was the voice of a teammate saying, "You okay, man?" Fuqua stood up, unsteadily. "Yeah, yeah." But the lightning kept flashing: flicker-flash, flicker-flash. In the huddle, Fuqua heard Bradshaw call out the formation, "Full right split," and as the huddle broke, Fuqua did not know the snap count, only that somewhere out there Willie Lanier lurked.

The most famous Steeler of the dynasty, now a television celebrity, Terry Bradshaw moves easily through the lobby of a Beverly Hills hotel where he has checked in under the pseudonym "Gary Cooper," a nice Hollywood touch. A concierge spots him, brightens, and says, "Welcome back, Mr. Cooper," and Bradshaw, in a loose-fitting Tommy Bahama shirt and jeans, smiles, and says, "Thank you very much." Bradshaw is six-foot-three and broad-shouldered, still identifiable as an athlete. In the hotel restaurant, a man at the bar calls, "Terry! Terry!" Bradshaw does not answer him. "TERRY BRADSHAW! I just want to shake your hand." Bradshaw looks at the man and then at his hand. He smiles wanly and shakes the man's hand, without making eye contact. A woman at the bar says, "You still got your quarter horses?" Now that topic will turn Bradshaw's head faster than a question about football. He stops to chat with her for several moments. Then he sits at a table near the front, by the window. His eyes are a liquid blue-green, his jaw massive. He is expressive in conversation and tactile, often slapping my right shoulder with the back of his left hand, each time as if to say, "Know what I mean?" His laugh is genuine, countrified, a half cackle. I hand him a team photograph from December 1999—the twenty-fifth reunion of the Steelers' first Super Bowl–winning team. Bradshaw was unable to attend that event, one of many that he has missed through the years. In the photograph, his former teammates and coaches pose in three rows wearing black-and-gold letterman jackets—except for Lambert, who wore a coat and tie, and Ernie Holmes, who wore a copper-colored suit because none of the jackets was big enough to fit the player known as Fats, five hundred pounds by then.

"Holy cow!" Bradshaw says as he studies the photograph. "Look at Ernie. He takes up two chairs! *Two Chairs Ernie!*"

Then Bradshaw turns serious: "Ernie's dead, you know?"

As his eyes move across the rows of faces—Noll, Gilliam, Mel Blount in his cowboy hat, Dwight White—Bradshaw does a play-by-play of time passing:

"Dwight White's death—that was shocking."

"Look at all the gray hair."

"Hanratty!"

"Golly, everybody's shrunk."

"Bobby Walden. Roy Gerela. Kiss my grits. Bud Carson. Dead. Dick Hoak."

"Boy, you look at this bunch and you wonder how we won a game!"

His index finger touches Stallworth in the photo, the Hall of Famer wearing glasses and a big smile. Bradshaw remembers his wide receiver's demeanor in the huddle. Warming to the memory, he becomes the quarterback again, mimicking Stallworth's high-pitched call for the football: *"Braaaaaaad, I'm open!!! Braaaaaaddd!"* Bradshaw squeals with delight.

When his players were still in their twenties, Noll often told them to think about their *life's work*. The phrase wasn't his. He'd first heard it from Cleveland coach Paul Brown, for whom he played during the 1950s. When Brown was about to release a player, he'd say, "If you were my son, I'd tell you to get on with your life's work."

To Noll, football wasn't a player's life's work. That work came later. When Noll told his Steelers, "Maybe it's time to get on with your life's work," some players took it as a coldhearted threat, or worse, their football career death knell. The phrase, acid poured over their dreams, meant they were done with the Steelers. Others accepted it as a call to deeper thinking, and action. Football is a savage game, a giant threshing machine that cuts down men in the physical prime of their lives. Studies in the 1970s showed that the average length of an NFL player's career was only about four years. From 1970 to 1980, the average annual salary for an NFL player grew from $23,000 to $78,000, though some of the Steelers' biggest stars made considerably more; during the early 1970s players commonly worked off-season jobs, including running back Rocky Bleier as an insurance salesman for Mutual of New York, Russell as a securities broker, and Greenwood as a junior high school teacher. Noll was telling his men that retirement might be only a play away. He wanted his Steelers to think about life's meaning and purpose. Noll knew he would release his players one day and so he related to them only at a distance. No Rockne pep talks, no coddling. Greenwood spent thirteen seasons with Noll and had only one conversation with him—when Noll told him he was being released. Lambert said he exchanged about eleven words with Noll during eleven seasons, which Lambert, an independent spirit, liked.

To Noll, preparation in life was, as in football, everything. He had many phrases familiar to his players. Chuckisms, they called them. "Win the battle of the hitting" was one, an intellectual approach to a brutal task. "Whatever it takes" was another. Some of his life stories confounded, like the one he told about the man who saved all his life for retirement. "He finally got to retirement," Noll said, "and died." End of story. Fuqua didn't get it, not until ten years later, when Russell explained it to him. "Chuck was telling us, 'Don't hold anything back,' " Russell said. To which Fuqua replied, "Ohhhhhh!"

But nothing Noll ever said to his team reverberated down through the years like *your life's work*. Even when Noll retired as coach in December 1991 after twenty-three seasons, the *Pittsburgh Post-Gazette* headline read, "Steelers' Noll decides it's time to get on with life's work." The phrase was deeply ingrained. Noll was saying there would come a time, even for future Hall of Famers, when the game would end and the rest of their lives would begin. *What will you do then?*

He didn't get into the specifics. He didn't say that nearly two-thirds of

NFL players left the game with a permanent injury, or that nearly 80 percent suffered emotional trauma during the transition to the rest of their lives, denial, grief, and then reluctant acceptance that their football careers were done, similar to the emotional responses to dying.

They would have to figure out *that* on their own.

In their physical primes, they were men of steel, and then the injuries came—to Greene's neck and shoulder, Lambert's toe, Ham's foot, Fuqua's wrists, and Bradshaw's elbow; for Swann, too many concussions. Now more than a few of the Steelers are men of titanium, their knees, hips, and shoulders replaced. Some seem fit—Ham and Blount look ready to suit up. Others wonder if their ailments and their memory losses are due to football. Some admit to fear of brain damage revealing itself in old age. I found pieces of the team's legacy in surprising places: in a bowl of blueberries; a number registered on Joe Gilliam's cell phone; in the research done by a Nigerian-born forensic pathologist who once thought football players in helmets looked like extraterrestrials; in a lyric from a lovely church song ("I'm Just a Nobody Trying to Tell Everybody About Somebody Who Can Save Anybody"); and in the sauna at the remembered Three Rivers Stadium.

Almost to a man, the old Steelers light up, and the years fall away, when they talk about the empire. Psychologists say there is a memory phenomenon known as the *reminiscence bump*, and it explains why adults often remember more vividly events from their formative years in their teens and twenties, important life markers for who they become. Some of the 1970s Steelers recount moments on the field and in the locker room, supplying details and context, as if they happened yesterday. In the 1970s they were young and invincible. They carried themselves like kings. It was a feeling almost none of them would know ever again.

In the pre–free agency era, these Steelers spent about ten years together. Stallworth, Bradshaw, Swann, Shell, Greene, Greenwood, Lambert, and Ham played a combined one hundred NFL seasons—every one of those seasons with the Pittsburgh Steelers. As athletes and as men, they knew each other intimately and intuitively, their strengths, weaknesses, and personality tics. They knew their favored brands of cigarettes and beer, and the music they liked best. They saw each other broken and bloodied, exultant and triumphant. They were all accountable to the greater cause, winning, which made them accountable to each other.

Their story is football's story. Today, amid mounting concern over brain injuries, the sport is being questioned for its violence. NFL commissioner Roger Goodell has spoken of the need for a cultural shift to change the "warrior mentality" of players who refuse to admit when they are injured in order to keep playing. Football's future appears more uncertain than at any time since 1905, when eighteen college and amateur players died on the sandlots and President Teddy Roosevelt called the coaches of Harvard, Princeton, and Yale to a White House summit in hopes of saving the game. Among the more than 4,300 retired professional football players who have sued the NFL over a lack of warning about, or protection from, traumatic brain injuries are twenty-five who played for the 1970s Pittsburgh Steelers in the days of empire.

Who better to address football's outsized grandeur, its danger and long-term physical implications, than the men I met in Latrobe more than thirty years ago who played for the greatest professional football team I ever saw? They knew they were extraordinary. I sensed it that day in Latrobe in their banter and in the way they moved. They seemed lit from within. They had created a mystique, and though they knew in 1981 that the empire was no more, they carried themselves like royals still. Now, having entered the fourth quarter of their lives, they are as well positioned as anyone to provide illumination, and to answer hard questions, about their game.

Their story has deep roots, and it begins with the Chief as a young man on the make, in the long shadows of the Great Depression, at a racetrack.

II

WHEN THE CHIEF WAS YOUNG

Did you ever notice, my friend, in the race track's grotto of tears,
How many go to the seller's maw—how few to the lone cashier's?

Did you ever notice, old pal, in the race track's dizzy spin
There are ninety ways that a horse can lose—with only one way
to win?

—Grantland Rice, sports columnist, "Maxims from Methuselah"

CHAPTER 1

THE CHIEF AT THE RACETRACKS, 1937

ART ROONEY WAS MOST COMFORTABLE in a crowd, blending in, just another man beneath another fedora. Horse track gamblers preferred it that way, to move, like spies, with stealth. Besides, Rooney had not a particle of pretense or self-importance. His sensibilities were working class, Irish Catholic. "I'm no big shot," he said. Physically, at thirty-six, there was little impressive or memorable about him. He stood five-foot-eight in his wingtips and carried about 150 pounds. Too many breakfasts at the stables with trainers and jockeys (steak, creamed potatoes, cornbread) brought middle age to his midsection sooner than planned. Examine the puff in his coat pockets more closely, though. That's where he kept his office. There, rubber-banded together, were scraps of paper with names and numbers, racetrack programs on which he detailed winnings for his tax man, and a thick notebook to keep track of his business affairs, jammed alongside his rosary beads, and a ready supply of cigars, some to smoke and others to give away as calling cards. He also stuffed a handful of postcards into those pockets, picked up and stamped that morning, ready to go. He learned about postcards, and other tricks of the politician's trade, from his friend Jim Farley, Franklin Roosevelt's postmaster general, a chesty, garrulous Irish Catholic. Here, in essence, is what Farley taught him: If someone's brother or uncle dies, be sure to attend the wake or funeral. And whenever possible send handwritten postcards to friends, acquaintances, *constituents*, just to say, "Hello, the sun is shining here at Aqueduct, and how's your day?" If the postcards were handwritten, Farley said, people would remember you on election day, and every day. Rooney took the advice to heart. Attending wakes and dashing off postcards became part of his routine—he said his hellos with postcards and his good-byes at wakes.

Everything about Rooney said *Pittsburgh*. He sounded like Pittsburgh with his *youse* and *yunz* and the way he said downtown as *dahntahn* and Billy Conn as *Billy Cawn*. He even looked like the steel city: in his dark, formless suit, he was stubby, tough, thick-necked, and perpetually covered in smoke, that from his cigars. He didn't mind if the steel mills pumped black particles into the fiery sky and left his white-collared shirts speckled with their residue. "When you see these skies red, and the smoke goin'," he liked to say, "things are in good shape." He rooted for the unions, Harry Greb, and Honus Wagner, and believed that if he spat into the Allegheny River his city was vulnerable to flooding. *Pixburgh*, from *E'Sliberty* to the *Norse Side* to the coloreds' Hill District, was his town. The city meant everything to him—it *was* everything to him. Once he crossed the rivers, usually bound to another horse track in Ohio, West Virginia, or beyond, he might as well have been in Egypt or Madagascar.

His Irish ancestry was a source of enormous pride. In 1930, 35 percent of Pittsburgh's 670,000 residents had foreign-born parents, Rooney among them. He'd been named for his paternal grandfather, the first Art Rooney to reach Pennsylvania, a steelworker who raised his gun against the Pinkertons hired by Carnegie and Frick as they barged up the Monongahela in 1892 in a failed attempt to bust the Homestead strike. The young Art Rooney heard these stories from his own father, Dan Rooney, a North Side saloonkeeper who claimed Ireland as home, even though he was born in Wales, where his father had gone from Ireland to seek work. But old Dan Rooney reasoned that he was Irish, by God, saying, "If a cat gave birth in an oven, would you call her kittens *biscuits*?"

In summer 1937, Art Rooney still moved like the athlete he once was. But there was something essential about him that the eye missed: his resourcefulness. That was his defining quality, his towering strength. He found a way. Horse players needed to be resourceful. The best approached their work as a craft, and applied a studied discipline to their wagers. They needed to lose before they learned to win. They needed to develop a touch with horses, and with people. In the latter regard, Rooney was masterful, a quick study. He sized up people, and their motives, at first meeting. His memory astonished. He remembered every name and every detail: your hometown, the name of your kids. He was, in that way, uncanny. He was also old school. He believed in the sanctity of a man's handshake. He carried a wad of bills, even during the Depression, and handed out five-dollar bills at the track, to restaurant maître d's, and to those in need. He had the Irish gift for gab, and little regard for convention. Art Rooney got by doing things his own way, even if it meant moving through a few shadows.

He had been ever so resourceful as a young ballplayer on Pittsburgh's sandlots, as a nimble leather-headed quarterback, and as a base-stealing leadoff hitter. He revered the Pirates' shortstop Honus Wagner ("The greatest of the great!" he said), but as an outfielder he played more like a young Cobb. Rooney teamed as player-manager with his younger brother Dan on the Wheeling (WV) Stogies of the Middle Atlantic League in 1925, playing against future Hall of Famers Joe Cronin and Rip Collins. Rooney hit .369, second in the league, and stole a league-best fifty-eight bases. Before that he had been an amateur welterweight boxer and twice had defeated Sammy Mosberg, the gold-medal winner in the 1920 Olympics at Antwerp. A photo from the period shows Rooney with gloved fists raised, his wavy brown hair parted down the middle, his eyes with a murderous look. In the aftermath of the Great War, one writer watched Rooney in the ring and likened his determination and hand speed to a "whippet tank going for one of Jerry's pill boxes."

Raised above his father's brawling saloon, Rooney honed his instincts and his left uppercut. On Saturday nights, Dan Rooney walked upstairs to the family apartment, where his wife and nine children watched him change his shirt, on occasion three or four times in a single evening, because it had been ripped, or splattered with some Irishman's blood, during fights that broke out beside his mahogany bar. "Lads, when you grow up and make your fortune," Dan Rooney told his sons, "go back to Galway to see what makes these harps tick."

Art Rooney ran errands for local politicians and carried bets on the horses from the men on his father's bar stools, and in the card room in back, to the bookies. His father took him to see his first horse race, at Cleveland's Randall Park Race Track, and though still a boy Rooney was swept up by the roar of the crowd, the explosiveness of the horses, and the thrill of wagering real money. The men at the saloon talked about politics, sports, women, and the unions, and Art Rooney heard every word. In such a world, his fists enhanced his reputation. At seventeen he fought as a 130-pounder at the Americus Republican Club and won a gold watch. He fought against stiffs at local carnivals for three dollars per round, and in tournaments in New York and Canada. When Prohibition shut down the Rooney saloon in 1920, the North Side filled with bathtub gin, the rackets, prostitution, and speakeasies. Rooney had close friends deeply involved with all of that. Those illegal mysteries were but an arm's reach away.

He passed through Georgetown, Duquesne, and Washington & Lee Universities, and never allowed his studies to get in the way of his ball games or bouts. He spent only one day of his young adult life in a real job—at a blast furnace—or, to be accurate, less than a day. Many local families, his included, had spent generations at the iron furnaces or in the soft coal mines in the Old World and in Pittsburgh. But Art Rooney quit just after lunch.

He and his brother Dan intended to become major-league ballplayers and reveled in the camaraderie they shared with the boys on the Wheeling Stogies—the jokes, the late nights out, the ball busting—even as they pushed their broken-down touring cars over the Alleghenies. Occasionally they crossed the color line to barnstorm in small Pennsylvania towns against black teams with stars such as Smokey Joe Williams, Martin Dihigo, and Oscar Charleston. They played the House of David teams, too. As a young man, the Chief fully marinated in Pittsburgh's melting pot.

We see the Chief as a young man in the Jazz Age, his world perfumed by nickel beer, backroom cigar smoke, ballpark hot dogs, and serenaded by the pounding hooves of racehorses. By the end of the dry decade, the Rooney brothers' big-league aspirations faded with their youth. His brother Dan turned from baseball to become a Franciscan priest, sent off to China as a missionary. Art Rooney turned to sports promotion— boxing, semipro football (the Hope-Harvey Football Club sponsored by the Majestic Radio Company), and Negro Leagues baseball. With two powerhouses, the Pittsburgh Crawfords and the Homestead Grays, Pittsburgh was becoming a celebrated hub of the Negro Leagues with luminaries such as slugger Josh Gibson, Cool Papa Bell, and Satchel Paige. Rooney knew them all. At a more private moment a decade and more later, Rooney would walk into the famed Crawford Grill restaurant and jazz club in the Hill District and place a paper bag on the table for his old friend Gus Greenlee, the cigar-chomping "Big Red" who ran an illegal numbers racket, owned the financially strapped Crawfords, and was being chased by the Internal Revenue Service. Inside the bag was $20,000 in cash, a gift from Rooney, no strings attached.

Of course, Kathleen ("Kass") McNulty's father didn't trust him. He made pickle barrels for the Heinz factory and didn't like it one bit that his daughter, a clerk at the Joseph Horne department store, was dating a man like Rooney, who ran with gamblers and thugs, and used his fists to solve problems. She noticed that Rooney seemed to know everyone in town, politicians, ballplayers, Jews, blacks, and Italians. Kass and Art slipped away to New York in 1931 and married in defiance of her father. Rooney whisked his new wife off to the Belmont Stakes, and then to racetracks all across the country, even to a racetrack out of the country, in Tijuana, Mexico, where they stayed too late, after the border patrol had closed for the night. Kass Rooney learned then just how resourceful her new husband was. She held fast to her dress as she and her man slid beneath the fence between countries.

Rooney hardly flinched when he put down $2,500 to buy a franchise in the National Football League in 1933. He was betting more than that on a single horse race. In fact, five years earlier, as a bookmaker working Hialeah Park in South Florida, Rooney had lost a $20,000 bankroll in a single afternoon. At the Fort Pitt Hotel in Pittsburgh he met with George Halas, George Preston Marshall, Bert Bell, Charles Bidwell, and Tim Mara, all NFL franchise owners. Rooney thought pro football might be a good investment, though he would've preferred to buy a major-league baseball team. He even leaned on the local baseball name in christening his new NFL team the Pittsburgh Pirates. He wouldn't change the name to Steelers, in honor of his city's defining industry, until 1940.

✦ ✦ ✦

The most pivotal week of Art Rooney's professional life came in summer 1937 and established him as one of America's leading horse players. It also would secure his family's future and make it possible for the Pittsburgh Steelers to remain his for the next half century. Decades later, the Chief answered the charge that he was merely a lucky bettor during this life-shaping week, saying, "That was a lot of bunk—I was no farmer. I may have been more reckless in betting in those days than I am today, but I wasn't an amateur."

It began, late night, on Friday, July 23, 1937, in Harrisburg, Pennsylvania, when Rooney left a plumbers' union gathering with his friend, a former Pittsburgh middleweight named Buck Crouse. Together, leaving a trail of cigar smoke, they made their way to the Empire City Racetrack in Yonkers, New York. A dapper dresser, usually with a boutonniere in his breast pocket, Crouse was a genuine character, typical of those Rooney would collect through the decades, an odd assortment of Runyonesque fighters, detectives, and childhood chums who kept him company at his office and in his car on drives to horse tracks and boxing matches here and there. A cagy, scientific fighter, Crouse had fought the Pittsburgh Windmill, Harry Greb, at Pittsburgh's Exposition Hall in 1917, but was unable to answer the seventh-round bell, sitting on his stool with a busted lower lip, his face puffy from inflammation and his mouth full of blood. He met Rooney, naturally, through the fight game.

On the final Saturday of the three-week meeting at Empire City, with Crouse by his side, Rooney won nearly $20,000 thanks in part to another win by his favorite Thoroughbred, Seabiscuit, with jockey Red Pollard aboard. The day was a portent of what was to come.

That night, Rooney and Crouse stopped by Joe Madden's speakeasy in Manhattan. Once a longshoreman named Joseph Penzo, Madden had wanted an Irish name when he turned to boxing. He liked his drink and his cigars, he wrote a few plays, and truly he was a Runyon character— Damon Runyon had lionized him as a Broadway original. Rooney told Madden he was headed back to Pittsburgh, but Madden convinced him to push his luck at Saratoga. So Rooney put down $150 for a 1928 model car, and with Crouse and Madden drove the nine-year-old vehicle the 180 miles to the famed horse track. They suffered a flat tire along the way, and reached Saratoga late on Sunday night. Rooney stayed up until four a.m., doping the Monday races. A little sleep and he was up to watch the horses' morning workouts, and noted the times recorded on stopwatches. He studied the post positions, the jockeys' riding tendencies. He talked with trainers over breakfast at the stables, passed out a few cigars in exchange for information. He spotted his friend Tim Mara, a bookmaker and owner of the New York Giants of the NFL. "He gets me to mark his card for him," Mara said days later. "I said, 'All right, sucker. Go ahead and blow your dough. I'll be here when the races are over if you want carfare back home.' " Rooney placed his bets as if the Depression didn't exist. He watched the races calmly, as was his custom, his fingers rubbing smoothly across the ten beads on his rosary ring. Between races he even sold ten-cent raffle tickets in the grandstands to help his brother's church in China. "He was making Christians out of the boys," Mara said with a laugh. After one race Madden burst into the men's room to tell Rooney that his horse had won in a photo finish, only to find his friend calmly explaining to "the colored groom the difference between the single wingback and [Pop] Warner's double-wing." Mara said, "When the races were over I asked [Rooney] how he made out. 'Pretty well,' he said. 'I won $108,600. How'd you do?' I didn't tell him, but I'd lost close to three grand on the day."

After his big day, New York's turf writers couldn't get enough of Rooney. Writers followed his every move in Saratoga, to a restaurant, a movie house, and even to the track's men's room, where Rooney noticed a young sportswriter standing behind him. *Just staying after my assignment*, the writer explained. It was a downturn year in the Depression, and the writers painted Rooney in soft, adoring colors, a lovable underdog hero from the steel town, a maverick horse player, churchgoer, and family man (he and Kass had two sons now) who possessed a spark of gambling genius.

"The plucky little plunger," the turf writers at Saratoga called him, and "Roll 'Em High Rooney." Columnist Bill Corum of the Hearst chain wrote, "Rooney is 'Rooneying'—if that one isn't too tough—the betting ring. He's not afraid to press his luck. He 'sends,' as the saying goes, and he sends at the right time, when he's winning." The *New York Post* added, "The casinos were licking their chops in anticipation of the new plunger. But Rooney never touches the dice, cards, or wheels. It's against his principles; it's gambling."

Runyon, the syndicated columnist who was only getting to know Rooney, didn't think much of the hullabaloo: "Mr. Rooney is perhaps too young to have heard the immutable law of the turf: 'All the horseplayers die broke.' "

Crouse announced to sports columnists that at morning Mass he prayed for Rooney to win. In time Crouse would slide into what one forensic pathologist in 1928 defined as *dementia pugilistica*—a neurodegenerative disease known as the boxer's punch-drunk syndrome. He had been punched in the head too often. Sometimes Crouse believed he was St. Francis of Assisi. On that Tuesday morning, Rooney attended Mass and then scored in the first four races, which, according to Corum's accounting, made "his total winnings for 18 successive races $148,180." At this rate, Corum surmised, Rooney soon would "wind up with the bookmakers' limousines, Skidmore College, the Canfield Museum and the New York State reservation and Roosevelt Baths."

By nightfall on Tuesday, stories circulated that Saratoga officials offered Rooney a cadre of Pinkertons or a Brink's armored truck to carry his cash back to New York City. The estimate of his winnings over three days, including one at Empire City, ranged from $200,000 to $380,000. The latter figure is more likely, and carried the same buying power as more than $6 million in 2013. The Chief himself never provided an exact figure, but years later told his son Art Jr. that he had won more than the writers estimated.

He sent $10,000 from his winnings to China, where his brother Dan, known now as Father Silas, needed to build a new roof for his mission house. It was reported that Rooney put $100,000 of his winnings into annuities, saying, "They'll never get that back." He gave Tim Mara $50,000 in cash to take back to New York City. "I may show up at Aqueduct next week and if I do I'll need something to work with," he said.

The following month the Chief returned to Saratoga, where he reportedly won $50,000 more in a single afternoon, leading one sportswriter to exclaim, "That fellow, Rooney, has horseshoes in both hands!" Soon turf writers hyperbolized that the size of Rooney's bets had not been seen since the wild days of the 1920s and the wagers of Arnold Rothstein, reputed fixer of the 1919 World Series.

On August 8 Kass delivered their third son, Timothy, named in honor of Mara. The New York papers reported that Rooney would soon send Kass, four-year-old Danny, two-year-old Art Jr., and the baby on a lengthy vacation to Bermuda, while he, naturally, would return to the tracks. On his immediate return home to Pittsburgh, though, the Chief had emptied his pockets, looked at Kass, his Irish eyes lit like fancy chandeliers, and told her they wouldn't ever have to worry about money again.

III

ASSEMBLING THE PIECES

CHAPTER 2

THE ROONEYS

THE TWINS ARRIVED IN MARCH 1939, and hours later so did the Chief's telegram to Kass from an NFL meeting in Chicago. He apologized for his absence and professed his love. Their marriage would last a half century and more, their roles well defined. The Chief, as provider, chased after his horses, football team, boxing promotions, and investments. Kass ran the home; her sister Alice McNulty moved in after the birth of the twins, and became her companion when the Chief was away. With her husband, Kass held her own. The Chief snapped at her once for tossing away a used tea bag. "Use it again," he insisted. To which Kass replied, "You want me to dry it and use it for snuff?" On another occasion she told him, "Why don't you just piss in your hat and pull it over your ears?" They were well suited for each other, if not entirely alike. She tipped modestly; he was a big tipper. (Once, the Chief didn't have money in his pockets to tip a delivery boy so he found a cigarette lighter featuring the Steelers' insignia, handed it over, and said, "This okay?" and the delivery boy was deliriously happy.) He never cursed; when Kass's temper got the best of her, she cursed like a salty seaman. The Chief winced and said, "Don't used that language in front of me," and never mind that the boys heard, too, and hid their smiles. He didn't drink alcohol; she did. "Have your belt," he would say to her at a restaurant, "and then let's eat." The boys respected their father and adored their mother. "He was Mister Rooney," Art Jr. said, "and she was Mom."

The Chief had given Kass carte blanche to look for a bigger house, as long as it was in the First Ward. She put down $500 in summer 1939 for one only a stone's throw away, an old house, built just after the Civil War, on a street filled with mansions that had lost much of their earlier luster. In one of the first defining moments in his young life, seven-year-old Dan Rooney walked out of the back of his house on Western Avenue, across an alley, and into the back of his new home at 940 North Lincoln Avenue.

In winter, the Chief froze the backyard so the boys could play ice hockey and skate there. In summer, a time for the Chief's beloved baseball, he smacked hard grounders that ricocheted off the backyard's unseen rocks as welts formed on his sons' shins and arms. "You're not crying, are you?" the Chief would say. "He thought we should be as good as he was," Dan remembered. As the boys grew older, the Chief sometimes chided them for their mistakes, saying, "You're brand new!" or, "You're unwrapped like a box! You don't have any experience." He wanted them tough, just as tough as he had been as a boy. The Chief didn't want his boys gambling on the horses, though. "I'd rather have you guys be dopes or drunks than have this as a scourge on you," he warned them. The Rooney sons grew up proud to be Pittsburghers and proud to be Rooneys, and the North Side became the midpoint on their life's compass.

Danny emerged as their leader. As the firstborn son and the first grandson in the extended Rooney family (per Rooney custom, the Chief named his first son "Daniel" after his father, his second son "Art Jr." after himself), he understood that he was "the cock of the walk." John Rooney, seven years younger, said, "He was like a man compared to us. He sort of ran the works when the old man wasn't there." John recalled Danny leading the boys in the family rosary, each saying their Hail Marys and Holy Marys. The twins were too young to keep up, though, and Tim, the third brother, howled, "Hey, Dan, that's ten!" But Danny shook his head: "You didn't say them in unison!" And so he added another, and made his brothers start from the beginning.

Football quickly got into Danny's bloodstream. He made a few road trips with his father's NFL team, and on the train the players helped him with his homework. He wanted to be with the players, and one day become just like them. It didn't matter that the team, from 1933 through 1950, had but four winning seasons, or that the Chief tended to hire his cronies as head coaches, including Walt Kiesling three times, and gave them a free hand to run the team as they saw fit, or that catcalls rained down on his Steelers from all across Pittsburgh. Danny knew what he wanted. In 1940, when he was eight, rumors swirled that the Chief was about to sell the team, and Danny got worried, until Kass finally told her husband, "You better talk to Danny," and the boy said, "Dad, what are you doin'?" and the Chief said not to worry, he wasn't selling. The boy had his whole life to lead, and yet already he began to envision himself with the Steelers.

Times got harder for the NFL during the war years due to player shortages. The Chief, struggling to survive, merged his Steelers with the Philadelphia Eagles in 1943 to become the Phil-Pitt Steagles, and then a year later with the Chicago Cardinals as Card-Pitt. Following the war, he attended only three of Danny's football games in four seasons at North Catholic High, including one against Boys High, a fund-raiser. "That was a civic thing," Dan said. "So he *had* to go to that game." Danny played quarterback, and broke his arm that day, but the Chief didn't see it happen because he had left at halftime. Back home, Kass asked, "Well, how was it?" and the Chief answered, "Danny is the same with his football team as he is here. He runs everything." As a senior in 1949, Danny Rooney was chosen among Pittsburgh's Catholic schools' all-star performers, second team, behind the St. Justin's quarterback, Johnny Unitas.

Danny went off to college to study accounting at Duquesne, married a local girl in 1951, and returned to the neighborhood to coach the St. Peter's Church youth football team. When it came time for him to think about his future, the Chief suggested a small construction company he owned, but Dan said no thanks to that, and the Chief asked him about working at the horse tracks, but Dan said no thanks to that, too.

But football . . .

Through history, Pittsburgh's industrial life had experienced both darkness and light. English novelist Anthony Trollope visited in 1862 and called Pittsburgh "without exception, the blackest place which I ever saw," and six years later biographer James Parton, writing in the *Atlantic*, termed Pittsburgh "Hell with the lid taken off." The city became home to the banking Mellons, and the place where Andrew Carnegie, George

Westinghouse, and H. J. Heinz began their ascents. "This used to be some town," the Chief said. "I remember coming in on the train with Halas from Chicago to New York, we came by Pittsburgh at night and those mills lit up the rivers all the way along."

Now dark clouds rolled up the Monongahela, like an enemy army massing, snowflakes the size of fifty-cent pieces falling in the gloom on Pittsburgh's metal bridges. The downtown skyline, built of brick, steel, and muscle—proof to civic-minded Pittsburghers that theirs was a great and important American city, not to mention the city that built the armaments that saved democracy—blurred to black-on-gray in silhouette. In the mist, the bustle of downtown life played across banks, restaurants, hat stores, and trolley cars, perhaps no place more harried, frenetic, and smoky than the Chief's ground-floor office in the Fort Pitt Hotel, an old pile of bricks on the corner of Pennsylvania and Tenth. Rather than take the long way through the lobby, visitors moved in and out through floor-to-ceiling windows that opened to the street. Someone always seemed to be sitting on the windowsill. The Chief's office filled with sounds: horns honking, and phones ringing, calls coming in from Halas, Bert Bell, sportswriters, fight managers, Aqueduct, his stockbroker (the Chief was big into commodities), and Shamrock Farm, the 350-acre stud farm in Maryland he purchased in 1947 to breed and train racehorses. Day to day, a parade of regulars entered, each there to loaf with the Chief, smoke a cigar, swap stories, tell a few lies, and talk about business or the old days: Billy Conn; horse players; down-and-outers in search of a few bucks or help getting a job; Mayor David Lawrence; and Dago Sam Leone, an old friend from the North Side with an affinity for dice games and the horses. Pie Traynor, the great Pirate third baseman and former manager, did plenty of loafing in the Chief's office. A master of the malapropism as a local radio man, Traynor reported scores on air, calling Niagara "Nicaragua" and Junianta "Juanita" and Ursinus "Urenzus." The sound of Framingham, Massachusetts, was in his voice, and at the Chief's office Traynor greeted arriving guests, *"How-ah-yuh, muh-boy!"* Years later, when the Chief moved his office to the fourth floor of the nearby Roosevelt Hotel, Traynor refused to visit, fearing he'd think he still was on the ground floor. "I'm not going to be the first guy to forget myself and duck out a fourth-floor window," he said.

The Chief found relative quiet at home, apart from his perpetually ringing telephone, and he imposed a rule that his five boys knew too well: after the Steelers lost a game, no one, including Kass, was allowed to mention the team for the next two days. He didn't want to read about the Steelers' defeat in the newspapers, either. "I don't want to have anybody tell me," he said, "that we gave it a good try." An early rendition of the Rooney Rule, it made for a quiet dinner table on Mondays and Tuesdays in autumn.

But the Chief's rule couldn't save Art Jr. from having to answer for the Steelers' failings when he was a student at Saint Vincent College in Latrobe. College humor could be raw and vicious. There in 1953, atop a chair, stood Art Jr. as a freshman, wearing a beanie, one pant leg rolled up, and a sign on his back that read, I'M ART ROONEY JUNIOR. He delivered a speech entitled "Why the Steelers Stink." The Steelers were in their twenty-first year of existence, and moving confidently toward their twenty-first consecutive season without winning a playoff game, let alone a title. In his speech, Art Jr. presented the same litany of excuses that he had presented to his high school friends. *Some of our key players are injured.* And: *We've had some illnesses on the team.* And: *Our draft choice should've come with us, but he thought he should be an officer in the army.* The Steelers' performance embarrassed him.

In a distant day Dan and Art Jr. would play central roles in the creation of the 1970s Steelers dynasty. Separated by three years, they were so different in appearance and personality as to prove the vastness of the gene pool. Dan was smaller, thinner, with angular features. He was more self-contained, secure with his place in the family, and always playing the role of signal caller. In his oversized black-rimmed glasses, Art Jr. was bigger, with rounder features, an offensive tackle on the football field ("a fat-ass," he said in a self-assessment, "without any lateral movement"), more expressive and expansive, and determined to gain his father's respect.

"As different as two brothers can be," their younger brother John would say. "Growing up they weren't alike at all. They never were. . . . Art was more of a student than Dan. We all got home from school and changed into play clothes. Art never changed his clothes. He studied."

The Chief pulled strings to help Artie, as he was known in the family, gain admission to Georgetown Law School. But Art Jr. had other ideas. He wanted to break away, forge his own identity. He wanted to try acting.

Acting? The Chief rolled his eyes. It wasn't the most masculine profession, but he supported the boy's attempt, anyway. Art Jr. gathered his courage and auditioned at the Carnegie Tech Drama School. He went onstage frightened half to death. He projected. He acted. He placed his foot on a stool, just as he had seen suave professional actors do, except that his leg trembled from nerves and the stool wobbled and made a loud noise in the stage microphones that sounded like a freight train crashing into the studio. Later, he stood before the judges. "You are worse than raw," one said. But the woman in charge told him, "You don't realize it, but your voice is a gift. You have a tremendous Irish lilting voice. We could really work with you." He stayed for a semester and then moved to New York to study Method acting, hoping to make it to the Actors Studio, a would-be Method actor's dream. He made it there finally, but only to move furniture. At least he got to see Broadway shows for free, and meet famous actors such as John Gielgud and Helen Hayes. Once, he got the Chief three great seats (ten rows back, center aisle) to see the distinguished British actor Eric Portman in Eugene O'Neill's *A Touch of the Poet.* The Chief showed up with his brother Jim and Dago Sam Leone. Bored, the threesome walked out before the first act ended. Portman was appalled. "Nobody—I mean *nobody*—has ever walked out on me before," he said after the show. The show's business manager, one of the Chief's old friends, calmed Portman. "I know those three guys. They are ignoramuses from Pittsburgh," he said.

Art Jr. didn't find his future onstage.

Forbes Field, 1950s. The Chief understood why Steeler fans booed. "After the people fight the traffic jam and then get to Forbes Field, which isn't good for football, they have to be in a bad mood," he said. "Then they take it out on our players." Jack Butler, a defensive back, stepped from the Steeler locker room as a rookie in 1951, and as he prepared to run out onto Forbes Field, a veteran teammate shouted, "Okay, put on your helmets!" Just then Butler heard the hollering and boos, and the sky filled with objects thrown by fans. Then, out on the same field where

Ty Cobb and Honus Wagner met for the only time in their careers, in the 1909 World Series, Butler stumbled in pursuit of ballcarriers over the hilly pitcher's mound, which the groundkeepers never leveled properly, and made tackles on an infield that sent sand flying beneath his jersey. To make ends meet, Butler held other jobs in the off-season, working a jackhammer and selling cemetery plots.

It wasn't much easier for Ed Kiely, the Steelers' publicist and jack of all trades. Kiely tried to spread Steelers' goodwill to US Steel, Alcoa, and other local corporations, and sell a few season tickets in the process. But he found that the local football allegiances remained with the college game, the University of Pittsburgh and Duquesne. "I had no real pitch," Kiely recalled. "I told them this sport would grow. What could I say? Some were just nice to me because I was probably interrupting something they were glad not to be dabbling with. Others wouldn't see me."

There was unanimity on at least one point: the Steelers needed better players. In this regard their future was in the hands of Ray Byrne, an undertaker at his family's funeral home who, when he wasn't answering death's call, managed the Steelers' college drafts. Byrne was small and cheerful. He read all the national football magazines, subscribed to all the newspapers, and diligently phoned college coaches across the nation to ask, "Who d'ya got?" and, "Whaddaya think?" He kept meticulous notes and records on index cards. In terms of scouting in the NFL, the early 1950s was the era of the Model T. Lou Spadia, an executive with the San Francisco 49ers, kept watch on Redskin owner George Preston Marshall on draft day in New York. "Marshall was the worst. He would peek over your shoulder and steal a name from your list," Spadia said. "It was like a men's club: a bunch of guys with drinks on the table, and looking at sports magazines." Because of Byrne's family profession and the Steelers' inability to win consistently, the jokes around Pittsburgh flowed: "What are you doing, drafting a bunch of stiffs?"

The jokes intensified during the middle 1950s, and for good reason. From 1955 through 1957, the Steelers' judgment of football talent was unbelievably, and catastrophically, inept. It wasn't only the players they failed to draft, but a few they did and chose not to keep. In 1955, the Steelers drafted in the ninth round quarterback Johnny Unitas, a local boy who played at the University of Louisville. The Steelers then cut

Unitas without playing him for a single down during the preseason, even after Tim Rooney, the Chief's third son, wrote his father an impassioned twenty-two-page letter urging him to keep Unitas. But the Chief, as always, deferred to his head coach, Walt Kiesling. So Johnny U was gone, a mistake that long remained in the Steelers' institutional memory.

A year later the Steelers had the "bonus pick"—the first overall selection in the NFL draft. They might have selected Penn State running back Lenny Moore but instead picked an obscure defensive back from Colorado named Gary Glick, a player they had only read about but never seen. Their draft-day catastrophes played on: in 1957 the Steelers might have drafted Syracuse running back Jim Brown but instead took Purdue quarterback Len Dawson, a fine choice. Even Paul Brown, picking next, desperately wanted Dawson, and punched his fist on the table in frustration when the Steelers took him, knocking books to the floor. But Pittsburgh subsequently traded Dawson. Buddy Parker had been hired in 1957 as the Steelers' head coach. A tough, hard-drinking southerner whose views tended to be set in cement, Parker wanted veterans and had no time or patience for rookies. He would trade draft picks so indiscriminately over the next seven years that in 1959 and 1963 the Steelers' first selections came in the eighth round.

Ernie Accorsi spent forty years in the NFL, the last nine as the New York Giants' general manager, and said with amazement, "Do you realize that the Steelers could easily have had a backfield of Johnny Unitas, Lenny Moore, and Jim Brown?"

In casting aside players who would become the game's most elite running back (Brown) and quarterback (Unitas), along with all-pros Moore and Dawson, the Steelers cast aside four future Hall of Famers who would amass a combined 68,000 passing yards, 20,000 rushing yards, and 27 Pro Bowl appearances.

The Chief, always candid, said many years later: "There were three main things the public knew about us. They knew we were Rooneys, they knew we were dumb, and they knew we were cheap."

The Chief groomed Dan as his heir apparent. The process wasn't formal; nothing with the Chief ever was, it just sort of happened over time.

"Nobody was worrying about titles," Dan said. He took Dan to NFL meetings and allowed him to run the Steelers' day-to-day operations. The Chief was gone most of the time anyway, and Parker thought the business side of football a necessary evil, so any calls that came from the league office, or from an executive from another club, went to Dan. When NFL owners met at the Kenilworth Hotel in Miami in January 1960 to choose a new commissioner, and the balloting deadlocked after twenty-two rounds, a new name was put forth: Pete Rozelle, the Los Angeles Rams' young general manager. "Who is this guy? Do you know him?" the Chief whispered to Dan, then twenty-seven. "I know him," Dan replied. "He's a good guy. I think he can do the job." Dan got involved in the league's conversations with the players' union, and in internal discussions about how to ward off the rival American Football League. When President Kennedy was murdered in November 1963, Rozelle, as NFL commissioner, decided to press ahead with NFL games on Sunday as scheduled. "Okay, Pete, I disagree," Dan told him, "but I'll support you." Dan stood atop the Forbes Field roof two hours before kickoff against the Bears that Sunday. There, he pressed a transistor radio to his ear and learned that Jack Ruby had shot Lee Harvey Oswald.

An actor no more, Art Jr. joined the Steelers soon after, getting a job, with encouragement and help from Kass, selling tickets, a formidable task because no one in Pittsburgh wanted them. The twins, Pat and John, manned the office phone at the Steelers' office at night, ostensibly to sell tickets, a job the Chief gave them. While waiting for the phone to ring, John recalled, "we played basketball in the garbage can against each other." He added, "The only one who ever called was the Chief to see how we were."

Art Jr. wanted to give scouting a try. Ray Byrne had left the Steelers to become a full-time undertaker. In 1964 Art Jr. asked his father about it. "Sure, you can become a scout," the Chief said. Why not? A scout was the low-man on the Steelers' totem pole, and Parker had made scouting all but superfluous. But Art Jr. saw the role as an opportunity to develop the team and his own career. Scouting would provide a niche for him, a way to prove himself and maybe earn the Chief's respect. Art Jr. was twenty-nine, married. He had hopes, dreams, a family to feed.

Scouting had entered a new age, and Dallas became the cutting-edge leader. The Cowboys made a fetish of building through the draft, selecting and then shaping players as their own. Dallas's young personnel director, Gil Brandt, was quoted everywhere, and soon the team added a new analytical component, the IBM 360 mainframe computer. The Cowboys inputted scouting statistics and assessments, and the computer made cataloging and retrieval fast and easy. "We might look for all linebackers with a competitive-aggressiveness factor of six-point-five or better," Brandt said. "We could do that manually with cards, but that might take us a day. On the computer, we've got the list in fifteen seconds." At first, Lombardi and other NFL traditionalists mocked the Cowboys' computer use as futuristic blather. "Everybody laughed," Brandt recalled, "and said, 'You've got to be kidding. How can a machine do the job of a man?' " But by the time Dallas vaulted into the 1966 NFL title game against the Packers, Lombardi told the Cowboys' hierarchy he was interested in joining their computer venture.

Art Jr. took the more traditional approach to scouting and soon was on the trail, in an old Packard with veteran scout Will Walls, nine hours up to Buffalo for a college all-star game, the raconteur Walls telling stories the entire way. Walls worked for the scouting combine to which the Steelers subscribed, BLESTO, an acronym for the Bears, Lions, Eagles, Steelers Talent Organization; each of the teams in this cooperative received the same stacks of assessments of college players. Walls was a genuine character. Part Native American, and a full-blooded Texan, Walls had been Sammy Baugh's favorite receiver at Texas Christian, played briefly for the New York Giants, appeared in a few Western films in Hollywood, and as a longtime scout drove his Packard about 50,000 miles a year, trolling the Southwest and West for college football talent. His Packard was crammed with such essentials as hot plates, movie projectors, coffemakers, a still camera (Parker wanted a photograph of every college prospect), 100-watt lightbulbs (motel room lights were too dim to read by), big bars of soap (Walls said motels had little bars for "skinny-assed folks"), and his .38-caliber pistol (just in case). Walls had strong scouting beliefs and sayings. "Artie, did you see that fella flinch there?" he said once, reviewing a game film. He showed the play again. "Remember, Artie: 'Once a flincher, always a flincher.' " Walls had his own code to designate a player's race: there were "Captains" (the letter *C* for "Colored") and "Winners" (the letter *W* for "White"). Walls introduced him to college coaches from the Southwest, and BLESTO's Jack Butler, the former Steeler, introduced him to coaches from the East and North. Butler mentored Art Jr., instructing him about what made good prospects and good organizations. Leaving his young family behind, traveling far and wide, gone for days on end, college football game films whirring through his projector in South Bend, Tallahassee, Shreveport, and Los Angeles, Art Jr. soon learned to grade a player's quickness, strength, balance, and speed.

Buddy Parker threatened to quit once too often. Dan, in a bold stroke, accepted his latest threatened resignation before the 1965 season. The Steelers hired another coach, and then another, Bill Austin, a Lombardi assistant, in 1966. Lombardi offered his recommendation of Austin in a phone conversation with the Chief as Dan and Art Jr. silently listened on other lines. The Chief hung up, Lombardi's word his gospel. He told Dan, "There's our coach." But Dan said he had other coaches on his list yet to interview. The Chief waved him away. "I don't need to talk to anybody else," he said. Dan had a theory: you do not hire people based on recommendations. *Recommendations create your list.* "The interview with the coach is the important thing," Dan said, "and it's not just one interview." But the Chief would not be dissuaded. Austin got the job. The Steelers continued to sag, 11-28-3 over the next three seasons.

Summer 1967. America's black ghettos erupted in violence: Washington, Montgomery, Louisville, Cleveland, Omaha, forty-three dead on the streets of Detroit, twenty-six in Newark. When the Kerner Commission issued its report on civil unrest in March 1968, it emphasized that the nation rapidly was becoming two nations, one black, one white. "What white Americans have never fully understood—but what the Negro can never forget—is that white society is deeply implicated in the ghetto," the commission reported. "White institutions created it, white institutions maintain it, and white society condones it."

On the scouting trail, Art Jr. was learning about race in America, each day bringing a new insight. He gave a box of cigars as a gift to John Merritt, coach at Tennessee State University, a football powerhouse among the black colleges. A folksy storyteller who weighed nearly three hundred pounds, Big John Merritt perspired so profusely at practices that he wore a towel around his neck. He liked to call his players *Baby*—as in, *"Hey, baby!"*—in part because he couldn't always remember their names. His fondness for cigars was well known to NFL scouts. Beside Merritt's desk, gifts of cigar boxes stacked up. "Rooney, I want to tell you something," Merritt said. "Never, ever trust a black man with gray eyes." Merritt explained why: "They are not black. They are not white. They are not trustworthy." *What a peculiar thing to say*, Art Jr. thought. Even so, he naively took this advice to heart. He began to study the eyes of the black players he scouted, searching for gray as a telltale sign of trouble.

As race relations in America smoldered, Dan read the sports pages of the *Pittsburgh Courier*, the city's historic black newspaper, and spotted the annual Black Colleges All-America football team created by editor Bill Nunn Jr. Dan wondered about the players on this list. *Why don't we know more about these guys?* He hadn't seen Bill Nunn in ages. He decided to find out why Nunn had stopped showing up at Steelers games.

CHAPTER 3

THE MAN FROM THE *COURIER*

BILL NUNN JR. HAD HIS reasons for avoiding the Pittsburgh Steelers. He had been victimized by too many slights that carried the whiff of unprofessionalism, if not prejudice, and he was fed up with it. He saw the Steelers grant passes to writers from daily newspapers and not to writers from weeklies such as the *Courier*. But he knew that writers from *white-owned* weeklies got press passes when he did not. The Steelers were hardly alone in this regard. Nunn had similar problems with the Pittsburgh Pirates and other white-owned professional teams. Even when the Steelers gave him a press box pass, they made him feel as if they were doing him a favor when, in fact, he thought it was the other way around.

To Nunn, the slights went deeper. For seventeen years he had been selecting the annual Black Colleges All-America football team in the *Courier*. Not once had the Steelers expressed interest. In recent years his list had become a primer for NFL teams preparing for the college draft, and some of those teams phoned him in search of insight. They respected Nunn and saw real value in his list. But the Steelers—the team in his hometown—never called and, even worse, didn't seem to care about players at the black colleges.

The slights cut deeper yet, dating at least to the locker room presence of Wallace "Boots" Lewis. In his cap and baggy clothes, Lewis was a likable, slightly stooped shoe-shine man, and a valet of sorts for Coach Buddy Parker from 1957 through 1964. Parker referred to him as "my good luck charm." A headline in the *Tuscaloosa (Ala.) News* in August

1963 trumpeted that fact: "Boots The Negro: A Good Luck Charm."
Lewis ran errands for Parker, shined the shoes of Steelers players in his
spare time (tips accepted), and sometimes retrieved sandwiches for them.
Lewis struggled to remember names. He called Dan Rooney "Marooney,"
the Chief was "The Boss Man," and Parker "The Man." Cynically, *Courier*
sportswriter Ric Roberts once said, "Boots looks like the guy hitting the
cymbals, and moving back and forth, one of those wind-up toys." More
than forty years later, Nunn still had difficulty discussing Lewis. "I don't
want to talk about that guy," Nunn said. "He was trying to make a living.
That was part of the times. But what Buddy Parker did with him"—Nunn
shook his head—"was something else."

Bill Nunn Jr. had his reasons for avoiding the Pittsburgh Steelers, and
if anyone asked, he would tell them what the reasons were. Even without
the Steelers, he had plenty of sensational black athletes to write about.
In January 1966, Nunn harkened to the sports pages' Golden Age in the
1920s, announcing to *Courier* readers a new "wave of burnished, bronze
superstars [who] roared across those same pages with unbelievable brilliance. Willie Mays, Arthur Ashe, Cassius Clay, Kipchoge Keino, Jimmy
Brown, Gayle Sayers, Zoilo Versalles, Roberto Clemente, Tony Oliva,
Mike Garrett, Mudcat Grant, Paul Lowe and the vanishing Sugar Ray
Robinson stood out in a galaxy of greats."

As Nunn saw it, the problem was not his. The problem belonged to
the Pittsburgh Steelers.

The sportswriter's life had grown on him. For that matter, so had the
Pittsburgh Courier. Its offices and printing presses on Wylie Avenue were
in the heart of the Hill District, historically the hub of black life in Pittsburgh, an area teeming with churches, small businesses, and nightclubs,
and later dramatized onstage by one of its most famous residents, play-
wright August Wilson. Nunn's father, Bill Sr., had dedicated his life to the
Courier as a proud race man crusading for civil rights through its pages.
Now it was his son's turn, and he would do it in his own way, carrying on
the fight through his columns and reportage in the sports pages. At forty-
two, Bill Jr. was still fit, trim. Everyone knew him, and he knew them,

their families, and where they'd gone to high school. He eased comfortably through the Hill District nightclubs, and often in the company of
local or nationally known black athletes, flashing his incandescent smile,
a gap between his front teeth. You might have seen Nunn at the bar at
Stanley's, chatting it up with boxer Ezzard Charles, or deep in conversation with Roberto Clemente at the Crawford Grill, where onstage the Er-
roll Garner Trio played "Misty," the remarkable five-foot-two Garner, like
Nunn, a graduate of Westinghouse High, sitting atop two phone books at
the piano and perspiring profusely in his tuxedo.

Nunn wrote a provocative sports column, and often with a sharp
edge. His writings adhered to the higher purpose of the *Courier*, and of
the black press—the still-unfinished business of bringing true freedom
to black Americans. "When St. Louis outfielder Curt Flood ran into difficulty trying to move into a home in Martinez, Calif. last week," Nunn
wrote, "he, like so many others, discovered being a well-known athlete
can expose you to the same type of discrimination faced by the average
man whose skin happens to be black." And: "Jackie Robinson has the
makings of a good major league manager." And: "[Eldridge] Dickey, it
says here, is one of the best. But his biggest drawback could be his ability to play quarterback. In the past the professionals have run away from
Negro quarterbacks as though they've had the plague."

Nunn's conversational breeziness made it easy for athletes to talk with
him. He developed closeness with some of the black athletes he covered,
their race a bonding force. The Pirates' Clemente was a star, a handsome
Puerto Rican with the muscled physique of an ebony god. Clemente
didn't speak English fluently, but got his points across. He told Nunn in
confidence about some of the racial slights he'd received in earlier years
from white players who were now his Pirates teammates. Nunn didn't
write about that. Neither did he write what he had learned about private
indiscretions committed by the players. Sportswriters didn't pry into
athletes' personal lives in the 1960s as they would later. Nunn lived only
four blocks from Clemente in the Schenley Heights area of Pittsburgh,
and their friendship was such that in the Forbes Field locker room after
game seven of the 1960 World Series, Clemente asked Nunn for a ride to
the airport; Nunn gave it to him, but only after first escorting him, inch

by inch, through adoring fans to his car. In his column, Nunn observed that Clemente enjoyed his celebration with the crowd more than with his teammates.

As the *Courier*'s sports editor, Nunn had sat ringside to cover the fights of Cassius Clay and Floyd Patterson. He wrote an exposé about segregated living conditions at the 1961 Pittsburgh Pirates' spring training camp in Fort Myers, Florida. He also served as ghostwriter for the "Jackie Robinson Says" column in the *Courier*. He interviewed Robinson occasionally at his home in Stamford, Connecticut, or in his office at Chock Full o' Nuts, to find out what was on his mind and then crafted the column in Robinson's voice, though more often than not the column's words and thoughts were entirely Nunn's. "Basically I would watch him during the week, and create things I felt that he might want to say," he said.

Each week during the fall, Nunn traveled to cover a high-profile game: Grambling State against Southern, or Morgan State against Virginia State. Invariably coaches such as Grambling's Eddie Robinson, Southern's Ace Mumford, and Morgan's Earl "Papa Bear" Banks were thrilled to see him. To their football players, Nunn was a kingmaker. He could help smooth the path for their professional deliverance. The white press largely ignored the black colleges' games, but Nunn shined a light on them. Through Nunn and the *Courier*, coaches at the black colleges got headlines and their players got noticed. These players coveted Nunn's attention and desperately hoped to be included on his annual Black Colleges All-America team, a much-anticipated listing his father had started as a *Courier* sportswriter during the mid-1920s. Players at the black colleges could recite the names of NFL players who earlier had been so honored: Roosevelt Brown (Morgan State, 1952), Willie Davis (Grambling, 1955), Willie Galimore (Florida A&M, 1956), Johnny Sample (Maryland State, 1958), Buck Buchanan (Grambling, 1963), Leroy Kelly (Morgan State, 1964), and Lem Barney (Jackson State, 1966), among others. In some segregated southern towns, Nunn struggled to find lodging. In Louisiana to cover Grambling, Nunn sometimes stayed at Coach Robinson's house.

Only now, in 1967, did Nunn realize that he had been groomed for his role, the pieces of his life suddenly fitting together logically and delivering him to this moment. His father, Bill Sr., spent more than forty years at the *Courier* and served as the *Courier*'s managing editor for a quarter century, until 1963. A leading light of the black press during many of those years, the *Courier* had fourteen national editions in the 1940s, and a reported circulation of more than 330,000. Nunn's father, a short, squat man with a deep, expansive voice that filled the newsroom, fought hard against racial injustice. He pushed for the integration of blacks into the American armed forces, and later raised funds to help attorney Thurgood Marshall of the National Association for the Advancement of Colored People argue *Brown v. Board of Education* before the US Supreme Court. He fought for the inclusion of blacks in major-league baseball, and dispatched *Courier* sportswriter Wendell Smith to cover Jackie Robinson as he broke the color barrier with the Brooklyn Dodgers in 1947. Smith roomed with Robinson on road trips that season.

The Nunns lived in the Homewood section of Pittsburgh, a predominantly white, middle-class neighborhood. Because of his father's important role at the *Courier*, Bill Jr. grew accustomed to seeing celebrated black Americans passing through his house: Count Basie, saxophonist Jimmie Lunceford, Lionel Hampton, Billy Eckstine. Arriving home after school, Bill Jr. never knew who might be playing the baby grand piano in the living room. His father had been a star athlete at Westinghouse High, and its first black football player. He played baseball and football on the local sandlots, and later served as secretary for baseball's Negro National League, cofounding the annual Negro Leagues' East-West All-Star game in 1933.

A basketball star in high school, Bill Jr. was set in 1943 to attend Long Island University to play for Coach Clair Bee. But his father intervened, insisting that he attend a historically black school. "What are you talking about?" Bill Jr. asked.

"I think you need to find out more about your own race," Bill Sr. said.

The son shook his head. He would attend LIU, he insisted.

"That's fine," his father said. "Where are you going to live?"

Bill Jr. wasn't ready to pay his own way.

Soon after, Wendell Smith convinced him to try his own alma mater, West Virginia State University, a historically black school. There, Nunn played on the basketball team as a six-foot shooting guard. As a senior, he starred on a team that won all twenty-six of its games. Upon his gradu-ation in 1948, the Harlem Globetrotters wanted him. But he knew too much about the Globetrotters' day-to-day existence. "All that bus trav-eling," Bill Jr. said, "it was just a hard life." The Basketball Association of America and the National Basketball League—predecessors of the National Basketball Association—weren't viable options. They had not yet desegregated, and wouldn't, as the NBA, for two more years. When Wendell Smith left the *Courier* in 1948 for the *Chicago Herald-American*, Bill Jr. saw his opportunity and took it.

When in 1967 *Courier* staffer Ric Roberts told him that Dan Rooney of the Steelers was asking about him and wondering why he never showed up at the team's headquarters or games, Nunn muttered, "Tell him as long as the Steelers have the approach they have to black athletes, they never have to worry about me being down there."

Dan called him, though, and Nunn reluctantly agreed to meet at the Steelers' offices at the Roosevelt.

Now, face-to-face, Dan asked, "How come we never see you down here?"

Nunn didn't mention the bygone days of Boots Lewis, or state his grievances as boldly as he might have. He spoke in more general terms. He cited his troubles securing press passes. Then he said, "I don't know if you guys understand the situation."

"I turn out an All-America football team every year," Nunn added, "and nobody from the Steelers has ever contacted me." He spoke carefully but firmly, and with conviction.

"Your team is not that good," Nunn said. "I don't think you'll ever be a winner."

A different man might have been so offended as to send Bill Nunn Jr. away. But Dan reacted differently. He said he would straighten out these problems and then he said, "Why don't you help change it? Why don't you join us, scout for us?"

"I've already got a job," Nunn replied.

"Work for us half-time, then," Dan said. "Look at the games, take notes on the players, and send us reports. Tell us what you think."

The Chief joined their discussion. He had known Nunn's father for more than forty years. They had played sandlot baseball against each other long ago. They had talked sports and politics at the Crawford Grill with their mutual friends Gus Greenlee and Cum Posey. The elder Nunn had helped the Chief locate housing for several black Steelers during exhibition games played in the South during the 1950s.

Bill Jr. knew about Lowell Perry. A black All-American wide receiver at the University of Michigan, Perry was the first black player ever drafted by the Steelers, in 1953, and the team had great expectations for him. Only six games into his career, though, Perry suffered a crushed pelvis and fractured hip on a reverse play when hit by New York Giant star Roosevelt Grier and another defender. Perry spent thirteen weeks in a Pittsburgh hospital, and the Chief and Kass visited him nearly every day; Kass baked several pies for him. Doctors told Perry that he could play football again eventually but might risk permanent damage. The Chief told Perry, "As long as I own the Pittsburgh Steelers, you will have a job with us, if you want one." A year later, Perry retired as a player and became the NFL's first black assistant coach of the modern era with the Steelers. When Perry told the Chief the following year that he wanted to pursue law school, the Chief hired him as a Steelers scout, effectively paying for his education, first at Duquesne University School of Law and then at the Detroit College of Law. Perry had told Nunn stories about the Chief, and raved about him. Nunn knew the Chief was a fair and honorable man.

Finally, Dan suggested that the *Courier* columnist talk to his brother Art Jr., who headed the Steelers' scouting department. Nunn agreed to talk, nothing more.

Now, in a conversation enriched by Pittsburgh history, two sons of locally prominent men raised on different sides of town, their jobs and their names gifts from their fathers, Art Rooney Jr. sized up Bill Nunn Jr. *Here's one of these smart-aleck, black-guy writers. What the hell does he know about scouting?*

Art Jr. had been working tirelessly to bring discipline and order to his Steeler scouting department. He reorganized files, films, and priorities. His department was virtually a one-man operation, though the Steeler coaches scouted some, too, and the team still subscribed to BLESTO. But Art Jr. had a more personal stake in his job. Scouting was *his* area, and the last thing he needed was top-down interference from his father or older brother. He didn't want anyone dictating the scouts he would hire, even if only a part-time scout. "I was pissed purple," Art Jr. said. As he studied Nunn from across his desk, he thought, *I know what he's thinking about me: this rich guy, his old man got him his job!* Nunn wasn't thinking that at all, though he sensed that Art Jr. was anxious and that the idea of hiring him as a scout was being imposed upon him.

Art Jr. understood that the Steelers needed entrée into the black colleges. He had visited those colleges, and been forced to wait for interminable periods in the hallways or outside the head coaches' offices. He had not developed relationships at the black schools, not yet. Dallas had hired Dick Mansperger in 1964, and as he scouted the black colleges it took him years to build a cross-race familiarity and trust with black coaches. A handful of professional teams already had hired black scouts, the most well known among them Lloyd Wells of the Kansas City Chiefs, a part-timer with a wealth of contacts, though Wells soon would leave the Chiefs to join Muhammad Ali's entourage. Art Jr. understood that the talent at black schools was impressive and abundant, and that times were changing in the nation and the NFL, and fast. He also knew about Bill Nunn's Black Colleges All-America team and about the accompanying banquet the *Courier* held each year in Pittsburgh.

Now Nunn began to talk about the black colleges, and the coaches, athletic directors, and presidents he knew at those schools. Art Jr. listened closely. Art Jr. offered his own impressions, the lessons he had learned after a few years on the scouting trail. There was, it seemed, a genuine meeting of minds.

Nunn agreed to work for the Steelers part-time while continuing his full-time job at the newspaper. He would meet with Art Jr. at the Roosevelt Hotel at night after finishing his work at the paper. He would share observations and insights with him about the black college players he had just seen, and review game films as the NFL draft approached. The two men engaged in animated conversations about the science of scouting and how to judge toughness, football intelligence, and potential.

From this point forward, when Nunn showed up at the black colleges, he would represent the *Pittsburgh Courier* and the Pittsburgh Steelers. To players at the black colleges who craved a shot at the NFL, Nunn became just about the most important man on the planet.

April 4, 1968. On assignment for the *Courier* at Maryland State College along the Eastern Shore, Nunn took a call from John Sengstacke, his publisher: the Reverend Dr. Martin Luther King Jr. had been shot in Memphis. He asked Nunn, his managing editor, to return to the newsroom at once, and so Nunn got in his car and rushed back to Pittsburgh. Nunn's fifteen-year-old son, Bill III, saw rioting break out later that day on Centre Avenue in the Hill District. Rock throwing led to gunfire, and one bullet passed perilously close to the teenager as he sprinted away. Art Jr. was on a scouting trip in Ohio that day, bound for the University of Cincinnati. His wife, Kay, watching on television as violence broke out in American cities, urged him to come home without delay, and so did the Chief. Art Jr. cut his trip short.

Back in the *Courier* newsroom, facing a seminal story with only a small staff, Nunn asked his retired father to help with the coverage. Bill Nunn Sr. went to his typewriter, and the old newsman's words burned with anger: "Even as the Rev. Martin Luther King is making his final journey, an assassin walks the streets of America, unchallenged, unguarded and untamed. Determined at all costs to beat back the American Negro's struggle for freedom, this ominous degenerate is represented by that portion of white America whose bigoted notions have made us the shame of the free world."

That summer, on the medal stand at the 1968 Olympics in Mexico City, American track stars John Carlos and Tommie Smith bowed their heads and held up black-gloved fists in protest of racism in America. Bill Jr. was amazed. *That took courage*, he thought. *They're willing to make a stand*. What Carlos and Smith did in Mexico City made him proud. In the battle for racial freedom and equality, Nunn believed, there were important stands to be made, even in sports.

✦ ✦ ✦

Dan wanted Nunn to work full-time for the Steelers, and his offer became increasingly difficult for Nunn to turn down. The steep decline of the black press, including the *Pittsburgh Courier*, pained Nunn. Few black journalists were getting jobs at white-owned newspapers. In 1969, Nunn finally agreed to join the Steelers, but he deferred leaving the newspaper for one year, to give Sengstacke more time for the transition. The Steelers permitted Nunn to continue to write his sports column for the *Courier*. As the league's sixth full-time black scout, Nunn would have a dramatic impact as the Steelers, during the next six years, would turn to players from historically black colleges as never before, at Southern, Arkansas AM&N, Prairie View, Grambling, Texas Southern, South Carolina State, Alcorn, Mississippi Valley, Alabama A&M, and Tennessee State. The Steelers drafted eleven black-college players from 1969 through 1971, after having drafted none in the previous two years. They weren't alone in this regard: the Miami Dolphins drafted ten black-college players during the same period. "I almost felt this was an untapped source, almost like Branch Rickey going into black baseball and finding all those players," Nunn said. He would miss on some of his assessments, but Nunn would also help land some of the empire's defining players, including Mel Blount, L. C. Greenwood, John Stallworth, Joe Gilliam, Frank Lewis, Donnie Shell, and Ernie Holmes.

He immersed himself in the art of scouting. As he sized up college athletes, he started with their feet. Athletes must move, change direction, bend. Footwork was paramount. Nunn always recorded an athlete's shoe size in his notes. To him, that detail was important. ("I'm a size nine and I weigh two hundred and fifty!" Art Jr. once told him. "From what I hear," Bill Jr. replied, "you couldn't run either.") Then there were the intangibles: intelligence, toughness, heart. Find a player with heart, and you can teach him fundamentals, Nunn believed. There were different types of intelligence; athletes could be book smart or street smart. To Steeler coaches and scouts he explained, "I can take you into the Hill District and show you a player there who might have a hard time reading a book, but you put him in a craps game and he'll win." It was not always possible to interview athletes on scouting trips. Perspectives from coaches could be helpful, though often they required corroboration from others. Some college coaches lied, or embellished, to increase the allure of their players.

As if the white-owned motels in the South weren't difficult enough to figure out.

Too many times Bill Jr. was given rooms in these two-story motels on the top floor, in the back, farthest from the swimming pool. Issuing his own challenge, Bill Jr. began to ask at motel front desks for a room downstairs that faced the swimming pool. Then he studied the reaction of the white clerks, noting their tension and their silence.

This was the scout's life.

CHAPTER 4

NOLL & MEAN JOE

THE TWO MEN ARRIVED IN Pittsburgh in January 1969 only twenty-four hours apart. Coach Chuck Noll showed up on Monday, January 27, and Mean Joe Greene was drafted on Tuesday, the twenty-eighth. After thirteen head coaches and nearly thirteen thousand days of Steeler stumbling—thirty-five years without a single playoff victory, from FDR through LBJ—here came, as if factory-ordered, the head coach who, through the force of his conviction, would lead the team's transformation, and the defensive tackle on whose broad back the dynasty would be constructed.

Noll was an apple rolled not far from a mighty football tree, Paul Brown of Cleveland, for whom he played seven NFL seasons. Brown was like the Benjamin Franklin of pro football, a founding father and peerless innovator. He was at least forty-five minutes ahead of everyone else in the game. Brown created the draw play. He created the playbook. He put the classroom in football, as his former player Don Shula liked to say. His ego was the size of the solar system's tenth planet. In politics, he was conservative. In football, he was a pragmatist. Brown kept himself at a remove from his players, who feared his wrath. Noll had a smaller ego, kept the same distance from his men, and was every bit Brown's equal as a football pragmatist. Noll emphasized organization, structure, fundamentals. He didn't believe in pep talks or false chatter.

Mean Joe Greene was Pittsburgh's second coming of Joe Magarac. A Bunyan-like folk hero to immigrant steelworkers, Magarac (pronounced *mah-gah-rats*) was said to have risen from an iron ore mine as a man made of steel. Tall as a smokestack, with shoulders as wide as a steel mill door, Magarac bent red-hot iron ingots with his bare hands, and walked along the furnace rims as the greatest Pittsburgh steelworker that ever lived. Joe Greene stood six-foot-four, 275 pounds, shoulders as wide as a steel mill door, and he moved through the line of scrimmage like a Texas windstorm sweeping across the prairie, a swirling force of destructive energy. Other defensive linemen were bigger, some were faster, and in the weight room more than a few could outlift him. But Greene had a compensatory quality: a state of mind, an attitude. He played with rage.

The signature traits of Noll and Greene were evident long before they arrived in Pittsburgh. You just had to look hard, and in obscure places, to find them.

Cleveland 1958: snow, wind, a parked car, engine running. On the practice field, the Cleveland Browns muttered about their fate and their coach, Paul Brown. In the heated warmth of his automobile parked alongside the field, PB sipped hot cocoa from a thermos, careful not to burn his lips, and watched his players, wet and chilled, and enjoyed their misery. Now, the messenger guard on offense, the rotating emissary between PB and quarterback Milt Plum, pulled up to PB's passenger-side door: number 65, Chuck Noll. An undersized technician, determined, quiet, and studious (he attended law school classes at night), Noll absorbed everything. At twenty-six, and in his sixth NFL season, Noll was a thoroughly competent guard, though not a star; sometimes he played linebacker, too. In the draft's late rounds, PB often selected a few local boys, as he did with Noll from the University of Dayton with the 239th overall pick. He didn't expect Noll to make the team; no one did, except Noll. PB met some kids from Dayton, and they asked, "How's the Pope doing?" He realized they meant Noll, and asked why they called him by that name. "Because he can do no wrong," one replied. Noll's college coach had given him that nickname for his technical proficiency.

PB rolled down his car window. Noll felt the blast of warm air, like a Caribbean visit, a pleasant thought. He smelled hot cocoa, brown and chalky, on PB's breath. PB, his face in a sneer, called out the next play, phlegm in his husky voice: "Thirty-seven! GIVE IT TO THE BIG MAN!" He rolled up the window, no time for questions or conversation. His windshield steam-clouded from the hot cocoa. Noll ran from the cocoa and the Caribbean warmth back to the offensive huddle, snow falling. He repeated the emperor's directive: "Thirty-seven. GIVE IT TO THE BIG MAN!" The big man, Jim Brown, an exceptional, explosive runner, would rather be anywhere but on this practice field. Chuck Noll, on the other hand, would rather be nowhere else.

Postgame, Coy Martin's Diner, Temple, Texas, autumn 1963: seventeen-year-old Joe Greene of Dunbar High School and a few of his teammates walked into the diner, just a few blocks from where Greene lived. They came for burgers and malts. At the counter they saw players from the opposing team, Waco Carver, which had just put its usual licking on Dunbar. Defeat brought out the worst in Greene. Defeat antagonized him. It diminished him. A man-child linebacker of nearly 250 pounds, Greene was kicked out of every game as a sophomore for his on-field conduct and nine games more as a junior. He was known to run over referees *intentionally.* He grew up fatherless, and his mother worked long hours as a domestic for white families. As a youth, Greene had picked cotton and pecans, and at thirteen, already grown into a man's body, he'd turned to construction. On his family's small black-and-white television he watched the resistance to Dr. Martin Luther King's civil rights movement, the fire hoses and attack dogs. And when Greene went downtown, he saw the water fountains marked "Colored."

Segregation shaped Greene's football experience, too. Dunbar played its games across town at an all-white high school, a superior facility, though Dunbar's players never went into the locker room there. They dressed at Dunbar and bused to the games. At halftime they sat in the end zone and discussed strategy as the bands marched next to them. The black schools played on Thursdays or Saturdays in Temple; the more glamorous Friday nights were saved for the white schools. Neither could Greene read about his games in the local newspaper. The *Temple Daily Telegram* hardly acknowledged games played by black high schools.

Now, at the diner, Greene would salvage defeat as only he could.

He snatched an ice cream cone from the hand of an opposing player and smeared it in his face. The player did not retaliate, he knew better, but cursed loudly at Greene as he stepped outside and onto the Waco Carver team bus. Greene followed him with the swagger of a desperado and moved toward the bus. From inside, a player called out to Greene and threw a soda bottle at him, but it struck the closed front door and shattered. In a rage Greene stormed ahead, one man ready to take on an entire team. With his massive hands he pried open the door, though it took some doing. By the time he stepped inside, the opposing team was gone, having escaped the bus through its rear emergency door. A Dunbar teammate grabbed Greene and talked some sense into him. He didn't pursue the opposing players.

No one yet called him Mean, but he was.

The Steelers fired Bill Austin after the team finished 2-11-1 in 1968, a classic "same old Steelers" kind of year. The Rooneys tried to hire Penn State's Joe Paterno as their new head coach. In December 1968, Dan and the Chief met Paterno for breakfast. They brought Vince Lombardi along to help sell Paterno on the pro game. Catholics all, Lombardi spoke about the strength of his faith. The Chief mentioned that his brother Dan was a priest and that two of his sisters were nuns. Paterno said his mother was so devout that each day she prayed for his Nittany Lions to the Infant of Prague and to St. Anthony. He admitted his mother's power of prayer must be really something, since his team had won eighteen games in a row.

The Steelers' sales job didn't work. Paterno decided to stay at Penn State, and the Rooneys turned to several other candidates, including Noll, the Baltimore Colts' young defensive assistant. In the Orange Bowl against Kansas a few weeks later, Penn State failed to convert what would have been a game-winning two-point conversion in the final seconds. However, referees flagged Kansas for having twelve men on the field, and so with no time left on the clock, the Nittany Lions ran another play, and this time scored to win 15–14.

The Chief couldn't resist. He sent Paterno a postcard: "Will trade my brother and two sisters for your mother."

✦ ✦ ✦

In a Madison Avenue moment, with a record 54 million television viewers, Broadway Joe Namath led the New York Jets of the rival American Football League to a 16–7 victory over the NFL's Baltimore Colts in Super Bowl III in Miami. The merger between leagues had been formally signed several years earlier, though still was a year from realization. With this defeat, the Chief and other NFL owners swallowed hard. In the postgame lights, Namath, the game's most valuable player, smiled broadly and mocked the sportswriters who had made the Jets heavy underdogs, saying, "I hope they all eat their pencils and pads." Back in Pittsburgh, Steeler center Ray Mansfield, a veteran known as the Old Ranger, gathered with linebacker Andy Russell and guard Bruce Van Dyke. They saw Namath's performance through the hollow tunnel of the Steelers' season just ended. "It just seemed kind of hopeless," Mansfield would say. "We were saying, 'We'll probably never see the Super Bowl.' "

The defeat was still in Chuck Noll's eyes the next morning. From across the breakfast table, Dan thought that Noll appeared enervated and still angry, but there was a set to his jaw that reflected conviction and strength of character. In this job interview, Noll talked about his working-class upbringing on the East Side of Cleveland. He had grown up in an integrated neighborhood—half of his youth football team was black—in the same house in which his mother had been raised with twelve siblings. Noll's father, a butcher, suffered from Parkinson's disease and often had been unable to work. Times were spare, difficult. Noll's mother worked for a florist, and Noll got a job at a meat market while attending Benedictine High School. The job paid fifty-five cents an hour. At Benedictine, in a class of 252, Noll graduated 28th. He might have played football for Notre Dame but suffered an epileptic seizure there during a practice before his freshman season. Noll went to play at Dayton instead.

Noll spoke frankly about his perceptions of the Steelers, a team the Colts had pounded 41–7 in September. He told Dan the Steelers lacked talent. Deficiencies, he said, existed in all areas. The words that rang in Dan's ears after the interview ended were the corrective measures through which Noll proposed to lead the team into the future: *fundamentals, teaching, building through the draft.* Dan thought Noll impressive, perhaps even extraordinary. He had one concern: Noll was young, maybe too young, just thirty-seven. Then again, Shula was just thirty-three years old when the Colts hired him as head coach in 1963, and a year later Shula had the Colts in first place. Back home, Dan told the Chief, "Let's keep Noll on our list." He continued to move through his process. He interviewed ten candidates. Cleveland assistant Nick Skorich was high on his list, but Browns owner Art Modell said his aging head coach, Blanton Collier, had developed hearing problems and that he intended to promote Skorich when Collier stepped aside.

The Steelers might have considered Lombardi. The night before Super Bowl III, Lombardi, the Packers' general manager, had dinner in Miami with Washington Redskin owner Edward Bennett Williams. EBW knew that Lombardi wanted to return to coaching after a year away, and that his wife, Marie, a New Yorker, wanted out of the Wisconsin cold. That night over dinner, EBW made his pitch to Lombardi. He offered him the Redskins' head coaching job, spiced with the dual role of general manager, a big salary, stock options, and a driver. "You know," Williams said, "you're the only one I want." The Chief never would pay so much to a head coach, not even to Lombardi. Besides, in Pittsburgh, Lombardi would have to start virtually from scratch. The Steelers' cupboard was nearly bare. Lombardi accepted EBW's offer before month's end.

In the meantime, Noll came to Pittsburgh for a second interview, meeting with the Chief and Dan. The Chief liked Noll's composure, his values, his intensity, and, perhaps most importantly, his apparent appreciation for Pittsburgh. Art Jr. horned his way into their conversation. He had questions about scouting. He asked Noll for his views about black players and if he had a quota system in mind. Both Dan and the Chief stared coldly at Art Jr., but Noll didn't hedge in his answer. "I don't care what color my players are," he said. "You find good players where they are."

Noll's teammates with the Browns during the 1950s could have vouched for him, and his work ethic. "Chuck was the kind of player that just kept working at it," his old Browns teammate linebacker Walt Michaels said. "He was just very quiet, very meticulous, very dedicated." Dedicated, maybe, but not fast on the field. The Cleveland Browns in the late 1950s had future Hall of Famers Jim Brown and Bobby Mitchell in their backfield, placing a premium on the mobility of their linemen. "Jim Brown and I spent all our time pushing him," Mitchell recalled, "and saying, 'Chuck, get out of the way! GET OUT OF THE WAY!' and just running over him, you know?" Mitchell laughed. "He was always where he was supposed to be, but he was also in your way!"

His toughness on the field was unquestioned. Once lined up at nose tackle for a punt, Noll delivered a blow to the head of Philadelphia's all-pro center Chuck Bednarik, whose helmet flew off as he crashed to the ground. Bednarik, known as Concrete Charlie, later said, "I saw these little black dots and the yellow thing." Bednarik also saw the jersey number 65. To Noll he sneered, "I'll get you!" Vengeance came four seasons later. With Noll walking off the field, helmet in hand, Concrete Charlie delivered a blow to Noll's head that dropped him. The league fined Bednarik for his actions, and encouraged him to apologize. Bednarik tried, approaching Noll later and saying, "I want to apologize for what happened in Philadelphia," at which point Noll's face drew close to his, only inches apart. Noll's eyes lit with fury as he said, *"Bull . . . shit!"*

Noll's seriousness and single-mindedness seemed a natural outgrowth of his upbringing and his postwar seasons with the Browns. The Cleveland players were a tough-minded lot. Some of Noll's older teammates had fought in World War II, others in Korea. Most football players liked to tell war stories, but those told by Noll's Browns teammates were real war stories, or, as Michaels said, "at the end of these stories you were either dead or alive." Tackle Lou Groza had served in the army in Okinawa, center Frank Gatski as an infantryman in Europe, and end Dante Lavelli in Bastogne during the Battle of the Bulge. "Dante told us he broke the forty-yard-dash time when the German Tiger tanks were coming," Michaels said. Four of Michaels's older brothers fought in World War II, and one, a marine, was killed at Guadalcanal. Sixty years later, Michaels could still hear his mother's pained cry when the telegram arrived. Even Paul Brown, commissioned in 1944, served as a navy lieutenant at Great Lakes Naval Training Station. "If you went through that period of World War Two, when you knew that it was either us or them, or else they were going to control the world," Michaels says, "it just created a different dedication."

Epilepsy shortened Noll's NFL playing career. Years later, Brown explained to Cincinnati sports columnist Tom Callahan why Noll's playing days with the Browns ended prematurely, in 1959, when Noll was just twenty-seven years old. Noll suffered an epileptic seizure on the team plane. He told Brown that he had medication to prevent another episode. But Brown worried that Noll might have a seizure on the football field. Brown couldn't, and wouldn't, allow that to happen, and so, in a professional football player's rite of passage, it was time for Noll to move on and think about his life's work.

Noll pondered his future. He had been married three years, and he told his wife, Marianne, that his heart was not in law, that what he knew best was football. He warned her about the coaching life. It was intense, full immersion. With her consent, he became a defensive assistant to Sid Gillman of the Chargers, whose teams during the next six seasons would win five division titles and one AFL championship. Not only did Noll demonstrate techniques for his players on the practice field, he also explained them in detailed writing—how to backpedal, the cornerback's proper posture and positioning while covering a receiver. In 1966 Noll joined Shula's Baltimore Colts and helped direct one of the NFL's premier defenses. Dan examined Noll's career scorecard: sixteen seasons in pro football as a player and assistant coach under three of the game's finest heads coaches; eleven division titles and four league championships won. He acknowledged that Noll's character references from Brown, Gilman, and Shula were A-plus, but what most impressed him was "the man himself."

With the 1969 NFL draft fast approaching, and Buffalo and New England both in pursuit of Noll, and Noll seeking assurances that the final say on draft day would be his, Dan hired him as the fourteenth coach in the Steelers' history. Art Jr. liked Noll but wanted the final say on draft day himself. But the Chief told him, "The coach is the one who's going to get fired if he doesn't win, so he should be the one making decisions on his players." Art Jr. fell in line, but he would be no one's flunky.

Noll arrived in Pittsburgh for the press conference on January 27, looking like a husky, young, sandy-haired executive in suit and tie. Longtime *Pittsburgh Press* sports editor Les Biederman was captivated, writing, "He's a good speaker, gives you the idea he's a solid man and appears to be confident without being boastful."

One reporter asked if his goal was to make the Steelers respectable.

"Respectability?" Noll said. "Who wants to be respectable? That's spoken like a true loser."

Another reporter that day told Noll, "This is the city of losers." Noll's look was serious when he replied, "We'll change history."

Jess Thompson, the BLESTO combine scout in the Southwest, had been in the football business forty-two years. He had a way with phrases in his written reports about college players, among them "He runs like a chicken with frozen feet," and "He's as fat as a town dog," and "He couldn't break a dish with a ball peen hammer in both hands." About Joe Greene of North Texas State, Thompson turned to capital letters: "AGILE, MOBILE & HOSTILE AS HELL . . . He is definitely my kind of football player." At defensive tackle, Greene coiled up at the line of scrimmage and, at the snap, physically overpowered men in front of him, often breaking through double teams. With hands like waffle irons, he head-slapped offensive linemen who thought they'd been struck by baseball bats. Greene saw himself cut from the mold of the Dallas Cowboys' all-pro Bob Lilly. As a senior, Greene was named the nation's best college lineman, which meant, come NFL draft day in 1969, he would not sneak up on anyone. Greene's college coach, Rod Rust, described him, evocatively, as "a fort on foot."

Art Jr. liked what he saw in Greene. He made multiple scouting trips to Denton, where the North Texas State team nickname—"the Mean Green"—would over time attach naturally, and rhythmically, to Greene. Thus was the name Mean Joe Greene born. After examining North Texas State game films on November 13, 1968, Art Jr. wrote of Greene, "Quick as a big cat. Forces opponents to double team him. Use of hands ok, should be able to develop a fine use of hands and arms. Does a real good job of rushing passer. Puts out all the time. Would give us the inside pass rush we have been looking for."

Noll had scouted Greene for the Colts the previous spring. He watched game films, saw Greene practice, and then interviewed him afterward. "There was no doubt in my mind that this guy loved to play football and wanted to play very badly," Noll said. The Steelers, picking fourth, knew Buffalo would take Southern Cal running back O. J. Simpson with the draft's initial pick, and that Notre Dame tackle George Kunz would go to Atlanta with the second. But not until Philadelphia took running back Leroy Keyes of Purdue with the third choice were they certain that Greene was theirs. Never mind that most Steeler fans had never heard of Greene, or that many of those fans preferred Notre Dame quarterback Terry Hanratty from nearby Butler, Pennsylvania. As it happened, the Steelers got Hanratty in the second round anyway. In Greene, the Steelers got, according to Art Jr., "the most important guy we ever drafted."

His rage . . . where did it come from?

He was so big as a toddler that his aunt playfully suggested that he might become the next Joe Louis, and so she began to call him Joe, and everyone else did, too. He was in grade school before he realized his given name was Charles Edward Greene. He often wondered how different his life might have been with a father in the house. As the biggest student in his elementary school class, older boys targeted him for fights. He suffered his bruises and defeats. "Everybody wanted to beat up the big young kid," Greene said. He didn't fight back. Sometimes he ran. He got faster as a result. "I had seven or eight ways to get home," he said. This was before football. "When I started fighting back," Greene said, "then I got the reputation of being a bully."

Football is a game of pain. *Controlled violence*, Lombardi called it. Lombardi knew from experience that many boys from turbulent backgrounds excelled at the game. As a parochial school football coach in Englewood, New Jersey, during the 1940s, he tapped local police as informal scouts, asking them to identify borderline juvenile delinquents who might be prospects.

In Greene there was turbulence. By ninth grade he weighed 203 pounds. Something inside of him was changing, too, something that schoolmate Leonard "Speedy" Vance didn't recognize, and he would pay for it. Though football teammates and friends, Vance often intimidated Greene and whipped him in neighborhood fights, embarrassing him in front of friends and girls. Several years older than Greene and nearly as big, Vance finally pushed him too far. He stole five dollars from atop Greene's family television set, money that Greene's mother had saved to pay for insurance to allow her son to play high school football. The next afternoon, Greene confronted Vance. "Yeah, I took it," Vance said. He jutted his chin forward and said, "Whatcha goin' to do 'bout it?" Greene punished Vance for his transgression. "I popped him on the side of his head as hard as I could. And I kept popping him," Greene said. It was over quickly. "I must've mopped the floor with him that day," Greene said decades later. "I gave him a good beating." The fight had a transformative effect on Greene. "I wasn't afraid anymore . . . I was able to find myself as a man after that fight."

Though he drew little interest from coaches at major colleges, Greene became increasingly compelled by football. He drove to Denton to introduce himself to coaches at North Texas State University, the alma mater of Kansas City Chief running back Abner Hayes, the 1960 AFL Player of the Year. Greene thought to wear a jersey with sleeves cut off at the biceps. He did so as part of a grand plan: before meeting the coaches, he stopped in a bathroom down the hall and put himself through several dozen push-ups, the blood rush expanding his biceps. "Those coaches, their eyes just got so big," Greene said, "they jumped out of their seats."

He was big and country strong, with soulful eyes. A freshman coed from Dallas noticed him on campus. She saw him dance the Philly Dog at a party. Greene was so massive she assumed he must be a senior. (He was only a sophomore.) Her heart was aflutter. "I was like Diana Ross when she saw Billy Dee Williams in *Lady Sings the Blues*," Agnes Greene recalled with a laugh about the man who became her husband. They began their courtship, and oftentimes Greene, safety Chuck Beatty, and a few others piled into a teammate's old Chevy and drove the twenty-eight miles to Agnes's parents' house in Dallas. Her father, known as Daddy-O, wasn't smitten with football, or with the men who played it, and he grew even less smitten when he looked into his refrigerator one morning and realized that the food he expected to find wasn't there because those football players had eaten it the night before. Not to mention the clothes they wore! Those wild colors! Those hats! Those boots! Beatty, Greene's college roommate who would also be drafted by the Steelers in 1969, showed up once in a red leather suit. Daddy-O said, "These guys dress awfully peculiar!"

A year later, still in school, they married at Agnes's sister's house in

Dallas, the irrepressible Beatty, no red leather flash this time, standing beside Mean Joe as best man and calling the groom's mom "Mother Dear." Money was tight for the newlyweds, but Joe and Agnes Greene had dreams as big as Texas. After the honeymoon, Joe even bragged to his father-in-law, "I took Agnes all the way to Fort Worth!"

Training camp, Latrobe, Pennsylvania, summer 1969. Amid the lush rolling hills of the Laurel Highlands, forty miles from Pittsburgh's smokestacks, the Steelers set up camp at Saint Vincent College, where sixteen years before, Art Jr. stood on a chair, wearing a beanie, a pant leg rolled up, delivering his speech "Why the Steelers Stink." Chuck Noll, another new head coach, was arriving, the team's fourth in six years, which was no big news to Andy Russell and Ray Mansfield. Drinking buddies in Latrobe, the two Steeler veterans were fast becoming locker room griots, keepers of the old stories. In 1963 Russell was congratulated by a University of Missouri teammate for "getting drafted." "What are you talking about?" Russell replied. "I'm ROTC." Russell thought he was bound for Vietnam. "No, I mean the Pittsburgh Steelers drafted you," his teammate said. Russell showed up to the Steelers' practices at South Park, a field inside a horse track where rookies were made to walk in a line each day picking up the little rocks they found along the way. *So this is the NFL!* Russell thought. Mansfield was a kindred spirit, a bad-bodied center, smart, physical, and well versed in the tricks of his craft, claimed by the Steelers in 1964 for $100 off the Eagles' waiver wire. The two players first met in 1963 as NFL opponents in an exhibition game in Bethlehem, Pennsylvania, Russell on kickoff return, dropping the oncoming Mansfield with a block at his ankles. "Nice block, asshole!" Mansfield said from the ground, and when he got up he dug his elbow into Russell's stomach.

Russell and Mansfield listened closely as Noll, speaking plainly and without emotion, addressed the Steelers for the first time. Noll said he had studied all the Steeler game films from 1968. He knew why Pittsburgh lost. It wasn't attitude. The players just weren't any good. They lacked size, speed, and, worst of all, their techniques were tragically flawed. Noll explained his approach. He said he would not make pep talks before games.

He wanted men whose motivation came from within. Thus, to transform the Steelers into a winner, he said, he would need to get rid of nearly every player. It was time to move on. Players shifted uncomfortably in their chairs. That afternoon, they bounded onto the practice field, hooting and howling, as was their custom, until Noll silently held up his hand. "You do not win games," he told them, and not for the last time, "with false chatter." By the time the Steelers would reach their first Super Bowl five years later, only five players from Noll's first team survived his purge, including Russell and Mansfield.

On the practice field in Latrobe, and in meetings, players began to hear their new coach's catchphrases. There were many. To linemen: "Play with leverage. Strike a rising blow." To ballcarriers: "When you break into the open, always look for the low numbers [smaller defensive backs] because you may be able to break their tackles." To the team at large: "You can't win with dummies." "Football is a game of habits." "If we do this right, we will be greater than the sum of the parts."

Noll said "the battle of the hitting" was the game's essence. "You hit him where he is soft. . . . If you do it right, you feel good. If you do it wrong, he feels good." Russell noticed Noll's devotion to the game by the meticulous way he taught the finer points of the three-point stance, and blocking and tackling techniques, even with free-agent rookies who had little chance of making the team. Noll appreciated Russell's intellectual approach. Even so, he probed deeper in conversations with his linebacker, wanting to know Russell's thought process on certain plays. No coach had ever asked Andy Russell about that.

Joe Greene didn't hear Noll's first speech. He was a contract holdout, which infuriated the Chief. "Who is he, anyway?" the Chief huffed to Art Jr. "I don't know that he's so good." But when Greene finally met the Chief, the defensive tackle never would have known how angry the Steelers' owner was. Greene and his agent, Bucky Woy, negotiated with Dan at the Roosevelt Hotel, the offers going back and forth. "Let's go talk to my father," Dan said. Greene saw Dan approach the Chief in his office and quietly explain the impasse in the negotiations. The first words Greene heard the Chief say were, "Oh, give it to him!" Greene signed a five-year deal reportedly worth, with incentive bonuses, nearly $250,000, an average of more than $45,000 per year. "Pretty snappy for a defensive tackle," Woy crowed. The Chief shook Greene's hand and gave him his first cigar.

At Latrobe, Noll put Greene to the test immediately. He ran "gassers," fifty-three yards across the width of the field, four at a time. Out of shape from inactivity during his holdout, Greene labored to complete the drill as a young boy stood at the sideline, heckling him: "C'mon, Joe! A number one draft choice ought to be in better shape than that!" Greene considered flattening the kid on his next turn but thought better of it. Next, Noll called for the Oklahoma Drill, a Steeler favorite, in which a defensive player faced off against a blocker, both starting from three-point stances. Typically an assistant coach handed off the ball to a running back, and the defensive player had to slip the blocker and tackle the running back within a confined space. The drill showcased strength and technique, the combat cheered by the entire team. Veteran offensive linemen couldn't wait to dismantle Greene. They lined up to get a shot at him, blood in their eyes. "To me, he's just another big, fat-butted defensive tackle," Mansfield said.

Greene had high regard for his own ability but little respect for anyone else's. No matter what an offensive lineman might try—a move he hadn't seen, illegally holding him—Greene would take care of him, and maybe punish and humiliate him in the process. The Old Ranger went first, winking at other veterans. A symbol of the old guard, Mansfield got tossed by Greene, who then slammed into the running back. *My God!* Mansfield thought. No hoots or howls from teammates. Greene's strength, his violence, and the sight of the fallen Old Ranger produced a teamwide silence. Greene took on each offensive lineman, Van Dyke, Sam Davis, and the others, and bent them all to his will. "It was," said Hanratty, "a thing of beauty to watch." Running back Dick Hoak overheard one offensive tackle say to another, "We might as well pack our bags. . . ." Beatty smiled, having seen it all before, at North Texas State.

Rookie defensive end L. C. Greenwood, one of Bill Nunn's early finds at the historically black Arkansas Agricultural, Mechanical & Normal College in Pine Bluff, Arkansas, said, "Joe was nasty. He kicked them all over the place." Greenwood noticed the veteran offensive linemen, initially eager for their turn with Greene, suddenly backing up and moving to the end of a different line, hoping no one noticed. In time Greene and Greenwood would become close friends, half of the Steel Curtain front four, but now "Joe was a first-round draft choice and I was a number ten, so Joe wasn't messing with chumps like me. He was with the big boys, and he was one of the big boys."

"You've got to be able to get into the minds of your people," Noll told the press, "and sell what you are doing." In Latrobe, he encouraged Greene to express his physical force on the field. But when his top draft pick kicked down the locked door of an equipment room at Saint Vincent to get his gear, Noll stopped by Greene's room later that night. From the doorway Noll said, "That will be five hundred dollars," and then he left.

The Steelers won the opener in 1969, and then lost the remaining thirteen games—their 1-13 kerplunk, the worst record in franchise history. They suffered lopsided embarrassments, a 38–7 defeat to the Bears at Wrigley Field, and 52–14 to the Vikings at Metropolitan Stadium. Noll bit his lower lip on the sideline as he watched the unwatchable, staying his course, unloading players who didn't fit his system, determined to make the Steelers his. The mounting defeats drew out the violent storms from within Greene. He acted like a vigilante seeking his own form of justice. At Yankee Stadium he chased the Giants' scrambling quarterback Fran Tarkenton all across the Bronx without catching him, Tarkenton infuriating him by teasing him after each escape. Finally Greene got him in the third quarter. "I hit him as hard as I could hit him," he said. But a yellow penalty flag flew, and hit Greene in the helmet. Tarkenton teased, "Guess what, Joe? We're out of bounds!" Greene got ejected for this malicious late hit more than five yards beyond the sideline.

The nickname Mean Joe took flight in the sports pages. In grandstands around the league, Greene began to see effigies—"these grotesque figures"—carrying the name "Mean Joe." "I didn't like it," he said. "I didn't like it at all." More than once, Dan heard people say, "You can't have a guy like this. He's undisciplined," and each time he responded, firmly, "Hey, he is the guy!" In the debacle at Minnesota, referees flagged Greene for another late hit near the Vikings' bench. At one point, Greene rushed to the nearby Steeler bench, grabbed trainer Ralph Berlin's tape-cutting scissors, and briefly chased after an opponent. At Wrigley Field, Chicago linebacker Dick Butkus, blocking for punt returner Gayle Sayers, blind-sided the oncoming Greenwood, knocking him unconscious near the Steelers' bench. Butkus stood over the fallen rookie like Ali stood over Liston. Onto the field stepped Greene. Eye-to-eye with Butkus, Greene threatened him and spat in his face. "Butkus was standing there with this [spit] thing hanging down his face mask," Mansfield said. Mansfield thought, *This is going to be the greatest fight in the history of the NFL!* But Butkus turned and walked away. Decades later, Mansfield said, "That was the beginning of the end of the Pittsburgh Steelers' problems." Greene kept ripping through offensive lines as if they were made of papier-mâché, and won the NFL's Defensive Rookie of the Year award.

The Steelers and Bears shared the worst record in the league, and so Pete Rozelle tossed a 1921 silver dollar in the air to determine the first choice in the 1970 draft. The Bears called heads, but it came up tails. The Steelers wanted Terry Bradshaw, Louisiana Tech's strong-armed quarterback, six-foot-three with an expansive chest, a player of impressive physical skills. One scout told Art Jr., "This guy's like buying Xerox. There might not be another one like him for twenty years." Noll wanted to see Bradshaw for himself, and after reviewing game films admitted, "Boy, he has a real rifle arm!" "You kind of feel 'em or smell 'em" is how BLESTO's Jess Thompson described rare prospects such as Bradshaw. "A pro all the way." Several NFL teams offered the Steelers multiple veteran players in a trade for the rights to draft Bradshaw, but they wouldn't bargain.

They chose Bradshaw in the first round, and on Nunn's recommendation, defensive back Mel Blount from Southern University in the third round. The next year's draft brought seven future starters: linebacker Jack Ham, receiver Frank Lewis, guard Gerry "Moon" Mullins, tight end Larry Brown, safety Mike Wagner, defensive end Dwight White, and Texas Southern's bearish defensive tackle Ernie Holmes. These players reported for physicals at the Pittsburgh Hilton, where Art Jr. heard a knock on the door of his suite, a soft-spoken fellow in blue slacks, a white golf shirt, and light jacket, saying, "I'm looking for Mr. Rooney." Impatient, Art Jr. asked, "Do you have a message for me?" "No," he said, "I'm Jack Ham." Art Jr. blushed with embarrassment. Ham looked so small out of uniform.

The puzzle pieces began to fit. In his continuing anguish, Greene wondered about Noll's methods. *Damn, why are we still doing these things when they're not working?* "But as we evolved and got better players, we kept doing the same things and they started working," Greene said. In the final game of the 1970 season, the Eagles rallied to beat the Steelers 30–20 at Franklin Field, ending the Steelers' season at 5-9. In his frustration in that game's final minute, Greene picked up the football at the line of scrimmage as the Eagles' offense approached. He heaved it on a high arc, deep into the grandstands, and walked off the field. The game and season were not done, but he was. "The ball went far," Dan would say, still seeing the mighty arc. "I mean faaarrrrr! It was like Bradshaw threw it."

Privately the Chief kept saying that Chuck Noll was remarkable, for though he lost games, he never lost his team.

The Chief felt the stirrings of bigger moments yet to come.

CHAPTER 5

THE ROCK & THE FRENCHMAN

ON THE FIELD THE STEELERS played to crowds in the tens of thousands, and via television in the millions. In the locker room, they played to each other, knowingly and unknowingly providing antidotes to the game's sufferings. In personality, running backs Rocky Bleier and John "Frenchy" Fuqua could not have been more different: one understated, the other full of pageantry; one often as the butt of jokes, the other as a teller of jokes. What linked them was that on that smaller stage both did vital work. They kept the Steelers laughing, and the team's heartbeat steady and strong.

Players sensed the gravity in Noll's voice at an evening team meeting in Latrobe in August 1969. Rocky Bleier, Noll said, had been wounded by an exploding grenade and shot through the thigh in a Vietnamese rice paddy. According to reports, Noll said, Bleier was "pretty lucky" to survive. A Steelers special teams player, Bleier had received his military induction notice in the mail at Pitt Stadium during the 1968 season, imperiling his pro football dream. In the next game, against Cleveland, he ran downfield in kick coverage like a crazy man, hurling his body horizontally into the Browns' blocking wedge, hoping to break a rib or some other bone that would cause him to fail his army physical. He got up, unscathed. As Namath created his legend in Super Bowl III, Bleier watched on television from his army training barracks in Georgia, spit-shining his boots.

Bleier was an overachiever, a favorite among the Steelers, especially the Chief, who mailed newspaper clippings, Steeler game programs, and postcard well-wishes that Bleier read in Vietnam. The Chief and Bleier had similar story lines: as Catholics who grew up above their father's saloons, and as small running backs who played football with aggression. The Chief liked to tell the story of how he had visited Bob and Ellen Bleier's crowded bar in Appleton, Wisconsin, in 1968 when the Steelers were to play the Packers in an exhibition game thirty miles away, in Green Bay. He introduced himself to Ellen Bleier as she busily served workers from nearby paper mills who came for their boilermakers after their shifts finished. She welcomed him and then handed a number to a man not accustomed to waiting. Bleier's was a working-class saloon, with an ornate wooden bar, a tin ceiling, private booths with curtains that dated to Prohibition, and fish fries on Fridays. In Appleton, Senator Joseph McCarthy's hometown, residents tended to be conservative, God-fearing, and Lombardi-loving. Bob Bleier was proud of his son as a football hero. When his boy was yet in a crib, he had taken a few customers in back to see him, saying, "Son of a bitch looks like a little rock!" Rocky Bleier starred at Notre Dame, and was team captain when the Fighting Irish won the 1966 intercollegiate national title. Once, at the Left Guard, a supper club in Appleton owned by the Packers' Fuzzy Thurston, the Green Bay running back Donny Anderson was brought to the table to meet Bleier, newly crowned as NCAA football champion. Anderson, blond and handsome, smiled and congratulated Bleier, then held up his hand, showing off his Super Bowl ring, and said, "But I'll bet you don't have one of these!"

On August 15, 1969, with the 196th Light Infantry Brigade, Company C, in Chu Lai, on the coast of the South China Sea, Bleier sent birthday greetings to his younger sister Pamela: "I've been talking to God a lot, and He's taking good care of me." Then he added, "Take care and remember my platoon motto: 'Eat shit; a million Vietnamese flies can't be wrong.' " Five days later, he helicoptered with his platoon into the Que San Valley. He carried a rocket launcher, and marched through the jungle's elephant grass and dense underbrush, water splashing over his boots. As Viet Cong snipers and machine guns did their killing work, Bleier crawled on his stomach through a rice paddy, and a bullet ripped through his thigh. Later that day, crouched behind his captain, a lobbed grenade hit the captain's back and tumbled like a football, end over end. Bleier saw it and sprang out of his crouch just as the grenade exploded. Shrapnel scattered and tore into Bleier's right leg and foot, soaking his pants with blood. He hobbled, crawled, and then was carried through enemy fire toward a medevac helicopter. His dangling legs catching on trees and bushes, it took six hours to cover two miles. Over the final segment, in the night darkness, a black soldier whose name he did not know carried him fireman-style over his shoulder. Fearful that he would be left behind for the Viet Cong, Bleier heard the black soldier softly encourage, "We're going to get there," and they did, the black soldier disappearing from Bleier's life forever.

In a Tokyo military hospital, doctors told Bleier that one day he would walk again. He asked about football. No, they said, impossible. We're sorry. The grenade had gashed his right foot in three places: along the instep to the ball of the foot, beside the big toe, and below the second toe. His body was, by US Army definition, 40 percent disabled. War correspondents, always in search of human interest stories, found Bleier: the Associated Press, United Press International, and NBC television. In Appleton, Ellen Bleier learned that her son had been wounded and refused to leave her apartment, upstairs from the bar. She feared the worst, a mother's prerogative. Telegrams kept arriving, the local police accompanying them, and each time she held her breath. The telegrams reported her son's condition as improving. She reserved judgment, also a mother's prerogative. When she saw a newspaper photograph of him, the Rock in bed at the Tokyo hospital, his left leg wasn't visible and she knew with absolute certainty that his left leg was no more. It must have been blown off or amputated, and she wept.

Another postcard from the Chief arrived at the Tokyo hospital: "Rock. The team's not doing well. We need you. Art Rooney." Back in Pittsburgh, the Chief pointed at Bleier's old cubicle in the Steelers' locker room and told equipment manager Tony Parisi to make sure no one else got it. "That's Rocky's locker," the Chief said.

Bleier returned to Pittsburgh that fall. Much thinner and wearing a handlebar mustache, a pale version of the powerful running back he once was, Bleier limped slowly onto the Pitt Stadium field, using a cane.

A thunderous war hero's ovation washed over him, the Chief and a few Steeler players brought to tears.

Nearly every morning the following summer, Bleier's sister Pamela accompanied him to a local track in Appleton, stopwatch in hand. Bleier, with shrapnel in his right foot still, tried to sprint, but fell to the ground in pain. He started again, Pamela pressed the stopwatch, and he fell again, his right foot throbbing. *Oh, God!* Pamela thought. *This is such a waste of time.* She admired her older brother's determination, but this was hopeless. At that moment her view was the same as the Pittsburgh Steelers': as a professional football player, big brother was finished.

Every day John Fuqua had a new story to tell, or an outrageous garment to wear, each more memorable than the last. He turned the Steelers' locker room into his campfire, his arrival announcing to teammates and sportswriters, "Gather 'round, boys!" In his best story, Fuqua was a French count who fell asleep while sunning on the French Riviera. When he awoke, he discovered that he had turned black, and so he lived his life as Negro royalty. The Pittsburgh press ate it up, especially the Steelers' radio man Myron Cope, who took to calling him Count Frenchy Fuqua. "I played soccer in the old country," Fuqua said once. Then, turning in a new direction, he said, "My father came down from Quebec and married my mother. I haven't been back to Quebec since he passed."

Arriving in 1970 in a trade with the New York Giants, Fuqua was a locker room vaudevillian with a comic's touch. He spoke through a bemused smile and with a slight lisp. Teammates loved his sense of theater, and grew accustomed to seeing him driving Cadillacs or Lincolns, and seeing bill collectors show up at the locker room seeking to reconcile his overdue payments. Every morning at six thirty at training camp in Latrobe, Fuqua turned up the volume on his Bose speakers in his dormitory room and blasted *In-A-Gadda-Da-Vida* by Iron Butterfly. Joe Greene and others threatened to throw cold water on Fuqua, but he locked his door and kept the volume high. Noll occasionally visited him late at night in his dorm room to listen to classical music on Fuqua's headphones, while across the room Fuqua, eager for his coach to leave, pretended to read his playbook. The Frenchman ran hard, both on the field and off, and rushed for a club-record 218 yards in a 1970 game against the Eagles. Once he asked Bleier to check outside the locker room's front door to see if Fuqua's wife was waiting for him in their car. "Yeah," Bleier said, after he had looked, "she's out front." "Thanks," Fuqua said, and Bleier saw Fuqua finish dressing and go out the back door.

In truth, Fuqua had been raised in the Detroit ghetto known as Black Bottom, only a block from the New Bethel Baptist Church, where he heard the explosive singing voice of Aretha Franklin, the minister's daughter, nearly blow down the steeple. He was not yet five years old when his mother chased off his father. "Your daddy wanted to run in the street," his mother explained years later, her way of saying that his father liked the ladies. He cried when his daddy left, though soon the father arranged to call his boy every Wednesday night at eight o'clock. On the phone he wowed his son with big stories, science fiction his favorites. Fuqua graduated from Eastern High School and played college ball at Morgan State.

His Steelers legend took shape the day he walked into Our Father's Son boutique in Pittsburgh. In high school Fuqua got a new suit at Easter, and in college he bought two sports jackets to wear while traveling to away games. But now, with a little NFL money in his pocket, this boutique stirred his imagination like his father's stories about Martian ray guns. "Some of the strangest stuff I'd ever seen," he would say, meaning gorgeous bell-bottomed pants, jackets with rhinestones, bright red stretchy pants that squeezed the contours of the hamstrings and calves; a Superstar jacket, black with red stars; and musketeer hats with plumes that might make the Frenchman look just like d'Artagnan.

Count Frenchy Fuqua had found himself. He bought it all, or at least what he could afford. Yet to his dismay, he showed up before the next game and discovered that his roommate, L. C. Greenwood ("We're both Virgos!"), and Chuck Beatty were dressed almost exactly as he.

Myron Cope called for a Steelers' Dress-Off. Small and frenetic, Cope was a talented national magazine writer and before that a staffer at the *Pittsburgh Post-Gazette*, whose city editor suggested a byline other than Myron Sydney Kopelman since, he said, the paper already had too many Jewish-sounding bylines. As a radio commentator and TV personality in Pittsburgh, Cope became like a barking schnauzer in the Steelers' front yard. His nasal tone often was likened to Howard Cosell's, though Cosell said Cope's voice sounded more like "a busboy's squealing cart." Cope liked to say that he was part of a trend toward the obnoxious.

A master of shtick, Cope searched for new angles or colorful gags as fodder to fill airtime on his evening WTAE radio show, *Myron Cope on Sports.* Once he strenuously promoted a streaker, a man who ran across the field at Steelers games, and across local bridges, wearing almost nothing at all. The Chief, at an impromptu press gathering, turned on Cope. "Myron, you are so out of line. That guy is an absolute nut," the Chief said. "You better knock that off," and then he turned on his heels and left. Art Jr. shook his head, smiled, and said, "Congratulations, Myron. He only talks that way to his five boys. You're one of us now." But Fuqua and a few other Steelers reveled in Cope's dress-off idea and readied for a showdown.

The Steelers' locker room became a cavalcade of personalities, no player immune from ribbing. Bleier made it back to the roster, the result of tireless training. In 1972, bigger and faster than before his Vietnam injury, Bleier raced seventeen yards in his only carry of the season, prompting the irrepressible Hanratty to post a small sign at his locker: "Only 983 more to 1,000," a playful jab that would make Hanratty seem a prophet several years later. Dwight White poked fun at Bleier, too, the Mad Dog in the locker room bellowing, "Rock didn't have any real guns over in Vietnam! Rock wasn't in the battles. He was eatin' sushi. Rock was over there with the girls PROPAGATIN' THE RACE!!" Once, White and Greenwood taped Bleier to a goalpost after practice. Another time, they taped him inside the team's dirty-laundry shopping cart and pushed it into Noll's office. (Noll saw Bleier immobilized and smiled.) The locker room provided a racial awakening for some, as the number of black Steelers on the opening day roster grew from thirteen in 1968 to nearly double that amount in the early 1970s.

Players such as Greenwood, Blount, Frank Lewis, and Ernie Holmes had never had white teammates, and Bradshaw had never known a black teammate. Racial boundaries were playfully pushed. At parties Bradshaw's black teammates sent their wives over to dance with him. Bradshaw, blushing, assumed Joe Greene was behind that. Fuqua, meanwhile, teased punter Bobby Walden, a South Georgian, about growing watermelons for him on his farm. Walden teased back, "You people will just steal 'em from me." Pranks eased but did not erase racial divisions. When Joe Gilliam Sr., assistant coach at Tennessee State University, visited his son Joe Jr. at his first Steelers training camp in 1972, he noticed the black Steelers sitting on one side of the cafeteria and the whites on the other. "Joey," the father said later, "I don't want you ever again to sit with those black guys to eat." He ordered his son to sit with Bradshaw, Hanratty, Russell, and other white players. "Daddy, I don't know if they want that," the son replied. "You're the quarterback, and you do it," the father admonished.

Only a handful of Steelers participated in Cope's dress-offs but the team earned a reputation in the league for its mod urban glamour, heavy on leather, capes, and bright colors. In terms of black cultural expression, the Steelers had traveled far in the eight years since Boots Lewis had served as Buddy Parker's valet. As Greenwood said, "People would go out to the airport to see us off, or see us come in. They knew it was a fashion show." Late one night before a game in Houston, Beatty, in three-inch heels, raced down the hotel hallway trying to beat curfew. For the next three weeks his knees pained him, and so trainer Ralph Berlin advised, "Chuck, you need to get out of those heels."

The absurdity was glorious, and part of the essential work of team-building. In one dress-off, Fuqua wore a skin-tight lavender jumpsuit, with a rhinestone-studded silver belt ("over my stomach and right above my privates"), white buccaneer boots, a floor-length lavender cape, musketeer hat, and he carried a glass cane. Fuqua had a broad back that sloped to a small dancer's waist. He wore a size forty-six jacket, and pants with a thirty-two-inch inseam. "Man, Beatty can go in a store and see a bad outfit and wear it right off the rack," Fuqua bemoaned. "My stuff . . . they have to let it out." When *Esquire* magazine named "The Ten Best-Dressed Jocks" in 1972, Fuqua's name wasn't on the list, and he ripped off a letter to the magazine's editor saying the list "makes me think your fashion editor wears white socks and a key chain. [St. Louis pitcher] Bob Gibson in that blue single-breasted looked just right for attending a funeral. . . . I do not know which is more embarrassing—to have been omitted, as I was, from your picks or to have been included among that motley crew." At a party, a man told Fuqua he ought to get a pair of goldfish shoes. "What are those?" Fuqua asked. Platform shoes, the man explained, with clear heels filled with water and live goldfish. They'll swim as you walk, the man explained. Intrigued, Fuqua gave the man his card ("Count Frenchy Fuqua, Three Rivers Stadium, Pittsburgh, Pa."), and the man sent him four pairs, but in the wrong size: ten-and-a-halves instead of elevens. Fuqua bought goldfish, but they died on his way home. He decided to save the too-small shoes for special public appearances. He would buy more goldfish later.

At the great dress-off showdown in the locker room, the Steeler players and Cope crowded around. Beatty wore an Afro wig and a little Red Riding Hood suit, the six-foot-six Greenwood a powder blue jumpsuit and white boots punctuated with a beanie and small wand. "We put up Jim Clack," Bleier said, "as our white hope." Clack, a guard, wore a vest, bow tie, velour pants, and a cap—"not as outlandish as the brothers," Beatty assessed. Then the Frenchman went to work, moving with suave confidence and playing to his crowd, his every turn scripted, dressed ghetto-chic in a full-length white fur and white suit, his teammates shrieking. It was the red snap-brim hat that Bleier would not forget, and the way the Frenchman narrated the finishing touch: the proper way to handle such a hat, breaking down its lid just so, with a sweeping motion and a *Snap!* The Steelers erupted with cheers for the master showman, who bowed, victory his. The Frenchman loved center stage. After games, he said, "I just feel good—when we win—from the top of my gorgeous head to the bottom of my curly toes. I hear the fans chanting when I come out of the locker room, 'Frenchy's comin', Frenchy's comin', what's he got on?' I sign autographs from different poses, so everyone can get a good look at me." A man of flourish, Fuqua understood his role, off the field and on, the small stage informing the big one.

In one dress-off display during the 1972 season, Count Fuqua entered the locker room, and a teammate walked several steps behind, carefully holding the showman's cape, as if it were the American flag, keeping it from dusting the floor, a chore for a rookie, this one a fellow running back by the name of Franco Harris.

CHAPTER 6

IMMACULATE

THE STEELERS NEARLY DID NOT draft Franco Harris. Across the NFL, scouts voiced concern that Harris lacked the necessary toughness and that he was too sensitive and moody. At six-foot-three and 225 pounds, he did not run over people, he ran around them, a novel approach for a fullback. Though big, he lacked muscular definition. When he removed his shirt, scouts weren't impressed. Some NFL teams preferred his smaller backfield teammate at Penn State, Lydell Mitchell. Their coach, Joe Paterno, described the difference between them: if, on the next play, he asked them to run through a brick wall, Mitchell would. But, Paterno said, Harris first would approach the wall, count the number of bricks, and only then would he run through it. On the field, Paterno was saying, Harris was more thoughtful and deliberate, and visualized not just an oncoming tackler but the entire field. Harris had extraordinary promise. In game films, scouts saw glimmerings of greatness, nimble cutbacks, and bursts of breakaway speed. They saw that not on every play, but every fourth or fifth play.

As the draft approached, opinion among the Steeler hierarchy was split. The consensus was to take cornerback Willie Buchanon of San Diego State in the first round. If Buchanon was already selected (as he would be), then the Steelers would choose a running back, and Noll preferred the University of Houston's five-foot-ten, bowling-ball runner Robert Newhouse instead of Harris. But Art Jr. wanted Harris and held his ground, his position more confident and immovable than ever before.

Art Jr. had read all the reports and had scouted Harris himself. So had Steeler scout Dick Haley, an indefatigable worker, meticulous with his written reports, hired from BLESTO in 1971. Haley, who would prove invaluable in building the empire, quickly learned that the biggest mistake made by NFL scouts was in overestimating a college player's toughness. In his report on Harris, Haley wrote, "No doubt that he has great ability," but he warned that he "doesn't push himself in college—very little 2nd effort—just doesn't run tough . . . has strength—but doesn't run tough inside." Many scouts missed something fundamental in Harris, who would continually surprise throughout his career, but Art Jr. was not among them.

On the eve of the NFL draft, Colts scout George Young asked Art Jr., "Is Chuck giving you the business again?" Art Jr. had told him that Noll wanted Newhouse, not Harris. Both Art Jr. and Young, a former high school history teacher, were devotees of history, and often talked about military battles when they met along the scouting trail: Trafalgar, Gettysburg, Midway. "You tell Chuck for me," Young said, "that that question was settled over two thousand years ago when Socrates said, 'A good big man is better than a good little man any day.' "

In the months leading up to the draft, Art Jr. drove himself hard. At home he became tense, abrupt. As he saw it, the NFL draft was a referendum on Art Rooney Jr. It alone determined whether he was a success or a failure. He wanted Franco Harris, and to strengthen his case, he audiotaped BLESTO scouts, and others, praising Harris and his skill set, and then played the smoothly edited tape for Noll and his assistant coaches.

He got his wish. The Steelers drafted Harris in the first round with the thirteenth pick, Noll telling Art Jr., "You'd better be right." Noll phoned Harris right away to welcome him to the Steelers. After the brief call, he returned to the draft room and said that Harris sounded lifeless, without energy. Dan Radakovich had been at Penn State with Harris as an assistant coach and replied, "Chuck, he's just a quiet kid, and smart. You'll like him." Dan Rooney told reporters that the Steelers would have selected four or five players ahead of Harris if they hadn't been drafted already by other teams.

Harris didn't want to come to Pittsburgh in the first place. He wanted to see the world, or at least warm weather. Dallas, Miami, or Los Angeles would have been nice. But he made an important decision even before the NFL draft: "Wherever I go to play, I want to live in that city and get involved in that city, become that city."

That summer, after observing Harris's first few days in Latrobe, Steeler coaches second-guessed their selection. Harris didn't seem to run hard. With the ball in his hands, he did more thinking, and searching for openings, than instinctive running. It was as if he were trying to translate a foreign language. Joe Greene said, "He had an odd way about him. He'd run up to the offensive line. He'd stop and he'd peek around." "He picked holes," receivers coach Lionel Taylor said. "Franco would pick it and slide." The other running backs in camp impressed Harris with their talent and intensity. *No way I'll make this team*, Harris thought. *What am I doing here?*

True to his nature, he asked a lot of questions. Dick Hoak, the Steelers' running backs coach, said, "You could say, 'Franco, we want you to do this.' He'd say, 'Why?' And then you had to tell him why." Privately a few Steeler veterans approached linebacker Jack Ham, who had been Harris's teammate at Penn State. They asked him about the rookie, namely, "What gives?" Some guys are practice players, Ham told them, and others are game players. "Just wait until the games start," Ham said. In the first preseason game, in Atlanta, Harris ran left and then, with seemingly no place to go, suddenly cut to his right and burst into the open field. He ran seventy-six yards for a touchdown. To Hoak, this run showed that Harris had great explosiveness, but also great peripheral vision, and a runner's innate feel for oncoming tacklers, ideal traits for the Steelers' trapping game. And even better, Hoak realized, none of the Falcons' little defensive backs caught Harris from behind. Hoak turned giddy. *Oh, boy! We've got something here!*

Sportswriters stumbled over adjectives in their attempts to describe Harris's biracial lineage. He was alternately tan-skinned, coffee-colored, muttonchopped, regal, sharp-featured, a mulatto, Othello-like, a Barbary Coast pirate, a Franciscan monk, and a gloomy, morose mope scowling from behind a well-trimmed, fierce-looking beard. These were more clumsy examples of a nation's struggle to come to grips with race.

✦ ✦ ✦

As a teenager walking along a beach boardwalk in New Jersey, Harris was stopped by a gnarled old man seemingly homeless. The man said he was crippled and asked for coffee. Harris bought a cup and handed it to him. The old man eyed him intently and said, "You've got a Roman nose. You've got a Roman eyebrows. You've got a Roman face. But you're black. I don't understand." Harris felt no need to explain and walked off, but he remembered the exchange, knowing the old man simply had said what many others thought.

Soon after Harris's arrival, the Steelers' publicist Ed Kiely asked him how he wanted to handle questions about his mixed-race parentage. The subject came up a lot in media queries. "That's no problem," Harris said. If he had to choose, Harris said with a shrug, "I'm black." As a young teen, Harris had spit-shined shoes in the Fort Dix barracks, learning the proper ratio of polish to water, making his biggest money on Sundays. His first name, and those of his eight siblings, spoke to a complex lineage: Giuseppe, Mario, Daniella, Marisa, Alvara, Luana, Piero, and Michele. Their father, Cadillac Harris, a black supply sergeant born a Mississippian, belonged to an army unit that chased the Nazis north through Italy. Along the way, at a dance in Pisa, where the tower famously leans, he met a local Italian, Gina Parenti, just seventeen. A courtship blossomed. He would bring her home as a war bride, and they would raise their family near the army base in Mount Holly in a racially diverse neighborhood. "We didn't look at color or nationality," Franco Harris said. His friends were half Filipino, half black, half German, half Catholic, half something.

Gina Harris visited Tuscany in 1969, and on a whim, Franco, a sophomore at Penn State, joined her. First he flew to Germany, where he visited castles and locals asked him if he was Egyptian or Indian. He took a train to Pisa, where he met his mother. They'd never really talked much about her war experiences. He knew only that the Parentis had faced the Nazi horror. Now, Gina Parenti Harris showed him her birthplace in Pietrasanta ("sacred rock"), home to exquisite marble, some said to have been used by Michelangelo. They went on to Viareggio on the Tyrrhenian Sea, where she had attended school through the fourth grade. She told him how in autumn 1944 the Nazis had massacred hundreds of Italian villagers and refugees nearby in Sant'Anna di Stazzema, including more than one hundred children, throwing hand grenades into locked basements, and killing the rest by machine gun in the open air. Then they burned the bodies and she saw the smoke curling into the sky over Sant'Anna. Her own mother had died years earlier, she explained, and when the Nazis came, she and her brother Alvaro hid with their father, in churches and in the nearby mountains, constantly on the run. During one escape a bullet grazed Alvaro's head and left him a marked man. The Nazis later found him. "If you are wounded, they know you have been somewhere that you shouldn't be," Franco's mother explained. Alvaro Parenti was taken to a slave labor camp. In time, a box arrived in Pietrasanta, in it Alvaro's remains, and the remains of others. The memory of her brother stirred emotions decades old. "She gets emotional," Franco Harris said years later, "but what Italian doesn't?"

Art Jr. and Haley were driving through the mountains between Penn State and Pittsburgh in October 1972 when they heard a radio report that running back Preston Pearson had suffered an injury and that Harris would get his first start that Sunday against Houston. In response, they did something silly. "We stopped the car," Haley said, "and did a little cheer." Against the Oilers, Harris rushed nineteen times for 115 yards, a breakout performance. Driving out of the stadium long after that game, Hanratty and his wife spotted a hitchhiker who looked just like Harris. *It was Harris.* They pulled over, and offered to drive him home. Harris said he would accept only if it wouldn't take the Hanrattys out of their way. "Can't you buy a car?" Hanratty asked, once Harris was in the backseat. "I'll get around to it," Harris replied. He usually took a public bus to practice, the 76 Hamilton, or he rode his bicycle. Joe Greene once spotted Harris on his bike trailed by a slew of neighborhood kids riding their own bikes.

In a boisterous locker room, Harris preferred to listen than talk. He had a charisma and presence, like a quiet storm. Fuqua also noticed his work ethic. "I had never seen anyone condition himself in the manner he did," Fuqua said. After the team finished its training camp workouts, Harris put himself through his own intensive jump-rope exercise regimen. After the team lifted weights, Harris remained to lift more weights, alone. "Franco was a thinker," Fuqua said. "But he wasn't what I would call a quick thinker. You'd proposition him about something and he'd think about it for two days." During the players' weekly poker games, Harris pondered his cards, and his next play, at great length. Fuqua said, "He'd make us mad because he'd say [aloud], 'Well, let's see, the jack has been played and . . .' "

Harris rented an apartment in Bloomfield, on the East Side of Pittsburgh, and by the middle of the 1972 season a forty-two-year-old pizza man from nearby East Liberty drove up once or twice a week and dropped off two Italian hoagie sandwiches (prosciutto, capicola, provolone), and a half gallon of Pepsi, gratis. You might say that the pizza man was just another Steelers fan, but that would be like saying that Franco Harris was just another Steelers running back.

Al Vento, pizza man, had been a Steelers season-ticket holder since the '50s at Forbes Field. Through the years he'd experienced Steeler frustrations so deep that he and his cousin, baker Tony Stagno, second-generation Italians, occasionally cheered for the opposition. "Just so we could be with a winner once in a while," Vento said. The two men, burly and animated, embraced their Italian heritage. Their fathers in 1927 were among the founders of the Spigno Saturnia Italo-American Beneficial Society of Pittsburgh, which drew its members from the Spignesi, those whose ancestry could be traced to a small village between Rome and Naples. Inducted as members at sixteen, Vento and Stagno played bocci and drank wine at the club and celebrated its annual old-fashioned night, I Paesani, singing and dancing while dressed in Old World attire. Vento opened his pizza shop late in 1950 and soon Stagno's nearby bakery was making the dough balls for his pizza shells. East Liberty long had been the center of Pittsburgh's Italian immigrant life, though during the 1950s blacks displaced by urban renewal projects began to move in. Tensions between the groups peaked in April 1968 after the murder of Dr. King, when blacks turned their violence on area homes and businesses owned by Italian Americans.

In 1971, a friend at Three Rivers Stadium had made a passing remark to Stagno: "It'd take an army to move this crowd." Stagno boldly replied, "Then we'll be the army." A year later the two cousins decided they needed a new Steelers hero. *But who?* The answer played out before their eyes as Franco Harris became the unstoppable running back whom Art

Jr. had envisioned. In late October 1972, in the season's seventh game, Harris rushed for 138 yards against Buffalo. In the next game he went for 101 against Cincinnati, and then 134 against Kansas City, 136 at Cleveland, 128 against the Vikings, and 102 at home against the Browns. The Steelers won five of those six games as Harris tied an NFL record with six consecutive games with at least 100 yards rushing held by Noll's former teammate Jim Brown. When Harris broke off a long run against Minnesota, sweeping around the right side, Dan Rooney sensed a new day dawning for the Steelers. The playoffs seemed possible.

Vento and Stagno knew that Harris was half Italian. "And so we said, 'That's our hero!'" Vento said. The cousins decided to create a new fan club galvanized around the rookie running back. They would call it Franco's Italian Army. First, though, they wanted Harris's approval. In early November, through a stadium guard who broached the concept to Harris, they got it.

The cousins let their creativity run wild. Into Three Rivers they came, initially with two dozen friends and more, neighbors with surnames such as Zottola, Danzilli, and Signore. They marched behind banners that read FRANCO'S ITALIAN ARMY and RUN, PAESANO, RUN! The cousins met before games at Vento's pizza shop, where they prepared two dozen hoagies. With these Italian sandwiches they would need Italian wine—their preferred choice, two-dollar bottles of Riunite. To sneak their wine into the stadium, they became agents of deception. They hollowed bread from some of the hoagies and hid bottles inside. As they approached Section 29 near the thirty-yard line, Vento distracted stadium guards and ushers (*"How 'bout that Franco Harris?"*) as his cohorts sneaked past with the wine. They also brought salami, provolone, gnocchi, olives, eggplant, and small red-white-and-green Italian flags. From a friend who worked at the Hunt Armory, they got surplus green army helmets on which they painted the Italian flag and FRANCO'S ITALIAN ARMY. On the back they stenciled their names. They made Franco a five-star general; Stagno took four stars, Vento three. Soon, as its popularity grew, the Italian Army added an Israeli Brigade; a Canine Corps (the cousins put a helmet on a Great Dane for the march into the stadium); and for women, a nurses' division. At the ballpark, army members teased one another as they toasted, "When Franco's good, he's Italian, and when he's not, he's on his father's side." They met Harris in the stadium parking lot after one game, shook his hand, and told him he was paesano.

On November 19 in Cleveland, Franco's Italian Army marched laps around Municipal Stadium before the game, drinking wine, taking no guff, Vento and Stagno happily leading, "Hup-three, hup-four." Occasionally Stagno turned to Italian sorcery to help the Steelers, waving what appeared to be an oversized red pepper from his seat. It was a *corno*, thought by Italian immigrants to ward off *mallochio*, or the evil eye, and inside was a small hunchbacked man carved from ivory. When the Steelers had the ball, Stagno removed the little man from the corno and waved him in the direction of the goal line, placing a curse on the opposing defense. "The wildest, swingingest, most intriguing fan club that ever honored a star," Pat Livingston of the *Pittsburgh Press* wrote. The national press rushed in to tell the army's story, which was emblematic of a larger story—a steel town awakening to rally around its football team whose lightning rod was a biracial running back.

With a 10-3 record, the Steelers needed a victory at San Diego in the season's final regular-season game to capture the first division title in their forty-year history. At Noll's insistence, they practiced that week in Palm Springs, California, to acclimatize to warm weather in December. Stagno playfully gave Cope an order: in Palm Springs, find Frank Sinatra, the desert's most famous and reclusive resident, and induct him into Franco's Italian Army. As it happened, Cope spotted Sinatra walking into a restaurant in Rancho Mirage with baseball's Leo Durocher and golfer Ken Venturi. Cope scratched out a short note on a table napkin, inviting Sinatra to come to the next day's Steelers practice and be inducted. For effect, he added, "P.S. Franco's from Hoboken"—Sinatra's hometown, and never mind that Franco was from Mount Holly. Sinatra came to the table where Cope sat with a group of Pittsburgh writers and Steelers officials. He agreed to come to the practice.

The late-night calls went out to Pittsburgh. Stagno and Vento caught flights west. The cousins stood beside the practice field wearing their army helmets and holding their two-dollar Riunite bottles. When Sinatra appeared, Cope lost his sideline decorum. He rushed out to the field, interrupting the Steelers' practice, and yelled, "Franco! Get over there. The man's here!" Harris hesitated and looked at Noll, who halted practice. As players gathered in a half circle, the cousins gave Sinatra his own helmet, called him "*Com'pad*," kissed his cheeks, and made him drink their wine, not the expensive wine he had brought. "It was like kissing God," Stagno said.

The Steelers defeated San Diego 24–2 on Sunday and carried Noll off the field on their shoulders. A group of sailors showed up with a sign proclaiming, FRANCO'S ITALIAN NAVY. Meanwhile, back in Pittsburgh, at the weekly meeting of a local Black Nationalist group known as Black Brother on Black in Black, an animated discussion broke out over how local Italians were trying to *steal* Harris. Old racial and ethnic tensions bubbled up. "It's a grave situation," the group's chairman said. He drew his line: "We must preserve blackness." At the next Steelers game, he said, the group would bring its own red-black-and-green black liberation flags in celebration of Harris. "We'll take the north end, of course," he said, "and give the south end to the Italians."

Three Rivers Stadium, December 23, 1972. Forty-three degrees, overcast, and damp at kickoff. The Oakland Raiders, with a villainous reputation, dressed virtuously in white, except coach John Madden, who wore long sideburns, a black jacket, gray slacks, and black Adidas sneakers. Here, for the Steelers' first home playoff game in a quarter century, was a panoramic view: $10 tickets scalped for $100; Raiders quarterback Daryle Lamonica, fighting a flu, hung in effigy in the crowd; the Chief, his fat cigar already soggy from twisting in his saliva, telling sportswriters in the press box before the game that Pittsburgh fans suddenly thought he was a genius. Just three seasons old, Three Rivers Stadium was a cookie-cutter structure, formidable in its way, built for utility, its playing field covered with an artificial turf. To the Chief, who had spent too much time in too many rickety old stadiums, Three Rivers was like heaven, clean, spiffy, and modern, especially the plush Allegheny Club, where black waiters were heard to cheer for Franco Harris, "That a way, soul brother!" The deposed Forbes Field would stand for sixty years, Three Rivers for only half that long. In its time Three Rivers would host two World Series, concerts by Bruce Springsteen and the Rolling Stones, and crusades by Jehovah's Witnesses and Billy Graham, but it would be remembered, above all, for one moment, freakish and heroic, on this day.

Nearly three hours into this divisional playoff game, the Steelers' magnificent defensive performance and 6–0 lead dissolved with less than two minutes to play. The Raiders' backup quarterback, Ken Stabler, eluded the pass rush from the Pittsburgh thirty-yard line, broke containment, and hobble-raced down the left side as the ghosts and goblins of Pittsburgh's past whispered, "Same Old Steelers! Same Old Steelers!" Greene and Greenwood were unable to catch Stabler from behind; neither could Ham nor reserve defensive tackle Craig Hanneman. Only safety Mike Wagner had an angle, but just as he put his mitts on Stabler, the quarterback lunged into the end zone for a touchdown. On the Oakland sideline, receiver Cliff Branch sprang up in celebration, lifting his legs high and wide, kangaroo-like, once, twice, seven times. Madden pumped his meaty fist. The Raiders led, 7–6; the stadium clock read "1:13."

Seventy-three seconds.

Now came a moment that sports produces best: a communal experience that merges adrenaline and hope against logic and history to produce a civic rush in an economically depressed town. It would have a startling diversity, forever bonding in lore a black running back from Detroit claiming to be French royalty, a Jewish sportscaster with an Anglicized surname, two second-generation Italian Americans from East Liberty drinking Riunite wine and waving a corno to ward off the mallochio, and a biracial running back whose Italian mother had escaped Hitler and now was at home in New Jersey, watching on television with his African American father. Deflated by the Steelers' sudden deficit, Gina Parenti Harris stepped into her garden in Mount Holly and then came back inside. Asking for intercession for those who have waited so long, totally without hope, she put a record on her phonograph—Beniamino Gigli's arresting "Ave Maria." A few hours later, in a downtown Pittsburgh bar, a Steeler zealot would stand atop a chair and call out to the Virgin Mary in his own memorable way.

No one felt it coming, not after three hurried Bradshaw incompletions had left the Steelers in supplication, down to a final chance: fourth and ten from the Pittsburgh forty with twenty-two seconds to play. Even the

Chief gave up. He left his upstairs box, bidding adieu to his priest and his driver, and stepped into the elevator, joined there by the part-time ball boy, Bill Nunn III, and others, their heads down, not a word spoken. At ground level, Nunn turned right, toward the field, the Chief to the left, toward the Steelers' locker room. There, he waited for the inevitable silence to fill his stadium, intending to tell his players, as he had so many times since 1933, that they had put up a good fight.

If only Bill Mazeroski were here . . .

Mazeroski's home run in the bottom of the ninth inning that defeated the New York Yankees in game seven of the 1960 World Series at Forbes Field was the last sports event to send Pittsburgh into the purest form of euphoria. Bill Nunn Jr. saw that home run—he gave Clemente a ride to the airport from the clubhouse after that game—and now he sat in a box upstairs with Art Jr., furious at the Steelers' defense for the breakdown that permitted Stabler's score. Mazeroski's seventeen-year baseball career had ended in October and now he was thirty miles away, at home in Greensburg, listening to the Steelers on radio, like most of Pittsburgh, because this game was blacked out on local TV.

On the Oakland sideline, Madden gathered his offense, and receiver Mike Siani heard him say what he, and the other offensive players, already knew. "We will get the ball back," Madden said, "and run out the clock." His players had a secret nickname for Madden—Pinky—because when he erupted with anger, his face turned bright crimson. At this moment, Madden was serious, focused, white-faced. Two Raider rookie linemen, Dave Dalby and John Vella, roommates, stood together farther back. Neither had played much, a few moments on special teams. Dalby said, "J.V., can you believe how much money we'll make from this game?" The answer, both knew, was $7,500. "And even if we lose the next game," Dalby said, "we'll get fifteen thousand dollars." That would nearly double their first-year salaries.

From the sideline, Noll sent in the play, "Sixty-six Circle Option," a pass play designed for rookie Barry Pearson, a receiver just inserted into the game and known for his fine hands. His job was to run a post pattern downfield, angling toward the middle, and get a first down and more, in hopes of setting up a game-winning field goal try by Roy Gerela. Bradshaw had completed just ten of twenty-four passes, not good. From the sideline, Ham could not watch. "I'm a realist," he said, and he began to cut the tape from his wrist, his back turned to the field. Bleier felt resigned to defeat, too. He thought, *I can't watch the disaster that's about to take place.* He didn't want the season to end. In case someone was watching him, Bleier walked from the sideline to a nearby table and reached for a Gatorade he didn't want. Joe Greene, an eternal optimist, stood nearby with cornerback John Rowser, and told him, "This season has been too good. It ain't gonna end this way."

In Section 29, near the Oakland thirty-five-yard line, Stagno waved his red pepper–like corno, putting a curse on the Raiders. Now, with fourth down calling for dire measures, he pulled out the little hunchbacked man carved from ivory, but it slipped through his fingers and fell to the ground. Vento reached down to get it for him.

Michael Ord, a thirty-year-old marketing consultant and Steeler zealot, sat in his usual seat near the fifty-yard line, in the upper deck, close to the stadium's upper rim, nearest to God. He loved his view of the field from here, and the savory smell of a turkey or chicken cooking on a fan's small grill perched on the stadium's top ledge. Sometimes a cooked drumstick or thigh was passed to him. With his girlfriend, Sharon Levosky, and his father, Ord stood.

All eyes on Bradshaw.

The Raiders showed a four-man rush, though defensive tackle Art Thoms would become a "spy," holding his place, in containment, in case Bradshaw tried to run. Now Bradshaw scrambled to his right with the Raiders' massive linemen Horace Jones and Tony Cline in pursuit. Instinctively, Bradshaw stopped and pivoted, slipping Jones. He did not see Pearson, but downfield, near the Oakland thirty-five-yard line, he spotted the Frenchman breaking into the clear. His pass to Fuqua, a laser beam, was released just as Cline lowered his shoulder into him, knocking him to the ground. Bradshaw would not see what was about to happen. Watching from the sideline, Steelers trainer Ralph Berlin said, "That's it. We're done," and he began to walk toward the end zone where he saw Parisi, the equipment manager, carrying in the water buckets.

There was a celebrated Raiders style, swashbuckling rogues and headhunters playing with a dark fury and recklessness. Safety Jack Tatum made that style his. One of the game's hardest hitters, Tatum was a feared tackler who threw forearm shivers and was known to his teammates as the Assassin. In a 1977 preseason game, Tatum would make a hit that paralyzed New England receiver Darryl Stingley from the chest down. Now, as Bradshaw's pass came to Fuqua, so did Tatum, from behind. The Raider safety had three options: (1) attempt to deflect the pass; (2) tackle Fuqua near the Raiders' thirty-five-yard line, leaving the Steelers with only a few seconds to try a long field goal; or (3) make like the defensive assassin he was and, as Raider linebacker Phil Villapiano would say, "Just knock the fucker out!" True to character, Tatum chose the third option, throwing his shoulder violently into Fuqua's upper back, near his left shoulder. "That's the way Jack played it and every one of us Raiders loved him for that," Villapiano said. "It was a perfectly clean hit. He overdid stuff a lot of times, and it was due to backfire." Moving behind Tatum, cornerback Jimmy Warren raised his arms in celebration, but only for an instant.

Franco Harris, a thinking player, the very trait some pro scouts had criticized, was called to block for Bradshaw on the play. Villapiano shadowed him, grabbing Harris's jersey. But when Bradshaw scrambled from the pocket, Harris reacted and moved downfield. At Penn State, Joe Paterno had implored his players, including Harris, "Go to the ball! Go to the ball!" Harris did just that now. Villapiano saw Bradshaw throw and thought, *The coaches will grade this film. If I stand here, I'll get a minus.* So he let Harris go and moved toward Fuqua when suddenly Tatum struck Fuqua from behind and the football whiplashed back over Villapiano's head. The linebacker's first thought: *Oh, fuck!*

Near the stadium's upper rim, Ord's father, Barney, a postal supervisor, saw the pass deflected. He covered his face with his hands, a debacle revealed, and sat in his seat with a feeling of despair.

From the ground, Fuqua, knocked woozy, looked up and saw Tatum smile wickedly. Yet so violent was their collision, the ball fluttered more than seven yards in the other direction, toward the oncoming Harris, who bent forward and scooped it from the air, near his shin. "If I had stayed with him," Villapiano lamented, "the ball would've come to me, because I was on the inside." Now Harris broke to his left, a $30,000 running back carrying the hopes of steelworkers who, if still employed, made, on average, less than a third of that amount.

In Section 29, where Franco's Italian Army massed, Vento located the fallen hunchbacked man on the ground, beneath a seat, and handed it to Stagno. Then Vento looked to the field, stunned by what he saw.

Up in the press box, Dick Hoak, the Steelers' running backs coach, sitting with fellow assistant coaches Bud Carson and Babe Parilli, leaped onto a table and shouted, "Keep going, Franco! Keep going!" Scout Tim Rooney sat in a different box with his cousin and boss, Art Jr., and Bill Nunn Jr., and when Harris made the catch, they all rose from their chairs. As Art Jr. stood, his chair's leg dug into cousin Tim's new Cordovans, mutilating the left one and gouging his toe. Sitting in the stands with his wife, Haley, who had expressed concerns about Harris in his scouting report a year earlier while noting "there is no doubt that he has great ability," saw his last point proven. "A phenomenal play by Harris," he decided, "to have the skill level to go down and catch that ball and keep running. A lot of guys would have gone to the ground to make the catch." Greenwood, meanwhile, had been moving slowly along the Pittsburgh sideline toward the locker room, appreciative of the Steelers' season that was ending. When he heard the crowd roar, he half turned and saw Harris sprint past him at the thirty-yard line, with the ball in his hand. It confused him. Near the stadium's upper rim, Barney Ord, seated with his head in his hands, was confused by the roar, too. He smacked his son Michael in the side, stood up, and asked excitedly, "What's happening? What's happening?"

Only one Raider had a chance to stop Harris, Warren, who angled toward him near the eleven-yard line. But Harris stiff-armed him, and Warren slipped from the back of Harris's moist jersey and crashed to the turf. Harris ran along the sideline, and just inside the pylon, to score a touchdown with five seconds to play. He casually dropped the ball in the end zone, as was his style, while dozens of fans leaped over the grandstand walls and rushed to slap him on the back. Greene, his eternal optimism affirmed, ran along the sideline in pursuit of Harris and victory. Bradshaw ran into the end zone, too, holding his head in disbelief, looking skyward, and accepting hugs from fans as if they were old friends, and imploring, "Somebody tell me: What happened?" Art Rooney II, Dan's twenty-year-old son, stood beside the Steelers' bench and tossed a water bottle in the air. It took about twenty minutes for that bottle to come down, or so it seemed. Just then, from out of the stands, the former Steelers defensive back Brady Keys appeared and bear-hugged the young Rooney, jumping up and down, and squeezing him so tight that Art II felt close to passing out. In Section 29, Franco's Italian Army danced and kissed cheeks, convinced of the power of their hunchbacked man. Near the stadium's upper rim, Michael Ord answered his father's question, saying, "Franco caught it!" And then, moments later, as he crossed the goal line: "Thank God!" And then speaking for all of Pittsburgh: *"Finally!"*

In the press box, sportscaster Curt Gowdy of NBC television told viewers, "You talk about Christmas miracles. Here's the miracle of all miracles!"

Back at the thirty-five-yard line, Tatum pointed at Fuqua, still on the ground, and shouted, "You touched that ball!" Fuqua denied it.

Here was the all-important question: did the ball touch Tatum? NFL rules forbade an offensive player from catching a pass if another offensive teammate had already touched the ball. However, the rules also stated that once a defensive player touched a pass, the ball could be touched by all eleven offensive players, and then legally caught by one of them. If Harris's catch was disallowed, the Raiders would take possession at the Pittsburgh forty-yard line, holding a one-point lead with five seconds to play.

Back judge Adrian Burk signaled a touchdown when Harris crossed the goal line, but referee Fred Swearingen did not. A red-faced Madden screamed for justice, Pinky being Pinky. Swearingen gathered his crew of officials on the field, asking each of his five cohorts, as was routine, "What did you see?" Burk said he was positive that Tatum had touched the ball. Umpire Pat Harder, positioned in the middle of the field, also believed that Tatum had touched the ball. Their conference stretched on, confusion among the hometown fans becoming agitation. From the Raiders' sideline, center Jim Otto noticed how close the grandstands were to the Oakland bench. He thought, *If the officials call this for the Raiders this place will explode and I'm going underneath those stands and getting out of the way.*

Swearingen broke from the group of officials and disappeared into the Pirates' dugout. From there, he phoned up to the press box to the NFL supervisor of officials, Art McNally. Madden later would charge that McNally had seen television replays on closed circuit in the press box (he had) and then, in that phone conversation, told Swearingen what he had seen. McNally said that wasn't so. In an interview nearly forty years later,

McNally said his phone conversation with Swearingen, lasting only seconds, totaled twenty-two words.

Swearingen: "Two of my men ruled the ball was touched by an opposing player."

McNally's nine-word reply: "Okay, Fred, you are fine. Go ahead and go."

And then, he said, Swearingen hung up.

After the game, in a car ride back to the Pittsburgh airport with a few of the officials (though not Swearingen), McNally asked, "Why the long delay in the conference?" One official replied that as Swearingen interviewed each man on the field, "he wanted to be sure" the correct call was made. McNally recalled, "Then someone in the crew—I never found out who it was—said to Swearingen, 'Well, there is one person here who can help and he is up in the press box.' He meant me." In his weekly review of the game's officiating filed with the NFL office, McNally said he awarded "a negative grade for the idea of coming for assistance on a call that should be made on the field." Soon after, McNally said, "I made it clear to my officials: I don't EVER want an official on the field to even attempt to make a phone call like that. That is your responsibility and you call it as you see it."

Returning to the field, Swearingen faced the press box and raised both arms to signal a touchdown. More than fifty thousand fans, including large groups milling about on the field, erupted as one, and Madden turned pinker with rage. It took more than ten minutes to clear the field. Gerela kicked the extra point to give the Steelers a 13–7 lead. With five seconds to play, Wagner, the Steelers' safety, suddenly had a big problem. When he returned to the sideline from the end zone celebration, his helmet was gone. A fan had stolen it. He borrowed guard Gerry Mullins's helmet, which was too large. Now Wagner worried, *I've got this big bucket helmet on, and it'll be just my luck that Stabler will throw the ball my way and this helmet will pivot around and I'm not going to be able to see and we'll lose!*

That didn't happen. Stabler's one last deep throw, for tight end Raymond Chester, fell incomplete, the Raiders done, stunned, and enraged. The Chief heard the earlier crowd roar, whereupon a stadium guard had rushed toward him, shouting, "You won it! You won it!" The Chief asked

if he was kidding. "No, listen to the crowd!" The Chief said later that he had never waited so long for a photo finish result at a horse track. Punter Bobby Walden was the first player to reach the Chief in the locker room afterward, and he hugged the old man. As a boy, Bradshaw had thrown a football off trees, his bedroom ceiling, the roof, his brother's swing. He thought he'd seen every possible weird bounce, but when he saw the replay, he admitted that he'd never seen anything like it. A security guard approached Wagner in the locker room and returned his helmet. "Some guy was trying to get out of the stadium with it," the guard said. Wagner smiled. "Well, thanks," he said. "You probably should have let him keep it." In games past, the Chief had approached Fuqua in the locker room, passing off compliments such as, "You made a great move, Frenchy. It reminded me of Johnny Blood." To Fuqua, there was nothing better than a postgame handshake and kind word from the Chief. Now he saw Art Rooney Sr. and said, "Should I tell you what happened?" The Chief shook his head, saying he had no real need to know, telling the Frenchman, "It's your secret."

From Penn State, Joe Paterno couldn't resist. Three years earlier, his Nittany Lions had won the Orange Bowl in a dramatic finish, and when Paterno said his mother had prayed for his team, the Chief dropped him a line playfully offering to trade his brother, Father Silas, and two of his sisters (both nuns) for Paterno's mother. Now Paterno sent the Chief a telegram. "It's a deal. You can have Mom," he wrote. "Send me your sisters and brother."

In Pittsburgh, all heaven broke loose.

On the streets of downtown, Ord and Levosky heard car horns honking, streetcar bells ringing, fire truck sirens blaring.

Twelve years before, after Mazeroski's homer at Forbes Field won the World Series, Ord, still a teenager, drove his convertible through these streets and saw bottles of wine and booze tossed happily from hotel windows. But this jubilation felt different to him. This was more intense. The difference, he decided, was in the depth of western Pennsylvania's devotion to football versus baseball. Ord and Levosky walked into the Interlude, a tavern on Court Street. Ord heard the sizzle of steaks and chops on the downstairs grill as he muscled his way upstairs to the crowded bar. He was a regular here and knew all the bartenders, but he had never seen the place so raucous and rowdy. He ordered a drink, and then another. A thought came to him, or an inspiration, a play on words too good to keep to himself. All around him, the bar was abuzz over Franco and the Steelers. The alcohol flowed, life was good, and Ord figured he would be able to talk coherently for only a little while longer. He would take advantage of his inspiration now because it might not return anytime soon.

He stood on a chair beside the bar and tapped a spoon against his glass, just as he'd seen others do at weddings. The bartenders shouted, "Shuddup, everybody! SHUDDUP!!" Ord's moment came, and now his Catholic school education and his marketing man's creativity melded, washed over by drink. Proudly he told the crowd, "From this day, today will forever be known as the 'Feast of the Immaculate Reception.' "

The response was instant and authentic: loud cheers, clapping, salutes, a miniroar, laughter, backslaps, more drinks. The crowd at the bar began chanting in singsong fashion, "Immaculate Reception! Immaculate Reception!" and marched out into the streets.

Back at Levosky's parents' home in Highland Park later that night, Ord had another brainstorm. "Sharon," he said, "call Myron Cope." Ord wanted all of Pittsburgh to know about his creation, *The Feast of the Immaculate Reception*. Ord knew that Cope was Jewish. He worried the sportscaster might think the phrase in poor taste, and possibly offensive to Catholics. "If he questions it, just tell him, 'It's okay, Myron,' " Ord told Levosky. A few minutes before the start of WTAE television's eleven o'clock news, Cope, about to go on the air, took Levosky's call. She told him about the Interlude and Ord's phrase. Cope laughed and told Levosky, "I don't know if I can say that on TV."

Ord and Levosky figured that was the end of it, but then they watched Cope say on the air that he'd just received a call from "a good Christian lady." (Levosky said she and Cope never discussed her religion. She assumed he was merely trying to soften the phrase and deflect possible criticism.)

Then, with Pittsburgh listening, Cope took Ord's phrase and, like Franco Harris, ran with it.

✦ ✦ ✦

Too often memories are wrapped around emotions, not facts. Decades later, as the particulars of the Steelers' dynasty merged and blurred, the Immaculate Reception immediately preceded the team's first Super Bowl victory. It wasn't so.

In the days that followed Franco's catch, the Christmas cards atop the mantel at 940 North Lincoln were joined by telegrams of congratulation from Jim Farley (once FDR's postmaster general), Charley Finley, Bill Veeck, and the widow Marie Lombardi. On the following Sunday, though, the Miami Dolphins defeated the Steelers 21–17 in the AFC title game at Three Rivers Stadium en route to the NFL's first-ever 17-0 perfect season. At game's end, the Steelers muttered about getting beat by, of all things, a fake punt. It had the whiff of S.O.S.: Same Old Steelers.

The day before that game had presented a bad omen. Franco's Italian Army had hired a prop plane to drop two thousand leaflets on the local hotel where the Dolphins were staying. The leaflets read, "Surrender now and enjoy life with your loved ones rather than face destruction on the field of battle at Three Rivers Stadium."

But the Fates conspired and the leaflets missed the mark, fluttering all over the Chief's town.

IV

AN EMPIRE BORN, 1974

CHAPTER 7

IN THE FILM ROOM

WHAT IS IT ABOUT FOOTBALL coaches? That's what J. T. Thomas wanted to know. Even as Noll kept an emotional distance from his players, Thomas felt the force of his coach's will. Mystery attached to Noll. He was a riddle for Thomas and the other Steeler players to solve, his detachment from them a distant echo from his postwar NFL days in Cleveland with the imperious Paul Brown and with teammates who had fought in Okinawa and Bastogne. The 1970s Steelers were part of a generation that challenged authority, and if they didn't confront Noll directly, they talked, and groused, about him among themselves in the locker room.

The Steelers' 1973 first-round draft pick from Florida State, Thomas had felt the weight of football coaches before, and even more than that, the weight of his family and of race relations. As a boy in Macon, Georgia, Thomas met the Reverend Dr. Martin Luther King Jr. in church, and sat at his feet as King told stories to gathered children about the promise of the future. At thirteen Thomas marched in civil rights demonstrations in front of Macon's hotels and restaurants. Angry whites spat at him and his group as they sang the freedom song "Before I'll Be a Slave, I'll Be Buried in My Grave" (*"No more weepin'... no more tommin'..."*). In August 1965, Thomas was among seventeen black students chosen to desegregate Macon's all-white Sidney Lanier High School. Each morning for a month, authorities taped numbers to the backs of these students (Thomas wore number 17) to monitor them as Georgia state troopers and German shepherds escorted them past NAACP monitors and into class.

Deeply spiritual, Thomas, a musician, played the piano at his church. He turned to football only as a matter of self-preservation. He saw his father physically threaten his mother at home, and vowed to protect her the next time it happened. He noticed that his high school's football players were big, and nearly as strong as his father. "So I'm kind of looking at football as strength and power," Thomas said. "My whole ambition from about seventeen years old was to take my father out. Football was my means to doing that." The inevitable confrontation came: a son, in defense of his mother, stepped in front of his father.

"Who you talking to?" the father asked.

"You," the teenager replied.

Thomas saw his father's hand reach to his pocket where, he knew, he kept a gun. But his father did not draw the weapon. Their confrontation ended in a standoff, and tensions at home soon eased.

Thomas went off to college in Tallahassee and in autumn 1970 was about to become the Seminoles' first black player ever to play in a varsity football game. But he wasn't thinking about being a pioneer in the opener, against Louisville. He was too furious with a Florida State assistant coach who had mocked him in front of his teammates at practice a day earlier. "Thomas, you ain't showing me shit!" the coach had screamed. "You call your mama and tell her to send me some of those newspaper clippings and some of those damn trophies because I ain't seeing a god-damned thing here!!!" Years later, Thomas said, "It was so quiet on the field that you could hear a cockroach pissing." Thomas thought, *He's calling me out. And he's calling out my mama! You don't EVER do that to a brother!* Thomas seethed all through that night and into the next day, one of the biggest days of his life. In the pregame locker room their eyes met. Thomas wanted to rip the assistant coach's head off. A short while later he stood with his Florida State teammates beneath the goalpost, his name about to be announced to a capacity crowd. Suddenly Thomas put aside his anger at the assistant coach and remembered his historic role on this day. The game's outcome was not determined until the final seconds, when Louisville's kicker lined up for a game-winning field goal. Thomas rushed in from the left side and blocked the kick and the home crowd roared, but referees penalized Thomas for being offside. The kicker lined up again, and remarkably Thomas blocked his next kick, too, preserving Florida State's 9–7 victory. In the postgame locker room, once more Thomas faced the assistant coach: Bill Parcells. In a distant day Parcells would win two Super Bowls as the New York Giants' head coach. Now Parcells smiled broadly, and embraced Thomas in an affectionate bear-hug. Only then did Thomas understand that Parcells had kept the focus on him rather than on racial history.

Noll was much different than Parcells. As Thomas saw it, Noll didn't hug you, or light your fire with pep talks. He just figured you out. He figured out your button, and pushed it, sometimes subtly. In a locker room with forty-seven players, there might be forty-seven individual buttons to push. To make his larger thematic points, Noll addressed his team in full and told stories—parables, really. In these instances he talked not about football, but life, or *your life's work.* Thomas noticed how Noll sometimes communicated nonverbally—to praise, or worse. "I mean, he could question your parenthood just by looking at you," Thomas said. He knew that Noll was satisfied with him when he passed off a certain look, brows arched, accompanied by a nod. With Joe Greene, Noll used a different approach, Thomas noticed. He pulled a chair in front of Greene's locker room cubicle—he was nearly *inside* the cubicle—and spoke softly to his star defensive tackle, face-to-face, man-to-man. With Dwight White, Thomas saw Noll turn playful and once—Thomas couldn't believe this— Noll went head-to-head with White in The Dozens, an insult-swapping game with deep roots in black culture. White cracked about "Jazz to Chaz," and Thomas heard Noll return fire, with rhythm and spunk, about White and "yo' mama." White broke up laughing. A self-controlled man, Noll pushed these buttons to extract a better performance, greatness.

At times Noll loomed above the fray, more like a corporate chieftain than a football coach. Steeler scouts, assistant coaches, and office staff also found him less than approachable. His door was always open, but his personality was closed. He seemed unwilling to share himself, and his deeper thoughts and feelings. Noll didn't laugh often, or easily. In conversation, you gave, he took.

Once, while reviewing special teams films in a darkened room, Noll said, "J.T., who is that running at L-three? Is that YOU?" Thomas snapped to attention and said it was. Noll ran back the film, all eyes focused on the third Steeler from the left on kickoff coverage. Noll: "I don't see that 4.4 speed going down there." Noll rewound the tape again, Thomas's stomach in knots. Noll: "No, I don't see that 4.4 speed, and I know that you've got it." Noll knew Thomas was a member of the team's Bible study group, and now he pressed his button. "But you know what they say," Noll said, seemingly to no one in particular. "The meek shall inherit the earth."

Thomas's eyes grew wide. He knew that phrase. It was from the Beatitudes, Matthew 5:5—"Blessed are the meek, for they shall inherit the earth." The reference stunned Thomas. *The meek shall inherit the earth? That has nothing to do with this!* Dozens of players sat in the film room, and Thomas knew that he was alone in understanding this reference.

Thomas couldn't believe it.

Chuck Noll went biblical on him!

CHAPTER 8

THE 1974 DRAFT

THE STEELERS' CROWNING ACHIEVEMENT OF the 1970s didn't happen in a Super Bowl. It didn't even happen on a field. It happened in a meeting room at Three Rivers Stadium where seven coaches, the Chief, Dan, Art Jr., and his scouts sat at tables pushed together in a T-shape for the NFL draft, January 29–30, 1974. To a wall, they had taped the names and ratings of top college players. On easels, they listed players by position, and in the Steelers' order of preference. Next to each player was BLESTO's numerical rating, and next to that, the Steelers' own rating. Seventeen rounds over two days, the Steelers, in less than optimal position, picking twenty-first among twenty-six teams. Lowering expectations, Noll told sportswriters that he saw real value in only the players drafted in the first round and a half.

Scouts had spent three years following this crop of college players. They had read BLESTO reports. They had watched countless college practices and games. They'd reviewed films and written their own reports. Noll and his assistants had attended the college postseason all-star games to qualify and quantify the scouts' earlier assessments. In the draft room, Noll sat with assistant coaches Bud Carson, George Perles, Woody Widenhofer, Lionel Taylor, Dick Hoak, and Dan Radakovich. Art Jr. surrounded himself with scouts Haley, Nunn, and Tim Rooney, his cousin. The scouting department had created a "200 List"—the most talented two hundred players in the draft. As soon as the draft ended, the Steelers would dispatch team officials to sign as free agents any players on that list who were not drafted, rushing to get to them ahead of representatives from other NFL teams. Every man in the draft room understood that the final say on all selections belonged to Noll. During the two days, the Chief, meanwhile, wandered into and out of the room, occasionally asking Art Jr., "What did you take that guy for?" and then, in the later rounds, as was his habit, to ask if the Steelers might choose a player with an Irish name. He meant it.

This 1974 draft would prove defining for Art Jr. and for the franchise. He had been an NFL scout for a decade. His long absences from home had made it difficult on Kay and the children. But Art Jr. couldn't scout from home. And, besides, he would say, "Football was like a narcotic to me, and I got addicted." For him each year's NFL draft became like planning the Normandy invasion. He needed scouting files, phone numbers, open phone lines, a Steelers representative in New York, another at BLESTO headquarters, a stack of contracts for free agents to sign. He designated a small room near the Steelers' draft room for private one-on-one conversations with Noll or Dan. That room also would serve as "the phone room," where publicists Joe Gordon and Ed Kiely, among others, would call college players the Steelers were about to draft to let them know what was coming, and to ask if they'd suffered any recent injuries, or if they had an agent, or about any changes in their military status.

Seventeen draft picks, and Art Jr. didn't want to waste a single one. He did not want to disappoint his father or Dan. His ambition was to deliver too many great football players to the coaches. *No easy cuts.* This ambition set him on edge. Once, in the draft room, trainer Ralph Berlin stood on a chair to tape a prospect's name high on the wall. But he placed the name in the wrong position, and Art Jr. bellowed, "RAAAAAALLLLLLPPPHH!" Startled, Berlin nearly toppled from the chair. On draft day, Art Jr. felt as if the Rooney name was his to carry.

He worked harder and more efficiently now than earlier in his scouting career, his self-confidence growing with the Steelers' winning percentage. The Steelers had made the playoffs in 1972 and 1973. They were on the cusp of a breakthrough. His friend the Baltimore scout George Young spoke as his conscience, needling, "Arthur, the question now is, 'Can you beat the big boys? Can you get to the Super Bowl? And then can you win the Super Bowl?'"

In the draft room, Art Jr. answered to Noll. He never felt at ease with him. Art Jr. was chatty, and gave freely of himself in conversation. He loved intellectual engagement, or just to BS. His humor was self-deprecating. "I got my job the old-fashioned way," he liked to say, "pure nepotism!" A good laugh line, but it didn't humor Noll, an up-from-the-bootstraps Clevelander. Art Jr. thought Noll a commanding presence, worthy of respect. Noll was forty-two years old, only three years older, but sometimes Art Jr. felt as if he were talking to someone from the Chief's generation, or even to the Chief himself. Both the Chief and Noll intimidated him. Noll challenged Art Jr. much as he challenged his players. Once he told Art Jr. he wanted to see college transcripts for all prospects. In Baltimore, Noll said, pushing a button, the Colts always had gotten transcripts. Accepting the challenge, Art Jr. returned to his office and screamed at secretaries, "Baltimore is getting more transcripts than us! We have to have more! MORE! Write to the schools, call them!!"

A few years earlier, Noll had told Art Jr., "Your problem is that everything is personal. You have to get over that. When you talk to these college coaches, polish up the old brass balls. You've got to talk to them." At another moment, Noll said, "The only reason teeth stay in our mouth is because we grind our upper teeth against our lower teeth, and that strengthens them. That's like the relationship between coaches and players and scouts. You've got to say your piece." Confrontation, Noll seemed to be saying, was part of life. Rise up to it.

In this draft the Steelers would collect the final defining pieces of their 1970s dynasty by choosing four future Hall of Famers in the first five rounds: Swann, Lambert, Stallworth, and Webster. The 1974 NFL draft would produce five Hall of Famers in all, and Pittsburgh got all but Oakland tight end Dave Casper. What made this haul all the more remarkable was that in the draft order Pittsburgh picked twenty-first. Only one other team in modern NFL history had chosen as many as three future Hall of Famers in a single draft: Dallas, picking fourth overall in 1964, chose defensive back Mel Renfro; receiver Bob Hayes; and, in the tenth round, Naval Academy quarterback Roger Staubach, who spent the next five years completing his military commitment before joining the Cowboys in 1969 as a twenty-seven-year-old rookie. Additionally, within twenty-four hours of this 1974 draft, the Steelers signed as free agents safety

Donnie Shell of South Carolina State, a player Nunn admired and urged the Steelers to grab and who would play in Pittsburgh for fourteen seasons and make five Pro Bowls, and tight end Randy Grossman of Temple, who would play for the Steelers for eight seasons. Among them, Swann, Lambert, Stallworth, Webster, and Shell would make twenty-nine Pro Bowl appearances.

"If you get one Hall of Famer in a draft, you've done tremendous," Charley Casserly, an NFL scout and executive for nearly a quarter of a century, would say. "Getting two Hall of Famers is off the charts. But four? That's incomprehensible."

Much later, Bill Walsh said, "Maybe the best draft ever."

Five weeks earlier, the Steelers' 1973 season had ended in Oakland with a 33–14 loss to the Raiders in a divisional playoff game. The Raiders' offensive line, with Jim Otto, Gene Upshaw, and Art Shell ("They were awesome . . . and that's an understatement," Andy Russell said in the locker room), neutralized the Steelers' front four. Joe Greene said afterward, "I'd hate to think we got fat. I'd hate to think *that*." In this 1974 draft, then, the Steelers' goal was to tweak and fortify the roster and perhaps even, in some small way, reinvent it.

Noll had defined the type of player he wanted. "Don't be afraid," he told scouts, "to get excited about a guy like L. C. [Greenwood], a big guy we can put on weights and who has all the other stuff." In this draft, especially, the Steelers would adhere to that concept. They would draft players who lacked heft or height but who possessed other qualities, including intangibles, and who could be taught, developed—reengineered. They could, with Noll's teaching and sculpting, be made.

One by one, the Steelers' top prospects were chosen by other teams. Now, with the twenty-first pick, their time had come. In the draft room, with the cigarettes, cigars, and coffee, there was consensus about Swann, a graceful, big-play performer from Southern Cal. Some had expressed earlier concerns about Swann's size (just five-foot-eleven, 180 pounds) and his speed, 4.6 seconds in the forty—good enough, but not great. Art Jr. had scouted Swann, and ridden in a golf cart around the practice field with USC coach John McKay. In the Steelers' draft room now he told coaches and scouts what McKay had said that day about Swann: "This guy here is one of the greatest competitors that I've ever had. He has uncanny jumping ability, and he has an ability to make the big plays at the big time." Lionel Taylor, for one, had zero concern about Swann. Returning from the Senior Bowl, Taylor, the Steelers' receivers coach, gave this report: "The only thing I know about Swann is this: the sumbitch gets open and catches the football."

But Noll liked Stallworth even more. Here was a moment when Bill Nunn's connections with the black colleges paid a huge dividend. As Dallas's Dick Mansperger, a white scout who covered the black colleges for the Cowboys, said, "The role Bill played was historic and positive. For that time, it was a great edge to have a guy like that working for them. He had those contacts. We didn't have those contacts. It's not that [Grambling coach] Eddie Robinson ever lied to me, but I don't think there is any question that Eddie told Bill Nunn things that he didn't tell me." Dick Haley said, "Bill Nunn was one of the best moves the Steelers ever could have made. All of a sudden, to all of the great black players in the country, the Steelers were one of the premier teams."

Nunn was a people person, smooth and likable, and now as a Pittsburgh Steelers scout he leveraged his relationships. Stallworth was a relative unknown, playing in obscurity before 1,500 fans a game for Alabama A&M in Huntsville. Nunn had worked out Stallworth. He had seen Stallworth cutting to ribbons the Tennessee State secondary. Nunn borrowed that game film from Alabama A&M coaches and promised to return it to the school in a week. The film showed Stallworth as a dazzling performer, and Nunn made certain every Steeler coach and scout saw it. Even the Chief looked at it. On the film, Art Jr. thought, Stallworth looked like the next Don Hutson, Hall of Fame–bound: he blocked, he caught, he ran, he scored. Art Jr. asked Nunn to return the film at once, otherwise "we'll have no credibility at that school." It was the only film Alabama A&M had of that game. But Nunn was in no hurry to give other NFL teams a chance to see Stallworth's artistry. In the Steeler offices Nunn became the greatest salesman that John Stallworth ever had.

In the draft room, Noll was torn: Swann or Stallworth, with the Steelers' first pick? He liked both, but preferred Stallworth. In Dallas, personnel director Gil Brandt wanted Swann with the very next pick, and told his team's representative at NFL draft headquarters, "Have Swann's name on the card and as soon as the [Steelers' allotted] fifteen minutes is up just rush up there and make the choice for us." Brandt thought the Cowboys would get Swann. The clock was ticking: teeth-gnashing time in Pittsburgh. To pass on Swann in the first round would mean to lose him. The Steelers knew that Swann was too well known to be missed by other teams, and if the Steelers chose Stallworth in the first round they wouldn't choose another receiver with their second-round selection because they had needs to fill at other positions. Nunn told the group he believed Stallworth would still be available when the Steelers came up in the fourth round, and Art Jr. and Haley agreed. Their voices rising as one, the scouts insisted to Noll that waiting on Stallworth was a gamble worth taking. With only a few seconds remaining in their allotted time, Noll made the decision to choose Swann. "Then Chuck sulked around," Art Jr. said.

The Steelers' focus in the second round shifted to linebacker, and the choices narrowed to UCLA's Cal Peterson and Kent State's Jack Lambert. Peterson had played in the big time, the Pacific 8 Conference. Lambert was tall and lean, just 203 pounds, and had played in a smaller conference. Art Jr. had visited Kent State when a muddy field moved the team's practice to a nearby parking lot with cinders. There, he watched as Lambert made a crunching tackle, and then got up with his face and arms full of cinders. Art Jr. liked that. The play said plenty about Lambert and his toughness. But what happened next was even more remarkable: Lambert left some of the cinders stuck in his face and arms. He didn't brush them off, at least not at first. It was as if he didn't notice they were there. *How odd! How revealing!* For Art Jr., the image of those cinders was seared in his memory.

Among NFL scouts, Lambert's toughness was hardly a secret. The Cowboys inputted Lambert's player traits into their IBM 360, on which they rated players in categories such as character, mental alertness, explosion, and competitiveness. "As a competitor," Brandt said many years later, "Lambert was as close to perfect as you could get." Other Steeler scouts had watched Lambert in game films against Akron, Bowling Green, Louisville, Toledo. Haley hated that Lambert wore high-topped shoes. "When a guy wears high-tops he doesn't look as quick as a guy wearing low-cuts. *It's an illusion!*" Haley said. But he had no doubts about

Lambert's intensity: "ag-
hit." With the seconds
nd-round choice, Noll
ach, and said, "Woody,
like?" Widenhofer said
antage to Lambert, say-
at special teams player."
Lambert.
ird-round pick, though
ey would have to wait
th. Noll's mood soured.
round." Art Jr. would
." Five receivers would
orth—Louisiana Tech's
State's Gerald Tinker,
ore. When the Steelers
eighty-second overall
erably: "He got kind of
got lucky," Nunn said.
fensive back, with their
and final round of the
he number of available
several players, includ-
rong recommendations
nference coaches with
that Webster, at six-
ry to play in the NFL.
center, and its report
on't get much bigger—
college all-star games,
hilate highly regarded
eir asses. His blocking
cise. The Steelers made
raft's 125th pick.
elers' haul had been "a

draft of exceptions." Art Jr. knew
Draft.' You had Swann as 'too sma
Stallworth was 'an unknown.' And

The *Pittsburgh Press* sportswrit
wrote, "They got a kid who figure
spire some bad jokes [Swann]; a li
cue [Lambert]; a receiver they did
guys [Allen, Webster] who seem too
gage." By Musick's figuring, the S
the ball during training camp."

The next night, his pro football
a few friends, drowned his sorrow
University's undersized tight en
drafted by an NFL team. Live and
television station with sportscaste
wide receiver Billy "White Shoes"
ment when two local Philly boys
waited. Finally, in the fifteenth
Grossman, there came more waiti
Grossman said. When a Tuskegee
final, player selected in the draft
Grossman stared at the floor. At t
a call from his parents. They'd bee
gested they phone the bar. The Pi
said excitedly, "and they want to
agent contract." Grossman had h
in his law office the next mornin
Steelers. He wore dark glasses, a
fob, and had a fat cigar stuck in hi
of money and of the big time. He
fessional football team, so Grossn

He wasn't. Standing before hir
one of a handful of team officials

has uncanny jumping ability, and he has an ability to make the big plays at the big time." Lionel Taylor, for one, had zero concern about Swann. Returning from the Senior Bowl, Taylor, the Steelers' receivers coach, gave this report: "The only thing I know about Swann is this: the sumbitch gets open and catches the football."

But Noll liked Stallworth even more. Here was a moment when Bill Nunn's connections with the black colleges paid a huge dividend. As Dallas's Dick Mansperger, a white scout who covered the black colleges for the Cowboys, said, "The role Bill played was historic and positive. For that time, it was a great edge to have a guy like that working for them. He had those contacts. We didn't have those contacts. It's not that [Grambling coach] Eddie Robinson ever lied to me, but I don't think there is any question that Eddie told Bill Nunn things that he didn't tell me." Dick Haley said, "Bill Nunn was one of the best moves the Steelers ever could have made. All of a sudden, to all of the great black players in the country, the Steelers were one of the premier teams."

Nunn was a people person, smooth and likable, and now as a Pittsburgh Steelers scout he leveraged his relationships. Stallworth was a relative unknown, playing in obscurity before 1,500 fans a game for Alabama A&M in Huntsville. Nunn had worked out Stallworth. He had seen Stallworth cutting to ribbons the Tennessee State secondary. Nunn borrowed that game film from Alabama A&M coaches and promised to return it to the school in a week. The film showed Stallworth as a dazzling performer, and Nunn made certain every Steeler coach and scout saw it. Even the Chief looked at it. On the film, Art Jr. thought, Stallworth looked like the next Don Hutson, Hall of Fame–bound: he blocked, he caught, he ran, he scored. Art Jr. asked Nunn to return the film at once, otherwise "we'll have no credibility at that school." It was the only film Alabama A&M had of that game. But Nunn was in no hurry to give other NFL teams a chance to see Stallworth's artistry. In the Steeler offices Nunn became the greatest salesman that John Stallworth ever had.

In the draft room, Noll was torn: Swann or Stallworth, with the Steelers' first pick? He liked both, but preferred Stallworth. In Dallas, personnel director Gil Brandt wanted Swann with the very next pick, and told his team's representative at NFL draft headquarters, "Have Swann's name on the card and as soon as the [Steelers' allotted] fifteen minutes is up just rush up there and make the choice for us." Brandt thought the Cowboys would get Swann. The clock was ticking: teeth-gnashing time in Pittsburgh. To pass on Swann in the first round would mean to lose him. The Steelers knew that Swann was too well known to be missed by other teams, and if the Steelers chose Stallworth in the first round they wouldn't choose another receiver with their second-round selection because they had needs to fill at other positions. Nunn told the group he believed Stallworth would still be available when the Steelers came up in the fourth round, and Art Jr. and Haley agreed. Their voices rising as one, the scouts insisted to Noll that waiting on Stallworth was a gamble worth taking. With only a few seconds remaining in their allotted time, Noll made the decision to choose Swann. "Then Chuck sulked around," Art Jr. said.

The Steelers' focus in the second round shifted to linebacker, and the choices narrowed to UCLA's Cal Peterson and Kent State's Jack Lambert. Peterson had played in the big time, the Pacific 8 Conference. Lambert was tall and lean, just 203 pounds, and had played in a smaller conference. Art Jr. had visited Kent State when a muddy field moved the team's practice to a nearby parking lot with cinders. There, he watched as Lambert made a crunching tackle, and then got up with his face and arms full of cinders. Art Jr. liked that. The play said plenty about Lambert and his toughness. But what happened next was even more remarkable: Lambert left some of the cinders stuck in his face and arms. He didn't brush them off, at least not at first. It was as if he didn't notice they were there. *How odd! How revealing!* For Art Jr., the image of those cinders was seared in his memory.

Among NFL scouts, Lambert's toughness was hardly a secret. The Cowboys inputted Lambert's player traits into their IBM 360, on which they rated players in categories such as character, mental alertness, explosion, and competitiveness. "As a competitor," Brandt said many years later, "Lambert was as close to perfect as you could get." Other Steeler scouts had watched Lambert in game films against Akron, Bowling Green, Louisville, Toledo. Haley hated that Lambert wore high-topped shoes. "When a guy wears high-tops he doesn't look as quick as a guy wearing low-cuts. *It's an illusion!*" Haley said. But he had no doubts about

Lambert's ferocity. In his reports, Haley wrote of Lambert's intensity: "aggressive and reckless in his play" and "will really hit." With the seconds ticking away for the Steelers to make their second-round choice, Noll turned to Widenhofer, the young linebackers coach, and said, "Woody, you worked out both of these guys. Who do you like?" Widenhofer said he liked Peterson and Lambert, but gave the advantage to Lambert, saying, "With his personality, he's going to be a great special teams player." With the forty-sixth overall pick, the Steelers took Lambert.

Earlier the Steelers had traded away their third-round pick, though they had two choices in the fourth round. They would have to wait thirty-six more selections to get a shot at Stallworth. Noll's mood soured. He muttered, "We'll never get him in the fourth round." Art Jr. would say, "Chuck was pissed. He was REALLY pissed." Five receivers would be selected by other NFL teams ahead of Stallworth—Louisiana Tech's Roger Carr, Tennessee State's John Holland, Kent State's Gerald Tinker, Alabama's Wayne Wheeler, and Florida's Nat Moore. When the Steelers selected Stallworth in the fourth round with the eighty-second overall pick, Art Jr. noticed that Noll brightened considerably: "He got kind of light on his feet." The scouts' gamble paid off. "We got lucky," Nunn said.

The Steelers chose Jimmy Allen, a UCLA defensive back, with their next pick in the fourth round. Then, in the fifth and final round of the draft's first day, they examined their 200 List. The number of available players on it had dwindled. They had their eye on several players, including Mike Webster, Wisconsin's center, who had strong recommendations from Perles and Widenhofer, former Big 10 Conference coaches with deep connections in the conference. All agreed that Webster, at six-foot-one and 225 pounds, lacked the size necessary to play in the NFL. BLESTO rated him as the nation's eleventh-best center, and its report stated Webster's downside bluntly: "Well built. Won't get much bigger—Strong for size but just too small for big people." In college all-star games, though, Noll and Steeler scouts saw Webster annihilate highly regarded opponents. One by one, he knocked them on their asses. His blocking technique, especially his leverage, was textbook-precise. The Steelers made Webster the third center selected overall, with the draft's 125th pick.

At day's end Noll told local reporters the Steelers' haul had been "a draft of exceptions." Art Jr. knew what he meant: "It was the 'Undersized Draft.' You had Swann as 'too small and slow.' Lambert was 'too skinny.' Stallworth was 'an unknown.' And Webby was a 'midget.' "

The *Pittsburgh Press* sportswriter Phil Musick was unimpressed. He wrote, "They got a kid who figures to play some good football and inspire some bad jokes [Swann]; a linebacker built along the lines of a pool cue [Lambert]; a receiver they didn't expect to get [Stallworth]; and two guys [Allen, Webster] who seem to fall under the heading of excess baggage." By Musick's figuring, the Steelers got Webster "primarily to snap the ball during training camp."

The next night, his pro football dream crushed, Randy Grossman, with a few friends, drowned his sorrows at a local bar in Philadelphia. Temple University's undersized tight end had harbored big hopes for being drafted by an NFL team. Live and on camera, Grossman had sat in a local television station with sportscaster Tom Brookshier and Widener College wide receiver Billy "White Shoes" Johnson, waiting for that proud moment when two local Philly boys got their good news. They waited. And waited. Finally, in the fifteenth round, Houston selected Johnson. For Grossman, there came more waiting. "I'm just sitting there like a chump," Grossman said. When a Tuskegee defensive back became the 442nd, and final, player selected in the draft, Brookshier looked at Grossman, and Grossman stared at the floor. At the bar, the suds flowing, Grossman got a call from his parents. They'd been trying to reach him, and a friend suggested they phone the bar. The Pittsburgh Steelers had called, his parents said excitedly, "and they want to meet with you tomorrow to sign a free-agent contract." Grossman had hired an attorney to represent him, and in his law office the next morning they met the man from the Pittsburgh Steelers. He wore dark glasses, a three-piece navy blue suit, a gold watch fob, and had a fat cigar stuck in his mouth. To Grossman, this man reeked of money and of the big time. He certainly *looked* like the owner of a professional football team, so Grossman naively assumed that he was.

He wasn't. Standing before him was Ralph Berlin, the Steelers' trainer, one of a handful of team officials dispatched, posthaste, to sign undrafted players. Berlin was known in the Steelers' locker room as the Plumber. When Steeler coach Bill Austin and his staff were fired after the 1968 season, and Noll and his new assistant coaches arrived, they peppered Berlin with questions ("What about this? What about that?"), until finally Berlin tossed up his hands and said, "Hey, don't ask me! I'm just the plumber." And to the Steelers he would remain the Plumber forevermore. His fat cigar had a story, too. He had been smoking inexpensive Hav-A-Tampa cigars. But when the Chief spotted him with those cheapies, he told Berlin, "If you are going to work for this organization, you better smoke better cigars." Now he did.

Contract negotiations with Grossman did not get far before Berlin asked Grossman's attorney to borrow a phone. Berlin went into a back room and called Dan. "You want me to sign this guy?" he asked, his voice a whisper. "The guy's no bigger than I am!"

"Well, we need someone," Dan replied, "who can bang around in training camp."

"All right," Berlin said. "I'm not going to give him any money."

Grossman got the usual free-agent salary, $15,000 in his first year, plus three $1,000 incentive bonuses. The Steelers also gave him a check for $500 to buy an airline ticket to Pittsburgh and cover some expenses. Grossman cashed it in instead, figuring he could drive the three hundred miles.

That spring he got a part-time job on a landscaping crew. During a break he told coworkers he had a college degree. "So what are you going to do?" one asked. Grossman answered, "Play professional football." As he pulled weeds from the ground, Randy Grossman noticed that his answer surprised them.

In August 1974, as President Richard Nixon, his political destruction complete, readied a helicopter to leave the White House, Franco Harris marched in Latrobe with a picket sign that read, ON STRIKE TO END OWNERS MONOPOLY. The NFL players' union struck in the name of free agency, and so, on the first day of training camp in 1974, when Mike Webster exploded like a meteor into the Steelers' consciousness, television didn't capture it. The cameras were fixed instead on the fringe of the Saint Vincent campus on the veteran Steelers and their picket signs. The Chief wasn't happy about the strike, but later, when he saw a few of his veteran players with their placards at the end of a road outside the Steelers' camp, he drove up, handed them a six-pack of beer, and said, "Thought you fellows might be awful hot out here."

The Steelers' rookies took part in the Oklahoma drill, which became a drama unto itself: a blocker and tackler at war, in the game's most fundamental battle. Once Webster leveraged a would-be tackler with his well-muscled arms, the battle was over. In one spirited matchup, he dropped fellow rookie Lambert, who later said, "Mr. Webster is one hell of a fine center." Sports editor Sam Bechtel of the *Beaver County Times* watched it happen and wrote, "Ray Mansfield and Jim Clack, if you are reading this, maybe you'd better start sweating the length of the strike. Mike Webster is a center."

Lambert soon created a training camp buzz of his own, stuffing ball-carriers, and ranging impressively far and wide in pass coverage. The understated Noll surprised beat writers by describing Lambert with superlatives such as *fantastic* and *sensational*. After two days of practices, Noll said, "He's something . . . a real pain-in-the-rear to our offense. We've tried to test him and he's done everything expected of him. He really zeroes in on the ball and doesn't let anything bother him." At the outset of camp each year, beat writers selected their own dark-horse candidate to make the team. "Who's your man?" Noll asked Bechtel at the end of the first day. "Webster," Bechtel replied. Noll grinned and said, "You're safe."

Three weeks later, the strike over, veterans reported. The usual hazing of rookies commenced. When the veterans told Lambert to sing the Kent State song, he snarled and said, "Kiss my ass."

A new day had arrived.

CHAPTER 9

QUARTERBACK CONTROVERSY: BRAD, RAT, OR JOE GILLIE?

ON MOST DAYS, THE CHIEF still had a retinue of curious local characters by his side. Among the regulars were his driver Richie Easton, who for a living drove a newspaper delivery truck; a police inspector from the South Side memorably named Iggy Borkowski; and Joey Diven, big and handsome, good with his fists, and all Irish. Diven was from nearby Oakland and once beat up the entire Pitt football team, or so the street legend went. He worked for a time as a doorman/bouncer for the Ancient Order of Hibernians on Oakland Avenue, up on the third floor, or, as Diven once said, "Up twenty-eight steps if you accidentally fell down them." Now he worked the Steelers' bench on game days, removing those who didn't belong. A fan stole Houston coach Bum Phillips's cowboy hat once as he walked off the field at Three Rivers Stadium, and so the Chief assigned Diven to serve as Phillips's escort on his next visit. As they walked off the field together, with fans tightly packed around them, Phillips still remembers: "A ten-foot ring opened up around us. They parted on both sides like the Red Sea. Never in my life had I seen anything as natural as that. Everybody knew who that guy [Diven] was, and they wouldn't get within ten feet of him. It was like a big wave coming. You could see it and it was unreal."

About the time the Steelers were ready to make their mark on history,

history paid a visit to their locker room in the form of the Chief and an old friend, the Pittsburgh Kid, Billy Conn. When Conn was with him, the Chief stood a little taller, and prouder. Conn, who named the Chief godfather to his first son, fought twenty-one world champions and defeated them all, except Joe Louis. The Chief was at ringside at the Polo Grounds in Coogan's Bluff in the summer of '41 when Conn had Louis outpointed on the scorecards, and his manager's voice in his ear, saying, "Stick and run. You got the fight won." But in the thirteenth round Conn defied orders and went for a knockout. Louis, with a thirty-pound advantage, saw an opening and struck a murderous right to Conn's jaw, and the Pittsburgh Kid, knocked out, drifted off to paradise. "I lost my head," Conn said in his locker room afterward, "and a million dollars." He also said, "What's the use of being Irish if you can't be dumb?" Now, as the Chief introduced Conn to a few of his Steeler players, Conn sensed they didn't know who he was. So he called across the room to several black Steelers. "Hey, blackies," Conn said, "you know who Joe Louis was?" They nodded. Conn looked back to several white Steeler players he had just met, shook his head in disbelief, and said, "And you sunsuvbitches don't know me?"

The week of the 1974 season opener, another local group paid homage to the Chief for his civic devotion. A local politician likened the Chief's many charitable acts to those of Richard K. Mellon, the local banker and philanthropist who had spearheaded the postwar Pittsburgh Renaissance urban revitalization movement. To the Chief, *that* was overdoing it. "[To] put me in a class with General Mellon that's it," the Chief wrote in a note to newspaperman Roy McHugh. With a touch of humor he added, "I didn't mind being with Gov. D. L. Lawrence because he was a horse player and a politician and I was a horse player and a ward heeler." Then turning to the Steelers' season, the Chief wrote, hopefully, "If they go all the way, Noll, the players, and Danny should be at the front table." Already he was quietly admitting that a Super Bowl victory was possible.

But the Steelers were suffering chaos at quarterback, no way to start an empire. "Somebody's got to take the bull by the horns," Noll said, and he would use this phrase often, through September, October, and well into November. The 1974 Steelers' quarterback controversy became high palace intrigue accompanied by big headlines, racial overtones, a plea to be traded, and death threats. If not for the strength of the Steelers' defense and running game, the quarterback controversy might have undermined their season.

Noll's quarterback options:

- Terry Bradshaw. He had sailed into harbor in 1970 like a proud high-masted ship, only to crash into the pier. After four NFL seasons, Bradshaw, at twenty-five, retained his impressive physical skills but was an emotional and statistical wreckage: a thousand passes thrown in the NFL with forty-one touchdowns and seventy-three interceptions, his inconsistency maddening, his vast potential unmet. Long ago, the Steelers had cut Johnny Unitas too soon. Their lesson learned, they exhibited more patience with Bradshaw, but even patience had its limits.

- Terry Hanratty. Known to teammates as the Rat (or Ratso Rizzo, from the movie *Midnight Cowboy*), Hanratty had a thick mustache, a prominent nose, and a magnificent sense of humor. The Rat also possessed the Chief's three favorite qualities: he was a local boy, Catholic, and a former all-American at Notre Dame—check, check, and check. The Steelers' game-day scorecard generously listed Hanratty at six-foot-one, and wearing a single digit on his jersey (number 5) made him appear smaller still. In five seasons with the Steelers, Hanratty had started sixteen games, his performance, at best, competent.

- Joe Gilliam. A black-colleges cult hero, he threw lovely forty-yard passes off his back foot. Six-foot-two and 180 pounds, Gilliam had the courage of Hercules but legs like swizzle sticks. When he scrambled he looked like Olive Oyl being chased by a team of Blutos. In his third season with the Steelers (including time on the taxi squad), Gilliam was vying to become the first black quarterback to start an NFL season opener and then keep his job. In college, Gilliam wore number 12 and white shoes, just like his hero, Broadway Joe Namath. As Namath was sometimes known as *Joe Willie*, Gilliam's Steelers teammates took to calling him *Joe Gillie*. Wearing his trademark Charlie Chan–style hat, Gilliam entered the locker room with a life-of-the-party personality. "Just the skinniest man," Fuqua said. "I thought he was too skinny to play football. I thought the first time he got hit he'd be broken in half. But he was a competitor." And he threw the football sweetly.

Ultimately, it was Noll's decision, his game to play. He'd fired assistant Babe Parilli as his quarterbacks coach after the 1973 season and made Parilli's job his. Now the quarterbacks answered directly to Noll each and every day. No one could accuse Noll of micromanaging his quarterbacks on Sundays: the old messenger guard allowed them to call their own plays (coach Paul Brown still called plays in Cincinnati and Noll termed him "the oldest quarterback in the league"). Neither could anyone accuse Noll of racial motivations. His racial bona fides were established long before. Even now, he chose Lionel Taylor, his only black assistant coach, as his roommate on road trips.

The Steelers' three quarterbacks genuinely liked each other. They knew each other's habits, weaknesses, the way they played cards. The three quarterbacks talked, laughed, commiserated. Noll lived in their heads. They feared him.

Somebody's got to take the bull by the horns.

Noll watched them, arms folded, lips pursed, like a grim gargoyle.

Among the three quarterbacks, Gilliam broke ranks with the striking veterans first, reporting to camp on July 29. He crossed the picket line after four weeks, as he explained to the team's veterans, because his position on the Steelers was already tenuous. He hoped they understood. "I feel sure Hanratty and Bradshaw will have no hard feelings," Gilliam said as he arrived in Latrobe. "I need some work and I came to camp to get it." Other players on the team and around the league were breaking ranks, too. On the same day Gilliam reported, so did Steeler defensive linemen Ernie Holmes and Steve Furness. Bradshaw reported a week later (sportswriters excitedly passing the news through camp, "The Blond Bomber's here!"), about the same time Cowboy quarterback Roger Staubach reported in Dallas.

No Steeler could remain angry with Joey Gilliam for long. He was fun, talented, a great teammate. Safety Mike Wagner said, "His vocabulary of foul expressions and foul words was the biggest I've ever seen. He'd say it, and he'd always be smiling. He was," Wagner said, "a lovable character." As a rookie in 1972, Gilliam had competed in the Cardinal Puff beer-drinking game at the 19th Hole, the Steelers' favorite watering hole in Latrobe. With Bradshaw sitting across from him and cheering his efforts, Gilliam choked on his beer and threw up in Bradshaw's face. A disgusted Bradshaw, who didn't drink, heaved and threw up on Gilliam, a true bonding experience. Beyond their camaraderie, Bradshaw and Gilliam shared a speed and crispness in the delivery of their passes that few could equal. When most NFL quarterbacks threw the ball, Taylor, the receivers coach, said, "You could *see* it travel. But when Joe [Gilliam] and Bradshaw threw it, it was just *there*."

Gilliam's task in the NFL was doubly difficult. He had to pick apart not only defenses but also stereotypes, namely that a black man wasn't smart enough to lead an NFL offense. More than a few talented black-college quarterbacks had been forced to change their position in the NFL to wide receiver or defensive back, the so-called speed or black positions, or else they went to Canada to play quarterback. Joey Gilliam's great-grandfather, known to the family as Pa Henry, was born into slavery in 1855 in South Carolina's upcountry. According to the family's oral tradition and research, when freedom finally came, Pa Henry's parents got forty acres and a mule and took on their master's name, Guillaume, slightly modified, to Gilliam—that is, *Gee-yahm* becoming *Gill-um*. When Pa Henry finally settled, he did so far away, in Steubenville, Ohio, north of the Mason-Dixon line, where his son would marry a third cousin, and work at a steel mill in the open hearth where, it was said, blacks had the constitution to better handle the fiery heat. Their son, the future Tennessee State assistant football coach, Joe Gilliam Sr., born in 1923, excelled as an athlete. He briefly played football at Indiana University, where against Michigan in 1945, his white teammates lodged at a local hotel while he and his black teammates slept on cots on plastic flooring at the 85,000-seat Michigan Stadium. Later Joe Sr. changed schools, and played shooting guard on the unbeaten 1947 West Virginia State University basketball team captained by Bill Nunn Jr. Joe Sr. earned a master's degree in education, and then made a career coaching football at black colleges, for decades as a no-nonsense defensive assistant to Big John Merritt at Jackson State and Tennessee State. From nearly the beginning, Coach Gilliam knew that Joey, the third of his four children, born in 1950, had a special athletic gift.

Joey Gilliam became a football star at Pearl High School in Nashville and then at Tennessee State, an All-American leading his team to the mythical national championship of the black colleges in 1970 and 1971. He threw often, whenever possible, the ball arcing in pretty spirals, but he hung in the pocket too long, taking hits. On the sidelines, his father whispered, "Joey, you've got to play-action or you'll get killed!"—spoken quietly enough so the offensive coaches wouldn't hear and think Coach Gilliam was meddling in their affairs. At the sunken W. J. Hale Stadium, which TSU players fancied as the Hole, twenty thousand fans chanted his name under the lights as he slew rivals such as Grambling, Southern, Prairie View, and Jackson State. At home, Coach Gilliam and his wife, Ruth, instilled middle-class values and the importance of education and discipline—or at least, with Joey, they tried. Merritt created a nickname for his dynamic quarterback, *Jefferson Street Joe*, a catchy acknowledgment of the thoroughfare that passed through campus and was the historic hub of black Nashville. Joey liked the nickname, favoring any link to Broadway Joe Namath. "But my wife highly resented it," Coach Gilliam said, "because the connotation of Jefferson Street is 'unruly, black thugs,' all that. Unsavory. Not too many good things go on there. I didn't care much for it, either. Merritt thought he was doing Joey a favor—make him famous."

Father and son had their battles. Once, Joey showed up late to practice at TSU. His father, as team disciplinarian, held him accountable. He made Joey do the "2-5-5s"—lying down and rolling the hundred-yard length of the field twice, then running five hundred-yard dashes followed by five fifty-yard dashes. That night Joey brought his soiled practice clothes home to be cleaned. Ruth said, "What's this?" Joey replied, "Daddy made me roll," and he explained how he was late to practice because he wasn't let out of class in time by his instructor. Coach Gilliam arrived home that night and his wife lit into him. "You rolled YOUR OWN CHILD in the mud?" she said. "That's YOUR CHILD!" Coach: "See, he was late to practice." Wife: "He said he was in class." Coach: "Baby, he

was telling a lie. I checked it out. He was talking to a girl and the time ran out on him." Wife: "And you ROLLED your own child? In the MUD?" Coach: "Yes." Wife: "See, I've always told you that football was going to make a damn fool out of you sooner or later! And now it finally did!" The coach knew his son. Years later he said, "Joey was secretive. He didn't let you know what he was doing. Joey would figure out ways to circumvent the regulations. He didn't mean any harm. That was just his nature."

Some black scouts in the NFL rooted hard for Joey Gilliam to succeed. He was a source of racial pride. Bill Nunn wanted him in Pittsburgh. Noll's old teammate with the Browns Bobby Mitchell, now a Redskins scout, wanted him in Washington. "This kid is sitting there on a keg of dynamite that is our history. That whole keg of dynamite is black history and he has it in his hands," Mitchell said years later. "I didn't want him to be wasting in Canada. He was just too good. Blacks folks, we *loooved* Jefferson Street Joe! We loved him to death. . . . And we knew that no matter how tough it got, he could work out of it on the field." Both Mitchell and Nunn rated Gilliam an NFL first-round pick based on talent. But because of racial stereotypes, Gilliam's slim physique, and because pro football had known only two black starting quarterbacks (Denver's Marlon Briscoe, later converted to a wide receiver, and Buffalo's James Harris, who started the opener in 1969 in his only start of that season), they knew he would be selected much lower than that. The Steelers, at Nunn's urging, selected him in the eleventh round of the 1972 draft. "He's the best player available," Nunn told Noll in the Steelers' draft room. "Sure, he's another quarterback, but he's still the best player available." Coach Gilliam served as his son's agent, and during negotiations accused Dan of offering too little. "You want to pay Joey *black quarterback* money," he charged, even though he knew that an eleventh-round pick had no bargaining leverage. Insulted, Dan snapped back, "I object to that!" Meanwhile, when her son left for his first Steelers training camp, Ruth Gilliam worried, "It's not going to work out. He's too immature. It's too much money, and Joey is indulgent."

Gilliam brought a supreme self-confidence to the huddle. During the 1974 season, he would tell Steelers rookie running back Reggie Harrison, who was about to run a medium flare route from out of the backfield, "I'm coming to you. Look for the strings. They are going to be at twelve o'clock." Harrison ran his route and here came Gilliam's pass with the strings on top. Twelve o'clock. *Holy mackerel!* Harrison took to calling Gilliam "Black Magic."

In a 26–7 victory over New Orleans in the exhibition opener, Gilliam excelled, completing eleven of nineteen passes for 158 yards. "You can't ask for any more than that," Noll said after the game. Gilliam's throwing style was unique: he held the ball low, near his right hip, and then, as if pulling it from his right pocket, flung it downfield with a dramatic snap action that was too quick for a camera to capture without his hand blurring. The strength of Gilliam's arm reminded center Ray Mansfield of Sonny Jurgensen's, the way "he'd field those high, soft bombs." Gilliam's performance sent an electrical current through camp. In subsequent exhibition victories over the Bears and Eagles, he outplayed Bradshaw, who suffered a forearm injury in the process. Then, against the New York Giants, Gilliam outplayed Hanratty, who threw ten passes with three completions and two interceptions.

One newspaper headline asked coyly, "Guess Who's Coming to Quarterback?"

"Right now it would be hard not to start him," Noll said of Gilliam after the victory over the Giants. "Right now it's very lopsided—extremely lopsided."

During a break in practice, Hanratty and Gilliam approached a water bucket. "Which side you gonna drink out of, Joe?" Hanratty said. "I want to know so I can drink out of the other side." Together, they laughed.

That was the Rat. He humored his way through the controversy. A salesman's son, he grew up thirty-five miles north of Pittsburgh in Butler, a town of steel, coal, Pullman-Standard (the nation's biggest maker of railroad cars), and football. "No one had a dime," Hanratty recalled, "or cared." So vast was the pool of football talent in the area that famous college coaches such as Paterno, Ohio State's Woody Hayes, and Michigan State's Duffy Daugherty became regulars passing through town. Hanratty met another high-profile college coach at lunch at the Pittsburgh Hilton, Notre Dame's Ara Parseghian. The Rat wanted to order a steak sandwich, but it cost three-fifty, too expensive. *He'll think I'm gouging him*, he thought. So he went for the buck-and-a-half club sandwich instead, and soon after accepted an offer to join the Fighting Irish. At Notre Dame he wore a crew cut, and each Friday players lined up and passed Parseghian in review, the head coach advising "shorter hair" or "shorter sideburns." Hanratty quarterbacked the Fighting Irish to the national title in 1966 with Bleier as a teammate. Hanratty appeared on the cover of *Time* magazine with receiver Jim Seymour, heady times for young ballplayers.

In Pittsburgh, Hanratty brought levity to the mix. As a scout team quarterback in practice, he once approached the line of scrimmage and blew kisses at the amped-up rookie Lambert. "Hanratty's up here blowing me kisses!" Lambert complained to coaches, to no avail. The Rat also hid cups of water beneath Lambert's shoulder pads in the locker room, and watched with glee as the rookie got drenched time and again. When Lambert suspected his trick was coming, Hanratty skipped a day, and then got him the next day, snickering, "You dumb bastard."

In the exhibition finale, in Dallas on September 6, Gilliam again showed his exquisite passing touch, completing ten of thirteen for 137 yards and two touchdowns as the Steelers beat the Cowboys 41–15 to complete the NFL's only 6-0 preseason record. Gilliam's older brother Craig, an assistant coach at nearby Bishop College, approached Gilliam after the game. "What are your chances to start this season?" Craig asked. The regular-season opener, against Baltimore, was just nine days off. "If I keep doing this," Joey Gilliam replied, "they'll have to start me."

A day later, Noll formally named Gilliam his opening-day starter. He was joined on the roster by fourteen rookies, nearly 30 percent of the team. Gilliam drew nearly all the media light. Dan Rather of the *CBS Evening News* reported, "There is a sociological aspect, a kind of sociological undertow to what the Steelers are doing."

If Hanratty was having his devil-may-care fun, Bradshaw was not. He was miserable, lonely, and alone.

Nearly everyone had expected Bradshaw to emerge as the Steelers' starting quarterback, a job that was his to begin with. He had the big name, the big arm, the big body, and a combined 20-6 record as starter during the two previous seasons. Plus, he was the Chief's boy, his teacher's pet status a subject of much teasing from teammates. The Chief would say that Bradshaw was like Babe Ruth and Jack Dempsey, an athlete for the ages, but he wasn't, at least not yet.

Before arriving in Pittsburgh, Bradshaw had never been booed or benched. He'd never seen a press conference, let alone participated in one. He'd never lived in a city with trolley lines and steel mills and black smoke. He'd never seen Pittsburgh, not even on television. He had never been skewered by the sports press or belittled (for poor scores on his college entrance exams) as Lil' Abner or a dunce. He'd never been divorced, as he was in 1973 after a brief marriage to a former Miss Teen America. He'd never thrown three interceptions in a second quarter (two returned for touchdowns), as he did in a 1973 exhibition game against the Giants at Yankee Stadium, or had his head coach berate him publicly, as Noll did on the sideline that day. Noll grabbed Bradshaw as he turned toward the water cooler and jerked him back to their conversation. One man in the press box who watched the scene through binoculars said, "Noll's not a swearer. And he said at least five 'fucks.' "

But the worst moment of all, Bradshaw's personal nadir, came later during that 1973 season, when he gained four yards on a quarterback sneak and a massive Bengals defensive tackle named Steve Chomyszak landed on his throwing shoulder. Trainer Ralph Berlin and equipment man Tony Parisi raced to the field to help. Bradshaw rose slowly to his feet and took a step toward the sideline, half bent, wincing in pain, pressing his left hand to his right shoulder, and that's when he heard it. Almost imperceptible at first, it grew in volume until it was unmistakable: Steelers fans cheering that their quarterback was hurt. "Almost made me sick," the Chief said. Greene called the cheers "vicious." Bradshaw felt pain in his shoulder, which was mildly separated, but a deeper pain in his heart. Later, some wondered if those hometown cheers were for Hanratty, about to return to the field. They weren't. Greene rushed to Bradshaw's defense, not for the first, or last, time, saying, "I'd be lying if I didn't say he doesn't tick me off sometimes. He does. [But] he needs to know he's our quarterback and that this team is behind him, and it is. . . . People don't realize the pressure on him to do good. They compare him to Joe Namath. But how many times did Namath foul up in his first four years? Plenty of times."

From the first, Bradshaw had a paragon's look. Punter Bobby Walden

had watched him throwing passes as a rookie in Latrobe in 1970 and predicted, "If he doesn't get hurt, in five years we'll be in the Super Bowl." A single play—the Immaculate Reception—had revealed multiple dimensions of Bradshaw's quarterbacking talent: his nimble footwork escaping the Raiders' pass rush; his courage to withstand an oncoming rusher's devastating blow as he threw; and his rocket release, evidenced by how the ball exploded into the collision between Tatum and Fuqua, and ricocheted to Harris.

Of course, Bradshaw also had what scouts called *rabbit ears*. He heard every catcall at Three Rivers Stadium, and each one wounded him deeply. "There's nothing dumb about him at all," Noll once told Art Jr. "He's just a flighty guy." Most critically, Noll believed that Bradshaw had yet to earn the trust, or confidence, of his teammates in the offensive huddle.

Now, with Gilliam named as the starter, Bill Christine, sports columnist for the *Pittsburgh Post-Gazette*, cracked, "Terry Bradshaw is the wrong guy to be living in a town with so many bridges. It's a good thing Bradshaw doesn't do any shaving commercials, because nobody would trust him with a razor blade in his hand. Nor would it be safe for Bradshaw to do any shilling for gas stoves."

Bradshaw wanted to be traded. Rumors surfaced that he was bound for the San Francisco 49ers in a trade, and so Bradshaw walked into the Steelers' locker room one day crooning "I Left My Heart in San Francisco." None of his teammates said a word. "Darn right. I'd love to be traded," Bradshaw told reporters. Gilliam had earned the starting job, he said, but sitting on the bench "would not only bother the hell out of me, it would be a waste of my time. . . . I don't feel any allegiance toward the Steelers, that's for sure."

Young, immature, and forever pampered in Louisiana, Bradshaw didn't understand Noll. At that moment, he despised him. In damage control mode, Dan Rooney met with Bradshaw the next morning, calmed him, and praised his determination and spirit. He said the Steelers would not trade him. Then Bradshaw met with Noll and told him, "I know there are teams that would like to have me. You obviously don't like me. Joe Gilliam is starting." Noll surprised him with kindness and flattery, complimenting his talent as never before. Listening, Bradshaw thought, *And I'm on the bench?*

An earlier football empire had handled a frayed relationship between head coach and quarterback in a more constructive way. In 1960, Lombardi, in his second season as Green Bay's head coach, had exploded at quarterback Bart Starr for throwing an interception during practice. Like Bradshaw in 1974, Starr was in his fifth NFL season, and already had been benched earlier that year. After practice, Starr paid a visit to Lombardi's office. Pointedly, he told him that the interception wasn't his fault, explaining that it had been tipped by a defender. Then Starr boldly told Lombardi that if he wanted him to lead the Packers, Lombardi could not chew him out like that in front of the team. "If you feel I have it coming, have at it. But please do it in the privacy of your office here," Starr said. Lombardi listened and nodded. "I hear you," Lombardi said. From that moment, Starr believed their relationship, and the Packers' fortunes, moved to a new and higher level. Bradshaw lacked Starr's confidence. Decades later, Bradshaw said, "I could never, nor would I, have gone in" to speak with Noll, as Starr had with Lombardi. "I was too afraid of my coach," Bradshaw said.

The Chief became Bradshaw's guardian angel. He invited him to dinner at 940 North Lincoln. They dined with Kass, and then the two men retired to the Chief's den, where they smoked cigars and watched *Monday Night Football.* There were long silences, cigar smoke curling toward the ceiling. They talked about their shared love of horses and about the pressures in Bradshaw's life. The Chief made him feel wanted, special. "Bradshaw may have a lot in common with this stadium," the Chief had said back in 1970 when Three Rivers was ready to open. "He'll be beautiful— when he's finished." He gave Bradshaw a key to his office at the ballpark, the only player given such access. At the Chief's invitation, Bradshaw helped himself to the cigars atop his desk. In his den at home, the Chief told him not to worry about Noll or the newspapers. He waved his right hand, as if brushing away all the naysayers, saying, "You're the best!" Then he brushed them away again and repeated, "You're the best!"

The Steeler players mostly kept quiet about the quarterback controversy. It was a tinderbox topic, and besides they had their own positions to worry about. Racial tensions might have torn a lesser team. Joe Greene made his voice heard. He stood behind Bradshaw consistently. "If we were

going to have a chance," Greene said later, "it was going to be with him." If anyone asked Greene, he would say, "Terry's the guy."

Living alone in a downtown high-rise, Bradshaw grew a beard and turned to the Bible. He arrived to Three Rivers Stadium early on many days and threw passes to members of the grounds crew, ball boys, or office workers, their fingers throbbing from catching his hard, tight spirals. He waited for his next chance.

"PITTSBURGH'S BLACK QUARTERBACK." Those words accompanied Joe Gilliam, taking the snap from center, on the cover of *Sports Illustrated* after Gillie shredded the Baltimore Colts' defense in a 30–0 victory in the opener, in Pittsburgh. Gilliam was masterful, throwing feathers and darts, completing seventeen of thirty-one throws for 257 yards and two touchdowns, one to Frank Lewis. His other scoring pass was a beauty to Swann. It traveled more than sixty yards in the air, the rookie receiver catching the ball without breaking stride at the five-yard line and taking it into the end zone. Harris and Fuqua also ran for touchdowns.

Before the second game, in Denver, Hanratty was being Hanratty, teasing Lambert about Denver's rookie linebacker Randy Gradishar, a glamorous star from Ohio State drafted in the first round. "All week long, I'm busting Lambert's balls," Hanratty recalled. " '*If Gradishar had been around we'd have taken him over your dead ass!*' And Jack says, 'Fuck you!' " In the tunnel at Denver, before the game, the Rat squeezed between teammates until he found Lambert. "We'd be a walk if we had Gradishar," Hanratty said wishfully. Before kickoff Hanratty saw Gradishar approach Lambert and introduce himself, "I'm Randy Gradishar," and then heard Lambert reply, "Who gives a fuck?" In what became the first regular-season overtime game in NFL history, the Steelers and Broncos tied, 35–35. Gilliam threw fifty passes and completed thirty-one, both club records, for 348 yards. He spread the ball to eight different receivers in what Denver coach John Ralston called "possibly the finest performance I've ever seen by a quarterback." Noll saw it differently. Gilliam was throwing too often for his liking. Noll wanted more running and ball control in his offense. With fifty seconds remaining in overtime, the Steelers took possession on their own sixteen-yard line. Gilliam, call-ing the plays, threw incomplete to Swann. Then Noll sent in Bleier with explicit instructions for the Steelers to run the ball twice more. He wanted to run out the clock and accept a tie. Gilliam followed orders.

He became a national news sensation. In interviews he brushed off questions about race as nothing more than "that rigamarole and razzmatazz in the press," no worry of his, except when his mail showed up at the stadium. One day at his locker, Gilliam handed a letter to Wagner. "Mike, look at this," he said. Wagner couldn't believe what he saw: racist venom spilled like blood across the page in red ink, "just a diatribe against him being black." Wagner asked, "You get a lot of this, Joe?" Gilliam nod-ded, sadly, and went home to his wife and their young daughter, Joi. "If the Lord chooses to take me out," he said dramatically once to his brother Craig over the phone, "He's going to take me out throwing the ball."

His mother and father paid a visit to Pittsburgh. "Come here, Daddy," Joey Gilliam said. He led his father to a closet with folding doors. He pulled out a square cardboard box, about three feet tall, filled to the brim with letters. "Read some of that," he said. Coach Gilliam read the racist bile, the violent threats creating sparks in his hands.

"We're going to kill you and your fucking Nigger family!" read one.

"WE'RE GONNA CUT YOUR DICK OFF!" read another.

One letter writer threatened to shoot him at Three Rivers Stadium.

"Who did you tell about this?" his father asked. Joey Gilliam said he had spoken about it with Noll and that the Steelers had spread security throughout Three Rivers Stadium. Coach Gilliam phoned Dan and Noll. They told him they were monitoring the situation. They had increased se-curity. That did not appease Ruth Gilliam. She was adamant, arms folded, saying, "He's got to leave here right now. I'm taking my son back home, or I'm not going back." Joey Gilliam replied, "Mama, I'm going to be all right." She said, "I'm taking you home!" Back and forth it went, deep into the night, until finally she relented. She seethed for the entire 570-mile drive back to Nashville, saying barely five words to her husband. Once home, though, she spoke her mind. "You've made mistakes with that boy," Ruth Gilliam began, and she ticked off those mistakes one by one, a familiar list. "And now you've made another mistake with him by allow-ing him to stay there!" Coach Gilliam said, "How are we going to take him back? Joey wants to stay!" Ruth Gilliam: "He's not mature enough to know what he wants to do. All he wants to do is play ball. But there is more to life than playing ball!" Her eyes grew wide with fear: "Don't you know that they will kill our son?!"

Pressure from family, pressure from racist letter writers, pressure from the quarterback controversy, now came the greatest physical pressure of all: the Oakland Raiders' pass rush. It pounded Gilliam into submission in the Raiders' 17–0 victory in Pittsburgh in week three. Gilliam threw thirty-one passes and completed only eight. He threw two interceptions. He looked lost, overmatched, once flung onto his left shoulder by defensive end Otis Sistrunk. It didn't help that Harris was sidelined with an injury, removing the Steelers' top running threat. The Raiders hit Gilliam hard and from multiple angles. That night Gilliam felt pain in his ribs, knee, ankle, and shoulder. He attended a party anyway, and made a decision there that would change his life.

He turned to heroin. Years later, he would say a man he had known, not a player, but someone on the periphery, offered to liberate him from his physical suffering, saying, "Look, snort some of this. It's going to make you sick, but you're not going to feel no pain." Gilliam did, and the heroin worked its magic. The dope man was right, no pain. In a phone conversation with his brother Craig a few days later he told him about how the dope man appeared and offered heroin, and how he took it and felt better. Now, he said, he could practice. He could be the Joey Gilliam he needed to be. "It hooked him," Craig Gilliam said. "I know that's where it began. If you know anything about drugs, and tootin' heroin, if you do any amount, and you are doing it every day, in two weeks you could be a junkie."

Slowly, Gilliam's performance began to erode. On October 6 the Steelers defeated the Oilers 13–7 in the Astrodome, where Gilliam completed half of his thirty-two passes, with two more interceptions. He overthrew receivers, misread defenses. In the days that followed the local press insinuated itself into the Steelers' huddle. "So, Will Joe Have to Go?" a headline in the *Post-Gazette* asked. With the Steelers scoring only one offensive touchdown in the past nine quarters, a sportswriter compared the offense to a sputtering old Model T. To Noll, the press was a necessary evil, a pack of prickly busybodies, always prying. He thought most sportswriters knew little about the game. He knew that opposing coaches read what Pittsburgh sportswriters wrote in the days before playing the Steelers, and Noll didn't want to provide them with any insights.

After the victory over the Oilers, Noll did not offer Gilliam a vote of confidence. "I don't know what's going to happen at quarterback," he said. "I'll make that decision later in the week." He went with Gilliam again anyway, and the Steelers defeated the Chiefs 34–24 in the rain in Kansas City, the Pittsburgh defense intercepting seven passes. Then the Steelers defeated Cleveland 20–16 at home, Gilliam completing only five of eighteen, his worst numbers of the season. A chant emanating in the upper deck during the second quarter spread across the far reaches of the ballpark: "We want Bradshaw!" In the second half that cheer returned, this time louder. The Steelers ran forty-five times against the Browns as Noll rotated the just-returned Harris, Preston Pearson, Fuqua, Bleier, and Steve Davis. The *Post-Gazette* put it this way: "Sp-Sputtering St-Steelers Win." Their record was 4-1-1, good enough for first place, but no one in Pittsburgh seemed entirely pleased.

Dan Radakovich, the offensive line coach, said, "Joe Gilliam had as much talent as any quarterback in the league as far as running, faking, throwing, coordination, quick release. He had it all. Smart learner, too, but not smart in how to run a game. He thought passing was his gig, and he threw the ball when he shouldn't have." Radakovich added, "I led the pack to get rid of him, and I liked him." Meanwhile, in Los Angeles, another black quarterback, James Harris, became the Rams starter and thrived.

As quarterbacks coach, Noll spent considerable time with Gilliam, in meetings and on the practice field. Gilliam's behavior changed subtly. For one thing, he showed up late to several team meetings, offering a different alibi each time. Acting on Gilliam's performance and his own wish to "return to the bread and butter," Noll named Bradshaw as his starter in week seven. That week's pregame conversation centered on Bradshaw, though it might have been focused on the new starting pair in the backfield, Harris and Bleier. After Harris ran for 141 yards and his lead blocker Bleier for 78 yards in a 24–17 victory over the Falcons, the Steelers' backfield was theirs for the rest of the 1970s. Against the Falcons, Bradshaw threw twenty-one passes (with just nine completions and two interceptions), and the Steelers ran the ball a startling fifty-two times, forty-three by Harris and Bleier, racking up 235 yards. Noll's bread and butter was a return to Paul Brown's three-yards-and-a-cloud-of-dust approach. "As long as we control the ball and score some points," Bradshaw told the press. "That's the way I've been schooled here." Music to Chuck Noll's ears.

Noll's overarching design for his team now was clear. He would let his defense and running game determine the Steelers' fate. He didn't trust his quarterbacks as passers. A week later, a 27–0 victory at home over the Philadelphia Eagles, the Steelers ran forty-eight times, their offensive line controlling the opponent and the clock, and diminishing the need for Bradshaw to pass. Bradshaw tried to remake himself into the self-contained, field-leader quarterback that Noll craved, and had known, as an NFL rookie in 1953, playing with Otto Graham. For Bradshaw, a cut-loose personality who loved nothing more than airing it out deep downfield, this was a struggle. "Bradshaw had a lot of talent but Rocky [Bleier] would be close, say, from here to the wall," Andy Russell said, pointing about fifteen feet away, "and Bradshaw would throw it one hundred miles per hour at him. Terry jokingly told me, 'Well, I don't want Noll to think I'm any good at those [shorter throws]. I want to go deep.' And I think he was semiserious."

On the carpet of Cincinnati's Riverfront Stadium in week nine, Bradshaw went to pieces in a nationally televised 17–10 loss to the Bengals, a loss to Paul Brown's team that churned acid in Noll's gut. Bradshaw threw into double and triple coverage, missed receivers in the clear. His misguided throws sailed too high or wide. It wasn't only that twenty-two of his thirty-five passes fell incomplete, but he also suffered by comparison to Cincinnati's Ken Anderson. Under assistant coach Bill Walsh, even then developing what would become known as the "West Coast offense," Anderson threw often to his running backs and completed all but two of his twenty-two throws, including fifteen in a row. A day later, in the conference room at Three Rivers, a reporter asked Noll if he would switch back to Gilliam for the next game, in Cleveland. "I'll have to make that decision after I'm out of this room," Noll said.

He chose Hanratty, and what followed in Cleveland was a 26–16 Steeler victory before nearly 78,000 fans at Municipal Stadium. But the win was grotesque in its offensive ineptitude, with a combined eleven turnovers, a game that Phil Musick of the *Pittsburgh Press* suggested "only a mother could've loved. Knute Rockne's mother." "Weird" is how Noll described a game the Steelers had entered as seventeen-point favorites, "but nice weird." Hanratty was worse than terrible. Battered by a pass rush that bruised his ribs and hand, he threw fifteen passes with more interceptions (three) than completions (two). He played like a quarterback who had been standing on the sidelines for the previous nine weeks and who had not started a game in about a year. The Rat qualified his performance as only he could: "I felt strange out there without my baseball hat on." When the Rat suffered leg cramps late in the game and with the Steelers leading by ten points, Gilliam replaced him, not Bradshaw.

No play-calling conservative, Gilliam immediately threw four consecutive passes, only one caught. Combined, he and Hanratty completed only three of nineteen passes for eighty-one yards. The defense again rescued the day for the Steelers. Joe Greene intercepted a pass and recovered a fumble that he lateraled to J. T. Thomas, who ran the final fourteen yards for the game-breaking touchdown. Afterward Noll deadpanned, "Joe Greene got the offensive game ball for his broken-field running." The Steelers were 7-2-1 and still in first place by a game and a half over Paul Brown's Bengals.

Noll's silence tore at Bradshaw's insides. Gilliam told local writers that he was "staying cool. My chance will come one of these days." As Hanratty saw it, "It hasn't hurt us too much. We're in first place." Columnist Bob Smizek of the *Pittsburgh Press* wondered, "Is Noll spiting Bradshaw, and possibly Gilliam, at the expense of the team? Such a thought seems ludicrous, but Noll invites such speculation with his illogical silence on the matter."

"Somebody's got to take the bull by the horns," Noll said again.

The *Pittsburgh Post-Gazette* did, publishing a quarterback poll, asking readers to make their choice. Nearly 3,500 replied, and Bradshaw won with 41 percent of the vote; Hanratty came next, with 32 percent; and Gilliam got nearly 20 percent. It couldn't be taken too seriously since, among others receiving votes, were Barbra Streisand, Raquel Welch, Lawrence Welk, and *Deep Throat* porn star Linda Lovelace. Still, the poll grated on Noll, more proof of the press being busybodies. One reader said the sportswriters should be "dropped off the Fort Pitt Bridge." No doubt Noll agreed.

Hanratty had much the same idea. He ran an ad in the *Post-Gazette*, with Brad and Gillie offering their laughing support, asking readers to vote for their favorite *Post-Gazette* sportswriter. Hanratty howled when he found out the cost for such an ad was $240. But Dan Rooney, unhappy with the quarterback poll, encouraged him to do it, and paid for it.

Noll turned to Bradshaw in the regular season's final month. His season statistics were roughly the same as Gilliam's. "Terry was going to be the quarterback," Hanratty said years later. "It was just a matter of when he broke out." Dick Haley, the personnel man, said, "We could have put anybody at quarterback and won some games. We didn't even have to throw it. You could have just run the ball and played defense. [But] there was nobody in the league that should have played ahead of Terry Bradshaw."

To the gathered press, Noll put it like this: "We've got to keep our defense playing good offense."

CHAPTER 10

THE STEEL CURTAIN

DWIGHT WHITE, ERNIE HOLMES, L. C. Greenwood, and Joe Greene shared in the violent execution of their craft. To a man, they believed defensive linemen the essential warriors of the game. Out on the periphery, a glamorous wide receiver might not get hit, *really* hit, during an entire game, but a lineman got hit on every play, sixty or seventy times a game. A lineman did not need to look for battle. It was right in front of him, 270 pounds, coiled, and less than a foot away. Like long-horned rams butting heads in explosive two- and three-second Darwinian struggles, the Steelers' front four physically overpowered offensive lines week after week. They attacked with different methods, White with a bull rush, Greenwood a slip move, Holmes a forearm club to the head, their task made less onerous by Mean Joe, in the middle, often drawing double teams. Pittsburgh's fifty-two quarterback sacks and forty-seven turnovers would rate most in the league in 1974, and by a good distance.

At times the Steelers' front four did more than overpower. They humiliated opponents, standing over them as the ovations thundered from Three Rivers Stadium across Pittsburgh's North Side and rattled coffee cups at the Chief's house. "It was not so much what we did. It was the way we did it," White said. "We kicked their asses very thoroughly." Together, these four players became the point of the Steelers' sword, and the first dominant all-black starting front four in league history. On the cover of *Time* magazine in December 1975, a source of great pride to men

raised on the burrs of southern segregation, they were like Tuskegee Air-
men in cleats.

They created mayhem at the line of scrimmage and laid waste to opposing quarterbacks. Baltimore's Marty Domres was first. Domres threw
three passes in the season opener and then went down, caught between
two crashing cymbals: Holmes and White. Domres stumbled off the field,
his ears vibrating, his shoulder and ribs bruised. His replacement, Bert
Jones—"alligator mouth" to White, "just one of those guys we did not
like"—received even ruder treatment. Jones got sacked six times. "Rule of
Thumb," White said, " 'QBs, you shut up, okay? You let the big guys do
all the talking.' " A week later, in Denver, it was Charley Johnson's turn.
In locker rooms before games, Mean Joe studied photographs of the opposing quarterback. "He is my mountain," Greene said. "When I throw
the quarterback for a big loss, I know I'm on top of the mountain." As
the veteran Johnson released a third-quarter pass, Greene crashed into
him, the quarterback's arm still raised in middelivery. Greene's mountain
winced, and left the game with a sprained shoulder. In came his replacement, Steve Ramsey. Now Holmes slashed through the Broncos' line and
unloaded on Ramsey, forcing a fumble recovered by Greenwood. "I just
like to get a good lick and then pick the quarterback up with a smile on
my face," Holmes said, "so we know we've hurt his pride." Greenwood
thought there was more to it than that for Holmes. "Ernie wanted to see
blood," Greenwood said. "He wanted to beat on the guy until he started
bleeding, and if he did start bleeding, Ernie felt he had done a good
day's work."

What the trumpet was to Satchmo, the defense was to the 1970s Steelers. Its pass rush made the earth tremble. It had smart, mobile linebackers,
and an aggressive secondary willing to take risks. The Steelers' defense
featured two players so unique they played their positions in ways they
hadn't been played before: Mel Blount, a six-foot-three, 205-pound shut-
down cornerback, beat up receivers from the snap so devastatingly that he
caused the NFL to change its pass-coverage rules in 1978 to forbid bump-
and-run coverage down the field; and Lambert, tall and lanky, moving

laterally across the field to great effect, was agile enough to do what other star middle linebackers past and present (Ray Nitschke, Dick Butkus) couldn't, cover tight ends and fullbacks on pass routes. At six-foot-four, playing underneath in zone coverage in the middle of the field, Lambert forced quarterbacks to arc the ball over him, giving safeties Edwards and Wagner an extra split second to make plays. Ten of the eleven starters from the 1974 Steelers' defense would make the Pro Bowl at least once during their NFL careers—everyone except Ernie Holmes, and at times during the 1974 season, Holmes was the team's best defensive lineman, outperforming even the man to his left, Greene. During the 1974 regular season, the Steelers' defense was still in the process of becoming. Come the playoffs, it would be a finished product.

In Denver, running back Otis Armstrong, who led the league in rushing in 1974, ran wild for 131 yards against Pittsburgh. In the game's opening quarter, Bronco receiver Haven Moses beat J. T. Thomas for a seven-yard touchdown reception, ending a long drive in the thin air. Back in the defensive huddle, Greene jumped Thomas, saying, "If you can't cover nobody, then get out of here!" White stepped in and shouted at Mean Joe, "What are you jumping down on T for? If they had not been trapping your big ass, we wouldn't be down here in the first place." Chaos reigned in the Steelers' huddle on the next series when Greene opted not to rush, but to drop back in freelance pass coverage. Lambert ignited, demanding to know what was happening, and Greenwood, always calm, said, "Why don't y'all cut off all that noise. It's hard enough to breathe out here." At halftime, Noll pulled aside Thomas and asked, "What's going on out there? Are they pointing fingers?" Unsure what to say, Thomas just nodded.

After that 35-all tie, the Steelers' defense, in particular the front four, grew tighter, stingier. Kansas City managed just fifty-eight yards on the ground (two yards per carry), the Eagles sixty-six yards (barely three yards per carry), and New England seventy-nine yards. The front four viewed quarterbacks as trophies. The Steeler defense sacked Atlanta's Bob Lee seven times, Cleveland's Mike Phipps six times—thirteen trophies. Houston's young Dan Pastorini eluded Greene's grasp only to have White leap on his back, as if riding a bucking bull, White's 255 pounds forcing Pastorini to crumple to the turf, face-first. Greene penetrated the line of scrimmage repeatedly against the Chiefs, reaching running backs Ed Podolak and Willie Ellison just as they took handoffs. Against Cleveland, Greenwood got flagged for a roughing-the-passer penalty and Noll later said, "I'll probably suffer in the next world for what I said about that call." In the 27–0 victory over the Eagles in week eight, the season's second shutout, Greene recovered a fumble, and Edwards and Blount had interceptions, Blount returning his fifty-two yards for a touchdown. In week thirteen, pressure came to New England quarterback Jim Plunkett from all sides. He took hits, sacks. In this game, Ham noticed a remarkable occurrence: on one play the Patriots' offensive line blocked the Steelers' front four, but Plunkett, anticipating pressure, went down anyway, virtually untouched. Ham thought, *That was one where we got a sack purely on reputation.*

As the reputation of the Steel Curtain front four spread across the league, Greenwood said, "There were several games where you could just get down in your stance and look up at the [opposing] guy and see him shaking and you kind of knew that you could just go ahead and play because this game was already in the bag."

Back in sports' hyperbolic Golden Age, columnist Grantland Rice likened the Notre Dame backfield to the Four Horsemen of the Apocalypse. In an epic gush of hero worship at the Army–Fighting Irish football game at the Polo Grounds in October 1924, Rice transformed Stuhldreyer, Crowley, Miller, and Layden into demigods by likening them to Famine, Pestilence, Destruction, and Death. Never mind that none weighed more than 162 pounds.

Now, a half century later, here came the Steelers' front four with a combined weight of more than a half ton. The NFL had known other front fours with colorful monikers: Minnesota's Purple People Eaters and Dallas's Doomsday defenses featured talented fronts, though perhaps the most famous was the Rams' Fearsome Foursome in the 1960s.

Standing alongside Mean Joe were Fats, Mad Dog, and Hollywood Bags. They were on average six-foot-four, 260 pounds, tough against the pass, tougher against the run. "Fats," a nickname Holmes got from his family while growing up amid the timber fields and creeks in rural James- town, Texas, near the Louisiana line, was built like a John Deere tractor, as Dwight White liked to say, with massive thighs and buttocks. His father, the farmer Emerson Holmes, was a 300-pound boulder of a man, physi- cally powerful and self-certain, traits that Ernie Holmes shared. According to Holmes family lore, his college football coach at Texas Southern first saw Fats working in his father's field while in high school, picking corn and shelling peas, and a new world opened up for both the coach and for Fats. Holmes could lift a 270-pound opponent and throw him. Before games, he liked to boast to his line coach, Perles, "Jawge, I'm gonna get ya' thirteen sacks today," and Perles would smile and think, *That's my guy! He'll do anything to play this game!*

Moody and unpredictable, Holmes was prone to excesses—Courvoisier and barbecued meats topped his list, and he wore rubber suits at practice to sweat them out of his body, his wrists leaking perspiration like twin faucets. He ate a huge plate of deviled eggs before one Steelers practice at training camp and then, in the huddle that afternoon, vomited. His teammates saw the pile of hardly chewed eggs and gagged. Noll, miffed, stopped practice, saw the heap of deviled eggs, and said, "Let's just move over to the next field."

Holmes's personality was so complex as to seem simple. Holmes felt underappreciated, underpaid, and every bit as talented as Mean Joe Greene. Said Bill Nunn, "Joe Greene made a whole lot of people think they were better than they were." With his strength and his glower, Holmes frightened opponents and even teammates. Grossman likened him to Lennie, the man-child with brutish strength, in Steinbeck's *Of Mice and Men.* "Ernie was just a lovable, really nice guy but when he was beaned up or fired up, it was frightening," Grossman said. "He would be the only guy that I would be afraid of in any combative situation. Anybody else might beat the shit out of me but Ernie would really tear me up." Grossman laughed. "He would rip off pieces of me and throw them somewhere . . . *or eat them.*" Holmes struggled with his weight and with his words. He called his camera a "Kodiak" and his two-toned shoes "splats," and when he told J. T. Thomas once that he felt "can- nibalistic," Thomas thought it best to keep his distance. "Ernie was our

Norm Crosby," Hanratty said. Late one night at a Pittsburgh bar called the Red Door, guard Moon Mullins saw Holmes enter with a woman. Mullins tried to shield his identity—too late. "Hey, Moon-baby! How ya' doin'?" Holmes said. They sat at his table, and Fats ordered a bottle of Courvoisier. Mullins could tell it wasn't Holmes's first bottle of the night. "My lady here is pissed at me," Holmes said. "She says I was trying to run whitey down coming through town." Mullins said, "Ernie, I'm whitey!" "No," Holmes said, brightening, "you're Moon-baby!" In a few moments, Mullins announced that he had to go. "No," Holmes said, "you've got to stay. Have a drink." Moon-baby stayed, and drank, past closing time.

In college, Dwight White got the nickname "Mad Dog," and for many years when old friends phoned, his wife, Karen, took calls for her husband that began, "Is Dog around?" The son of a college-educated military man, White was hardworking, smart, often cynical, and uneasy with whites in social settings, at least during his early years with the Steelers. He intellectualized and personalized segregation more than his three defensive linemates, never forgetting that in Dallas he was made to read old textbooks handed down from the local white schools. He considered Pittsburgh "Up South" where, he said, racism flourished beneath the surface. White was loud and argumentative, and at the line of scrimmage the consummate trash talker who tried to motormouth his way inside an opponent's head, and often succeeded. In his three-point stance at the far end of the defensive line, Greenwood sometimes couldn't hear the quarterback's call over the chattering White. "Dwight's just constantly running his mouth. He's pass-rushing up the field and he's still running his mouth," Greenwood said. "He NEVER shut up."

Long and lean in the manner of a basketball player, Greenwood was, among the foursome, the tallest (six-foot-six), lightest (240 pounds), and fastest (4.7 seconds in the forty-yard dash). With his broad chest, narrow waist, and long arms, Greenwood was difficult to block. "You could only block half of him," White said, "because there was so much of him that you almost needed to say, 'You take this piece and I'll take the other piece.'" Raised in Canton, Mississippi, about twenty miles north of Jackson, Greenwood knew the local rules of race. "We didn't have any relationship with the white people, and they had no relationship with us," he said. "You knew not to go across the track unless you were working because the sheriff rode around with a shotgun rack in the back of his truck with loaded shotguns." His given name was L. C. Henderson Greenwood, though no one believed those initials were his given name (they were); once he told a writer his real name was Lover Cool. His father, Moses Greenwood, worked in a factory that made cabinets for TVs and radios. He placed high demands on L.C., the oldest of his nine children, typically a full list of chores, including paint the fence and clean the gravestones, or else. L.C.'s dream was to one day own a corner drugstore, with a malt soda counter, where he would serve as pharmacist, always glad to see you. He received a partial academic scholarship to attend Clark College in Atlanta, but football meant a full-ride scholarship, so he went to Arkansas AM&N. After the 1969 draft, Nunn arrived with a contract that insulted Greenwood, a tenth-round pick. Greenwood reconsidered the pharmacy, and teaching, but he went to Pittsburgh and made the team, and two years later White and Holmes showed up.

On the field, Greenwood, a speed rusher, wore gold-painted high-topped shoes, for which he was fined $100 per game by the league for deviating from his teammates' attire, a fine his shoe company happily absorbed. ("Cheap publicity," Greenwood said.) A Steelers assistant coach, Walt Hackett, first called him "Bag It," which Greenwood assumed came from the stylish leather shoulder bags he often carried. Hanratty abbreviated that to "Bags" and then made up a rumor that he and Greenwood were about to be traded together to Los Angeles, whereupon Hanratty began calling him "Hollywood Bags," an odd nickname that stuck.

In nearly every regard, Mean Joe was boss, and the others answered to him. Through physical gifts and force of personality, Greene made them submit to him, and they did, though not always willingly. When he thought the front four's performance lacking, Greene called for private meetings, players only. Once, in the huddle, he told Greenwood to cover the tight end, never mind that their coaches preferred a different cover scheme. "I'll handle the rush," he said. And so Greenwood covered the tight end. Berlin, the trainer, once saw Holmes standing next to Perles on the Steelers' sideline. "What in the hell are you doing here?" Perles asked, demanding to know why Holmes had just left the defensive huddle.

Holmes replied, "Joe threw me out of the game." Perles, incredulous, said, "What do you mean?" Holmes: "I wasn't playing the defense and Joe said if I wouldn't do it, to get the hell out." Perles: "Get the hell back in there!" Holmes: "Naw, I'm not going back. Not until Joe tells me it's okay." Greene became the team's de facto spokesman. In the locker room after games, the press went directly to him. "Joe was the best interview on the Steelers. He was honest," *Pittsburgh Press* sports columnist Roy McHugh said. "He didn't worry about the effect of what he said on teammates or the public or the owner. He said what he thought." Lambert wasn't always sure why the Steelers had won or lost. "I waited to read it in the paper on Monday as to what Joe had to say about it," Lambert said, "so I could understand what happened."

On the Steelers, as with most professional football teams, friendships tended to take shape along lines of race, position, age, marital status, and late-night social habits. Among the Steel Curtain front four, Green-wood, a go-with-the-flow sort, got along with everyone. Holmes was the odd-man-out renegade. The closest friendship among this foursome was shared by White and Greene. Initially they roomed together in a Pittsburgh apartment while Greene's wife and kids remained in Dallas. It worked for a while. White teased Greene about his driving, and complained that he played Marvin Gaye and the Temptations too loud and too late. Greene hid chocolate chip cookies sent by his mother, planting a small stash of them for White to find so he'd think he had found them all. (He hadn't.) As roommates they were, White said, "like two pit bulls," and so finally they got their own places.

On a visit to Dallas, and bound for dinner in the backseat of a car, Radakovich, the line coach, saw the mighty pit bulls clash. Mean Joe and Mad Dog argued in the front seat—two emotional alphas going at it, at high decibels—until White insisted Greene pull the car to the side of the highway to let him out. Greene pulled over, White stepped out, and Greene drove off. "You can't leave Dwight there!" Radakovich shouted from the backseat. Greene drove on. Radakovich: "YOU CAN'T DO THAT!" Silence. Radakovich: "Joe, you know what Texas is like." Finally Greene turned around and drove back to White, who walked along the roadside at dusk. Radakovich called for White to get in the car but White said, "The hell with you!" It took a while, but finally he got in.

Greenwood sometimes felt on the outside looking in at the other three, Texans all. But it was Fats Holmes, always Fats, who stood apart from the others. In March 1973, the Steel Curtain front four almost broke up, before it had really asserted itself, when Fats looked to the sky and fired gunshots at a helicopter.

Fats snapped. That's the simplest way to put it. His world closed in. His wife wanted a divorce. He feared losing their two young sons. He needed money, and fast, a loan maybe, and called Dan, who suggested he come to Pittsburgh for a talk. Holmes swallowed a handful of No-Doz pills and drove through the night in his green Cadillac from Houston to Pittsburgh, suffering from what a court-ordered psychiatrist later termed "acute paranoid psychosis." He didn't make it to Pittsburgh before the Steelers' offices closed, so he drove back out of town, into Ohio, feeling lost, frazzled, and alone. On the highway, trucks entered his space, or so he believed, and tried to drive him off the road. A deer hunter and marksman in the off-season, Holmes had brought a shotgun and a 9-millimeter pistol and, with the latter, he fired several shots at the tires of those trucks. Word of the shooting reached the local authorities. A chase ensued and Holmes—an erratic driver in the best of circumstances—drove at high speed off the highway, slamming onto a country road. He broke an axle in the process, and off spun a wheel. He pounded to a stop in a ditch. He ran for cover into nearby woods, carrying his shotgun and pistol. As he ran he broke his wooden clogs. Thorns entered his heels. An Ohio Highway Patrol helicopter appeared in the sky. Holmes heard it and fired at it, striking the ankle of an officer inside. He spotted a patrolman approaching from nearby woods, fired at him, or tried to, but his gun jammed. Patrolmen surrounded him, though Holmes didn't realize that until he felt the cool metal of a gun pressed to his back and heard a voice say, "Put your hands behind you, slowly." Later a law enforcement official said, "We could have killed him a dozen times."

Holmes faced federal and state charges: interfering with interstate commerce, assault with a deadly weapon. The Steelers got him an attorney and arranged for payment of his $45,000 bail. Letters from Texas testified to Holmes's character and noted he'd never had troubles before with

the law. The judge said Holmes needed to play football to provide for his family. He got five years' probation, plus a one-month stay, later extended to two months, in the Western Pennsylvania Psychiatric Hospital in Pittsburgh. Some protested that he'd received preferential treatment.

At the psychiatric hospital, in an antiseptic eight-by-eight room on the tenth floor, where all door locks mechanically clicked open and closed, Holmes received frequent visits from the Chief, who offered words of encouragement. Art Jr. stopped by, too, and brought Holmes a pocket-sized prayer book. Greenwood got a call from the Chief. "Why don't you go over there and see Ernie, and take him out?" As far as Greenwood knew, no other Steeler player had visited Fats, and the thought of being the first made him uneasy. He wondered "if Ernie had really lost it," but when he showed up Fats seemed genuinely happy to see him. They drove off and spent a couple of hours at Greenwood's place. "They got me in there saying that I'm crazy," Holmes said. "But I'm not crazy. They are!" Years later, Greenwood said, "I think Ernie's big issue was that he was paranoid."

That summer Fats Holmes returned to training camp, more fit and focused. He pledged his loyalty to the Chief forevermore, saying, "If someone saved your life, would you be loyal to them? . . . Mr. Rooney is a beautiful fellow. I dig the guy to the utmost."

His Fu Manchu mustache, gold tooth, and eight quarterback sacks weren't enough. In mid-October 1974, Fats Holmes wanted more recognition for being the player he was. So he shaved his head and left behind only a bit of hair in the shape of an arrow pointing forward, a new nickname born, Arrowhead Holmes. Following the 34–24 victory in Kansas City in week five, Holmes approached Perles before a meeting of defensive linemen. Perles saw the arrow. He heard himself gasp. Holmes said that everyone on the line had a nickname but him—Mad Dog, Mean Joe, and Hollywood Bags. Fats, he said, wasn't a real nickname since it dated to his childhood. "Jawge," he said, "I don't get any publicity because I don't have a nickname. From now on, my name is Arrowhead." The sportswriters loved the new look and nickname. Holmes explained the arrow pointed him toward the quarterback. He shaved his head twice weekly, neatly working the arrow's contours. "You have to be commercial in this business to get ahead. You need a gimmick," he said. "This way I have my goals set right up in front of me, and can keep pointing in the right direction."

The front four developed its own pass-rushing tricks. The left end, Greenwood sometimes turned inside and crashed into the guard, allowing Greene to sweep behind and take an outside path to the quarterback. Sometimes they did that move in reverse, Greene crashing into Greenwood's man, and Hollywood Bags taking an inside pass-rushing route. White and Holmes worked the same tricks on the other side. In practice, though, Greene tried something entirely new: instead of lining up directly over the center, he moved to the open space between center and guard, lining up in his stance at a ninety-degree angle. This forced the guard and center to double-team him, lest Mean Joe instantly burst through that gap into the backfield. "If you get penetration, eight times out of ten you will screw something up," White said. "When you do that, they're at the mercy of the defense." The double team left Lambert roaming free in the middle, with more time to decipher a play and more freedom to attack a ballcarrier. This also allowed Holmes to loop behind Greene and attack a part of the offensive line that Mean Joe already had reduced to ruins. The Steelers called this alignment the "Stunt 4-3." It was aggressive, proactive. It created problems for offensive lines and forced quarterbacks to take deeper drops—better targets for the onrushing ends, Greenwood and White.

The Steelers defeated Buffalo 32–14 in the divisional playoff game, the outcome essentially decided in the second quarter when the Steelers scored four touchdowns to take a 29–7 lead. Bradshaw played with confidence, passing for 203 yards in the game, and running for 48, his most complete performance to date as a Steeler. But it was O. J. Simpson, the Bills' great running back who had rushed for a league record of more than 2,000 yards a season earlier, who drew the attention. In this game Simpson got nowhere. He rushed fifteen times against the Steel Curtain for just 49 yards. In eight of those rushes, Simpson got stuffed for 2 yards or less. The Steel Curtain front four, shifting on Greene's audibles into the Stunt 4-3, caged Simpson, gang-tackled, and bludgeoned him.

Greene knew what came next: the Raiders, always the Raiders. This was how it worked in the AFC. It had worked this way for the 1968 Jets, the 1970 Chiefs, the 1971 Colts, and the 1973 Dolphins. To get to the

Super Bowl from the AFC, you had to defeat Oakland. The Raiders were the team the Steelers wanted to be, a perennial power, participants in two Super Bowls, and a winning record every year for a decade. The Steelers knew the Raiders would give them a physical game plus an occasional surprise.

The Steelers had run into a cul-de-sac in Oakland in a 33–14 defeat in a 1973 divisional playoff game. Earlier in that season, they had defeated the Raiders 17–9 in Oakland in a game that had more than a few surprises. Loud music piped into the visitors' locker room made it difficult for the Steelers to hear Noll's pregame and halftime talks. When Greene reached for the Raiders' offensive linemen early in that game, he found their jerseys slathered with Vaseline, his own fingers suddenly covered in goo. Mansfield felt like the straight-man for Raiders' jokes in that game. As long snapper on a field goal attempt, he reached for the ball and found it half deflated. He thought, *If I balance this football on my middle finger, both sides of the ball will hang down over my finger. It's that soft!* He complained, and a referee got him a different, fully inflated ball. Earlier Mansfield had found a message penned on the ball that read, "GO RAIDERS!!" It happened a second time, with a new message. "Hey, Bruce, look at this!" Mansfield said to guard Bruce Van Dyke. On the football someone on the Raiders had written, "FUCK YOU." The Steelers called it the Dirty Tricks Game. Now the Raiders would play the Steelers owning the league's best record (13-2), the homefield advantage, and secure in knowing they'd already shut out the Steelers 17–0 earlier in the season at Three Rivers Stadium.

Greenwood started on Fats Holmes immediately after the Bills game, saying, "Ernie, Eugene Upshaw's gonna beat your butt just like he always does!" Holmes brushed it off, certain he could handle the Raiders' all-pro guard without any ribbing, but Greenwood kept after him. Mean Joe and Mad Dog joined in until Fats Holmes couldn't take it any longer. "That got his juices going," Greene said. By Tuesday morning Fats Holmes was like a surly bear in full froth, exactly what his defensive linemates hoped for, and, come Sunday against the Raiders, exactly what they would need.

CHAPTER 11

STALL & WEBBY

THERE WOULD COME A TIME years later when Coach Lionel Taylor knew that he couldn't pull his coach's motivational ploy on his wide receivers anymore, that they had risen above it, and perhaps him as well. He would gather Stallworth, Swann, and Frank Lewis on the sideline during a game and excoriate them. "DAMMIT!!" Taylor screamed. "YOU GUYS MUST NOT BE AS GOOD AS I THOUGHT!! I NEED TO GET SOMEBODY ELSE!!" The three receivers would look at him, chins slightly raised, their confidence bordering on defiance. They were superior talents and knew it, and they knew that Taylor knew it. That ended that ploy. Taylor walked away, thinking, *Noll would get rid of me before he would get rid of them.*

But as the 1974 AFC title game in Oakland approached, Stallworth and Swann were only beginning their ascents as rookie reserves, replacements for Lewis and Ron Shanklin in the second and fourth quarters of each game. At this early hour in their careers, they remained vulnerable to Lionel Taylor's machinations, and so once more the receivers coach got out the film from the Raiders' 17–0 victory over Pittsburgh in week three, and made them watch it. They had seen it more than a few times already; Taylor had made sure of that. Whenever Taylor decided his two rookie receivers weren't working hard enough or thought too much of their own talents, he showed them the Raiders film. Stallworth and Swann had played poorly in that game, like rookies. Worse, Raiders safeties Jack

Tatum and George Atkinson physically overpowered them. Never let this happen again, Taylor told them in the darkness of the film room as he pressed Rewind.

Stallworth and Swann watched in silence.

Mike Webster, the backup center and the team's best long snapper, was enduring his own rookie sufferings. Early in the season, unhappy with his playing time, Webster had had enough, and rented a U-Haul. He intended to quit, pack up his things, and return home to Wisconsin. His wife, Pam, convinced him to stay. "What are you going to do back in Wisconsin?" she asked.

Webster had suffered a knee injury that would require off-season surgery, and as the playoffs approached Noll told Radakovich, his line coach, that Webster needed to be benched, or at least protected. "He's the only snapper we've got that's any good for punts. If we lose him, we're dead," Noll said. Players called Radakovich "Bad Rad," a nickname that suited a coach whose intensity and ingenuity made him seem a football mad scientist. Once, as a college coach, Radakovich had driven home, walked into the kitchen, put down his books, sat at the table, looked up, and saw two kids he didn't recognize and a woman in a housecoat with her hands on her hips who was not his wife. "What the hell is going on here?" he asked. "Where is Nancy?" Radakovich had entered the wrong house, three blocks from his own. He apologized, picked up his books, and left, thinking maybe he needed a vacation.

He admired Mike Webster's dedication and work ethic, they mirrored his own, and he knew that one day Webster would replace Mansfield at center. Even Mansfield knew that. Each year during training camp, Mansfield's business partner would ask, "Do you have any competition this year?" and Mansfield answered, "No, not really." But when Webster showed up in training camp in 1974, Mansfield, in his twelfth season, gave a different answer: "I've met my replacement. He's steady, and *he wants it so badly.*" Occasionally in 1974, Radakovich put Webster at guard, next to Mansfield, to get the rookie more playing time. Now he told Webster what Noll had said, that his playing time needed to be reduced, but he reassured Webster that he would play in goal-line and short-yardage situations. Webster was furious. "There's nothing you can do about it," Radakovich told him. "I've got orders from the head coach."

To Webster, playing the Oakland Raiders in the AFC title game meant playing Jim Otto, a fellow Wisconsinite, and the kind of center Webster wanted to become. Tough, inscrutable, and undersized, Otto was the Lou Gehrig of the gridiron, playing through pains that would have shattered most men. Otto had played 210 consecutive regular-season games for the Oakland Raiders dating to 1960, a league record. He had *never* missed a pro game.

As a high school senior in 1969, Webster had phoned Otto from his family's potato farm in Tomahawk, Wisconsin, and asked to see him. They met in Wausau, Otto's hometown, and that day Webster, bound for the University of Wisconsin, announced his dream to play in the NFL. "What do I need to do to get there?" Webster asked. Otto told him to work hard on the field and in the classroom, to stay out of trouble, and play football with a desire that would make his mother and father and his entire hometown proud. In the five years that followed, Otto lost track of Webster, never figuring that he would see him again.

But then in the third week of the 1974 NFL season, teammates Gene Upshaw and Art Shell walked past Otto during pregame stretches at Three Rivers Stadium and teased, "Mr. Otto! Mr. Otto!" Otto, deadly serious, snapped, "Knock it off!"

Just then he heard a voice calling to him from across the field: "Mr. Otto! Mr. Otto!" The old Raider saw number 52 of the Pittsburgh Steelers waving his arms and shouting to him: "It's me, Mike Webster! I made it!"

Amazed, Otto thought, *Yes, you did.* He waved back and called out, "Way to go, kid!"

As John Stallworth saw it, no matter what he accomplished on the field as a Steelers rookie in 1974, Lynn Swann loomed and threatened to eclipse him. Swann was his rival and his yardstick, and if he brought out the competitive best in Stallworth he also brought out Stallworth's deepest insecurities. Swann possessed qualities that Stallworth longed to have. Though a smallish five-foot-eleven, Swann seemed big in so many ways. He had a big personality, a big smile. He was from a big city (San Francisco) and a big school (Southern Cal), and he was a big-play guy, especially in big games. Whereas Stallworth excelled in digging out poorly thrown passes near the ground (a feat unseen by many), Swann leaped into the sky for all to see to catch passes thrown too high. Trained in ballet through his formative years, Swann was acrobatic, a midair Nureyev. At six-foot-three, Stallworth was considerably taller, and ganglier with a lean upper body and well-muscled legs. As blockers, Swann shielded defenders, while Stallworth knocked them down. In personality, they were as different as Hollywood and Huntsville. Swann was telegenic, glamorous, and spontaneous, gravitating naturally to the cameras, whereas Stallworth was shy, understated, and wishing sportswriters would give him a day or two to think about their questions so that he might offer a more well-considered response.

What framed the rookie Stallworth's context, and told him all that he needed to know, was that the Steelers had drafted him in the fourth round and Swann in the first round. That meant the Steelers thought Swann the better player, and that stoked Stallworth's competitive fires.

But really, it wasn't about Lynn Swann. It was about obstacles and overcoming them. As a boy Stallworth bore witness as his parents, Mary and David Stallworth, overcame obstacles through hard work, she as a domestic in Tuscaloosa who earned her high school diploma when she was in her thirties, and he as a laborer for a plumbing company working in ditches with pick and shovel and then studying to become his company's heavy machine operator, the man in the big rig. The Stallworths had known poverty—"At the end of the week," John Stallworth would say, "we had more week than money"—but there was no scarcity of love or faith or big dreams. For years, Stallworth had carried morbid fears. When he was only eight years old, after a day of play, he suffered chills, became feverish, and inexplicably became paralyzed on his left side. His paralysis lasted for days, and doctors feared polio. Stallworth stared at the sun through the hospital window and dreamed of running free. Through tears, he feared death, and even when his symptoms cleared, the fear of dying persisted. He made a silent vow to achieve in his life so that people would remember him. What that achievement might be he had no idea.

Football, maybe? At Tuscaloosa High School, as a running back on a poor team, Stallworth, like all local boys, dreamed of playing down the street, at the University of Alabama. He had watched Joe Namath and Ken Stabler play for the Crimson Tide, and imagined catching their passes. He had high hopes when Alabama asked to see his game films. But no offer came from coach Bear Bryant, who thought the lanky runner hit holes standing too upright, and so he went to Alabama A&M in Huntsville, a Division II school that became his springboard.

At the Steelers' training camp, waiting for the veterans to report, Lionel Taylor had put the fear of Mel Blount in him. As Stallworth and Swann easily outmaneuvered rookie cornerbacks in practice, Taylor told them, "You won't be able to do that once Mel gets here." Stallworth finally laid eyes on Blount on the sideline in New Orleans during the preseason opener, Blount in street clothes, still out on strike. "My jaw hit the ground," Stallworth said. "I thought, *No, he can't be a cornerback. Not that big!*" Upon his arrival in camp weeks later, Blount called out Stallworth, and every day thereafter, for the two-line passing drill, in which a receiver goes one-on-one with a defensive back. He shouted, "Stallworth, come on out here!" Stallworth was brave enough, or foolish enough, to answer Blount's challenge in front of the entire team. And he hated it.

Each time, Blount lined up in Stallworth's face. "He couldn't say anything that would scare me more than what I was feeling already," Stallworth said. "If Mel would've spread his arms, it would have looked like they would have gone on forever. He's standing there, and I'm thinking, *This man across from me knows exactly what he is doing. I, on the other hand, have no idea what I am about to do.*" Blount stood so close that Stallworth's first step could not be forward. He needed to sidestep Blount, though if Blount took his fake and leaned in the wrong direction, he was long enough to drape his arms over Stallworth to slow him down. Blount clung to Stallworth and bumped him hard all the way downfield, as rules then permitted. It was, depending on your perspective, beautiful or horrible to watch, scintillating or devastating. For Stallworth, Mel Blount became another obstacle to surmount.

Stallworth felt so in sync with Joe Gilliam. Maybe that's why he led the entire National Football League in pass receptions during the 1974 preseason. Gilliam and Stallworth understood each other. They talked.

Joe Gillie liked to let it fly. In the huddle, Stallworth told him to look for him downfield, and Gilliam did. When Bradshaw became the starter, that same feeling wasn't there. Stallworth couldn't talk to Bradshaw. It was as if they existed on different levels, Bradshaw the number one overall pick, Stallworth . . . from Alabama A&M.

Or was that all in Stallworth's head? Was that his insecurity creeping in? Many years later, he wondered. "Maybe it was, sorry to say, a black-white thing," Stallworth said. "Maybe it wasn't Terry at all. Maybe it was John. It took me time to develop, and to grow, and to be able to do that. I was used to black quarterbacks." He believed Swann had it easier in his relationship with Bradshaw, having come from USC. Against Cincinnati in the final game of the 1974 regular season, Stallworth, recovered from an arm injury, caught six passes for 105 yards, including a 5-yard touchdown from Bradshaw.

Between Stallworth and Donnie Shell, players from historically black colleges, a powerful friendship grew. As rookies in 1974, they struck a deal. They would observe each other's performance and then, after games, provide critiques of what they saw. Stallworth and Shell insisted on frankness over flattery. Stallworth made a great impression on Shell with his work ethic on the field, and, off the field, with the fine suits he wore and the way he carried himself like an executive. "Why are you dressing up like that," Shell asked, "and carrying that briefcase?" "Donnie, if you don't see yourself as successful," Stallworth advised, "you'll never be successful."

In the locker room Stallworth's comfort level grew. Once he turned up the volume on his boom box, blaring music from a local black radio station. A few white teammates complained, Lambert among them. They didn't like Stallworth's music. Fats Holmes got involved, rising to Stallworth's defense. One teammate, unseen, changed the station on Stallworth's boom box; another teammate unplugged it. Late in the season Stallworth returned to his locker and noticed that someone had cut the cord to his boom box. He demanded to know who had done it. The answer came: "Joe Greene cut the cord." Stallworth thought about taping the cord together, plugging his boom box in, and turning the volume even louder. But the better angels of his conscience prevailed. *Cutting the cord was probably the right thing to do. We don't need any division among us.* Besides, Stallworth thought it best not to mess with Joe Greene.

✦ ✦ ✦

What drove Mike Webster, his teammates weren't sure. Webster was quiet, and didn't reveal much about himself or his past. Obsessive in his workouts as a Steeler rookie, he pushed himself each day to the brink of physical collapse. Teammates wondered how he did it and why. They knew that he weighed 225 pounds, that he wanted to get bigger, and that he didn't like being considered an *undersized* center. But there seemed to be something else, something deeper, driving him. After practices, no matter how cold or wet, Webster took an extra fifty snaps at center, and then hit the blocking sleds, alone, refining his technique. He ran along the upper deck at Three Rivers Stadium, a grueling personal regimen. He ran twenty-four rows up, jogged across to the next section, then down twenty-four steps, and then up the twenty-four steps of the next section, all the way around the Chief's empty ballpark, his footfalls creating echoes. It wasn't about how long this took. It was about finishing. A weight room habitué, Webster lifted in the stadium's boiler room, staying long after teammates left. And on every offensive play, he broke the huddle early and sprinted to the line of scrimmage, a habit that dated to freshman football at the University of Wisconsin. Noll said, "Mike was fulfilled on the football field."

His wife, Pam, knew the general outline of his upbringing, or at least what he'd told her. It was complicated, with family dysfunction, divorce, a frightening house fire, and a spartan life on a potato farm near the pine forests of northern Wisconsin. Once when he was a boy, Webster told her, a drunken Native American broke into their house with a knife, and Webster protected his mother as the intruder ran off into the darkness. "A hard life," Pam said. "Mike overcame a lot of stuff." At Rhinelander High School, eighteen miles from the family farm, Webster joined the football team as a junior and played defensive tackle, forcing opposing offenses to run to the other side. His high school friend Bill Makris thought Webster humble, hardworking, a bit of a loner, and a prankster who threw a firecracker into the school auditorium once and got into trouble for it. Makris noticed that Webster had penned his personal goal in a notebook: "To become All-Big-10 Conference at defensive tackle." Right about that time, Webster went to see Jim Otto.

At Wisconsin, he struggled with schoolwork and changed his major several times. Greg Apkarian, his roommate, and teammate on the Wisconsin football team, watched Webster type papers for class, his fingers so thick he struck four keys on the typewriter simultaneously. One well-intended comment Webster made in a poetry class prompted the long-haired professor to glare at him as if he were a numskull, and Webster whispered to Apkarian, "I think I should drop this class, eh, Greg?" That Webster was a tough guy was unquestioned. In one game, he dislocated his thumb and ran past coaches and trainers on the sideline to Apkarian. "Greg! Greg! Pull it out! PULL IT OUT!!" Webster screamed. Apkarian saw Webster's thumb pushed back into its socket and became squeamish. "The only thing sticking out was his nail," Apkarian said. Trainers used special pliers to pull out Webster's thumb and, as an insight into his pain threshold, Webster returned to the game almost at once. "That's how intense he was," Apkarian said. On the field, Wisconsin coaches moved Webster from defensive line to center, and he flourished. He became team captain and later achieved his goal by being named All-Big-10 Conference.

"Mike was one of those people who when he got into something, he got into it in excess. It was never halfway," Apkarian said. "I really believe that Mike's workout ethic—his ability to work out—was kind of a drug to him." Apkarian said the physical release from football improved Webster's life outlook. "At times he would get very down and morose. He wouldn't talk. Then he would disappear for two or three days. I honestly don't know where he went. No idea."

During his senior season, Webster met Pam at the school's football office at Randall Stadium. He proposed about two months later, at his apartment, saying, "Oh, by the way, my dad gave you a Christmas gift and it's on the bathroom sink." There, on the sink, she found a small box with a diamond ring inside. Pam repeated loudly, " *'My dad gave you a Christmas gift and it's on the bathroom sink'?*" And then, "Could you be any more unromantic than that?" They married in Lodi, her hometown, in May 1974, and spent that night at the Aloha Inn in Madison. That was as close as they would get to a Hawaiian honeymoon. Webby was bound for his rookie season in Pittsburgh.

◆ ◆ ◆

On Monday, an off-day for the Steelers, with anticipation for the AFC title game in Oakland building, a handful of rookies, Stallworth among them, casually asked Tony Parisi, their equipment manager, for spare boxes. The rookies were planning ahead. They would need these boxes to pack up their locker room belongings once the Steelers' season ended. If they lost to the Raiders, they would return to Pittsburgh, quickly box up their personal items, and drive home for the off-season.

Suddenly the rookies heard a familiar voice, deep and resonant, the last voice on earth any of them wanted to hear, asking, "What do you want the boxes for?"

Joe Greene.

Greene didn't appreciate the lack of confidence their request for boxes suggested. It seemed as if they expected to lose in Oakland.

None of the rookies answered his question. How could they? Greene's value to the Steelers was nearly as great in the locker room as on the field. "Joe was dynamite in that locker room," Perles said. "That's what a lot of teams lack. They don't discipline themselves. They wait for the coaches to do it. When you have someone like Joe Greene, it makes it pretty easy for the coaches."

Facing the rookies, Greene did not yield. He asked once more, "What do you want the boxes for?"

Stallworth admired Greene. When Mean Joe spoke, there was wisdom, insight, and big-bodied intimidation. Teammates did not challenge or defy him, least of all rookies. Greene's leadership was unquestioned.

Standing there, with suddenly no need for a spare box, Stallworth thought, *Maybe we need to look at this a little differently.*

CHAPTER 12

1974 AFC TITLE GAME

CHUCK NOLL HAD NO SENSE of theater, not an ounce of Olivier in him. He was more like Paul Brown, a frozen lake in winter. In the Steelers' locker room before a game, the battle about to be waged, Noll was all focus and details. For him, emotion was anathema. It befogged the intellect, threatened a week's preparation. It got in the way of execution. Sunday's games, he said, were won on Wednesday, Thursday, and Friday, at practice. "Remember," Noll said flatly in more than one pregame talk to his players, "let's make Sunday Fun Day." But when he heard what John Madden said on television after the Raiders rallied to defeat Don Shula's Dolphins, 28–26, purging the two-time defending Super Bowl champion from the playoffs, Noll felt nearly jilted. He heard Madden say that the NFL's *two best teams* had just played—the Dolphins and the Raiders—and that comment struck Noll as unfathomably wrong. It stirred his inner Lombardi. And so on the Tuesday before the 1974 AFC title game, the Steelers' forty-seven players sat in chairs attached to small writing tables in their usual meeting room, expecting the usual tepid gruel from Noll. But Noll surprised them. He took his best shot, figuring it was early enough in the week so that an emotional rush wouldn't backfire. He told his Steelers what Madden had said and then, his eyes tightening at the corners, Noll said that Madden was wrong. "The best team in the NFL," Noll said, thumping his index finger on a table, "is sitting right here in this room."

It took his players a moment to react, to decide whether their coach had just said what he had just said. Then their reaction was like a small dam breaking, hoots and howls, broad smiles and hand slaps, and Franco Harris saying, "Yep!" No player reacted more demonstratively than Joe Greene. He stood so rapidly to pump his fist that his right thigh stuck in the small writing table attached to his chair, and the chair lifted from the floor and toppled.

Noll's speech ignited Greene. It was like additional gunpowder for an already explosive weapon. Much as he respected Noll, Greene had long craved more emotion from his coach—for his teammates, not himself—and now he had gotten it. It wasn't *what* Noll said in the meeting room, or *how* he said it. It was simply *that* he said it. It caught Greene, and the entire team, by surprise.

Greene would be voted the league's defensive player of the year in 1974, and now, at the pinnacle of his professional career, he entered a three-week period during which he terrorized playoff opponents. John Vella, a Raiders offensive tackle, studied Greene in game films prior to the AFC title game. "I looked at the way he carried himself. He was their leader," Vella said. Madden showed the Raiders films of Greene and Lambert acting as ruffians, shoving opponents after plays, pushing off their face masks to stand up. Madden didn't offer comments. He thought their actions spoke loudly. "You could tell how proud Joe was," Vella said, "and that the rest of the Steelers looked up to him for leadership." Raiders receiver Mike Siani had the same feeling: "Joe was a beast, an absolute beast. He was a destructive force." Radakovich later said that during the 1974 NFL postseason, "Joe Greene was the greatest defensive lineman that ever lived."

Oakland Coliseum, pregame. Long and lean, L. C. Greenwood stretched out on a folding chair in a hallway outside the visitors' locker room. There, on a small TV, he watched the Vikings and Rams in the other conference's title game. Just then, the Raiders' Gene Upshaw and Art Shell happened by, like two all-pro ships passing. "Whatcha watching, L.C.?" Upshaw asked. Greenwood had none of the puffed-up bravado of Fats, Mad Dog, or Mean Joe. But even Greenwood couldn't resist this one. "I'm just looking," he said, "to see who we're going to play in the Super Bowl." The Raiders' two all-pro ships passed without reply.

✦ ✦ ✦

Joe Greene vs. Jim Otto: here was the AFC title game's defining matchup, at the line of scrimmage, Greene at the apex of his career, and the Age of Otto, fading to darkness, in its fifteenth season and 223rd consecutive (and final) start. An opponent once said that looking through Otto's face mask was like looking at a gargoyle. Otto, the Raiders' center, had a massive Prussian head, a perpetual sneer, and dark, menacing eyes. His nose, broken more than twenty times, curved like the letter "S," and his wife sometimes rearranged it in the stadium parking lot after games as if it were living room furniture. He wore a size 8 helmet, big as a bucket, largest on the Raiders, a battlefield relic with the signature Pirate with an eye patch on its side covered over by a white splotch—the paint scratched off from Otto's violent collisions with the likes of Curly Culp, Ernie Ladd, Buck Buchanan, Merlin Olsen, and Mean Joe Greene. Greene once railed at Otto on the field and Otto simply said, "How's your wife and children, Joe?" This was Double O's way of saying, "Shuddup and play!"

As Otto said years later, "It was like war out there and in war there is no Geneva Convention." So deep was Otto's immersion in football, his wife once heard him calling out line signals in his sleep. He was the quintessential Raider, the standard-bearer who insisted on holding the football in every Raider team photograph from 1960 through 1974, reminding young teammates that centers were supposed to hold the football. Early on he asked the Raiders for jersey number "00" because, he said, his last name began and ended that way (aught-oh). Double O became his moniker, and the zeros on his jersey looked like two eyes opened wide. He wore a face mask with two simple horizontal bars, a look more common to wide receivers and quarterbacks, none of that cagelike protection many linemen used. Opponents gouged his eyes, and after some games Otto looked in the mirror and thought he'd been in a knife fight. But he was wily, a tactician, and through the years he doled out more pain than he received. Siani saw Otto return to the sideline once in 1973, his forehead oozing blood that streamed over the bridge of his nose, a screw inside Otto's helmet the cause. The team trainer approached Otto to help stop the bleeding. "Get away from me!" Otto growled. Siani thought, *Double O likes it! He thinks the blood will intimidate his opponent!* It intimidated Siani.

For six seasons, Greene had done battle with Otto. "I mean, you hit him in the head and your helmet would just . . . *ring*!" Greene said. "You had to deliver a blow with your helmet and hitting him with your helmet was not something that you cherished. First, you had to *get your mind right*, as we say."

Otto had stayed too long. A week shy of his thirty-sixth birthday, his younger teammates deferentially called him Pops. His body had been shattered by the game. He had endured nine knee surgeries. The interior of his knees grinded, bone-on-bone. Surgical scars crisscrossed his legs like train tracks. He suffered terrible pains in his back. His fingers, stepped on too often, were misshapen and throbbed. He'd grown nearly dependent on the painkiller Darvon and muscle relaxers. During the latter half of the 1974 season, ligaments pulled and creaked in his right knee, which trainers drained thrice weekly. Doctors told him the knee needed a bone graft reconstruction. Otto went home to bed after practices and his wife iced his legs. She awoke in the darkness of three a.m. and put more ice on his legs. Then Otto got up at seven, the swelling much improved, and headed off to practice. Tackle John Vella said, "His leg and knee didn't look like a leg and knee. It looked like a blob, just one continuous leg with no form. I'd see that and think, 'That's kind of where his knee should be.' " Each week in the training room Vella saw bloody fluid form on Otto's knee and couldn't bear the sight. Vella: "You couldn't believe what he put his body through to play. Then he would do the same thing the next week. It was like you thought to yourself, *Are you really going to complain about anything physically when you see what Otto is going through?*"

As the playoffs started, Dan Jenkins wrote in *Sports Illustrated* that the Steelers were the "only playoff team without a quarterback," another dig at Bradshaw. Approaching the AFC title game, the Steelers' offensive strategy was simple: they would run the ball. All week they had studied films of how other teams had pounded the run against the Raiders, the Dolphins for 213 yards, the Cowboys for 144, and Denver for 292. The Steelers would run Harris and Bleier over and over, leaning on tackle traps, using the mobility of Jon Kolb and Gordon Gravelle. Bradshaw, with a sixteen-day growth of red beard, would throw minimally, perhaps fifteen times. "All of them ran on Oakland," Bradshaw said, "so we knew we could, too."

On the Raiders' first play from scrimmage, Fats Holmes didn't bother with the defensive huddle. He stood over the football at the line of scrimmage, all wired up, and howled at his Raiders opposite. "Hey, EUGENE!!" No response. "EU-GEEEEEENNNEEE!" Nothing. "Hey, UPSHAAAAAAAW!!" From the offensive huddle, Gene Upshaw looked at him. "I'M GONNA KICK YOUR ASS!" Holmes shouted. In the defensive huddle, Greenwood laughed, knowing that his weeklong teasing had worked. "Far out, Ernie!" Greenwood said.

Oakland running back Clarence Davis took the first handoff and ran left, behind Upshaw. Holmes slammed into the running back. Davis gained four yards, and it would be the Raiders' longest run of the day. For good measure, in a pile of players, Holmes spat in Upshaw's face. Two plays later, on third and five, Greene aligned in the Stunt 4-3, threw Otto to the ground with one hand, leaped with both arms skyward to block a pass that Stabler opted not to throw, and then grabbed the quarterback by his right hip pad and spun him to the ground for an eleven-yard loss. As was their habit, the Raiders continued to run left during the first half, behind Upshaw and Shell. That sent the action toward Holmes, White, and Russell; each time, the Raiders' runners got mauled by gang tackles. In the huddle, Ham playfully told Russell that he was bored. "Let me take a few shots over on your side," Ham said, though his own big moments were soon to come.

Greene played as if a Super Bowl appearance depended on him, and him alone. After one run, Greene, consumed by emotions, turned on Otto. He kicked him in the groin and dropped him. *In war there is no Geneva Convention.* Once, in an earlier game between the teams, Raider guard George Buehler's hand had snagged accidentally inside Greene's jersey. Mean Joe believed Buehler was holding him and took corrective action, kicking wildly at Buehler. Pops Otto had rushed in that day, protectively, saying to Greene, "Knock that off!" But now it was Pops's turn, and this time Greene's swift cleated kick did not miss its mark. Beneath his breath Otto muttered, "You dirty . . ." Otto was on the defensive, vulnerable. His injured right knee ruined his blocking posture and balance. Greene, meanwhile, complained to officials that Otto was holding him. Otto replied with a snarl: "The only person I hold is my wife!" In the week leading up to this game, Buehler had prepared only for Greene.

"I didn't hear anything anybody was saying," Buehler said. "I just watched films and thought of Joe." Now, with the Raiders intending to send running back Marv Hubbard up the middle, between Buehler and Otto, Greene moved into the gap between them in the Stunt 4-3 and took his three-point stance, his nose inches from the ground. "I knew I had to get to Joe quickly because he was my assignment," Buehler said. "But Joe leaped back and I went falling on my face, and Hubbard told me, 'I've never been hit so hard.' "

The Steelers took a 10–3 lead midway through the second quarter—or so they thought—when Bradshaw lobbed an apparent eight-yard touchdown pass to Stallworth at the far left edge of the end zone. Cornerback Nemiah Wilson held Stallworth's right hand as he trailed half a yard behind, and Stallworth made a one-handed catch, cradling the ball with his left hand. But the head linesman ruled Stallworth out of bounds, a call TV replays proved incorrect (the NFL did not allow instant replay reviews at the time). "I don't mind another player shaking my hand, but not when I'm trying to catch a pass," Stallworth said after the game. Bradshaw threw an interception two plays later, and Stallworth, still furious over the earlier call, got penalized for a late hit on the interception return. The Raiders drove to the Steeler twenty-three and, with a minute left in the half, Stabler threw a twenty-two-yard pass to receiver Cliff Branch, who beat Blount, and stepped out of bounds at the one-yard line. As Otto had set up for pass protection on the play, pain shot through his right knee. He lifted his right leg, and tried to balance himself on his left leg while stopping Greene's furious rush. Greene fell over him, and Otto was penalized for tripping, negating the gain and costing the Raiders a possible touchdown before the half. Madden said the Raiders hadn't been cited for a tripping penalty in five years. Lambert blocked George Blanda's thirty-eight-yard field goal attempt, and so the half ended at 3-all. In the first half the Raiders' offense managed just two first downs and sixty-five total yards.

The Steelers' defense continued to punish Oakland running backs in the third quarter. By game's end, the Raiders would gain only twenty-nine yards on twenty-one rushes, a stunning performance by the Steelers' defense. "They stopped Oakland's running," *Oakland Tribune* sports editor Bob Valle would write, "with a Steel Curtain the Russians couldn't penetrate." But the Steelers' offense wobbled, keeping the game close. When Branch, the Raider receiver who led the NFL with thirteen touchdown catches, turned Blount inside out and caught a thirty-eight-yard touchdown pass from Stabler, the Raiders led 10–3 with five minutes left in the third quarter.

Then the Steelers opened up the ground game, their offensive line asserting control, Harris and Bleier running eight times in a time-consuming nine-play drive. Harris ran for a touchdown from eight yards on a tackle trap, tying the game at 10 early in the fourth quarter.

Now came Ham's big moment. With Russell, Lambert, and Edwards blitzing, Ham cut in front of running back Charlie Smith to intercept his second Stabler pass of the game, this one at the Oakland thirty-four. He returned it twenty-five yards to the Oakland nine. Up in the press box, the Chief, wearing his lucky cap and his favorite old overcoat, studied the replay on the television monitor, without comment. Bradshaw, three plays later, lasered a six-yard touchdown pass to Swann slicing across the middle for a 17–10 lead. The Chief watched the replay of that one, too, the cold stub of his cigar stuck in his mouth. He revealed no emotion, though his insides roiled.

Carson, the Steelers' defensive coordinator, mixed coverages and blitzes that confused Stabler all afternoon. But Branch beat Blount again, this time for a forty-two-yard gain. Had Lambert not tackled Branch in the open field at the Steelers' twenty-four he might have scored the game-tying touchdown. Carson snapped. He benched Blount for the remainder of the game, replacing him with rookie cornerback Jimmy Allen, who fared well against Branch. Blanda's field goal cut the Steelers' lead to 17–13.

Bradshaw would throw only seventeen passes in this game, completing eight, for ninety-five yards. By design, he put the ball in the hands of Harris and Bleier. Harris would run for 111 yards, Bleier for 98. On one sweep, Gravelle found himself at the bottom of a pile in front of the Raiders' bench and got an earful of Madden screaming at officials. As he excavated himself from the tangled players, Gravelle saw Madden, in midtirade, look at him, smile, and wink, and then resume screaming at officials. "I thought to myself," Gravelle said, "*I like that guy!*"

Stabler got one last chance. Trailing by four points with a minute forty-eight to play, he needed to cover nearly seventy yards for the winning touchdown. On first down, Greenwood, in his gold high-tops, flashed into the pocket and sacked him for a nine-yard loss, but cornerback J. T. Thomas was called for holding on the play. In the ensuing defensive huddle, Russell told Thomas, "Don't let the officials intimidate you. Keep playing your aggressive game." On the next play, Stabler's pass protection collapsed at the Oakland thirty-two, a blitzing Russell closed in on him, and he lofted a pass downfield that Thomas intercepted. With arms and legs pumping, Thomas raced down the left side, past a forlorn Madden, thirty-seven yards to the Oakland twenty-four. Moments later Harris shot up the middle, past Mansfield and Clack, for a twenty-one-yard touchdown with fifty-two seconds left. The Steelers' 24–13 victory was sealed, as was their date in Super Bowl IX against the Minnesota Vikings at Tulane Stadium in New Orleans two weeks hence.

The most important victory in the Steelers' forty-two-year history, the 1974 AFC title game offered important insights and glimmerings of what was to come. On offense, Harris and Bleier proved well matched, complementary pieces. Bleier was a fireplug lead blocker, willing to donate his body for the greater cause (Noll likened him to "a third guard"), and Harris was one of the league's elite runners, a one-thousand-yard rusher in 1974, a statistical summit he would reach in each of the next five seasons. Swann and Stallworth revealed exquisite big-play promise, their breakouts only a matter of time. Bradshaw made some big throws—and some unforgivable misreads. The Steelers won in 1974 because of Bradshaw and in spite of him. He would be their starting quarterback from this point forward, even as Noll gnashed his teeth over his inconsistencies, over Bradshaw being Bradshaw. The rookie Webster, playing as long snapper, and in short-yardage and goal-line situations, witnessed the end of Otto, his role model from Wisconsin, not yet knowing that Otto's consecutive-games streak, and NFL career, were, at long last, finished. History would reveal Pops Otto as a cautionary tale for Webster in ways that he, as a young player, couldn't begin to understand. On defense, the Steelers' front four, all muscle and violence, dominated, and the linebackers showed startling versatility. Lambert made an athletic tackle of a little receiver (Branch) in

the open field to save a touchdown, and also blocked a field goal, revealing his impressive combination of speed, range, instinct, and power. Ham had none of Lambert's showmanship, none of the stamping feet or the lion-in-the-jungle roar. Ham played linebacker with an understated efficiency and grace. Said to be the fastest Steeler in five- or ten-yard bursts, Ham sprinted laterally to his right twenty-five yards across the field to make his first interception of Stabler, who could not have known that Ham would be anywhere near his intended receiver, running back Pete Banaszak.

An empire was building.

Many years later Joe Greene would say that only once in his thirteen-year NFL career had he and the Steelers' defense been *in the zone*—where the unit could do no wrong—and that was during the 1974 AFC title game. Twenty-nine yards in twenty-one carries, an average of 1.4 yards per carry, became a statistic he would never forget. "The zone is a place that you rarely visit. It's not someplace you go every week," Greene said. "The zone is sacred ground." Harris would remember his own nervousness during this game, even when the Steelers were ahead. Harris thought, *God, we're just one half from the Super Bowl!* And then: *We're just one quarter from the Super Bowl!* He had promised a few teammates that after they defeated Oakland and flew back to Pittsburgh, he would host a champagne breakfast with steak and eggs. But years later Harris said, "I just remember having butterflies in my stomach for three and a half quarters, still feeling nervous that our job isn't done."

In the postgame locker rooms, Madden said, "Defeat is a bitch," and Tatum said, "We felt this was it. This was our year." Mean Joe said, "The Raider offensive line got so frustrated it lost its poise. . . . I kind of felt sorry for those cats." Stallworth said the referee stole a touchdown from him: "I was so far inside the end zone it was ridiculous." There were a few bursts of candor by the Steelers, admissions that times hadn't always seemed so glorious. Bradshaw admitted Noll had told him four weeks earlier, after the loss to Houston, that he would give him "one more chance" as quarterback. Bleier admitted that Noll had wanted him to retire after 1970. None of that mattered now.

The press rushed to the Chief, bound for an NFL championship game at long last. "In the old days we'd have a great celebration," the Chief said, "but I took the pledge about fifteen years ago, and things are different now." He said he looked forward to the Super Bowl. "I'll go there like a big shot," the Chief said, hardly meaning it. United Press International sports columnist Milton Richman interviewed Rooney outside the Steelers' locker room. Rooney told him, "This has been my life—sports. You learn to accept the bad with the good. No matter how bad it got sometimes, you always lived in hopes that next year would be the year. What would I have said had we lost today? I'd have said, 'Well, we'll get 'em next year.' " In his syndicated column, Richman waxed on about his old friend, his tone every bit as fawning as most sports columns written about the Chief on this day: "They just don't make 'em like Art Rooney anymore. He's God's gift to the human race, a natural winner. That goes no matter how his team does against the Vikings two weeks from now."

Dwight White phoned his girlfriend and future wife, Karen Farmer, back in Pittsburgh. She had taken him and Greene to the Pittsburgh airport, and now she would pick them up after midnight. Super Bowl–bound, White gushed into the phone, "You know what I really want tonight? Some fried chicken!!" She didn't think of herself as much of a cook. But White played on his charm: "Karen, would you go to the store and fry up some chicken for me for when I get back home?" Reluctantly, she agreed: "Okay, Dwight, I'll do it for you."

On the plane flight home, White took to the airplane's PA system and said, as only he could, "Mr. Rooney has something to say in the jubilance of what we've done." The Chief professed his joy over the Steelers' performance, thanked the fellas, and at thirty thousand feet in the air they cheered for him. When they stepped into the terminal at Greater Pittsburgh International Airport at one o'clock in the morning, ten thousand fans awaited them, chanting, "We're number one!" and "Dee-fense! Dee-fense!" Spotting the Chief, a band struck up "When Irish Eyes Are Smiling." Pittsburgh mayor Peter Flaherty presented the Chief with a key to the city. The Chief, all bundled up, stepped to a microphone and thanked the crowd for showing up. Sixty Allegheny County sheriffs escorted the team through the adoring crowd, Greenwood later saying, "I got more beat up by them than I did in the game. When I got in the car finally, I

just sat there for a minute. People were banging on my windows. 'Open up, we're your fans!' I said, 'Yeah . . .' "

Later that morning, Franco Harris, a man of his word, hosted several teammates at his home for a celebratory breakfast of steak, eggs, and champagne. Karen Farmer, a woman of her word, had made fried chicken and drove Dwight White's car to the airport. White and Greene were still in high spirits when they climbed inside the car. Greene, always in charge, took to the wheel and said, "C'mon, Dwight. We're going out to celebrate!" Then he suggested, "Why doesn't Karen take your car back home, and we'll go out?" It was nearly 2:00 a.m. now, and Karen understood this was the boys' big night. The Super Bowl was next, after all. Even so, she reminded, "Dwight, I cooked that chicken for you."

Mad Dog said, "Yeah, but . . ."

"Duh-wight," she said, turning one syllable into two for added effect, "I went to the store. I stayed up. *I cooked that chicken for you.*"

The Mad Dog said he was going out with Mean Joe. Karen Farmer wouldn't hear of it. "Duh-wight, guess what? You are going to come and eat that chicken."

Back and forth they went, Mean Joe growing impatient, same as he did when Jim Otto held him. Finally he snapped, saying, "Get it under control." He drove to his apartment complex, the lovers' spat between Mad Dog and Karen Farmer at full throttle. The boys' planned celebration of the AFC title game victory suddenly seemed in jeopardy.

Arriving at the entrance to his apartment complex, Mean Joe did not wait for the traffic arm to lift. He crashed Dwight White's car right through it, a loud bang in the night that reduced the wooden arm to splinters. Mean Joe and the Mad Dog didn't much care about that, or about White's car. The night was young, and so were they. They had big plans.

But on an evening when the nation began to see the Chief and his Pittsburgh Steelers in a new light, perhaps even as NFL champions, and when the Steel Curtain front four had dominated Jim Otto and the Oakland Raiders, Dwight White relented. Mad Dog returned home and ate fried chicken.

It was in the locker room at Oakland, though, when the AFC title game victory was brand new and the team's joy was at its purest, that these

Steelers hugged and preened and busted each other's chops, the camaraderie that was always the most satisfying antidote to the game's sufferings.
Finding his way to the cameras, Swann said, "Going to the Super Bowl
feels like a million dollars. Wait, make that twenty-five thousand dollars,
to be exact." Hanratty let loose a few happy roars and then later, always
the jokester, said, "I think I'll report to the trainer tomorrow and soak my
vocal cords in the whirlpool."

The Chief, naturally, searched for Joe Greene. He reached for Mean
Joe's hand. "Congratulations, Joe," he said. "No, Chief," Greene replied.
"Today the congratulations go to you."

CHAPTER 13

SUPER BOWL IX

AMERICA WAS ABOUT TO BE introduced formally to the Chief. He was a few weeks shy of his seventy-fourth birthday, and with his shock of white hair, craggy eyebrows, and dark-suited portliness, he looked like a bishop. All those racetrack victories through the decades had belonged to him alone. But a Steeler victory in Super Bowl IX, should it come, would occur on a stage unlike any he'd ever known, the world and the electronic media growing around him and the NFL in ways that would have seemed unimaginable to him a generation before. To an old horse player, nothing could have been bigger than Seabiscuit outracing War Admiral in 1938 with forty million Americans listening on radio. But now seventy-one million people—roughly a third of the nation's total population—would tune in on television to see the Steelers and Vikings at Tulane Stadium in New Orleans, and the Chief himself would become the game's lead protagonist.

His many friends in the press box made sure of that. He was a sports-writer's dream, always available. His tales filled their notebooks. He gave them cigars, complimented their columns, and sent them occasional postcards from the road. If they were Irish, or liked horse racing, or wrote in New York, the Chief was even more inclined to like them. Whereas in the old days, his press box friends were the likes of Grantland Rice and Bill Corum, now they were Jim Murray in Los Angeles; Blackie Sherrod in Dallas; Red Smith, Dave Anderson, and Dick Young in New York; Bill Gleason in Chicago; Pat Harmon in Cincinnati; John Steadman in

Baltimore; and all the boys in Pittsburgh. Even as the sports press became harder-edged and more cynical in the 1970s, the stories about the Chief remained valentines and puff pieces, all. From New Orleans, he was lionized as a gentleman and a gentle spirit. With a Steeler victory his legend would explode into Super Bowl–sized hyperbole: a lovable loser for forty years transformed into a *great American sportsman.* The Chief's devotion to the men of the fourth estate was authentic. Rather than sit in owner's boxes, he preferred to watch NFL games, including Super Bowl IX, from the press box, among friends.

A few days before flying to New Orleans, the Chief and Kass invited Joe Greene, Franco Harris, and Dwight White to dinner at 940. The Chief sat at his dining room table that night, held up his fork, and said, "I believe if we can hold this club together, I think it will be a strong ball club for five or six years." Some of the newer Steelers had missed the franchise's darker days. Harris had been a Steeler for only three years, all playoff seasons. Rookies such as Stallworth and Webster reached the Super Bowl in their first year. But every Steeler knew about the Chief's personal odyssey. *Was there a soul in Pittsburgh who didn't?*

Super Bowl IX promised to be the Chief's moment, and television's moment, too. TV cameras brought out the best in the Chief, the bright lights softening his features, making him seem vulnerable, a sage, old Irish Everyman. His self-deprecating humor played well on camera, too. "When you win you are smart and so I was the only dumb person left in our league," he said, sitting on a couch, in an interview with Jeannie Morris of NBC Sports. "I'd like to get that stigma off me."

He was a feel-good story and a curiosity piece. To New Orleans he brought his history, his anecdotes, and a chartered jet for 192 stadium and office workers from Pittsburgh plus writers and guests from Yonkers Raceway in New York and Liberty Bell Park near Philadelphia, horse tracks he owned and that his sons Tim, John, and Pat operated.

Some sportswriters weren't sure what to make of the Chief, or the curious Pittsburgh characters surrounding him.

Atop that list was Joey Diven. As the Chief unlocked the door to his suite at the Fontainebleau Hotel, a voice urgently called out to him from behind, "Wait a minute!"

It was Diven, his hand held up.

The former Billy Conn bodyguard, who patrolled the Steelers' bench during games and helped Houston coach Bum Phillips protect his cowboy hat at Three Rivers Stadium, would shadow the Chief in New Orleans during Super Bowl week. He would watch for evils that lurked. Some mistook Diven as the Chief's bodyguard, but he was just an old pal, another fistic character in the Chief's inner circle.

Now Diven entered the hotel suite alone. He peeked inside empty closets, poked his head into bathrooms. He searched for mischief. "C'mon, Joey!" the Chief said, standing by the front door with Kass, Art Jr., and his wife, Kay. But Diven would not be deterred. He walked slowly through the suite, room to room. Diven, big and broad, his gray hair slicked back, finally gave the all-clear sign. He said he wasn't worried about hoodlums. "But you can get these nuts hiding in here," he told the Chief, "who want your autograph or their picture taken with you."

As true celebrity came to him, the Chief rolled his eyes and said, "C'mon, Joey!"

Diven turned his palms up and said, "Just making sure."

Noll gave his men the first two nights without curfew. They were free to roam New Orleans into the wee hours. Joe Greene arrived with the team at the Fontainebleau, threw his bags on the bed, gathered Fats, Hollywood Bags, and Mad Dog, and, in short order, taxied with them to a seafood-and-oyster bar on Bourbon Street. There, amid great fanfare, the foursome drank rows of Heineken beer and ate baskets filled with crawdads and peel-and-eat shrimp. Their thousand-pound presence drew a crowd, stares, flashbulb photographs, and respectful applause. The bar soon ran out of Heineken, and an employee rushed out to get more for the Steel Curtain front four, and fast. Fats's eyes grew slanted (from alcohol), his belly full (from shrimp he didn't bother peeling), as self-satisfaction surged through him. Mean Joe felt something approaching joy. He reveled in the closeness he shared with Dwight, L.C., and Ernie. Together they had limited O. J. Simpson to forty-nine yards rushing, and the Raiders to twenty-nine. Ranging in age from twenty-five to twenty-eight years old, the members of the Steel Curtain front four were at the height of their physical, and reputational, powers. As Greene saw it, ever since Noll's speech before the Raiders game ("The best team in the NFL is sitting right here in this room"), the Steelers were cresting. Their practices had been sharp and focused. The adrenal rush produced by the victory over the Raiders was, to Greene, indescribable. He felt himself riding atop a wave. That oddsmakers favored the Steelers in Super Bowl IX, and that the Vikings had lost two previous Super Bowls, meant nothing to Greene. Sitting in the seafood-and-oyster bar with his linemates, Greene expected to win. Suddenly, his reverie shattered, Mad Dog announced that he felt ill, a sharp pain in his chest, a fire in his lungs. He couldn't breathe. He felt nauseated. Mean Joe feared that Dwight White had been sabotaged; poisoned, maybe. He helped White out of the bar and into a taxi. They sped back to the Fontainebleau. Before the night was done, White was hospitalized, weak, his temperature rising, intravenous fluids pumping into him; his diagnosis, viral pneumonia and pleurisy. His game-day status was uncertain. If he couldn't play, Steve Furness would replace him.

Six days later, on the eve of the game, his weight down eighteen pounds, Mad Dog remained hospitalized.

Along the banks of the Mississippi, in a convention hall, a tanned and smiling Pete Rozelle eased through the room like Caesar. An army of more than 1,500 media members, a PR man's dream, feasted on muffulettas, gumbo, jambalaya, and an ocean of alcohol at the NFL commissioner's annual Super Bowl party. Eight years before, the Super Bowl was born, its name coined by Kansas City Chiefs owner Lamar Hunt, who noticed his young daughter playing with a bouncy rubber toy, the Super Ball; the name grew creatively from that. In the week preceding the first Super Bowl, in January 1967, the Packers against the Chiefs in Los Angeles Memorial Coliseum, sportswriters interviewed players informally, sometimes one-on-one, in their hotel room or at poolside. It was all so intimate. But the game had grown into a Barnum-like sensation, a cultural spectacle launched by television and fueled by hyperbole. To sportswriters, the Super Bowl became a plum weeklong assignment that offered visions of warm weather in January, fine dining on expense accounts, and an array of free gifts from the NFL (bags, pens, shirts, hats).

"What kind of grades did you make?" a reporter asked Bradshaw during a press conference. He replied, "I beg your pardon?" Reporter: "What kind of grades did you make?" Bradshaw: "That's none of your business." Bradshaw became like a laboratory rat dissected under the microscope all week. Never mind that, unlike many NFL quarterbacks, Bradshaw called his own plays. "I've been labeled 'Ozark Ike' and 'Dummy' and 'Country Bumpkin' and I hate it," Bradshaw said. "You don't have to be an Einstein or a magna cum laude to be a good quarterback. You just have to have good football sense." Mel Blount created sparks and headlines when he termed defensive coordinator Bud Carson's reasons for benching him in the AFC title game "stupid." Blount also said that four quarterbacks in the AFC were superior to the Vikings' Tarkenton. Noll's disdain for the media was obvious. In each exchange he was guarded and on the brink of irritation. After Noll had told his players not to be intimidated by the press, Mansfield saw his opportunity and seized it. During one interview session in a hotel ballroom, the Old Ranger sat at a table with Russell, the two players on the Steelers with the most seniority. Asked to provide their firsthand contrast stories—the Steelers' modern ascension as opposed to their ineptitude during the '60s—Mansfield rolled out his best old stories and told them with energy and spunk. "We had two toilets in the club-house but only one of them worked," Mansfield began. "You had to chase the rats out to take a shower. . . ." And: "I remember one time the new coach, Chuck Noll, came down and said he had good news and bad news. 'The good news is that you're going to get to change socks and jocks. The bad news is, Mansfield, you change with Andy Russell. Russell, you change with Mansfield.' " Steelers publicist Joe Gordon announced the interview session at an end, the cameras and microphones turned off, and Mansfield climbed atop the table and bellowed: "I've been in this league twelve years and I've never had this much attention. I've got some things to tell you. SO GET YOUR ASSES BACK HERE!!"

Other Steelers proceeded more quietly. Glen Edwards, the team's safety and a devastating hitter, sat alone at his table, not a media member in sight. "Nobody wants to talk to a muffucker like me," he grumbled to the writer Roy Blount of *Sports Illustrated*. Between these two men, Roy Blount was the bigger celebrity, his book on the 1973 Steelers, *About Three Bricks Shy of a Load*, released only a month earlier. Blount had spent the previous season embedded with the Steelers, given access by the Rooneys and Noll. Blount later wrote, "While I was with them, [Steeler players] had tended to forget I was a writer because I was always drinking with them and eating chowder and playing liar's poker instead of taking notes. I knew that what I had written had hurt the feelings of three or four players I liked, and that made me feel bad." That included Fats Holmes, who didn't like a quote Blount attributed to him about how he prayed from the moment he entered a locker room until game's end, "with the mind of a child and the brains of a sixty-year-old warrior." Blount thought the quote poetic. Holmes didn't. "Said I had the mind of a six-year-old," he growled.

Holmes turned frisky during Super Bowl week. Once, at a small gathering at the Fontainebleau with Joe and Agnes Greene and a few others, music played, camera flashbulbs popped, and beer, bourbon, and Mateus wine flowed. As Holmes danced the Bump with Agnes, others took photos and shouted to her, "Get *down*, Texas!" On the dance floor Holmes playfully began to bump his head against her hip, Agnes Greene shook her head, no-no, and Fats apologized.

When Holmes spotted Roy Blount in New Orleans before Super Bowl IX, he greeted him with a Sonny Liston glower, and said, "Hello, Archenemy."

On Sunday morning, game day, White phoned his girlfriend, Karen Farmer. "I'm gonna play," he told her. "You're kidding," she replied. White told her that he would play even if it killed him because he might never get another chance to play in a Super Bowl.

Super Bowl IX was a cultural phenomenon interrupted by a physical phenomenon—the Steel Curtain defensive line, four black southerners riding into football lore as the modern-day Four Horsemen of the Apocalypse.

It was cold and gloomy, just forty-six degrees, and players slipped on the rain-slicked Poly-Turf surface as seventeen-mile-per-hour winds whipped through the concrete-and-steel hulk of Tulane Stadium. Kass Rooney, in her mink coat, shivered among the eighty thousand in the

grandstands as she sat with her son Art Jr.; his wife, Kay; and BLESTO scout Jack Butler. Dreamily, Kass said, "What I wouldn't do for a shot of Canadian Club." Like pennies from above, several glasses filled with Canadian Club were passed to her from fans in nearby seats. Gratefully, Kass partook. On television, sportscaster Curt Gowdy said, "Yesterday more money was spent in New Orleans than on any day since V-E Day!" Madison Avenue advertisers ponied up a record $107,000 for thirty-second television commercial spots during the game. Joe Garagiola trumpeted Pinto and Vega automobiles, McDonald's spun its Big Mac jingle ("Two all-beef patties, special sauce, lettuce, cheese, pickles, onions, on a sesame seed bun!"), and a tantalizing trailer touted the movie *Earthquake* "in Sensurround and starring Charlton Heston and a superb cast!" Viking quarterback Fran Tarkenton, in a public service announcement, reminded viewers of the energy crisis. "Drive under fifty-five miles per hour," he said. "Keep your thermostat under sixty-eight degrees."

The two teams massed in the tunnel, ready to rush onto the field. In the tunnel of his thoughts, Bradshaw, a consummate worrier, fretted: *Don't you lose this game! DON'T YOU DARE LOSE THIS GAME!* Just then Bradshaw saw a fan, bare-chested and wearing a plastic Viking helmet with horns protruding from the sides, collapse and fall to the ground only a few feet away, dead by heart attack. In the tunnel, Glen Edwards sidled up to an old friend who played for the Vikings, wished him well, and in return received a cold stare. Edwards said, "Hey, bub: you *know* me!" His friend didn't respond. "Okay, then," Edwards warned, "buckle up!" Hearing this, Joe Greene laughed. The Chobee Kid, with his straight-from-the-swamp manner of speech, had that effect on him. Greene led the Steelers onto the field, and he flashed a number one sign as he ran. Noll dressed fully in black—black jacket, black slacks, black sneakers. In the press box, the Chief gave away a few cigars to sportswriters and took his seat between Dan and the columnist Jim Murray.

Noll had embraced the underdog position. He'd known the other side. His Baltimore Colts, as heavy favorites in Super Bowl III, lost to Namath and the Jets. Noll had a plan, well established throughout the season, for this game. On offense, Bradshaw would pass infrequently lest he become the bull's-eye in the target of Viking pass rushers Alan Page and Carl Eller.

The Steelers would run Franco Harris often, and mix in runs by Bleier. They would run suckers and draws, influence plays with the movements of offensive linemen intentionally misleading Viking defenders. The rest Noll would leave to his defense.

In Super Bowl IX, the Steelers' front four painted a masterpiece of mayhem. They beat the Vikings' offensive linemen off the snap, slipped their blocks, and physically handled them. As his pass protection disintegrated, Tarkenton scrambled wildly, as if escaping a burning building. No time to search for receivers downfield, his view obscured by the onrushing Steel Curtain, Tarkenton settled for short throws to his running backs and tight ends. He completed fewer than half of his twenty-seven passes and threw three interceptions. The front four batted down four passes, three by Greenwood. Greene angled into the space between Minnesota guard Ed White and center Mick Tingelhoff (a surname Holmes couldn't pronounce all week, calling him "Ticklehoff"), and created confusion and chaos. Mean Joe recovered a fumble, and intercepted one of the passes that Greenwood tipped. Running backs Chuck Foreman and Dave Osborn discovered the growling Ernie Holmes to be like an impenetrable stone wall, the arrowhead of his haircut pointed, for them, in the wrong direction. Dwight White played nearly the entire game. Each time he returned to the sideline, the Steelers' medical staff and assistant coaches surrounded him, asking, "You okay? How's your breathing?" And each time Mad Dog replied, "Fine, fine. Leave me alone." White even scored the game's only first-half points. The Vikings botched a handoff on their own ten-yard line, the fumbled ball unwittingly kicked backward off one of Greenwood's gold shoes. Tarkenton fell on it near the goal line and rolled into the end zone, whereupon the onrushing White simply touched him for a safety, and the Steelers led 2–0.

Up in the press box, the Chief knew Tarkenton's pain. He winced and Jim Murray heard him say of the opposing quarterback, "He's playing his heart out." At the time, Tarkenton had completed just three of twelve passes, and the Steelers had outrushed the Vikings seventy-four yards to one. Shanklin got hurt, and the Steelers let their rookie receivers, Swann and Stallworth, play the rest of the game, Stallworth making three catches for twenty-four yards, Dandy Don Meredith, on TV, telling America, "He's got the best hands of anybody in the league. I'm told that by Terry

Bradshaw." With Minnesota driving late in the half, receiver John Gilliam slanted over the middle and reached high overhead for a pass at the Pittsburgh five-yard line. There he met Edwards, angling in for the kill shot. "*Hey, bub, you* know *me! Okay, then, buckle up!*" His teammates later would vote Edwards the Steelers' most valuable player of the 1974 season, and this play typified why. Edwards delivered a two-forearm blow beneath Gilliam's chinstrap. As Gilliam dropped to the ground, the ball fluttered from his hands high into the air, and Mel Blount intercepted near the goal line.

In the halftime locker room, Bradshaw, upbeat, called for more: "We're whipping their asses off and still ain't got but two points!" Trusting in the defense, Mansfield couldn't resist. "Hey, Brad," he said, "that's good. Maybe that's all we'll need." In an adjacent room, trainer Ralph Berlin cut the tape from Lambert's injured ankle. Through pain and gritted teeth, the rookie loosed some curse words. "Shoot me up!" Lambert insisted. But so painful was his ankle, Lambert couldn't stand and balance himself. The team doctor feared that he'd broken it. (He had.) Ed Bradley would take Lambert's place. Then, in the third quarter, Russell got leg-whipped and tore his hamstring. He limped off, gone for the game, replaced by Loren Toews. That two of three starting linebackers had left the game might have troubled other defenses. But Bradley and Toews played exceptionally and such was the dominance of the Steelers' front four that the absence of Lambert and Russell mattered hardly at all.

Harris began to pile up big yardage. Early in the third quarter, on a Counter-15 Special, he ran nine yards around the left side, where Moon Mullins's lead block leveled linebacker Wally Hilgenberg. Harris's sixth touchdown in three postseason games gave the Steelers a 9–0 lead. Later in the quarter, the Vikings' Matt Blair swept in unblocked from the right side to block Bobby Walden's punt, the loose ball recovered by the Vikings in the end zone for a touchdown. The extra point missed, the Steelers led 9–6 with more than eleven minutes left.

Bradshaw responded. Neither Einstein nor magna cum laude, he showed *good football sense* in directing an expansive eleven-play drive that covered sixty-six yards and swallowed more than seven minutes. He mixed eight running plays between Harris and Bleier, and passed only as needed. On third and goal from the Minnesota four-yard line, executing a play suggested from the sideline by Joe Gilliam, Bradshaw rolled right and threw a dart into the chest of tight end Larry Brown for a touchdown. To Mean Joe Greene the ball struck Brown's chest with the resonance of cannon fire. The scoring drive produced a 16–6 Steeler lead and consumed with it the Vikings' last hopes. With little more than three minutes to play, Tarkenton still running for his life, and Harris rushing past Larry Csonka's Super Bowl record with 158 yards on thirty-four carries, the Vikings were effectively finished, losers of a Super Bowl for the third time in six years. That reduced Page, their star defensive tackle, to tossing his elbow pads in the air, and saying to the Steelers' Jim Clack, "Hell, Clack, I'm all through." On the Steelers' sideline, as the clock wound down, Clack thought of euphoric fans back home in Pittsburgh and said to Mansfield, "I'll bet the 'Burgh looks like Hiroshima." Mansfield found his old friend Russell, the two survivors from the Steelers' shipwrecked days. "We made it," Mansfield said. They were older and more beat up than the others, nearer to the end of football, and closer to their life's work. They became emotional and embraced.

In the press box, all eyes were upon Art Rooney Sr. Sitting beside him, Jim Murray noticed that the Chief had "watched the game with a kind of bemused detachment." The columnist wondered if the Chief had grown so accustomed to defeat through the decades that he identified more with Tarkenton than with his own team's victory.

Attention always made the Chief chafe, and television, that boxy machine, confounded him. The Chief was rooted in an earlier time, as a fight promoter working with his old friend Jake Mintz, posting flyers on barroom walls about an Irishman pitted against a Jew, an Italian against a Pole, or they might introduce a colored boy to give white crowds at Duquesne Gardens someone to boo. But TV connected the entire nation to the Super Bowl. There was no need to post flyers now. Privately, the Chief worried that television made the NFL seem so much more important than it had a right to be. There was so much money in the game now, in network revenues and players' contracts, that it created so many new complications. The Chief liked to ask his players, "What are you going to do when they turn that little red light off—when TV goes on to new sensations? Are you still going to play football for one hundred dollars a game?" They laughed, but he meant it.

The Chief during the years of empire.

Joe Greene, Dwight White, and Ernie Holmes (left to right) at training camp in Latrobe, Pennsylvania.

Terry Bradshaw, Joe Gilliam, and Terry Hanratty at Super Bowl IX.

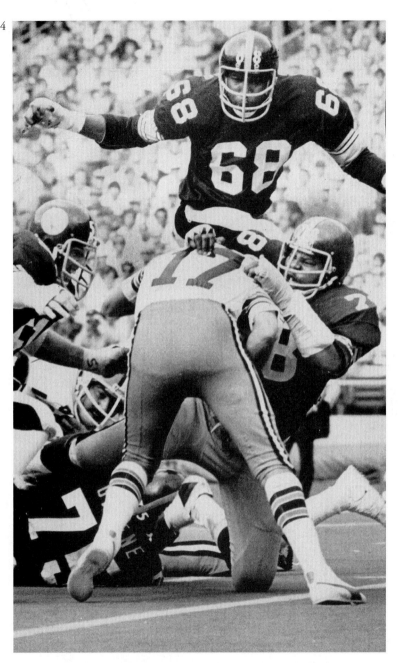

Dwight White sacks Cleveland quarterback Brian Sipe
as L. C. Greenwood (68) swoops in, 1976.

5

Chuck Noll and Terry Bradshaw.

Lynn Swann and John Stallworth, rookies, 1974.

Immaculate Reception 1: The Raiders' Jack Tatum blasts into John "Frenchy" Fuqua near the Raiders' thirty-five-yard line. The X marks the spot where the ricocheted pass came into Franco Harris's hands during the 1972 AFC divisional playoff game.

Immaculate Reception 2: The Raiders' last hope, defensive back Jimmy Warren, fails to bring down Franco Harris.

Franco Harris re-creates his pose and Fuqua laughs in front of the Immaculate Reception monument commemorated on the fortieth anniversary of the famed play, 2012.

The Frenchman, ready for the dress-off.

11

John Stallworth, 1974 AFC title game.

12

Noll gets a victory ride after Super Bowl IX from
Franco Harris and Joe Greene.

The Chief and his five sons.

The Chief and Dan, draft day, 1970.

NFL commissioner Pete Rozelle presents the Lombardi Trophy to the Chief after the Super Bowl IX victory.

LEFT: Bill Nunn, 2006.

BELOW: Bill Nunn, Art
Rooney Jr., and his
cousin Tim Rooney
in the Steelers' draft
room, 1976.

The Chief and Mean Joe, postgame, 1972.

Chuck Noll and Joe Greene, Latrobe.

20

21

ABOVE: Terry Bradshaw and Joe Greene, 1976.

LEFT: Mike Webster (52) and Steve Courson.

22

Jack Lambert.

23

L. C. Greenwood at his final training camp in Latrobe, 1982.

Ernie Holmes greeted by Dan Rooney at the opening of the Western Pennsylvania Sports Museum in Pittsburgh, 2004.

Ernie Holmes, aka Arrowhead.

26

Franco Harris, 2012.

27

At Heinz Field in Pittsburgh for the fortieth anniversary of the Immaculate Reception in 2012, former Steelers teammates line up (from left to right): Franco Harris, Frenchy Fuqua, Mike Wagner, Andy Russell, Gerry "Moon" Mullins, Jon Kolb, L. C. Greenwood (with Santa hat), Joe Greene, Larry Brown, and Rocky Bleier.

28

On Lynn Swann's induction day at Canton, John Stallworth (left) served as his presenter, 2001.

29

Chuck Noll and
Terry Bradshaw at
the annual Dap-
per Dan banquet in
Pittsburgh, 2003.

30

Joe Greene at the
Steelers' seventy-fifth-
anniversary gala, 2007.

31

One more center snap at the Pro Football Hall of Fame for Mike Webster and
Terry Bradshaw, 1997.

32

Terry Bradshaw hugs Pam Webster, as Mel Blount looks on, at Mike Webster's funeral, 2002.

The time for his official coronation had, at long last, arrived. With three minutes to play, the Chief headed down to the Steelers' locker room. He said he needed time to comb his hair.

Hot dog wrappers blew in the wind as Noll was lifted onto the shoulders of Franco Harris, voted the game's most valuable player, and Mean Joe Greene. It made for a fitting image, the coach sitting atop the offensive and defensive pillars on which this Super Bowl IX victory rested. Cameramen encircled them. Flashbulbs exploded. The writer Roy Blount had sneaked onto the Steelers' sideline near game's end, tossed all objectivity aside, and celebrated with Steeler players, hugging them and happily slapping their shoulder pads. Blount noticed Noll's broad smile as he rode off on his players' shoulders. "I had never seen Noll's mouth so wide open," Blount wrote later. "It was as though the Dragon Lady had gone all soft around the eyes and said, 'Oh, baby.' "

Bill Nunn wasn't about to venture down to the field, or into the Steelers' locker room. That wasn't his style, though it was Lloyd Wells's way, and Nunn often kidded the Kansas City Chiefs' black scout, "All you want is for somebody to take your picture." Nunn had just driven in from Mobile, where he had scouted the Senior Bowl. Now he took in the victory scene from the grandstands, where he sat with other Steeler officials. He felt enormous satisfaction. As a *Courier* sportswriter he had been around other champions—Sugar Ray Robinson, Ezzard Charles, Roberto Clemente—and so his reaction was professional, understated, as if he'd seen it all before: "You win, you feel good about it, and you go on." Besides, he believed that moments such as this belonged to the players.

Among the first to reach the locker room, Bleier saw the Chief, his white hair combed neatly now. The darkness of what happened in the Vietnamese rice paddy seemed as distant to Bleier as the Steelers' decades of failure seemed to the old man. They hugged. Mike Webster entered, clapping in celebration, and was followed by Dwight White, who had lived for a week on little more than water and sleep. Carson, the defensive coach, was asked about Joe Greene. He shook his head in amazement and said, "I'll tell you, Joe Greene is . . . the best I ever saw. I just didn't think he could be any better. Only he was."

One statistic shimmered more than all the rest: the Vikings ran for only seventeen yards in twenty-one attempts. As dominant as the Steelers' front four had been in limiting the Raiders to twenty-nine rushing yards in the AFC title game, this performance was even more definitive, the Vikings managing less than a yard per carry, averaging just 2.4 *feet* per carry. Hearing the rushing statistics, Mad Dog White, enervated, chimed, "Wowie!" Greene bemoaned a mixup with Greenwood on one pre-snap stunt, their confusion leaving a wide opening for Foreman to run for twelve yards, the Vikings' longest carry. Subtract that play and the Vikings managed only five yards on their other twenty rushes, a gleaming monument to run defense and a mathematical marvel—an average of nine *inches* per carry.

Nine inches.

From the press box, Murray typed happily of the Steelers' victory, "It was like one of those hokey, old three-handkerchief Warner Bros. movies." Murray cited Bleier and his Purple Heart from Vietnam, "a little guy knocking down people twice his size"; and White for rising from his hospital bed to stop the Vikings cold; and the Chief, the man sitting to his left in the press box, "the kindly old owner with the Coke-bottle glasses . . . who lost and lost and lost for 42 years and hired all his pals and flew in every nun and priest north of Maryland for this game at his expense." The game had nearly everything, Murray added, "Everything but Lassie, right?"

The Old Ranger saw the game ball on the field at game's end as players and fans rushed past it. "It looked kind of sad," Mansfield said. He picked it up and gave it to Russell. The postgame role for the Steelers' captains was to award symbolic game balls to offensive and defensive players. Russell intended to honor Mean Joe, but as he walked to the center of the cramped locker room, teammates surrounding him, he noticed the Chief standing quietly in back, behind a few sportswriters. *That's the guy who created all of this*, Russell thought. He changed his mind. He would apologize to Greene later. He called to Art Rooney Sr., "Chief, c'mon up here!" The Chief stepped forward. He wore a yellow sports shirt, his tie loosened at the collar, an overcoat, and one of the fifteen woolen caps his son Tim had brought him from Ireland (he gave away all the ones with tassels, leaving two or three for himself). The Chief also had a cigar in his mouth, naturally. Russell held aloft the game ball. "This one's for the Chief," he said. "It's a long time coming." The Chief came to the locker room hoping not to weep, but as his players roared their approval, his glasses misted over.

A few moments later, in an adjacent room, Bradshaw sat on a stool beside sportscaster Charlie Jones. Bradshaw stroked his beard as he considered Jones's question about whether his performance would forever squelch the mocking of his intelligence. Bradshaw played a mistake-free Super Bowl. He completed nine of fourteen throws for ninety-six yards and a touchdown and ran for thirty-three yards more. "I'd like to say that it's all said and done and in the past," Bradshaw said. "But Super Bowl or not, it's just something that I'm going to have to live with." Harris took Bradshaw's place on the stool. He held a cigar, symbolic of victory. Handsome, bushy-haired, and speaking softly, Harris praised Bleier's blocking. "Rocky was just hurtin' guys, punishing them," he said. Mean Joe replaced Harris on the stool beside Jones. He wore a black-and-gold ski cap. He beamed. "This is beyond my wildest dreams," Greene said. "I didn't think I could get this big a charge out of it." Later, off camera, Greene told sportswriters, "A great part of me would've died if we had lost."

Rozelle stood beside the Chief in the Steelers' locker room, holding the Super Bowl trophy named for Vince Lombardi, a friend the Chief had greatly admired. On camera, speaking to seventy-one million viewers, Rozelle praised the Steelers' performance and gently placed his left hand on the Chief's shoulder. He handed him the gleaming trophy. (Joey Diven loomed inches behind them, peeking over the commissioner's shoulder.) Dan, the managerial architect of this team, remained far from the camera, believing his father deserved all attention and credit. Even farther from the spotlight, Art Jr. shared the postgame celebration in the grandstands with his wife and mother. Years later Rozelle would call this trophy presentation his fondest memory from nearly thirty years as NFL commissioner, so deep was his respect for Art Rooney Sr. The Chief's players shouted, "Speech! Speeeeeeeeccccchhhh!" The Chief wouldn't look directly into the camera, his eyes red-rimmed from emotion, his glasses fogging over again. "Thanks, Pete," he said. He looked toward his ballplayers. "They are a great bunch of fellas," he said. "I'm not a bit surprised."

✦ ✦ ✦

From Shreveport came the Bradshaw family and friends, about thirty in all, and that night in a hotel suite they celebrated the Super Bowl with champagne. This might have been the greatest night of Terry Bradshaw's life, but for migraine headaches. He sat up in bed, his head throbbing, as his family sang and cheered all around him, his mother happiest of all, because of the triumphant way her boy had responded to the meanness of a badgering press.

On the plane flight home the next day, Harris, Swann, and Greene played with, and wore, plastic Viking helmets with silly horns. These were more than souvenirs. The spoils of war, they called them. Just as he had in the postgame locker room, Greene pulled out his Nikomat camera on the plane and happily snapped photos of teammates in high spirits.

One hundred twenty thousand fans in Pittsburgh braved the twenty-five-degree chill, lining the expressways and downtown streets as the Steelers' motorcade passed. One new fan club announced itself with a placard as "Bradshaw's Brains." Dwight White headed directly to a local hospital, where he spent the next two and a half weeks recuperating, visited each day by the Chief and Kass.

The Chief had left Tulane Stadium in the darkness, the streets empty. He couldn't find the chauffeured limousine he had rented, so a New Orleans policeman hailed a taxi. He climbed inside the taxi with the Pittsburgh columnist Roy McHugh. "This is better anyway," the Chief said. "I never feel comfortable in those limousines." The Chief's sons gathered with him in his suite that night at the Fontainebleau. The Chief had removed his press pass and tossed it on the ground, and Art Jr., with his devotion to history, picked it up. "Hey, Dad, this is a collector's piece. Sign it," he said, and his father did. Forever a creature of habit, the Chief sat at a desk in his hotel suite and dashed off a large batch of postcards, mostly to his horse-track friends. They knew his understated nature and must have laughed when they read in his cursive scrawl, the old man at the football mountaintop, announcing, "We're in the big time!"

V

STEEL EMPIRE

CHAPTER 14

DAYS OF EMPIRE: 1975–1981

NOW THE CHIEF AND HIS Steelers were writ large across America's sports pages. At the White House in May 1975 to watch the long-ago Steeler receiver Lowell Perry sworn in as chairman of the Equal Opportunity Commission, the Chief stood behind the ropes in the Rose Garden. Perry walked directly to him after the ceremony to shake his hand and to once more thank the man who helped pay for his law school education nearly twenty years earlier. President Gerald Ford came by, an aide whispering in his ear, "There's Rooney," and Ford, once a University of Michigan football player, stopped to shake the Chief's hand. They got along famously. Ford told Rooney that he'd always wanted to meet him, and had watched the Steelers' Super Bowl victory. The president talked on and on, the Chief mostly listening, until finally the Chief said, "Look, Mr. President, there are a lot of your friends waiting here. You better go back to work."

It was all so unexpected. The Steelers won back-to-back Super Bowls after the 1974 and 1975 seasons, then missed for two years, and then won back-to-back Super Bowls again after the 1978 and 1979 seasons, four in six years, and it was said that the road to the Super Bowl ran through Pittsburgh. The 35–31 victory over Dallas in Super Bowl XIII after the 1978 season carried symbolic import. Both teams had won two Super Bowls and vied to become team of the decade. After this third Super Bowl victory Noll told reporters, "We haven't peaked yet," and he was right. Dwight White cherished such wins over America's Team in his own inimitable way: "We'd say, 'After we beat the Cowboys, *what we really want are those cheerleaders.*'" Fifteen different Steelers were selected to the Pro Bowl during these days of empire, Bradshaw for first time in 1976, his seventh NFL season. When the league tightened rules on pass coverage in 1978, outlawing the bump-and-run (aka the Mel Blount Rule), the Steelers' passing game opened up during the next two seasons. Stallworth and Swann electrified by catching a combined 213 passes for thirty-three touchdowns, and Bradshaw flourished as never before, becoming at long last the quarterback the Chief always imagined. Every Steeler home game sold out, a streak that continues to this day. The Steelers won thirteen of fifteen playoff games from the 1974 through the 1979 seasons. They lost once to Oakland in 1976 due to injury, when neither Harris nor Bleier could play, and once to Denver in 1977 due to three Bradshaw interceptions and a case of misguided vigilante justice, when Greene complained to referees about being held by Denver's offensive linemen, to no avail, and then threw one punch at Bronco guard Paul Howard, and another at center Mike Montler. That ignited the Broncos and the Mile High Stadium crowd and nearly led to a fistfight between Perles and Denver coach Red Miller as the teams shoved their way to the locker rooms at halftime.

More than 330 million viewers watched on television as the Steelers won Super Bowls IX, X, XIII, and XIV, including more than 97 million against the Rams in January 1980. How grand it was to be a sports fan in Pittsburgh in 1979. The Pirates won the World Series that year, their wives dancing atop the dugout to Sister Sledge's "We Are Family!" Fewer than a hundred days later the Steelers won their fourth Lombardi trophy. As Green Bay claimed the moniker of Titletown USA, now Pittsburgh became the "City of Champions." The two teams, whose locker rooms were separated by less than a hundred feet, became a mutual admiration society, feted together at the Jimmy Carter White House in March 1980. Kicker Matt Bahr sometimes put on a glove and shagged flies during Pirates batting practice at Three Rivers. In L. C. Greenwood's kitchen in Squirrel Hill, neighbor Willie Stargell spent hours, and a deep friendship developed. As the steel industry withered, these two teams became emotional life rafts to a region.

To the Steelers came the spoils of celebrity. Twenty-one of them made national commercials: Samsonite luggage, Ford's Fairlane, Uniroyal's new

Steeler tire, 'Lectric Shave, Red Man chewing tobacco. *Advertising Age* marveled that athletes no longer needed to play in New York to catch the eye of Madison Avenue: "The Steelers have, in fact, become football's version of the pin-striped New York Yankees of old." Bleier wrote his life story, and it became a TV movie with Art Carney as the Chief, Robert Urich as the Rock. Bradshaw sang country songs, went on a national tour for Terry Bradshaw Peanut Butter, and got himself in movies. Joe Greene won advertising's Clio award for his Coke commercial.

Virtually half the team, twenty-two men, would win four Super Bowl rings with the Steelers. A brotherhood developed among them, its depth unattainable in most walks of American life, and perhaps akin to author Sebastian Junger's definition of the camaraderie shared by a military pla-toon in battle: "As a soldier, the thing you were most scared of was failing your brothers when they needed you, and compared to that, dying was easy."

The celebrated brotherhood of the '70s Steelers was evident at all those Super Bowls. But the brotherhood that mattered most to them was not shared with millions of Americans watching on television at home. Their brotherhood lived in smaller moments, shared only by them. They saw Webster leave a hospital shortly after knee surgery following Super Bowl IX and go directly to Three Rivers Stadium. There Radakovich heard someone yell, "Webster's already in the fuckin' weight room!" Downstairs, in the stadium's boiler room, Webster, a weight-room fanatic, was work-ing up a sweat, the stitches in his knee still fresh. Bad Rad shouted, "Well, get him the fuck out of the fuckin' weight room!" Donnie Shell, trying to get some shuteye before an afternoon practice at Latrobe in 1977, saw his roommate, rookie defensive back Tony Dungy, rewinding the game-film projector one more time in their dorm room. "If you don't put that projector away . . . ," Shell threatened. To which Dungy replied, "Just one more look, Donnie!"

Whatever teammates were—brothers, soldiers under the same flag, bloodied men sharing a common goal—the defining bonds were made as much off the field as on. The Chief had players for dinner at 940 North Lincoln. Boys being boys, players threw a bachelor party for Ernie Holmes that none ever forgot. They did all this out of sight, did it only for themselves and not the fans, and they did it in ways that brought together white and black, old and young, men and women, with wives, siblings, and parents sometimes carried along on the ride.

The Sauna

It was their most cherished space, no matter how spare or small, no matter if the coals were hot and steam poured forth, no matter that only a pale ambient light filtered through the small window in the door. The sauna in the back of the Steelers' locker room at Three Rivers Stadium, near the showers, was the players' postgame sanctuary and decompression chamber. It contained plain wooden benches, enough to seat seven or eight big men, plus the real drawing card, an oversized plastic trash can that Parisi filled with ice and beer. In the locker room three and a half hours earlier, before kickoff on an NFL Sunday, their nerves and adrenaline kicked in and players dealt with anticipation in their own ways, their stomachs churning. A few bent over toilets and vomited. After they waged battle against the Chiefs or Oilers or Browns or Raiders, they returned to the locker room, bruised and lacerated, heard Noll say, "Job well done," or the opposite of that, and then together on bended knee recited the Lord's Prayer, the Chief usually at their side. Then the locker room door swung open, the sportswriters poured in, and with their questions nibbled at the players' insecurities the way mice nibbled at cheese.

Then came that special time: the players' thirty-six-hour grace period. Monday was an off-day before Tuesday morning's review of game films, when Steeler coaches nitpicked and pointed out every little thing players had done wrong. After that film review and a light workout, a group of Steelers usually met at Franco Harris's place for the Tuesday-afternoon game of poker: Mean Joe, Moon Mullins, the Frenchman, Sam Davis, the Plumber, and, on occasion, Swann, Stallworth, or Bradshaw.

If the three hours on the field each Sunday represented the most important and hyperfocused three hours of their lives, then the postgame sauna was how a rational man sought a return to normalcy. It was like the start of shore leave.

For Steeler players, the postgame sauna was a hideaway, a refuge from the press and coaches, off-limits to the rest of the world, except on those rare occasions when an invitation was extended to an opposing player they admired and respected. Noll never went near the sauna. He understood what that postgame gathering was really about—player unity, camaraderie, building an esprit de corps. It had happened when he was with the Browns in a similar way, in the locker room, with Groza, Gatski, and Lavelli telling their war stories about Okinawa, the infantry, and the Battle of the Bulge. What forms at such times, Noll understood, was a common purpose and a deeper bond among men. Besides, what Noll didn't know, or hear, wouldn't hurt him. His players gathered in the sauna while their wives or girlfriends waited for them in the stadium lobby.

The sauna was the place where Steeler players could be together, and be themselves, and say what needed to be said. The pressure was off, the next game a full week away. They crammed into the sauna together for their postgame beer and stood side by side, or squeezed onto the wooden benches, ten or twelve players in all, like a crowded subway at rush hour. Some wore towels around their waists, some T-shirts and uniform pants, others a jockstrap and nothing more. They opened their beers, sat down, and removed tape from their ankles, the smell of sweat oppressive. A few moved in and out quickly, such as Harris and Swann, en route to the nearby shower. (The sauna wasn't for everyone. The old veterans Russell and Mansfield, preferring vodka to beer, showered and headed upstairs to the stadium's Allegheny Club.) Occasionally a Steeler might hide from the press in the sauna, but only until publicist Joe Gordon rapped on the door and pleaded, "Come on out for interviews! They're waiting!" In the days of empire, winning bred a generosity of spirit—they were, after all, on top of their game, their league, and the world—and in the sauna players' petty differences and frictions disappeared or at least were forgotten for the moment. They had been sculpted into a great team, and they knew that and proved it on Sundays, and when the game and the day were won, they reveled in their great fortune to be together.

In the sauna, their comments crackled:

"Oh, man, I fanned on that blitz. And I knew it was comin'!"

"You see me tag whatshisname? He was up in the air!"

Hollywood Bags stepped inside the sauna, shirtless, lean, wiry-strong, the muscles of his upper torso taut. L. C. Greenwood liked hearing teammates talk about what had or had not happened in that day's game, and engage in an honest discussion about what should have happened.

In the sauna Bleier sensed a pure moment: "It wasn't fabricated. It was honest, unvarnished. It just *was*."

The regulars in the sauna? "Whoever drank," Parisi said with a laugh. Lambert, Webster, and defensive tackle Gary Dunn were the mainstays. They'd spend an hour in there, sometimes two hours, more. Usually the steam was turned off, but once or twice Parisi warmed the sauna to more than one hundred degrees and players poured their beers over the hot coals. Together they stood, they sat. They needled, they laughed. They elevated bullshit to high art. They talked of blocks and tackles made, and blocks and tackles missed. Stripped of bravado, stripped bare, they achieved a level of honesty with each other that wouldn't be equaled at any other time or place.

Look at Webster reclining on the sauna's wooden bench, his back against the wall, five or six Iron City beers deep into the conversation. Bare-chested, he wore only his black-and-gold uniform pants, and sweaty tape on his wrists and mangled fingers. "Webby, how in the world did they get all that pressure on Brad?" Dunn asked. Webster became like a gridiron professor as he explained the stunts, blitzes, and zone coverages used by the opposing defense, and the Steelers' failure to handle them. Webster loved these conversations, lived for them.

Decades later, as the Steelers remembered their times together in the postgame sauna, they smiled and laughed, and in their recollections Lambert, always Lambert, loomed largest and loudest. If the sauna represented the 1970s Steelers' version of King Arthur's court, then Lambert was Arthur. "It was Jack Lambert's haven," Mullins said. "He'd be the first one in and the last one to leave." Dunn remembered that after one loss, pin-drop quiet in the sauna, Lambert stared at the floor, and no Steeler said a word. And then, after their second and third beers, their tongues loosened, and Lambert turned to Bradshaw and asked why he threw into double coverage on third and twelve, and then Bradshaw turned to Lambert and asked how he missed that tackle on Earl Campbell. "And then," Dunn said, "it would be *on*"—a candid free-for-all, everyone venting. Deeper truths emerged. Once, in the sauna after a poor performance, Bradshaw said to J. T. Thomas, "T, you guys can lose with me, but you can't win without me." Thomas thought about it, laughed, and said, "Brad, you're probably right." In the sauna following a 1979 game, Donnie Shell asked Thomas, who had missed the entire 1978 season due to an inflammatory disease, "You were on the outside looking in last year. What did that look like?" And Bradshaw chimed in, "Yeah, how was that?" Thomas knew they all dreaded retiring from the game, and their question, to him, "was like the anticipation of a death." He told them he saw the game—and himself—differently, and that he returned knowing the game was terminal, that all football careers die. "I returned," Thomas told them, "so I could exit properly."

Lambert was like the Steelers' version of Ernest Hemingway, a genius at his craft and an unforgettable character, but in personality so prickly and boorish that some teammates swore it had to be an act. No one could be *that* obstreperous. Lambert's closest friends in the organization were the guys in the equipment room, Parisi, Jack Hart, and Rodgers Freyvogel. His teammates didn't understand him, or at times even like him. For the most part, they kept their distance. Lambert hosted a party at his Fox Chapel home each year for the linebackers and defensive backs known as the Chobees, named in jest for Edwards and Lake Okeechobee in Edwards's native Florida. Since most of the Chobees were black, there was a playful undercurrent of racial humor. As Thomas, Blount, Edwards, and Shell arrived at Lambert's house one year, Lambert was heard to say, "Oh, shit, here come the Chobees and I haven't nailed down all my stuff!" Once, the Chobees parked their cars on Lambert's lawn, their headlights illuminating the house, and Lambert showed up on the porch, shotgun in hand, calling out that they had ten seconds to get off his lawn, and they did. The Chobees brought a boom box to one of Lambert's parties, and as their music played loudly, Thomas couldn't believe what he saw: "Jack didn't like the music, so he pulled out a pistol and shot the boom box. It was loud in there anyway, and then '*Pop! Pop!*' What the hell, that's Lambert." Or, as linebacker Dennis Winston, a regular at Lambert's party for the Chobees, would say, "When he got to playing with those guns, it was time to go. He had a house full of 'em."

His teammates respected Lambert for the way he played and for how much winning meant to him, and come Sunday they were thankful he was a Steeler. He played the game exquisitely. In the sauna, "Jack would hold court," Bleier said, adding, "and Jack held people accountable." Lambert could be especially critical of fellow defenders. In the sauna he'd poke fun at Ham or Wagner, and he would point fingers of blame sometimes, too. Bleier heard Lambert tell a teammate, "I don't even know why you showed up today. You didn't have any impact on this game at all," and he meant it. That was Jack Lambert, curmudgeon. But Bleier also heard Lambert tell a teammate, "We couldn't have won this game without you," and he meant that, too. "That was a big part of Jack's life—those locker room moments after a game," Bleier said. "He would just bust your balls about the way you played. . . . He *loooved* that! And I think we loved it, too. Everybody wanted to be recognized, or picked on. Jack was willing to do that, and more times than not, Jack was right in his analysis."

On occasion Lambert or Webster invited an opponent to join them in the sauna before the team bus left for the airport. Once it was Cincinnati quarterback Ken Anderson, who stepped inside the sauna, sat down, and said words Lambert would remember, "God, you guys are awesome." To get such an invitation, a high honor, an opposing player had to be respected, and tough, and, in the best case, a roguish character. Jack Rudnay of Kansas City, an all-pro center and noted clubhouse prankster, fit that bill. Once, at midfield after the pregame coin toss, instead of shaking hands as opposing team captains, Lambert and Rudnay exchanged several violent smacks on their helmets as officials rushed in to separate them. Their exchange was done in fun, but only partly. They were warriors sending signals they were ready for battle. Rudnay laughed as he jogged back to the Kansas City sideline, and a rookie teammate, wide-eyed over what he'd just seen, asked, "Holy shit! Is that the way it's going to be today?" Rudnay smiled and said, "Strap up, young man!" Now, at Three Rivers, an equipment room worker escorted Rudnay through the Steelers' locker room to the sauna. Fully dressed, his Chiefs bag in hand, Rudnay stepped inside and sat with Webster, Lambert, Ham, and a few others; they handed him a beer. They exchanged pleasantries, asked about each other's families, Rudnay saying to Ham, whose wife he had watched dance up a storm at a Pro Bowl, "How's Disco Lady?" Webster told Rudnay he was impressed with some of the Chiefs' young players, Lambert threw a few verbal jabs, and they all laughed. "It's counterintuitive that you can try to kill each other on the field and be best friends after it," Rudnay said. "I really was honored to share that time with them." One beer led to an-

other and another, and Rudnay discovered that the Chiefs' team bus had left for the airport without him, Coach Marv Levy apparently in a dither about his absence. Sweeping into action, Parisi threw car keys to another clubhouse man and instructed him to drive Rudnay to the airport post-haste. The driver did great work because Rudnay was sitting in his seat on the airplane before his Kansas City teammates arrived, and in his bag he discovered several gifts, including Steeler T-shirts for his daughters and several beers for himself.

After another game, long after most Steelers had left the stadium, Dunn stepped from the sauna, put on a shirt, and walked outside the locker room to find his mother. She'd had a long wait, and Dunn told her that he planned to sit with his teammates in the sauna a while longer. "Well, then can I come in there and have a beer with you?" his mother asked. Dunn thought it a bad idea ("The sauna is not a place for *your mother*," he would say) but he reconsidered, and told her that he would find out. "Jack, Brad, do you guys care if my mom comes in and has a beer with us?" he asked. Lambert and Bradshaw thought the idea of Gary Dunn's mother joining them in the sauna hysterical and preposterous, and so naturally they consented, saying, "Bring her in, buddy!" In she came. The topic of conversation in the sauna shifted, naturally, Lambert and Bradshaw needling Dunn without mercy, asking his mother, "How in the world did you give birth to *that*?" And: "He must've had some real problems in his childhood, didn't he?" Lambert and Bradshaw treated Dunn's mother with kindness. She never forgot the experience, and celebrated afterward with a tour of the field given by her son. As the beers took effect, she pretended in the darkness to be a drum majorette marching alone down the field at Three Rivers Stadium and tossing an imaginary baton high in the air. Grounds crew members turned from their work to watch. Dunn asked grounds crew chief Dirt DiNardo, "Can you turn on some lights? Mom can't see her baton," and so DiNardo flipped on the field lights. As his mother marched from the forty-yard line to midfield, her legs kicking high, Gary Dunn decided, *This is awesome!*

"It was our escape, and nobody could get to us," Bradshaw said. He loved those days and nights in that sauna. "That was the most fun we ever had."

Being Bradshaw

Surely the great Terry Bradshaw didn't want to socialize with a mere rookie defensive tackle, or so John Banaszak assumed. But then Bradshaw asked him in the locker room one day in 1975 if he wanted to play golf. Banaszak thought, *Me play golf with Terry Bradshaw?* Humble and hardworking, Banaszak was a former US marine teased by Rocky Bleier for never having made it to Vietnam. (Banaszak teased back: "Yeah, Rock, well, if you were a marine, you never would have been wounded!") Signed out of Eastern Michigan as a free agent by the Steelers, Banaszak phoned home to Cleveland to share the good news with his father, a factory worker and devoted Browns fan who hated the Steelers. "Dad, I just signed with the Pittsburgh Steelers," he began. His father said nothing and hung up. Banaszak phoned back and his father spoke finally, saying, "How am I going to tell your mother? How am I going to tell my friends? And how am I going to go to work tomorrow?" (In time his father got over it.) Banaszak spent the afternoon golfing with Bradshaw and punter Bobby Walden. Afterward, Walden left and Bradshaw asked the rookie, "You want to go to dinner?" Giddy, Banaszak said he'd love to go to dinner. From the restaurant he phoned his wife to say, *"I'm having dinner with Terry Bradshaw!"* After dinner, Bradshaw asked, "You want to go to the mall with me?" Banaszak replied, "Sure, I'll go to the mall with you, Terry." In a pet shop there, Bradshaw eyed the puppies, the shop's workers amazed to see the Steelers' Super Bowl–winning quarterback in their midst. It struck Banaszak that for all his celebrity Bradshaw, between marriages, was lonely and alone. Bradshaw bought a puppy, and when Banaszak got home late that night, his wife was not happy with him even as he defended himself by explaining the magnitude of what he, a mere rookie defensive tackle, had just accomplished: *"I was with Terry Bradshaw!"*

At times in Pittsburgh, Bradshaw felt like an animal in a zoo, caged and observed, people talking about him, and at him, as if he couldn't hear or understand them. When he looked in the mirror, he saw a different Terry Bradshaw than fans saw. They saw a Super Bowl champion. He saw scars from the lashes of earlier seasons, from fifty thousand hometown fans cheering his shoulder injury, from his lost battles with Noll, and from the way the nation's sportswriters ridiculed his southern accent and his intelligence. Two headlines spoke volumes: "Is Bradshaw 'Too Dumb' to Be Super?" and "Li'l Abner Finally Makes It Big," and these weren't from tabloids trying to stir the pot, they were from bedrocks of the sports press, the *New York Times* and *Sports Illustrated.* Bradshaw's insecurities eclipsed his victories. "When he did win them over," Greene said of Steeler fans, "it went right over his head. He wasn't aware of it." Bradshaw retreated inward, and to avoid crowds, became like a hermit. He didn't have a wife, or head coach, to lean on, intimates who might have served as sounding boards for his troubles. He might have found safety and strength in his Steeler teammates—he held his own in the locker room, and they liked his sense of humor—but Bradshaw wasn't one for developing deep personal connections and keeping them.

On television before Super Bowl X, even actor Burt Reynolds poked fun at Bradshaw's intellect. Then Bradshaw threw *that pass* to Lynn Swann. With the Steelers leading Dallas 15–10 with three minutes to play and facing third and four from the Pittsburgh thirty-six and trying to keep the ball from Dallas quarterback Roger Staubach, a Franco Harris run seemed a logical and likely play. But Bradshaw called an audible at the line of scrimmage, 69 Maximum Flanker Post. With Dallas blitzers bearing in on him, he cut loose with a downfield pass just as defensive tackle Larry Cole slammed his helmet into Bradshaw's. Bradshaw's pass rose on an arc and then it was as if rocket boosters kicked in, propelling it higher and deeper, across the galaxy like a shooting star, more than seventy yards in the air, all those long-ago college scouting reports ("This guy's like buying Xerox. There might not be another one like him for twenty years") and the Chief's unwavering support ("You're the best!") becoming prophecy. At the far end, there was Swann, racing on a post pattern, a step ahead of cornerback Mark Washington, no need to break stride as the ball arrived over his left shoulder. Washington swiped at it in vain and then crashed to the ground, Swann catching it (or did *it* catch Swann?) at the Dallas five-yard line, and taking it in for the game-breaking touchdown. "I've always seen myself as put to music," Swann once said, and here was his sweet song. Swann raised both arms like the game's MVP he was. Lambert got to him first in the end zone celebration, and grabbed him at the waist and lifted him as guard Gerry "Moon" Mullins pumped a fist nearby. The Steelers led 21–10, a second Super Bowl about to be theirs.

Seventy-three million people watching on TV saw Swann's catch but Bradshaw did not. He was on the ground, concussed, knocked woozy by Larry Cole, helped off the field by Wagner and Bleier, and then into the locker room before game's end, his thoughts popping like champagne bubbles. Up in the press box, Dan Jenkins of *Sports Illustrated* wrote that Bradshaw "seems to collect concussions and championship rings with equal facility." Everyone kept telling him what a godly pass he had thrown, but Bradshaw couldn't quite see it or remember it.

Cashing in on his celebrity after that game, Bradshaw stepped from a small private jet, Moon Mullins by his side. They were escorted into a red 1973 Cadillac El Dorado, a longhorn on the front grille, the car's horn the sound of a cow mooing—definitely Nashville. Mullins was by his quarterback's side, same as Banaszak and the puppy at other moments, for a good reason—Bradshaw didn't want to be alone. He told Mullins that he was about to cut a country record, said a promotional tour was being arranged, and asked him to serve as his road manager. Mullins said he didn't know the quarterback could sing ("Oh, yeah, I used to always sing in the shower," Bradshaw said), and he didn't know what a road manager was supposed to do. But Mullins decided that since he was young and single, he'd have an adventure with Bradshaw for a few weeks. At a Nashville recording studio, a backup group waiting, an engineer asked, "What songs are you going to sing, Terry?" He had no idea so he thumbed through a songbook and picked the Hank Williams hit "I'm So Lonesome I Could Cry" and another song. After Bradshaw's studio performance was done, Mullins thought, *Pretty good*, though privately he was grateful sound mixers made Bradshaw seem even better. Together they flew back to Pittsburgh and watched Bradshaw's single improbably rise up the country charts.

With Mullins along for company, Bradshaw made a handful of promotional appearances, *The Mike Douglas Show* in Philadelphia, *The Dinah Shore Show* in Los Angeles, and a few live performances in country bars. As Bradshaw performed onstage, Mullins sold records at the bar, or at least he made his best attempts. After a live debut at the Palomino Club in North Hollywood, where the likes of Johnny Cash, Merle Haggard, and Patsy Cline had headlined, one reviewer wrote, "Bradshaw stood alone on stage for 40 minutes shaking in his cowboy boots, hopelessly trying to pass himself off as a country and western singer. . . . By the time he had butchered the final note, the only thing Bradshaw was to be admired for was his courage."

That night at the Palomino Club a gift arrived: a lovely set of carnations arranged in the shape of a horseshoe, with ribbons and a note asking for forgiveness and signed "Burt Reynolds." Off camera a few days before, Dinah Shore had told Bradshaw that Reynolds, her beau, wanted to apologize to him in person, insisting his joke about Bradshaw's intelligence had been the work of some gag writer. Shore invited Bradshaw to meet Reynolds at her home. With Mullins, Bradshaw drove to Beverly Hills and stopped at Shore's electronic front gate. A butler stood at the front door and led them into the front foyer where a maid—"Dressed like a real maid. It was amazing!" Mullins said—asked Mullins if he would like a drink. To Mullins, a middle-class kid from Anaheim, this was the big time. Bradshaw thought Shore remarkable. "So classy, a southern gal," he said. "She had a mom's attitude toward me." They connected in friendship as southerners. ("You don't think Elizabeth Taylor would invite me over, do you?" Bradshaw said years later.) Then Reynolds appeared, walking down the staircase, wearing a sports shirt and ascot, rendering Mullins speechless. Reynolds and Bradshaw had much in common. Both southerners, they were involved with horses and registered cattle, and Reynolds had played college football.

Later that night, Bradshaw's girlfriend, JoJo Starbuck, skated in the Ice Capades show in Los Angeles, and Bradshaw and Mullins attended a late-night party hosted by Starbuck's mother. At about 3:00 a.m., Mullins whispered in his ear, "Terry, we've got to get up in a few hours." Bradshaw had a gig scheduled at a country bar in Albuquerque that night. "We'll just catch a later flight," Bradshaw replied. They would arrive in New Mexico only a few hours before his evening performance, only to discover that a crowd, including the mayor and a band, had been awaiting his arrival at the airport for several hours. The country bar owner who had arranged this reception was furious. Bradshaw, apologetic, said to the gathering, "I love New Mexico!" and he performed onstage that night as Mullins stood by the bar and did his best to sell a record or two. By night's end the country bar owner was deliriously happy, his arm draped around Bradshaw's neck.

After a few weeks with Bradshaw, a sleep-deprived Mullins had lost more than fifteen pounds. "Terry, we've got to part ways," Mullins said. Bradshaw pleaded, "Aw, c'mon!" Mullins said he needed some rest. First, though, they went to the Florida Keys, where Bradshaw appeared on television's *The American Sportsman* on a fishing expedition with sportscaster Curt Gowdy. When a fish pulled the rod from his hands, Bradshaw dove into the water to retrieve it. "He blew up about five thousand dollars' worth of sound equipment," Mullins said. "They were all laughing their asses off."

Bradshaw married Starbuck at a Bel Air hotel that June, and *People* magazine would liken their marriage to a "DiMaggio-Monroe union," though, to hear all the dumb-blonde jokes, Bradshaw might have been Monroe. Together the couple read from the Bible, Bradshaw called her an angel, Starbuck bought him his jeans, they lived in a penthouse apartment near Three Rivers Stadium, and then their careers began to pull them apart. Mel Blount visited Bradshaw at his 440-acre ranch in Grand Cane, Louisiana. There, they rode horses, worked out together, jogged across the property, and Blount couldn't help but notice Starbuck's cultural isolation. "JoJo was a city girl just sitting out there on the farm and figuring it all out," Blount said. "Kind of like the *Green Acres* type, asking, 'What am I doing here?' "

One night in Pittsburgh, Dwight White invited Bradshaw to his house for a barbecued ribs dinner. White had been talking about these ribs for months and had them flown in from Texas. Joe Greene showed up, too, because White surely couldn't have ribs flown in from Texas without having Greene there to help eat them. The three teammates had a few drinks, and Bradshaw teased Karen White about pursuing her master's degree in public administration and international affairs. "Why would a woman want to go to graduate school?" Bradshaw asked. He insisted that the best education for a woman was to go out in a field and birth a cow. They ate their ribs and laughed. Before the night ended, though, Bradshaw turned somber, and apologized that Starbuck had been unable to join them. He said she was on the road again. "I don't have anybody to hug," Bradshaw said, "but the dog."

A moment of terror: Cleveland, October 1976. Browns pass rusher Joe "Turkey" Jones wrapped his arms around Bradshaw's waist, the quarterback fighting, as he always did, to keep his feet. Against the full-throated roar of the crowd at Cleveland Stadium beside Lake Erie, unable to hear the official's whistle that signaled the end of the play, Jones spun Bradshaw, and in one motion lifted and flipped him, spiking the top of his helmet, like a pile driver, into the earth. Bradshaw's body flopped over, onto his back, his hands falling to his sides, palms up, his body inert, the appearance that the Plumber, rushing onto the field, most feared. Doctors strapped Bradshaw to a spine board, immobilizing him, and rushed him to a local hospital. Later that night they brought him to the airport tarmac, and several men carried him up to the back door of the team plane bound for Pittsburgh. The Steelers' medical staff wondered how to ease Bradshaw into the rear of the plane, where they would lay his spine board across the middle aisle. Fats Holmes rose from his seat. He stepped forward, and without a word, took hold of Bradshaw's spine board from the men. He lifted it with both arms, his massive biceps straining, and alone carried the 215-pound quarterback onto the plane, delicately, as if he were carrying a royal feast on an expensive platter. Holmes spoke not a word as he looked down at the quarterback. Bradshaw had suffered another concussion, and he would return to the field in three weeks, but none of that was evident at this moment. Teammates and coaches watched from their seats in silence, marveling at Holmes's strength and fearing for Bradshaw for the head and neck injury he had suffered. A shiver passed down the plane's main aisle.

Burt Reynolds still was making amends. His manager took Bradshaw to the set where the movie *Hooper* was being filmed. Seeing his new friend, Reynolds pointed to the script and told director Hal Needham, "I don't know who we've got for this role here, but get rid of him." Reynolds looked at Bradshaw. "Terry, read this line." Bradshaw read it, unsure how or if to perform. "That's as good acting," Reynolds said, "as I've ever seen." Bradshaw got the part, his first small step toward his life's work. Playing the role on camera, Bradshaw wore a blond hairpiece with bangs and ambled into a country bar. "Hey, Granddad," he said as he approached a table where Reynolds, playing an aging stuntman, sat with friends. "I've got fifty cents in that jukebox and all I can hear is your mouth flappin'." An old-style barroom fight broke out among twenty people and more, fists striking jaws, table turning over, Reynolds punching Bradshaw in the mouth, Bradshaw spitting out one of his front teeth, smiling like a jack-o'-lantern. When Bradshaw lifted Reynolds over his head during the fight and said, "You ain't ever gonna learn, are ya, dummy?" few viewers recognized it for the payback that it was.

Dinner at 940

Kass worried about him. She knew the Chief's vision and hearing were beginning to fail him, and that, at seventy-six, he was depressed about it and had grown more withdrawn. He'd recently stopped going to Steelers home games, instead choosing to watch on television in his den at 940. She encouraged him to attend NFL owners' meetings because there he would be among friends and in his element, but he had stopped going to those, too. At NFL meetings typically each franchise got one chair at the table, and the Steelers' chair was for Dan. Of course, if the Chief showed up, beloved as he was by the younger generation of NFL leaders, they would pull another chair to the table for him, or someone would give up theirs. But at a time when many old men gave in to the frailties of age, the Chief proved resilient. He rallied. He began joining Dan at NFL meetings once again, and returning to his old seat at Steeler games, beside a priest.

He drew strength from being around his players, and not only the more celebrated ones. Sometimes he played gin rummy with obscure special teamers amid the smell of sweat and balm in the Steelers' trainer's room at Three Rivers Stadium.

And he still invited his favorites to occasional dinners at 940: Bradshaw, Greene, Harris, Dwight White, and their wives. It was hardly common practice in the steel mills or the coal mines or in any other American industry for an owner to invite employees to dinner in his own home. In the NFL it happened only in Pittsburgh. In a booming multimillion-dollar sports entertainment industry, the Steelers remained a mom-and-pop franchise, and Kass and the Chief were mom and pop.

Before dinner, the men gathered with the Chief in the den, and the women with Kass in the living room. The Chief and Kass were old-fashioned in that way. Their longtime maid, Mary Roseboro, passed through the rooms, serving drinks to guests. Kass, dressed impeccably, her hair styled, sitting upright and tall in a living room chair, the epitome of a lady, led conversation among the women. In the den, the Chief sat in his leather recliner, sucking on his cigar, surrounded by his men. As Joe Greene sized up the Chief, he noticed how quiet he had become, and he wasn't sure why. But Greene also sensed the man's impressive pride and power.

At 940, his players and their wives were on their best behavior and careful to call their hosts "Mrs. Rooney" and "Mr. Rooney." Agnes Greene had been apprehensive the first time she dined at the Rooneys'. *I'm just a girl from Dallas, Texas*, she had fretted. That night she was served a steak too rare for her liking. In her seat at the Rooneys' dining room table, she agonized over what to do. *Should I say something? I don't want to eat a steak like this.* Finally, she summoned the courage to say, in a small voice, "May I have my steak a little more well done?" A moment passed, Agnes Greene on edge. Then Kass swept up that steak and Agnes Greene with it, and said, "I hate those steaks rare, too!" and she brought them into the kitchen and, with her sister Alice McNulty, cooked it a little longer until it was just right. Everyone laughed as Mrs. Mean Joe Greene exhaled.

Now, as the women chatted in the living room, a chess set on a nearby table caught the eye of Karen White. The chess pieces were carved as football players and painted in the Steelers' black and gold, each with a different jersey number. She thought, *Now, this is real interesting. What happens if the piece with your number isn't on the board? Does that mean you are . . . gone?*

The Chief hadn't consumed a spot of alcohol in decades—he said alcohol had caused the undoing of too many of his relatives and Irish ancestors—but his players liked their liquor. In his presence at 940, they drank discreetly, if at all. Roseboro delivered to Joe Greene a Canadian Club whiskey, the first time he had ever tried it, and he announced, "You know, I kind of like this." The Chief offered his players cigars. White didn't want to turn him down. He'd smoked one of the Chief's cigars before, though, and, "Woo!" he said years later, it "knocked the hair out of your nose. You've got to be a seasoned veteran to deal with one of these bad boys." This cigar he accepted graciously and told the Chief he would smoke it later.

Harris had brought his girlfriend and future wife, Dana Dokmanovich, an Eastern Airlines stewardess. He moved cautiously through these evenings, which was his way. The first time he'd had dinner at 940, as a rookie in 1972, Harris came alone. He couldn't believe that the owner of the Pittsburgh Steelers would invite to dinner a rookie and no one else. Harris pressured himself that night to say and do the right things. "I didn't have much training in formal dining," he said. "Not that this was formal, but I don't think I'd been to anybody's house on that scale." As he grew more comfortable at 940, Harris playfully recited the special grace said at his family's table back home in New Jersey. "In the name of the Father, the Son, and the Holy Ghost, whoever gets here first eats the most." The Chief loved that one. From the very first, Harris sized up the Chief and Kass: "Good people."

In personality the Chief stood apart from other owners of professional sports teams. In Chicago, Bear players thought owner George Halas a screamer and skinflint, tight end Mike Ditka once famously saying, "He tosses nickels around like manhole covers." In major-league baseball, the Oakland Athletics won three consecutive World Series from 1972 through 1974 even as the players united in their dislike for owner Charles Finley, a quirky, creative micromanager who loved nothing more than to see his name (not theirs) in headlines. The Chief was removed from the muck of contract negotiations, Dan handled that, so players who had hoped for more money didn't blame the Chief. What they knew about the Chief was that he always passed along kind words and good vibes in the locker room, and that he remembered the names of their wives and children, and sometimes even their birthdays. They thought the old man cool.

They'd all experienced his random acts of kindness. "Joe, my boy," the Chief would say to Greene, approaching him after practice and placing a hand on the big defensive tackle's shoulder, "how's Aggie?" That was his nickname for Agnes. And now, as they all sat at the dining room table beneath a chandelier of cut glass, the firelight from the candlesticks illuminating a dinner of steak, peas, corn, and salad, the Chief looked across the table to Mean Joe and said, "You've got a fine wife, Joe!" Agnes glowed. Karen White remembered how she'd been hospitalized with a virus—doctors feared it might be Legionnaire's disease—and how the Chief had visited her at Divine Providence nearly every day. Once he brought his brother, the priest known as Father Silas. They began praying, without telling her why, and so she feared the worst. "I thought there was something they were not telling me," she said.

The Chief had passed Dwight White's racial litmus test early on. White bore the scars of his upbringing in segregated Texas. To Pittsburgh he carried a skeptical view of whites: they had to prove their essential decency and fairness to him. One evening after practice, in the Mexican War Streets district of Pittsburgh's North Side, White and some friends noticed a black Buick driving toward them, headed the wrong way on a one-way street, and inside the car were the Chief and Father Silas. White heard the black folks on the street calling out happily, as if to an old friend, "Hey, Mr. Rooney!" He thought, *This guy must be pretty big. He can go up a one-way street and nobody says anything about it.* Much later White shared breakfast with the Chief at a North Side diner, just the two of them, and he had a similar thought. *It's so cool for a guy of his stature to be able to walk around in this community like that.* Even now, over dinner at the Rooneys' house, he noticed the way the Chief and Kass interacted with Mary Roseboro, their black maid, and he sensed a genuine good feeling. "I don't think it was a swinging door over there," White said. "I think there was some chemistry there."

In 2002, White would tell the University of Pittsburgh historian Rob Ruck, "I've been in Pittsburgh thirty years and to this day I can't say I know Mr. Rooney." But White said he had learned enough. "The Rooneys didn't come over here with a silver spoon in their mouth. This guy grew up, rolled his sleeves up, socked a few people in the nose, probably got socked a few times in the nose," he said. All things considered, Dwight White said, the old man sitting across the dining room table was exceptional: "This was my kind of guy."

Unanswered Question

Sometimes it takes an outsider to see the inside. In 1976 a Boston journalist reported on the Steelers in ways new to them, new even to the NFL. Clark Booth did it for the *Real Paper*, a counterculture weekly and journalistic gadfly near Harvard Square in Cambridge, Massachusetts. He wanted to probe the hidden costs of professional football, in particular the rising number of severe injuries. A local TV sportscaster in Boston with an English literature degree from Holy Cross, Booth was a newspaperman at heart, an old-style gumshoe reporter with a lyrical writing touch and the sensibilities of an Old Testament prophet. In addition to covering thirteen World Series, Booth moved outside of sports to cover national political conventions and religion, making nine trips to the Vatican. Occasionally he sharpened his pen for special-assignment freelance stories for Boston newspapers, magazines, and weeklies. He wrote these stories with an edge. He attended Super Bowl X in Miami, not as a card-carrying member of the football writers' lodge, but, as he would write, "seeking the darkest secrets of life in the National Football League."

Carrying his tape recorder, Booth posed his penetrating questions to Steelers and Cowboys, surprised by how responsive, or evasive, they were in interviews and by how haunted they seemed by the specter of serious injury. Dallas tight end Jean Fugett put it like this: "Look, football players approach injuries the way most people look upon the idea of death. You know you're gonna die someday. But you don't think about it. *Do you?* Injuries are just like death to a lot of players . . . death of a career . . . death of all that a lot of them really want in life. So you say . . . 'I'm not gonna worry about dying. I'm gonna go ahead and live!' "

Booth asked Dwight White how he had managed to play nearly all of Super Bowl IX while suffering from pleurisy and pneumonia. "Did the doctor say you could play?" Booth asked. "I don't think I want to answer that," White told him. But Booth continued to probe and Mad Dog said, finally, "Listen, God takes care of fools and little babies and I'm no baby."

A pinched nerve in his neck and shoulder had diminished Greene's strength, and his performance, during the 1975 regular season. He tried to play through it but missed four games. Booth put his question to Greene: "How is it possible to ignore the fact that you could be damaging your body for life?" Greene leaned across the table and told him, "Hey, man, what are you trying to do? Hasten my retirement?" Their conversation ended there.

In his cover story, "Death & Football," Booth painted a vivid tableau of gridiron pain, suffering, and rationalizations, including a memory of violence that lived like an apparition in Andy Russell's head. In 1963, Russell's first season with the Steelers, he'd seen an Eagles running back put his helmet into the throat of the Steelers' oncoming tackler, linebacker John Reger. Reger dropped to the ground, his body limp, as the stadium fell deathly silent. Reger had swallowed his tongue and stopped breathing. From the Steelers' bench, Russell saw Reger's body suddenly convulse and as he approached Reger he saw blood oozing from his nose, his eyes rolling to the back of his head, his skin turning blue. A frantic attempt was made to save him, a rescuer using a scissors' sharp edges to bang out Reger's front teeth to free his tongue, blood spurting in all directions, a rescuer pounding on his chest, an ambulance arriving, Russell seeing it all, and thinking, *God, what a brutal game.* Reger was saved (he returned to the field weeks later), and the Steelers' coach, Buddy Parker, a tough ol' cuss, told Russell to enter the game in his place at linebacker. Russell told Booth, "I'm more scared of Buddy Parker" than of what he had seen happen to Reger, and so play he did.

Booth asked Rocky Bleier to compare survival in football to survival in war. Bleier said: "The experiences and the reactions are quite the same. In battle action, you're concerned with something more than where you got shot. You're concerned with finding cover. You're concerned with where the enemy might be. You want to know where you are. You could be shot in the stomach. Your leg could be broken and you wouldn't even know it. You would go on."

Bleier pointed at Booth: "Now you could twist your ankle and not walk in a week. I could play on that ankle a whole week. The focal point of my attention is not on that injury, it's on getting back into the game. It's the intensity of what's happening at the moment. It's the hostility of the moment. Medically, I can't understand it. But psychologically I can."

Lynn Swann evaded the subject of injuries much as he would a defensive back. Two weeks earlier, against the Raiders in the AFC title game, Swann had been drilled in the back of the neck by safety Jack Tatum, and later driven headfirst into the icy field at Three Rivers Stadium by safety George Atkinson. Swann was knocked unconscious on that play and in one of the most enduring images of the Steelers' empire, Greene stepped from the sideline, lifted Swann in his arms, and carried him from the field, the receiver's body limp and childlike in his grasp. (When Swann later thanked Greene for what he'd done, Mean Joe said, true to form, that he'd only done it to keep the Steelers from having to waste a time-out—then he smiled.) Swann suffered a severe concussion, spent two days in a hospital, and missed the next week's practices. Doctors warned him that another such blow could be dangerous. The Dallas safety Cliff Harris told reporters during Super Bowl week, "Getting hit again while he's on a pass route must be in the back of Swann's mind. I know it would be in the back of my mind." Swann gave serious consideration to retiring. Egged on by Harris's comments, though, he opted to play in Super Bowl X even as team doctors, after each day's practice, searched deep into his eyes with small flashlights. Come game day, as the Goodyear blimp flew over the Orange Bowl and filmed crowd shots for the movie *Black Sunday*, Swann put forth the most dazzling and remembered performance of his career, catching four passes for 161 yards and the game-winning touchdown, becoming the first wide receiver ever named the game's most valuable player. But when Booth had interviewed him several days before the game about the possible consequences of playing, Swann held up his hand and said, "I'll say this about it and that's all I'll say. First you get well. Then you forget about it. That's the only way to deal with it.

"If you continue to worry about it, then you quit. It's as simple as that. And that's all I'm going to say about it."

Black Magic's Vial

Only three weeks before Clark Booth's reporting, Joey Gilliam held a vial. Whatever was in it, he handled it delicately, expertly, as if it were a precious substance. From across the hotel room, Reggie Harrison saw a powder that looked like salt and pepper. "What is that?" he asked. Gilliam, fingers at work, deep in concentration, said, "Doogie." They were road roommates, both with big personalities, Harrison known to teammates as "Boobie" for his resemblance to Cincinnati's bullish runner Boobie Clark, the nickname a gift from Dwight White who, upon seeing Harrison in the Steelers' locker room for the first time, announced, "Oh, man, we got us a Boobie now!" Black Magic, that's what Harrison called Gilliam for his passing skill. But in personality, too, Gilliam was like a street Houdini, now-you-see-him-now-you-don't, a teammate of mystery, lovable, cool, incandescent, a bullshit artist. Gilliam tipped his head forward, put what looked to be a hollow ink pen to his nostril. Harrison heard a loud *Snnffffittt!* The heroin did its mysterious work on Black Magic, a warm, euphoric flush. The 6:00 p.m. kickoff against the Rams at Los Angeles Memorial Coliseum was hours away, the 1975 regular-season finale meaningless. The Steelers at 12-1 had clinched their spot in the playoffs, and so had the Rams at 11-2. Gilliam hadn't thrown a pass in a game for two months, but Noll told him he would play the second half against the Rams. The Steelers were Bradshaw's team now. By design, Bradshaw would play only the first half. This would limit his exposure to the Rams' murderous pass rush.

Gilliam had other names for his Doogie. He called it Boy and he called it Girl, street names for heroin that Harrison had never heard. *Snnffffittt!* Watching, marveling, Black Magic so serene, Harrison said, "God damn!"

Harrison said, "Man, let me try some of that."

"No," Gilliam said. "Don't ever fuck with this."

In the Los Angeles Memorial Coliseum locker room, the visiting team's cubicles aligned in numerical order: 5 (Hanratty), 10 (Gerela), 12 (Bradshaw), 17 (Gilliam). Pregame, Bradshaw noticed Gilliam, in his cubicle, snorting powder. He'd never seen anyone do this before. Quietly, he asked Hanratty about it. The Rat said Gilliam must be using drugs. Some of the Steeler players had suspected as much. Gilliam had been late to team meetings all season, his excuses legendary and great fodder for locker room gossip. Noll fined him for each tardiness and used the money Gilliam paid in fines to buy him a reel-to-reel projector to review game films at home. Before the season opener, in San Diego, Gilliam didn't attend the pregame meal at the team's hotel. Noll asked Harrison, "Where's Joey?" Harrison, with a shrug, said, "I got him up." Gilliam finally appeared just as position meetings were ending. Noll asked him in the hallway for an explanation. Harrison, Fuqua, and others overheard Gilliam's answer: "I got up and asked the maid what time it was. She didn't speak no English so I went back to bed." Fuqua and Harrison tried not to laugh. In time, Noll would instruct his secretary to phone Coach Joe Gilliam Sr. in Nashville. "You need to call Joey and talk with him," the secretary told the father, without elaboration.

"He was in denial," Coach Gilliam said many years later. "Joey had his story ready: 'It's hard, Daddy.' " Coach Gilliam added, "How do you know what's in their heart and mind and what motivates them to do certain things? You don't." This was the deeper truth of Joey Gilliam: he lived as he played, with an element of risk and danger. If he could have arranged it, he would have thrown seventy-five passes every game, none shorter than twenty yards. That was the Jefferson Street in Joe. Noll was a fair-minded man—race meant little to him, the better man would play—but risk was unnecessary to him. The 1970s Steelers might have been Joey Gilliam's to lead. But already he was tobogganing out of control down an icy slope. Art Jr. put it like this: "Bradshaw, when he had his tough times, he'd read his Bible and let his beard grow. Joey would have a problem, he'd go out and find a good strong drug."

A 3-all tie against the Rams at halftime, Gilliam entered in the third quarter and moved the Steelers downfield. He threw an interception, and then another. He misfired with his passes again and again: eleven passes, only two completed, for twenty-nine yards. He was worse than terrible, his movements slow, no resemblance to the famous snap release of Jefferson Street Joe. Hanratty, his elbow injured and unable to play, told Noll he would give it a try, but Noll, furious and suspicious, said of Gilliam, "Let *him* play." The Rams' pass rush pancaked Gilliam. He went down and stayed down. Bradshaw reentered. Black Magic's head cleared, and he returned to the huddle. Then the Rams' defensive end Jack Youngblood caught him flush in the face. *Where is Joey's three-step drop and quick release?* Harrison wondered. He saw his roommate go down again, and stay down. Once Harrison had heard trainer Berlin say that when a Steeler went down, but was still moving, that was one thing. But when an injured Steeler didn't move, that's when the Plumber got worried. From the sideline, Harrison saw that Gilliam wasn't moving. It looked like Youngblood might have killed him.

Frightened, Harrison thought about what he had seen Gilliam doing with his vial. "Oh, God!" Harrison said aloud. Next to him on the sideline, Greene said, "What's wrong?" Harrison said, "Man, I've got something to tell you." Harrison could not hold it back. "He's fucked up, man. He's been snorting that shit all day." Joe Greene was like the team sheriff, the locker room his county. He played hard, lived clean, and was all for the team. If a Steeler teammate needed to be straightened out, Mean Joe did the straightening, and for that Noll and his coaches were grateful. The Rams won, 10–3. "Whatever Joe told Chuck, they kind of put the eye on Joey after that," Harrison said. Greene said of Gilliam, "I used to talk to him about being a man, and being stand-up." Gilliam would be the only Steeler on the roster not to play in Super Bowl X, and the following June, after missing several more team meetings, he would be released. Once, Harrison and Fuqua saw Greene confront Gilliam about his drug use, Mean Joe looming over him, Gilliam telling Greene to mind his own damn business, and Greene grabbing him by the scruff of his collar and sternly saying, "This isn't just you. *It's the team.*"

A Criminal Element

Oddly, the Steelers' idea of a brotherhood came under its sternest test not on a football field but in a courtroom. That test became a morality play in one act about football and violence, the value of a man's good name, and the intensity of the blood rivalry between the Steelers and the Raiders. Chuck Noll became a defendant in a $2 million slander suit filed by the Oakland safety George Atkinson. It was not a good moment for pro football, or for Noll. Beginning with the Immaculate Reception in 1972, the Steelers played the Raiders in an elimination postseason game for five consecutive seasons—1972 . . . 1973 . . . 1974 . . . 1975 . . . 1976—the Steelers winning three, the Raiders two. Then came 1977, and contract holdouts during training camp by Lambert, Holmes, and Blount. "Our distraction year," Donnie Shell would call it, and the Noll trial, three thousand miles from home, created the biggest distraction of all.

Scene: July 1977. The seventeenth floor of the US District Court building in San Francisco: carpeted, well lit, sterile, Judge Samuel Conti presiding, a large green blackboard on wheels rolled in. On it, names would be written, and those names would tighten the vise on Noll and provoke the biggest stir of this nine-day trial—and the ire and wrath of Mel Blount. For the sports press, the trial of Noll presented a procession of colorful personalities, plus charges and countercharges made with oratorical flourish by high-priced attorneys on both sides. These attorneys turned their superheated rhetoric against the game, describing professional football's "love of blood" and "wanton violence." One after another, players from the Steelers and the Raiders stepped away from training camp and paraded earnestly onto the witness stand: Bradshaw, Swann, Russell, Otto, Villapiano, Upshaw. Private correspondence between Rozelle and the two teams appeared in the courtroom for all to see on poster boards eight feet high—like dirty sheets hung on a clothesline. Feeling pestered and morose, Dan testified, and so did Rozelle and John Madden. On the witness stand, Al Davis, the Raiders' managing partner, wore a white shirt, gray tie, and black suit that one of Noll's attorneys cynically called his "sincere suit." The conspiracy-minded charged that the Atkinson lawsuit was another behind-the-scenes attempt by Davis to disrupt the harmony of the Steelers' training camp, and another of his attacks against his personal rival Rozelle. That Davis often passed notes to Atkinson's attorneys during the trial further fueled this theory. The Atkinson legal team, meanwhile, suggested to jurors that it was squaring off with the manipulative and almighty NFL establishment led by Rozelle and the Rooneys. The six jurors (four women, two men) knew nothing about Davis and almost nothing about football. They required explanations of terms such as "punt returner" and "line of scrimmage." Attorneys showed many film clips of savage hits in NFL games, causing a few jurors to gasp audibly.

To get in this predicament, Noll, through gritted teeth, had done what he almost never did—lose control—and it happened at a press conference one day after the Raiders' 31–28 win over the Steelers in Oakland in the 1976 season opener. He'd had time to study the film of Atkinson slamming his forearm into the back of the head of the unsuspecting Lynn Swann, the two players in open space, no other player near them on the field. As the play unfolded, Bradshaw had scrambled and completed a pass to Franco Harris, who ran for a thirty-five-yard gain. Just as Harris caught the ball, about fifteen yards away, Swann moved laterally across

I'm receiving is a direct result of the statements of Coach Chuck Noll." Atkinson said he delivered his hit only because he thought Swann had caught the pass.

Other players had their say. Otto said in his fifteen NFL seasons he had "suffered every possible illegal blow." Villapiano said, "The hit by Atkinson was not that unusual. I've seen plenty worse than that." Bradshaw said he felt Atkinson had "deliberately clobbered" his receiver. Swann said he considered retiring after Atkinson's first hit even though he had played only two NFL seasons. "He completely, unwarrantedly, violently, maliciously hit me from behind and allowed Franco to run right by him," Swann said. Jurors learned that Rozelle had fined Atkinson $1,500 for the hit, and on a poster board they read a portion of Rozelle's letter to Atkinson explaining the fine: "In sixteen years in this office I do not recall a more flagrant foul." They also read Rozelle's letter sent jointly to the two teams' head coaches, Noll and Madden: "A full review of the available films and television tapes of your Sept. 12 game indicates that your 'intense rivalry' of recent years could be on the verge of erupting into something approaching pure violence." Jurors heard that Rozelle had fined Noll $1,000 for publicly criticizing a player. On a poster board they read Dan Rooney's blistering response to Rozelle, in which he called Atkinson's hit "a cowardly act," and wrote, "I also believe, because of the number of Oakland Raider players making such attacks on Lynn, the Raiders must have an opinion that Lynn is vulnerable and can be forced out of the game, which makes such acts premeditated and involves the Raiders' coaching staff as well as the players."

Noll lost control, in a tactical sense, in the courtroom, too. Though a skilled witness and former law school student, Noll became a dupe for opposing attorney Daniel Mason, who was more skilled at the legal craft. Mason led Noll into a trap, and used the blackboard to do it. First he instructed Noll to diagram the play in question on the blackboard. Mason then erased Noll's carefully drawn Xs and Os and wrote on the clean board, "NOLL'S NFL CRIMINALS." Beneath this heading he wrote the name "George Atkinson" and left space to add more names. Noll parried skillfully with Mason. He said he hadn't branded Atkinson, but that Atkinson's style of play had branded him. He asserted that he had not used the term "criminal element" in a legal sense, only as it applied to football.

the middle and then slowed down, when suddenly Atkinson,
his man, accelerated and swung his right arm, striking Swann
of his helmet. Swann crumpled to the ground with a concussi
would miss the next two games. No official saw Atkinson's b
penalty was called. The game was nationally televised, though,
ers inundated the NFL office with complaints about Atkinson's
eight months earlier, in the 1975 AFC title game, Atkinson had
Swann unconscious with another brutal strike. Noll had time to
his words carefully this time and, in a press luncheon in Pittsb
pressed his outrage by saying, "You have a criminal element in e
ety and apparently we have it here in the NFL, too. George Atki
on Lynn Swann was with intent to maim and not with football
I'd like to see those guys thrown out of the league." For these w
kinson sued Noll for slander.

"One of the morals in this case is that, in real life, Mr. Atkin
be a charming young man," James MacInnis, Noll's attorney, sai
opening argument. "You may safely invite him to your drawing r
your home. But you may not with equal safety encounter him
line of scrimmage on a football field, particularly if your name
Swann and your back is turned. . . . Professional football, as outli
afternoon, may appear as a primitive game to those who do not fo
It may appear as gang warfare conducted in uniform, and it may b
to all that is violent within any one of us. But there are rules, and w
those rules in football the strong devour the weak and professiona
ball would destroy itself within a short period of time."

In his opening statement, Atkinson's attorney, Willie Brown, a
ismatic future mayor of San Francisco, called the Steelers "the l
cheap-shot artists in pro football" and "a team trying their best to d
Mr. Atkinson's career. . . . I'm out to make Chuck Noll just what he
a man who talks too much." Later Brown added, "I think when we f
finish, the question of pro football—as we know it—continuing
played may very well be in doubt." Outside the courtroom, Brown
reporters, "This is pro football's Watergate."

On the witness stand, Atkinson said, "I'm labeled for the rest of
life, you know?" He said, "There are two types of publicity. Charles M
son received publicity. Sirhan Sirhan received publicity. The publi

"If I had meant that I probably would have said 'thrown in jail' instead of 'kicked out of the league,' " Noll said. For the next eight hours, Mason interrogated him. Their exchanges grew abrupt, argumentative, repetitive, tense. Mason hammered away at the innate brutality of the sport, emphasizing that Atkinson couldn't possibly be alone among 1,200 NFL players as the league's "criminal element." To prove his point, Mason showed film clips of other violent hits in NFL games. He wrote a new name on the blackboard based on Noll's judgment of one of those clips: "Jack Tatum." Then jurors saw films of Greene kicking a Cleveland Browns guard in a 1975 game, Glen Edwards striking a blow at a Cincinnati Bengal in 1974, and Blount hitting the Raiders' Cliff Branch in the back of his helmet after the whistle had blown in another game. In such instances, Noll said from the witness stand, he typically spoke with his team to let his players know "it wasn't an act I approved of." Under pointed questioning, Noll defined "criminal element" as "a player who willfully and wantonly violates the rules on the football field." Now Mason created a powerful visual for jurors. He added new names to the blackboard: "Joe Greene, Glen Edwards, Mel Blount." They, too, he said, belonged among "NOLL'S NFL CRIMINALS."

"You didn't tell the press that there was a criminal element when Mel Blount did it, did you?" Mason asked.

"No," Noll said, though he agreed that Blount's hit on Branch qualified under his definition.

Mason suggested that in the future Noll ought to announce to the press "criminal element" violations by his own players, and Noll coldly replied, "You're trying to drive a wedge between me and my players." A wedge materialized when Blount, furious that his own coach had labeled him part of a *criminal element*, announced that he would file a $5 million slander suit against Noll. Blount said he would never play for Noll again.

Noll's relationship with players was old-school, built on respect and fear. Communication was never his strongest suit. Like many football coaches, Noll was clumsy in the way he showed love for his players. But he succeeded in creating a shared purpose among them. His leadership style brought his team together, if not his players closer to him. That was a price, he thought, worth paying. In this instance, he had attempted to stand up for Swann, but doing so cost him Blount, at least for a time.

The trial had a whirlwind finish. Willie Brown said Atkinson was a "rag-tag kid brawling with the Establishment," the NFL being "second only to the US government in terms of power, scope, and potential." His emotions running hot, Brown said, "This young man has been labeled for life!" But one of Noll's attorneys told jurors that, in the past, Atkinson had experienced trouble with the law for carrying a concealed weapon and for once threatening to castrate a man, and "since injury to reputation is the gist of slander, a bad reputation must be considered by you."

The jury deliberated four hours, rejected Atkinson's arguments, and determined that Noll had not committed slander. Atkinson said all he ever really wanted was for Noll to retract his comment anyway. Blount patched up his differences with Noll and played another seven seasons in Pittsburgh.

The Steelers' insurance company had tried to convince the Rooneys to settle with Atkinson for $50,000 in advance of the trial. Dan refused. To settle, he said, would mean that every time an NFL player was criticized he would file a lawsuit. "We felt we had to go to court to save the game," he said. Noll's victory in the Atkinson trial didn't feel like much of a victory to Dan. He said, "This trial has been the most depressing thing I have ever done."

Fats Holmes's Bachelor Party

There was only so much room on the Pittsburgh Steelers' marquee. When sportswriters wrote of the team's heroics, they singled out the stars. But Ernie Holmes wanted his name in bright lights, too, and he wanted the big money that came with that. He wanted to be viewed, apart from the other Steel Curtain defenders, for being an annihilative force at the line of scrimmage. His teammates knew that Fats craved recognition, and so when they could, they acknowledged him, as their brotherhood demanded, for being unique and special.

Since Holmes was getting married again, this time in midseason, November 1976, it fell to Frenchy Fuqua to design a bachelor party that would please his friend. Fuqua rounded up many of the Steeler players on a Friday night and brought them to the twenty-fourth floor of the Pittsburgh Hilton, a glassed-in penthouse suite with breathtaking views of the Allegheny and Mount Washington, and enough space to set up a few poker tables and ten bottles of Courvoisier neatly stacked upward in a 4-3-2-1 pyramid. Fuqua told Noll about the party. "With Chuck you don't sneak," Fuqua said. "You tell him. You just don't mention the cognac." Fuqua told players he would arrange for two women to pop out of a cake, except, he decided, there would be no cake, just two women. According to his plan, these two women would arrive at the end of the party and entertain Fats on his last night as a bachelor. As every moment with Ernie Holmes was memorable, this night would be remembered by nearly all in attendance, at least in bits and pieces. "He did scare me that one night," Franco Harris said. "Oh, my!" John Stallworth said with a laugh when asked to recall the night. "Uhm . . ."

A team's "chemistry" is the sum of individual personalities. Whatever events, thoughts, and adventures brought these Steelers together, they seemed, perhaps more often than was healthy, to include Holmes. Everyone had Holmes stories. Most could be cataloged under three headings: "Mood Swings," "Eating to Excess," and "Courvoisier." There, for instance, was Randy Grossman, celebrating with his wife hours after Super Bowl X, walking down a hotel hallway in Miami just as Holmes approached from the other direction, a woman on each arm, a bottle of Courvoisier cognac in each hand. Holmes suddenly grabbed Grossman's wife, lifted her onto his own shoulders, and began to walk away. If it had been Joe Greene or Dwight White or Jack Lambert, Grossman told himself later, he would have fought to protect his wife's honor. "But short of an elephant rifle," Grossman said of Holmes, "there is no way that I'm going after this maniac." After half a dozen steps Holmes lowered Grossman's wife to the floor, roared with laughter, and walked off. Grossman didn't bother to explain to his wife the danger she had just escaped.

The Eating to Excess stories were the stuff of legend, like the time Joe Greene's mother made an enormous pot roast and baked a lovely pie at home in Texas, but Mean Joe and Mad Dog went hungry because Fats ate the entire roast and the entire pie. Then, later that night, on the plane flight home to Pittsburgh, Mad Dog watched Fats eat three meals more. Or the time Reggie Harrison, at a team picnic, saw Holmes eat twelve plates of spaghetti with meatballs the size of softballs, plus two plates of potato salad and a plate of ribs, and then heard him complain that he couldn't get a diet soda. Or the most legendary Eating to Excess story of all: that night in 1976 when Perles brought his defensive linemen to a local restaurant for a feast of roasted suckling pigs. When all the eating was done, Holmes took another swig of Courvoisier and then cracked a knife handle against a pig's skull. He dug his fingers deep inside, scooped out small pieces of the pig's brain, and ate them with delight. "Where I come from," Holmes gushed, brain matter splotching his cheek, "this is a delicacy!" Furness and Banaszak blanched. Perles would laugh and say, "Fats sucked those eyeballs out, and he ate the head! *Hee-hee-hee.*" Greenwood shook his head and said, "Ernie was a real piece of work when it came to eating."

Holmes had met his new wife at a Christian athletes' association meeting. "He's just the opposite of the publicity he gets. I see a side of him the public never sees," she told *Jet* magazine. Fats said, "She helps keep my shoulders straight. As for religion, I'm a kid nourishing on the milk of the Bible. I've been making mistakes, but not like I used to." Facing cocaine possession charges in Texas, Holmes would be exonerated following the 1976 season after a trial in which Noll, Dan, and Andy Russell testified to his character.

At the bachelor party, the Steelers sat at poker tables, shuffling cards, bluffing in the usual ways, and drinking beer. Music filled the suite. Outside, lights danced across the Pittsburgh skyline. All seemed right until Fats sidled up to Fuqua at the card table and muttered, "You ain't got me no ladies?" Fuqua eyed his cards and said, "Be patient." Then Dwight White saw Fats guzzling Courvoisier from a bottle and said to Fuqua, "Don't let him drink any more!" Banaszak heard Fats in the suite's bedroom, on the phone, arguing with someone, perhaps his fiancée, Fats's voice exploding through the closed door the way Fats exploded through some of the NFL's best offensive lines. Banaszak heard sounds that suggested Fats was throwing objects in anger. When Fats emerged from the bedroom, Fuqua poured him a soft drink and told him to be careful with his cognac consumption or else "by the time your surprise gets here you'll already be sleeping."

Fats drained another cognac bottle. "When he took the top off, the top never went back on," Reggie Harrison said. "He was a force to be reckoned with." Holmes's eyes grew sleepy and slanted. His mood swung from right to left, like a pendulum, from disappointed to offended to surly to enraged. Fats addressed the entire room, saying, "You sonsabitches ain't shit!" This was his last night as a free man, he bellowed. He was drunk, and furious at his teammates. "He was acting like a complete fool," Fuqua said. As host of the party, Fuqua tried to calm him, saying, "Let me make a phone call." He called the two women and asked them to come earlier than planned—like now. Fats howled on. He said his teammates didn't care about him even as he played hard for them. As he spoke, his hands moved in dramatic arcs and then, with the sound of a gunshot, his Courvoisier bottle exploded against the edge of a table as the neck of the bottle shattered. Holmes didn't care. He drank from the broken bottle even as Fuqua pleaded, "Don't do that. There's broken glass inside!" Fuqua opened another cognac bottle and presented it to Holmes, who continued his oration, drinking as he ranted.

Danger was in the air. Players looked to the door. Harris already had sneaked out. "I saw how narrow Ernie's eyes were getting," he would say. Stallworth and cornerback Jimmy Allen ducked out, too. Banaszak noticed that Holmes became even more riled up when he realized that a few teammates had left. Holmes was, by nature, tactile and physically intimidating. When he horsed around with teammates in the locker room, he sometimes hurt them without meaning to. Fuqua thought about that as he looked at all the windows in the suite. *If he grabs me and throws me out the window, I'm going to fall twenty-four floors!* Fats prattled on and on and on. He blocked the front door and told teammates, "Ain't nobody going nowhere!"

"I bust my ass for you guys!" he said. His anger intensified as he said Mean Joe, Dwight, and L.C. got all the credit and he got none. "They never mention my name," he said of the sports press. "I'm playing my ass off every game." Another glass broke, shards on the floor, tensions rising, teammates wanting out. Fats's eyes grew so slanted that Fuqua said he "looked like a Chinaman." The Steelers had seen and heard this all before.

Fuqua watched Fats take another long swig of Courvoisier. Then Fats wavered and fell to the floor. His teammates did not rush to help him. They rushed for the door to *escape* him. Holmes was out cold. Fuqua enlisted help from several teammates, and together they dragged him into the suite's bedroom, no small task. They couldn't lift his enormous body onto the bed, so they left him kneeling beside the bed, with his head and arms resting on it.

The next morning at seven thirty, Fuqua returned to the hotel to awaken Holmes. But Holmes already was sitting at a table in his suite, smiling and drinking coffee. He said, "I had a good time last night!" Fuqua decided that Holmes didn't remember any of his bachelor party. It was just as well. Fuqua would handle the cleanup details, including the bill from the hotel to pay for broken glass.

The Frenchman drove Holmes to Three Rivers Stadium, and they arrived in the locker room two hours before players were required to show up for a walk-through practice.

"The reason I came early for you," Fuqua told Holmes, "is so we can go sit in the sauna.

"Because if Noll smells this shit on you, we're all going to be in trouble."

Merry, Moody, Massive

A piece of the team's chemistry was pharmaceutical. Some Steelers used anabolic steroids. The NFL had not yet banned steroids, and did not begin year-round random testing for them until 1990. Unchecked, steroid use in the league flourished during the seventies as players grew bigger and faster. Over time, the 1970s Steelers would develop a reputation as a steroid team, the subject like a steady, if distant, drumbeat across the decades. In the early eighties, several Pittsburgh linemen dominated the NFL's Strongest Man competitions, and from these muscle-bound, made-for-television events, whispers and innuendos about steroids grew. In 1990, when Dallas's all-pro defensive tackle Randy White admitted that he'd started using steroids in the late 1970s, he told author Skip Bayless, "Man, I'd look across the line at those Steelers with their sleeves rolled up on those huge arms and, well, I had to do something. I figured they were

using steroids, too." In 2005, New Orleans coach Jim Haslett, a former linebacker who entered the league in 1979, said of the presence of steroids in the league, "It started, really, in Pittsburgh. They got an advantage on a lot of football teams. They were so much stronger [in the] '70s, late '70s, early '80s. They're the ones who kind of started it." Dan called Haslett's charge "totally false." Haslett admitted using steroids as an NFL player, and Dan suggested "maybe it affected his mind." In 2009, Fran Tarkenton, in a radio interview, made a passing reference to the Steelers' use of steroids, saying, "It made a difference. It increased their performance."

But nothing advanced the 1970s Steelers' reputation as a steroid team more than when one of their own, guard Steve Courson, his conscience stirred and his heart damaged, turned whistle-blower, first in a 1985 *Sports Illustrated* article and then in a 1991 book. Courson pointed a finger at himself and more broadly (without mentioning names) at some of his former Steeler teammates. He wrote that Steeler offensive linemen often talked confidentially about their sexual conquests, their jobs, and their steroid use, and agreed that steroids helped their explosiveness at the line of scrimmage but also created problems with acne, water retention, and a rage difficult to control off the field.

Courson was a steroid creation, merry, moody, massive, his body miraculous. Whenever he removed his shirt—either quietly in the Steelers' locker room or to raucous cheers as he stood atop a bar in Pittsburgh and tensed his upper-body muscles in the bodybuilder's crab pose—it was impossible not to stare. His six-foot-one physique was like cut marble, so big as to be nearly cartoonish, with a twenty-two-inch neck, twenty-inch biceps, a thirty-eight-inch waist, and a chest that expanded to fifty-eight inches. At a Halloween party in 1979 he slathered himself in green paint to fittingly become the Incredible Hulk. When Courson arrived at training camp in Latrobe in 1977 as a fifth-round draft pick from the University of South Carolina, he had just finished a six-week cycle on the anabolic steroid Dianabol, taking fifteen milligrams daily in three small pills. He weighed 265 pounds then and would add 30 pounds more, and ran the forty in 4.6 seconds and would get faster still. In the bench press he lifted nearly 500 pounds, already one of the strongest players on the team. He also had an intellectual side impossible for his new teammates to miss. He studied German on Berlitz tapes, often listened to classical music while driving, and read voraciously about ancient Grecian and Persian wars and American military history.

A rowdy night owl, Courson shared some of his most memorable social adventures with the garrulous Gary Dunn at his side. After Steeler victories at Three Rivers Stadium, he and Dunn celebrated at the bar in a nearby Marriott hotel, where they were treated like heroes and young women set their skirts for them, and the bar manager arranged platters piled high with shrimp and cheese at their usual table. When the two Steelers arrived, they tilted their heads back as a bartender poured vodka, Cointreau, and lime juice into their mouths, and then they stood upright and swallowed as loud cheers erupted from onlookers; this sequence was repeated several times. On occasion they substituted margaritas for kamikazes, and the bartender salted their lips. Courson luxuriated in the muscleman's light, even as he suffered moodiness, irritability, and an increased desire for sex, all side effects, he believed, from his steroid use. Bar-hopping on one Saturday night, Courson turned his Chevy Blazer into a battering ram and flattened nearly every stop sign on his way home. To him it felt like a 'roid rage, and later he agreed to pay for the damage.

Courson barely hid his steroid use. Wearing a tank top, gym shorts, and a Super Bowl ring, he drew stares once as he left a Pittsburgh pharmacy with a shopping bag full of steroids (Winstrol, Dianabol, Deca-Durabolin, Anavar) and other compounds, including human chorionic gonadotropin (HCG), which he used at the end of his steroid cycles to stimulate testosterone production. At Courson's apartment, Banaszak watched Courson inject himself with syringes. "He was banging himself in the legs, his butt," Banaszak said. "He knew what he was doing. Everybody would ask him. He wouldn't cycle off of it. He was an absolutely massive man." When Courson pulled a hamstring muscle during one training camp, he heard Noll angrily shout at him, "All you want to do is body-build and take steroids!"

Noll knew about steroids, and had for a long time. Way back in 1963, as a Chargers assistant coach on Sid Gillman's staff, he had observed as Gillman hired pro football's first-ever strength coach, Alvin Roy, a former trainer for the US Olympics weight-lifting team. Ron Mix, a Chargers offensive lineman on that team, remembered Roy telling Chargers players,

"I learned a secret from those Rooskies," and then Roy held up a bottle of pink pills—Dianabol. Mix said these pills soon showed up at their training table in cereal bowls. In 1970, Noll hired the Steelers' first strength coach, Lou Riecke, a weight lifter from Louisiana and friend of Roy's who had worked out in Roy's gym in Baton Rouge. Riecke had competed as a thirty-eight-year-old weight lifter on the US team at the 1964 Tokyo Olympics after taking Dianabol at a doctor's suggestion and experiencing a sudden surge in his results. Noll discouraged Steeler players from using steroids. In testimony before a Senate panel in 1989, Noll said "steroid use has grown in direct proportion to the money to be made in football," a trend he termed "megadoses in pursuit of megabucks."

When Courson told *Sports Illustrated* in May 1985, "Seventy-five percent of the linemen in the NFL are on steroids and 95 percent have probably tried them," it was as if a meteor exploded on the page, readers awakened to a new truth in pro football. By this time, Courson's seven-year tenure with the Steelers was done, he'd been traded to Tampa Bay, and his NFL career hung by a thread. He told the magazine he had no regrets about his steroid use. "It's very easy for people on the outside to criticize. But it's different when it's your livelihood, when it's your job to keep a genetic mutation from getting into your backfield."

In his Steelers prime, Courson's personality was as gargantuan as he. He painted his Chevy Blazer in camouflage and put a Corvette's mighty engine inside. Before one game, he picked up his buddy Dunn, who stepped from his house into snow flurries and twenty-five-degree cold, and saw Courson sitting behind the wheel of his Blazer, shirtless, and wearing camouflage paint on his face and torso, ready for battle.

"How we doin'?" Dunn said, climbing inside.

"We're gonna go hunting some Jets today!" Courson roared.

As they sped down I-79 toward Three Rivers Stadium, snow swirling into the Blazer through a broken side window, Courson blasted a tape of Wagner's "Ride of the Valkyries." The two Steelers arrived at the stadium hours before kickoff, the Steeler Nation tailgaters already massed. Courson, ever a showman, climbed atop the hood of his Blazer and flexed this way and that, a muscleman preening, his upper-body muscles rippling. The way the tailgaters roared in approval, you might have thought the Steelers already led by two touchdowns.

Mrs. Rooney Goes to Canton

Kass Rooney was the Steelers' matriarch, a lofty title much too preten-
tious for her liking. Though she never played a down of pro football, as
the Chief's wife she had seen and heard it all since the beginning, back
when the team was known as football's Pittsburgh Pirates. She had the
Irish storytelling gift, always did. As a boy, Art Jr. had visited her and her
sister Alice in the kitchen at 940 and listened to their stories about family
and the old days, gossipy tales about hushed-up scandals, richly expressed.
Their stories fired a boy's imagination. And now, in her seventy-seventh
year, Kass would matter-of-factly tell a story from 1933 or 1947 or 1962
about Whizzer White, Charles Bidwell, or George Halas that startled her
five boys. They thought, *How does she know that?* But they didn't ponder
the question for long before the realization came. *Oh, yeah, she was there.*
Kass Rooney had spent her entire adult life surrounded by men. Apart
from her sister, there was the Chief, their five sons, and nearly half a century of football players and coaches and boxers and promoters and horse
players . . . all men. Her directness might have been a product of that,
a way for a woman to hold her own, to survive. Like the poet Dorothy
Parker, she could sting with her words, the Chief her usual target. Once,
noticing that his well-worn suit had turned shiny, she asked him, "Are you
planning to die soon?" "Why?" the Chief asked. Kass shook her head, and
said, "You could use a couple of new suits." John Rooney said, "I never
saw my mother and dad have an argument. My mother knew what her
position was—and my father certainly knew what his was—and so there
were no mixups." Kass had great insight, and intuition, and sometimes,
especially when she had a Canadian Club or an Old Fashioned in hand,
her stories poured forth.

In 1981, Kass, the Chief, Art Jr., and Kay drove to Canton. Per usual,
they stopped along the way at a small restaurant, the Chief ordering ham
freshly sliced off the bone on Jewish rye bread with chocolate cake for
dessert. They arrived unannounced at the Pro Football Hall of Fame, and
the staff made a big fuss when the Chief appeared. Kass slipped away
with Art Jr., moving into the silence of the great hall that featured bronze
busts of pro football's most illustrious figures. She stood in front of the
Chief's bust—ART ROONEY SR.—depicted in midlife, no glasses, no cigar.

He had been enshrined in 1964 as part of the Hall's second induction class. Kass didn't think his bronze bust much resembled him, then or now. She patted it on the head, as if to say, "Poor Arthur," and moved on to others.

"Well, here's Johnny Blood!" she said of the Steelers' legend of the 1930s, narrating to Art Jr. as she went. "He was some guy. Kind of a wild man, but I didn't see that all the time."

Next up was the former Steelers coach from the war years, Walt Kiesling. "Such a great friend of ours," Kass said wistfully. "You knew he had to get into this Hall of Fame as a player." She paused, smiled, and finished the thought: ". . . because he could NEVER get in as a coach."

The bronze likeness of the founding owner of the New York Giants came into view: "Tim Mara! He was a great friend of your dad's. You know that your brother Tim is named for him?" She looked at Art Jr. with arched brows and asked once more, "You do know that, don't you?" He did.

Down the line of bronze busts she went. "Now here's one! You didn't want to be left in the room with him. He'd grope you!" His mother's narration led Art Jr. to an epiphany. He realized more powerfully than ever before that the Rooneys were a part of a cultural phenomenon, professional football in America, and an important part at that, as a founding family. As his mother filled him with the intimate history of a sport that had defined his family's life and his own, Art Jr. thought, *Jiminy, this is like being at Mount Vernon with Martha Washington and listening to her tell stories about Lafayette!*

Tears, Sunglasses

In at least one respect, Pam Webster and Debbie Furness were like most of the wives of Steeler players. They saw and heard a lot. At home they listened to their husbands' dreams and grumblings, dodged their mood swings and defeats, nursed their welts and bruises, and happily shared in the Steelers' magic carpet ride. As football wives they inhabited an all-consuming man's world, existing on its periphery but drawn into its emotional vortex. They saw the Steelers' years of empire through the prism of their husbands' performances. Each year the playoffs seemed a given and, in capturing four Super Bowls, the postseason money rolled in. They grew to expect that money, which provided welcome security for their young and growing families. Around Pittsburgh being a Steeler's wife during the late 1970s offered celebrity, cachet. Some wives embraced that; others didn't. As Joe Greene said, speaking generally about professional football players' wives, "The wives like being Mrs. NFL probably more, or as much, as the husbands enjoy being a football player." The reason, Greene said, were "some of the benefits that go with the social scene."

Pam Webster and Debbie Furness stayed mostly in the background. So did their husbands, Mike Webster and Steve Furness, a center and defensive tackle, respectively. Growing up in Wisconsin and watching Lombardi's Packers, Pam Webster had kept her eye on Ray Nitschke, Green Bay's snarling middle linebacker. With a laugh she said, "Everyone else had a crush on [running back] Donny Anderson. I had a crush on Ray Nitschke." Debbie Furness didn't feel entirely comfortable in the Steelers' fold. She knew the team's Christian athletes shared regular prayer meetings and Bible studies. She was Jewish, and though her husband was not, they agreed to raise their kids in the Jewish faith. "Sometimes," she said, "I felt a little on the outside looking in."

Their husbands had roomed together at training camp. Like Mike Webster, Steve Furness embraced the underdog role. Selected from the University of Rhode Island in the fifth round of the 1972 NFL draft, Furness spent two years on the Steelers' reserve taxi squad and then became the team's primary backup on the defensive line. In 1977 he led the team in sacks and the defensive line in tackles. Because Webster and Furness slavishly devoted themselves to weight lifting in the underground strength gym at the Red Bull Inn in suburban Peters Township, they moved their families close by. Steeler wives understood that football came first, that football was *everything*. To keep up her husband's weight, Debbie Furness, a gourmet cook, made enough food each night for six people, even in the early years "when there were just two of us." He would eat two dinners, the second just before bedtime.

As the friendship between Pam Webster and Debbie Furness blossomed, they looked for each other at Steeler gatherings. The Furnesses had married in 1973, the Websters a year later. They had their first children at

about the same time (the Banaszaks, Toewses, and Bleiers had babies during that period, too). Their friendship might have grown deeper if Pam Webster had gotten out more often. But she mostly stayed home, where she felt most comfortable. She rarely attended games at Three Rivers Stadium because Mike Webster preferred her to be home with their young children. That was his protective nature. Knowing that his children were safe at home, he told her, freed his mind to play football. So she watched most Steeler games on television, confident her husband would prevail. Debbie Furness went to games, and with other Steeler wives, including her friends Mary Banaszak and Vanessa Brown (wife of tight end Larry Brown), often drove out to the Pittsburgh airport to see the team off, and return, no matter the hour. The Furnesses attended team-only celebrations at Jack and Joanne Ham's house. When a group of Steeler players got together at a teammate's house to watch an important NFL game on television, Debbie Furness and other wives joined their husbands there and brought plates of food. After one big victory, the popular downtown nightclub Heaven closed to the public and allowed the Steelers and their wives to celebrate in privacy. That was a night, Debbie Furness would remember, for "everybody to let their hair down, relax, and reap the rewards of the season."

Mike Webster typically returned home long after home games and drank a few beers as he watched old movies of his cowboy hero, John Wayne. Sometimes Pam watched with him: *True Grit, McLintock!,* and her favorite, *Rooster Cogburn (. . . and the Lady),* costarring Katharine Hepburn. The Websters memorized lines from these movies and sometimes recited them aloud just before Wayne and Hepburn did. At one moment, Cogburn, riding in a wagon, asked Eula Goodnight (Hepburn), "How old are you?" and Hepburn said, "Shall we say it has already struck midnight." That exchange was one of the Websters' favorites.

The inevitable came in training camp in August 1981, Furness in his tenth season with the Steelers, Webster his eighth. The Steelers had failed to make the playoffs in 1980 for the first time in nine years. Bleier and White retired after the season. The reputational jewel of the Steelers—the Steel Curtain front four—was in steep decline. Holmes was three years gone, and Mean Joe and Hollywood Bags were nearing the end of their careers. In 1980 the Steelers registered only eighteen quarterback sacks, lowest in the league. Pittsburgh's coaches wanted the defensive line to get quicker and younger.

In Latrobe, Furness found out he'd been traded to Tampa Bay for a draft choice. The news, and its finality, devastated him. He'd given his life to the Steelers, and his body and the numbers bore that out: nine seasons, thirty-two sacks, four Super Bowl rings. He had replaced the injured Greene in Super Bowls X and XIII and performed admirably. He loved Pittsburgh. "He was recognizable there," his wife said. Packing personal belongings into his car at training camp, Furness told reporters what players usually tell reporters at such moments. "I'm unhappy about it," he said, "and I guess I'll be bitter for a long time, but that's the way it goes." Perles said, "It was a very tough decision because Steve and I came in at the same time. It's emotional but you do what you have to do." Webster drove by and saw Furness with the reporters. He pulled over and stopped. "Furnie, where are you going?" Webster asked. "Tampa Bay," Furness said. "No!" Webster said, with a look of shock. The two men spoke quietly, shook hands, and Webster said, in parting, "If there's anything I can do, let me know."

Pam Webster heard about the trade that afternoon. To her it was like a death in the family, a safety net tearing. She stopped by the Dairy Bar & Market in McMurray and there happened to see Debbie Furness. For a moment she considered what to do, what to say. Finally she approached her friend. She saw tears behind Debbie Furness's big sunglasses. "I'm sorry," Pam Webster said with real feeling, "about what's happened." Debbie Furness felt for her husband, his battered pride. He had been happy as a Pittsburgh Steeler, and thought he was an asset to the team still. She felt for herself, too. She had a job, a young family, and comfort with their life in Pittsburgh, a life that was about to change. Tearfully, she told Pam Webster that she couldn't talk about it, and left.

Pam Webster knew that one day the football life would end for her family, too. The thought chilled but didn't seem applicable or real. It seemed far away.

VI

THEIR LIFE'S WORK

CHAPTER 15

BAR SCENE AT PRO BOWL, 1982

AT THE TIME OF THE Immaculate Reception, Ronnie Lott was a Jack Tatum fan, drawn to his toughness. But as the football ricocheted from the colliding Tatum and Fuqua and into Franco Harris's hands, Lott sensed the fighting spirit of the Steelers kicking up like a monstrous sandstorm. Watching on television at home with his father in Rialto, California, Lott, an eighth grader, was only thirteen years old, an impressionable age. From the moment Harris made his catch, Lott felt in the Steelers an impressive quality—an aura, really—that was much bigger than the players themselves.

As a freshman at USC five years later, Lott listened closely as Coach John Robinson told him about one of those Steelers, Lynn Swann, and the former Trojan's outsize competitiveness. "Lynn would go anywhere on the field here to catch the ball. He would actually get up the goalpost—and get to the top of the goalpost—to catch the ball," Robinson said. Lott imagined Swann leaping into the sky, over airplanes and cumulus clouds. "Ronnie, if you are going to be like Lynn," Robinson said, "not only do you need the desire, you need the competitive spirit."

Four years later, here came Swann onto the field at Three Rivers Stadium during pregame warm-ups, November 1, 1981. He approached Lott, the San Francisco 49ers' rookie free safety. Swann, injured and unable to play, knew that Lott was part of the USC football family and joked, "Man, I don't know if you guys would've wanted some of me today!" Swann gave that pretty-boy smile, but Lott didn't know what to say, so he just smiled and left it at that. To Lott, playing the Pittsburgh Steelers in 1981 amounted to playing soccer's Manchester United, or the 1927 New York Yankees or Bill Russell's Boston Celtics. They were one of the greatest assemblages of talent the sport had ever known. Lott studied the history of football. He cared about it, and hoped that one day he would find his own special place in it. By the time his Hall of Fame career was done fourteen years later, Lott would be known as one of the most devastating hitters in pro football and would accumulate more than 1,100 tackles, sixty-three interceptions, and ten Pro Bowl appearances. He was acutely observant, on the field and off. He noticed small details. As a rookie at Three Rivers Stadium, he looked across the field and saw Greene, Lambert, Blount, Harris, and Donnie Shell. He noticed the way they had entered through the tunnel, and how they carried themselves on the field, with a certain pride and swagger. On television he'd noticed the Steelers' camaraderie, it was unmistakable, and he'd seen the Chief, "the old man with the cigar hugging those guys." Lott even studied the Chief's hugs. "I got that sense of him letting his guys in," Lott said, "just in how he held them." Nearly awestruck by the Steelers' presence, Lott conjured the notion of royalty. He thought about how British subjects, upon meeting their queen or prince, bowed in their honor. Standing on the turf at Three Rivers, he nearly felt as if he ought to bow in the direction of the Steelers' sideline. He decided that, in the pantheon of pro football, *The Packers created the foundation, and the Steelers created the pillars.* The 49ers, young and ascendant, defeated the Steelers 17–14 that day, and their victory transformed the way they were perceived in the NFL and the way they perceived themselves. It validated who they were, especially for Joe Montana, who hailed from western Pennsylvania, and for team owner Eddie DeBartolo, an Ohioan. The 49ers would win their first Super Bowl that season.

Lott and three teammates were off to Hawaii for the Pro Bowl, and there found themselves in esteemed football company, living a dream. It was all too much for a rookie to process. As Lott sat at a hotel bar with 49ers receiver Dwight Clark, small pineapples and plastic umbrellas in their tropical drinks, a waitress placed two more drinks on their table. "Where did these come from?" Lott asked. With a wave of her hand, the waitress said, "From those guys over there." Lott looked at a far table and saw several Steelers: Lambert, Ham, Donnie Shell, and Webster. To Lott this was a great and humbling gesture, four-time Super Bowl champions welcoming first-timers to their club, the 1970s passing a baton to the 1980s. "My first encounter with true greatness," Lott called it. This was how champions were supposed to act, Lott decided. He made eye contact with Lambert and nodded to him, an understated way to thank the Steelers, and for more than just the drinks. Lott felt almost like royalty when the great Lambert nodded back.

CHAPTER 16

MEAN JOE

FOR THIRTY-FIVE THOUSAND DOLLARS, Mean Joe Greene became an actor for a few days. He drove to an old municipal football stadium in Mount Vernon, New York, in May 1979 to film a Coca-Cola commercial that would change the way he was perceived in ways he couldn't have imagined.

Greene got the part for a good reason. A copywriter for the McCann Erickson advertising agency, Penny Hawkey, had worked on an array of campaigns for L'Oréal, Tab ("A Beautiful Drink for Beautiful People"), Gillette, and the New York Racing Association. Recent Coke commercials—happy-pappy people on a beach, turning sideways into the sunset, drinking Coca-Cola, and serenaded by great tunes ("I'd Like to Buy the World a Coke")—were effective, lovely, and memorable. In this Coca-Cola commercial, though, Hawkey aspired to create on camera what none of those ads ever did, a relationship using dialogue. Through multiple drafts, she imagined a child making a grand gesture by offering a Coca-Cola to a downcast superstar, thus reviving him. This was David and Goliath stuff, classic plot development, a little guy helping a big guy. Her motif became football, and the Coca-Cola Company suggested using Terry Bradshaw as the superstar. But as the conversations at McCann Erickson and the Coca-Cola Company deepened, Hawkey would say, "we realized there would be more empathy and more surprise and more delight and more contrast and shock with the great big sort of threatening presence of Mean Joe Greene."

Greene was apprehensive as the film shoot approached because Coke was a famous worldwide brand, and, "well, heck, I'm a ballplayer, not an actor." On the set in Mount Vernon, he met his nine-year-old support-ing actor, Tommy Okon. He expected filming to take only half a day, but it lasted three full days. For each take, Greene downed a bottle of Coke, more than twenty bottles in a single day, and because his hands were un-usually large, McCann Erickson had bigger bottles specially made for the commercial. Because of lighting problems and the boy's botched lines, the commercial required 128 takes. Greene's stomach grew bloated, he belched several times on camera, and each time he did, Okon laughed and said, "You fumbled!" Greene might have spat the mouthful of Coke into a bucket provided for that purpose, but his manners wouldn't allow that. "I'm endorsing this product," he recalled, "so that didn't seem right."

Hawkey watched Greene on the set with a mixture of satisfaction and awe. "Mean Joe had this amazing aura about him," she said. The com-mercial's pairing of a small white boy and a black man was unusual for its time, though Hawkey said "the only thing about it that was racial was the little boy was sort of pale by contrast to the beautiful, robust, giant of a black man who was extraordinarily kind and articulate." When finally they'd gotten their performances just right—Greene guzzled a Coke, and as a show of gratitude, called out to Okon, "Hey, kid, catch!" and flung his jersey into the boy's arms—Hawkey felt "that little tiny transformation that had been at the heart of the Coke brand since it was created."

Greene burped his way back to Pittsburgh. He got the impression the commercial must have been good because after it was shown to Coca-Cola bottlers, he received a case of champagne at home. "And it wasn't Dom Pérignon," he said, "but one slightly *above* Dom Pérignon." He heard that the bottlers had responded to his commercial with a standing ovation.

The ad aired for the first time during the baseball playoffs that Octo-ber. The next day, Greene walked into the Steelers' locker room and team-mates applauded, slapping him on the back, proud of his acting work, though needling him still. "*'Hey, kid!'*" Dwight White teased, and then said, "Yeah, right . . ."

The commercial won a Clio award, advertising's Oscar, and Greene won a Clio for best actor. The public response overwhelmed Coke.

"Women just fell for it," Hawkey said, especially mothers. African Americans cheered, too, for the integration of a black athlete into an advertising campaign for a famous brand.

That little tiny transformation worked for Greene, too. Suddenly fans seemed less fearful about approaching him. He saw it, felt it. "Little old ladies," Greene said with surprise, "saying, 'Hi, Mean Joe!'" After a practice for the 1980 Pro Bowl in Hawaii, Greene stood beside Earl Campbell and other AFC running backs and quarterbacks, "the glamour guys, the guys who score touchdowns," and a herd of kids rushed onto the field right past them on their way to Greene. They asked him to toss his jersey their way. In TV commercials years before, Joe Namath had famously endorsed panty hose and Noxzema shaving cream (with Farrah Fawcett lathering his face), and in the process burnished his reputation as a ladies' man. But no athlete's persona was so profoundly transformed by a commercial as Mean Joe Greene's, and no one could have played the role, with that look and that presence, as well as Mean Joe himself. Franco Harris once said about Greene as a player, "He's just the ultimate because he brings the whole package, the mental attitude, the physical attitude, the joy of it, the sorrow of it. He just brings it, brings it all." That's what Hawkey felt on the set: Greene bringing the power and charm of his personality, the intimidation and sensitivity, bringing it all, to the camera.

In a parade through the streets of Canton in 1987 when Greene became the first player from the 1970s Steelers inducted into the Pro Football Hall of Fame, kids and adults ran up to his car to hand him bottles and cans of Coke. Some sports stars might have brushed them off. In 1960, baseball's Ted Williams homered at Fenway Park in the last at-bat of his career, and fans urged him to step from the dugout to acknowledge their cheers, but he refused. Novelist John Updike was there and later wrote, "Gods do not answer letters." But Mean Joe Greene, a football god, accepted his letters at the Hall of Fame parade—Coke bottles and cans— and he acknowledged them all, smiling broadly, fully transformed. It was, he said, "something special."

On a bright winter day near Dallas in 2011, Mean Joe's physique fills the front doorframe of his fine two-story brick home in a gated golf community about twenty minutes from Dallas/Fort Worth International Airport. Married for more than forty years, longest among the 1970s Steelers, Joe and Agnes Greene were always Texas. "Good afternoon," Agnes says, stepping forward to greet me in her black Steelers T-shirt. Mean Joe wears a black, zipper-down shirt, too-loose jeans that occasionally require him to hitch up, and comfortable slippers. He leads me into the family room beside the kitchen, where he falls back comfortably into a leather couch. The room, designed in soft tones, has a warm, lived-in family feeling. Photos on the walls and on shelves feature their three children and seven grandchildren, plus a few of Joe with Franco Harris. Greene adores his grandkids—seven more chances, he says, to become an active dad. "I think that I missed my three kids [growing up]," he says with regret. "Agnes was with them a great deal more than I was."

At sixty-five, Greene, in conversation, is engaged and engaging, his eyes alight. He gives himself fully to our conversation for more than four hours, energized by talking about the 1970s Steelers. A big man still, he carries his weight well and moves through the room with little noticeable effect from a life in football. Greene underwent hip replacement surgery in 2006 and admits to occasional pain in his back, shoulder, and neck. But he points out that some friends his age have endured worse physical troubles and they never played a day of pro football. He says he has had no troubles with his knees, a remarkable feat given how often NFL players sneaked from behind and cut down the knees of opposing linemen. "Yeah," Greene tells me, "but usually they do that when they think there is no risk"—of retribution, he means.

In 2010, NFL Films created a list of the greatest one hundred players in pro football history. "You know your number on that list?" I ask. "Thirteen," Greene answers without hesitation, and he doesn't sound happy about it. Four of the 1970s Steelers joined him on this all-time list: Lambert (29), Blount (44), Bradshaw (50), and Webster (68). Then, as if to question the list itself, he says, "I don't think *anybody* was better than Jim Brown." Brown ranked second on the NFL Films list behind Jerry Rice. "Yeah, a wide receiver," Greene says, doubt in his voice. "Why do you say it that way?" I ask. "I probably said it the way I meant it," Greene replies. "That's not disrespect to the person, for sure. It's more about the position." Greene holds his hands wide apart. "They [wide receivers] are out there—*way out there.*" He moves his hands close together, his palms nearly touching. "And the ball is in *here.*"

It's always difficult, regardless of the sport, to watch the gradual demise of the great ones. They get hurt. They grow old. They lose a step. Long before the Coke commercial, the perception of Greene as a player had begun to change. He wasn't as dominant as before. By 1975, his seventh season, he could no longer alter the course of a game by himself. A nerve problem in his neck and shoulder persisted, causing weakness in his left side. At times he seemed to be playing with only one arm. It pained Art Jr. to see Greene's decline. He told the Chief that Greene played "team defense," and the Chief, never wanting to hear an unkind word about Greene, embraced that phrase and repeated it often, and each time he did Art Jr. thought, *That's beyond Joe now, too,* but instead he said, "You're right, Dad. Joe plays team defense." Injury-free until 1975, Greene said, "I had no respect for anyone's ability then because I had so much regard for my own. . . . [But] it was like I had been running wild for all those years and someone said, 'Hmmm, let's humble this boy.' " Greene didn't want sympathy. He continued to make the Pro Bowl, ten times in all, a few on reputation alone. At the line of scrimmage he funneled plays now to teammates.

When Andy Russell retired after the 1976 season, Noll elevated Greene to defensive captain. Greene took his new role, as he took all things, seriously. Sportswriters went to him at nearly every turn now, surrounding his locker after games. In all ways Greene led. Once, after an exuberant Gary Dunn sacked Joe Namath, Greene pulled him aside after the game and advised, "Hey, Gary, we don't hit Joe that way. Just put him down. Don't hurt him." At another moment, a troublesome Steeler rookie had rudely treated Berlin and the men working in the equipment room. Sitting in a closed bathroom stall, Berlin heard Greene's threatening voice. Berlin opened the door of the stall slightly and, peeking out, saw that Greene had the troublesome rookie up against the wall, his hands at the rookie's throat. "You don't talk that way to those people! They are important to us!" Greene said. Mean Joe gave the rookie three choices: "Number one, you go in and apologize to them. Number two, you pack your bags and get the hell out of here. Or number three, I kick the shit out of you." The rookie offered his apologies to Berlin and the equipment men.

He still had his mean moments. Once, in 1977, he railed against NFL officials, saying, "If I get half a chance, I'll punch one of them out." In a skirmish against the Browns in 1977, he kicked Cleveland tackle Bob McKay in the groin and stomach, "my most embarrassing moment," Greene said later. In a 20–17 defeat to the rival Oilers in 1979, Houston lined up with only seconds to play near the Steelers' goal line, the victory already in hand. Greene pointed angrily across the line of scrimmage at quarterback Dan Pastorini. "If you come into this end zone, I'll beat the crap out of you!" he warned. "I'm gonna kill you!" Pastorini answered, "Joe, I'm going to fall on the ball! I swear to God!" Pastorini took the snap and dropped to his knee, ending the play and game. Afterward Greene laughed and told him, "I knew you weren't going to do it." Pastorini, relieved, said, "Man, don't ever do that to me again. You scared the hell out of me."

The Steelers finished out of the playoffs during Greene's last two seasons, 8-8 in 1980 and 9-7 in 1981. The phrase "One for the Thumb in '81," an allusion to winning a fifth Super Bowl ring, was Greene's creation, his wish unfulfilled. Greene called Gordon to his Houston hotel room on the morning of December 20, 1981. "I'm retiring," Greene told the team publicist. Gordon replied, "It's up to you, Joe." In the Astrodome that day, with both teams out of the playoffs, the thirty-five-year-old Greene played his 181st regular-season game. He became wistful as he took in the scene one last time. He realized this game carried no real meaning other than being his last. Greene thought, *Can you imagine playing games like this your whole career? What a sad statement that would be.*

At the press conference announcing his retirement, Greene sat beside Agnes, the Chief, Dan, and Noll. "I'm a non-combatant now," Greene said. Noll told reporters, "There will never be another Joe Greene." A reporter asked Greene how he wanted to be remembered. "What is this, a wake?" Greene said. "Just remember Joe being a good football player," he said, "and not really mean."

He struggled to find his life's work. He opened two restaurants in Texas, and then a third, but they failed. CBS hired him as a commentator on NFL games, but that lasted for only a year. He did not finish his degree at North Texas State. "I tried, but my heart wasn't in it," Greene said, though much later he became a member of the school's board of regents. He trained in insurance, got his real estate license in Texas, but his heart wasn't in those professions, either. In 1987, his future uncertain, Noll and the Steelers brought Greene back as defensive line coach. With his emotions, he captured the attention of his Steeler players. He slammed his headphones into the turf during games and wouldn't talk to his players for a series or more. During the week he ejected them from defensive line meetings. "[Joe] used to absolutely terrify us," Steeler nose tackle Gerald Williams once said, adding, "This is before he realized that we weren't all Joe Greene." No, Greene says to that charge, it wasn't that. He simply felt that they exhibited a lack of effort. "Over the years, I began to understand what having the right attitude meant. It meant everything to me," Greene says. "That was the separation for me. That allowed me to play."

Dan interviewed Greene but did not hire him as the Steelers' head coach to replace the retiring Noll after the 1991 season. Bill Cowher got the job. That wounded Greene's immense pride, but later he said he understood that as a defensive line coach for four years he'd never coached more than eight or so players during a season, and he figured that if he coached fifty-three players and more, and dealt each day with the media, he'd explode more often than Chicago Bears coach Mike Ditka ever did. Greene moved on to Miami as an assistant coach for Don Shula. When Shula retired in 1995, Greene moved to the Arizona Cardinals for eight years to coach the defensive line for Coach Dennis Green. His defensive linemen lived in fear of him and called him Dante's Peak, after the 1997 disaster movie about an erupting volcano. As a coach, Greene tried to emulate Chuck Noll in the way he taught his men to be professionals. But Joe Greene couldn't be Chuck Noll, any more than Chuck Noll could be Joe Greene.

The Steelers brought the fifty-eight-year-old Greene back into the fold in 2004 as a special assistant for pro and college personnel, and he remained there, in a warm black-and-gold embrace, scouting, advising, and simply being Joe Greene, until he retired, after twenty-seven years with the franchise, in May 2013. When he had arrived on college campuses to scout, coaches often asked him to address their teams. "Joe still has that effect of grounding people in what we are about," Art Jr. said. "He still brings that sense that we are something special."

He grew to love Pittsburgh and its people. "This is an *oooold* town. It's a workingman's town," he tells me as we sit in the bar of the William Penn Hotel one night, Greene sipping Pellegrino. "There are sections in this town where you can find some of the poorest people, and there are sections you can go in and find some of the richest people, and they all have one thing in common: they love the Pittsburgh Steelers. One of the best feelings I have is when I can walk down the street in Pittsburgh and someone can say, 'Hey, Joe!' They don't want to ask for an autograph, they don't want to say anything other than, 'Hey, Joe!' And that's good. Those are my favorite people."

The Steelers now refer to the Super Bowls won during the 1970s as *the early four* since the team won two more, in 2006 and 2009. It is only fitting that of all the men who played for the Steelers during the days of empire the only one with six Super Bowl rings is Joe Greene.

The members of the Steel Curtain front four got another chance to be together more than a decade after they'd broken up. They joined forces in the early 1990s on the card show/sports memorabilia circuit, signing autographs and posing for photos with fans, each man sometimes earning $10,000 or more for appearing. Individually their names still carried strong recognition, but together as the famed Pittsburgh Steelers Steel Curtain, they drew even bigger crowds.

Mean Joe, Fats, Mad Dog, and Hollywood Bags met several times each year at signings in convention centers and hotel ballrooms in Colorado; Florida; Virginia; Chicago; Cleveland; Edison, New Jersey; Los Angeles; and San Diego. They shared breakfasts and dinners in each city, and there was joy in being together again, telling old stories and old jokes, and in watching Fats eat, as Greenwood said, "a steak, two steaks, and then everything on the table." Once he became ordained as a minister in 2006, Fats prayed for the group at each meal they shared. "I'm gonna pray for you, Greene," he said. "You go ahead and pray for me, then, Ernie," Mean Joe answered. They talked about their kids, Greene talked about his NFL coaching and scouting, Fats talked about Jesus, and in his hotel room worked on his sermons. Mad Dog discussed the business at hand, their group signings. White had good business sense and an ability to pull them together. He discussed future possibilities for the group, money to be earned.

They assumed their old roles, and inevitably old tensions cropped up, usually between Greene and Holmes. "Ernie was just *different people*," Greenwood said. "Joe was always trying to get things right, as they should be. Ernie didn't want to listen. And Dwight would say, 'Screw it,' and get out of there."

The lives of Mean Joe, Mad Dog, and Hollywood Bags had been relatively straight lines: Greene as a football lifer; White in the investment business in Pittsburgh and actively involved in his city's philanthropic life (he and his wife, Karen, helped raise more than $36 million as cochairs of a capital campaign for the August Wilson Center for African American Culture in Pittsburgh); and Greenwood running an electrical supplies business, with a storefront set up in nearby Carnegie.

"I happen to think that the ultimate test is not to play football, but to be something after football," White said. "It's a real challenge to wipe out that image, that stereotype." Perhaps because he had managed to do this successfully, White added, "I'm more impressed with Wall Street than Three Rivers Stadium."

Holmes's life continued to be as colorful and dramatic as his NFL career. He was traded to Tampa Bay for two lowly draft picks before the 1978 season, Noll explaining, "Ernie is very much like Pittsburgh—much better than its reputation," and then, in short order, his football career was at an end. For a time he moved out west, to California. He became a wrestler and shaved his hair again into the shape of an arrowhead. He made an appearance in WrestleMania 2. He worked as a bodyguard; when the Reverend Jesse Jackson came to Jasper, Texas, in the summer of 1998 to officiate at the funeral of James Byrd, a black man dragged to his death along an asphalt road from the back of a pickup truck by three white men, Holmes, seemingly as immovable as a mountain, stood beside the Reverend Jackson. Holmes also became a bit actor, seen in an episode of television's *The A-Team* and on the big screen as a bouncer in the horror movie *Fright Night*. In that film a vampire grabs Holmes by the neck and throws him across the floor, a scene that, back in Texas, reportedly made

his ex-wife cheer. Near his small East Texas ranch in Wiergate, he opened a nightclub known locally as the Yellow Banana. His club was little more than a roadside shack with thin walls, a strobe-lit dance floor, and a lengthy bar, and painted bright yellow on the outside; ergo, the Yellow Banana.

Later Holmes became a 688-pound Baptist minister. "That's what he told me on the phone," Greenwood said. "He said he weighed 'six-eight-eight.' " Greenwood didn't believe it until he saw Holmes. Fats developed troubles with his legs, had a knee replaced, and walked with a cane. Later, he told Greene, he lost 250 pounds, the majority of that after gastric bypass surgery.

"It shocked me, too," Roderick "Byron" Holmes said when he learned that Ernie Holmes, his father, was becoming a minister. Byron Holmes earned a doctorate as a mathematician and became an assistant professor of mathematical sciences at Texas Southern, his father's alma mater. Raised by his mother (Holmes's first wife), Byron Holmes likened his father's complexity to that of the late rapper Tupac Shakur: "It's like Biggie [Smalls] said in the movie *Notorious*, 'You ask ten people about Tupac and you get ten different answers.' " Ernie Holmes was like that, his son said. "He had his crazy moments," Byron Holmes said with a laugh. "But that same zeal he had toward football he showed toward the church. He talked about Jesus all the time."

Holmes preached sermons in small churches across Texas. Byron Holmes sent me a CD of one of his father's sermons. On it, the Reverend Ernie Holmes's voice explodes from the pulpit, and a small congregation calls back to him in the tradition of the Southern Baptist black church. He cites biblical passages and defining moments in his life, including that day in March 1973 when he fired at trucks on an Ohio highway and law enforcement chased him. He blew out a tire on his Cadillac, crashed, threw one gun out the window, grabbed another and some shells, ran through a field, and jumped a fence. Says the preacher, his voice strong and resonant:

> So I went out and set up camp to do battle with them . . . and then all the sudden this little kid called me and he said, "I'm cold." I took my jacket off. I put it on him. . . . This helicopter flew over and I shot that

helicopter. Now, look . . . I'm telling you the truth. I ran after I shot that helicopter, through some briar. . . . And when I dove, a marksman shot at my head. . . . I put that barrel underneath my chin and rolled back and I shot at that marksman. . . . [But] the gun jammed. I threw the gun away and I sat [and called out], "Tell them to stop shootings." . . . Then, all the sudden, I felt this guy [and he said], "Put your hands behind your back." There was a state trooper standing behind me. And he said, "There are another fifteen men looking at you with twelve-gauge shotguns," [and they were] pointing at the middle of my back. He asks, "Who else is out here with you?" I said, "That little boy." He said, "What little boy?" I said, "That little boy that put my jacket on." They went over there. He says he sees my jacket but there ain't no little boy. . . . Thank you, Jesus. The jacket was on this live oak tree with the limb sticking out. I said, "Thank you, Jesus. Thank you, Lord. You saved me." They said, "How did he look?" I said, "I couldn't tell you how he looked. The sun was so bright until I could not see his face but I put that jacket on him." And that is the godforsaken truth. They wouldn't put that in the paper. Because they ain't gonna let you know how God saved [me]. . . . They ain't gonna let you know that when you need somebody, you just say, "Jesus, help me!"

In his sermon, Holmes talks about his Steeler teammates, too. "We loved each other," he says.

"YEAH!" a man in church calls back.

"And that bond that you made," the Reverend Holmes says, "is a bond between soldiers."

"He loved those guys," Byron Holmes tells me as we drive through East Texas, referring to the other members of the front four. "He talked about them all the time."

On January 18, 2008, a Friday morning, Greene's home phone rang in Texas, Dan Rooney on the line, saying, "Joe, I've got bad news for you. Ernie had a car accident and he's gone." On a dark night near Beaumont, Texas, Holmes's SUV suddenly had bolted from the road, careened into a ditch, and rolled over several times, killing him at age fifty-nine. Holmes had complained to family members recently about chest pains, and they were left to wonder if he had suffered a heart attack while driving alone in the night.

Pittsburgh Steelers were dying at an alarming rate. In July 2006, the *Los Angeles Times* reported that of the seventy-seven NFL players from the 1970s and 1980s who had died since 2000, sixteen—more than one in five—were Steelers. "I like us to have records," Franco Harris told me, "but I don't want *that* record. That's very disturbing." Of the sixteen, ten were from the 1970s empire—Ernie Holmes became the eleventh—and all died before age sixty. The old whispers of rampant steroid use on those Steelers Super Bowl teams resurfaced. But Stallworth brushed those away. "Fate" was his explanation for the deaths. Stallworth noted the widely varied causes and circumstances of the deaths. A few died from disease: Ron Shanklin at fifty-four from colon cancer, guard Jim Clack at fifty-eight from throat cancer, and receiver Theo Bell at fifty-two from scleroderma and kidney disease. Defensive backs Ray Oldham and Dave Brown, single-season Steelers, died from heart attacks. The Old Ranger, Ray Mansfield, a bad-bodied center, had died even earlier, in 1996, from a massive heart attack while hiking in the Grand Canyon with his son. Mansfield, fifty-six, was buried with a cigar in hand. "If you saw Ranger's body, you knew," Stallworth said with a laugh, referring to possible steroid use. "Not him."

Mean Joe, Mad Dog, and Hollywood Bags sat together at the funeral for Fats in a high school gym that overflowed with more than five hundred mourners, an old-fashioned home-going that lasted four hours and more. As the hearse carrying Holmes passed through the streets of Jasper, local police officers removed their hats, and placed their hands over their hearts. Mel Blount and J. T. Thomas attended the funeral, too, and so did Art Rooney II, Dan's son, the Steelers' president. In the front row, Greene, White, Greenwood, Thomas, and Blount sat together in folding chairs, so closely bunched their knees touched, and that closeness gave Thomas a heightened sense of comfort.

"You can see a person grow up," Greenwood said, "and go from one extreme to another extreme. The transformation Ernie made, there was seriousness to it." Greene spoke at the funeral, though no one had told him in advance, so he hadn't prepared any comments. He spoke briefly, from the heart, about the brotherhood of the Steel Curtain front four.

Later he tells me, "I don't do funerals real well. I'm an emotional person, you know? I care about people more than I let them know." He sat in the gymnasium that day, head bowed, "just reminiscing about Ernie, about all of us. We won't see him again. I'm sad for his family. I'm sad for myself."

White returned to Pittsburgh from that funeral a changed man, a new and deep spiritualism flowing through him like music. He heard a church song at Holmes's funeral, "I'm Just a Nobody Trying to Tell Everybody About Somebody Who Can Save Anybody" by Lee Williams and the Spiritual QCs. It affected him, played through his thoughts, and often in his car, too, on a CD. Greene noticed a change in White; they all did. "I get it now," White told his wife, Karen. "I get this whole thing about life."

On his trips to Pittsburgh, Greene nearly always paid visits to Mad Dog's house. Together they grilled steaks, smoked Excalibur No. 1 cigars, had a few drinks, and talked about the past, and now they reminisced about Fats as well. They knew it wouldn't be the same at card shows with the Steel Curtain front *three*. White broached the idea of leaving a vacant chair at future signings to honor Fats, or perhaps setting aside money to give to Fats's church or Texas Southern or his children. They never got the chance to implement these ideas.

Several months later, White underwent lower back surgery for a herniated disc. Greene phoned him from Texas a few days later to ask, "How you doin'?" Recuperating at home, White growled that he felt poorly and said, "Man, I've got to apologize. I can't talk to you. I've got to go." Greene went off to a scouting event, where he received a call later from Greenwood. "Dwight's back in the hospital," Greenwood said, "and it's not looking good."

Doctors diagnosed White with a pulmonary embolism, a blood clot in the arteries of his lung. Greenwood sat at White's bedside in the intensive care unit of a Pittsburgh hospital. "Hooomes," White told him, dragging out the syllable, "I'm in a lot of pain." White always called him Home Boy or Homes or Hollywood Bags or H.B., but to Greenwood this sounded more dire than ever before, and it scared him. As White groaned, and faded into and out of awareness, Greenwood encouraged his old teammate, kept talking softly to him, to be sure he felt his presence. A nurse appeared. "Can't you give him something," Greenwood pleaded in a whisper, "for the pain?" She did, and White chattered on for some time, the meaning of his words not entirely clear, until finally he eased quietly into his medication. Greenwood waited another ten minutes, watching over him, and then left.

Franco Harris became Greene's information point man. Harris and his wife, Dana, as great friends of the Whites, visited the hospital daily. In the ensuing days there was hope that White's condition might stabilize. Harris phoned Greene to say that doctors were about to remove White from a ventilator. *Was it just a few hours later that Harris called back?* It was, and his voice was pale and hollow as he told Greene, "He didn't make it." Dwight White was dead at fifty-eight, the twelfth member of the 1970s Steelers Super Bowl teams to die before sixty.

Stunned, Greene phoned Karen White and wept. In time his sadness turned to anger. How could this have happened? At Ernie Holmes's funeral, Thomas had observed the new spiritual electricity in White. "Joe, you can be angry, but the Lord's will is the Lord's will," Thomas said. "Dwight was ready." But Mean Joe was not. He asked Thomas, "Do you think Dwight got in?" Thomas didn't understand the question, so Greene clarified, "Did he get his act together with God?" Thomas said softly, "I don't know."

More than a thousand people filled the church in Pittsburgh for White's funeral—bankers, lawyers, politicians, and many former Steeler teammates, a testament to a full life. Governor Ed Rendell spoke, and so did Greene. Delivering his second Steel Curtain eulogy in five months, Mean Joe spoke of his friendship with Mad Dog, just two ornery Texas guys, and about how his kids adored Uncle Dwight. White's funeral was a respectful farewell, with less of the overheated emotion that charged Holmes's funeral. "I guess there is a Texas way of doing things," Greenwood said, "and a Pennsylvania way of doing things." At one point during the funeral, Thomas smiled and whispered to Greene, "Dwight got in," the notion of heaven comforting to both.

Outside the church, Greene and Greenwood embraced. They felt more vulnerable than ever before. "We were the first to come," Greenwood told him, "and we're the last standing." Much later, Karen White said, "Dwight's death is really tough on Joe. He even has trouble talking to me. And I know what it is. He calls me and cries. He loved Dwight—and Dwight loved him—and he misses him."

✦ ✦ ✦

May 2009: Joe and Agnes Greene stepped from a taxi in front of the White House. The Steelers had won Super Bowl XLIII over Arizona 27–23 three months earlier, and now the team came to meet President Barack Obama. The Greenes traveled apart from the team, and at the front gate they discovered that no one had left their names with security. Not a good start. Finally, they were allowed into the Rose Garden with other Steeler staff and family members. There they saw and embraced Karen White. Greene had missed the Steelers-Pirates ceremony with President Jimmy Carter twenty-nine years before. Agnes convinced him not to miss this one. Greene was brought inside the White House, where current Steeler players and coaches began to line up in rows for a photo op with the president. Greene brought his camera, took pictures, and then Obama appeared, jaunty and well pleased, calling out to the team, "Hey, guys, what's up?" Obama told the Steelers that he'd grown up in Hawaii without a local football team to cheer and during the 1970s he fell in with the Pittsburgh Steelers' dynasty "led by Terry Bradshaw, Franco Harris, the Steel Curtain, and Mean Joe Greene." At the mention of the last name a murmur passed through the players, one finally saying, "Mr. President, Joe Greene is right there." Greene, in a blue suit and blue tie, stepped forward. Obama smiled and shook his hand heartily. It was all very informal. Greene told Obama that he was proud of him and that he'd been emotional the night Obama was elected president. It was, he knew, a watershed in American race history. About Obama, Greene said, "I watched him during the [2008] campaign and if I put myself in his shoes I saw many times where I would've gotten angry. And he didn't. I definitely would've gotten angry with Sarah Palin. My goodness!"

That the president of the United States knew his name, and had rooted for him long ago, didn't surprise Greene. Once, he tells me, he'd been in a men's room in Florida, and a Pittsburgh Steeler fan entered and wanted to shake his hand and take his picture. "While I'm in the men's room!" Greene says. He makes a larger point. "Pittsburgh Steelers fans are all over the place. Including the White House." He shrugs. "Maybe I expected it."

✦ ✦ ✦

"Do you take sugar?" Agnes Greene asks. She pours coffee and returns to the living room recliner, a comforter warming her. I had brought a DVD of the 1974 AFC title game against Oakland, and now Mean Joe, TV remote in hand, rises from the couch to point out blocking schemes on the screen. I mention that, in this game, he kicked Jim Otto between his legs. "Joe would never do that! NEVER!" Agnes says, "and especially to somebody like Jim." Mean Joe stares at the screen, saying nothing.

He recalls his recent conversation with a woman at a banquet. She had asked him what he thought about football now. "I told her, the problem with a lot of people who play this game is that they think it's a game. It's not a game. It's war, without the bullets. I mean, it is a fight all the way through. You've got to go in with the mind-set that you are going to beat the crap out of those guys. If you are not thinking that way, you are probably going to come up on the short end of the stick. It's a mind-set. You are going out there to win the game, and your mind-set is that you are trying to hurt them. You are trying to hurt them physically, mentally, and emotionally. You are trying to take away their will—within the rules—if they allow you to."

Next we watch a DVD of the Steelers' Super Bowl IX victory over Minnesota. Somehow, Greene says, he has never seen film of this game. Seeing himself young again on the screen, in his physical prime, and destroying the Vikings' offensive line surprises and delights him. With a sparkle in his eyes, he acts like a youngster, whooping and cheering certain plays. It all comes back to him, and he likes what he sees, especially when number 75 runs onto the field before the game. "See that!" Greene says. "I never ran onto the field with my finger up, 'number one.' This was the only time I ever did that." And then he says, as if talking to the younger version of himself on the screen, "Go get 'em! FIRED UP!

"That's one of the joys of being on a good team and winning championships," Mean Joe tells me. "It never gets old. I can revisit them and feel really, really good about them. Just like it was yesterday. The guys that you do it with are very, very special. You can't take it away."

When Holmes makes a jarring tackle early in the game, Greene shouts happily from the couch, "ERNIE!" and on TV the broadcaster Al DeRogatis marvels, "We're seeing just beautiful defense."

Greene gets up, puts the DVD on Pause, and says, "I've got to go to the little boys' room." When he is gone, Agnes says, "Joe remembers every play." In a few moments he returns, and on the screen Glen Edwards delivers his two-forearm shot to the chinstrap of Viking receiver John Gilliam, and Blount makes the goal-line interception. "HOOOO!" Agnes howls, flinching at the blow. Mean Joe says simply, "The Chobee Kid!"

Mean Joe: "Now this shot right here [by Edwards], guess what? Today that is a penalty! That's terrible. That's a big play for us. Imagine what would've happened if they had called a penalty on that!"

He emphasizes the point: "I can understand trying to change some of the rules that directly affect concussions and head injuries. But you can't take football out of football. . . . When the body is elongated and you have a clear target, and you choose to hit the man high in the head, *that* is enforceable. That's right [to ban such a hit]. That's fair. But some of this other stuff? It's not.

"Now, the hypocrisy in all of this is that hits to the head—between the tackles—happen on every play, and are more violent between offensive linemen and defensive linemen, and between linebackers and running backs. So how are we going to avoid those? We can't unless we change the game."

Greene believes he might have suffered one concussion as an NFL player, in Super Bowl XIII, when Dallas's pulling guard Burton Lawless hit him in the chin. Greene remained in the game, though he wasn't clearheaded for at least two defensive series. He says the NFL had multiple motives in creating more protective rules in today's game: "What they are trying to do—well, first of all, they are trying to cover their asses from these lawsuits. That's the bottom line." Agnes cautions him to be careful what he says, but Joe holds his ground: "If I can't say that— That's what I feel. I believe that."

On the screen, Rozelle hands the Vince Lombardi Trophy to the Chief in an emotional scene. From the couch, Mean Joe begins to chant: "Here we go, Steelers, here we go!" Then Franco Harris sits beside broadcaster Charlie Jones for a postgame interview. "That," Mean Joe says, pointing at number 32, "is a special young man there." Bradshaw appears, and Jones asks him about the Super Bowl week criticism of his intelligence. "No one on the team EVER felt that Terry was a dumb guy," Greene says from the couch. "History will tell you that he is far from that, right?"

Suddenly, Mean Joe Greene's eyes grow wide. "Oh, boy! Where did you get THAT from?" He sees himself on the screen sitting on a stool next to Charlie Jones and wearing a black-and-gold ski cap. Greene is twenty-nine years old on the TV screen, one of the fiercest players in the game's history. His postgame smile is broad and authentic. "In my wildest dreams I didn't think I would get this big a charge out of this," he tells Jones. "It's even bigger than I thought it would be."

I ask, "Joe, what do you see—and feel—as you look at yourself at Super Bowl IX all these years later?"

"Well, I look a lot younger, that's for sure. And I like that number seventy-five in white," he says. "My enthusiasm is real. That was the greatest feeling I ever had other than getting married and having kids. . . . I enjoyed that stretch of football because it was so new, and our determination was right where it needed to be."

Returning to the room just then, and seeing her young husband on the screen, Agnes says, "Who is THAT young man? Is that my Billy Dee Williams?"

She giggles and Mean Joe rubs his gray-flecked beard as he studies the screen. "Why did I put that stocking cap on? I'm not a stocking cap guy. My hair must've been in pretty poor shape."

CHAPTER 17

BRAD

"LISTEN," TERRY BRADSHAW SAYS, AND he holds up his index finger as if to push back against history, "you are the last one I am going to talk with about this stuff."

I know that isn't true. He would talk about it again and probably many times because that is who Terry Bradshaw is. He is a talker. He is a Hall of Famer, a sportscaster, an *entertainer* who talks about football, the Steelers, and himself for a living. Still, whenever the subject turns to his relationship with the Steelers and Noll—especially Noll as the coach who never gave him the affection or positive reinforcement that he craved and who once suggested that maybe it was time for the first quarterback ever to win four Super Bowls to get on with his life's work—I watch Bradshaw suffer a chemical reaction. He says, "It's like I told you on the phone, this stuff is *buried*. I move on. I have to. I've got children. I've got jobs. I've got responsibilities. I keep being drug back into the past after I've already healed certain wounds."

Thirty years ago I interviewed him in his training camp dormitory room in Latrobe, and he was frisky and fun. "Have I changed?" he asks.

His familiar face has yielded to the passing years, the lines deeper around his eyes and mouth, his baldness beyond disguise with silly blond hairpieces, the chin still dimpled and the eyes an iridescent aqua blue. He thwacks my shoulder with the back of his hand a few times during the conversation, as if to say, "Know what I mean?" He remains an energetic interview, I tell him. "That's why the writers always used to say, 'Go talk to Brad,' " he says. "Ten guys would talk to me, and ask me the same question, and they'd get ten different answers! I wanted everybody to have a scoop. Nothin' wrong with that."

For Bradshaw an interview remains a performance, and he gives himself to his role completely. He vibrates energy. There is drama in his Steelers story, a bittersweet narrative as he tells it. Whereas his teammates look back and see the gleam of their four Super Bowl rings, Bradshaw sees something different—the same four rings, only with a more complicated resonance and perhaps some rust. His teammates live with a warm after-glow, while Bradshaw suffers from something like post-traumatic stress disorder. But to listen closely to Bradshaw's old stories is also to hear his joy, and the purity of his laughter, as he tells of Stallworth's high-pitched voice, and his times in the postgame sauna with Lambert ("Lambert was a badass. Lambert was the best"), and the way the Chief always told him everything would be fine (*"Hey, you're the best!"*), and of the irrepressible Hanratty as his roommate. He laughs so hard telling these stories that his body shakes, and he seems young again.

I tell him that, for most of his teammates, the Steelers' empire of the 1970s provided their finest moments in life, and he says, "Absolutely, I've never been able to match it." He says, "Ninety percent is fond memories."

But then he spins in a different direction, storm clouds in his expression, and says, "I mean I don't have any rapport with Pittsburgh. There's no need for me to have one. I have no business there, unless we're covering a game there and I need to do an interview or something. It's like everything else: you move on with your life. That was *a stage* in my life. That isn't *my life*. It was a stage. Hey, you look over your shoulder, I don't look over mine, okay? I'm sorry. It's not a good trait of mine. It doesn't serve me well."

"It may be protection," he says.

Look at number 12 now. He has proven the lie in Fitzgerald's dark view that there are no second acts in American lives. Bradshaw has his own star on the Hollywood Walk of Fame. Once, on a USO tour in Afghanistan (he'd already been to Qatar and on ships in the Mediterranean), he suddenly broke into song, "God Bless America," and his longtime broadcast

colleague Howie Long stared out into the eyes of a hangarful of US ser-
vicemen "and there's not a dry eye in the place."

On the speaking circuit Bradshaw rubs elbows, including the damaged one that ended his Steelers career, with impressive company. In
October 2009 at a motivational speaking event in Fort Worth, Texas,
Harry Rhoads Jr., head of the prestigious Washington Speakers Bureau
that represents George W. Bush, former British prime minister Tony
Blair, former New York mayor Rudy Giuliani, and Bradshaw, among others, said, "Would you like to meet the president?" and Bradshaw replied,
"Would I!" Rhoads took him down the hall and there Bradshaw told the
forty-third president of the United States that he loved his speech just
after he had returned home to Texas from Washington. "If you had been
giving those kinds of speeches all of the time, I'm tellin' you, as many
people that loved you," Bradshaw told Bush, "twice as many would have
loved you because that was just off-the-cuff, good-ol'-boy, normal." Later
that day, Bradshaw followed Bush onstage and told a packed arena, "Not
everybody can say they had the president of the United States be their
opening act. . . . *How'd he do?*"

For a speech folksy, ironic, self-deprecating, and designed to inspire,
Bradshaw makes big money. He rates in the highest tier among Washington Speakers Bureau clients, which starts at $40,000 per speech and
moves upward. With a booming economy, Bradshaw said he'll make fifty
speeches or more in a year. (Add that up: if paid $40,000 per speech that
equals $2 million.) But in 2010, the economy in steep recession, he made
only eight such speeches. He stays clear of partisan politics. Once he was
a registered Republican, he says, but now he's an independent. His real
fun comes from joshing with other speakers, such as when President Bush
invited him to his dressing room in Orlando to say, "Are you big-dogging
me now? You won't come down and say hello to me?" Bradshaw laughed
and replied, "Are you shittin' me? You're the president of the United
States. I'm just going to come down and say [gruff voice], 'Hey, George,
how ya' doin'?' " Bush told him that's exactly what he ought to do. Standing with friends, Bradshaw once saw Giuliani, a presidential candidate at
the time, step from a limousine, and he called out to him, "Roo-die Giu-
li-ah-nee! Boy, I hope you runnin' for president because my ass, and so is

these people's, we are votin' for YOU!!" Giuliani, his back turned, didn't respond, so Bradshaw hollered, "That's right. Don't even acknowledge us!" Giuliani turned, saw Bradshaw, and laughed.

"Yeah," Bradshaw says, reliving that moment happily, "it's that little boy in me."

It's no surprise that the quarterback remains the most famous Steeler of all, the only member of the empire with squatter's rights on center stage. Bradshaw always had the knack, and the need, for celebrity.

For years he absorbed mocking attacks that he was a dumb southerner, Huck Finn in shoulder pads, including the most memorable jolt of all, at Super Bowl XIII, from Dallas linebacker Thomas "Hollywood" Henderson, who said, "Bradshaw couldn't spell 'cat' if you spotted him the 'c' and the 'a.' " It didn't matter that Henderson was abusing cocaine then, and even snorted it through his Vicks inhaler on the sideline during the second half of that game, or that in 1989, a decade later, he would apologize to Bradshaw. Bradshaw's CBS broadcasting partner and friend Verne Lundquist would say, "Terry wore that like the 'A' in *The Scarlet Letter.* That whole Hollywood Henderson thing was seared in his soul."

Bradshaw says, "As much as I hate people saying that I'm dumb and stupid, the facts are that I flunked the ACT [standardized college admission] test, okay? Now, let's get real here for a second. Aren't there a lot of people in this world who are not good testers? Okay, I'm one of them. I'm also ADHD. There was no cure, there was no pill, there was no doctor. The deal was, when you talk about it—'He's a *Hy-puh* boy'—and I sat all my life up by the teacher's desk because that *Hy-puh* boy was always making people laugh. My ass sat up front."

Bradshaw made a calculated career decision. He couldn't fight the stereotype, so he would roll with it and use it to his advantage. He crafted a persona of a simple guy, proud to be southern, and so uninhibited that he'd say almost anything. That persona has proven bankable. His popularity and earnings soared. He won Emmy Awards in the Outstanding Sports Personality/Analyst category in 1999 and 2001 and was voted America's Favorite Sportscaster in a *TV Guide* readers poll. At ninety-three, the distinguished former Pittsburgh columnist Roy McHugh couldn't explain Bradshaw's popularity except to shrug and say, "Why was Red Skelton popular?"

We're sitting at a table in a posh Beverly Hills hotel restaurant talking football when suddenly, as if from nowhere, Bradshaw tells me, "I just got a German shepherd from Czechoslovakia." It sounds like the beginning of a comedy routine, and I soon discover that it is. He says he named the dog Cash to honor singer Johnny Cash, but the problem was that Cash had been trained with German commands. *Aus*, Bradshaw learned, meant "out." *Platz* meant "down" or "stay." *Sitz* meant "sit." "So I put him in attack mode yesterday," Bradshaw says. "It was scary. He nailed this guy. But what if I go up there and get my wallet out"—he acts as if hurriedly rummaging through his wallet—"and I'm going, 'What's that term?' as this guy is bleeding to death and I'm going, *'Platzis!'* and, *'Auuuus!'*" Bradshaw laughs, and so do I. He says, "I'm going to do some of this on the *Tonight Show* next Friday. I'm working up a little routine." I am his trial audience, perhaps one of many. Sure enough, six days later there he is on Jay Leno's couch, wearing a black cowboy shirt and exchanging quips with Leno, *Brad being Brad*, as his Steeler teammates used to say, and doing his German shepherd routine. He tells Leno, "I got this sucker to keep people just like you from coming around." Leno asks why people came around Bradshaw's house. "Because I'm a sex symbol, Jay!" Bradshaw says, and Leno nods and says, "That's why you got a male dog." And soon Bradshaw is waving his hands wildly and shouting, *"FASS! Daaash! Platz! Sitz!"* and the in-studio audience loves it.

Bradshaw's personality is complex. He's emotional, a quality that at times served him well as a leader in the huddle. He has a palpable charisma, a politician's gift. When he enters a room, you know it, and then you hear it, his ol' boy persona kicking in. He built a multipronged career. He has written books, recorded records, endorsed an array of products (Nurtisystem, Paxil, recreational vehicles), costarred in the film *Failure to Launch* with Kathy Bates and Matthew McConaughey (and showed his naked buttocks on camera), and reportedly earns more than $2 million annually as a studio analyst on *Fox NFL Sunday*, where his comments tend to spark controversies that keep him in the news, which is good for the Terry Bradshaw brand. His controversial comments about football attract headlines and seem neatly spread out, as if preplanned to make certain he never fades from the news for too long. He sat on Leno's couch for the forty-ninth time in June 2012 and said that if he had a son he would not allow him to play football, and predicted that growing concerns about head injuries would launch the popularity of basketball, soccer, and baseball past football within ten years. He has a business manager, agents, an outside marketing firm that promotes him, a home in Florida, and a ranch in Thackerville, Oklahoma, where he breeds quarter horses.

"Get this," he says, "I'm sixty-three years old and I don't need to work another day in my life. I mean, I don't have all the money in the world. People say, 'Well, now football season's over so you can take a break.' *Are you shittin' me?* I haven't had any time off yet. I've been traveling all over the country giving speeches, buying up houses, starting businesses. My agent goes, 'Why are you doing this? You've made your money.' [But] for me to have a private jet and for me to fund my kids and to go see them, and help them on, help them get new cars and new homes, and to take care of my mom and dad, I've got to work. I *like* to work. Billy Graham says, 'You don't ever retire because when you retire you probably die.' I don't want to retire. I want to retire when I go *uhhhhhh* [Bradshaw makes a choking sound, as if dying]."

As a boy in Shreveport, he watched broadcasters Dizzy Dean and Pee Wee Reese on TV on Saturday afternoons. *"Heeeyyy!"* Bradshaw does a reasonable imitation of Dean's baseball play-by-play with an exaggerated southern drawl. *"Curve ball right there looked like my hand slippin' off an udder when I was milkin' my mother's Jersey cow. Falstaff beer. Hey, friends, here's ol' Dizzy with Pee Wee Reese."* But Bradshaw says he never gave a thought to becoming a sportscaster. He knew the long history of athletes turning to Hollywood: Olympic swimmer Johnny Weismuller as Tarzan, baseball's Chuck Connors in *The Rifleman*, bodybuilder Arnold Schwarzenegger as an action hero, and a number of NFL players, too, including Jim Brown, Merlin Olsen, Fred Williamson, Bubba Smith, and Ed Marinaro. But, Bradshaw says, "I wasn't trying to be an actor."

He is a natural entertainer. Upon retiring from football, he gave speeches for $1,000, building his storehouse of anecdotes, though ad-libbing mostly. He also did three-minute segments of commentary on KDKA-TV in Pittsburgh and tried to be creative and funny. As he embarked on his sportscasting career with CBS, Bradshaw received sage advice from Don Meredith, another southern quarterback, who had parlayed his ol'-boy routine into a lengthy career as Dandy Don on ABC's *Monday Night Football.* "Be yourself," Meredith advised. "Don't worry about what they say. The critics are going to hammer you because you've got a southern drawl." Bradshaw developed his own approach: "It's just a friggin' game, folks, get over it. Let's have some fun here. I put in my fourteen years [in the NFL]. I'm going to just present it to you in a good old-fashioned homespun way where you can understand it."

He began in 1984 at the bottom of the CBS broadcasting hierarchy. Among the eight NFL broadcast teams, the team of Lundquist and Bradshaw rated eighth. They didn't get plum assignments. They got Detroit, New Orleans, and Tampa. Bradshaw worked hard, sweated profusely. He searched for gimmicks that worked. During one telecast he asked Lundquist to help demonstrate a point on camera, and so Lundquist, in coat and tie, bent over in the press box and lowered his rear end to the camera to simulate Mike Webster's low stance, and then raised his rear end to simulate Vikings center Kirk Loudermilk's higher set. Lundquist said, "I wished away all my dignity." According to Lundquist, Bradshaw decided that few viewers knew or cared about special teams players, other than kickers and returners, so he created a fictitious one, Willie Anderson of Colby College. With a great sense of fun, for a brief time, no matter which NFL teams were playing, Bradshaw said, "That tackle was made by Willie Anderson, free agent from Colby College." It was a joke and no one in America seemed to notice, except for an official in the athletics department of Colby College, who sent some T-shirts as a show of gratitude. "Willie died a natural death," Lundquist said, "at the end of the season."

Lundquist sensed Bradshaw's growing frustration that, no matter how good they became as a CBS broadcast team, they would never replace Pat Summerall and John Madden at the top. "Ultimately that's what drove Terry to the studio," Lundquist said. Beginning in 1990 with CBS, and then with Fox, Bradshaw moved from the press box into the studio, and there, for more than two decades, he has thrived with jokes about his disappearing hair, his three failed marriages, and also by creating controversies with his tough-minded opinions about the NFL, including those about Brett Favre's annual retirement dramas and Ben Roethlisberger's off-the-field conduct. "I knew that's where he would make his mark," Lundquist said. "He is so physical. Terry gestures with every word. He's very animated in person. That's why he is making a heck of a living as a motivational speaker. What he has to say is accepted more readily if you can see him make his presentation, rather than as a voice over a picture."

Bradshaw admits that his celebrity's life was made possible by football. He says the game gave him plenty—"Everything I have." Without football, he says, "I don't have Fox. I don't have ranches. I don't have money. I don't have fame. But it didn't give me happiness. I earned that."

But football took a lot from him, too.

"It didn't *take* anything from me," Bradshaw clarifies. "I gave it freely." He laughs hard at that. "I'm proud that I'm all beat up. That means I was a warrior! You can't walk out of this game, if you competed hard, and not be messed up, right?

"I'd hate to be sitting around with my fifty-two brother teammates, and they are having hip replacements and knee replacements, and all kinds of stuff going on, and I'm sitting there dancing and doing back-flips."

Here's one way to quantify Bradshaw's NFL career: in fourteen seasons in Pittsburgh, he threw 212 touchdown passes and 210 interceptions. He won four NFL championships, second only to Bart Starr's five, and two Super Bowl most valuable player awards. Here's another way to quantify Bradshaw's NFL career: the physical price paid.

"Where do you want me to start?" he asks.

He suffered seven concussions, perhaps more. He has undergone five surgeries on his wrist. He still endures sharp pain in his neck from compression and bone spurs, the product of the vicious sack by Cleveland's Joe "Turkey" Jones. "I get this horrible nerve pain [from the neck] that makes me sick in my stomach," he says. One day, he says, he'll have surgery to fix that. He has virtually no cartilage left in his knees. He has undergone two foot surgeries due to dislocated toes. He's had arthroscopic surgery on both shoulders. His right elbow is a mess of knots and lumps, ravaged by the game. "This," he says, pointing to those knots and lumps, "is where they put a needle in, and went in and crunched the bone to stimulate blood flow, and I didn't tell anybody [with the Steelers]. And this here is where they tied the muscle together. I need the Tommy John [surgery] right here."

He hadn't given much thought to those seven concussions until late in the 2010 NFL season, when he suffered short-term memory lapses on the Fox studio set. He couldn't remember players' names or statistics he'd studied the night before, and he feared being embarrassed on air. It scared him, made him jittery. It took nine days to memorize a ten-page speech and he knew it should have required only a day or two. Even his hand-eye coordination suffered, and he wasn't sure why. All of this on top of his 2003 announcement that he'd suffered bouts of depression through much of his adult life. After some Steeler games, he said then, he'd been reduced to sweats and crying jags.

He spent a weekend at the Amen Clinic in Newport Beach, California, in 2011 undergoing brain scans and diagnostic testing. "Upside down, inside out," Bradshaw says of his testing. He passed most of the cognitive tests at the clinic. "Not as bad as they thought [but] memory loss was a big key." Now he takes multiple pills. "I have a power boost, a mood boost. I take one, two, three, four, plus Omegas, plus really good vitamins," Bradshaw says. "I'm sharp as a tack now, quick." He downloads brain puzzles from the Internet and to help his hand-eye coordination he bought two Ping-Pong tables.

"At what point in your football career," I ask, "did you realize that you would be giving pieces of your body to the game?" He says, "But you don't think about that. That's not a concern. We're not the smartest people in the world to want to do something that we can only do for probably ten or twelve years, max. We truly do have to go to work. So why are we so upset when they say, 'Get into your life's chosen work,' when, in fact, when we get drafted, which is a miracle, and we make it past five years—four years is the average—and we make it to ten or twelve years—which your average life expectancy is, like, what, fifty-two, if you start ten years? You die young! I'm a miracle. *You are talking to a fuckin' miracle!!* So, would I do it differently?" He laughs. "No!"

✦ ✦ ✦

It was only a formality in 1989 that Bradshaw would be elected to the Pro Football Hall of Fame in his first year of eligibility. The previous summer, he told Lundquist over dinner that he'd been thinking about who might present him at Canton. The Chief, his obvious choice, was in poor health and wasn't an option. Bradshaw said he didn't get along with Noll, and wasn't close with his former Steeler teammates. He considered asking his father, but he didn't want to put the pressure of the public spotlight on him. So Bradshaw looked across the table at Lundquist and said, "Bubba, it might be you."

Lundquist was honored and stunned. They'd worked together for only two years, and now were beginning a second stint. "I knew and liked him," Lundquist said years later. But, and here he hesitated, "I didn't think we were that close."

"I don't think that would go down well in Pittsburgh," Lundquist told Bradshaw that night. "You really need to think about that."

It had not ended well for Bradshaw in Pittsburgh. He had surgically repaired a torn ligament in his right elbow after the strike-shortened 1982 season. He rushed his recovery and missed nearly the entire 1983 season. Noll suggested maybe it was time for the thirty-five-year-old Bradshaw to get on with his life's work. Bradshaw played in only one game in 1983, for sixteen minutes, and threw two touchdown passes to spur a victory over the Jets. But he left the field after the second scoring pass holding his arm and wincing in pain. His elbow felt like it was about to explode. He returned the following May for the Steelers' minicamp and threw passes like missiles, the young Bradshaw reborn. The following day, though, he couldn't toss a Wiffle ball, so severe was his elbow pain. His final locker room exchange with Noll: "I just shook his hand and said, 'I'm finished.' He turned and walked, and I walked. I got on a plane, came home, and never went back. But that's okay. That's who I am, that's who he is."

Noll avoided personal good-byes with his players, and always had. When the Steelers traded tackle Gordon Gravelle to the Giants in 1977, Dan Radakovich asked Noll to speak with Gravelle, reminding, "He's a guy we won Super Bowls with." But Noll said, "I'm not talking to him. You talk to him." Radakovich phoned Gravelle and as Noll walked past, he handed him the phone, saying, "Chuck, it's Gordon. Talk to him."

Radakovich heard Noll make all the right comments: "You were great for us. You've won Super Bowls. It's another opportunity in your life. We had to make some decisions." Radakovich said, "Chuck was really good at it. It wasn't something he couldn't do. It was something he didn't want to do. . . . Chuck wasn't real good at personal relationships with the players."

Today, when Bradshaw recalls the Steelers' days of empire, his first thought seems to be not of teammates, the Chief, his two Super Bowl MVP awards, or of Three Rivers Stadium and the fans who filled it. He thinks of Noll, and the thought pains him. The Chief died in late summer 1988, and Bradshaw skipped the funeral. His absence was much commented upon in Pittsburgh. Most saw it as an unforgivable act. Bradshaw later admitted he'd made a mistake, and regretted it. But his absence was a clear sign of his inner turmoil about all things Pittsburgh. So when it was announced a year later that he'd selected Lundquist to present him at the Hall of Fame, it was seen in Pittsburgh as another example of his embitterment and his estrangement from the team and the city. Mullins called his choice "tragic," but added, "I'm not going to question it." The press asked about it once more in Canton, and Bradshaw bristled: "What is it with you people? My choice is very simple. For all you Pittsburghers, listen one more time and see if y'all can't get this through your heads. Art Rooney is gone. He was my presenter. He's dead, people. That's the only person that would've represented me. The reason is, he and I were close, and I am the type of person, in an event like this, that I am not going to have some coach or athlete I'm never going to see again come up here and do this."

On induction day, Bradshaw didn't use his prepared speech. He winged it, and the performer performed, saying, "Thank you, number eighty-eight, Lynn Swann. Thank you, number eighty-two, John Stallworth. Thank you, Franco Harris. Thank you, Rocky Bleier." He pointed at the sky and said, "Art Rooney, boy, I loved that man. I know you're watching, Art. I love ya'. You were always, always by me. I love you so much." In the massive crowd, Steeler fans chanted and cheered (Mel Blount was inducted on the same day), and when Bradshaw said, "What I wouldn't give right now to put my hands under Mike Webster's butt just one more time," there came a roar from the crowd and from the depths of the old empire.

His bronze bust was unveiled. It showed Bradshaw with furrowed brow and total focus, as if pondering a calculus equation. The sculptor, Blair Buswell, used calipers to measure Bradshaw's nose, mouth, and ears. Then he set up the bust on a pedestal in Bradshaw's house in Dallas, and they worked together for seven hours. "He's an antsy guy," Buswell said, "can't sit for very long." Bradshaw suggested they take a break, go outside, and throw a football. Buswell had played running back at Brigham Young University and caught passes from Jim McMahon, but not passes like these. "No rise or fall or wobble," Buswell said. After twenty minutes, they returned to the sculpture. "My hands were red and throbbing," Buswell said. He showed Bradshaw an array of photos of the quarterback with different facial expressions. "How do you want to be portrayed?" he asked. "Do you want to be intense? Happy? Calm?" Bradshaw studied the photos and chose a look of deep concentration, a look that defied his *Hee Haw* caricature.

"I wish I'd a hell got out after the last one," Bradshaw tells me. He meant after the 1979 season, when the Steelers won their fourth Super Bowl. "That's when I realized that we, as a bunch, it was over. We were a football team built on defense, and our defense was starting to show some age. Our offense wasn't as dominating in the running game. And we were pretty much a passing team, which wasn't what we were really geared for. We didn't run the West Coast offense." The pressures of the game wore him out. "One of the things I thought would have been cool: play nine years, win four Super Bowls, because that's like Jim Brown. I just wanted to move on. . . . I was totally overwhelmed by what we had accomplished. Can you imagine this: you build the greatest—*you are Steve Jobs!*—honest to God, man, when are you just going to let it go and enjoy the fruits of your labor?"

It's curious to think of the 1970s Steelers in a huddle without Terry Bradshaw, though in a sense it has come to that. Through his comments and actions across the years, Bradshaw has separated himself from his team. Mike Wagner said, "Here you have one of the great sports heroes in Pittsburgh history and he's not comfortable here. Terry articulates it real well: 'I'm afraid they are going to be mean to me.' What did he do to deserve that? *Oh, let's see, he didn't win SIX championships.*" Art Jr. said, "He was a playoff player, a Super Bowl player. But I always felt kind of sorry

for him. . . . Then I found out when he was all through that he was clini-
cally depressed. I wasn't smart enough to pick that up myself. But I picked
up that there was something that made him unhappy. He was truly one of
the great, great athletes."

Some of his old Steeler teammates miss him. "Hell, I'm on TV," Bradshaw says with a laugh. "I'm not hard to find!" Unlike most of his former
teammates, his days with the Steelers seem far from his thoughts. He's oc-
cupied with being famous. Besides, he says, he is not in total Steeler isolation. "I do have Franco and I do have a relationship with Joe Greene," he
says. "And then I occasionally see the other players [and] . . . I'm thrilled
to see them, as I should be. We had great moments together. I hadn't seen
Bobby Walden in fifteen years and I talked to him two days ago.

"Let me tell you something about the Steelers," Bradshaw adds.
"While I love seeing them, there wasn't the closeness that you think. . . .
When we left, you may have had your one buddy, and that's your only
connection. I mean, Lambert is where he is. Wagner is where he is. Ham
is where he is. Franco, Swannie, Stallworth. The list goes on and on. But a
real love for a friend—*love!*—love is very special and very rare." He makes
his point with conviction. "So don't be surprised that you don't have the
bond that you are looking for as you write this. It's not there. You will find
it isolated with certain people. [But] some of it is bullshit and you'll be
smart enough to see through it."

This statement, like many Bradshaw has made over the years, is frank,
and blasphemy to Steeler Nation. It is also, in part, true. The Steelers'
days of empire carry different meanings to the men who lived it. Some
of their bonds of friendship have endured, and profoundly so (the Steel
Curtain front four, for instance), while others have not. For Donnie Shell,
who remains close with Stallworth, Dungy, and Blount, this is akin to
the biblical Gospels of Matthew, Mark, Luke, and John, and how they
convey portraits of Jesus from different perspectives. "So that's the way
[Bradshaw] saw it. That's the way he feels about it," Shell said. "I didn't
see it from that perspective. Everybody has their own opinion." Shell
added, "If they are true relationships they last a lifetime. But you've got
to be committed in any relationship. And John [Stallworth] and I made
that commitment to one another to stay in touch. To have friends . . . you
have to be a friend. A relationship is built. It doesn't just happen." Perhaps

to credibly accept the idea that the 1970s Steelers—or any professional sports teams—once were *like family* is to acknowledge that all families have some dysfunction. That Bradshaw isn't close with any former Steeler teammates today seems more his doing than theirs. To a man, they want him back in the fold, and to see him more often at team reunions and charity events. But he is busy, and he is wounded. "I call him occasionally," Greene told me. "But I haven't been able to reach him for the last year or so." Franco Harris said, "I'm reaching out to Terry now a lot more frequently. But for years . . ." Harris shook his head.

For Bradshaw, the turmoil comes back to Noll, always Noll. Once he called his coach "a jerk," and as the Steelers struggled during the 1980s he questioned Noll's commitment and said, "So now that *we're* gone, what have *they* done lately? Not a whole hell of a lot." Later Bradshaw said he'd like "to patch it up." Noll's response never varied. "There is nothing to patch up from my standpoint," he said.

"The way he treated me," Bradshaw says, shaking his head at the memory, "I hated him—and I mean, HATED him. He is the only person that I can truly say I hated. But when I grew up, he was the reason I grew up. He made me a man. And then I understood it. I needed to be toughened up. I'd been loved on and pampered at [Louisiana] Tech when I finally became the starter there. And I was immature. He recognized that."

At the 2003 Dapper Dan banquet in Pittsburgh, after Noll presented Bradshaw with an award, the quarterback publicly apologized to him "for every unkind word and thought I ever had." Bradshaw attributed those comments to "my wrong, my childness [*sic*], my selfishness. Having said that it kind of cleanses me." Seventeen hundred people in a hotel ballroom stood and cheered those words as Bradshaw threw his right arm around Noll's shoulder. When Bradshaw was guest of honor at a 2004 fund-raiser for the Mel Blount Youth Home, he privately told Noll that night that maybe they'd get together, play golf.

But they haven't spoken in the years since.

"[Noll] makes you uncomfortable," Bradshaw says. "He's not a warm guy. His vibe doesn't say, 'Come love me. Hug me. Praise me.' Athletes want to love their head coach. We love our position coaches. But head coaches, he's the guy that brings your ass in after fourteen years, and you've given him everything you had, and he says, 'You've got to get on with your life's chosen work,' and you are like, 'But I helped you win all these Super Bowls. I played hurt. I took injections and da-da-da,' and [he says], 'Yeah, and we're thankful. Thank you.' Athletes have a hard time with that.

"But we shouldn't."

This is why Bradshaw chose no one from the Steelers to present him at the Pro Football Hall of Fame in 1989.

"Do I know him, really?" said Lundquist, his presenter at Canton. He answered his own question: "I've seen Terry once in the last twenty years."

Bradshaw was anxious and worried, and Joe Gordon knew it. The retired Steelers publicity man had worked with Bradshaw in the best, and worst, of times. He knew how to read Bradshaw's looks. Gordon had just toured Bradshaw's parents through the Steelers' new South Side facility, and now, at a downtown hotel late in the afternoon, he saw worry in Bradshaw's face. For the first time in nineteen years, since his last game as a player in 1983, Bradshaw would appear on the field at a Steelers game in Pittsburgh, before kickoff against the Colts on Monday night, October 21, 2002, and again at halftime, and he expected the worst from sixty-two thousand Steeler zealots at Heinz Field.

"They're going to boo me," Bradshaw told Gordon. They would boo him, Bradshaw knew, because he had criticized Noll . . . and Steeler Nation . . . and the city . . . and the current Steelers . . . and because he'd missed the Chief's funeral and Steeler reunions. He'd given them plenty of fodder. Years later, Dan Rooney would put it like this: "Terry shouldn't say some things, like giving Ben Roethlisberger advice." This much Terry Bradshaw knew: Pittsburgh Steeler fans would skewer him, and maybe they had a right to do it.

"Hey, are you crazy?" Gordon replied. "They love you! You won't believe the reception you'll get. They've been waiting for this."

Bradshaw had arranged his own Steel Curtain defense. He brought his two daughters, Rachel and Erin, just fifteen and thirteen, and they would walk onto the field with him, perhaps as his security blanket. No one would boo a father in front of his two daughters, would they?

As he ran off the field after the coin toss, Bradshaw waved to the crowd, and there was a stirring, a chant forming: "Ter-ree! Ter-ree!"

At halftime, in a ceremony at midfield, Dan and his son Art II presented Bradshaw with a new number 12 Steelers jersey, which featured an "AJR" patch honoring the Chief. A video tribute played on the big screen, and with it, for the two millionth time, the Immaculate Reception, Bradshaw evading Raider tacklers and throwing a missile downfield, Tatum slamming into Fuqua, and then Franco, with the ball in his hands, running downfield. This image pulls on the heartstrings of Steeler Nation much as the Iwo Jima monument pulls on the heartstrings of military men. Now the fans at Heinz Field responded by waving their Terrible Towels.

Bradshaw stepped to the microphone, his daughters by his side. The chant began anew, "Ter-ree! TER-REE!"

"Believe me when I say this," Bradshaw said. "I have missed you all very much."

"TER-REE! TER-REE!"

His daughters beamed. He became emotional. "It's good to be home," he said, and the stadium erupted, tumultuous cheers washing over Bradshaw.

You can see the 1890s New York City streetscape on the back lot of the 20th Century-Fox studios in Century City where *Hello, Dolly!*, starring Barbra Streisand, was filmed in 1969. Colorful murals of Julie Andrews in *The Sound of Music* and Darth Vader and Luke Skywalker fighting with lightsabers in *Star Wars* play across the sides of adjacent buildings.

On the main set of *Fox NFL Sunday*, television's top-rated pregame show, host Curt Menefee and his four studio analysts sit in their usual chairs as makeup artists sweep through for final touch-ups, a lint roller pushed across Jimmy Johnson's chest, and powder dabbed heavily onto Bradshaw's nose and bald head. Long, a Hall of Fame defensive end, had back surgery a few days earlier and looked impeccable in his suit. Out of camera's view, though, his shirttail hung loose and he wore shorts and sneakers. Michael Strahan studied his note cards. To no one in particular, Bradshaw asked, loudly, "Hey, how did *The X Factor* do this week?"

Suddenly, all quiet on the set: "Twenty seconds!" came the call. "Ten seconds!" "Five!" Bradshaw gave last-second, good-luck handshakes to Menefee and Long. On the set, music rose along with bright yellow-orange lights. The show opened with a video tribute to Al Davis, who had died a day earlier. Long, a former Raider, honored his old boss with a few stories, and turned to Bradshaw and Strahan, a former New York Giant pass rusher, and said, "You guys would've been great Raiders," and they nodded.

Long has been on the studio set with Bradshaw for nearly two decades, their on-air rapport, he said, "a yin-and-yang, that kind of Martin-and-Lewis deal, where I'm the straight man just reacting off what Terry does impromptu." "Terry is our quarterback," Long said. "If it were a cast of a movie, the name above the title would be Terry's." That was appropriate, Long said, because Bradshaw appealed to a broad spectrum of Americans. "I call it the Saran Wrap Factor. You are who you are, and inevitably that will show up on the television that's in your family room. People will either like you or they won't. You can't mask who you are." Long added, "When the light goes on, Terry is just brilliant." He said Bradshaw performed at his best each year at the postgame Super Bowl trophy presentation, a test of nerve and focus. "It's kind of a melee, it's mass chaos," Long said. Operating on instinct, with more than one hundred million viewers, Bradshaw often didn't know which player he would interview next, or his earpiece malfunctioned, cutting off communication with the truck, or a broadcast assistant waved at him frantically as he conducted an interview to indicate that only five seconds remained until a commercial, and he better not miss a commercial that costs several million dollars. "Terry just does it," Long said, "time and time and time again—flawlessly."

Now, at the first commercial break, Bradshaw teased Strahan, saying, "As you get older, your head will get bigger and your teeth are gonna spread out even more!" Bradshaw squealed with laughter, and Strahan, accustomed to being teased about his gap-toothed grin, laughed with him. Bradshaw got more powder on his head and nose. He sat tall in his chair, as did Long and Strahan. Next to those three big men, the former coach Jimmy Johnson looked like a wind-up toy.

Back on air, Strahan couldn't resist: "Terry told me on break that my gap is getting bigger." Behind them, in a high-tech flurry, colorful graphics appeared, showing quarterbacks Drew Brees and Cam Newton.

Now Bradshaw was saying on air, "Well, my brain starts working when I get up. And it doesn't stop . . . until I get to the office."

It was time for analysts to make predictions on the day's games. Staring into the camera, Bradshaw said, "The Steelers are beat up. Love my team, but I think they are going down today. I'm going with Tennessee."

"Oooohhh!" Menefee said.

But Pittsburgh won 38–17 that day as Roethlisberger threw for five touchdowns. Bradshaw got it wrong. But his prediction shouldn't have been a surprise.

Just Brad being Brad.

CHAPTER 18

FRANCO

FRANCO HARRIS, THE MOST UNCONVENTIONAL Steeler, never forgot the pizza man who led his Italian Army. Year after year, he spent Christmas Eve with Al Vento and his extended family. Over the Feast of the Seven Fishes, they hugged like good Italians, and they laughed and they ate and they sang songs with gusto and yuletide spirit accompanied by the living room piano. "My nieces are good singers," Vento said. "And Franco loves to sing!" At eighty-four, Vento was old enough to be Harris's father. Their friendship harkened to a bygone time when it wasn't so unusual in Pittsburgh for a football fan to be on a first-name basis with his Steelers hero, or maybe even for the fan to drop off gratis hoagies and Pepsi at his hero's home once or twice a week. Through the decades Harris invited Vento to local charity events and placed him at his table, beside his wife, Dana, and son Dok. Harris stopped periodically at Vento's Pizza in East Liberty, where the neon sign in the front window announced HOME OF FRANCO'S ITALIAN ARMY and the walls held photos and sketches of Stargell, Billy Conn, and of the Italian Army on that glorious day in 1972 when its leaders met Frank Sinatra. Each time Harris showed up at the restaurant, without fail, Vento watched him slip twenty-dollar bills into the hands of the hired help.

Harris's loyalty to friends, and devotion to teammates, might be his most towering quality. When Joe Gilliam, addled by drug addiction, reached out to him in the late 1990s, Harris reached back, and flew several times to Nashville to participate in Gilliam's football camps. To Mike

Webster, addled with cognitive problems, Harris once discreetly handed an envelope with a $5,000 personal check. Webster almost never accepted handouts, but from Franco he did. "He's a guy I don't think I've ever, ever seen mad," J. T. Thomas said. "Time is just time to Franco. He's not concerned about time. Most people are so time-conscious. If he's there, it's going to be a while. He's not going to rush you, or rush it." Thomas went deeper, saying, "I look at a friend like, 'When you are down to the last point of life, who would you look to?' For me, it would have to be Franco Harris."

Harris's enduring friendship with Vento was evident at the Heinz History Center in November 2007, when Dan Rooney appeared before a capacity crowd, Steeler Nation turning out in force, to talk about his new memoir that covered his seventy-five years with the team. The event was televised locally, and a number of the 1970s Steelers stars showed up onstage, Mean Joe, Franco, Dwight White, and even Bradshaw among them. When Dana Harris spotted Vento sitting with his wife in the back, she insisted they join her up front, and from the stage Franco flashed Vento a thumbs-up sign. Later that night, Vento wandered upstairs to the Western Pennsylvania Sports Museum. There, various artifacts dramatized the region's rich athletic past: the golf bag and shoes of Latrobe's Arnold Palmer; Satchel Paige's baseball glove from the Pittsburgh Crawfords; Honus Wagner's wool Pirates jersey; and the trunks worn by Ezzard Charles in his heavyweight title fight against Jersey Joe Walcott at Forbes Field in 1951 (a fight promoted by the Chief and his brother-in-law Barney McGinley). Vento also saw some of the memorabilia he had donated years before—the green Franco's Italian Army helmet he wore to every game until Harris's last with the Steelers in 1983, his Franco's Italian Army scarf, and the Italian Army seat cushion that Franco had autographed. But nothing made him quite as proud that night as when Franco Harris interrupted a story he was telling onstage about his affection for the Rooney family by saying, "By the way, we've got the number one fan in the city of Pittsburgh here, General Al Vento of Franco's Italian Army!" The cheer that filled the room was the kind a pizza man didn't often get.

◆ ◆ ◆

In his public life, Harris sometimes made bold, unequivocal stands, ironic given that his football critics often said that he avoided confrontation on the field by veering away from would-be tacklers for the safety of the sideline.

Late on a spring afternoon in 1997, Harris sat alone, leaning against a stone pillar of the City-County Building on Grant Street in downtown Pittsburgh, his emotions aflame over a Ku Klux Klan demonstration scheduled for the following afternoon. As a counterprotest he came to this spot to stage a one-man sit-in. He intended to spend the night, and had brought a few provisions (water, some food, a jacket), and a self-made placard: KEEP AMERICA AMERICAN. NO NAZIS.

City Hall was already on a high alert. Three hundred officers—in riot gear, on horseback, and in SWAT vehicles—would be deployed the following afternoon, blanketing the demonstration area. The Klansmen would be literally fenced in, with access to their area controlled by police. The last thing City Hall needed was Franco Harris, the famously biracial Mr. Immaculate Reception, in the middle of a race riot with Klansmen in downtown Pittsburgh. Even without a riot, City Hall feared that Harris's presence might turn the demonstration into a national news event. Franco Harris's face was as familiar in Pittsburgh, after all, as the metal bridges that spanned the rivers. A call was put in to Dan. "This could be a bad scene," a mayoral staffer told him. "Would you come over and talk with Franco?"

In short order, Dan sat beside Franco, the two men sharing a pillar. They had shared much over the past quarter century, extraordinary highs, and that last failed contract negotiation in 1984 that both knew never should have happened even as it did. As different as they were, they were much alike with their deep sensitivities, high principles, and in the way they viewed Pittsburgh as not only home but nearly sacred.

The Klan demonstration stirred emotions so deep in Harris that he struggled to contain them. It was as if a dam had burst within him, and in the surging emotion was his family's past: the Klan in their hoods marching alongside the Nazis with their swastikas, the prejudices his father faced as a black man in Mississippi, and those his mother faced as a young woman in Italy, fearful of the Nazis and on the run from them, her brother Alvaro Parenti—the uncle Franco Harris would never meet—

wounded, captured, sent off to a slave labor camp, his remains sent home in a box. "This is wrong," Harris said. "They shouldn't be allowed to do this." Then Dan heard him say, "My mother shouldn't have suffered," and, "Why are they letting this happen here in Pittsburgh?" and, "I want to make a statement, and want them to know this," and, "We can't let hate or evil take over or predominate." Harris was standing up for Pittsburgh, for America, and for all that he was. Already some local reporters had gotten to him, and Harris had told one, "I have a hard time letting Nazis take over America."

"Franco, I'm one hundred percent with you," Dan said. "I'll back you on this. But there is a better way to do it." He reminded Harris that religious leaders planned an anti-Klan rally at Market Square the next day and said that rally would offer a better forum for Harris to speak his mind rather than take on the Klan on these steps. Dan said he would go to that rally with Harris. He left a short while later, still uncertain what Harris might do. At that moment, Harris, preparing for an all-night vigil, faced the challenge of the thoughtfully principled. He asked himself, *Do I do nothing here or make a stand?* And that question raised others. What was required of him? How could he be most effective? Harris left quietly not long after Rooney, and the next day both spoke at the anti-Klan rally.

Only thirty-nine Klansmen participated in the demonstration. They wore robes and hoods, waved Confederate and Nazi flags, and denounced blacks, Jews, gays, and liberals. Across the barriers a crowd of more than two thousand booed, threw rocks, and chanted, "Klan go home!" "I came here for one reason," one Klansman said, "to start a race war, a holy race war." Using megaphones, the Klan was heard to vilify the Reverend Jesse Jackson and Franco Harris.

Fifteen years later, Dan considered this experience and what it said about Harris: "Just how sincere he is, and what a good person he is," he said. Through the years, Dan knew, Franco hadn't changed one iota. He was as principled as any Steeler he'd ever known, perhaps to a fault.

Do you remember how odd Harris looked in that Seattle Seahawks uniform with the royal blue jersey and silver pants, and that angry bird on his helmet? Even his number, 34, wasn't right. It was like watching other

NFL greats limp into the sunset wearing unfamiliar colors, Unitas with the Chargers, Namath with the Rams. Harris needed only 363 yards to pass Jim Brown as the NFL's all-time rushing leader at 12,312 yards, but he didn't make it. Instead, the Bears' Walter Payton rushed past Brown. At thirty-four, the second-oldest running back in the league behind the Redskins' thirty-five-year-old John Riggins, Harris didn't look the same with the Seahawks, or run the same. He didn't have the old giddyup or the deft cutbacks. He played eight games for Seattle, ran for 170 yards on sixty-eight carries—2.5 yards per carry, by far the lowest of his career—and was released.

The slow fade-out of the 1970s Steelers continued. The city still held strong emotional ties to the starring players who won four Super Bowls, but the players grew old, their skills diminished. Proud champions were always the last to recognize their own athletic mortality; their coaches became the bearers of bad news. Jack Ham played two seasons after he had dislocated his foot in a pile beneath running back Earl Campbell. Watching game films in 1982, his last season, Ham saw the painful truth. He wasn't the player he'd once been. "Tape doesn't lie," Ham said. Bradshaw had retired in the spring of 1984, following Greene, White, Ham, Blount, Greenwood, and Bleier, and now it was Harris's turn. Lambert, suffering from painful turf toe, would be next. It was like watching the back-row pieces captured in a game of chess, still regal in their bearing but banished to the side of the board, irrelevant to the game at hand. Through it all, Noll coached on, keeping his stiff upper lip and his distance.

But the Chief didn't. He couldn't. At a family dinner at the St. Clair Country Club, he rose from the table several times and walked across the room to the bar. There, he stared up at the TV to watch the Seahawks and Harris. At eighty-three, the Chief stood as close as one could to the screen, his vision poor. Besides, he couldn't believe what he was seeing. *Franco with the Seahawks!* There was sadness in his old, rheumy eyes. "I just felt so sorry for him because he loved Franco," Art Jr. said as he watched his father that night. "You want the legends to go out with dignity."

As the most celebrated running back in Steelers history, Harris ran for more than twelve thousand yards in his NFL career, scored one hundred touchdowns, and made nine Pro Bowls. He withstood the rigors of the game better than most. In his final nine seasons in Pittsburgh he missed only five games. Art Jr. considered him the Steelers' equivalent of the naval Battle of Midway during World War II. "Before the Battle of Midway we never won a [naval] battle. After Midway, we never lost," he said. With Harris, Art Jr. said, "We played from 1972 to 1983 and never had a losing season." In Harris's dozen seasons in Pittsburgh, the Steelers made the playoffs ten times. Beyond that, he was a symbol of strength. Said Ham, "What Joe Greene meant for the defense, setting the tone, that's what Franco did for our offense. The constant became our running game."

In 1984, as the Summer Olympics played out in Los Angeles, Harris became a contract holdout. He was due to earn $385,000 in his option year, but he wanted considerably more. His holdout stretched a month, and more. Noll didn't like holdouts—they threw wrenches into his training camp engine. Tensions rose on both sides. From retirement, his old friend Dwight White supported Harris. "It's unfair," White said, "because of his contributions to the team and to the city." White called Harris the Steelers' historic "pivot point." Of course, some in the organization felt Noll had shown too much loyalty to White by keeping him in 1979 and releasing draft pick Dwaine Board, who then played ten seasons for the 49ers as the Steelers' pass rush withered. Beat writer Vito Stellino privately began calling Noll "Closet Nice Guy" when he decided the coach also had kept a few other stars from the 1970s on the roster a year or two too long. Perhaps. Art Jr. said, "Chuck thought [NFL] records took care of themselves, and that the main thing was winning and losing. He told Hoak [the Steelers' running backs coach], 'You've got to talk to Franco to say, 'You better retire.' Chuck wanted Hoaky to tell him. But Hoak said, 'You or the Rooneys should do it because he's a superstar.' "

Instead, the Steelers reportedly offered Harris a one-year contract for $557,000 plus an option year. Mel Blount called Dan and offered to intervene. He wanted to help. "If you can, that's great," Dan said. Blount phoned Harris, and then phoned Dan to say, "I talked to Franco and it's going to be okay." Relieved, Dan phoned the Chief, and Noll, and told them the deal was done. "Just make sure that Franco is there tomorrow morning," he told Blount. "He's got to be at practice." But Harris didn't report.

Joe Gordon phoned Harris and encouraged him to talk with Noll in person. "By this point," Gordon said of the negotiations, "Chuck was a stubborn German, which he is." Gordon convinced Harris to set up a meeting at Noll's house in Upper Saint Clair, and gave him directions how to get there. "Call me when you get home," Gordon advised.

Gordon hoped for the best, and waited. Left to his own imaginings, Gordon thought the two men might share a conversation in Noll's living room or perhaps the kitchen. Being together, face-to-face, might produce a mutual good feeling, he thought. They might let bygones be bygones and get the deal done. But Gordon also knew that both were bullheaded: the opaque principles of Noll facing off against the transparent principles of Harris didn't make agreement seem especially likely.

Two hours later, Harris hadn't called, so Gordon phoned him.

"What happened?" Gordon asked.

Harris said, "Nothing happened."

Gordon: "Did you go?"

Harris: "Yeah."

Gordon: "How long were you there?"

Harris: "Five minutes."

Gordon: "And nothing happened?"

Harris: "Nothing happened."

"At that point," Gordon said, "I knew it was a lost cause, we were done."

Noll poured out his frustration in two words. Asked by sportswriters about Franco, he replied, "Franco Who?" This remark still burned in Harris's memory nearly thirty years later, Harris saying "that was pretty stupid to make a statement like that." On August 20, 1984, Dan announced in a press conference that the Steelers had severed their relationship with Harris. In Pittsburgh, this was unthinkable, like Clemente playing for the Reds. "Franco told us what it would take, and we thought we gave it to him," Dan said decades later. "That was extremely hard."

Harris's enduring closeness with the Rooneys through the years affirmed Karen White's belief that "Franco is forgiving, just turn the other cheek." But Harris has been less forgiving toward Noll. "We had someone who really didn't connect with you while you were playing, or even after you were playing," he said of his head coach. "With all of this greatness that we have, I feel that really leaves a void." Harris lives in suburban Sewickley, not far from Noll's condominium, but said he couldn't remember the last time he'd seen Noll. When Bradshaw spoke critically of Noll, it was as if a blast furnace door had opened. But Harris, true to his nature, chose his words carefully, and winced as he spoke, as if in pain. "I really shouldn't say that," he said, but he allowed his words about Noll to stand.

During the Christmas season in 1985, more than a year after Harris was cut loose by the Steelers, Art Jr. brought his children to 940 to visit the Chief. What he saw there startled him: Franco sitting beside the Chief on a bench pulled close, and his son Dok on a nearby chair. This scene moved Art Jr., brought him nearly to tears. The Chief had invited Harris. "Hey, I had twelve great years with the Steelers," Harris said. "The twelve great years to me is more important than what happened at the end."

"Franco's a tremendous guy," Art Jr. said. "To bury that hatchet and come out and see the old guy. You know, if you wait with old people, it can be too late. I was just so impressed with Franco from what I was see-ing. He's a very sensitive guy, very much a right-and-wrong guy, with a sense of fairness. My dad had that."

Harris arrives at a hotel near the Pittsburgh airport on a Sunday morn-ing forty-five minutes behind schedule, per usual, though his wife, Dana, graciously had phoned me to say he was running late. His Ralph Lauren shirt hangs loosely over blue jeans. His hairline has receded, at least to the opposing thirty-yard line, the Super Bowl IX Afro gone with the years. He looks tired, and says he arrived back in town late the night before from a family graduation in Colorado.

We sit together in a comfortable concierge room filled with tables, chairs, and a couch. After a while two young men sit at a table next to ours, typing on their laptops. Harris whispers to me, "You know what? I don't know this guy here. Do you know this guy?" I shake my head and say they look like young businessmen. "Oh, okay," Harris says. But their presence bothers him, makes him suspicious. "Let's go over here," Harris says finally, and we move to a chair and couch across the room. He would spend nearly four hours there, talking about the past, in no hurry to get up. I think about what J. T. Thomas had said: *Time is just time to Franco. . . . If he's there, it's going to be a while. He's not going to rush you, or rush it.*

For breakfast Harris orders blueberries with his French toast. For the past decade, he explains, he has eaten blueberries, and taken fish oil, nearly every day. "That's for the brain," he says. Some research suggests blueberries and fish oil help memory, and delay cognitive aging in middle-aged men. "I do think that all of us have brain damage," Harris says, referring to former NFL players. "There are just no two ways about it. I mean, there is no doubt that a lot of football players die young. And a lot of them have a lot of chronic and other problems. We all know about the concussions. I don't think I'm going to get away from all this stuff. But my whole thing is: Can I do things to delay it?" Forty-five minutes later, a waitress eyes his plate and asks, "Can I take this away?" "Yeah," Harris replies, "but leave the blueberries."

He says he suffered at least one concussion as an NFL player. He apologizes to me later for not remembering certain moments from the past. "But I've *always* had a bad memory," he says, inferring that head injuries on the football field hadn't caused his forgetfulness. He says he exercises regularly, on treadmills, and occasionally the tennis court. "I've been very lucky," he says.

Or maybe it wasn't luck. Jim Brown, among others, criticized Harris in 1984 as he approached his NFL rushing record, for running out of bounds to avoid contact and to prolong his career. "The only reason to run out of bounds," said Brown, an attacking runner who never missed a game in nine NFL seasons before he retired at twenty-nine, "is to stop the clock." But the Raiders' linebacker Phil Villapiano waved away such criticism: "The smart guys who stay around know when to take a hit, or deliver a hit. I give Franco credit for that. Anybody who says he was soft needs to go tackle him a few times."

Decades later some of Harris's fellow Steelers running backs understood the wisdom of his evasive running style in ways they hadn't as active NFL players. Fuqua, a straight-ahead runner, said, "Franco played thirteen years and I played nine, and the last two I was on injured reserve. It isn't one game that puts you out. It's an accumulation of the blows. Why take that lick that you don't have to? If I had to do it over, I would have run out of bounds a lot more. Every player I know who had to make a decision between sideline or contact and chose contact can barely walk today." Reggie Harrison, a bullish runner who navigates his home now with the help of a motorized chair and special ramps, agreed. "I was the one that wanted to run over people. I took the head shots," he said. "Look at me! Look at Earl Campbell! And Jim Brown can't walk now. I saw him on TV and he's [walking] with a cane. Franco is still walking around, man! I see him at golf outings and say, 'This is the smartest dude that I've been around!' "

Harris has heard it all before. "As the Persian general said, 'On contact with the enemy all the plans evaporated,' " he says. "So that means I'm running according to *what*? Now some guys run straight ahead to where the hole should be, no matter what. I read my keys." I ask him about Jim Brown's criticism. "I mean, I'm fine with Jim. Jim said that just to say it, and everybody else ran with it. The press ran with it. But I loved my running style. If we needed short yardage, I'd get short yardage. If we needed third and one or third and two, was there a time that I didn't make it? *You know what I mean?*"

Like so many of the 1970s Steelers, Harris stayed in Pittsburgh after football to pursue his life's work. At Penn State he had earned a degree in business administration and food services and he put that to good use creating Super Bakery, Inc., which has sold nutritionally enriched doughnuts and bakery goods to schools and hospitals for more than twenty years. More recently he cofounded SilverSport, a company that makes antimicrobial exercise products. He also adhered to the vow he made before the 1972 NFL draft: "Where I go to play, I want to live in that city and get involved in that city, become that city." He has been involved in so many charities and causes in Pittsburgh that Jack Ham said, "I swear, I think he's cloned." Dan recalled Ernie Stautner's voluminous work in the community years ago, and even before that, the charity work of the irrepressible Johnny Blood, who also often went onstage at local theaters to recite Shakespearean verse or to sing with famous baritones, but Dan said no Steeler had ever been as actively committed to Pittsburgh as Franco Harris.

Harris has been a stalwart in the city's philanthropic community, his attendance at charity events coveted, his active participation even more so. His name resonates in Pittsburgh as few others do. The more causes he joined, the more other causes sought him out. He became a quintessential celebrity about town, at benefits, groundbreakings, and at head tables at charity events. The Chief's deep involvement in Pittsburgh, he will say, served for him as a powerful model. He won the NFL's Man of the Year award in 1976 for his community service, and he never turned back. More recently, Harris served as a director of the Heinz Endowments; chairman of the Pittsburgh Promise, a nonprofit scholarship program for students in the city's public schools; and as a cochair of the Western Pennsylvania Sports Museum. At the nearby August Wilson Center for African American Culture, the conference room and stage carry his name in recognition of his financial contributions. He has been spokesman for a federally funded low-income energy assistance program, and a regular at the annual Mel Blount Youth Home Celebrity Roast, except for when he has been out of town or, in one instance, at another charity event in the city introducing actor Michael Keaton, a Pittsburgh native. His name has popped up in politics and business. Democratic kingmakers in Pittsburgh and across the state have encouraged him to run for office, but he never has or will. In 2008, he waved a Terrible Towel across western Pennsylvania campaigning for Barack Obama, altering the usual Steeler chant by saying, "Here we go, America, here we go!" He served as an Obama elector at the Democratic National Convention in Denver. In 2010 he joined a small group of private investors and three nonprofits that purchased the historic Crawford Grill, the shuttered jazz club in the Hill District, with plans to refurbish it. And with the Immaculate Reception statue at Pittsburgh International Airport that stands beside General George Washington, he might as well serve as the city's unofficial greeter, too. "He's the best PR man we have," Vento said.

Harris has done virtually everything in Pittsburgh but run for mayor, and his son tried that. In 2009, Franco Dokmanovich Harris, aka Dok, just thirty, a graduate of Princeton University who had scored a perfect 1600 on his college boards and later earned a joint law/business graduate degree from Pitt and Carnegie Mellon, ran as an independent against Luke Ravenstahl, the Democratic incumbent. Franco and Dana Harris, common-law husband and wife for decades, became actively involved in their son's mayoral campaign. Franco called on some of his former Steeler teammates for help, and they responded in force. J. T. Thomas, Mike Wagner, Robin Cole, Moon Mullins, and others bused to different neighborhoods, handed out campaign leaflets, and marched in a parade in the cold and rain for Dok Harris.

"I knew that politics would be a little sticky. But they were very supportive," Franco said of his former teammates. "It was a nice time being together. Those bus trips were fun. There were a lot of laughs." Wagner had always thought Franco Harris quiet, but no more. "He went to introduce his son and we couldn't get him to shut up," Wagner said with a laugh. "We said, 'Hey, you are not the candidate!' " Dok Harris commercials on television and the Internet tapped into the Steelers' days of empire, one featuring Vento, and another with Bleier and Franco Harris standing beside the candidate, and Dok Harris saying, "I think you both know what happens when they say things can't be done. . . . A good thirtysomething years ago they said the exact same thing about a team that had never won. . . . You guys came together, brought the right leadership and the right people. What happened? You changed football, you changed Pittsburgh, and in a certain way you changed the entire country." Franco: "We need that type of leadership that will demand that excellence because we are a great city and we should expect nothing less." Bleier: "And that's what you're doing here. It's about time." Despite an energetic campaign, Dok Harris got only 25 percent of the vote and finished a distant second to Ravenstahl, who captured 55 percent.

Some of Franco Harris's personal loyalties have been challenged, and pushed to the limits. He was close with Swann, for years his Steeler roommate. Swann presented him in 1990 at his Hall of Fame induction. But when Swann told Harris that he intended to run for governor of Pennsylvania in 2006 as a Republican challenger to Democrat Ed Rendell, Harris did not offer his support. "In running against Rendell and the machine, I told him he didn't have a chance," Harris says, adding, "It just wasn't a good time to support a supporter of Bush. Even though I really care for him [Swann], there was no way that I could support him in that situation. I mean, any other time." Rendell defeated Swann easily, and Harris's friendship with Swann had changed. "Since the election me and Swann really aren't . . ." He shakes his head, and demonstrates their separation by moving his hands far apart.

He stood up for Joe Paterno. In the face of public outrage over the Jerry Sandusky child sexual abuse scandal at Penn State, Harris led a strenuous public defense of Paterno, his former college coach. Harris met with Paterno and his family, and later with PSU students. He waged his own media campaign. In firing Paterno, Harris insisted, the university had been guilty of a rush to judgment. After Paterno's death, he criticized the investigative report issued by former FBI director Louis J. Freeh as flawed, misleading, one-sided. Franco Harris didn't run out of bounds on this subject. He took it on. Once, with a laugh, Paterno had described Harris's running style by saying that, asked to run through a brick wall, he would, but only after counting each brick. No more. In his skybox at Penn State's stadium for one game in 2012, Harris stood up a life-sized cardboard cutout of Paterno holding a sign: DUE PROCESS FOR PSU JVP, the latter initials for Joseph Vincent Paterno. His words of support for Paterno created headlines, led television news programs. "No way would Joe ever cover up anything like this," Harris said in one interview, vowing to fight to clear Paterno's name. "No way would Joe protect Sandusky or protect the football program."

His comments created a backlash. They cost Harris his job as a spokesman for the Meadows Race Track and Casino near Pittsburgh, which cut ties with him, and prompted Mayor Ravenstahl to call for Harris's resignation as chairman of the board of the nonprofit Pittsburgh Promise. In response to Ravenstahl, Harris issued a statement saying of Sandusky's victims, "my heart aches for those young people and their families," while calling Paterno "a transformative and guiding influence in my life." "Helping people in need, especially those you care deeply about, is the basis of my expression for Joe Paterno," he said. Harris voluntarily stepped aside as chairman, though later was reinstated by supportive board members. His old teammates explained it easily enough: Franco was the most loyal guy in the world, and stubborn, too. If his sense of rightness was stirred, he would fight to the end of the earth, even if it damaged his own good name. "Franco looks at friends and life from a different perspective," Thomas said. "He looks at things on merit. He doesn't look at faults. That's what friends do. They help you when you have a need, not when the sun is shining, but in hurricanes and storms." The same loyalty principle worked in reverse in shaping his feelings toward Noll. "Loyalty has to be a two-way street," Gordon said. "When Franco was holding out and went to see Chuck at his house, Chuck totally dismissed him. Franco feels that was definitely a case of disloyalty on Chuck's part." Among the legions of players Paterno coached during his forty-six seasons at Penn State, none defended him more vigorously than Harris.

An archivist at the Western Pennsylvania Sports Museum brought in a new exhibit piece to show the gathered committee members. Mike Wagner, among dozens of former Pittsburgh athletes, sports executives, and sportswriters on the committee, saw the new piece carried in on a tray covered by white cloth. In a moment of suspense, as if the artifact had been excavated from a Peruvian cave, the white cloth was drawn back, and Wagner heard the archivist say, "These are Franco's shoes from the Immaculate Reception." Dumbfounded, Wagner thought, *What? WHAT? NO WAY!* Wagner knew that in 1972 Steeler players got only one pair of football shoes for the entire season. Wagner's shoes from those days were long gone. *How can these be Franco's shoes?* But then he decided that the Immaculate Reception had transcendent powers, so anything was possible, even this.

With Harris, it always comes back to the Immaculate Reception. How could it not? On December 23, 1997, its twenty-fifth anniversary, Harris hosted a private dinner party for some of his former Steeler teammates and their wives to honor that famous play and all that it symbolized. He did it again in 2002 and 2007 to commemorate the thirtieth and thirty-fifth anniversaries. Each time he rented one of Pittsburgh's best restaurants, ordered a six- or seven-course meal (twenty-two-ounce porterhouse steak, cedar-plank salmon, pan-fried chicken, strawberries dipped in a cascading chocolate fountain), showed a season's highlight film from the 1970s, and presented to his guests a special gift to remember their night together. For the thirty-fifth, he and Dana gave a pearl necklace to each of the wives in attendance. Swapping old stories that night were Bleier, Swann, Mullins, Wagner, White, Berlin, Parisi, and Vento. ("You are a part of the family, Al," Harris told him.) These dinners weren't fund-raisers. They were Harris's way of remembering a defining moment, and the defining people, in the defining period of his life. They were his way of saying thank you, and each time he footed the entire bill.

Myron Cope, the seventy-nine-year-old Steelers broadcaster who became a central figure in the naming of the Immaculate Reception, didn't RSVP for the dinner in 2007, and Harris found out why: Cope was hospitalized and slipping toward death. Harris asked to see him. He stepped into the ICU and saw the little man in bed, his face splotchy, tubes of all sorts connected to him. Cope's eyes opened and grew wide with disbelief. Seeing Harris, Cope beamed. Harris was his favorite Steeler, in part due to the Immaculate Reception. They'd both received so much attention from it. Harris leaned over the bed and hugged Cope, careful not to become entangled with the tubes. The two men didn't talk much but Harris's common touch won the moment. As Harris left the room of Cope, who died weeks later, an ICU nurse asked him if he wouldn't mind stopping in another room down the hall. A young woman there wanted Harris to say hello to her father, also an ICU patient. Harris stepped inside that room, held the man for a shared photo, and then he left.

I ask him about his Immaculate Reception anniversary dinners. "I need to do it more," Harris said. "It's about bringing back good memories, [and] a time to reflect," he said. After the fortieth-anniversary dinner in 2012, Harris planned to host the dinners more frequently. "See, I don't think it's too late," he says. "I've been thinking lately that I'll have it every year." He pops a blueberry into his mouth. "Because we are getting older," he says, "and five years is a long time to wait."

Typical Franco, Bleier said.

"Franco is big about getting together, and having dinners, as small as they may be, or large," Bleier explained. "Time is kind of running out as far as those memories are concerned. And people have a tendency to float away and not get together. If somebody doesn't do it, then it's not going to get done. I think Franco has kind of taken that on. It takes a star to be able to do that. Franco ultimately, among us, is that player. Bradshaw, Joe Greene, there are a few. Everybody looks up to Franco for what he has accomplished. Personalitywise, Franco is outgoing. He'll pull it together, and he doesn't expect anything from it. He won't say, 'It's going to cost you a hundred bucks to come.' He'll just fund it. And he wants it to be memorable."

To Harris, there remained at least one piece of unfinished business: Bradshaw's enduring estrangement. "I want to reconnect Brad to a lot of the guys. I think that's important," Harris says. "He left with a bitter taste in his mouth." He invited Bradshaw to the fortieth-anniversary dinner. Bradshaw had told me he wasn't sure if he could make it, given his hectic TV schedule during the football season. "Franco is one of my friends," Bradshaw had said. "I mean, I love him. I truly do love Franco."

Franco's private dinner party for the Immaculate Reception's fortieth anniversary on December 23, 2012, was his grandest to date, with about seventy guests at the Heinz History Center, beautifully appointed for the occasion. The menu featured lobster, steak, and pasta. Franco and Dana gave out elegant keepsakes, small glass footballs from Tiffany's inscribed "Immaculate Reception 40th Anniversary." To the offensive linemen from 1972 (Mullins, Kolb, Van Dyke, Larry Brown), Harris handed out small bronze statuettes. Harris moved through the room that night, holding a microphone, and used it to speak informally whenever he got the urge, once recalling how the Steelers had pulled together in 1972, no player worrying about individual accomplishments. He sang a Christmas carol solo, and then another, in duet, with Jan Bleier, Rocky's wife. Fuqua was there, telling his tales, and J. T. Thomas handled the invocation ("Don't make it too long," Harris instructed with a smile). A camera dangling from his neck, Joe Greene took photos of guests. "And we all talked about how good it was," Greene said, "to be a Steeler." Sitting with Dana, Dok, and Franco was the Raiders' Villapiano, friends now with the running back he was supposed to cover on the famous play. The next afternoon, at the very spot where Harris made the catch at Three Rivers Stadium— streetside now outside of Heinz Field—he and Fuqua, in front of nearly a thousand fans waving Terrible Towels, jointly unveiled an Immaculate Reception monument, the third in Pittsburgh, along with identical life-sized likenesses of Harris at the airport and the Western Pennsylvania Sports Museum. Later Vento stepped forward and, with a helmet liner and bottle of Riunite wine inducted Villapiano into the otherwise dormant Franco's Italian Army. Villapiano said Al Davis was probably turning over in his grave. "I guess I'm a Steeler now," Villapiano said.

Bradshaw didn't make it to the fortieth-anniversary dinner, which surprised no one. Harris had phoned him twice but never heard back from the quarterback. Harris said he will keep trying to bring Bradshaw back into the fold. "Franco got pissed off at me last year for busting Roethlis-berger," Bradshaw had told me months earlier. Bradshaw had criticized the current Steelers quarterback on the air. "Word got back to me. Franco knows my number. I called him." Bradshaw said Harris never mentioned Roethlisberger during their conversation, and he laughed over that.

Typical Franco, Bradshaw said. "Such a good guy. He is. A classy, classy guy."

CHAPTER 19

STALL

THE PLAY THAT BROKE THE Los Angeles Rams and won Super Bowl XIV was called 60 Prevent, Slot, Hook, and Go, football mumbo jumbo that essentially meant Get It to Stallworth. Set in the right slot, John Stallworth was to hook across the middle of the field, breaking double coverage, and then run deep, moving at a diagonal, along a knife's edge. In his NFL career, Stallworth would catch 594 passes, digging them out inches above the turf, one-handing them in the corner of the end zone, some of them aesthetic beauties. A big-play virtuoso, he set a league record with touchdown catches in eight consecutive playoff games. But because of the magnitude of the moment, this catch would become his signature, featured on the cover of *Sports Illustrated*, the catch forever imprinted in memory.

Lionel Taylor watched it happen from the Rams' sideline. Taylor had left his job as receivers coach for the Steelers three years earlier, though with a heavy heart. He loved coaching for Noll and the Rooneys. But anyone could coach the likes of Stallworth and Swann, Taylor told himself. He said, "I had to find out if I could coach." Two other Steeler assistants, Bud Carson and Dan Radakovich, migrated west and joined Taylor on Coach Ray Malavasi's staff. Thus the Rams had insight into the Steelers' tendencies. In essence they knew everything the Steelers did.

Though an eleven-point underdog, Los Angeles led 19–17 early in the fourth quarter. The Steelers, on their twenty-seven-yard line, faced third and eight. If Swann was like the sun among Steeler receivers with his big smile and Peter Pan–like aerial maneuvers, then Stallworth was like the moon, dependable, always there, even if his brilliance wasn't always recognized. The two receivers competed against each other, vying for Bradshaw's attention and for the football. "How many did you catch yesterday?" Swann asked Stallworth after a 1979 game. The answer was six, but Stallworth smiled and needled Swann by saying, "Four more than you." Still, Swann was Swann: he created light, drew light, and longed for the light. Even before kickoff of Super Bowl XIV, when actress Cheryl Ladd of television's *Charlie's Angels* sang the national anthem before 103,000 fans in the Rose Bowl, Swann, standing on the sideline beside Stallworth, flashed his big personality, saying, "John, watch this." As Ladd walked past them, Swann called out, "Hey, Cheryl, how you doing, sweetheart? Everything going okay?" He'd never met Ladd, and she didn't reply, just walked off, as Swann and Stallworth laughed.

On this game-turning play in Super Bowl XIV, though, Swann stood on the sideline, Steeler receivers Jim Smith and Theo Bell set up wide, and Stallworth asserted himself, the Steelers' moon shining brightly, and sportscaster Tom Brookshier shouted to his television audience, "What a catch! He had to take that over the wrong shoulder!" Lionel Taylor shook his head on the far sideline, as if he had known it all the time. "Greatest catch I ever saw," Taylor would say. "I almost died."

Now, more than thirty years later, Stallworth sits in a leather chair in a conference room at his office in Huntsville, Alabama. At sixty, he carries himself like an athlete still. Though he says one ankle creaks, a finger bends oddly out of place, and an unrepaired knee ligament remains torn, Stallworth says, "I really don't have anything that hurts." As a receiver, his approach to football differed from those of defenders such as Lambert, Greene, and Donnie Shell: "It was a part of who they were. Hitting people! Take a running start and just blow into someone. That is so far from my mentality. I don't live to hit people. I'd rather avoid them. I'll hit somebody if I need to. But take a running start and stick my head somewhere?" He shook his head. His facial features remain youthful and unmarked, his head shaved smooth and shiny, Mel Blount–like. But middle age caught up to Stallworth, even if the Rams' defensive backs didn't: his midsection has softened and filled out, his physique lanky no more. He wears wire-rimmed glasses, black slacks, a blue short-sleeved shirt, and an expression that suggests inner peace and a good life.

If Franco Harris is, to use Joe Greene's phrase, *Mr. Pittsburgh*, then Stallworth might be *Mr. Huntsville*, sitting on the boards of a local bank, a local medical center, a local botanical garden foundation, a local nonprofit designed to enhance development in the city's traditional downtown area, and serving as a deacon at his Baptist church. He swells with pride over his family: a namesake son working as an analyst for an international accounting firm, a daughter as a software safety engineer for a global aeronautics company, and four grandchildren who call him "Grandfather." He borrowed that name from *Heidi*, a Shirley Temple film from 1937, fifteen years before Stallworth's birth. He saw the movie as a boy and never forgot it. "I just liked the sound of 'Grandfather,' " he says. Smiling broadly, he adds, "And I wanted every bit of that."

On a laptop computer on the table, 60 Prevent, Slot, Hook, and Go plays, and Stallworth points to his accelerating image on the screen as it races past Rams cornerback Rod Perry. If he has seen this replay once, Stallworth says, he has seen it at least five hundred times.

"My first impression when I look back at the trajectory of the ball is, 'Bradshaw, dammit!! You've overthrown me!' " Stallworth speaks in the present tense, inhabiting the moment, exhilarated by it still. His hook fake is minimal—he doesn't want to break stride, lose momentum—so he merely leans to momentarily distract Perry. "Now I know that I've got to run. So I turn away from the ball and run, and turn back to gauge where it is." Thirty-five yards downfield, he has a step on Perry. "I'm moving like this," Stallworth says, his hand demonstrating a slash, "and then [he points at the laptop screen] Perry is here, so he's running and not looking for the ball. He's in position to knock it away." Bradshaw's pass, hardly overthrown, arrives over Stallworth's *other* shoulder, to the outside, away from Perry. At six-foot-two, Stallworth holds a five-inch height advantage over the Rams' cornerback, and he uses it. "He jumps to knock it away," Stallworth explains, pointing at the screen, "but the ball is here." Stallworth reaches up and catches it at the Rams' thirty-four-yard line and, as the leaping Perry crashes to earth, he sprints alone in long, loping strides into the end zone for a seventy-three-yard touchdown and a 24–19 Steelers' lead. Stallworth drops the ball casually in the end zone, no preening, no spike, understated always. The Steelers try the same play during their next series, but Bradshaw slightly underthrows the pass. With two defensive backs trailing him, Stallworth slows slightly, and looks back and up, as the football descends like a spaceship. He catches it *with his face mask.* Stallworth squeezes it there for an instant as the two Rams defenders jump on him, and he holds on to the ball for a forty-five-yard gain to the Rams' twenty-two. This play arranges big spoils for the Steelers: another touchdown, a 31–19 victory, and a fourth Super Bowl trophy, Joe Greene in the locker room afterward saying, "You can't beat talent," and "This game was an invitation engraved in gold"—an invitation, he said, when prodded by the press, "to immortality."

John Stallworth had been thinking about 60 Prevent, Slot, Hook, and Go—or something like it—for nearly his entire life, even before he got swept up at home in Tuscaloosa by Bear Bryant's Crimson Tide and the civil rights movement, even before his high school pep rallies crackled with the battle song "Dixie" and rebel flags waved, even before he and his white teammates at his recently integrated high school drank from the same water bucket. As an eight-year-old boy suffering inexplicably from paralysis on his left side that lasted for days, he had stared through a hospital window and dreamed of running free. He had made a silent vow that he would achieve in his life so that people would remember him. Later, in pickup football games on the playground, Stallworth imagined it would happen just like this: he would break into the clear and catch the big pass. "And the world is watching and for that play you are the hero."

But his silent vow, and soaring ambition, carried him far beyond football.

Stallworth's life's work has mirrored 60 Prevent, Slot, Hook, and Go, his work ethic and resourcefulness leading to big results. Look at number 82 now: a self-made millionaire who built an information technology and engineering company based in Huntsville and sold it in 2006 reportedly for $69 million. Then, in retirement, he became a limited partner of the Steelers, completing his personal odyssey with the team.

Among the 1970s Steelers, no player had worked harder at his football craft than Stallworth. As a rookie, he was acutely self-conscious. Once, before a preseason game, as trainers taped the ankles of barefoot Steeler rookies in a hotel lobby, Stallworth stood alone, apart from the rest. Art Jr. approached him to ask why he wasn't getting taped. "I'm not going out there in my bare feet," Stallworth replied, pointing to the lobby. Art Jr. didn't understand. Stallworth told him that he didn't want to look like some country kid from Alabama. Art Jr. shrugged, said that all of the other Steeler rookies were in bare feet, and so were the trainers and ball boys, "and, anyway, you *are* from Alabama." He considered Stallworth's reticence odd, but the more he thought about it, he decided it offered a penetrating insight into Stallworth's character. "There was something intrinsic about him," Art Jr. said. "He had a certain dignity about him."

Decades later the tuxedoed Stallworth stood at the dais in a Pittsburgh hotel ballroom before nine hundred guests, poking fun at a former teammate at the annual Mel Blount Youth Home Celebrity Roast, a fund-raiser for Blount's rural home for wayward boys. Stallworth delivered his laugh lines with confidence, poise, and a comic's timing. He was droll, ironic, in total command. Watching with amazement, Andy Russell leaned toward Chuck Noll and whispered, "That's a side of John I've never seen."

His teammates knew Stallworth as the consummate hard worker, a man of faith, and a spirited prankster, but his intellect and introspection largely escaped them. "I never saw John as an entrepreneur," Bradshaw said. But then he amended, deadpanning, "Well, I mean, he wore glasses. . . ." Dan said, "We've had players who have gone into business, even in the thirties, who ended up having nice businesses, but not in the class of John."

Mid-August, ninety-two degrees, a steam bath in Huntsville: so humid the brick walls drip sweat outside the two-story building near downtown that houses the John Stallworth Foundation. Stallworth created the foundation in 1980 to grant need-based scholarships to students at his alma mater, Alabama A&M. Inside, the offices are bright and airy, a colorful area rug thrown over a polished wood floor. Freeda McDowell, manager of the foundation office since 2004, watches on DVD as Stallworth and Swann slap hands on the Steeler sideline. She shakes her head. "I still have a hard time seeing John do that. It's foreign to me. He left that part of his life behind," she says. Unlike many of his former teammates, Stallworth keeps no Steeler memorabilia, or photographs, in his office, only a Steeler helmet on his desk, a recent gift from the broker who helped him buy into the Steelers, a gift Stallworth insists he'd rather not have anywhere in sight. "Because," he says, "that's not what we do here. The honest-to-God truth is I don't know what to do with that helmet. It's been sitting on my desk since I got it."

For a time, it seemed like his Steeler career might never end. Swann had retired after the 1982 season, his ninth. Stallworth suffered a series of injuries, including a broken fibula and broken ankle. In his biggest season, 1984, he caught a career-high eighty passes for eleven touchdowns and nearly 1,400 yards as the NFL's Comeback Player of the Year, and the following season he caught seventy-five passes more. At long last, he was the Steelers' primary receiver. In the locker room, he led quietly. "He was one of the guys who invited me to Bible study," said tackle Tunch Ilkin, raised a Muslim. "Here were these guys, Jon Kolb, Donnie Shell, Mike Webster, and Stall. I was so intrigued by their faith commitment and their love for each other, and yet they were men—men's men! It was really through those guys that I met Christ and became a follower."

The locker room had changed: the talent, the intensity, everything. As the 1970s stars fell away, the Steelers became merely an average team during the 1980s, with a 77-75 overall record. "Sometimes it doesn't hit you," Stallworth says. "For us, it hit us."

"I looked around and Joe [Greene] wasn't there, and Mel [Blount] wasn't there, and Lambert was gone, and Bradshaw was gone. The guys that replaced them weren't as talented, lacked some of the qualities these guys had. I thought for a lot of years, that when Joe Greene retired, the next year we were going to have a number one draft choice and we were going to draft a defensive tackle somewhere and he was going to replace Joe Greene. Then I realized, 'That ain't going to happen,' and how rare a Joe Greene is! . . . I knew that Joe Greene was one of the greatest defensive tackles to ever play the game. History was going to record that fact. But less evident to the world was his leadership qualities, and what he brought to the table in that regard." Stallworth felt similarly about Blount, Bleier, Bradshaw, Swann, and Lambert. "You don't realize the intangibles they brought along with them until they are gone."

Stallworth lasted fourteen seasons, a tribute to his work ethic. In 1987, his final NFL season, only three Steelers remained from the fourteen rookies who had made the team's 1974 opening-day roster: Webster, Shell, and Stallworth. All three, as team captains, crossed the picket line during the 1987 NFL players' strike, each man first phoning Ilkin, the team's union representative, to apologize and say, with their career nearing an end, they didn't have a choice. That season, rookie linebacker Greg Lloyd closely watched Stallworth, a role model he much admired. "Stall came in one game at halftime, took his shoes off, went in the corner, and started smoking a cigarette. I was like, 'What the hell?' " Lloyd said with a laugh. "I'm thinking Chuck will come in and rip him a new one. Then Stall goes out [during second half] and outruns everyone. I'm like *are you kidding me?!*" Stallworth participated in a thousand Steeler practices and more, and at his final one, he concentrated on every small detail—his locker room conversations with teammates, the way he taped his ankles and ran his receiving routes. His final wish was to catch the last ball thrown to him, and he did, making a difficult fingertip grab. But just then his great friend Shell, Uncle Donnie to Stallworth's two children, participating in his final Steeler practice, too, dropped Stallworth with a crushing tackle. Limping back to the huddle, Stallworth smiled and thought, *I guess Donnie got his last wish, too!*

The Steelers held a retirement luncheon for Stallworth and Shell. There, Noll pulled his receiver aside and told him that he felt emotional about the end of Stallworth's career. But, Noll said, he did not want to display that emotion. "That wouldn't be right, would it, John?" Noll said. Dutifully, Stallworth answered, "No, coach, it wouldn't." Stallworth believed that Noll had held on to some of the 1970s stars too long because he did not want to release them. True to his character, Stallworth said, "We had some guys who were around longer maybe than they should have been, maybe even me."

He had started to execute his plan for his life's work years earlier. Stallworth had returned to Alabama A&M in Huntsville and earned a master's degree in business administration. Living in an aerospace town, he began to think about creating a technology and government contracting corporation that would provide services to the US Army on missile systems in foreign countries. It was a good idea, he thought, and then a bad idea, and then an idea to put aside, and then, finally, a good idea. At his son's soccer game, he met a retired army engineer, and together, along with his wife, Flo Stallworth, they created Madison Research Corporation in 1986 with John Stallworth as majority owner and chief executive officer. Their corporation focused on prototype manufacturing, information technology, and logistics. "There were times," Stallworth says, remembering those early years, "when we looked at the phone waiting for it to ring."

Madison got its first contract with the US Army in 1987, Stallworth's last year with the Steelers. For $271,000, Madison built two stands with gauges for testing parts of the M1 tank. "We didn't make a cent on it," Stallworth said, but they delivered on time and at the projected cost, so "we had something to hang our hats on." Madison's name and credibility built over time, and soon it contracted to set up air-defense systems in Norway and for American troops in Afghanistan. It won contracts with the Department of Energy, the US Navy, and NASA. Madison also sold, and supported, technology for the Egyptian and Saudi Arabian governments. By 1992 Madison was winning prime contracts instead of subcontracts. Three years later, it won a $50 million contract to run a computer simulation center for the US Army's Space and Missile Defense Command. Through its developmental years, Madison gained advantage from the government's minority set-aside programs, but Stallworth said by about 2000 the company outgrew them. The number of employees grew from three to ten to twenty to two hundred to more than five hundred with operations in Florida, Georgia, Tennessee, Texas, South Carolina, and Washington, D.C.

To Stallworth, Madison was "another opportunity to do something to be remembered, but also to do something that's unexpected." He says, "Athletes are not supposed to be the most cerebral people in the world, football players in particular. Here I'm going in a totally different direction than what you would expect from an athlete into a field of engineers and chemists and computer scientists. It was an opportunity . . . to let folks know that I was more than just an athlete, that there was more to me than just being able to run and jump on the football field and catch a football."

At first, the army generals he met intimidated him, though his celebrated Steeler career helped him gain entrée. "I'd go to a meeting and all they would want to do is talk football," Stallworth says. Football became an icebreaker but nothing more. "I can't imagine a person who has to make the decision about a missile system that may help someone who is in conflict get out of harm's way or prevent someone from being in harm's way making a decision about whether they want us to do the work or not because I played with the Pittsburgh Steelers," Stallworth says. Football became an obstacle to overcome. He made a point not to wear a Super Bowl ring to business meetings, and removed from his office any Steeler mementos. He says, "I had to prove that I was intelligent and that the business was legitimate."

He created a corporate culture that drew heavily from his experience with the Rooneys, in particular from his fondness for the Chief. He says, "I modeled the way I wanted our employees to feel about me from the way that I felt about him." Stallworth habitually asked his employees about their families, and encouraged them to voice their opinions. He wanted his workplace relaxed. "I wanted the employees at our company to feel like the most important thing was what was going on at home, and how the family was doing," he says.

The Rooneys reciprocated that respect for Stallworth. In 2008, Stallworth walked across midfield at Heinz Field before a Steelers game, when a team escort told him that Dan wanted to speak with him, and then said, "Oh, there is Mr. Rooney right there!" They shook hands and Dan said, "We're looking to bring some partners into the organization and would like you to consider being a part of that." Stallworth was flattered, honored. Hockey's Mario Lemieux, basketball's Michael Jordan and Magic Johnson, and baseball's Nolan Ryan were among the few retired athletes to become minority owners of pro franchises. Much later, Dan said, "We wanted to bring in a minority and to bring in a football player. John was *the* guy, no question." Sitting in his foundation office, Stallworth measures his words carefully, saying, "What they think of me gives me a good feeling . . . that what I was about, and the way that I carry myself, was worthy of being a part of a very solid family-oriented, above-reproach kind of organization."

That Stallworth had become a minority owner of the Steelers made headlines in Pittsburgh, and his former teammates proud. "It's still in the family," Joe Greene said at the time. Mike Wagner said, "I mean, that's great that a former player could put himself in that position. He's a class guy, that's for sure."

Stallworth said he had purchased "just a small percent." When Reggie Harrison picked up his cell phone and heard his buddy Frenchy Fuqua say that Stallworth had bought part of the Steelers, he asked, "Are you out of your mind?" Fuqua said, "No, man, call yo' boy." And so Harrison phoned Stallworth and said, "Stall, Frenchy tells me you just bought part of the Steelers?" Stallworth said, "Yeah, I did." "Holy mackerel, man!" Harrison said. "That's great," and then Stallworth recounted how he'd been busy since his NFL days building Madison Research Corporation, and then, finally, selling it.

"John was a great worker," Harrison would say. "John had to work so hard that you knew, when [football] was all over, John was still going to be working hard."

For Stallworth, it always came back to Swann. The two receivers came in together and ascended together. "[It's] not like having one guy who is your big-time receiver and the other guy is picking up the change," Swann said. "Our team, we had two go-to receivers." As rookies in 1974, they bonded and developed a shared pregame mantra, "2 and 4! 2 and 4!"—a reference to the quarters they would play together in each game, alternating with the veterans Shanklin and Lewis. When the Steelers' defense was on the field that season, Stallworth and Swann usually sat together on the sideline, atop their helmets, sizing up the game and waiting for their next chance. Early on, during training camp and practices, Stallworth grew uneasy if he saw Swann talking privately with Bradshaw, and vice versa. Bradshaw playfully would say, "Watch this: I'm gonna go over and talk to Stall. Watch what Lynn does." Stallworth laughed and said, "Brad played it for all that it was worth." The two receivers' confidence grew into near hubris: once in 1976, when Bradshaw was injured and the Steelers threw even fewer passes, Stallworth and Swann sat together in the film room during a team meeting, and upon seeing a Steelers pass finally completed on the projector screen, both stood and playfully applauded. Stallworth saw Noll shoot them a cold look. They developed their own pregame ritual, pacing back and forth together in the end zone, uniting their thoughts, and creating a vision for the opposing team to see that Stallworth intended as a statement: "Here we are and it is something that you have to reckon with."

Even so, as teammates, a barrier remained between them. "I think the barrier was that we wanted the football. . . . We should've been a lot closer than we were," Stallworth says. "I wanted the best to happen for Lynn. I wanted him to catch as many passes as he could. But I wanted to catch one more than that." When Swann retired, that competitive barrier fell and their relationship deepened. They agreed it was time to cast their mutual competitiveness aside. "It was just a conscious acknowledgment that those feelings existed and that we are bigger than that," Stallworth says. "We just put it *over there.*"

In January 2001, Swann phoned Franco Harris from the United Airlines lounge at O'Hare International Airport in Chicago; he was en route to Hawaii to cover the Pro Bowl for ABC Sports. At long last, Swann had been elected to the Pro Football Hall of Fame after fourteen consecutive years as a finalist, a painful ritual every January that left him feeling deflated and rejected. "I'd become very callous about the whole thing," Swann said. Harris was a close friend and godfather to Swann's second son. Swann had presented Harris at his induction in Canton. Now, Swann called to explain to Harris that he'd struggled to choose his own presenter—Harris or Stallworth—and had decided on Stallworth. Swann wanted to be sure Harris was comfortable with that. "I think that's a great idea," Harris told him. "It will be terrific."

From his airplane seat, Swann then phoned Stallworth to ask him to present him at Canton.

"Swanny," Stallworth said, "you're kidding?"

From the instant Swann asked, Stallworth knew he would accept, but his emotions were complicated. Though excited for Swann, Stallworth, as a Hall of Fame finalist for the seventh time, felt small pangs of jealousy. "I wanted to go in, too," he said. Through comparative statistics, Stallworth could make a strong case that he deserved election before Swann. He had played fourteen seasons to Swann's nine, and caught two hundred passes more than Swann for thirty-three hundred more yards, and made four Pro Bowls to Swann's three. They had shared long discussions about the

Hall of Fame, and the painful process of *nearly* making it year after year. Seven of their teammates had been first-ballot inductees—Greene, Ham, Blount, Bradshaw, Harris, Lambert, and Webster—and some voters felt that was enough Steelers. From his long wait, Swann said he had developed a deep appreciation for how long Russell and Mansfield had waited to win a Super Bowl, and for the Chief's forty-year wait for an NFL championship. Patience created perspective, Stallworth believed. "He's been humbled a little bit," he said of Swann. "I do believe he's the better man for that."

Swann's request humbled Stallworth and intimidated him. Since Swann was a longtime ABC sportscaster, Stallworth figured he could have selected a superior public speaker as his presenter, "some very eloquent folks who could wax on for hours about him." But as he sat on a United Airlines jet, Swann told Stallworth that no one knew more about him as a player, or had shared more special moments with him on the field, than Stallworth. On the phone, Swann became emotional. "I don't know if John could sense it but I was crying on the phone because it meant that much to me," Swann said. As they talked, Swann's mind raced into the past and he considered the journey he had shared with Stallworth, battling through the competitiveness to a more mature appreciation of their unique talents. They had become teammates in the truest sense. Swann told Stallworth that he deserved induction into the Pro Football Hall of Fame, too, and that being onstage would remind voters of that. Presenting Harris in 1990, Swann heard the crowd chant, "Swann! Swann! Swann!" as he stepped to the microphone and it "renewed my spirit and confidence that one day I might be here." As his presenter, Swann wanted Stallworth to know that same feeling.

At Canton, Stallworth heard an enormous ovation when his name was called. He presented Swann, and closed by saying, "Please help me to bring forward one of the greatest wide receivers to ever play the game, my friend Lynn Swann." As cheers rolled across an audience filled with Steeler fans, the two receivers embraced, Stallworth saying, "I love you," and Swann answering, "I love you, too."

Their friendship reached a new summit. They began to talk by phone more frequently. In 2002, President George W. Bush appointed Swann as chairman of the President's Council on Physical Fitness and Sports, and

Swann soon moved from television to politics. He lost his Pennsylvania gubernatorial bid in 2006. ("He hit me up for money for the campaign," Stallworth said with a laugh.) Swann had his own marketing/communications consulting firm and was named to high-profile corporate boards such as the H. J. Heinz Company, Hershey Entertainment and Resorts, Caesars Entertainment Corporation, and Harrah's Entertainment. He became in 2009 one of relatively few black members of Augusta National Country Club, showing up on the famed veranda at the Masters in his green member's jacket and sunglasses. He traveled to Huntsville to play in the annual golf tournament for Stallworth's foundation. Together again, they talked about family, business, politics, gardening ("Lynn can't do a whole lot of that. He has deer."), and how far their friendship had come.

On his induction day in 2001, Swann said, "The man who introduced me today, John Stallworth, he and I battled day in and day out. . . . I could not be standing here if it were not for that competitive spirit that I learned from John Stallworth, for his trust and his faith in me as a wide receiver. . . . If we're going to call someone the best and if you think of me as being the best and I'm number one, well, you've got to broaden that thinking. There has to be one-A and a one-AA. I'm not saying who's one-A but John and I are one-A and one-AA, side by side."

And then Swann's voice rose in an act of friendship and devotion, saying, "If this is the greatest hour of my life, then I will tell you at this moment, this is only a half hour. It'll be the greatest hour when I can sit in that back row and John Stallworth is wearing a gold jacket and making this speech."

A year later, Stallworth stood in Canton at that same microphone wearing a gold jacket, a Hall of Fame inductee at long last, the ninth player from the Steelers' days of empire to be enshrined, and said, "And I say to Lynn here today, I am more than happy to complete that hour for him."

CHAPTER 20

WEBBY

PAM WEBSTER WAS NEVER IN it for the glamour. She didn't marry the quarterback, she married the center. She and Mike Webster made a handsome couple, young, blond, and upbeat, their marriage ascending at the same moment as the Steelers' empire. They were small-town midwesterners from Wisconsin, Green Bay Packers country, where life was lived on Lombardi Time, with Calvinist virtues, hard work, fidelity to family, blocking, and tackling. *So how did it go so wrong?* How did Webby get so angry at the Steelers, the NFL, and at her? In his rage, she saw him punch cabinets. She saw him punch the car. When times were hardest, he blamed her. He said it was her fault, all of it, and he said it so often that she began to believe it. It got so she could tell when he was angry with her. Entering the house, she looked at her photo on the desk: if he had turned it facedown, he was angry with her, and if it remained in its usual place, face up, he was not.

This was what became of the man of her dreams. She had never considered the amount of effort it would take, or what it would cost, to be Mike Webster. As soon as football ended for him, their life went to hell, and fast. It was as if someone had removed the governor that regulated his personality, initiating a sad slide into . . . *what?* Anger, confusion, aloofness, disorganization, fragmented thoughts, falsehoods, despair. He disappeared for days, weeks. Once, in anger, he told her that he'd thrown his four Super Bowl rings into the Allegheny. *You did what???* She didn't find out for years that he really hadn't. He stopped opening mail, and so unpaid bills piled up. He stopped paying taxes. Life became one surprise after another. At school a bully smacked a backpack against their son Garrett's head, and when Pam took him to the hospital emergency room, a nurse, looking into the computer, told her, "You have no medical insurance," and Pam replied, "But that can't be." She knew that opportunists with business propositions preyed upon Mike Webster, became his best friend, and he was led, as if on a leash, into investments she thought ridiculous. This caused the evaporation of about $2 million in assets. In Pam's hometown, Lodi, Wisconsin (population: 3,000), Mike pedaled around on a bicycle. He had given up his car, no money to pay for it, and everyone knew about his financial troubles. He was a shrinking football hero—shrinking, literally—his pallor gray, his body suffering from cellulitis, inflammation everywhere. She had to admit he looked pathetic on that bike. He was too big, the bike too small. The small-town gossipmongers whispered as he pedaled past, but they might as well have screamed because she heard what they said about him and so did the kids. *Mike Webster's on cocaine! Steroids did this to him! He's a drug addict! He's a loser!* The electricity was turned off at their Victorian house. They lost the house, foreclosed. They lost their family equilibrium. Stress became the norm, expected, accepted. Pam separated from him even though she loved him still. As she saw it, she had no choice but marital separation. He needed help, they all needed help.

Now that pro football was over, Iron Mike, who had played in more games than any center in Steelers history, spending seventeen NFL seasons at football's most vulnerable and unprotected position, had lost his daily tether, his regimen, his purpose. He moved back to Pittsburgh, though exactly where he was living, she had no idea. But over time Pam needed to know the following: *Why did the kids' college fund disappear? What about our annuities? What do you mean, "bad advice" on investments? A worm farm? Are you kidding, Mike? You invested in a worm farm?!! I mean, really? A worm farm?* He moved around, Kansas City, Pittsburgh, West Virginia, at Steve Courson's place, though Courson finally asked him to leave. He slept in his black Chevy S-10 pickup truck, its busted side window sealed with a plastic bag and duct tape. It took days for Webster to find out that he'd been named to the NFL's seventy-fifth-anniversary all-time team in 1994 because the Steelers couldn't find him to tell him the great news. His lawyer said the NFL pension board later would put a private investigator on him to see if he was earning wages, but how could an investigator find Mike Webster if Webster couldn't find himself? Pam got a job. She cleaned houses for a while. She cleaned up at a local restaurant. There, she wiped splattered ketchup from the floor. She replaced air fresheners in the men's room urinals. It had come to this. A woman needed to look after her kids. They needed the money. They needed the medical insurance. She heard that her husband was fixing his rotted teeth with Super Glue. *How did it all go so wrong?*

She sits with me at a Starbucks in suburban Moon Township near Pittsburgh International Airport on a Saturday morning in springtime, remembering it all, wiping away tears, her blue eyes like stormy seas. Her attire—if not the subject matter—is relaxed. She wears a casual oyster-colored sweater-vest layered over a soft blue and white paisley blouse and white T-shirt. A crucifix dangles from her necklace. Her blond hair pulled back, she fidgets with a few loose strands as she recalls that day when she looked to the sky, in supplication, and asked, "God, why? *Does one good thing ever happen?*"

For her, the epiphany would come much later, and it would shock her, because when she considered what it really meant, it was like staring into the center of the sun, a burst of light: the truth!

The truth pained her, and deepened her guilt, but it liberated her, too. It wasn't her fault, after all, or even his.

The fault belonged to football.

In the glory of his times, when Mike Webster was Mike Webster, the Xs and Os moved from the chalkboard through his mind with boldface clarity. He was like a quarterback among offensive linemen, quickly deciphering defensive fronts, stunts, and blitzes and communicating them up and down the line of scrimmage with his signals. Bent over, the ball in his hands, Webster once heard Bradshaw call an audible, turned his head, and shouted back, "You can't do that, Brad! Not against a strong safety blitz! GET OUT OF IT!"

Bradshaw snapped back, "Just run it!"

Webster: "GET OUT OF IT!!"

Bradshaw: "RUN IT!"

Webster: "GET OUT OF IT!"

Bradshaw called a time-out and in the huddle laughed at his center's stubbornness.

Webster was an archetype of the game, the quintessential gladiator, his trunk thick, his Popeye biceps erupting in the frozen December air, his eyes coldly searching for the next defender to knock flat. It was the look of Nagurski and Nitschke, the look of human granite. Webster stood in the huddle in black and gold, number 52, at the end of his fifteenth Steelers season, his blond hair thinned, his face pockmarked and worn like a seaman's, his arms and hands mummified with white tape wrapped around his elbow pads, his wrists, and a few fingers so gnarled from battle they pointed to every direction on the compass. Webster's jersey seemed too tight (it was) and his sleeves too short (they were), and this was all part of a covert operation run by equipment man Tony Parisi. The Steelers' offensive linemen began wearing smaller shoulder pads, and Parisi's mother-in-law, a seamstress, restitched their jerseys, pulling them up and back from the shoulder to make them snug yet still allow for movement. Parisi then secretly applied two-sided carpet tape so that the offensive linemen's jerseys stuck to their pads. The result: opposing defensive linemen couldn't easily grab their pads or jerseys. For Webster, showing off his bare biceps, especially in the winter cold, was a point of pride. "His muscles were like trees. He was a man and a half," George Perles said. And Tunch Ilkin, a teammate who viewed Webster as a hero, went even further: "Here is this guy with arms like legs and legs like . . . people. His hands were like giant vice grips, and his fingers like sausages." Webster sprinted from the huddle to the line of scrimmage on every play, a bold announcement to the defense ("Here I am, come and get me!"), though Ilkin kidded that Webster only wanted to get into his stance before anyone realized how short he was.

Webster played ten years without missing a game, and six of those years without missing an offensive snap. Spanning seventeen NFL seasons, he played more than 340 games (including pre- and postseason) and missed only 4, those at the start of the 1986 season due to a dislocated elbow. What drove him was fear of failure. He worried perpetually that another man would take his job. He brought a gung-ho spirit to weight training, practices, and to mastering his blocking technique, aspects of preparation most players viewed as football drudgery. Webster's workout regimen knew no off-season and bordered on manic. His kids watched him drive the blocking sled through their snow-filled yard, wearing only shorts, a shirt, and his helmet. They saw him walk up and down their backyard incline carrying heavy weights on his back, dipping down and exploding forward to strengthen his legs and hips. In the off-season, he ran with his father-in-law's Weimaraner along the railroad tracks in Lodi, five miles down, five miles back. In Pittsburgh, downstairs at the Red Bull Inn, he joined linemen Courson, Ilkin, and Craig Wolfley in the restaurant's boiler room, their bars bending, their weights clanking. His career lasted through the evolution of NFL defenses, from four-man fronts to three, meaning that instead of seeking out middle linebackers Webster had mammoth 325-pound nose tackles positioned directly in front of him; in battle he went at them helmet to helmet. Webster packed on forty pounds by the end of his career. At 260 he tried to keep up with the bigger linemen of modern times. In conversations with his son Garrett, Webster admitted to brief experimentation with steroids during the 1980s, though years later some of his teammates and opponents wondered if his experimentation had lasted much longer. "He saw it [steroid use] affecting his moods with the family, with his kids," Garrett Webster said. "He just stopped doing it."

His work ethic never wavered. After minicamp in 1987 at Three Rivers Stadium, Webster looked to rookie linebacker Greg Lloyd and said, "C'mon, rook, and run with me." He led Lloyd through his daily routine, running the steps of the stadium's upper deck. Up and down, section to section they went, all the way around the stadium. "It wasn't about how much time it took," Lloyd said. "It was just about finishing." To the twenty-two-year-old Lloyd it was grueling, torturous, like a death march. The burly thirty-five-year-old lineman finished three stadium sections ahead of him. "Mike was in incredible shape," Lloyd said. "I just wanted to keep him in sight."

As a player, Webster lived in the moment as if the moment would never end. Grossman called him "a high-end diesel tractor that is stuck on 'Go.'" He played hard and he played hurt. The Steeler quarterback who became the starter in 1984, Mark Malone, noticed Webster's intensity even in pregame warm-ups. "We'd be running plays against air and inevitably the first snap would just blow my hands apart and the ball would fly up in the air, his motor was running so fast," Malone said. Webster tore knee cartilage late one season. The knee swelled, locked up. He made the Pro Bowl. "Don't go," Berlin advised. "Let's get this worked on now." But Webster said, "I only have to run five yards" as a center, so he played in that Pro Bowl and, Berlin said, worsened his knee in the process.

Webster had a tough guy's droll sense of humor, often issuing what Ilkin called "The Webby Doom-and-Gloom Report." Stretching on the field before practices, Webster often turned to Ilkin and quoted John Wayne in *McLintock!*: "Pilgrim, if you say it's a fine day, I'm gonna shoot you!" His humor showed up during games, too. On Thanksgiving Day in 1983 in Detroit, the Steelers trailed the Lions 38–3 in the fourth quarter when quarterback Malone replaced starter Cliff Stoudt and enthusiastically burst into the huddle, saying, "C'mon, guys, we can do it!" Webster replied by saying what the others probably thought: "There's no way in hell we can do it!" On another occasion, moments before playing Dallas, Webster told the other offensive linemen to be respectful of the Cowboys' all-pro defensive tackle Randy White and not to block him at his knees. "Don't anybody cut Randy," he said. "Just leave him alone. It's preseason." But on the game's first play, White steamrollered Webster, who returned to the huddle and announced, "All right, cut the fuck out of him!"

Webster was a blocking technician, a master of leverage. He snapped the ball and quickly got his hands on the saddle horns of a defender's shoulder pads, the first stage of his blocking battle already won. Gary Dunn thought he had an understanding with Webster during one scrimmage in Latrobe in the early 1980s. Dunn had been moved to nose tackle that season and, facing Webster, whispered, "Hey, Webby, how about taking it easy on me? I need to look good here." Webster nodded and said across the line of scrimmage, "Okay, Gary. I'll take it easy." On the next play, Webster lifted the 258-pound Dunn and threw him backward against Lambert's legs.

"You sonavabitch!" Dunn muttered, and he knew he was in for it. Webster beat Dunn soundly throughout the scrimmage.

Humbled by the experience, Dunn drove his Jeep away from camp late that afternoon, bound for Pittsburgh on a rare off-night for players. On the Pennsylvania Turnpike, Webster suddenly appeared in his car, headed in the same direction. Dunn flipped his middle finger at him, and Webster smiled and shrugged. He motioned for Dunn to pull over. The two Steelers pulled their cars into a rest area beside the turnpike. Webster lifted his trunk, took out a few beers, and they talked about the scrimmage. "Naaw, you're going to be a good player. You just need to work on some things," Webster told him. Webster demonstrated what Dunn had done wrong in the scrimmage. They paired off again in the parking lot, in street clothes, pushing and maneuvering over an imaginary line of scrimmage. Dunn won several rounds, but then Webster said, "We need to do one more, and then I have to go." Then Webster did it: he re-created what he had done on the first play of the scrimmage. He lifted Dunn and threw him into a nearby guardrail. Webster got back into his car and drove off, laughing. Gary Dunn watched him leave and thought, *That sucker was probably just playing with me the whole time.*

It didn't end smoothly because it never does. Webster was the last active player among the twenty-two Steelers to win four Super Bowl rings. After the 1988 season the Steelers left him as an unprotected free agent, meaning the prideful Webster, approaching thirty-seven, was a Steeler no more. He burned in silence. Pam had begun to notice changes in his personality, the way he dealt with the kids, money. He seemed more distant, angrier.

If ever there was a cause for change in Pittsburgh, the 1988 season was it. The Steelers bottomed out with five wins and eleven defeats, the team's worst record in the twenty seasons since Noll's first in Pittsburgh. Noll was under attack. It was postulated in the sports press that he, Shula, and Tom Landry had lost touch with the modern-day player. The Steelers were ready to go with their young prodigy at center, Dermontti Dawson. The transition would be similar to 1976, when the Old Ranger, Ray Mansfield, gave way to Webster. Teammates held a retirement dinner for Webster, roasted him, and gave him a gold watch.

Webster hadn't planned for his life's work, but he had saved money and lived frugally through the years. He had purchased annuities, invested in some small businesses. He earned $350,000 during his last season in Pittsburgh, and there was a suggestion that he might serve as a coach

for the Steelers. But he felt spurned, discouraged. For fifteen years he had given himself to the Steelers. He didn't expect it to end this way or perhaps even to end at all. He needed to figure out what came next, as others had. At home, Pam held back her tears. She had expected, in some dreamy way, they might remain in the Pittsburgh Steelers family forever. She said, "It was like a death."

When the Kansas City Chiefs called with a coaching offer in February 1989, Webster accepted. He convinced himself that he would enjoy coaching, especially since teammates always said that he was like a coach on the field. But after coaching the Chiefs' offensive linemen for five weeks, Webster told Kansas City team president Carl Peterson and head coach Marty Schottenheimer that he wanted to play again, as a center for the Chiefs. "He wanted to prove it to the Steelers," Peterson said. "He felt that he had been thrown out with the wash." Playing center would give Webster structure, purpose, stature, and hope. That his move from assistant coach to starting center for the Chiefs would increase his salary from about $50,000 to $400,000 served as an incentive. Pam supported his decision, and she and the kids moved to Kansas City.

Webster returned to his old habits. In the weight room he worked himself to exhaustion. He arrived first to the Chiefs' team meetings, and sat in the front row each day, pen and notepad in hand. He studied game films deep into the night. He sprinted to the line of scrimmage during games, and at practices, and even from drill to drill. If a blocking drill came next, he grabbed the blocking bags—no need to wait for the equipment guys to do it!—and carried them himself. In private conversations in Peterson's office, Webster spoke with reverence of Noll, his no-nonsense approach, and how the Steelers had developed a world championship spirit. Webster wanted that for Kansas City, and wrote lengthy letters to Peterson about that, emphasizing commitment. The Chiefs signed veteran quarterback Ron Jaworski, who was thirty-eight, and with Webster would serve in 1989 as the NFL's oldest battery-mates since the Raiders' George Blanda and Jim Otto. Webster started all sixteen games in 1989 and played nine more games in 1990. He talked by phone with Ilkin each week and admitted that he didn't like the Chiefs' zone blocking scheme. "You are running to the sideline for five seconds," Webster said, "before you run into somebody!"

Otto stood on the sideline before a Raiders-Chiefs game in 1990. A Raiders executive wearing sports coat and tie, Otto spotted Webster, in his Chiefs uniform, walking toward him. They had much in common as undersized centers from Wisconsin who played through pain and built themselves into celebrated all-pros. They'd first met twenty-one years before, in 1969, when Webster was still in high school, and then five years later, when Webster, a Steelers rookie, waved to him from across the field during pregame warm-ups ("Mr. Otto! Mr. Otto!"). Otto played fifteen seasons, Webster seventeen. Football shattered Otto's body. He would endure fifty-three surgeries on his knees, including fourteen replacements. He surgically replaced both shoulders. He underwent four back surgeries and, during one, a steel rod was inserted. "I have so much metal in me," Otto said, "I'm a one-man Steel Curtain." He suffered an infection after one knee procedure, which prompted open-heart surgery. In 2007, his right leg was amputated. "Football took it," Otto said.

On the sideline that day in 1990, Webster greeted Otto as an equal. "Double-O!" Webster said, with swagger and a smile. They shook hands. "What are you going to do, Mike?" Otto said. "Wear the football out?"

"The thing about Webster and Otto, and that type of player, the famously tough guys," Michael Oriard, a former Chiefs center and now an Oregon State professor, said, " 'tough' is less in what they deliver than in what they absorb or withstand. . . . They are two really powerful, iconic figures of stoic toughness. Toughness is fundamental to football, and I don't disparage it. It just has its limits." Oriard added, "Webster didn't protect himself. The most obvious way [to do that] would have been to quit after ten years at the most."

In March 1991, Webster officially retired from the NFL after seventeen years. "One thing you learn in this game," he said at his press conference, "is reality."

That Webby was losing touch with reality soon became clear to Peterson from letters Webster sent him. They were longer and more rambling than before, written in longhand with a pencil. Passionate, yes, but they were beyond repetitive, Peterson said, "almost like an adolescent wrote them." Peterson had offered Webster a coaching job upon his retirement, but Webster declined. He moved to Lodi, saying he needed to repair his marriage. Peterson cared deeply about Webster and occasionally slipped him some money. Webster tried to earn a living. He promoted or invested in a variety of businesses that failed or never materialized. NBC Sports expressed interest in him as a sportscaster, but his scheduled auditions didn't happen. His name attached to multiple businesses, but without compensation. He received offers to join boards of obscure companies—people wanted to lay claim to his famous football name—and he was too nice, or perhaps too naive, to say no. His earnings dried up. He made less than $6,000 in wages in 1991, and no wages at all in 1992 and 1993.

In Pittsburgh, Webster met Bleier for lunch several times, always with a new business deal to discuss. He didn't seek Bleier's investment, just an ear to bend. To Bleier, Webster seemed clean-pressed and presentable. "But there was always something that wasn't quite right, and I couldn't put my finger on it," Bleier said. For one, he thought Webster's shirt was a little old. Webster paid a visit to Andy Russell, an investment banker. "He came to see if we could raise some money for a [business] project he had," Russell said. But Russell said he was unable to help. Webster approached Dan Rooney, too. "He acted strange even during the early period [after his NFL retirement]," Dan said. "He would have different problems and come to see me." Once, Webster wanted to borrow money for an investment in a worm business. "What do you do with worms?" Dan asked. Webster replied, "You fish with them." Dan shook his head and said, "Well, that's no business. I'm not giving you money for that."

Sitting across from Mike Wagner, Webster wanted to know if Wagner's company might invest in a manufacturing company developing a new product. Webster's appearance startled Wagner. He seemed small and shriveled. He didn't look healthy. "He was hard to engage," Wagner said. Wagner didn't have a good feeling about this manufacturing business, and he told Webster as much. Wagner thought, *I'm sitting here in this nice office, and I'm his old teammate, and I'm bringing him bad news.* He sensed Webster's embarrassment. "Mike, I did not want to tell you this," Wagner said. "I'll help you if you want some help." Webster's presentation puzzled Wagner. It was odd and suggested disconnect. It was the first indication to Wagner that maybe Webby wasn't right. "Mike, do you do a lot of these?" Wagner asked. From his briefcase Webster pulled out a handful of memorandums from business brokers. "Who makes these decisions for you?" Wagner asked. Webster answered, "I do. I look at all these things." Years later, Wagner said, "My relationship with him wasn't that good. I really couldn't give him, or wanted to give him, professional advice."

Webster's financial and marital strains intensified. He was in his early forties but looked at least a decade older. He suffered intense physical pain from sharp headaches, arthritic joints, a torn rotator cuff in his shoulder, from nerves activated by desiccated and ruptured spinal discs, from hands and fingers mangled and swollen from being bent and stepped on at the line of scrimmage, and a right heel that felt almost as if a spear were stuck in it. He saw doctors, got prescriptions, lived a nomadic life. He wrote copious notes on legal pads, his thoughts like bumper cars colliding. He ate poorly, if at all. From lack of care, his teeth rotted. He took a long list of prescribed medicines—Darvocet, Vicodin, Prozac, Ritalin, Dexedrine, Klonopin, Ultram, Paxil, and Lorcet—to combat pain, inflammation, attention deficit, anxiety, and depression.

Saying he wanted his players to see the look of a winner, Peterson brought Webster back to the Chiefs in 1994. He awarded him the title of assistant strength coach, though Webster's name wasn't listed in the team's media guide. Essentially, the job was a gift to a proud man, who insisted he wouldn't accept handouts. At the Chiefs' facility, Webster was cheerful, positive, and worked hard with young players in the weight room. During some practices, he bent over and made snaps to quarterbacks during seven-on-seven drills, a role often handled by equipment room workers. What many of the Chiefs players didn't know at first was that Webster was living at the Chiefs' facility, upstairs in a storage room between two racquetball courts. The room was spartan, windowless, and littered with pieces of broken furniture and broken weights. It was like a cell, with a sleeping bag. Word got out finally and players whispered among themselves, "Don't say anything—he's living up there." The response was always the same: "He's living up . . . *there*?" He became like Boo Radley, a ghostly, if friendly, figure. A team physician examined Webster and told Peterson that he suffered from liver and kidney problems that would only get worse in years to come. The physician prescribed new medication and encouraged Webster to take action. "Mike had such pride, he just refused to do that," Peterson said. Peterson instructed Webster to participate in the NFL Players Association insurance program but said Webster did not fill out the paperwork.

Safety Ronnie Lott was in the Chiefs camp early in 1995. At thirty-six, Lott was considered an old man of the gridiron. Unlike the younger Chiefs players, Lott knew Webster's herculean NFL accomplishments chapter and verse. When Lott first met Lambert, Greene, Harris, Swann, and Stallworth, those Steelers had commanded his respect through their presence alone. But that wasn't the case with Webster. "I could tell there was the heart of a champion there," Lott said, but "it was like looking at an old pair of Converse." Lott found Webster friendly but difficult to engage in conversation. He had a faraway look. "You could tell that the world of the [1970s] Steelers was far away," Lott said. Webster reminded him of Jim Otto. "Both of those guys exemplified something that football is about," Lott said. Football injuries were like badges of courage to them. To Lott, Webster and Otto represented both sides of the game, the light and the dark. "And," Lott said, "I think the dark sometimes, for them, is light."

The nomad moved on. Back in Pittsburgh, Ilkin got word that Webby wasn't right, and was living out of his car. He gathered with former team-mates Craig Wolfley and Ted Peterson and together they put him up at a motel in Greentree. He needed a physical checkup and dental work. "He just didn't want to do any of those things," Ilkin said. Even so, they enjoyed being with Webby again and sharing some laughs. "He would sound like the old Mike," Ilkin said, "but then he would say something really peculiar, kind of out of left field." The three former teammates searched for an apartment for Webster near their own homes, so together they might keep watch over him. But first they bought a plane ticket for him to return to Pam and the kids for Christmas; he stayed in Wisconsin for some time. When he returned, Webster grew increasingly suspicious of his former teammates' help. "He got really suspicious of me, and I couldn't believe it," Ilkin said. "And that hurt."

Other Steeler teammates tried to help, too. In phone conversations among Russell, Ham, and Wagner, an idea was broached to create a chari-table entity that would fund bill payments for Webster and other former teammates and their families. "A few of us would write checks," Wagner said, "but we were trying to decide whether to develop a program like a

Pittsburgh Steeler Dire Need fund, or something like that." They considered creating a fund-raiser for that purpose but, Wagner said, the concept never came to fruition. "We were kind of going, 'Well, who is going to donate money to old football players? They think you guys are all taken care of anyway.'" Wagner added, "We were concerned about [Webster's] kids. If he doesn't have enough money, then what about his kids?"

Bradshaw spoke with Webster a couple of times a year. In those phone conversations, Bradshaw asked, "What can I do for you? What do you need?" Each time, Webster's answer was the same: "Nothing." Years later, Bradshaw said, "The problem with men is pride. Webby wouldn't take anything from me. . . . Proud men don't want handouts. We do have to take care of them. But, golly, if they won't let us, what are we going to do?"

In August 1996, Joe Gordon hurried to the Amtrak station in Pittsburgh. The Steelers had received a call from the train station's night manager: a haggard-looking man had just spent the night sleeping in the train station, and that man looked a lot like Mike Webster. At Dan's suggestion, Gordon took $200 from petty cash at the Steelers' offices. He discovered Webster sitting in the station's waiting room, photos of Muhammad Ali, Arnold Palmer, and other famous athletes spread out before him on a table. Webster said he had obtained permission to market the photos. Gordon asked Webster where he was living. The Red Roof Inn, Webster said. Trying to help, Gordon arranged for him to spend the weekend at the Hilton, and gave him the $200. Webster would spend the next two months at the Hilton. The Steelers picked up the tab. Only after some cajoling by Gordon did Webster finally check out.

When Bradshaw first laid eyes on Webster at Canton in July 1997, he was shocked and alarmed. Webster's appearance was even worse than Bradshaw had feared. ESPN had aired a segment a few weeks before, revealing that Webster was homeless, struggling with cognitive issues, eating Little Debbie pecan swirls and Pringles potato chips from vending machines, and living out of his truck. Bradshaw wanted to get Webster's teeth fixed, but there wasn't time. He did what he could. "I got him a haircut," Bradshaw said. Others bought him new clothes. Webby had chosen his quarterback as his Hall of Fame presenter. As newspapers across the nation picked up on the story of Webby's plight, the *Pittsburgh Post-Gazette* said, "What will happen after Bradshaw introduces Webster is anyone's guess."

Webster didn't want to attend the ceremony. He wanted no part of the Hall of Fame, the Steelers, or the NFL. To Webster, they were moneymaking machines that cared little about him. Sunny Jani convinced him to go to Canton. Jani had become Webster's caretaker. Married with a young family, Jani ran a grocery store in the McKee's Rock section of Pittsburgh. A lifelong Steelers fan, Jani had met Webster at an autograph show in 1994 and befriended him. Soon Webster was sleeping in his pickup truck outside Jani's grocery store, and on the couch in the store's back office. Jani took Webster to doctor's appointments and autograph shows. If he earned $1,500 at a signing, Webster sent $1,000 of that amount to Pam and the kids in Wisconsin via Western Union. Once, Webster called Jani in the middle of the night to say he was in his truck, pulled to the roadside confused, and unsure of where he was. Jani drove nine hours, nearly to Milwaukee, to get him. Jani began to duct-tape money in hidden places in Webster's truck in case he got lost again.

Pam told her husband that she and the kids were broke and couldn't go to Canton "if you don't pay our way there." The Hall of Fame quietly made arrangements for their stay. For Webby, it was an uncomfortable weekend in Canton. "He ranged between timid and quiet," Joe Horrigan, the Hall's vice president of communications, said. "I thought of him being maybe just a little bit odd at times. He'd disappear and I'd look around and think, 'Where did he go?' He'd be off by himself."

Thinking of that weekend fourteen years later, Pam shakes her head. She had hoped for the best in Canton but feared the worst, knowing that Mike Webster was sick, angry, and unpredictable. "He was like a loose cannon," she tells me. "You didn't know what was going to happen." Her four children worried, too. She says, "We didn't want him to embarrass himself there. There were people that still loved him, and remembered him in a certain way, including us. It was really important to me that he wasn't going to be laughed at."

When Bradshaw stepped to the microphone, Pam and the kids were there, and so were some of Webster's former Steeler teammates. In his introduction, Bradshaw said, "He was the backbone upon which we were built. He was our spine. There never has been, and never will be, another Mike Webster." Webster stepped into the light. He brought a football and once again he and Bradshaw pantomimed the center snap for the crowd.

Wearing a yellow Hall of Fame blazer and black cowboy boots, Webster was well groomed, and fortified by an 80-milligram dose of Ritalin, which helped his concentration and mood. Sitting only a few rows from the speaker's platform, Pam braced herself. "We were all afraid what he was going to say," she says. "I mean, he had trouble completing a sentence, and thought."

"Giving Bradshaw a forum and a microphone," Webster began, "is like giving Visine to a Peeping Tom, you know?"

Webster spoke without notes. He thanked Steelers fans, his coaches, the Chief, and Kansas City owner Lamar Hunt. Then he addressed "the most important people in my life," saying, "I'd like the members of my immediate family, Pamela and the children, to stand." They did, along with his parents and siblings. Then Webby stepped from the podium and walked toward them. Pam tensed.

Absorbed by the memory of this moment, she says, "So Mike starts walking toward us and we were all like, 'What's going to happen?'" Webby stopped in front of Pam and hugged her, and then hugged their four children, one by one. It was heartfelt, unexpected, sad. "That just totally blew me away," Pam says. Sitting in a Starbucks, her body trembles at the memory, and tears come, same as they did in Canton. "It was like this man up there was a man I didn't know anymore," she says.

Instructed to limit his speech to less than ten minutes, Webster spoke for twenty-three. "If he would've just stopped at ten," said Ilkin, who sat in the crowd with Wolfley and Peterson. "He took a shot at Brad. It was really good. But then he started drifting." At one point Webster seemed to be speaking not only of football, but his life, when he said, "You only fail if you don't finish the game. If you finish, you win, okay? But you don't measure that in the middle of the second quarter, third quarter, you measure it at the end. As long as you keep going, you keep trying, you keep working at it, right?" He rambled on with no coherent narrative or theme.

"It went on forever," Pam says.

Ilkin: "He would say things that were Old Webby, sharp and articulate, and then he would go off in a direction, and you would go, 'Wow!' The longer it went, the harder it was to watch."

Bradshaw: "He was not right. I knew he wasn't right."

Pam: "I knew nobody would have the balls to go up and stop him. I was going to nudge [their son] Garrett if it kept going. It was obvious at that point to everyone that this wasn't the Mike Webster of the days of old."

When his speech was done, there was relief for Webster's family and friends. Photographers crowded around and asked for a family photo. As Mike and Pam and the kids pressed together and prepared to smile, Mike said softly to Pam, "This is probably our last family photo." It was.

They looked out the window and saw him sitting at the curb in his beat-up truck, which looked like it had played seventeen NFL seasons, too. "Mom," one of the kids would say, "Dad's outside again." It happened this way several times. It wasn't exactly that Webby would come home for the holidays. Instead, he would show up and sit in his truck in front of the house at the holidays. Pam saw him out there—he looked so alone and sad in the darkness—and the sight pained her. "My heart is breaking that he doesn't want to come in," Pam says. "I wanted him inside." They had been separated since 1992, but she told him he always was welcome at the house to spend time with their kids. Invariably his pride kicked in, and he wasn't thinking logically, or perhaps he was—"I know I caused him some pain by not being able to be so-called husband and wife," Pam says. "We lived apart for a lot of years"—and so he sat alone in the cold of his truck on Thanksgiving night. Pam sent out one of the kids to gauge his mood and his willingness to join the family. When he refused to come inside, she sent out a plate with turkey, biscuits, and gravy, and that pleased him. Sometimes he gave in and joined his family for a holiday dinner. Afterward, Pam says, he would head for Garrett's bed and sleep for a few days.

Constantly on the move, and misplacing his Ritalin pills, Webster made frequent stops at Pittsburgh-area drugstores for replenishments. In

February 1999, police arrested and handcuffed him in Beaver County and charged him with forging nineteen prescriptions for Ritalin. At a press conference, Webster put on a coat and tie, and choked with emotion as he read a statement, apologizing for what he'd done, and insisting that he would pay his debt to society. Bleier, Blount, and Grossman came to lend their support. Two doctors treating Webster told reporters that Webster's frontal lobe had been damaged from too many hard hits on the football field and that he suffered from a condition similar to dementia. It affected his moods, and decision making. He needed Ritalin, one doctor said, and asserted that Webster's brain injury could not be healed: "All you do is control symptoms."

Bob Fitzsimmons, a personal injury attorney from Wheeling, West Virginia, had arranged the press conference, brought in the doctors, and asked a few of the old Steelers if they would attend to give Webby some moral support. Dan had called Fitzsimmons before the press conference to see if he could help, too.

Fitzsimmons had begun to lay the groundwork for Webster to file a disability claim with the NFL. It took him nearly a year to gather Webster's medical records and employment history from the 1990s. He sent Webster to four doctors and they all agreed that Webster had suffered cognitive loss from repetitive head traumas on the football field. Webster was a poor historian of his own life. He wasn't even sure if he and Pam were still legally married. (They were.) Fitzsimmons developed a legal narrative about a rugged athlete brutalized by professional football and unable to earn a living or function normally in daily life. Sometimes Webster showed up for scheduled meetings two days late. He placed notes and letters on Fitzsimmons's car windshield, or against the front door of his law office. Fitzsimmons gave Webster use of an office in the basement to rest and clean up after another night sleeping in his truck. "The girls in the office made a big fuss over Mike and I think he liked that," Fitzsimmons said.

Webster grieved over his inability to provide for Pam and the kids. At one point, he decided to sell his five rings, four from the Super Bowls, and one from the Hall of Fame. Fitzsimmons urged him not to do it. He said in a short time Webster would begin receiving disability payments from the NFL. But Webster was adamant, saying the rings were only symbols.

"They don't mean anything to me," he said. Two potential buyers from New York showed up at Fitzsimmons's office. Fitzsimmons didn't like them. "They were there to make a quick deal and a profit," he said. He pulled aside Webster and convinced him not to sell. Then he told the buyers, "They aren't available." The buyers weren't pleased. The room grew tense. Much later Fitzsimmons said, "It's a wonder we didn't get shot."

Dan lobbied the NFL's pension board behind the scenes, and in November 1999 Webster began collecting partial disability payments of about $3,000 a month. He endorsed these checks and sent them to Pam and the kids in Wisconsin, taking just enough for himself to buy groceries. But then the Internal Revenue Service seized those checks, saying that Webster had not filed taxes in years. Other lawsuits against Webster cropped up. "Every time we receive news, it's another problem," Fitzsimmons said. "It all has to do with the ability [for Webster] to remember how to do certain things, like filing tax forms."

The league's pension board had granted Webster a disability plan for former players who developed injuries six months after they retired from football. But Fitzsimmons sought a more lucrative payment plan for those players totally disabled from the moment they retired from the league. And so Fitzsimmons began the appeals process, "fighting the big evil giant, the NFL Pension Board." Webster made him promise never to give up this fight to which he, too, was committed. Webster immersed himself, and as his suspicions and paranoia grew, it loomed as his final obsession.

His thoughts became like a dense forest that light couldn't penetrate. They lacked clarity, direction, conclusions. "It's like having ginger ale in my skull," Webster would say. His conversations became odder, more eccentric. With Fitzsimmons, he might begin talking about one subject (his medical condition) then stray to another (the Civil War) and then to another (Bill Clinton).

Late in 1999, he disappeared again. *Where is Webby now?* His older son, Colin, who would become a marine, hadn't seen him for two days. Father and son lived together near Beaver Falls, Pennsylvania, Joe Namath's hometown. Just out of high school, Colin had grown accustomed to his father's disappearances. Webby got lost frequently, even driving to the local store. Several times during winter, he had wrapped himself in an Indian blanket and walked shirtless and barefoot into the woods. There was no way to reach him during these absences, and he was gone for weeks at a time. In the woods, Webby told Colin, he thought more clearly.

On a hunch, Colin wandered into nearby woods, and walked alone into the deep-packed snow for some time, maybe a mile or more, searching for his father. He found a bare human footprint, a good sign. Up ahead, in a clearing, he saw his father, perspiring heavily.

"If there is meaning in life at all, then there must be meaning in suffering," Viktor Frankl, a Holocaust survivor, wrote in *Man's Search for Meaning*.

Frankl also wrote, "Abnormal reaction to an abnormal situation is normal behavior."

Both notions applied here.

Barefoot and shirtless, as before, and wearing only khaki pants, Webby held a sizable log in his hands. He smiled at Colin as if their meeting were planned. He dropped the log and it crashed to earth with a thud, creating a shower of snow powder. Colin had never seen him so thin. He was emaciated, though still a mighty force. His shoulder-length blond hair was matted, and the six-pack muscles of his abdomen revealed themselves impressively, especially for a forty-seven-year-old man. To Colin, who would write about this moment years later on a website for weight lifters, his father resembled a caveman. Suddenly he heard Webby's huff and puff as he power-snatched the log over his head, palmed it, and lowered it to his chest. Webby squatted up and down, an experienced weight lifter's moves. Colin thought it amazing but disturbing. He saw no sign of a campfire, no kindling, no food, only some large stones, a few logs, and his father's notebook and pen, a football Thoreau at Walden Pond. When Colin tried to lift the same log, he barely got it off the ground.

Later Colin read the notes his father wrote in the woods, and decided they made no sense, no sense at all. Yet he extrapolated a deeper meaning from what he had witnessed, and it soothed him. His father was happy and physically energized. That moment, abnormal as surely it was, provided Mike Webster a refuge and a release. It reaffirmed his lifelong love for the outdoors and for physically challenging his body in ways that would break most men. These woods became like surrogates for the Wisconsin northwoods of Webby's youth and for those spare, unadorned places where he lifted weights obsessively as a Steeler with Kolb and Courson and Ilkin and Wolfley—the boiler room at Three Rivers Stadium or in the basement of the Red Bull Inn.

The sight of his father lifting a fallen log like a modern caveman returned him, at least in his son's eyes, to greatness. Colin clung to this hope for without it there was nothing, and then the man really was crazy.

Webby's younger son Garrett wanted to be with him. So in 2000, after Colin had moved on, Garrett left Lodi, still furious about those rude small-town whisperers who had mocked his father, and moved into an apartment with Webby in Moon Township, near Pittsburgh International Airport. The IRS garnishments kept them virtually penniless. They had no furniture for a time, and slept on the floor, often surrounded by empty pizza boxes. The local pizza parlors knew about Webby's myriad troubles and gave them free pizza. Garrett put a small flag in the apartment's front window so that his father could identify which apartment was theirs.

Only seventeen, Garrett was like a man-child, six-foot-eight, 350 pounds. He played high school football, though without his father's dedication. Mike Webster attended his games, standing behind a fence, and interacting happily with people who approached him. To Garrett, he wrote pregame notes meant to inspire, quoting Churchill and Patton. These notes were as repetitive as his letters to Carl Peterson once had been. "Stay low on your blocks and have fun," he wrote in one, and by Garrett's measure there was but one lucid paragraph in eight pages.

At times it seemed Garrett was the father, and Webby his son. Garrett, Fitzsimmons, and Jani referred to themselves as the Team. Together they were to protect Mike Webster from anyone who threatened him, including himself. Garrett figured his father had about three good days a month during which he seemed normal, or at least normal for him. A fitful sleeper, Webby often sat through long nights in a chair, his body racked with pain, waiting for sleep to come. Sometimes he remained awake for two or three consecutive days before exhaustion finally brought sleep. Father and son shared some happy times together, shopping at Wal-Mart, testing their memories of lines from John Wayne movies. "Having him in my corner meant everything," Garrett said. "My dad was my whole world. He was my best friend. He was Dad."

He saw his father's pride rise up against his slow demise. When Bradshaw phoned him, Webster told Garrett, "Don't tell him anything. Tell him that I'm fine." That was his standing order, and Garrett followed it with everyone—former Steelers, the press, even his mother and siblings. He knew that this wasn't honest. "But that was under his directive," Garrett said. He added, "There are seven deadly sins. My dad's was pride."

Webby stayed up late at night poring over legal documents related to his case against the NFL. He absorbed little of what he read. One morning, Garrett saw him reading a book and late that night, still holding the same book, Garrett asked, "Dad, you goin' to bed?" Webby answered, "I only got through three pages today." In his readings, he immersed himself in conspiracies, his favorite the Kennedy assassination. "I'll tell you about this JFK stuff, but whatever you do, don't say it on the phone," he told Garrett. "Somebody could be listening." As the NFL pension board continued to reject his disability claim, Webby became increasingly suspicious that his phone was bugged and that someone was following him, and perhaps even looking through his trash. He wrote letters to Bill Clinton and George W. Bush, seeking their intervention in his case.

One moment brought intense discomfort to Garrett. His father asked Garrett to use his stun gun on him to ease his pain and to help him sleep. Garrett thought he was joking. He wasn't. Webby often used the stun gun on himself, holding it against his body and zapping himself over and over. Now he asked Garrett to press it against his side to stun him into unconsciousness. "It was supposed to paralyze [him] for like fifteen minutes," Garrett said. He didn't want to do it, though he did, because he would do anything for his father. He pressed it against his father's flesh, just above his hip, and watched the old football player's body shake from the electrical surge. "That's enough," Webby said finally. Garrett was aghast by what he'd seen and done, though the jolt seemed to help. His father closed his eyes, and rested for about forty-five minutes. When he awoke, he said he felt better. Webby never asked him to do it again.

✦ ✦ ✦

Pam stood alone in a Wisconsin courtroom in 2002. After a decade's separation, her husband of twenty-eight years didn't show up. The center who hardly ever missed a Pittsburgh Steelers game missed his own divorce proceeding. Pam had filed for divorce years earlier, though it didn't happen. Now, though, it had to happen, she needed to move on, past the rolling waves of distress, the financial uncertainties, the raw emotions, the frayed relations with her husband. She was exhausted by all of it.

Here was how the marriage of Mike and Pam Webster looked at its final hour: an empty Wisconsin courtroom but for the plaintiff, Pam Webster; her attorney; the recorder; and the judge.

No communication from Mike.

No lawyer for Mike.

No Mike.

It was as if no one cared, Pam thought. "One of the emptiest feelings I've ever had," she says.

The legal proceeding took only minutes. The divorce was issued by default.

At home in Wheeling, Fitzsimmons took the call from Garrett late at night on September 23, 2002. He heard the urgency in the teenager's voice. Webby was at Allegheny General Hospital and not doing well. Doctors said he'd suffered a heart attack. He underwent surgery and was on the brink. "Can you get here?" Garrett asked. Mike Webster's protectors—the Team—sprang into action. Fitzsimmons sped toward Pittsburgh and called the hospital for several updates along the way. Jani called Pam in Wisconsin and told her the situation was grave. With her daughters Brooke and Hillary, she, too, sped toward Pittsburgh. In the darkness, somewhere on Interstate 80 in Indiana, she took a call from Garrett. "He's gone," Garrett said, and their voices caught with emotion. She turned and faced her daughters. They knew. Pam said, "Daddy's gone." Fitzsimmons was only minutes from the hospital when he got word that Mike Webster had died. The attorney went inside and saw Webster's body on the table. Fitzsimmons was struck by its musculature, the huge chest, massive biceps and forearms. Webby's hair was long and unkempt, his facial features bony, yet prominent with that great, defined chin and jaw.

Here, then, was the shorthand of Mike Webster's life: retired after seventeen NFL seasons at nearly forty, he was dead at fifty, and in between he lost his money, his marriage, and—precipitating all of it—his mind.

Days later, at the small funeral home in Robinson Township, his 1970s Steelers teammates showed up in force, crowding in among the two hundred mourners. Swann delivered a eulogy. Beneath his cowboy hat, Blount wore a somber expression. Reconvening in Steelers brotherhood were Mullins, Kolb, Dunn, Thomas, Dwayne Woodruff, Courson, Bahr, Ilkin, Wolfley, and others. These men embraced, exchanged updated e-mail addresses and cell numbers, and discussed the importance of looking after their health. Harris heard former teammates saying privately that maybe they all ought to get medical checkups. Dan was there, and Art Jr., too; Dan sent a check to pay for the funeral. Chuck Noll, with his wife, Marianne, asked to see Garrett. In a side room at the funeral home, Noll told Garrett that there was no player that he had loved and respected more than Mike Webster, words that pleased the son.

Iconoclastic Steeler personalities revealed themselves anew: the colorful and massive Courson wore a sports coat, cowboy boots, and a white dress shirt with its sleeves cut off in a tribute to his old friend Webby. (Garrett said, "If Dad had been alive he would've laughed his ass off." Pam added, "Steve Courson looked like a Chippendale dancer.") Lambert, ever the soloist, did not attend the funeral, but arranged a visit to the funeral home after hours to pay his respects privately.

Bradshaw delivered a eulogy. He had missed the Chief's funeral fourteen years earlier. Not Webby's. He said, "We should never allow the passing of a loved one to be the drawing card to keep our family together," a thought that resonated with the 1970s Steelers in attendance. It was ironic that Bradshaw, of all Steelers, gave voice to this feeling, given his estrangement from the team. I asked Bradshaw about it. "When we are all together we realize how much we love and care about one another," he said, "and then the emotion of that moment dissipates and we move away, and the further we get away from that moment of love, we go right back into our lives. That was what that meant."

Dan Radakovich didn't make it to the funeral. He stopped by the funeral home the day before and spoke with family members. He dressed

for the funeral, had every intention to attend. But when he drove up and saw the people gathered outside, he drove off. I sat with Radakovich at a Moon Township restaurant nearly a decade later and asked him why he hadn't stayed. Tears filled Bad Rad's eyes. "Because he fucked up," he said of Mike Webster. He pounded his fist against the table four times. "Oh, God . . . ," he said. "It's hard." He had coached the Steelers' offensive line for four seasons and considered Webster "the epitome of a great player." But near the end of Webster's long NFL career, Bad Rad said, "He couldn't run across the field. You could see him struggling. He should've quit. He played at least three years too long, okay?" I asked him to explain the source of his tears. His answer sounded like a football coach's survivor guilt: "He was a hell of a player and you are pissed because you thought maybe you could've helped him at the end. Maybe I could've. Maybe somebody could've. His life got screwed up somehow. I don't know. I'm a football coach and I'm trying to figure out how he got the brain damage. He's a center. He could've gotten hit in the head many times. But we didn't block that way, didn't coach that way. . . . I devised this [blocking style] to hit with the shoulder, and come through with the hands."

For years Webster's plight confounded Franco Harris. "In the beginning, I wasn't sure what it was, but you'd help out," Harris said. "A lot of people tried to help, but it just wasn't—I mean the only way [to help Webster] was to put him in an institution or something like that. None of us really understood the full impact of his brain damage at that time." Harris admired Webster. "People have this image of him at the end of his life that's totally the opposite of the real Mike. Mike Webster was such a beautiful person. He was such a great human being." The weekend after the funeral, Harris made sure to attend Garrett's high school football game as a show of his continuing support.

The funeral was hard on Pam. She was the ex-wife now, and felt the tension of a divorce less than a year old. At the funeral, she says, one of her former in-laws told her to *rot in hell* for what she'd done to Mike. Pam sat apart from family, though Garrett moved to sit with her. Colin was a marine now, married with children, and about to ship to Iraq. Bradshaw, Harris, and other former Steelers approached Pam, expressed their condolences. Bradshaw hugged her, and held her for a few moments.

"I don't think any of them blamed me," Pam said, "which was a total relief, because I'm struggling in this war of words." Pam stared at all the former Steelers, overwhelmed by a solitary thought: "My God, you look good, your family is intact, you've got money. You've got a new career. *Why couldn't that be us?*"

She put a letter in Webby's casket to say that she was sorry and that she cared.

CHAPTER 21

THE ROONEYS

AROUND PITTSBURGH, NO ONE MISTOOK the Rooneys for Carnegies or Mellons. To become one of modern Pittsburgh's defining families, the Rooneys had not followed the late-nineteenth-century path of the titans through banking, railroads, and steel. They rose from a saloon on General Robinson Street and built their name through football, horse racing, and a common touch.

The Chief's personal story resonated in a workingman's town. He'd made it big, and on his own terms. Everything about the rumpled old man, the way he dressed, spoke, and carried himself, that he'd lived for a half century in the same old house (not a *mansion*) in a transitional area on the North Side, and even the way he proudly embraced the story about how his grandfather had raised his gun against Carnegie and Frick's Pinkertons in the Homestead strike of 1892, suggested that he was still *one of us.* Those who knew Art Rooney Sr. as the soft touch attending wakes of people he didn't know might have been shocked to see how demanding and dismissive he could be in private moments with his five boys even as they grew into civically devoted, self-respecting men.

In Pittsburgh, around the Chief, a powerful mystique grew.

By the middle 1980s Art Rooney Sr., a pudgy old leprechaun, was celebrated as a Pittsburgh treasure and his son Dan a civic pillar and custodian of the beloved Steelers. With his father's sense of noblesse oblige, Dan became a steward of Pittsburgh, involved in many local causes, and with a deep attachment to Ireland, the Rooneys' ancestral home. To their city and to pro football, the Rooneys brought their own brand of stability, civility, and humility. "They always said the right things," former Houston coach Bum Phillips observed of the Rooneys, "and never bragged on themselves."

After Kass died in 1982, the Chief remained in the old house at 940 North Lincoln as it filled with echoes. His five sons often brought some of his thirty-one grandchildren on visits. Once, in passing, the Chief wistfully told Art Jr. he might like to buy a minor league baseball team. The NFL was so big now, he said, and wouldn't it be fun to watch young ballplayers begin their long march to the big leagues! At times he became cantankerous with his sons. "You guys aren't taking care of me," he complained once. "I was keeping my father a lot younger than you are with me. And you don't have to keep me. *I'm still keeping you!*" He wasn't keeping them, of course. Time had sped past Art Rooney Sr. like one of his racehorses.

It was Dan's team now, and Dan's city. It was Dan's time, a generational passing. Dan was in his fifties, and his four younger brothers still remembered how, when they were boys and the old man wasn't around, Danny took charge, leading them in reciting their Hail Marys. If the Chief had taught his eldest son one overriding life lesson about what it meant to be a Rooney in Pittsburgh, it was this: you must keep the Steelers viable, *and in Pittsburgh*, and to do that you must help the league, and the city, remain viable.

In the NFL, Dan, in his nondescript suits, became like a five-foot-eight-inch Gibraltar, a pivotal figure in labor negotiations with the players' union, expansion, scheduling, realignment, the salary cap, and the selection of league commissioners, who then turned to him as a sounding board. Dan's great gift was in blending toughness and compassion, a chip off the old block in that regard. At league meetings, Dan channeled his father's voice, often saying, in carefully measured terms, "Gentlemen, let's discuss and think about what is best for the National Football League, and think about our individual franchises secondarily." He did not inherit the raconteur's gift of gab from his father—Art Jr. did—or radiate warmth and good cheer in the Steelers' locker room like the old man. But Dan looked after his Steelers players. When J. T. Thomas developed an inflammatory disease and missed the 1978 season, leaving his career in jeopardy, Dan privately reassured him that a job in the Steelers' front office awaited him if he was unable to return to the field, exactly as the Chief had done once with Lowell Perry and others. When NFL players went on strike in 1987, Dan pulled aside Ilkin, the Steelers' union representative, and instructed, "Tunch, keep them together." Dan heard that the striking Steelers needed a place to hold practices, and thought of the locked, fenced-in grass field a few blocks from Three Rivers Stadium. He phoned Ilkin to say that a key to that field could be found on his secretary's desk. "But," Dan added, a wink in his voice, "you didn't get it from me."

During the eighties, Art Jr. felt pressure to re-create the 1970s, as nearly everyone with the Steelers did, and when that didn't happen it began to feed on his insecurities. It was all so much harder now. League-wide, college scouting was vastly improved, more systematized with computer analyses. Teams poured big money into scouting. It was cut-throat. Art Jr. also faced heightened expectations. He had drafted nine Hall of Famers in a six-year period, including four in 1974. In Super Bowl XIV, against the Rams, not a single player on the Steelers' roster had ever played a down for another NFL team. An NFL champion 100 percent homegrown was unprecedented, a monument to scouting. He had proven to himself during the 1970s that he could do the job, and do it exceptionally well. But deep down he still was trying to prove value to his father, Noll, and Dan.

Increasingly, Art Jr. grew tense as drafts approached. His insides churned, he became difficult, obstreperous. Everything, and everyone, not central to the draft he pushed aside. Once, in a pique, his wife, Kay, told him the draft was more important to him than his wife and children, and her accusation stung because he knew she was right. They had four children, including an autistic daughter with special needs. While he was on the road scouting for days on end, Kay shouldered the burden at home, heroically. At the start of one draft, nerves overcame him, and Art Jr. rushed to the men's room at Three Rivers Stadium and threw up, blood everywhere. His doctor later told him it was stress. On another draft morning, a reporter he didn't know made a crack, "Well, it's draft time, and you've got your game face on!" and Art Jr. thought to give him a piece of his mind but instead turned and stormed off. It mattered that much to him and he knew it was unfair to Kay and the kids. She began to take them away for a little vacation a day or two before the draft, and return once it was over. It was better for everyone that way.

The Chief wasn't happy when local-boy quarterback Dan Marino slipped away from the Steelers in the 1983 NFL draft. The Steelers still had Bradshaw, plus big hopes for backup quarterbacks Cliff Stoudt and Malone. They picked sixteenth in the first round, with Marino, from Pitt, still on the board. But Noll wanted to rebuild his defense with a brawny tackle from Texas, just as he had in 1969 with Greene. Art Jr. didn't try to change Noll's mind, as he had once about Franco Harris. The Steelers selected Gabe Rivera, "Senior Sack," from Texas Tech. It couldn't have turned out worse. Rivera was paralyzed in an automobile accident that fall. Bradshaw played only one game in 1983 and retired the next season, and the two backup quarterbacks combined to win one playoff game for the Steelers. Marino, meanwhile, went to the Miami Dolphins, and threw for more than four hundred yards and four touchdowns to defeat the Steelers in the 1984 AFC title game en route to a Hall of Fame career. Whenever Marino's name arose in conversation, Art Jr. saw the Chief give him an icy stare. "I know he never forgave me for Danny Marino," Art Jr. said.

Art Jr. protected his scouting turf fiercely, and with Bill Nunn, Dick Haley, Tom Modrak, and others, scoured the nation for college prospects. The draft-day masterpieces were no more. Only five Steelers picked in the dozen drafts between 1975 and 1986 made the Pro Bowl. To Dan, it was as if his younger brother had sealed off his department, creating his own fiefdom. Dan wanted open lines of communication, and for Art Jr. to let him and Noll inside. The Steelers finished 7-9 in 1985, and began the 1986 season by losing five of the first six games. The days of empire seemed a hundred years gone.

October 14, 1986, Dan's office: a meeting between two brothers. They sat on opposite sides of a desk. Decades later this moment crystallized in a younger brother's thoughts as his loneliest hour, when all that he had accomplished in his professional life was ripped to pieces by his older brother. Art Jr. could still see the chairs they sat in—leather-upholstered with ultramodern cast-iron silver frames—and the office's gray carpeting, and on the wall the document the Chief had signed in 1933 buying the

Steelers for $2,500. He could still hear his brother's words, swift as a descending guillotine, "I want you out of the day-to-day business."

That was it; it was done. That quickly, he had been fired. He heard Dan say that he could enter one of the family's other enterprises and write his own ticket. Art Jr. got up, as if dazed, and walked down the hall into the Chief's office. He asked the man for whom he was named if he'd known that this was coming. No, the Chief said, he did not, but then he heard the Chief say, "There can only be one boss," and those words, delivered in an evenhanded way, left Art Rooney Jr. feeling profoundly alone. This was not just his job. It was his family, his blood, his life's work. Twenty years and more on the road, a scout's lonely life, driving to college towns, filing player reports across the 1960s and 1970s and 1980s, the music on the radio changing, America changing, and now the Rooneys changing. He felt shock, anger, and the deep embarrassment of being fired by his brother. A day later, back in the Chief's office, he heard his father say, "I can't make things happen anymore," and as he spoke the Chief looked old, tired, and sad. Then he repeated, "There can only be one boss."

By design, the firing of Art Jr. would not be announced until season's end, more than two months away. The next day, Art Jr. called Tim, John, and Pat, and told each of his brothers what had happened. Surprised, yes, but they were not shocked because brothers know brothers. They knew the personalities, the internal struggles.

The Chief called a meeting. "You two guys," he scolded Dan and Art Jr., "I didn't need you. I could have gone out and hired a general manager. You guys have to work this out." Art Jr. didn't have a reply. Dan could hold up to the Chief's scolding, Art Jr. never could. Years later, Art Jr. recalled, "That had been my life, scouting. I was very, very, *extremely* one-dimensional."

John Rooney, their younger brother, got involved at the Chief's urging. "My dad asked me and young Art [II, Dan's eldest son] to get that straightened out. It was terribly hard because I cared so much about both of them," John said. "I was sort of the *consigliere* of that deal. Young Art and I talked to both of them for months. There were a lot of fights and arguments."

Hearing of the tensions, George Young of the Giants told Art Jr.,

"You cannot have palace revolts. You guys have been so great at that. You've never had a palace revolt."

The Steelers finished the 1986 season with a 6-10 record. In the doldrums of early January 1987, the announcement came: Art Jr. was out, replaced by the promoted Haley. Publicly, Dan said, "Our object is to establish direct lines of communication and better internal communications. This will enable us to function more efficiently." Art Jr. later heard some suggest that Noll was responsible for his firing, but he didn't believe it. The firing, he knew, was his big brother's doing. By title, anyway, Art Jr. would remain as one of the team's vice presidents, but what he'd lost was his sense of purpose and identity, and that was irreplaceable.

More than twenty years later, Dan sits in his Steelers office. I ask about his brother's firing, and he stiffens noticeably. He says, "That was not an easy thing. But it was, I felt—and still do—necessary. You couldn't . . . have a separate place in the organization. The organization, it has to be together." Dan says he spoke about the firing with the Chief. "But let me say this to you: in all honesty"—the strength of his conviction surges— "I talked to him *after* I did it. I didn't talk to him *before* because I knew how he would've been. He would've been emotional, and said, 'You don't have to do this now.' But it had to be done now or we would not—it may have been the end of us."

Sibling conflicts arise often in family businesses. But no one in the NFL, or in Pittsburgh, expected that to happen to the Rooneys, the steady and practical owners of a storied franchise.

Art Jr. personalized his firing. At fifty-one, he was out of the only job he'd ever really known.

As the decades passed and his raw emotions subsided, Art Jr. saw his quarter century with the Steelers with greater clarity and context. After decades of defeats, the Steelers, beginning in 1972, had mounted thirteen consecutive nonlosing seasons and won four Super Bowls. And, for all that it wasn't, Art Jr. says, over dinner at the St. Clair Country Club, "The 1980s was like the second-best decade we'd ever had. But because we were so good [in the 1970s] everybody looked at us as being disasters. . . . You had three losing seasons in the decade. That's not bad. But, yeah, I guess it was perceived to be bad." Then he adds, "I got the job on the fix . . . and I did the job that I was asked to do, with the people I worked with and the coaches, better than it was ever done in history. . . . If you take our drafts from 1969 through 1974, I think that may have been—*I'm sure that it was!*—the best drafting there ever was by one team."

He worried about the future. He had three children in college, and an autistic daughter in need of professional care. The Chief phoned him during the turmoil and, as ever, got right to the point. "Artie," he said, "you'll never have to worry about money in your life." And he didn't.

Art Jr. holds a deep, abiding respect for Dan, but recently when someone asked, "Are you Dan Rooney's brother?" he answered, pointedly and loudly, "No, I'm Art Rooney's son."

The Chief died at eighty-seven in August 1988. In Latrobe, Steelers defensive line coach Joe Greene took it hard. He sat on a bed, clutched a pillow, and watched a montage of the Chief's life on television. He waved away sportswriters, too emotional to speak. Mike Webster, in his final Steelers season, said of the Chief, "He *was* the Steelers." The *Pittsburgh Press* editorial said, "He was the father figure of an entire region. Rich but unassuming, he was a workingman's millionaire." The *Pittsburgh Post-Gazette* columnist Gene Collier caught the spirit, writing, "The Chief has been to only a few thousand wakes in his day, but today he is at the wrong one entirely." About five thousand people paid their respects during visitation. St. Peter Roman Catholic Church on Arch Street overflowed for the funeral and, by one estimate, about fifty priests were on the dais; six of the Chief's grandsons served as pallbearers. Local television and radio carried live broadcasts from the church. As the funeral procession made its way to the cemetery, Dan saw everyday people step from their houses, wearing Steelers jerseys and holding up signs that read, GOOD-BYE ART. Decades later, Roy McHugh, the columnist who first met the Chief in Pittsburgh in the years following World War II, said, "I don't know if there will ever be another [sports franchise] owner accepted as a sort of civic jewel. It was almost thrust upon him, but he was prepared for it because he was such a genuinely unpretentious, honest, admirable person. You couldn't help but like him."

Art Jr. paid visits to 940 in the ensuing days, the erstwhile method actor walking alone through the vacant rooms, sitting in the Chief's favorite recliner in the den, overcome with devotion and emotion. He remembered so many of their conversations, and all the postcards he had received from his father ("Up here at Sainte-Anne-de-Beaupré. We prayed for you."). In the den he searched for his father's rosary beads, usually kept in an unused ashtray on the table, but they were gone. Then he had a thought: he reached into a crack in the old man's recliner, his fingers feeling deep into its upholstery, and found his rosary beads there. A gift from above.

The Chief's five sons gathered in the living room at 940 to divvy up some of their parents' possessions, a somber occasion. Their mother, Kass, dead nearly six years, had had little time for nostalgia. She once told her sons that when she and her husband were dead and gone, "Don't sell the house. *Just burn it.*" They were middle-aged men—brothers, from fifty-six years old to forty-nine. But being together in the old house with the old furniture and the old smells made them feel like boys again, reminders everywhere of their shared past. As in many families, the Rooney brothers were united *and* divided, depending on the issue and the brother.

The Chief had been a commanding presence in their lives, and his five sons had walked mostly a straight line, attending daily Mass, and the eldest two continuing the Rooney tradition of naming the firstborn son for the grandfather and the secondborn for the father, which assured a new generation of Art Rooneys and Dan Rooneys. (Their wives sometimes simplified matters by distinguishing *My* Art from *Your* Art, and *My* Dan from *Your* Dan.) The Chief used to tell his sons, "We're not big-time people," and they accepted that as fact, and conducted themselves, in the manner of the Chief, without pretense.

Their wives weren't invited to the gathering in the living room. That was how the Chief conducted business—no women, just men—and so his sons, even now, followed his lead. As the youngest son by two minutes, John negotiated for the first pick, and the others agreed to follow him in reverse birth order: Pat, Tim, Art Jr., and Dan.

The dispersal of possessions began. John chose a small stool his mother had crocheted. He also chose a little statue of a boy playing rugby, and a Chinese tea service that once had belonged to their maternal grandmother. Later, when he selected a large mirror in the hallway, Dan said in a huff, "That belongs here!" John shrugged and said, "Okay, keep it."

Dan had little patience for what was transpiring. "I felt we were tearing our history apart," he said. Divvying up these possessions was a travesty, Dan told his brothers, disrespectful to the house and to their parents. Besides, they hadn't decided yet what to do with the house. "I won't participate in this," Dan said finally. He left the living room, walked down the hall to the den where the Chief used to talk with Joe Greene and watch *Monday Night Football* with Bradshaw. He sat in his father's recliner, picked up his father's phone, and made a call, "just to get my mind off this." He left his son Art II, an attorney, to represent him in the living room. Dan didn't select any of his parents' possessions, and neither did Pat, who shrugged as he told his brothers that he didn't need anything.

It wasn't that Dan didn't want any of these possessions. To the contrary, he felt deeply connected to every photograph and every piece of furniture in the house, even the notes played by the front doorbell (Westminster chimes). When he learned later that one of his brothers had chosen a wooden chest from China that was a gift to his parents from the Chief's brother, the priest known as Father Silas, Dan insisted that it be returned to the house, and it was. The dispersal of possessions, Dan said, "just didn't go well with me. The other guys, it didn't seem to affect them."

The selections went on for some time, round by round, the brothers eyeing a certain piece in the house and calling it theirs. Tim selected the dining room table. They each took one of the Chief's humidors.

Art Jr. had prepared carefully for this event. He was good at drafting, after all, having once selected Swann, Lambert, Stallworth, and Webster on the same day. He had discussed this family draft with his wife, Kay, and drawn up their wish list in advance. He chose plates the Chief and Kass had bought to commemorate their fiftieth wedding anniversary. He also chose the Chief's black Buick automobile, which he would keep for a year and then give to Tim, who stored it at Yonkers Raceway. In the humidor he selected, Art Jr. found a handful of the Chief's cigars, which he wrapped in ribbons and presented as keepsakes to Steelers employees. Though he'd quit smoking cigars, Art Jr. saved one for himself, and would smoke it nearly thirteen years later, on St. Patrick's Day in 2001, in what would have been the Chief's centennial year. He got a sore throat from it, though, and never smoked a cigar again.

In this family draft, Art Jr. got the possession he most wanted: the

Chief's red, leather-bound prayer book, his name embossed in gold lettering on the cover, "Arthur J. Rooney." The Chief's good friend Father Jim Campbell had given him this prayer book for Christmas in 1954. To Art Jr. the prayer book was a miracle. "It was like—my father's life!" he said. On an inside page, the Chief had recorded his rosaries from 1955, fifty or sixty per month on average, a red line for each spoken aloud, and a blue slash noting the fifth in a set. Crammed inside the pages of the book were cards from wakes the Chief had attended, including those for his political mentor James J. Coyne (July 1954); his father, Dan Rooney (February 1956); 49ers owner Victor Morabito (May 1964); his old friend Governor David L. Lawrence (November 1966); Vince Lombardi (September 1970); and his beloved Kass (November 1982).

The prayer book was so worn from use it looked to Art Jr. like it might have been from medieval times. Its pages had rubbed thin, the moisture from the Chief's fingertips living at the edges. The Chief had prayed over his family, his friends, his horses, and, perhaps more than any Pittsburgher dead or alive, his Steelers. Art Jr. knew this book was important to his father. For thirty years and more the Chief had held it in his hands every single day. To Art Jr. the personal value of this prayer book was incalculable.

From the passing of the 1970s Pittsburgh Steelers, he had learned that not everything is replaceable.

Dan wrote three words atop his scripted comments for the press conference: "Don't Get Emotional." In December 1991, Chuck Noll retired after thirty-nine seasons in pro football, and twenty-three seasons as Steelers coach. During Noll's tenure in Pittsburgh, 170 head coaches had worked in the NFL, but only one, Miami's Don Shula, his former boss, had outlasted him. The Steelers had reached the playoffs just once in the past seven seasons, and had suffered losing marks four times. Even so, Dan, who fired his younger brother, would not, and *could not*, fire Noll. That very morning he had told Noll that he wanted him to return for the 1992 season, though with changes in his coaching staff, but Noll said he was finished.

Don't Get Emotional. Dan wrote those words because he was emotional. He and his wife, Patricia, shared a great friendship with Chuck and Marianne Noll, and he and Noll had won great victories together. When the press conference began, Dan said to the gathered reporters, "Ready? Because I don't think I can do this twice." Then, reading from his notes, he said, "It has been a wonderful twenty-three years. Chuck has been a great man and he hasn't changed since day one." He cited Noll's 209-156-1 record with the Steelers and ranked him with football's coaching greats, Amos Alonzo Stagg, Curly Lambeau, Halas, Lombardi.

At the press conference, Noll said, "You know, it's much easier coming in than going out. The emotions that build up and the attachments that build up over twenty-three years are tough to, I guess, sever." Just ten days shy of his sixtieth birthday, Noll said he wouldn't coach again. "I'll have to step back and see what the flowers smell like," he said. Noll said burnout hadn't caused him to retire from coaching. "Natural death," he said.

As patriarch of his family and team, Dan remained the Steelers' one enduring constant. Players came and went, even the Hall of Famers from the celebrated seventies. The Chief was gone, Art Jr. forced out, and now Noll had retired. Dan was born in 1932, a year before the football franchise started. It was difficult to pinpoint his start date with the team. Was it when he broke his wrist as a small boy playing with the Steelers' blocking sled stored in the basement at home? Or was it in 1940, when he was eight and worried about rumors that the Chief was about to sell the team and asked him, "Dad, what are you doin'?" Dan had been involved with the Steelers on a daily basis since his graduation from Duquesne in 1955, and would be at his Steelers desk still more than twenty years after Noll's retirement. Veteran NFL writers admired him, though not because he was a good quote—Dan Rooney rarely said anything colorful, and his spoken sentences often were tangled and poorly punctuated. Rather they admired him because he was a straight shooter. They accepted what he said as truth.

He professionalized the management of a franchise his father once ran from his coat pockets. The Steelers became a model of stability with only three head coaches in forty-four seasons, and sellout crowds at every game since 1972 in a city riven by economic hardship. Dan hired Bill Cowher to replace Noll, and Cowher coached the team for fifteen seasons, and won for the Steelers a fifth Super Bowl in 2006. Then, upon Cowher's resignation, Dan hired thirty-four-year-old Mike Tomlin as the team's first African American head coach. Tomlin won the Steelers' record sixth Super Bowl in 2009 and became the second black head coach to win an NFL championship. The first, Tony Dungy, had risen from the Steelers' defensive backfield to become in 1984 the NFL's first black coaching coordinator with the Steelers' defense, and though Dungy won the Super Bowl with the Indianapolis Colts, the Rooneys rooted hard for him. Art Jr. said, "It was like it happened to a relative."

As chairman of the NFL's Diversity Committee in 2002, Dan spearheaded the enactment of a new rule that required NFL teams to interview at least one nonwhite candidate for vacant head coaching positions, and later added senior front office positions as well. Designed to break down the league's good-ol'-boy network, it became known as the Rooney Rule. In 2002, the NFL had just two African American head coaches and one black general manager. A decade later, in 2012, those numbers had grown to eight black head coaches, including Tomlin, and five black general managers. Though named for Dan by the Fritz Pollard Alliance, which promotes diversity in NFL hiring, the Rooney Rule might have been homage to the Chief as well. Skip a rock across time to the 1930s, when the Chief promoted and funded Negro Leagues baseball in Pittsburgh, to 1946, when he served with Josh Gibson as honorary pallbearers at the funeral of their friend Cum Posey, owner of the Homestead Grays, to 1957, when he hired injured Steelers wide receiver Lowell Perry as the modern NFL's first black assistant coach. The Chief had built close friendships and goodwill in the Hill District for generations. Bill Nunn Sr. of the *Courier* told his son that much, and Dwight White had witnessed for himself years later how blacks in Pittsburgh's neighborhoods held the Chief in high regard. Though honored that the rule carried his name, Dan, deflecting the praise elsewhere, as he had been taught, would say, "I felt [the rule] was the important thing, and that what we had accomplished was important."

In 2008 Dan became swept up in Barack Obama's presidential campaign, and in the tide of race history. He surprised family members, and his Republican friends, by stumping aggressively for the Democratic candidate. No longer was Dan a young man. He was seventy-six, about two and a half years older than the Chief had been at Super Bowl IX, and he was frail, his posture increasingly hunched over. Yet he made about fifty speeches for Obama on the campaign trail in McKeesport, Altoona, and Johnstown, and in West Virginia and Ohio. He also hosted an Obama fund-raiser at 940. Michelle Obama was there, and so was Bill Nunn, still working for the Steelers forty years later, and reminiscing about how much the Rooney family had done for Pittsburgh and for race relations. "To me the legacy of the family is really outstanding," Nunn said. That Dan endorsed Obama didn't surprise Art II. "It wasn't like he was some true-blue active Republican," Art II said. "[But] as time went on, and he was going on Saturday mornings to rallies in little towns around western Pennsylvania, that's when I said, 'There's something very strange going on here.' " On the trail Dan campaigned with Franco Harris, Jerome Bettis, and governors. At a rally in Mellon Arena in Pittsburgh he presented Obama with a Steelers jersey.

Following his election, President Obama repaid him for his devotion, naming him US ambassador to Ireland. Dan had cofounded the American Ireland Funds, dedicated to building bridges of culture and peace in Ireland and Northern Ireland, and funded the annual Rooney Prize for Irish Literature, awarded to Irish writers younger than forty. He and Patricia had visited Ireland and now they would move to the American embassy in Dublin. His new boss would be Secretary of State Hillary Clinton. From Ireland he would watch Steeler games on specially ordered late-night television or through his computer on Slingbox.

He became Ambassador Rooney, an impressive capstone to his life's work. His succession with the Steelers had been secured in 2003, when he did what the Chief once had done: install his oldest son as team president and take the title of chairman for himself. Art II, who had served for many years as the Steelers' legal counsel, was cut from his father's mold: serious, civic-minded, and attuned to Rooney family history. Art II might have been a US senator from Pennsylvania, but declined an appointment to the seat of US senator John Heinz, who died in a 1991 plane crash. He had a young family and said the timing simply wasn't right. As a teen, Art II had traveled with the Chief to racetracks, horse auctions, and Catholic shrines, the Buick filling with cigar smoke, the Chief rolling down his window to spit or throw out his cigar, and Art II in the backseat ready to dodge if either flew in his direction. Once, when someone told Art II that he had big shoes to fill, the Chief pulled him aside and said, "Don't worry about filling anybody's shoes except your own."

At this generational passing, Dan's impressive football legacy came into sharp focus. By the time he left for Ireland, he had worked full-time in the NFL for fifty-four years, and his far-reaching contributions to pro football neatly complemented those of his father. When Dan entered the Pro Football Hall of Fame in 2000 (Joe Greene presented him), he and the Chief became the second father-son inductees in history following Tim and Wellington Mara. In Pittsburgh, the Chief made the Steelers viable, but Dan made them champions. Their legacies within the league could be seen in much the same way, though on a larger scale. The Chief, as a founding father, helped the NFL survive through payroll shortages during the Depression, and player shortages during the war years, and led the league, as if by stagecoach, into the modern day. Dan, as a shrewd modern manager, helped the NFL stave off opposing leagues and player strikes, tap into new revenues and markets, and mature into a gleaming American business enterprise, the league like a rocket ship bound for the stars, padded by billion-dollar television contracts, and with more than 111 million people across the planet watching the Super Bowl in 2012. Both were quintessential league men, steady and practical at owners' meetings, though the Chief always had one eye on the ponies, and football might have been only his third- or fourth-favorite sport. For Dan, pro football was full immersion, and he would be involved in virtually every important league decision dating to the days when Kennedy was in the White House and tossing a football with family members on vacations at Hyannis Port.

As he stumped for Obama in 2008, there remained one more great football challenge for Dan, and it would prove his most emotional as the Steelers' lead custodian—to keep the team in the family, and to keep the family as a team.

Behind the scenes, the Rooney brothers had been wrangling over the future of their storied franchise for nearly two years. Diverging interests, estate tax issues, and old sibling tensions arose, a scenario common among second- and third-generation owners of a family business. The Chief had given each of his five sons a 16 percent share in the team. The remaining 20 percent passed down to their cousins in the McGinley family. In 2006 NFL commissioner Roger Goodell approached Dan and asked that the Steelers comply with a league rule that required a single owner to hold at least a 30 percent stake, and also to divest from outside gambling operations that violated another league policy. Goodell encouraged Dan to buy out his brothers, a move that would satisfy both rules. It would separate the team from operations run by three of his brothers, the Yonkers Raceway with its recently added video-gaming slot machines, and the Palm Beach Kennel Club in Florida, which had a poker room.

It took some time before Dan finally offered his four brothers a debt-laden buyout deal that, presented by Société Générale, a European bank, valued the Steelers franchise at about $700 million—a healthy increase from the Chief's initial $2,500 investment in 1933, but still, his brothers thought, not a fair price. Dan told them, "Look, you are going to end up with a lot of money. I'm going to end up with a lot of debt." His brothers retained Goldman Sachs, which, in a secret valuation code-named "Project Newcastle," determined the Steelers franchise value at between $800 million and $1.2 billion, according to the *Wall Street Journal*.

Battle lines were drawn. "Once you go out and hire an investment bank and you hire lawyers, they find ways to make things difficult," Art II said. "There were rough moments when I was pissed off at them [his uncles], or they were pissed off at me. I suppose that was to be expected."

Dan put it more succinctly: "It was very tense."

Art Jr. warned Goldman Sachs about negotiating with Dan. "Do you know who you are dealing with here?" he said. "This guy deals with the scum of the earth—the worst lying agents in the world!—and he knows how to deal with them. You think you are dealing with just some guy, some Goody Goody Two-shoes? The most formidable guy you are going to deal with is Dan Rooney." Paul Tagliabue, former NFL commissioner, tried to help the Rooney brothers broker a deal among themselves. "He was trying to keep all of us away from each other's throats," Art Jr. said.

Another option emerged. Stanley Druckenmiller, billionaire chairman of Duquesne Capital Management, a hedge fund star and lifelong Steelers zealot, was interested in buying the franchise and offered to allow Dan and Art II to continue to run the team's daily operations.

Art Jr. suffered anxiety and heart palpitations. He couldn't sleep. He gained more than seventy pounds, ballooning past three hundred. A doctor suggested tranquilizers, but Art Jr. said he needed to remain clearheaded at all times. Once, he suffered a visual whiteout. An anxiety attack, a doctor said, and then advised, "How about losing about seventy-five pounds?" It was reminiscent of his firing in 1987, when Art Jr. felt as if an essential piece of himself—namely, the Pittsburgh Steelers—was being ripped from his chest. All five brothers felt pressure and stress, some more profoundly than others. Tim struggled with selling, too. The twins, Pat and John, though, were ready. "I wanted to divest myself, and try to get as much as I could into my kids' hands, and get my life in order," John said. "It was time." John knew that Dan desperately wanted to retain control of the team. "It's Dan's baby, and it always was."

Finally a deal was cut. Dan and Art II borrowed about $250 million, cobbled together a group of new investors, big and small, including John Stallworth, and won control of the Steelers with the full support of the NFL. Tim and Pat Rooney sold their 16 percent stakes and remained in the racing and casino businesses. Art Jr. and John each sold roughly half of their 16 percent.

"At the end of the day," Art II said, "everybody still speaks to each other. I don't hold any grudges against anybody. I think they did what they felt they needed to do for their families." Through the process, Art II gained new perspective about his father: "I learned that he has an emotional attachment to the Steelers that probably goes beyond him ever being able to make a rational business judgment. He wasn't prepared to sell the team under any circumstances, no matter what the offer was on the table."

Dan put it like this: "I think our legacy here—and this comes from my father—was to keep the team ownership, to be seen and recognized [for that] ownership, so that people knew what we did: went through tough times and stayed with it for all those years."

VII

EMPIRE IN TWILIGHT

CHAPTER 22

IT'S STILL THEIR TOWN

YOU FEEL THE 1970S STEELERS' presence at Heinz Field, a carnival setting, the fragrance of history mixing with grilled kielbasa. Game night, November 2011, tailgaters by the thousands along General Robinson Street, where a century earlier old Dan Rooney ran his saloon; an oversized American flag draped from the stadium's upper rim; a fan wearing a Polamalu jersey and black-haired wig swung a heavy mallet but failed to ring the bell. A street called Art Rooney Avenue, another Chuck Noll Way; a boy in a Webster jersey too young to have seen the center's bulging biceps with his own eyes. Memorabilia-filled lockers from Greene, White, Lambert, Harris, Fuqua, Stallworth, Russell, Swann, and others from the 1970s in the stadium's Walk of Fame, including a few unique items sealed inside glass: a seat back from Three Rivers Stadium signed by the Steel Curtain front four, the Frenchman's colorful brick-red shirt with glittering rhinestones in the shape of an *F*; Lambert's toothbrush inside field manager Jack Hart's coffee mug. An hour before kickoff, 133 fans streamed past Gate D wearing replica jerseys of the 1970s Steelers, nearly half (61) in Lambert's number 58, and about a quarter in Mean Joe's number 75. Fans queued up for photo ops in front of the Chief's statue nearby. Look at the Chief's bronze likeness: in coat and tie and tasseled loafers, seated on a low wall, a long cigar between his fingers, the raincoat he always misplaced draped over his knee. So often did he misplace that raincoat, his secretary Mary Regan thoughtfully clipped a note inside its collar: "This raincoat belongs to Art Rooney. If found please call Three

Rivers Stadium." Cell phone cameras clicked. Several women might have caused the Chief's likeness to blush, striking their pose by leaning back into his lap. Two men, in their thirties and smoking cigarettes, one wearing a Lambert jersey, the other a Greene jersey, approached the statue. "The Chief wears nice shoes," said one, and the other answered, "He always did. Okay, let's go." But the man in the Lambert jersey said, "No, dude. I didn't have my time with the Chief yet." He reached out with his right hand, took hold of the Chief's left hand, and stared intently into the statue's eyes. Then he bowed his head. He kept that silent pose for a minute or more, the waiting fans growing impatient. His ritual done, he released the Chief's hand and walked off.

For the Steelers themselves, the 1970s lived in a series of reunions celebrating yet another twenty-fifth anniversary of a Super Bowl victory. The first gathering, in 1999, for the team that won Super Bowl IX over the Vikings, brought three dozen and more 1974 Steelers for a cameo appearance on the field at Three Rivers Stadium. Seeing their old heroes in middle age, the home crowd erupted like old times, and *for* old times, its roar loud enough to be heard up the hill at 940.

At a private gathering, players reveled in their time together. They relived the old days, and measured which teammates had held up best and changed most, and how many were still married to the same wives. (Answer: not many.) "Contact sports is the best form of communication," J. T. Thomas would say. "In real life, you've got these masks you put on every day. You forget who you really are. But in contact sports every contact tells you who you are. We know through contact if you are scared or timid. Out there [on the field] it's like you become buck naked. Your teammates constantly affirm you. In the huddle, they'll say, 'Way to go, T-man! Way to kick his ass!' The different ways they affirm you is awesome. You don't hit a guy in the butt or grab him by the face mask in life to affirm him." Thomas relished Steeler reunions because each time, he said, "It's like the drought is ended." Along with coaches and training staff and their spouses, players met at a downtown hotel for dinner and several hours of reminiscing. Coach Bud Carson gave a big hello to Chuck Noll, except that it wasn't Noll. It was punter Bobby Walden, who bore a striking resemblance to the head coach. Years before, Walden had even signed autographs as Noll. Teammates raised a glass in memory of Ray Mansfield, the Old Ranger, the only player from the 1974 Steelers to have died. His death had struck Andy Russell particularly hard, the two having hiked mountains in the Far West together, and traveled across the world, after their NFL careers. What these Steelers couldn't have known was that within three years their group would suffer four more deaths.

A powerful fascination attached to three men, Lambert, Holmes, and Gilliam, though for different reasons: Lambert, because he had seemingly not changed one iota in a quarter century, still lean, blond, and brusque, a perfect contrarian whose bluntness always seemed worth gossiping about; Holmes because he was part man, part mountain, his weight exceeding five hundred pounds; and Gilliam because he looked genuinely happy and seemed to have righted a drug-addled life. Only a few years before, he had slept each night inside a cardboard box beneath a bridge in Nashville.

For a team portrait, Dan purchased special black-and-gold letterman jackets for each player and coach, but Lambert refused to wear his. The jackets had an embroidered *P* on the left breast and Lambert huffed that they were Pirates jackets, not Steelers jackets. In the portrait, he wore a coat and tie. His teammates hid their smiles: typical Lambert, they said. Lambert had become somewhat reclusive, building a home and raising his family in a wooded area about thirty-five miles northeast of Pittsburgh. For a time he had worked as a volunteer deputy game warden. He declined most media interviews, and often declined to show up for team reunions, too, though he readily appeared at card signings and speeches for which he was paid. His teammates and those who came after him on the Steelers knew Lambert as a curmudgeon. Greg Lloyd spent two hours once standing next to Lambert on a skeet shoot. "And he didn't say one word to me. People had warned me that he was missing some screws," Lloyd said. "To get something out of Lambert would be like trying to get grapefruit from corn." Lambert communicated on his own terms. Once, Wagner got a letter from him. Opening it, he saw a photo of Lambert on a motorcycle, with a handwritten note: "What do you think of my ride?" At the reunion's photo shoot, after Lambert said he wouldn't wear any damn Pirates jacket, no one in the room tried to convince him otherwise.

At the dinner, Dan welcomed the group, and asked players to say a few words about their lives. They passed a microphone around and each man spoke briefly. Then Ernie Holmes got his chance. *This is going to be really interesting*, Wagner thought. Holmes talked about his family and his faith. He turned a few biblical phrases and told his teammates how much he'd loved winning championships with them. He spoke for nearly thirty minutes. As he talked on, some teammates smiled and rolled their eyes. A few clinked spoons softly against their glasses as a signal for Fats to stop talking. "Some people are still afraid of Ernie. No one is going to go, 'Okay, Ernie, that's enough!'" Wagner said. "It's not like the Academy Awards, where the band starts playing." Finally Holmes gave up the microphone.

Joe Gilliam brought his new wife to the reunion and talked eagerly about his new life. The Steelers had released him before the 1976 season. "Joey, you behaving yourself now?" Ralph Berlin asked at the reunion. Gilliam understood the question's deeper meaning. "I've been clear of drugs for a long time," he replied. Stallworth had a good feeling after his conversation with Gilliam. It seemed to him that Gilliam, at forty-eight, was "married to a fine lady. He had kicked the drug thing. He was at peace." Through the years, Gilliam had borrowed money from teammates still suspicious he might be buying drugs. "Pay you back," Gilliam said, but never did. Some teammates gave, others didn't. "He was always short," Bleier said. "I sent him some money. It would be five hundred here, couple hundred there." At the reunion, Gilliam told Bleier about his years on the streets. "I'm not proud of my life," he said. Gilliam emphasized that Barbara, his fourth wife, had him on the straight and narrow.

Reggie Harrison knew Gilliam as few teammates did. He had seen the vial filled with heroin in 1975 in their hotel room, and all these years later still carried guilt for telling Joe Greene about that. Harrison knew that Gilliam was essentially shy, and that when he became animated and chatty, as he was at this reunion, it was a sure sign that he was using drugs. Harrison asked Black Magic about it, "Joey, are you using?" Gilliam, with downcast eyes, answered: "Not as much as I used to." Harrison knew the truth: Gilliam was using still.

As the microphone passed to Art Jr., he looked at the middle-aged men filling the room and felt awe. He said he had scouted them all when they were twenty-two years old, and they'd become such marvelous NFL players that they'd made him look, as a scout, like he knew what he was doing. "I remember seeing you all when you were kids," Art Jr. said, "and we had such great hopes. And those hopes were realized. Here we are twenty-five years later"—his voice choked with emotion, for they had ennobled him as a scout, a Rooney, and as a man—"and all I can say is 'Thank you.'"

Once a year, the brotherhood wears tuxedos. The old teammates do it, they'll say, "for Mel," and his annual Mel Blount Youth Home Celebrity Roast fund-raiser. Blount founded a home for troubled boys in 1984 in his native Georgia and then a second one five years later in a pastoral setting in Claysville, Pennsylvania. For this work, President George H. W. Bush in 1989 named Blount his 524th Point of Light, and *US News & World Report* later honored him among eight national heroes. Funding remained a challenge. When Blount turned fifty in 1998, his wife, Tianda, hosted a black-tie fund-raiser dinner, including a roast of her husband, with Bradshaw as emcee. It attracted seven hundred tuxedoed guests and raised about $250,000. Blount seized on the concept. He tapped into the 1970s empire, a celebrated heirloom to Pittsburgh, and each year selected an honoree with a name big enough to draw a crowd. He chose Noll, and Harris, and then Bradshaw, Bleier, Swann, Stallworth, Shell, and Dungy. Baby boomer fans in Pittsburgh turned out, and paid $350 per ticket, to reconnect with the football team that gave shape to their formative years. The old Steelers paraded into a hotel ballroom one at a time, entering from the back and walking from darkness into bright light. Starstruck, the audience seemed to see them not as men in their sixties with hobbles in their gait, but more reverentially as the transformative athletes they once were, part of the team that lifted their hometown when it most needed lifting.

From the dais, the 1970s Steelers have had their fun roasting each other through the years:

Andy Russell (on Bleier): "Rocky had deceptive speed. He looked a lot faster than he really was. . . . In 1976, Rocky became the only rusher in NFL history to gain a thousand yards without ever changing direction."

John Stallworth: "Rocky's hair loss is not natural. Rocky's hair loss comes from extensive blow dryer use during the 1970s. . . . There were two reasons that Rocky couldn't portray himself in his movie [*Fighting Back: The Rocky Bleier Story*]. The first was the hair issue and the second was that he was too short. He was too short to play himself in the movie."

Bleier (on Bradshaw): "Brad's just a good ol' boy, wasn't that smart to begin with. I mean, the only vices he had were chewing Red Man and collecting wives."

Bradshaw: "Can I sum up Tony Dungy? He's Chuck Noll minus the wild sense of humor."

Dungy (on Bradshaw, a Fox sportscaster): "Since we moved from Tampa to Indianapolis, we're in the AFC, so fortunately we don't get the Fox pregame show anymore. We get CBS, so I get to hear some intelligent commentary."

Stallworth (on Swann): "Lynn ran for governor. I thought I'd mention that because I looked at the final numbers and I don't think that a whole lot of people in Pennsylvania knew that."

And there is, always, the Frenchman talking about the Immaculate Reception. To visit him in his man cave is to think he scored the touchdown on the play that triggered the 1970s Steelers' avalanche. But he didn't catch the pass, or throw it. He took the hit, and if you count up all his retellings through the years onstage, at dinners, charity events, gatherings of Steelers fan clubs, and in impromptu conversations in bars, Jack Tatum has rammed into his back about a thousand times, and Tatum might hit him a thousand times more.

You'll find John Fuqua at home now in the South Rosedale Park section of Detroit, in a small brick house, usually downstairs in his basement man cave, his big-screen TV turned to the NFL, CNN, or a sci-fi thriller. His man cave has the feel of a 1970s Steeler shrine, with photos of Mean Joe, Andy Russell, Franco, Gerela, and many others covering the walls—he even put up a photo of Tatum—plus a few random pieces of African art he'd rather not have. "My wife picks that shit out," he tells me. Fuqua spent thirty years as a distribution supervisor at the *Detroit News*. He talks almost daily with his friend Kamal Ali Salaam-El (formerly Reggie Harrison), whose number he keeps on speed-dial. ("Our friendship will never die," Salaam-El says. "It will see us in the grave.") Fuqua underwent six surgeries on his wrists, the initial injury a result of a hard tackle by Cleveland defensive tackle Walter Johnson. Fuqua had bones fused and metal plates inserted. His surgeon told him in 1974, "This ought to last you thirty years," and exactly thirty years later he underwent new procedures on both wrists. He still can't turn a doorknob. As a result, his doors at home have latches. He doesn't go out much. "What is out there is cold, tragedies, crooks," he says. "I can be more content watching my sixty-five-inch TV, seeing everything that's going on in the world and knowing that I'm safe." After his NFL career ended in 1977 he wore to bars and clubs some of his mod Count Fuqua outfits, including his Superstar jacket and Cave Man getup. He gained weight, though, and broke zippers and split seams. His kids later wore his outfits on Halloween nights until finally he gave them all away.

At lonelier moments, Fuqua says he talks to the photos on his walls as if they are alive. To Greene: "Joe, you should've made that tackle!" To Franco: "Yeah, I'm going bald, but you are, too!"

"Am I crazy?" Fuqua says. "No. I talk to them, they talk to me."

On a team of natural-born entertainers, Fuqua might have been the most natural of all, as thespian and comic. What slipped from memory was that he was a productive NFL player, rushing for more than three thousand yards and scoring two dozen touchdowns. In his man cave, Fuqua wears a Steelers T-shirt, jeans, sandals, and a ball cap that reads, "RETIRED: Don't Ask Me to Do a Damn Thing." He holds a plastic cup filled with Jack Daniel's, his grip familiar. He says he didn't speak to Tatum for many years. But over time (and drinks) the two men finally talked, and though both held firm to their convictions about what really happened on the play, they developed a friendship. They appeared together at signings eleven times by Fuqua's count and autographed a poster with a sequence of photos from the Immaculate Reception. Fuqua told audiences, "Jack didn't know what was happening. It was cold. His brain was half froze!" "Yeah," Tatum countered, "but I knocked the hell out of you, didn't I? Do you still see me in your sleep?" Fuqua: "What really counts is who wins the game!" Tatum: "Yeah, but you didn't go to the Super Bowl." Fuqua: "We went the following year." Tatum: "Fuck-wuh, you touched that ball!" Fuqua: "Dirty Jack, you touched the ball! And what did the referees say?" And then they laughed.

When Tatum died from a heart attack at sixty-one in 2010 after years of suffering from diabetes, Fuqua felt a deep sense of loss and sent condolences to Tatum's family.

Fuqua developed a stock speech about the Immaculate Reception. It ran twenty-two minutes, though he modified and customized it, adding new twists. "You want to hear the whole show?" he asks me. I do. Without hesitation he rises from his chair, a showman always. He tells me to imagine that we are in Biloxi, where recently he had given a speech. Then, without notes, and with a quick swallow of Jack Daniel's, he begins, as if addressing a crowd:

> *I made a promise years and years ago to the Chief that I would never tell. I'm very proud of myself because in all these years I've never told a soul about the truth. But, you know, I'm not going to take it to the grave. And, hey, here in Biloxi, you guys got hit with that hurricane, and all they talked about was New Orleans. In the tour I was taken on yesterday, you guys got hit hard! Houses are gone! Businesses are gone! You don't have a beachfront anymore! But I'm going to do something for you: I'm going to tell you what happened in the Immaculate Reception. You know why I am telling you this right now? Number one [he holds up his cup of Jack Daniel's], "Jack" told me to. But number two, I'm a realist, and I know that when you two hundred and fifty people leave this affair tonight, no one will believe you. Hell, they didn't believe you when you said that you got hit by a HURRICANE! And I'll tell you something else: tomorrow morning when I wake up, I'll deny it to the press. But I'm going to tell you right now what happened on that cold December day was immaculate, and I'm going to take you through it step by step.*

Now Fuqua points across the man cave. "Excuse me, sir?" he says. He imagines a hotel staff member. "Would you please close the doors back there? [To the audience] I will tell you what happened and I will tell you only once. If I see you on the street tomorrow, I will deny it!"

He provides the context of the blood rivalry with the Raiders, the physical nature of that 1972 playoff game at Three Rivers Stadium, how Stabler had rushed for a touchdown that gave the Raiders a 7–6 lead with only seventy-three seconds to play, and how the Steelers were down to one last play. His voice suddenly quickening, Fuqua says, "I went into my hook." He says he saw Tatum break away from receiver Barry Pearson and move toward him. "Bradshaw didn't look at Barry Pearson. He looked at me. I saw his blue eyes, and I know that he saw my brown eyes. I knew the ball was coming." The safety Tatum, he says, was coming, too. "I could hear his footsteps." Fuqua pretends to hit a microphone several times and says, "*Boom, Boom, Boom, Boom!*" He says, "I started going faster. His footsteps got faster. First I could hear the footsteps, and now with only a millimeter of a second left [before impact] I could hear Tatum breathing—[he rasps here] '*Hunh, Hunh, Hunh!*' I know there is going to be contact. We got to that point, the same place. I dive, he hits me, I flip and I fell on the ground. The only thing that I caught was an expression and it was in slow motion, and that was Jack Tatum with a smile from ear to ear." But then Fuqua says he saw Tatum frown, and when he looked far across the field, Franco Harris, with the ball in his hands, ran into the end zone. "Jack reaches down and grabs me and he says, 'Frenchy, you touched that damn ball!' " Fuqua says the referees needed fifteen minutes to figure it out and then signaled: "Touchdown!"

As I listen, I realize that the Immaculate Reception became an important part of Fuqua's life's work. He was always a performer, in dress-offs, in the Steelers' locker room, at nightclubs. His performances got sportswriters, like me, through the day. He made writers smile, laugh, and filled up their notebooks. But now I understand that the Immaculate Reception is so much more to Fuqua. It is the prism through which he chooses to see his life. It makes him young and significant.

He moves to the payoff of his speech: "But tonight I'm going a step further than that because what I want to share with you is what really happened. I don't want to take this to my grave with me." Fuqua removes his cap. He tells me, "Hold on," and he yells upstairs to his wife: "Shree! Shreeeeeeeee! Call me on my cell. I'm doing the skit from the Immaculate Reception." In a moment Fuqua's cell phone's ring tone plays the *Monday Night Football* theme song. Fuqua says that when he removes his hat during speeches, that secretly signals his wife to call his cell phone, which he keeps in his pocket. Returning now to his speech, he pretends that Commissioner Roger Goodell is on the line. "Roger? No, Roger, I wasn't going

CHAPTER 23

THE LEGACY HAUNTED

A STARTLING DISCOVERY ATTACHED ITSELF to the legacy of the 1970s Steelers, and at first it seemed like a mere barnacle on the belly of a mighty leviathan. The discovery was made in 2002 beneath a microscope under the jurisdiction of the Allegheny County medical examiner's office in downtown Pittsburgh. It would prove a seminal moment in football history because nearly three dozen more cases just like it followed in the ensuing decade and threatened the future of the game.

The 1970s Steelers' special place in football history suddenly needed to be amended and requantified. In the archives of their legacy, next to those glorious highlight films, four Vince Lombardi Trophies, and twelve Hall of Fame busts, were stained slides that revealed brown splotches in neurofibrillary tangles in Mike Webster's brain.

The discovery was made by Dr. Bennet Omalu, a jaunty thirty-four-year-old forensic pathologist with a smooth ebony complexion. He was born in the Biafran jungle in 1968 during an air raid in the Nigerian civil war. In his forensic work, Omalu found answers and, in his curious way, spoke not only for the dead (often providing answers for family members left behind), but also to the dead. He arrived at the medical examiner's office on Saturday, September 28, 2002, and heard a commotion out front, noisy reporters saying that Mike Webster's body had arrived for autopsy.

"Who is Mike Webster?" Omalu said in earnest, and they laughed.

Omalu knew little about the Steelers, or football. He didn't understand the game, or watch it. He preferred soccer. NFL players in helmets looked to him like extraterrestrials. He had heard the news coverage about the death of a former Pittsburgh Steeler a few days earlier on CNN, ESPN, and all the local stations, namely that this former Steeler had been sad, angry, and depressed for years, had acted strangely and slept in his truck. Omalu knew that the human brain, floating inside the skull, was not designed to receive football's repeated forces. He wondered about *dementia pugilistica*, a famous case he had read from 1928 about punch-drunk boxers suffering forms of dementia. He hypothesized that Webster was a victim of football.

Omalu put on his scrubs, stepped into the back room, and saw Webster's embalmed body ready for examination: *Such a big guy!* Omalu was a Christian, and emphatically so. He thought now of the spirit, as he always did at such moments, and of the biblical gospel Luke 20:36—"Neither can they die anymore: for they are equal unto the angels." He believed in spirits. When a body was on the examination slab, he believed the spirit floated like an angel through the room. He talked aloud to that spirit, his two technicians hearing his words. "Mike, we need to prove them wrong," Omalu said. "You are a victim of football. But nobody accepts it."

He began his work, executing the science of his craft. First he cut a V shape to open Webster's chest. He examined the heart. It was enlarged and damaged, with dead cells and vessel occlusion, findings consistent with a man who had suffered a heart attack. Then, using a scalpel, Omalu cut from behind Webster's right ear across the forehead to the left ear, from mastoid to mastoid. With an electrical saw, he made an ellipsoid incision in the top of the skull, exposing the brain. From there he moved his way into football's darkest space.

Omalu estimated that he had examined thousands of brains during his career, including those of a 2-month-old fetus and of a 105-year-old. The brain was enigmatic to him, stirring his intellectual curiosity. It contained so many different parts, the hippocampus, the cornu ammonis, the dentate gyrus, and within that, the granule layer, two hundred billion cells, all interdependent, working together like a musical orchestra. The brain was roughly 85 percent water. Hold a fresh brain in your hand and it would fall apart. Now, as Omalu studied Webster's brain, it appeared normal. This surprised him, and so he asked aloud, "Mike, why are you letting me down? C'mon!"

Omalu received permission from his boss to conduct further tissue analysis and, through attorney Bob Fitzsimmons, obtained the required next-of-kin approval. Now Omalu became like one more Mike Webster protector, part of the Team. He brought Webster's brain in a plastic tub back to his condo in the Churchill district of Pittsburgh, and set up shop in his living room, working late into the nights. He did the bread-loafing of Webster's brain, cutting it into thin slices that he sent to the lab at the University of Pittsburgh where he taught in the Departments of Pathology and Epidemiology. Later, reviewing four hundred stained slides of Webster's brain under his microscope, he saw the brown splotches for the first time. They confused, amazed, and exhilarated him. *What have I just seen?* They resembled the markings of Alzheimer's, except the pattern was different. These accumulations, he knew, were tau proteins gunking up the cells in the brain regions that had controlled the way Mike Webster felt and thought and acted. Omalu showed these slides to his boss and to other specialists. None had ever seen anything like it. Omalu ordered more case studies and more journal papers. In bed at night, he sought to name this previously undefined neurodegenerative disease. He decided on Chronic Traumatic Encephalopathy, the last word suggestive of an abnormal brain. He liked its generic sound and its easy-to-remember acronym—CTE. In the July 2005 issue of *Neurosurgery*, a peer-reviewed medical journal, Omalu published an article titled, "Chronic Traumatic Encephalopathy in a National Football League Player." Mike Webster's name was not cited.

The NFL dismissed his findings. In a letter to the editor published in *Neurosurgery*, three scientists serving on the NFL's Mild Traumatic Brain Injury committee jointly called for a retraction of Omalu's article. They questioned his work and his interpretations. Omalu became dispirited. "I was like the lone voice in the wilderness," he said. "Nobody believed me. I was called a 'voodoo doctor.' "

Omalu obtained the brain of another NFL player who died young and tragically, a Steeler guard for eight seasons (1984–1991) by the name of Terry Long. Long had suffered his own troubles after football, pain and depression, and took a direct route to the hereafter: he drank antifreeze, dead by suicide at forty-five. Omalu found CTE in Long's brain, and published another article in November 2006. Then he got the brain of the Eagles safety Andre Waters, known as "Dirty Waters" for his aggressive style of play. Waters had suffered at least fifteen concussions in a dozen NFL seasons. In 2006 he put a gun into his mouth. He was forty-four. In Waters's brain, too, Omalu found CTE; he published a third article.

He studied more brain slides, read more reports. For a time, in a coat closet at his condominium, Omalu stored in separate containers the brains of Webster, Long, and Waters; later he moved them to West Virginia University. He pressed on, immersing himself fully in his craft the way Mike Webster once had in his.

A few months after the 2010 publication of his third article on CTE, Omalu greets me at his new office in Lodi, California, where he had become chief medical examiner of San Joaquin County. A small, energetic man, he wears a gray suit, bright yellow tie, big gold cuff links, and strong cologne. With his latest article, Omalu believes he has entered new scientific territory: "You see, in science, when you report one case it is a case report. You report the second case, it is [still] a case report. But the moment you strike the number three, it becomes a case series. What that means is that there is a trend."

In 2009, Omalu and Dr. Julian Bailes, a former Steelers team physician and chairman of neurosurgery at West Virginia University Hospitals, cofounded the Brain Injury Research Institute to study repetitive brain injury and CTE. Bob Fitzsimmons joined them at BIRI as a codirector. Garrett Webster joined them, too, as BIRI's family liaison responsible for acquiring brains for research purposes. "I call families to talk to them, and tell them my dad's story," he said, "and I talk about how important it is to continue brain research." A larger, better-funded program, the Boston University School of Medicine's Center for the Study of Traumatic Encephalopathy, later moved to the forefront of CTE research. The BU center has received brain-donation promises from more than five hundred athletes, and from the NFL, in 2010, $1 million in unrestricted funds for research purposes. Then, in September 2012, the NFL donated $30 million to the Bethesda, Maryland–based Foundation for the National Institutes of Health (NIH) for research into brain injuries, the largest donation in league history. That same month a study under the auspices of the Centers for Disease Control and Prevention revealed that a disproportionate number of men who played in the NFL from 1959 to 1988 developed Alzheimer's disease or Lou Gehrig's disease.

Through rule changes, the NFL has tried to limit damaging helmet hits to the head. When a league investigation revealed the New Orleans Saints had placed bounties on opposing players over a three-year period beginning in 2009, offering Saints defenders secret bonuses for knocking specific opponents from the game with hard hits, the NFL dealt suspensions and fines. The threat of brain injuries has trickled down to Pop Warner youth football, with its more than 285,000 players from five to fifteen years old, issuing an edict that limits full-speed collisions during practices.

The gunshots go off in the night, new names added to the list. As of January 2013, thirty-four former NFL players had been diagnosed, posthumously, with CTE, many of them having died in the throes of pain, depression, or forms of dementia, and more than a few by their own hand. They form a multibillion-dollar industry's collateral damage: *Mike Webster . . . Andre Waters . . . Terry Long . . . John Grimsley . . . Justin Strzelczyk . . . Shane Dronett . . . Lou Creekmur . . . Chris Henry . . . Dave Duerson . . . Tom McHale . . . Ray Easterling . . . Junior Seau.* In their personal odysseys these former NFL players shared plights of darkness, rage, and irrationality. Self-inflicted gunshots killed Easterling, Waters, Duerson, and Seau. Duerson fired a gun into his chest, explicitly telling his family in a suicide note that he wanted his brain examined posthumously for signs of football-related brain damage. Under the microscope Duerson's brain, with CTE, was exposed as another victim of the game. By spring 2013, more than 4,300 former NFL players, consolidated into more than 230 complaints, had filed lawsuits against the NFL and helmet-manufacturer Riddell, Inc., maintaining they knew that players were vulnerable to traumatic brain injuries on the field, and the physical pain and suffering that would ensue, but did little to warn or protect them. Among the names on the master list are twenty-five Pittsburgh Steelers who played between 1974 and 1980: Shell, Thomas, Dunn, Edwards, Banaszak, Fuqua, Hanratty, Kamal Ali Salaam-El (formerly Reggie Harrison), Frank Lewis, Sidney Thornton, Ed Bradley, Dennis Winston, Bennie Cunningham, Greg Hawthorne, Dave Reavis, Rick Druschel, Preston Pearson, Ray Pinney, Ron Johnson, Ted Peterson,

Fred Anderson, Larry Anderson, Marv Kellum, Neil Graff, and Zack Valentine.

"I believe every professional [football] player has a persistent sequela—a lasting adverse outcome from football," Omalu says. Those outcomes, he tells me, range from headaches to complete incapacitation.

One study suggested that for NFL players even more problematic than concussions was the accumulation of subconcussive hits—estimated at between 1,000 and 1,500 per NFL player each season, varying by position. By that standard, Mike Webster's brain received on the field between 17,000 and 25,000 subconcussive hits.

Speaking at conferences, Omalu began to describe CTE in a new way. As amyotrophic lateral sclerosis (ALS) became known as Lou Gehrig's Disease for the famous New York Yankee first baseman who suffered from it, Omalu coined a new name for CTE—Mike Webster's Syndrome.

The final legal victory for Mike Webster's estate came in December 2006, four years after his death, and seven years after he first filed a disability claim with the NFL. The US Court of Appeals for the Fourth Circuit, in Baltimore, upheld a trial court ruling that Webster had been totally and permanently disabled from brain injuries from playing in the NFL. This resulted in an award of more than $1.5 million for Pam and the Websters' four children. It was an important and symbolic victory for the family, though the award, split five ways, and with debts to pay off, hardly transformed lives.

For Pam, the scientific finding that her husband had suffered from CTE brought clarity and some comfort. "When you put that piece in there, it fits back into the puzzle and everything makes sense," she tells me. "I mean, living through it was hell. . . . But then you find out later on that he wasn't just pissed off and angry, he was brain-damaged." She shakes her head. "Boy, I'll tell you, that makes things clear!" Some guilt remains. She becomes emotional, brushing away tears, as she explains her decision to divorce Webster. "So many people thought I was a quitter," she says. "I didn't quit. I just didn't know. If somebody had told me what I know now, I would have done more."

She got in touch with her old friend Debbie Furness. They hadn't spoken for many years. Once they had lived around the corner from each other, and their husbands lifted weights together at the Red Bull Inn. Pam saw Debbie shed tears beneath her sunglasses in the market that day in 1981 when her husband was traded to Tampa. The old stories came back in their phone conversation. But they connected in a new way by swapping stories about their football afterlives, and the way their husbands' moods and personalities had changed so dramatically. It was as if their husbands had been combat veterans, and they'd seen them fight that combat with their own eyes. They'd also seen the resulting post-traumatic stress but couldn't do anything about it. Popular among his Steeler teammates, Steve Furness had a difficult time after football. He coached for a while, and then struggled to find work that motivated him. Alcohol became a recurring presence in his life. "When you have worked that hard [in football], and you've reached those goals, you always have to find new goals," said Debbie, who became a home economics teacher and guidance counselor. "But I don't think Steve found new goals." Their marriage foundered. Steve Furness died in 2000, two years before Webster, from a heart attack. Debbie said that his family had a history of heart troubles. Furness was just forty-eight.

When Pam told Debbie about how Mike Webster had become more angry and confused after football, and had struggled to function day to day, and how she learned after his death that he had been brain-damaged from football, Debbie wondered if her Steeler husband might have suffered any brain damage from football, too. But he was cremated, she told Pam, and so it was too late to find out. Pam noted their common ground: they'd both divorced their husbands not long before their deaths. "So we're cut out of their lives, cut out of the NFL, cut out of everything," she says. "It's like we were never married to them."

On NFL Sundays, Pam and Garrett still watch Pittsburgh Steelers games together. In front of the TV in Garrett's apartment, they wear their Mike Webster jerseys. Both still love football.

A year after the team's first twenty-five-year reunion, Joey Gilliam was still telling the same story about turning his life in a new direction, this time to Franco Harris as they walked off the field together with other former teammates at the last game ever played at Three Rivers Stadium, on December 16, 2000. Gilliam said he was writing a book about his life, and working on a movie about it, too. Then nine days later, on Christmas Day, while watching an NFL game on television at a friend's house in Nashville, Gilliam dropped dead of a heart attack on his friend's couch. He was forty-nine, and when the toxicology reports came back weeks later, his last lie was detected: cocaine was found in his system, his death ruled an accidental drug overdose.

Dan Rooney dispatched Joe Gordon to the funeral to represent the Steelers. The only player from the days of empire to show up was Franco Harris, who, as the conscience of the 1970s Steelers, nearly always answered the call of brotherhood. He looked in the casket and saw Joe Gilliam dressed in white, and escorted the widow, Barbara Gilliam, from the packed funeral at Kean Hall on the Tennessee State University campus. Harris's emotions were mixed. On the one hand, he believed that Gilliam in 1974 "wasn't a very strong person as far as character" and that his drug use had disrupted the team. But Harris also had his own regrets: "I wish I had tried to be a little more mature myself, and taken Joe under my wings then and really tried to work on his strengths."

Rocky Bleier suffered regret, too. Bleier might have been Gilliam's favorite teammate of all. To Gilliam, Bleier was tough, wise, and so helpful with his encouragement and advice. Late on Christmas Eve, Bleier's cell phone rang, and he saw Gilliam's name on his caller ID. It was nearly eleven thirty, and Bleier was wrapping Christmas presents for his kids. He and Gilliam had talked at Three Rivers Stadium eight days earlier, and Bleier assumed Gilliam was calling to talk about the book he was writing, or maybe to wish Bleier a merry Christmas. He figured he'd call Gilliam back later. But late on Christmas day, Bleier answered his cell phone and heard a woman's voice asking, "Who is this?" "Rocky Bleier," he replied. It was Barbara Gilliam, calling to say that her husband had died. Then she said, "And you were the last call he made on his cell phone." Bleier was left to wonder, *Would it have made a difference if I'd called him right back?*

Nashville's black community wondered how much more pain Gilliam's football coach–father could take, or if maybe he'd been too hard on Joey by providing the same tough love he'd given his football players for thirty-five years. On the day after his son died, Coach Joe Gilliam Sr.

sat at home, in deep grief, wearing his silk pajamas and robe, his phone ringing constantly, the Reverend Jesse Jackson calling, friends, and former players, too, expressing condolences. Coach Gilliam launched more than eighty Tennessee State University players into the NFL. When one of those players, defensive end Richard Dent of the Chicago Bears, entered the Pro Football Hall of Fame in 2011, Coach Gilliam presented him. So deep was the old coach's affection for the sport, he wrote instruction manuals on different aspects of the game. "He's like the black Paul Brown," Bobby Mitchell said.

How much more pain could the old coach take? "There are no secrets about me and my family in this town," Coach Gilliam tells me as we walk the TSU campus on a summer day in 2010. In 1967, his nineteen-year-old daughter Sonia, struggling with depression, fell to her death from the window of a dormitory beside the TSU football stadium. Eight local churches refused to hold her funeral, Coach Gilliam says, because she'd taken her own life. "I had given my damn life to this place and this city and their kids," he says, embers of old emotions still burning. "And this damn town told me that." Finally, a Presbyterian church stepped forward, the minister saying, "Why, sure, Coach, a man of your stature, we'll take that funeral." To show his gratitude, Coach Gilliam says he has donated $100 per month to that church ever since.

He had experienced firsthand his son's drug demons. "Go find Joey," his wife, Ruth, used to say, and the coach drove the streets of Nashville and entered the drug dens, seeing broken liquor bottles, used syringes, strung-out whores, despair everywhere. He called out, "Hey, I'm looking for Joey!" The drug denizens knew the coach, virtually everyone in Nashville did, and they answered, "Hey, coach, I saw him day before yesterday over there," or, "I saw him on the corner two hours ago." Occasionally he found his son and brought him home to Ruth. She stripped off his clothes, put him in the bathtub, and gave her forty-year-old son a good scrubbing. Their door was always open to Joey, the coach says, with only one rule to follow: "Be straight." The father tried to help in so many ways. In 1979, when Joey Gilliam was beaten nearly to death outside a liquor store in Baltimore, a nail protruding from a two-by-four pounded into his head, he awoke in a hospital several days later with his parents at his bedside. The old coach took him to drug rehabilitation centers in Shreveport,

Richmond, Houston. Sometimes he paid the bill for his son, other times the centers took him in, gratis, because of his famous football name. The quarterback's younger sister Kim worried for her parents, and at times became angry at Joey for what he was doing to them. "He was eating Daddy alive," she said. Her mother, Ruth, withdrew socially after a few close friends bluntly suggested that maybe she shouldn't be alone in the house with a drug addict. "We all recognized that Joey was our jewel, not just because of his talent. It was his presence, his aura. It was star power," said Kim Gilliam Grant, the youngest of the Gilliams' four children. "It's convenient to say something drove Joey to drugs. That's a narrative. But it's far more complex, far more nuanced. I'm perfectly comfortable with the idea that I'm not supposed to know."

The old coach escorts me onto the field at W. J. Hale Stadium, where the legend of Jefferson Street Joe was born. There he spots an old-time equipment man, and they share, in a musical call-and-response, a warm reverie about Joey cutting to shreds the defenses of Grambling, Southern, and Prairie View, just as he later did to the NFL's Colts, Broncos, and Chiefs.

Coach Gilliam: "Joey was in the pocket, guys hitting him, and he's still throwing."

Response: "Yes!" (hushed reverence)

Coach Gilliam: "He had too much damned courage."

Response: "Yes!"

Coach Gilliam: "He'd stay in that pocket, and they'd beat the devil out of him. He had a strong arm."

Response: "Yes!"

Coach Gilliam: "Those were good times."

Response: "Yeah, them was great days."

Coach Gilliam: "But they're gone. (wistfully) They're gone."

Joe Gilliam Sr. can't find the cemetery. We cross the Cumberland River and lose our way, the coach driving this direction and then that direction. Suddenly he seems uneasy and jittery. He apologizes. He says he hasn't visited Greenwood Cemetery in years. Finally, with directions from a service station attendant, he finds it. In his eighties, Coach Gilliam stands upright and proud, a walking cane his only outward concession to his advanced years. At the stadium, he had seemed formidable, but now as he approaches the gravesites of Ruth, Sonia, and Joe Gilliam Jr. he weakens visibly. It is August, and muggy in Nashville, mosquitoes flying crossing patterns through the air.

A gravesite tells the history of a life, usually in whispers. As research for my first book, a history of Atlanta and its racial conscience, I visited graves of Confederates and their slaves, Georgians and Tennesseans dead a century and more. I saw impressive obelisks on hillsides, unmarked graves in potter's fields, and long-forgotten tombstones of freedmen covered over by soil, vines, and time. I saw headstones standing upright, others embedded in the earth. These markers listed dates of birth and death, and sometimes epitaphs, only a few words to convey a full life.

In another two years, the old coach would die at eighty-nine, and nearly a thousand people would attend his funeral, including many of his former players, and he would be buried here, beside his wife and two children.

But now Coach Gilliam stares down at the grave of his son, whom Kamal Ali Salaam-El lovingly described as "one of the greatest quarterbacks that will never be known." The grave is marked with a decorative urn and a handsome bronze plate that carries an epitaph suggested by Ruth: HE WAS LOVED IN SPITE OF HIMSELF.

"If you live long enough," the old coach says, finally, "not all of your days will be happy."

When Coach Gilliam heard about what Bradshaw had done, it pleased him to know that an old Steeler—his son's quarterback rival, no less—had helped Joey in a time of need.

In the throes of addiction, Joey robbed a Church's Fried Chicken restaurant in Shreveport in 1991, and he did it alone, with a butter knife. Desperate for drug money, he walked up to the drive-through window, placed an order, and when the employee turned his back, Gilliam reached in with his butter knife and grabbed less than $100 in cash, and ran.

Police caught him a few minutes later. He received a suspended sentence, plus supervised probation and mandatory drug-abuse treatment. Years later, Coach Gilliam learned that Bradshaw, who seemed to know everyone in his hometown of Shreveport, had spoken to the judge as a character witness and former teammate.

I ask Bradshaw about it. "I just made sure that things were right," Bradshaw says. But he won't discuss it further, only to say, "It's nothing. I don't want a pat on the back."

As he talks about Joey Gilliam, Bradshaw's eyes mist over. "You know what," he said, recalling 1974, "I lost my job to a cool dude. I loved him. I really did."

Steve Courson picked up the *Washington Post* while sitting in the greenroom for on-air guests at CNN's studio in Washington on April 27, 2005, only hours before he would testify about steroid use in the NFL before a congressional panel. Courson read that a Baltimore federal judge had ruled in favor of Webby's family in its case against the NFL Retirement Board, and he was elated for Pam and the kids. Courson thought often about Webby, sometimes when taking long walks through the woods near his cabin in Farmington, Pennsylvania, with Rufus and Rachel, his two Labrador retrievers. The memory of Webby saddened Courson because the great Steelers center had paid the game's ultimate price. *A lonely way to die*, Courson thought.

From using steroids, and then turning whistle-blower against others who used them, Courson had paid his own steep price, but now he felt as if he'd regained his personal honor. He felt redeemed. He had beaten alcohol addiction, reaffirmed his faith, and restored his health. Only three years after leaving the NFL, he had been diagnosed, at thirty-three, with dilated cardiomyopathy, his heart enlarged and weakened. Placed on a heart transplant list and given perhaps five years to live, he blamed steroids for his fate. But through strict diet and exercise, he had returned to vibrant health. A treadmill stress test on his forty-ninth birthday produced results similar to those in his playing days.

Still, he felt sentenced to social isolation, frozen out by his old friends on the Steelers. To them, he had broken the locker room code of honor.

It was one thing to tell *Sports Illustrated* in 1985 that steroid use was rampant in the NFL, but entirely different to point his finger at his own team. In his 1991 book *False Glory: Steelers and Steroids*, Courson wrote that during his years in Pittsburgh between 1977 and 1983, 75 percent of the team's offensive linemen used steroids at one time or another and that half of the team's players in the power positions had experimented with them. Lambert had taken him on in 1988 in an open letter published in the *Pittsburgh Press*, his tone respectful but firm. Lambert wrote, "When it comes to your quote, 'If you're competitive, you've got no choice,' I beg to differ. . . . As a former 11-year NFL veteran who did not use steroids, I would like to think that if anything I was at least competitive." Lambert urged Courson to speak honestly to young athletes and not to say they needed steroids to be competitive. "That would be a lie," Lambert wrote.

Among the 1970s Steelers, admissions of steroid use came from only Courson and three other players: Rocky Bleier, Jim Clack, and Webster, and Webster's admission wasn't public. He had made private comments about his experimentation with steroids to doctors and to one of his sons. Denise Masciola, Courson's girlfriend, said, "Steve just wanted badly for [Steelers teammates] to come out and admit it themselves. He felt, 'Why live a lie?' "

Courson knew they feared he might one day mention their names. But he told Masciola he would never do that. No matter how conflicted, bitter, and betrayed he felt that his Steelers teammates wouldn't stand with him and publicly admit to steroid use, or how they'd acted like they'd had no idea what he was talking about, he admired and loved them still. Courson believed he hadn't broken the bond, or any code of brotherhood, he'd simply answered to a higher truth. He remained in touch with a few Steelers, including Dunn, who asked, "Why did you write that?" Courson answered, "I'm just trying to clean up the league."

In 2004, Courson and Masciola attended a twenty-fifth-anniversary dinner for the Steelers team that defeated the Rams in Super Bowl XIV. Courson wanted to show his old friends that he'd restored his health and risen above their past tensions. But apart from Dunn and Bleier, Masciola sensed that the others treated Courson coolly. "They weren't avoiding us like the plague," Masciola said. "But I could tell—being an outsider, looking in—they weren't as close with Steve as they were with the others. They would just say a couple little words to him and that was it."

Courson continued to speak out against steroids to youth groups, making as many as one hundred speeches a year. He had a slide show, a story to tell. By nature analytical and introspective, he had also taken to writing about his life experiences.

"Football with drugs or without drugs is society's drug," Courson wrote in 2005.

"The part that is upsetting to me is the realization now that I had to defend myself for almost 20 years for telling the absolute truth."

"We all are accountable for, and face a reckoning for what we do," he wrote, "if not in this world surely in the next."

At the moment his chainsaw cut into a forty-four-foot tree on his property in November 2005, Courson harbored aspirations to move west and start life anew. He thought he had lived an American nightmare for too long. At fifty, he told friends, he was ready to chase the American Dream. As the tree began to fall, a gust of wind blew it in a different direction—toward Rufus, his beloved old dog. Courson raced to save his Lab, moving into the path of the falling tree. Rufus became tangled in Courson's legs and was spared. But the tree struck Courson in the back, crushed his chest, and killed him, as his chainsaw whirred on.

The funeral was held in Gettysburg, where Lincoln famously spoke about binding up a nation's wounds. The Steelers sent flowers but no official representative, a sign of Courson's alienation from the organization. The team also paid for a bus that brought about a dozen former players, Gary Dunn among them. On the bus ride from Pittsburgh, these players told their best Courson stories, about long-ago games, and bars and women, and a Chevy Blazer painted in camouflage. No one mentioned steroids.

In the quiet of night, the game called out for payment. The players felt it in their muscles and bones. They all lived with some pain, differing by degrees. As Franco Harris takes blueberries and fish oil each morning to slow brain damage he believes that he, and every other NFL player, has suffered, Kamal Ali Salaam-El takes OxyContin and other medications for head, back, and leg pain, and whisks through his northern Virginia home on a motorized scooter. As Fuqua needs latches on doors at home because his surgically repaired wrists can't turn a knob, Russell gets occasional massages, whereupon deep pains in his legs trigger deep memories. *Ouch! That one's from the Cincinnati Bengals in 1968. Ouch! That one's from getting leg-whipped in Super Bowl IX.* Greenwood can't recall exactly how many back surgeries he's had. Fourteen? Fifteen? "I feel like I've been rode hard and put away wet," he says. Shell, one of the Steelers' hardest hitters, says his memory isn't what it once was. The reason? "I'm quite sure it's football," he says. Dunn underwent ten knee surgeries. He also suffers pain from bulging lumbar discs, which doctors treated with cortisone shots and by burning nerves in his lower back, with mixed success. Some days Dunn can't walk, some nights he can't sleep.

For many of these Steelers, pro football had provided a way up from difficult circumstances early in life. Today, as they measure what their Steelers years gave and took, to a man they all say they would do it again, even those who suffer daily for it.

"No, I don't regret it," Dunn said. "But the older I get, and the more messed up I get, I might be a little more hesitant to say that. In other words, I think about it more now that I feel so bad. . . . I played for a great organization. It was a great time. Do I wish I wasn't so screwed up because of it? Yes. But not everybody is as messed up as I am, and some people are worse."

Downstairs at his northern Virginia home, Kamal Ali Salaam-El sits at the front edge of a recliner—the opposite of reclining. He holds the chair's left arm for balance as his body lists far to the right, like the *Titanic* just before it disappeared beneath the water's surface. His gray hair has receded enough to fully expose the *V* branded in the center of his forehead from savage hits against his helmet, hits that caused cognitive deficits and prompted him in 2006 to enroll in the University of North Carolina's memory recovery program. He hardly resembles the running back formerly known as Reggie Harrison. As Kamal Ali Salaam-El, his names translate to "Greatness" and "Exalted" and "Peace." A Christian still, he legally changed his name in 2000, he says, to embrace Moorish American citizenship at a time when he was angry with his ex-wife, the judge in their divorce proceedings, the court system, and the United

States of America. His life has been filled with surprises, even that moment in Super Bowl X that belonged to him when, as a Steelers special teams kamikaze, he broke through the Dallas line to block Mitch Hoopes's fourth-quarter punt, the ball bouncing out of the end zone for a safety. He got so close to Hoopes on the play that the punter's foot busted him in the mouth on his follow-through, splitting open Harrison's tongue, blood gushing from it. But Fats Holmes, so cheerful on the sideline, reminded him that with the money they would get from winning the game, "You can buy yourself a new tongue."

It was the head-on collisions that Reggie Harrison loved best. He was a 218-pound battering ram, his self-described running style "beastly." He liked collisions on kickoff and punt returns best. "You go thirty-five or forty yards and it's a blast! Let me tell you something: IT IS A BLAST! No matter what, God dang it, you are going to get that ass tore up, man! That's the way it is." Even so, he says, he carries no regrets: "If you played *that* game you are going to hurt. Still, I can slip on one or two Super Bowl rings, and there is something there for me." Banaszak, too, relished the big hits. He saw one recently on television and replayed it for his wife. "See that?" he said. "That's what I miss right there! That one shot where you know that you've—it's hard to describe—but that feeling that you've just annihilated someone." Banaszak, who coaches football at Robert Morris University, said, "When you see it happen on television, you know you'd like to be in that position again. But it's not going to happen. I'd be crippled now if I hit people as hard as I did back in the day, and I wasn't a vicious hitter." Even so, Banaszak said, wistfully, "I wish I could buckle that chinstrap one more time."

It is a young man's right to play pro football. His mind-set is worth exploring. He straps on his helmet and accepts the possible long-term breakdown or failure of his body in return for a chance at fame and glory. He is drawn in by the game's aphrodisiacs. He loves football, its athletic artistry, the high-speed collisions, the pageantry, the spoils of money, women, and celebrity. At twenty-two he is invincible. He sees himself at the age of fifty or sixty through the lens of a telescope. Fifty is a faraway planet, his father's world.

Thirty years later, long-retired NFL players will explain past behaviors, including their decision to continue to play the game through pain, and apply their reasoning in retrospect. To say playing in the NFL was all a mistake would be to invalidate an essential part of their lives. But if players really understood at twenty-two that they would suffer daily pain or struggle to walk in their fifties or perhaps even suffer and die, as Mike Webster did, as a direct result of playing pro football, would they play the game? It's a different hypothesis when they answer that question much later in life, in middle age. At twenty-two no such internal conversation takes place. It's an ex post facto conversation that old football players have.

"I mean, you can't *not* get your head banged when playing this game," Stallworth said. "I think the options are, for a player, it's either you play and realize the potential [for injury], or you don't play at all. I think the integrity of the game is that it is 'hit and be hit.' My philosophy—and the philosophy in Pittsburgh on the football teams I played for—was you win football games when you hit the other guy harder than he hits you. And you do that on a consistent basis."

There was another compelling reason they played, Randy Grossman said. They all had unique physical gifts. "It's what separates you from the faceless crowd," Grossman said. "It's the one thing that [we] are amazingly special at. The recognition and self-worth that comes with being special is special."

NOLL & THE AMBASSADOR

"IS THAT NOLL?" WHISPERING AMONG themselves, the autograph collectors can't be certain, even those wearing Steelers colors. Age has transformed him. A lion in winter, here is Chuck Noll in his eightieth year: as his stomach cascades over his belt line, he walks at a steady clip, a metal cane in each hand, head down, moving past the customers at a sports collectors' show in 2011 in a warehouse-like building near Dulles International Airport in northern Virginia. One man claps as Noll walks by, solitary echoes at first. Then more join in, clapping respectfully, as if honoring a passing former head of state. Noll does not acknowledge the applause. Head down, his canes' tips pounding the concrete floor, he keeps walking. Two steps in front, Marianne Noll, his wife of half a century and more, serves as his shield and protector, her full-time role now.

Noll settled into retirement comfortably. When Lombardi stopped coaching at Green Bay, he became the Packers' general manager, and loomed over his replacement, Phil Bengtson, and then left a year later to coach the Redskins. Noll wasn't the looming type, nor did he ever coach again. At eighty-seven years old, Bum Phillips, Noll's coaching rival in Houston, still welcomed and hugged some of his former Oiler players on visits to his ranch in Texas. "I'm like their daddy," Phillips said. But Noll's players mostly keep their respectful distance, and Noll never was the hugging type. Jack Ham sometimes sees Marianne in the village in Sewickley Heights, not far from where the Nolls own a condo and live for much of the year. "But Chuck is a private man for the most part," Ham explains.

Among Noll's players, there is an abiding respect, but a residual fear, too. Ilkin laughs and says, "Chuck had that way about him. He could look at you and make you lose bladder control." Noll wasn't good at small talk, or with sharing his emotions. Even the Chief, who prided himself on being able to talk with anyone, said he couldn't make a conversation with Noll. Noll's assistants Perles and Widenhofer hadn't seen him in years, and made separate visits to Florida, where the Nolls winter. From Noll, Perles had learned, "Work hard, keep your mouth shut, and good things will happen." "That's something he preached all the time," said Perles, who thanked Noll for changing his life. Lionel Taylor, another coaching assistant, stopped by, too, and shared a bottle of wine with Noll. "Marianne wouldn't let us have another bottle," Taylor said. "We didn't talk football. We lived it. We just socialized."

In retirement, Noll was heard to joke that he wakes up each day with nothing to do and usually only accomplishes about half of it. He did occasional charity work for years, and then his health declined. Now he sleeps a lot, does jigsaw puzzles. He suffers back troubles, and while a back doctor suggested surgery, his heart doctor said that wouldn't be a good idea. Medication shifts caused him to gain weight. He suffers from mental decline suggestive of Alzheimer's. At a restaurant, just after ordering dinner, he might say, "When are we going to order?" Sometimes he whistles or recites lengthy poems from memory. On a good day, he might recall an anecdote from working at a butcher shop as a teenager in Cleveland. His greatest pleasures include eating, and drinking fine wines. When fans, especially children, approach him at a restaurant, he greets them warmly and with a grandfatherly smile, though without small talk. He hardly ever watches football on television. He doesn't much like talking football at all. Day to day he seems happy.

Noll has not been a regular at sports collectors' shows. In this crowd there is quiet talk that this might be his last show ever. "You've got to get him now," one collector tells another, "if you are going to get him." Collectors pay $75 for Noll's signature on a small flat item, or $95 for him to sign a jersey or helmet. Among the many sports figures appearing at this show only Joe Montana draws a larger crowd. Noll's paying customers exceed those of Kevin McHale, Robert Parish, John Havlicek, Paul Warfield, Sonny Jurgensen, Nate "Tiny" Archibald, and Meadowlark Lemon.

For a couple of hours' work, smiling for photographs and for signing one thousand items (some done earlier at home), Noll is paid $25,000. The written directions to autograph collectors are explicit: "Mr. Noll will include 1 inscription (HOF 91 or 4x SB Champs) per item as requested. Limit of 1 per item." His rare public sighting here is captured on television camera and shown on the evening news in Pittsburgh.

A few of his former players show up to sign, too, including Swann, who charges more than double Noll's rates for his signature. Swann shakes Noll's hand, and pats him on the back in a perfunctory way. Mike Wagner shakes hands with his old coach, though their conversation is brief. "I didn't know Chuck did these shows. Typically he keeps such a low profile," says Wagner, who hadn't seen Noll in about eight years. Once he and Noll were neighbors—Wagner and his wife had bought a house in Upper St. Clair, about a block from the Nolls—and at practice one day Noll said to him, "I understand you're bringing up the property values." As he sits at his own table at the sports collectors' show, memories of Noll flood Wagner's thoughts. He was a fair coach, Wagner believes, and not a nitpicker. "He let us live our lives. What he cared about was for us to be at meetings on time and to play great football." As Wagner signs autographs and poses for photos, he thinks again about Noll: "Then, when I looked up, he was gone."

His players remember many Chuck-isms, though none more vividly than, "Football is what you are doing now, but it's not your life's work." Tony Dungy spent ten seasons with Noll in Pittsburgh, including eight as a defensive coach. He often thought about that phrase, and on occasion Dungy wrote, "It occurred to us that he had been in football for such a long time that it certainly seemed to be his life's work, but I don't think anybody ever had the guts to say it."

Yet Noll still lives within his players in impressive ways. In October 2012, when Stallworth brought Greene, Blount, and Dungy to a Legends Round Table onstage in Huntsville for a discussion designed to inspire high school and college athletes, Greene was struck by how often each of the four Steelers spoke of Noll and the power of his leadership. No matter the question, Greene noticed, their answers always came back to Noll. Greene thinks of Noll nearly every day now, especially his Chuck-isms: " *Focus. Pay attention to the details. Whatever you are facing, good or bad, meet the situation.*' They come off as clichés but they became a way of life. It's the simple things." Greene smiles. "Chuck told me once when I was late that I had *a history* because one time creates a history." Greene remains indebted to Noll. "Some of that roughness that I brought into the profession, Chuck, in his own way, understood. He allowed me to grow as a person and as a football player without quashing it. He didn't browbeat you. He just told you the way it should be. Any one guy on a football team can derail it. You need good people and you must control them. They need to know who the bosses are. And there was no doubt Chuck was the boss."

At his final press conference in 1991, Noll had revealed much about himself, though in his usual cryptic way. "Probably the thing I appreciate most about football is that it teaches humility, because as soon as you start thinking you're pretty good things can get tough," he said. A sportswriter asked if he had regrets about the way his relations had soured with Bradshaw and Harris at the end of their Steeler careers. "Termination is not easy, it's not usually smooth," Noll said. Then he quoted Emerson: "'Your actions speak so loudly that I cannot hear what you say.' And I'd like to keep it that way," Noll explained. Later he said, "Reminisce? When we get in rocking chairs, we'll probably do that." But twenty years later he still hadn't reminisced much with his former players.

When linebacker Greg Lloyd approaches his table at the collectors' show, Noll doesn't recognize him at first, perhaps because of Lloyd's newly shaved head. As they chat amiably for a few minutes, Lloyd tells Noll that he is working with the Tampa Bay Buccaneers' linebackers, and teaching martial arts, too. Then Lloyd remembers one of Noll's favorite lines—if he heard it once, he heard it a thousand times—and says with a broad smile, "I'm finishing my life's work."

Lloyd still ponders that thought as Noll leaves the building in a wheelchair.

"Dan has my seat!" Barack Obama said in Ireland as he boarded *Marine One*, the presidential helicopter, in spring 2011. As US ambassador to Ireland, Dan knew Obama's humor and playfulness almost as well as he had come to know the president's maternal Irish ancestry. The helicopter set down on a rain-soaked field in Moneygall, an Irish village with fewer than three hundred residents. From there in 1850, a nineteen-year-old shoemaker named Falmouth Kearney, the great-great-great-grandfather of the forty-fourth American president, fled the Great Famine for America; at about the same time, James Rooney, Dan's great-great-grandfather, left for the New World from Newry, in what is now Northern Ireland. Dan visited Newry but found no Rooneys there, and now Obama came to experience a connection made by a genealogist in 2007, and verified through painstaking clerical study of old parish records.

In Dublin, Obama said in a speech, "My name is Barack Obama, of the Moneygall O'bamas. I've come home to find the apostrophe that we lost somewhere along the way."

Amid light rain and waving American and Irish flags, the president and Michelle Obama walked down Main Street in Moneygall, shaking hands with the crowd. Dan had done months of advance work for this visit. "We did so much preparation," he said, "you couldn't believe it." From the instant he arrived on the job in Dublin, he had been an active ambassador, reaching out to the people, visiting all twenty-six counties in Ireland, and several in Northern Ireland.

During the 2008 campaign, Obama came to understand Dan's understated style. What Obama didn't know was how much of that style Dan had inherited from the Chief. Obama noticed how Dan seemed to walk nearly everywhere (so had the Chief), and how once, as they moved through a Pittsburgh hotel during a campaign event, Dan greeted janitors and security guards with a consummate common touch. Obama noted, too, how Dan sent him handwritten postcards from Ireland. "Old-fashioned," Obama said. "[He] just writes on the postcard saying, 'How are you doing? We are all thinking of you here, and can't wait to see you.' " And Obama added, "He probably stamps them himself." The two men talked plenty about the Steelers. "[Obama] knows everything that's happening," Dan said, "guys that were injured, guys we drafted."

Their Moneygall visit ended in a Main Street pub, the proprietor, Ollie Hayes, behind the bar, handing a pint of beer to Obama, and the president insisting, "We have to get a Guinness for the ambassador." The president and his ambassador clinked their glasses in a toast to homecomings.

✦ ✦ ✦

Above the fireplace in the den at 940 is a painting of Abraham Lincoln sitting at a table with his secretary of state, William Seward, and his Union generals, McClellan across the way, and the bearded Meade, standing. "What I like about this is that Lincoln is not at the center," says Dan, who, in his own life's work, had scrupulously remained near, but never in, the spotlight.

He finished his work as ambassador to Ireland in December 2012 and returned home to Pittsburgh, the Steelers, and to 940, this time to stay. After the Chief had died in 1988, Dan had his parents' house appraised, and then purchased it from his brothers. Keeping the house in the family—the continuity of it—pleased him. In 1993, after living twenty years in Mount Lebanon, he and his wife, Patricia, moved in. "We'd raised our family for the most part," Patricia explains. "I kept saying that I wanted to move back into the city." With a smile, she adds, "Heinz Field being just two blocks down, that's been great for the men in the family." They renovated the interior at 940, pulled up the old carpet in the hallway to reveal handsome wood floors, added an expansive conservatory, and living space above a new two-car garage. Time has not been as reinvigorating to North Lincoln Avenue. Some of the grand old homes were subdivided into apartments, and, now, across the street from 940, is a parking lot and a Subway sandwich shop. For years Dan walked to Steelers home games, past a closed-up gas station and underneath an overpass.

Sitting in the den late on a Sunday morning, the ambassador wears a dark Pendleton shirt, suspenders, and sneakers. The den has been transformed since the Chief's time, including the installation of an elegant new mantelpiece the ambassador designed himself. He incorporated symbols of ancient Ireland, from the *Book of Kells*, and others suggestive of Ireland's promising future. A formidable bookshelf lines one wall, Irish books on the left, American history books and Lincoln biographies on the right. Dan wants to add another bookshelf, but Patricia shakes her head. "We are in a bit of a discussion about that," she says with a raised brow.

In the hallway, by the staircase, they mounted a composite of old photographs that reveals, generationally, the vibrant life of the Rooney family:

of Dan and Patricia at 940 on their wedding day; of their nine children, and seventeen grandchildren, at Halloween, in Ireland, and skiing in Colorado; of the Chief with his five boys, and sitting alone in the den; of family members with Ethel Kennedy, two popes, Obama; of Dan with his small airplane; of Chuck Noll; and of Joe Greene with Patricia's mother. (Patricia: "They all love Joe; one of our daughters wanted him at her wedding and so he came.")

On a crystalline autumn day, the trees in high color across western Pennsylvania, the ambassador steps into his stylishly manicured backyard, which features a lovely Japanese maple, some oaks, and the peaceful sound of a waterfall. One section of the yard's back wall showcases his artistic talent: small embedded stones in an abstract design, and a piece of wood angled horizontally. "We get everybody to guess what this is. You've got twenty questions," Dan tells me. "You'll never get it." A few moments later, he points to the wall and narrates: "This here is the Christ child. That's Mary reaching to him. And that's St. Joseph on this side."

Walking through the yard, he waves his hand in the direction of a bush. "It must be a hundred years old," he says. As boys nearly seventy years earlier, he and his four brothers dug trenches around that bush as if they were soldiers in World War II. Beside that bush, the Chief belted hard ground balls that struck wildly off his sons' shins. "We did more things to that bush," Dan says, "but it's still makin' it!" He says the gardener has been warned, "Don't touch it!"

A child's knock at the front door: a Rooney grandson pays a visit as 940 North Lincoln Avenue thrums to life. A gorgeous light warms the oaks' red-orange leaves. The ambassador returns to his den, where Bradshaw and Mean Joe once sat with his father, and he hears Patricia say how the smell from the Chief's cigars hung heaviest in this room, and took years to dissipate. Dan has an admission to make: the cigar smell in the house is so familiar to him that he never noticed it.

CHAPTER 25

THE SAUNA, ONCE MORE

BECAUSE A MAN IN HIS twenties doesn't have the depth of experience or wisdom of a man in his sixties, John Stallworth can see now what he couldn't see then. In quiet moments when he reminisces about the days of empire, Stallworth thinks not of the big catches or the roar of the crowd or the Super Bowl rings. He thinks of teammates and of the brotherhood they share. The 1970s Steelers get together occasionally now, usually at charity events, but nearly always with fans tugging at them. Rarely do they have an opportunity for meaningful, uninterrupted conversation.

In his dreamy imaginings, Stallworth brings back the 1970s Steelers, all of them, even those who have died, for one more shared conversation. The imploded Three Rivers Stadium necessarily rises from rubble and smoke to stand again, and they gather, out of sight from the press and coaches, in their favorite protected haunt and private postgame space, the sauna. There, each man knows who he is, and speaks honestly, nothing fabricated, the conversation between teammates more pure there than at any other place. In the postgame sauna, as Bleier had said, "It just was."

Stallworth imagines it will play out this way: inside the sauna they laugh, share old stories, tell old jokes, talk about key moments in key games, and revel in the greatness of their shared experience. Attendance is mandatory, so Mad Dog and Fats are there, and so are Brad and Webby, Furness, Mean Joe, Hollywood Bags, Courson, Bleier, Lambert, Franco, Swann, and the rest.

Stallworth insists on ground rules. Foremost, they must catch up on their lives since they were all last together without interruption. When was that? The early eighties? Thirty years ago? To each man, Stallworth asks, "What's going on in your life? What makes you happy these days, or sad?" These are the questions that, as teammates, still in their twenties, the 1970s Steelers never thought to ask because they were still proving themselves as football players and as men, competing against the Raiders, the Oilers, and each other. But now, in his sixties, and a minority owner of the team, John Stallworth imagines asking each man, "How are you *really?*"

He knows how Dwight White answers. Mad Dog rails in the sauna about some injustice in his life, and wants Stallworth to feel every bit of that injustice. His brow furrows as he rants, as it always did, and so Stallworth reaches up with his index finger and pokes White in the space between his brows, as if to smooth out the wrinkles, and to say, "Loosen up, Dog!" Just thinking about this makes Stallworth happy, wistful.

The last time he saw White was in 2007, for the celebration of the Steelers' seventy-fifth-anniversary all-time team. Mad Dog often spoke profoundly, and he did that night as well, when he said to his old teammates, "We ought to take this in because we may not all be here the next time," and Stallworth thought, *Yeah, he's right*, but then pushed that thought aside until eight months later, when he heard that White had died.

Stallworth knows that the transition from football to life's work was difficult for Webster, and that so much of Webby's life was football, and that he suffered in his final years as a result of football. In a last conversation in the sauna, Stallworth hopes to hear Webby say that somehow he is okay. From Fats Holmes, Stallworth wishes for reassurance that the inner demons are purged finally, and that Ernie Holmes, six-hundred-pound preacher man, has achieved true contentment in his life.

He remembers Bradshaw's laughter and jokes, moments when he seemed truly happy, and he hopes for much more of that for his quarterback. As teammates, he'd watched Bradshaw try to become what the fans in Three Rivers Stadium desperately wanted: a franchise savior on the field, who was more like them off the field, resilient, approachable, no-nonsense. But Bradshaw needed more space between him and the fans, and they wanted to collapse that space. Alabama Stallworth knew

Loo'siana Bradshaw. He was a southern boy, country, and there was nothing wrong with that, and once Brad understood that it was okay to be true to who he was, things got better for him. Now Stallworth hopes that Bradshaw lets go of any remaining negative thoughts about his years in Pittsburgh and about Chuck Noll, and rejoins the Steelers' huddle.

Time is sliding past the 1970s Pittsburgh Steelers, and as Stallworth considers what football did for them, and to them, he decides that now, as grandfathers in their sixties, they need to cherish not only the time they spent together, but the time they have left. They need to cherish each other and to say perhaps what they'd long thought about saying but have left unsaid. He wants to know what makes them happy these days. He is eager to hear what they have to say. Their conversation starts with the question "How are you *really*?"

MORTAL IMMORTALS

WE ALL PAY COSTS FOR the lives we choose. We make compromises, give up time, money, our health. We ask, Was it worth it? What about these Steelers? What would we have given to be a part of their storied magnificence? Would we pay in lasting pain for the fame, the wealth, the feeling of teammates having our backs on a long, hard journey against sworn enemies? I suspect we would.

At twenty, a kid just beginning an adult's life in 1981, I saw the Steelers of Mean Joe Greene as armored gods. I cared about the game then. But now, past fifty, with a life's experiences, I care about the lives. The Steelers of grandfatherly Joe Greene have become a rich and revealing expression of pro football's gifts and costs. The gifts came in their twenties, the costs in their forties, fifties, and sixties. With the game's violence under scrutiny, the attention now is on brain injury, surely football's highest cost. But many former NFL players in midlife also suffer daily debilitating pain in the hips, shoulders, knees, and backs. These costs are real and lasting. Still, the 1970s Steelers were a force of nature, and even in the twilight of their lives, the memory of their sheer power shines brilliantly.

It's that brilliance that draws me back to pro football. The spectacle is irresistible, with its sensory overload of sights and sounds, frenzied crowds, extraordinary athletes performing at the highest levels of talent and craft. But the game itself leaves me confused. More than ever, it is frighteningly physical. Today's players are bigger and faster. In 1970 one NFL player exceeded three hundred pounds; in 2009 more than 390 players did. Watching NFL games now we see injured players carted off. We know that some play into their midthirties even after suffering six or eight concussions. I wonder how many know Mike Webster's story. A better question: does Mike Webster's story even matter to them?

Still, the game is more than simple violence. There is skill, camaraderie, art, strategy. Football demands talent, courage, dedication, and determination. I admire how NFL players, at their physical zenith, push the human body to its limits. The respect I had for the 1970s Steelers when I first met them in 1981 has multiplied. They chose a brutal game and played it as well as any team ever has. They also made unseen gestures that honored their opponents (Lambert inviting the Chiefs' Rudnay into the postgame sauna, Greene advising the rookie Dunn how to sack Namath, "Just put him down. Don't hurt him."). They doled out punishment and absorbed it. They paid a physical price. For the most part, they endured quietly and nobly.

Their run during the seventies was historic, and they cling to every aspect of it—the intellectual, the tangible, and the emotional. Franco owns the trademark on the phrase "Franco's Immaculate Reception." He drove to Three Rivers Stadium just before it was demolished in 2001 and asked that the piece of turf covering the precise spot on the field where Bradshaw's deflected pass came into his hands be cut out and saved for him, and it was. The emotional connection of these Steelers is to the men they once were, and to each other. When Tony Dungy's eighteen-year-old son James committed suicide in 2005, his Steelers teammates of long ago reached out to him. Joe Greene, Franco, and Donnie Shell sat among 1,500 mourners at the funeral in Tampa. Shell's knees had buckled when he first heard the news, but he believed that Dungy, coach of the Indianapolis Colts and Shell's long-ago Steelers roommate, would emerge from the depth of his sorrow even stronger. Shell had seen Dungy rise before. In 1978, Dungy missed several weeks of training camp due to mononucleosis, and feared the Steelers would release him. Shell challenged him to put God before football, and Dungy did. He led the team in interceptions that season while clinging to the words of Matthew 16:26: "And what do you benefit if you gain the whole world but lose your own soul?" As

Dungy spoke to Shell and other friends outside the funeral home, Shell saw his towering faith and grace. Proud to know Dungy, Shell felt as if they were teammates still.

Only now do I understand that these Steelers believe it was worth the physical price they paid. To be Franco Harris—reaching to catch Bradshaw's deflected pass at the Raiders' forty-two-yard line, and then scoring the touchdown that would become the identifying marker in his life—wouldn't that be wonderful? Forty years later, because of the Immaculate Reception, Harris is a football immortal. You pay a price in pain, you're rewarded with the romance of the game. Harris was twenty-two years old when he caught that pass, and forty years later he is a statue. What would you give to have achieved so greatly that people wanted to remember you forever? And there is this: of the more than 22,000 players in the NFL since 1920, only 247 have been elected to the Pro Football Hall of Fame—little more than 1 percent—and the 1970s Steelers contributed nine of those players.

As Noll told his men, football was not their life's work. The tension between football and life's work would strain, rend, inform, and empower his 1970s Steelers. Some moved on from football and achieved success in finance, technology, entertainment, philanthropy. Thirty years later, the 1970s Steelers remain compelling and likable as interview subjects, and, more importantly, as men. Now their armor is gone. They are us.

I think of the author and rugged individualist Jack London. Just weeks before his death in 1916, London was interviewed by a San Francisco journalist, who quoted him as saying:

> *I would rather be ashes than dust! I would rather that my spark should burn out in a brilliant blaze than it should be stifled by dry-rot. I would rather be a superb meteor, every atom of me in magnificent glow, than a sleepy and permanent planet. The function of man is to live, not to exist. I shall not waste my days trying to prolong them. I shall use my time.*

The 1970s Steelers players lived in a magnificent glow and used their time for rare achievement. For some, the price was higher than for others. At the time, they paid willingly, even eagerly. Now they live with it.

ACKNOWLEDGMENTS

OVER THE PAST THREE YEARS I traveled to meet with the 1970s Pittsburgh Steelers and their families in Texas, Alabama, Michigan, Virginia, California, Tennessee, and Pennsylvania. I conducted interviews in their living rooms, dens, and offices, at hotel coffee shops, restaurants, country clubs, a Starbucks, and in Frenchy Fuqua's man cave. Once I drove around in a golf cart with L. C. Greenwood as he played in a tournament for charity. Each time Greenwood climbed behind the driver's seat, in between shots, I turned on my tape recorder and asked questions. My aspiration was to gauge the full measure of pro football, its gifts and costs, by chronicling this historic team's movement across the decades as the players advanced into middle age and beyond. Thus this book became a hybrid of history and journalism. In all, I conducted more than two hundred interviews, including multiple sessions with key figures. From the 1970s Steelers I interviewed twenty-three players, six Rooneys (Dan, Patricia, Art Jr., John, cousin V. Tim, and Art II), five coaches, four scouts, two publicists, one trainer, and an equipment manager. My initial circle of interviews rippled outward to include wives, siblings, NFL opponents, league officials, sportswriters, and others. Foremost, I'm indebted to the Rooneys and their former players for sharing their personal stories.

In his Pro Football Hall of Fame induction speech at Canton in 1993, Chuck Noll said, "I can't tell you how much you can gain, how much progress you can make, by working as a team, by helping one another. If there is anything the Steelers of the seventies epitomized, it's that teamwork."

Book-writing is, by nature, a solitary pursuit. But it was my great fortune during this project to join forces with a remarkable book team. Foremost among teammates was senior editor Thomas LeBien of Simon & Schuster. Once, we walked 9.4 miles together along the Tomales Point Trail near Point Reyes, California, where tule elk roam and the Pacific surf pounds. We talked (and talked!) about football, narrative structure, and life. A week later, we reprised our walk through New York's Central Park, continuing our dialogue. With editor's pen in hand, Mean Tom LeBien is a Hall of Famer. And so, too, is David Black, my literary agent and short-yardage blocker for the past twenty-seven years. At his agency, David Larabell, Gary Morris, Susan Raihofer, Antonella Iannarino, Sarah Smith, and Joy Tutela are longtime friends. At S&S, Brit Hvide, LeBien's assistant, kept the chains moving for this book with efficiency and grace.

For each of my five nonfiction books, I've assembled a panel to read early drafts of my manuscript. I've asked them to point out any missteps I've made and to challenge my interpretations. I thank my early readers for this book: Ernie Accorsi, who spent forty-seven years in the NFL, the last ten (1998–2007) as general manager of the New York Giants; Vito Stellino of the *Florida Times-Union*, an NFL writer of four decades, who lived the Steelers' empire day to day during the 1970s as beat writer for the *Pittsburgh Post-Gazette*; R. B. Brenner, my teaching colleague at Stanford University's Graduate Program in Journalism, and formerly Sunday Editor and Metro Editor at the *Washington Post*, where he served in 2007 as one of the primary editors of the paper's Pulitzer Prize–winning coverage of the Virginia Tech shootings; Andy Mathieson, friend and neighbor, who hails from Pittsburgh, and as a sixteen-year-old sat with his father at Three Rivers Stadium on December 23, 1972, and saw firsthand the Immaculate Reception; and Dave Kindred, forty years a sports columnist and a member of the National Sportscasters and Sportswriters Association & Hall of Fame. "He can run but he can't hide," Joe Louis once said about Billy Conn. Same goes for Kindred. He moved during this book project from rural Virginia to Carlock, Illinois. He could run from me, but he couldn't hide. By e-mail and phone, I found him to discuss this book: once, twice, ten thousand times.

I'm indebted to others as well. For years, the Steelers' Joe Gordon was one of the best PR men in the NFL. I phoned the since-retired Gordon at home in 2009 to discuss my project. He became my point man, helping me reach out to the old Steelers.

ACKNOWLEDGMENTS

OVER THE PAST THREE YEARS I traveled to meet with the 1970s Pittsburgh Steelers and their families in Texas, Alabama, Michigan, Virginia, California, Tennessee, and Pennsylvania. I conducted interviews in their living rooms, dens, and offices, at hotel coffee shops, restaurants, country clubs, a Starbucks, and in Frenchy Fuqua's man cave. Once I drove around in a golf cart with L. C. Greenwood as he played in a tournament for charity. Each time Greenwood climbed behind the driver's seat, in between shots, I turned on my tape recorder and asked questions. My aspiration was to gauge the full measure of pro football, its gifts and costs, by chronicling this historic team's movement across the decades as the players advanced into middle age and beyond. Thus this book became a hybrid of history and journalism. In all, I conducted more than two hundred interviews, including multiple sessions with key figures. From the 1970s Steelers I interviewed twenty-three players, six Rooneys (Dan, Patricia, Art Jr., John, cousin V. Tim, and Art II), five coaches, four scouts, two publicists, one trainer, and an equipment manager. My initial circle of interviews rippled outward to include wives, siblings, NFL opponents, league officials, sportswriters, and others. Foremost, I'm indebted to the Rooneys and their former players for sharing their personal stories.

In his Pro Football Hall of Fame induction speech at Canton in 1993, Chuck Noll said, "I can't tell you how much you can gain, how much progress you can make, by working as a team, by helping one another. If there is anything the Steelers of the seventies epitomized, it's that teamwork."

Book-writing is, by nature, a solitary pursuit. But it was my great fortune during this project to join forces with a remarkable book team. Foremost among teammates was senior editor Thomas LeBien of Simon & Schuster. Once, we walked 9.4 miles together along the Tomales Point Trail near Point Reyes, California, where tule elk roam and the Pacific surf pounds. We talked (and talked!) about football, narrative structure, and life. A week later, we reprised our walk through New York's Central Park, continuing our dialogue. With editor's pen in hand, Mean Tom LeBien is a Hall of Famer. And so, too, is David Black, my literary agent and short-yardage blocker for the past twenty-seven years. At his agency, David Larabell, Gary Morris, Susan Raihofer, Antonella Iannarino, Sarah Smith, and Joy Tutela are longtime friends. At S&S, Brit Hvide, LeBien's assistant, kept the chains moving for this book with efficiency and grace.

For each of my five nonfiction books, I've assembled a panel to read early drafts of my manuscript. I've asked them to point out any missteps I've made and to challenge my interpretations. I thank my early readers for this book: Ernie Accorsi, who spent forty-seven years in the NFL, the last ten (1998–2007) as general manager of the New York Giants; Vito Stellino of the *Florida Times-Union*, an NFL writer of four decades, who lived the Steelers' empire day to day during the 1970s as beat writer for the *Pittsburgh Post-Gazette*; R. B. Brenner, my teaching colleague at Stanford University's Graduate Program in Journalism, and formerly Sunday Editor and Metro Editor at the *Washington Post*, where he served in 2007 as one of the primary editors of the paper's Pulitzer Prize–winning coverage of the Virginia Tech shootings; Andy Mathieson, friend and neighbor, who hails from Pittsburgh, and as a sixteen-year-old sat with his father at Three Rivers Stadium on December 23, 1972, and saw firsthand the Immaculate Reception; and Dave Kindred, forty years a sports columnist and a member of the National Sportscasters and Sportswriters Association & Hall of Fame. "He can run but he can't hide," Joe Louis once said about Billy Conn. Same goes for Kindred. He moved during this book project from rural Virginia to Carlock, Illinois. He could run from me, but he couldn't hide. By e-mail and phone, I found him to discuss this book: once, twice, ten thousand times.

I'm indebted to others as well. For years, the Steelers' Joe Gordon was one of the best PR men in the NFL. I phoned the since-retired Gordon at home in 2009 to discuss my project. He became my point man, helping me reach out to the old Steelers.

At archives and libraries across the land, I was treated with kindness and extraordinary professionalism. I'm especially grateful to: David Plaut, Bob Angelo, and Chris Willie at NFL Films in Mount Laurel, New Jersey; Joe Horrigan, Pete Fierle, and Jon Kendle at the Ralph Wilson, Jr. Pro Football Research and Preservation Center, Pro Football Hall of Fame in Canton, Ohio; Alexis Macklin at the Heinz History Center in Pittsburgh; Burt Lauten, Ryan Scarpino, Dave Lockett, and Mike Fabus of the Pittsburgh Steelers; Joe Browne and Dan Masonson at the National Football League offices in New York; Ted Ryan (who handed me thick folders of materials on Joe Greene's famed Coke commercial) at the Coca-Cola Company archives in Atlanta; and University of Pittsburgh historian Rob Ruck, coauthor of *Rooney: A Sporting Life*, a biography of the Chief. Ruck shared a few lengthy conversations with me about the Chief, the Steelers, and Pittsburgh, including one on the Pitt campus.

My indebtedness extends to George Solomon and Len Shapiro, my long-ago sports editors at the *Washington Post*, who threw me into the waters—or at least sent me to Latrobe—as a summer intern in 1981 to write about the Steelers' crumbling dynasty. That assignment planted the seed for this book. I'm lucky to have worked for Solomon and Shapiro at the start of my writing career. They pushed me hard as a sports journalist and set the bar high.

By the time I started this book, our sons, Ross and Win, had flown the coop, the former with his college degree and pitching in independent pro baseball, the latter off to study business as an undergraduate. That left my wife, Carrie, and our daughter, Leigh, to bear the brunt of a grumpy author who came home at night to watch DVDs of long-ago Super Bowls and AFC title games, and kept muttering about the blood wars between Mean Joe and Jim Otto. At the dinner table, I diagrammed for them the Immaculate Reception, the salt shaker as Tatum, the pepper shaker as Fuqua. Narrative nonfiction is full immersion—for them, too. I owe Carrie and Leigh and love them greatly.

NOTES

Epigraph

PAGE

xi *"What has the game given me?"*: John Banaszak interview.

Introduction: Reverie & Reality

PAGE

3 *favorite black leather recliner*: Dan Rooney, Art Rooney Jr. interviews.

3 *played a semipro football game against Jim Thorpe*: Rob Ruck, Maggie Jones Patterson, and Michael P. Weber, *Rooney: A Sporting Life* (Lincoln: University of Nebraska Press, 2010), p. xxiv.

4 *"Thanks, Mike. I needed that"*: Reggie Harrison (known today as Kamal Ali Salaam-El) interview.

4 *toddler granddaughter calls him Gumpa*: Joe Greene interview.

5 *"I'm gonna tackle that fuckin' airport statue"*: Phil Villapiano interview.

5 *"almost like living in a wonderland"*: Randy Grossman interview.

6 *He used terms like* yeggs, greasy bums: Roy McHugh interview.

7 *"If you hold me"*: Jack Rudnay interview.

7 *"I would love to have a chance to hold"*: Ibid.

7 *"Can you imagine if you could create"*: Ronnie Lott interview.

7 *"Glen had—it wasn't a speech impediment"*: Mel Blount interview.

7 *drank Michelob beer in bottles (never cans)*: Jack Ham interview.

8 *"HE'S GONNA HAVE A BAD DAY!"*: Dwight White interview with Keith Cossrow of NFL Films, October 6, 2006. NFL-161516.

8 *"And Lambert: oh, my God!"*: J. T. Thomas interview.

8 *"Just leave him out there!"*: Ibid.

8 *"I'm coming right over your ass!"*: Ibid.

8 *"We saw you go home"*: Coach Joe Gilliam Sr. interview.

9 *the shoe-shine man at the Hotel Northland*: David Maraniss, *When Pride Still Mattered: A Life of Vince Lombardi* (New York: Simon & Schuster, 1999), p. 239.

9   *"I liken it to the Big Bang theory"*: Dwight White interview with Keith Cossrow of NFL Films, 1999. NFL-80189.

9   *"Best team ever!"*: Gordon Gravelle interview.

10 *"It just goes 'Click' "*: Pete Cronan interview.

11 *"What is old? Chronologically we are old"*: *Washington Post*, August 4, 1981.

11 *"I don't mean to brag"*: Ibid.

12 *"Who know the conflict, hand-to-hand"*: Walt Whitman, *Specimen Days & Collect.* (New York: Dover Publications, 1995), pp. 35–36.

12 *"It all depends on what you prefer"*: Reggie Harrison (known today as Kamal Ali Salaam-El) interview.

12 *"You're going to set the head-butt record"*: Gary Dunn interview.

13 *voice of a teammate saying, "You okay, man?"*: John (Frenchy) Fuqua interview.

14 *"Look at Ernie. He takes up two chairs!"*: Terry Bradshaw interview.

14 *"If you were my son, I'd tell you"*: Paul Brown with Jack Clary, *PB: The Paul Brown Story* (New York: Signet, 1979), p. 163.

15 *salary for an NFL player grew from $23,000*: Tom Van Riper, "The NFL's Truly Most Valuable Players, www.Forbes.com, December 22, 2006. See also *New York Times*, January 29, 1982.

15 *had only one conversation with him*: L. C. Greenwood interview.

15 *Lambert said he exchanged about eleven words with Noll*: Jack Lambert interview with Bob Angelo of NFL Films, October 25, 1994.

15 *"He finally got to retirement"*: John (Frenchy) Fuqua interview.

15 *"Steelers' Noll decides it's time"*: *Pittsburgh Post-Gazette*, December 27, 1991.

17 *NFL commissioner Roger Goodell has spoken*: *New York Times*, November 16, 2012.

17 *since 1905, when eighteen college and amateur players died*: John J. Miller, *The Big Scrum: How Teddy Roosevelt Saved Football* (New York: HarperCollins, 2011), p. 11.

17 *Roosevelt called the coaches of Harvard, Princeton*: Ibid., pp. 184–90.

Chapter 1: The Chief at the Racetracks, 1937

PAGE

21 *"Did you ever notice, my friend"*: Grantland Rice, *The Tumult and the Shouting: My Life in Sport* (New York: A. S. Barnes, 1954), p. 266.

23 *"I'm no big shot"*: John Rooney and Art Rooney Jr. interviews.

23 *(steak, creamed potatoes, cornbread)*: Rob Ruck, Maggie Jones Patterson, and Michael P. Weber, *Rooney: A Sporting Life* (Lincoln: University of Nebraska Press, 2010), p. 121.

23 *scraps of paper with names and numbers, racetrack programs*: Gerald Holland, "The Winning Ways of a Thirty-Year Loser," *Sports Illustrated*, November 23, 1964, p. 90.

23 *be sure to attend the wake or funeral*: Ed Kiely interview.

24 *"When you see these skies red"*: Dan Rooney interview.

24 *In 1930, 35 percent of Pittsburgh's*: Samuel P. Hays, ed., *City at the Point: Essays on the Social History of Pittsburgh* (Pittsburgh: University of Pittsburgh Press, 1989), p. 10.

24   *"If a cat gave birth in an oven"*: Art Rooney Jr. interview. Also Art Rooney Jr. with Roy McHugh, *Ruanaidh: The Story of Art Rooney and His Clan* (Pittsburgh: Geyer Printing Company, 2010), p. 5.

25   *"The greatest of the great!"*: Art Rooney Jr. interview.

25   *"whippet tank going for one of Jerry's pill boxes"*: Ruck, Patterson, and Weber, *Rooney: A Sporting Life*, p. 33.

25   *"Lads, when you grow up and make your fortune"*: Draft of Dan Rooney speech in 1990. Dan Rooney files, Ralph Wilson, Jr. Pro Football Research and Preservation Center, Pro Football Hall of Fame, Canton, Ohio.

25   *his first horse race, at Cleveland's Randall Park Race Track*: Ruck, Patterson, and Weber, *Rooney: A Sporting Life*, p. 134.

26   *one day of his young adult life in a real job*: Dan Rooney as told to Andrew E. Masich and David F. Halaas, *My 75 Years with the Pittsburgh Steelers and the NFL* (New York: Da Capo Press, 2007), p. 12.

26   *had spent generations at the iron furnaces*: Dan Rooney and Art Rooney Jr. interviews.

26   *pushed their broken-down touring cars*: Ruck, Patterson, and Weber, *Rooney: A Sporting Life*, pp. 49–50.

27   *Inside the bag was $20,000 in cash*: Ibid., pp. 69, 235–36.

27   *Kathleen ("Kass") McNulty's father didn't trust him*: Ibid., p. 74.

27   *She held fast to her dress*: Ibid., p. 84.

27   *Rooney had lost a $20,000 bankroll*: New York Post, June 2, 1938.

28   *"That was a lot of bunk"*: New York Post, December 12, 1966.

28   *Rooney left a plumbers' union gathering*: Ruck, Patterson, and Weber, *Rooney: A Sporting Life*, p. 117.

28   *A dapper dresser, usually with a boutonniere*: Pittsburgh Post-Gazette, July 21, 1956.

28   *Once a longshoreman named Joseph Penzo*: Ruck, Patterson, and Weber, *Rooney: A Sporting Life*, p. 119.

28   *So Rooney put down $150 for a 1928 model*: New York Post, July 28, 1937.

28   *Rooney stayed up until four a.m., doping*: Ibid.

29   *"He gets me to mark his card"*: New York World-Telegram, August 30, 1937.

29   *"the colored groom the difference between"*: John Lardner, *It Beats Working* (Philadelphia: J. B. Lippincott, 1947), pp. 57–58.

29   *"Roll 'Em High Rooney"*: Evening Journal and New York American, July 27, 1937.

29   *"Rooney is 'Rooneying' "*: Ibid.

30   *"Mr. Rooney is perhaps too young"*: Ruck, Patterson, and Weber, *Rooney: A Sporting Life*, pp. 126–27.

30   *Sometimes Crouse believed he was St. Francis of Assisi*: Art Rooney Jr. interview.

30   *"his total winnings for 18 successive races $148,180"*: Evening Journal and New York American, July 28, 1937.

30   *"wind up with the bookmakers' limousines"*: Ibid.

30   *The estimate of his winnings over three days*: Interview with Art Rooney Jr. Also Art

Rooney Jr. with Roy McHugh, *Ruanaidh*, p. 38. Also see Roy Blount Jr., *About Three Bricks Shy . . . and the Load Filled Up* (Pittsburgh: University of Pittsburgh Press, 2002), pp. 199–200.

30   *"They'll never get that back"*: *New York World-Telegram*, August 13, 1937.

30   *"That fellow, Rooney, has horseshoes"*: *Evening Journal and New York American*, August 31, 1937.

31   *on a lengthy vacation to Bermuda*: *New York Post*, July 28, 1937.

Chapter 2: The Rooneys

PAGE

35   *He apologized for his absence*: Rob Ruck, Maggie Jones Patterson, and Michael P. Weber, *Rooney: A Sporting Life* (Lincoln: University of Nebraska Press, 2010), p. 155.

35   *"Use it again"*: Art Rooney Jr. interview.

35   *"This okay?"*: Ibid.

35   *"Don't use that language"*: John Rooney interview.

35   *"Have your belt"*: Lou Spadia interview.

36   *She put down $500*: Dan Rooney as told to Andrew E. Masich and David F. Halaas, *My 75 Years with the Pittsburgh Steelers and the NFL* (New York: Da Capo Press, 2007), p. 18.

36   *an old house, built just after the Civil War*: *Pittsburgh Post-Gazette*, November 6, 1993.

36   *seven-year-old Dan Rooney walked out of the back*: Dan Rooney interview.

36   *he smacked hard grounders*: Dan Rooney and Art Rooney Jr. interviews.

36   *"You're not crying, are you?"*: Ibid.

36   *"I'd rather have you guys be dopes"*: John Rooney interview.

36   *"the cock of the walk"*: Dan Rooney as told to Masich and Halaas, *My 75 Years with the Pittsburgh Steelers and the NFL*, p. 13.

36   *"He was like a man compared"*: John Rooney interview.

36   *"Hey, Dan, that's ten!"*: Ibid.

37   *"You better talk to Danny"*: Dan Rooney interview.

37   *"That was a civic thing"*: Ibid.

37   *"Well, how was it?"*: Ibid.

37   *"without exception, the blackest place"*: Anthony Trollope, *North America*, vol. 1 (Philadelphia: J. B. Lippincott, 1863), p. 75.

38   *"This used to be some town"*: Roy Blount Jr., *About Three Bricks Shy . . . and the Load Filled Up* (Pittsburgh: University of Pittsburgh Press, 2002), p. 14.

38   *Someone always seemed to be sitting on the windowsill*: Lou Spadia interview. Also *Chicago Tribune*, September 26, 1970.

38   *an affinity for dice games and the horses*: Art Rooney Jr. interview.

38   *Niagara "Nicaragua" and Junianta "Juanita"*: Roy McHugh interview.

39   *"I don't want to have anybody tell me"*: Art Rooney Jr. interview.

39   *"Why the Steelers Stink"*: Ibid.

39   *"As different as two brothers can be"*: John Rooney interview.

40   *"You are worse than raw"*: Art Rooney Jr. interview.

40   *"Nobody—I mean nobody"*: Ibid.

40   *"After the people fight the traffic jam"*: *Baltimore News American*, December 14, 1962.

40   *"Okay, put on your helmets!"*: Jack Butler interview.

41   *"I had no real pitch"*: Ed Kiely interview.

41   *He read all the national football magazines, subscribed*: Art Rooney Jr. interview.

41   *"Marshall was the worst"*: Lou Spadia interview.

41   *"What are you doing, drafting a bunch"*: Art Rooney Jr. interview.

42   *wrote his father an impassioned twenty-two-page*: Tom Callahan, *Johnny U: The Life & Times of John Unitas* (New York: Three Rivers Press, 2006), p. 50.

42   *Even Paul Brown, picking next, desperately wanted Dawson*: *Pittsburgh Press*, April 23, 1989.

42   *"Do you realize that the Steelers"*: Ernie Accorsi interview.

42   *"There were three main things"*: *Pittsburgh Press*, August 25, 1988.

43   *"Nobody was worrying about titles"*: Dan Rooney interview.

43   *"Who is this guy?"*: Dan Rooney as told to Masich and Halaas, *My 75 Years with the Pittsburgh Steelers and the NFL*, p. 94.

43   *"Okay, Pete, I disagree"*: Ibid., p. 104.

43   *"we played basketball in the garbage can"*: John Rooney interview.

44   *"We might look for all linebackers"*: Gil Brandt interview.

44   *" 'How can a machine do the job of a man?' "*: Ibid.

44   *hot plates, movie projectors, coffeemakers, a still camera*: Art Rooney Jr. interview.

44   *"Artie, did you see that fella flinch there?"*: Ibid.

44   *"Captains" (the letter C for "Colored")*: Ibid.

45   *"I don't need to talk to anybody else"*: Dan Rooney interview.

45   *"What white Americans have never fully understood"*: Gary M. Pomerantz, *Where Peachtree Meets Sweet Auburn: The Saga of Two Families and the Making of Atlanta* (New York: Scribner, 1996), p. 354.

46   *He liked to call his players Baby*: Coach Joe Gilliam Sr. interview.

46   *"Never, ever trust a black man"*: Art Rooney Jr. interview.

46   Why don't we know more about these guys?: Dan Rooney interview. Also Dan Rooney as told to Masich and Halaas, *My 75 Years with the Pittsburgh Steelers and the NFL*, p. 134.

Chapter 3: The Man from the *Courier*

PAGE

47   *He saw the Steelers grant passes to writers from daily*: Bill Nunn Jr. interview. For context about the treatment of black sportswriters during this era see A. S. (Doc) Young, "Black Athlete in Golden Age of Sports: The Black Sportswriter, Part IX," *Ebony*, October 1970, pp. 56–57.

47   *Lewis was a likable, slightly stooped shoe-shine*: *Tuscaloosa (Ala.) News*, August 23, 1963.

48   *"Boots The Negro: A Good Luck"*: Ibid.

48   *He called Dan Rooney "Marooney"*: Ibid.

48   *"Boots looks like the guy hitting the cymbals"*: Art Rooney Jr. interview.

48   *"I don't want to talk about that guy"*: Bill Nunn Jr. interview.

48   *"wave of burnished, bronze superstars"*: *Pittsburgh Courier*, January 8, 1966.

49   *"When St. Louis outfielder Curt Flood"*: Ibid., November 7, 1964.

49   *"Jackie Robinson has the makings of a good"*: Ibid., June 4, 1966.

49   *"[Eldridge] Dickey, it says here"*: Ibid., January 6, 1968.

49   *some of the racial slights he'd received*: Bill Nunn Jr. interview.

49   *Clemente asked Nunn for a ride to the airport*: Ibid.

49   *escorting him, inch by inch, through adoring fans*: *Pittsburgh Courier*, October 22, 1960.
      Also David Maraniss, *Clemente: The Passion and Grace of Baseball's Last Hero* (New
      York: Simon & Schuster, 2007), p. 135.

50   *"Basically I would watch him during the week"*: Bill Nunn Jr. interview.

50   *Nunn sometimes stayed at Coach Robinson's house*: Ibid.

51   *Nunn's father, a short, squat man with a deep, expansive voice*: "Bill Nunn Sr., Former
      Courier Editor, Dies," *Jet*, December 4, 1969, p. 48.

51   *celebrated black Americans passing through his house*: Bill Nunn Jr. interview.

51   *"I think you need to find out more about your"*: Ibid.

52   *"Tell him as long as the Steelers have the approach"*: Ibid.

52   *"Why don't you help change it?"*: This scene is drawn from interviews with Dan Rooney
      and Bill Nunn Jr.

53   *elder Nunn had helped the Chief locate housing*: Dan Rooney interview.

53   *Kass baked several pies for him*: Maxine Perry interview. She is the widow of Lowell
      Perry.

53   *"As long as I own the Pittsburgh Steelers"*: Ibid.

53   Here's one of these smart-aleck: Art Rooney Jr. interview.

54   I know what he's thinking about me: Ibid.

54   *it took him years to build a cross-race familiarity*: Dick Mansperger interview.

55   *Nunn took a call from John Sengstacke*: Bill Nunn Jr. interview.

55   *one bullet passed perilously close to the teenager*: Bill Nunn III interview.

55   *His wife, Kay, watching on television as violence broke out*: Art Rooney Jr. interview.

55   *"Even as the Rev. Martin Luther King"*: *Pittsburgh Courier*, April 13, 1968.

56   *he deferred leaving the newspaper for one year*: Bill Nunn Jr. interview.

56   *As the league's sixth full-time black scout*: Peter King, "The Steel Age," *Sports Illustrated*,
      January 22, 1990, p. 66.

56   *The Steelers drafted eleven black-college players*: Ibid.

56   *"I almost felt this was an untapped source"*: Ibid.

56   *"From what I hear"*: Bill Nunn Jr. interview.

56   *"I can take you into the Hill District"*: Ibid.

Chapter 4: Noll & Mean Joe

PAGE

59 *In the heated warmth of his automobile*: Bobby Mitchell interview.

59 *PB often selected a few local boys*: Paul Brown with Jack Clary, *PB: The Paul Brown Story* (New York: Signet, 1979), p. 232.

59 *"How's the Pope doing?"*: Ibid.

60 *"Thirty-seven! GIVE IT TO THE BIG MAN!"*: Bobby Mitchell interview.

60 *Greene was kicked out of every game as a sophomore*: Roy Blount Jr., "He Does What He Wants Out There," *Sports Illustrated*, September 22, 1975, p. 103.

60 *Greene had picked cotton and pecans*: Joe Greene interview.

60 *he saw the water fountains marked "Colored"*: Ibid.

60 *The black schools played on Thursdays or Saturdays*: *Temple (Tex.) Daily Telegram*, February 5, 2007.

60 *The* Temple Daily Telegram *hardly acknowledged games*: Ibid.

61 *He snatched an ice cream cone from the hand*: Blount, "He Does What He Wants Out There," p. 104.

61 *a player called out to Greene and threw a soda bottle*: Joe Greene interview.

61 *They brought Vince Lombardi along to help sell Paterno*: Rob Ruck, Maggie Jones Patterson, and Michael P. Weber, *Rooney: A Sporting Life* (Lincoln: University of Nebraska Press, 2010), p. 368.

61 *"Will trade my brother and two sisters for your mother"*: *Dallas Morning News*, August 29, 1988.

62 *"I hope they all eat their pencils and pads"*: *Wisconsin State Journal*, January 13, 1969.

62 *"It just seemed kind of hopeless"*: Ray Mansfield interview with Noah Lerner of NFL Films, January 19, 1996.

62 *half of his youth football team was black*: Tom Danyluk, *The Super '70s: Memories from Pro Football's Greatest Era* (Chicago: Mad Uke Publishing, 2005), p. 51. Paul Zimmerman, longtime NFL writer for *Sports Illustrated*, conducted an interview with author Danyluk about Noll and the 1970s Steelers on March 6, 1998. Zimmerman spoke of an earlier interview he'd conducted with Noll.

62 *in the same house in which his mother had been raised*: *Cleveland Plain Dealer*, December 27, 2008.

62 *in a class of 252, Noll graduated 28th*: Ibid.

62 *He might have played football for Notre Dame but suffered an epileptic*: Ibid.

62 *Noll spoke frankly about his perceptions of the Steelers*: Dan Rooney interview. Also Dan Rooney as told to Andrew E. Masich and David F. Halaas, *My 75 Years with the Pittsburgh Steelers and the NFL* (New York: Da Capo Press, 2007), pp. 125–26.

62 *He told Dan the Steelers lacked talent*: Ibid.

63 *He had one concern: Noll was young*: Ibid.

63 *"Let's keep Noll on our list"*: Ibid. Also Dan Rooney as told to Masich and Halaas, *My 75 Years with the Pittsburgh Steelers and the NFL*, p. 126.

63   *"You know," Williams said, "you're the only one I want"*: David Maraniss, *When Pride Still Mattered: A Life of Vince Lombardi* (New York: Simon & Schuster, 1999), p. 453.

63   *The Chief liked Noll's composure, his values*: Dan Rooney interview.

63   *"I don't care what color my players are"*: Art Rooney Jr. interview.

63   *"Chuck was the kind of player"*: Walt Michaels interview.

64   *"Jim Brown and I spent all our time pushing"*: Bobby Mitchell interview.

64   *"I saw these little black dots and the yellow thing"*: NFL Films video interview with Chuck Bednarik: http://www.youtube.com/watch?v=Up2FvxA5UQ8.

64   *"at the end of these stories you were either dead"*: Walt Michaels interview.

64   *"Dante told us he broke the forty-yard-dash"*: Ibid.

65   *Noll suffered an epileptic seizure on the team plane*: Tom Callahan interview.

65   *He warned her about the coaching life*: Pittsburgh Press, December 8, 1974.

65   *what most impressed him was "the man himself"*: Ibid., January 28, 1969.

65   *"The coach is the one who's going to get fired"*: Art Rooney Jr. interview.

65   *"He's a good speaker"*: Pittsburgh Press, January 28, 1969.

66   *"This is the city of losers"*: Ibid.

66   *"He runs like a chicken with frozen feet"*: George Plimpton, "Rubies and Diamonds," Sports Illustrated, February 9, 1970, p. 24.

66   *"AGILE, MOBILE & HOSTILE AS HELL"*: BLESTO scouting report on Joe Greene filed by Jess Thompson, October 1, 1968, from Denton, Texas, BLESTO Reports, 1968–1975, BLESTO Reports Collection, Ralph Wilson, Jr. Pro Football Research and Preservation Center, Pro Football Hall of Fame, Canton, Ohio.

66   *cut from the mold of the Dallas Cowboys' all-pro Bob Lilly*: Joe Greene interview.

66   *"Quick as a big cat"*: Pittsburgh Steelers Senior Scouting Report on Joe Greene filed by Art Rooney Jr., November 13, 1968, from Denton, Texas, Pittsburgh Steelers Scouting Reports Collection, 1968–1975, Ralph Wilson, Jr. Pro Football Research and Preservation Center, Pro Football Hall of Fame, Canton, Ohio.

67   *his aunt playfully suggested that he might become the next Joe Louis*: Joe Greene interview.

67   *"Everybody wanted to beat up"*: Ibid.

67   *he tapped local police as informal scouts*: Maraniss, When Pride Still Mattered, p. 300.

68   *"Whatcha goin' to do 'bout it?"*: Joe Greene interview.

68   *"I popped him on the side of his head"*: Ibid. Also see Ron Cook, "Yesterday's Heroes," Football Digest, July/August 1987, p. 84.

68   *"Those coaches, their eyes just got so big"*: Joe Greene interview.

68   *She saw him dance the Philly Dog at a party*: Agnes Greene interview.

68   *"I was like Diana Ross when she saw Billy Dee"*: Ibid.

68   *"These guys dress awfully peculiar!"*: Ibid.

69   *calling the groom's mom "Mother Dear"*: Charles Beatty interview.

69   *"I took Agnes all the way to Fort Worth!"*: Joe Greene interview.

69   *"What are you talking about?"*: Andy Russell interview.

69   *"Nice block, asshole!"*: Ibid.

70   *he would need to get rid of nearly every player*: Ibid.

70   *"You hit him where he is soft"*: Roy Blount Jr., *About Three Bricks Shy . . . and the Load Filled Up* (Pittsburgh: University of Pittsburgh Press, 2002), pp. 96–97.

70   *wanting to know Russell's thought process on certain plays*: Andy Russell interview.

70   *"Who is he, anyway?"*: Art Rooney Jr. interview.

70   *"Oh, give it to him!"*: Joe Greene interview.

71   *"Pretty snappy for a defensive tackle"*: *Pittsburgh Post-Gazette*, February 11, 1976.

71   *"C'mon, Joe! A number one draft choice"*: Joe Greene interview with Keith Cossrow of NFL Films on February 22, 2006. NFL-145346.

71   *"To me, he's just another big, fat-butted"*: Ray Mansfield interview with Jonathan Hock of NFL Films on June 6, 1994.

71   *"a thing of beauty to watch"*: Terry Hanratty interview.

71   *"We might as well pack our bags"*: Dick Hoak interview.

71   *"Joe was nasty"*: L. C. Greenwood interview.

72   *"Joe was a first-round draft choice"*: Ibid.

72   *"That will be five hundred dollars"*: Joe Greene interview.

72   *"I hit him as hard as I could hit him"*: Joe Greene interview with NFL Films on July 21, 1994.

72   *"Guess what, Joe?"*: Ibid.

72   *"these grotesque figures"*: Joe Greene interview with Steve Sabol of NFL Films on November 29, 2004. NFL-135139.

72   *"You can't have a guy like this"*: Dan Rooney interview.

72   *grabbed trainer Ralph Berlin's tape-cutting scissors*: Andy Russell interview.

73   *"Butkus was standing there with this [spit] thing hanging"*: Ray Mansfield interview with Jonathan Hock of NFL Films on June 6, 1994.

73   This is going to be the greatest fight: Ibid.

73   *"That was the beginning of the end"*: Ibid.

73   *"This guy's like buying Xerox"*: Roy McHugh, "The Making of the No. 1 Draft Choice," *Sport*, May 1970, p. 80.

73   *"Boy, he has a real rifle arm!"*: Ibid.

73   *"You kind of feel 'em or smell 'em"*: Ibid., p. 27.

73   *"I'm looking for Mr. Rooney"*: Art Rooney Jr. interview.

74   Damn, why are we still doing these: Joe Greene interview.

74   *"The ball went far"*: Dan Rooney interview.

Chapter 5: The Rock & the Frenchman

PAGE

75   *hoping to break a rib or some other bone*: Rocky Bleier with Terry O'Neil, *Fighting Back* (Pittsburgh: Rocky Bleier, Inc., 1975), pp. 62–63.

75   *Bleier watched on television from his army*: Ibid., p. 65.

76 *He introduced himself to Ellen Bleier*: Ellen Bleier, Rocky Bleier, and Pamela Bleier interviews. Pamela Bleier is Rocky Bleier's sister.

76 *"Son of a bitch looks like a little rock!"*: Bleier with O'Neil, *Fighting Back*, p. 10.

76 *"But I'll bet you don't have one of these!"*: Rocky Bleier interview.

76 *"I've been talking to God a lot"*: Bleier with O'Neil, *Fighting Back*, p. 85.

76 *As Viet Cong snipers and machine guns*: Rocky Bleier interview. Also Bleier with O'Neil, *Fighting Back*, pp. 93–103.

77 *Bleier heard the black soldier softly encourage, "We're going to get there"*: Bleier with O'Neil, *Fighting Back*, pp. 102–3.

77 *His body was, by US Army definition, 40 percent*: Ibid., p. 121.

77 *Telegrams kept arriving, the local police*: Ellen Bleier interview.

77 *she knew with absolute certainty that his left leg was no more*: Ibid.

77 *"Rock. The team's not doing well"*: Rocky Bleier interview.

78 This is such a waste of time: Pamela Bleier interview.

78 *"I played soccer in the old country"*: John Fuqua interview.

78 *blasted* In-A-Gadda-Da-Vida: Ibid.

78 *Noll occasionally visited him late at night in his dorm*: Ibid.

79 *Bleier saw Fuqua finish dressing and go out the back*: Rocky Bleier interview.

79 *"Your daddy wanted to run in the street"*: John Fuqua interview.

79 *"Some of the strangest stuff I'd ever seen"*: Ibid.

79 *the paper already had too many Jewish-sounding bylines*: Myron Cope, *Double Yoi!* (Champaign, Ill.: Sports Publishing, 2002), p. 34.

80 *"Myron, you are so out of line"*: Art Rooney Jr. interview.

80 *"Only 983 more to 1,000"*: Terry Hanratty interview.

80 *"Rock didn't have any real guns over in Vietnam!"*: J. T. Thomas interview.

80 *At parties Bradshaw's black teammates sent their wives*: Terry Bradshaw with Buddy Martin, *Looking Deep* (Chicago: Contemporary Books, 1989), p. 65.

80 *"You people will just steal 'em from me"*: Bobby Walden interview.

81 *"I don't want you ever again to sit with those black guys"*: Coach Joe Gilliam Sr. interview.

81 *"Daddy, I don't know if they want that"*: Ibid.

81 *"Chuck, you need to get out of those heels"*: Ralph Berlin interview.

81 *"over my stomach and right above my privates"*: John Fuqua interview.

81 *"Man, Beatty can go in a store"*: *Beaver County (Pa.) Times*, October 23, 1972.

81 *"makes me think your fashion editor wears white"*: John (Frenchy) Fuqua, "Sour Drapes," *Esquire* 78, no. 5 (November 1972): 20.

82 *"We put up Jim Clack"*: Rocky Bleier interview.

82 *"I just feel good—when we win"*: *Rome (Ga.) News-Tribune*, January 7, 1973.

Chapter 6: Immaculate

PAGE

83   *Harris first would approach the wall, count*: Mickey Herskowitz, "Rebel with Cause," NFL *GameDay (Raiders vs. Chargers)*, September 18, 1977, p. 120.

84   *"No doubt that he has great ability"*: Scouting report on Franco Harris filed by Dick Haley of the Steelers, December 4, 1971, from University Park, Pennsylvania, Pittsburgh Steelers Scouting Reports Collection, 1968–1975, Ralph Wilson, Jr. Pro Football Research and Preservation Center, Pro Football Hall of Fame, Canton, Ohio.

84   *"Is Chuck giving you the business again?"*: Art Rooney Jr. interview.

84   *"You'd better be right"*: Ibid.

84   *"Chuck, he's just a quiet kid"*: Dan Radakovich interview.

85   *"Wherever I go to play"*: Franco Harris interview.

85   *"He had an odd way about him"*: Joe Greene interview with Keith Cossrow of NFL Films on February 22, 2006. NFL-145346.

85   *"He picked holes"*: Lionel Taylor interview.

85   No way I'll make this team: Franco Harris interview.

85   *"You could say, 'Franco, we want you'"*: Dick Hoak interview.

85   *"Just wait until the games start"*: Jack Ham interview.

86   *Harris was stopped by a gnarled old man*: *Provo (Ut.) Daily Herald*, December 25, 1972.

86   *"That's no problem"*: Ed Kiely interview.

86   *Harris had spit-shined shoes*: *Provo (Ut.) Daily Herald*, December 25, 1972.

86   *His friends were half Filipino, half black*: Franco Harris interview with Keith Cossrow of NFL Films, July 20, 2005. NFL-143735.

86   *Gina Parenti Harris showed him her birthplace*: Franco Harris interview.

87   *"If you are wounded"*: Ibid.

87   *"She gets emotional"*: Ibid.

87   *"We stopped the car"*: Dick Haley interview.

87   *"Can't you buy a car?"*: Terry Hanratty interview.

87   *He usually took a public bus to practice, the 76 Hamilton*: *Philadelphia Daily News*, November 14, 1972.

87   *"I had never seen anyone condition himself"*: John Fuqua interview.

88   *"He'd make us mad because he'd say"*: Ibid.

88   *dropped off two Italian hoagie sandwiches*: Al Vento interview.

88   *"Just so we could be with a winner once in a while"*: Ibid.

88   *drew its members from the Spignesi*: Nicholas P. Ciotola, "Spignesi, Sinatra, and the Pittsburgh Steelers: Franco's Italian Army as an Expression of Ethnic Identity, 1972–1977, *Journal of Sport History* 27, no. 2 (Summer 2000): 273.

88   *Tensions between the groups peaked in April 1968*: Ibid.

88   *"It'd take an army to move this crowd"*: Dave Anderson, "Breakthrough in Pittsburgh: Franco Harris & His Italian Army," *Sport*, November 1973, p. 71.

89   *"And so we said, 'That's our hero!'"*: Al Vento interview.

89   *neighbors with surnames such as Zottola, Danzilli*: Ciotola, "Spignesi, Sinatra, and the Pittsburgh Steelers," p. 275.

89   *They hollowed bread from some of the hoagies*: Al Vento interview.

89   *"When Franco's good, he's Italian"*: Ibid.

90   *thought by Italian immigrants to ward off mallochio*: Anderson, "Breakthrough in Pittsburgh," p. 62.

90   *Sinatra walking into a restaurant in Rancho Mirage*: Myron Cope, *Double Yoi!* (Champaign, Ill.: Sports Publishing, 2002), p. 167.

90   *"P.S. Franco's from Hoboken"*: Ibid., p. 168.

91   *"It was like kissing God"*: Ibid., p. 170.

91   *"It's a grave situation"*: Ciotola, "Spignesi, Sinatra, and the Pittsburgh Steelers," p. 282.

91   *Pittsburgh fans suddenly thought he was a genius*: *Oakland Tribune*, December 24, 1972.

91   *"That a way, soul brother!"*: *Detroit News*, December 22, 1972.

92   *Gina Parenti Harris stepped into her garden*: Undated United Press International story from January 1975. Franco Harris file, Pro Football Hall of Fame, Canton, Ohio.

93   *At ground level, Nunn turned right*: Bill Nunn III interview.

93   *he sat in a box upstairs with Art Jr., furious at the Steelers' defense*: Bill Nunn Jr. interview.

93   *at home in Greensburg, listening to the Steelers on radio*: Bill Mazeroski interview.

93   *"We will get the ball back"*: Mike Siani interview.

93   *"J. V., can you believe how much money"*: John Vella interview.

94   *"I'm a realist"*: Jack Ham interview.

94   I can't watch the disaster: Rocky Bleier interview.

94   *"This season has been too good"*: Joe Greene interview.

94   *Stagno waved his red pepper–like corno*: Al Vento interview.

94   *savory smell of a turkey or chicken cooking on a fan's small grill*: Michael Ord interview.

94   *tackle Art Thoms would become a "spy"*: John Vella interview.

94   *"That's it. We're done"*: Ralph Berlin interview.

95   *"Just knock the fucker out!"*: Phil Villapiano interview.

95   *"Go to the ball!"*: Franco Harris interview.

95   The coaches will grade this film: Phil Villapiano interview.

95   *"If I had stayed with him"*: Ibid.

95   *Vento located the fallen hunchbacked man on the ground*: Al Vento interview.

96   *"Keep going, Franco!"*: Dick Hoak interview.

96   *his chair's leg dug into cousin Tim's new Cordovans*: Tim Rooney interview.

96   *"A phenomenal play by Harris"*: Dick Haley interview.

96   *he half turned and saw Harris sprint past him*: L. C. Greenwood interview.

96   *"What's happening?"*: Michael Ord interview.

96   *"Somebody tell me: What happened?"*: Terry Bradshaw with Buddy Martin, *Looking Deep* (Chicago: Contemporary Books, 1989), p. 13.

96   *tossed a water bottle in the air*: Art Rooney II interview.

97   *Brady Keys appeared and bear-hugged the young Rooney*: Ibid.

97   *"Franco caught it!"*: Michael Ord interview.

97   *"You touched that ball!"*: John Fuqua interview.

97   *"What did you see?"*: Art McNally interview.

97   *Burk said he was positive that Tatum*: Ibid.

97   If the officials call this for the Raiders: Jim Otto interview.

98   *"Two of my men ruled the ball was touched"*: Art McNally interview.

98   *"Then someone in the crew"*: Ibid.

98   *"a negative grade for the idea of coming for assistance"*: Ibid.

98   I've got this big bucket helmet on: Mike Wagner interview.

98   *"You won it!"*: *Oakland Tribune*, December 25, 1972.

99   *never waited so long for a photo finish*: *Washington Post*, December 26, 1972.

99   *He thought he'd seen every possible weird bounce*: Terry Bradshaw with Buddy Martin, *Looking Deep*, p. 2.

99   *"Some guy was trying to get out of the stadium"*: Mike Wagner interview.

99   *"It's your secret"*: John Fuqua interview.

99   *"It's a deal"*: Rob Ruck, Maggie Jones Patterson, and Michael P. Weber, *Rooney: A Sporting Life* (Lincoln: University of Nebraska Press, 2010), pp. 414–15.

99   *saw bottles of wine and booze tossed happily*: Michael Ord interview.

100 *"From this day, today will forever"*: Ibid.

100 *"call Myron Cope"*: Sharon Levosky interview.

100 *"If he questions it"*: Michael Ord interview.

100 *"a good Christian lady"*: Sharon Levosky interview.

101 *telegrams of congratulation from Jim Farley*: *New York Daily News*, December 25, 1972.

101 *hired a prop plane to drop two thousand leaflets*: Ron Reid, "Sweet Sixteen on a Super Trip," *Sports Illustrated*, January 8, 1973, p. 17.

101 *"Surrender now and enjoy life"*: Ibid.

Chapter 7: In the Film Room

PAGE

105 *Angry whites spat at him and his group*: J. T. Thomas interview.

105 *Georgia state troopers and German shepherds escorted*: Ibid.

106 *He saw his father physically threaten his mother*: Ibid.

106 *"Thomas, you ain't showing me shit!"*: Ibid.

107 *Now Parcells smiled broadly, and embraced Thomas*: Ibid.

107 *"J. T., who is that running at L-three?"*: Ibid.

Chapter 8: The 1974 Draft

PAGE

109 *On easels, they listed players by position*: Art Rooney Jr. interview.

109 *he saw real value in only the players drafted in the first round*: *Pittsburgh Press*, January 30, 1974.

110 *"What did you take that guy for?"*: Art Rooney Jr. interview.

110 *Steelers might choose a player with an Irish name*: Ibid.

110 *"Football was like a narcotic"*: Tom Danyluk, *The Super '70s: Memories from Pro Football's Greatest Era* (Chicago: Mad Uke Publishing, 2005), p. 3.

110 *"RAAAAAALLLLLLLPPPHH!"*: Art Rooney Jr. interview.

110 *"Arthur, the question now"*: Ibid.

111 *"Baltimore is getting more transcripts"*: Ibid.

111 *"Your problem is that everything"*: Ibid.

112 *"If you get one Hall of Famer in a draft"*: Charley Casserly interview.

112 *"Maybe the best draft ever"*: Peter King, "The Steel Age," *Sports Illustrated*, January 22, 1990, p. 70.

112 *"They were awesome"*: *Pittsburgh Press*, December 24, 1973.

112 *"I'd hate to think we got fat"*: Ibid.

112 *"This guy here is one of the greatest competitors"*: Art Rooney Jr. interview.

113 *"The only thing I know about Swann"*: Lionel Taylor interview.

113 *"The role Bill played was historic"*: Dick Mansperger interview.

113 *"Bill Nunn was one of the best moves"*: Dick Haley interview.

113 *Even the Chief looked at it*: Bill Nunn Jr. interview.

113 *"Have Swann's name on the card"*: Gil Brandt interview.

114 *Nunn told the group he believed Stallworth would still be available*: Bill Nunn Jr. interview.

114 *"Then Chuck sulked around"*: Art Rooney Jr. interview.

114 *Lambert left some of the cinders stuck in his face*: Ibid.

114 *they rated players in categories such as character, mental alertness*: Michael MacCambridge, *America's Game: The Epic Story of How Pro Football Captured a Nation* (New York: Random House, 2004), p. 325.

114 *"Lambert was as close to perfect"*: Gil Brandt interview.

114 *"When a guy wears high-tops"*: Dick Haley interview.

115 *"aggressive and reckless in his play"*: Pittsburgh Steelers Senior Scouting Report on Jack Lambert filed by Dick Haley, March 13, 1973, from Kent, Ohio, Pittsburgh Steelers Scouting Reports Collection, 1968–1975, Ralph Wilson, Jr. Pro Football Research and Preservation Center, Pro Football Hall of Fame, Canton, Ohio.

115 *"will really hit"*: Pittsburgh Steelers Senior Scouting Report on Jack Lambert filed by Dick Haley, November 28, 1973, from Kent, Ohio, Pittsburgh Steelers Scouting Reports Collection, 1968–1975, Ralph Wilson, Jr. Pro Football Research and Preservation Center, Pro Football Hall of Fame, Canton, Ohio.

115 *"With his personality"*: Bob (Woody) Widenhofer interview.

115 *"We'll never get him"*: Art Rooney Jr. interview.

115 *"We got lucky"*: King, "The Steel Age," p. 70.

115 *"Well built. Won't get much bigger"*: BLESTO scouting report on Mike Webster filed by Lou Blumling, April 24, 1973, from Madison, Wisconsin, BLESTO Reports,

1968–1975, BLESTO Reports Collection, Ralph Wilson, Jr. Pro Football Research and Preservation Center, Pro Football Hall of Fame, Canton, Ohio.

116   *"It was the 'Undersized Draft' "*: Art Rooney Jr. interview.

116   *"They got a kid who figures"*: *Pittsburgh Press*, January 30, 1974.

116   *"primarily to snap the ball"*: Ibid.

116   *"I'm just sitting there like a chump"*: Randy Grossman interview.

116   *"and they want to meet with you"*: Ibid.

117   *"Hey, don't ask me!"*: Ralph Berlin interview.

117   *"If you are going to work for this"*: Ibid.

117   *"You want me to sign"*: Ibid.

117   *That spring he got a part-time job*: Randy Grossman interview.

117   ON STRIKE TO END OWNERS MONOPOLY: *McKeesport Daily News*, July 30, 1974.

118   *"Thought you fellows might be awful"*: King, "The Steel Age," p. 75.

118   *"Mr. Webster is one hell of a fine center"*: *Beaver County (Pa.) Times*, July 16, 1974.

118   *"Ray Mansfield and Jim Clack"*: Ibid.

118   *"He's something . . ."*: Ibid.

118   *"You're safe"*: Ibid.

118   *"Kiss my ass"*: Terry Bradshaw with Buddy Martin, *Looking Deep* (Chicago: Contemporary Books, 1989), p. 69.

Chapter 9: Quarterback Controversy: Brad, Rat, or Joe Gillie?

PAGE

119   *once beat up the entire Pitt football team*: Ron Fimrite, "Two Champs from the City of Champions," *Sports Illustrated*, December 24, 1979, p. 41.

119   *"Up twenty-eight steps if you accidentally"*: Frank Deford, "The Boxer and the Blonde," *Sports Illustrated*, June 17, 1985, p. 76.

119   *"A ten-foot ring opened up"*: Bum Phillips interview.

120   *"What's the use of being Irish"*: Deford, "The Boxer and the Blonde," p. 76.

120   *"Hey, blackies"*: Ibid., p. 101.

120   *"[To] put me in a class"*: Art Rooney Sr. letter to Roy McHugh of the *Pittsburgh Press*, September 16, 1974. From the personal files of Roy McHugh.

120   *"If they go all the way"*: Ibid.

122   *"Just the skinniest man"*: John Fuqua interview.

122   *"the oldest quarterback in the league"*: Roy Blount Jr., *About Three Bricks Shy . . . and the Load Filled Up* (Pittsburgh: University of Pittsburgh Press, 2002), p. 185.

122   *"I feel sure Hanratty and Bradshaw"*: *McKeesport Daily News*, July 30, 1974.

122   *"The Blond Bomber's here!"*: *Pittsburgh Post-Gazette*, August 6, 1974.

123   *"His vocabulary of foul expressions"*: Mike Wagner interview.

123   *Gilliam choked on his beer and threw up*: Blount, *About Three Bricks Shy*, p. 81.

123   *"You could see it travel"*: Lionel Taylor interview.

123   *Pa Henry, was born into slavery in 1855*: Coach Joe Gilliam Sr. interview. Coach Gilliam

said he studied his paternal family history late in life, exploring it with the help of a genealogical researcher.

123 *he and his black teammates slept on cots on plastic flooring*: Coach Joe Gilliam Sr. interview.

124 *"Joey, you've got to play-action"*: Ibid.

124 *"But my wife highly resented it"*: Ibid.

124 *"You rolled YOUR OWN CHILD"*: Ibid.

125 *"Joey was secretive"*: Ibid.

125 *"This kid is sitting there on a keg"*: Bobby Mitchell interview.

125 *"He's the best player available"*: *Pittsburgh Post-Gazette*, September 16, 1974.

125 *"You want to pay Joey* black quarterback*"*: Coach Joe Gilliam Sr. interview.

125 *"I object to that!"*: Ibid.

125 *"It's not going to work out"*: Ibid.

125 *"I'm coming to you"*: Reggie Harrison (known today as Kamal Ali Salaam-El) interview.

126 *"You can't ask for any more than that"*: *Pittsburgh Post-Gazette*, August 5, 1974.

126 *dramatic snap action that was too quick for a camera*: Blount, *About Three Bricks Shy*, p. 190.

126 *"he'd field those high, soft bombs"*: Ray Mansfield interview with Jonathan Hock of NFL Films, June 6, 1994.

126 *"Guess Who's Coming to Quarterback?"*: *Beaver County (Pa.) Times*, August 26, 1974.

126 *"Right now it would be hard not to start him"*: Ibid.

126 *"Which side you gonna drink out of, Joe?"*: *Pittsburgh Post-Gazette*, August 30, 1974.

126 *"No one had a dime"*: Terry Hanratty interview.

127 *"shorter hair"* or *"shorter sideburns"*: Ibid.

127 *"Hanratty's up here blowing me kisses!"*: Ibid.

127 *"What are your chances to start this season?"*: Craig Gilliam interview.

127 *"There is a sociological aspect"*: "Joe Gilliam: What Could Have Been but Never Was," Dexter Rogers, writer and producer. This is an eleven-minute documentary on Gilliam, available at http://www.youtube.com/watch?v=oTZ0idRGDjc.

128 *"Noll's not a swearer"*: Blount, *About Three Bricks Shy*, p. 110.

128 *"Almost made me sick"*: Ibid., p. 179.

128 *"I'd be lying if I didn't say he doesn't tick"*: *Pittsburgh Post-Gazette*, November 4, 1973.

129 *"If he doesn't get hurt"*: Bobby Walden interview.

129 *"There's nothing dumb about him at all"*: Art Rooney Jr. interview.

129 *"Terry Bradshaw is the wrong guy"*: *Pittsburgh Post-Gazette*, September 8, 1974.

129 *"Darn right. I'd love to be traded"*: Ibid., September 10, 1974.

129 *"would not only bother the hell out of me"*: Ibid.

129 *"I know there are teams that would"*: Terry Bradshaw interview.

129 And I'm on the bench?: Ibid.

130 *"If you feel I have it coming"*: David Maraniss, *When Pride Still Mattered: A Life of Vince Lombardi* (New York: Simon & Schuster, 1999), pp. 256–57.

130   *"I was too afraid of my coach"*: Terry Bradshaw interview.

130   *the two men retired to the Chief's den*: Ibid.

130   *"Bradshaw may have a lot in common"*: Maury Z. Levy and Samantha Stevenson, *"Play-boy* Interview: Terry Bradshaw, a candid conversation with the Steelers' country-boy Christian quarterback," *Playboy*, March 1980.

130   *"You're the best!"*: Terry Bradshaw interview.

130   *"If we were going to have a chance"*: Joe Greene interview with Steve Sabol of NFL Films on November 29, 2004. NFL-135139.

131   *"All week long, I'm busting Lambert's balls"*: Terry Hanratty interview.

131   *"Who gives a fuck?"*: Ibid.

131   *"possibly the finest performance I've ever seen"*: *Pittsburgh Post-Gazette*, September 23, 1974.

132   *"that rigamarole and razzmatazz in the press"*: "Joe Gilliam: What Could Have Been but Never Was," http://www.youtube.com/watch?v=oTZ0idRGDjc.

132   *"You get a lot of this, Joe?"*: Mike Wagner interview.

132   *"If the Lord chooses to take me out"*: Craig Gilliam interview.

132   *"Read some of that"*: Coach Joe Gilliam Sr. interview.

132   *"He's got to leave here right now"*: Ibid.

133   *"He's not mature enough to know"*: Ibid.

133   *He turned to heroin*: Craig Gilliam interview. Joe Gilliam described to his older brother his injuries from the Oakland Raiders game and his use of heroin at a party later that same night.

133   *"I know that's where it began"*: Ibid.

133   *"So, Will Joe Have to Go?"*: *Pittsburgh Post-Gazette*, October 8, 1974.

134   *"I don't know what's going to happen at quarterback"*: Ibid.

134   *"We want Bradshaw!"*: *Pittsburgh Post-Gazette*, October 21, 1974.

134   *"Sp-Sputtering St-Steelers Win"*: Ibid.

134   *"Joe Gilliam had as much talent as any quarterback"*: Dan Radakovich interview.

134   *"return to the bread and butter"*: *Pittsburgh Press*, October 22, 1974.

135   *"Bradshaw had a lot of talent"*: Andy Russell interview.

136   *"only a mother could've loved. Knute Rockne's mother"*: *Pittsburgh Post-Gazette*, November 18, 1974.

136   *"Joe Greene got the offensive game ball"*: Ibid.

136   *"staying cool. My chance will come"*: *Pittsburgh Press*, November 18, 1974.

136   *"It hasn't hurt us too much"*: Ibid.

136   *"Is Noll spiting Bradshaw"*: *Pittsburgh Press*, November 22, 1974.

136   *"Somebody's got to take the bull"*: Ibid., November 18, 1974.

136   *Bradshaw won with 41 percent*: *Pittsburgh Post-Gazette*, November 25, 1974.

137   *"dropped off the Fort Pitt Bridge"*: Ibid.

137   *the cost for such an ad was $240*: Terry Hanratty interview.

137 *"Terry was going to be the quarterback"*: Ibid.

137 *"We could have put anybody at quarterback"*: Dick Haley interview.

137 *"We've got to keep our defense playing"*: *Pittsburgh Post-Gazette*, November 18, 1974.

Chapter 10: The Steel Curtain

138 *White with a bull rush, Greenwood a slip*: "Half a Ton of Trouble," *Time*, December 8, 1975.

138 *"It was not so much what we did"*: Dwight White interview with Keith Cossrow of NFL Films, October 6, 2006. NFL-161516.

139 *"alligator mouth"*: Ibid.

139 *"He is my mountain"*: Barry Abramson, "Sports Mini-Profile: 'Mean Joe Greene,' " *Family Weekly*, November 25, 1972, p. 23.

139 *left the game with a sprained shoulder*: *Pittsburgh Post-Gazette*, September 23, 1974.

139 *"I just like to get a good lick"*: *Pittsburgh Post-Gazette*, September 18, 1974.

139 *"Ernie wanted to see blood"*: L. C. Greenwood interview.

140 *"If you can't cover nobody, then get out"*: J. T. Thomas interview.

140 *"Why don't y'all cut off all that noise"*: Ibid.

140 *"What's going on out there?"*: Ibid.

141 *"I'll probably suffer in the next world"*: *Pittsburgh Post-Gazette*, October 21, 1974.

141 That was one where we got a sack: Jack Ham interview.

141 *"There were several games where you could"*: L. C. Greenwood interview.

141 *Rice transformed Stuhldreyer, Crowley, Miller*: *New York Herald Tribune*, October 19, 1924.

142 *saw Fats working in his father's field*: Roderick (Byron) Holmes interview.

142 *"Jawge, I'm gonna get ya' thirteen sacks"*: George Perles interview.

142 *wore rubber suits at practice to sweat them*: Mike Wagner, Ralph Berlin, and Terry Hanratty interviews.

142 *His teammates saw the pile of hardly chewed eggs*: Gary Dunn interview.

142 *"Let's just move over to the next field"*: Ibid.

142 *"Joe Greene made a whole lot of people"*: Bill Nunn Jr. interview.

142 *"Ernie was just a lovable, really nice guy"*: Randy Grossman interview.

142 *his camera a "Kodiak" and his two-toned shoes*: Terry Hanratty interview.

142 *he felt "cannibalistic"*: J. T. Thomas interview.

143 *"Hey, Moon-baby!"*: Gerry (Moon) Mullins interview.

143 *"Is Dog around?"*: Karen (Farmer) White interview.

143 *in Dallas he was made to read old textbooks handed down*: Ibid.

143 *"Dwight's just constantly running his mouth"*: L. C. Greenwood interview.

143 *"You could only block half of him"*: Dwight White interview with Keith Cossrow of NFL Films, October 6, 2006. NFL-161516.

143 *"We didn't have any relationship"*: L. C. Greenwood interview.

144   *he told a writer his real name was Lover Cool*: Roy Blount Jr., *About Three Bricks Shy . . . and the Load Filled Up* (Pittsburgh: University of Pittsburgh Press, 2002), p. 34.

144   *His father, Moses Greenwood, worked in a factory*: L. C. Greenwood interview.

144   *a fine his shoe company happily absorbed*: Ibid.

145   *"Joe threw me out of the game"*: Ralph Berlin interview.

145   *"Joe was the best interview on the Steelers"*: Roy McHugh interview.

145   *"I waited to read it in the paper on Monday"*: Jack Lambert interview with Bob Angelo of NFL Films on October 25, 1994.

145   *Greene hid chocolate chip cookies sent*: Joe Greene interview.

145   *"You can't leave Dwight there!"*: Dan Radakovich interview.

146   *His wife wanted a divorce*: Roderick (Byron) Holmes interview.

146   *Holmes swallowed a handful of No-Doz pills*: L. C. Greenwood interview.

146   *court-ordered psychiatrist later termed "acute paranoid psychosis"*: Undated Associated Press story. Scrapbook of press coverage from 1973 Pittsburgh Steelers' season. Pittsburgh Steelers media relations office.

146   *Holmes heard it and fired at it, striking the ankle*: *Valley News (Pa.) Dispatch* and *Pittsburgh Press*, July 31, 1974.

146   *"We could have killed him a dozen times"*: Undated *Pittsburgh Press* column by Phil Musick. Scrapbook of press coverage from 1973 Pittsburgh Steelers' season. Pittsburgh Steelers media relations office.

147   *brought Holmes a pocket-sized prayer book*: Art Rooney Jr. interview.

147   *"Why don't you go over there and see Ernie"*: L. C. Greenwood interview.

147   *"They got me in there saying that I'm crazy"*: Ibid.

147   *"I think Ernie's big issue was that he was paranoid"*: Ibid.

147   *"If someone saved your life"*: *Valley News (Pa.) Dispatch*, July 31, 1974.

147   *"I don't get any publicity"*: George Perles interview.

147   *"You have to be commercial in this business"*: *Beaver County (Pa.) Times*, November 2, 1974.

148   *"If you get penetration"*: Dwight White interview with Suzanne Morgan of NFL Films on July 19, 1996.

149   If I balance this football on my middle finger: Ray Mansfield interview with Jonathan Hock of NFL Films on June 6, 1994.

149   *someone on the Raiders had written, "FUCK YOU"*: Ibid.

149   *The Steelers called it the Dirty Tricks Game*: *Pittsburgh Post-Gazette*, November 13, 1975.

149   *"Ernie, Eugene Upshaw's gonna beat your butt"*: L. C. Greenwood interview.

Chapter 11: Stall & Webby

PAGE

150   *"YOU GUYS MUST NOT BE AS GOOD"*: Lionel Taylor interview.

150   Noll would get rid of me: Ibid.

151   *Webster had had enough, and rented a U-Haul*: Pam Webster interview.

151 *"What are you going to do back in Wisconsin?"*: Ibid.

151 *"He's the only snapper we've got"*: Dan Radakovich interview.

151 *"Where is Nancy?"*: Ibid.

151 *"I've met my replacement"*: Ray Mansfield interview with Noah Lerner of NFL Films, January 19, 1996.

152 *"There's nothing you can do about it"*: Dan Radakovich interview.

152 *"What do I need to do to get there?"*: Jim Otto interview.

152 *"Mr. Otto! Mr. Otto!"*: Ibid.

153 *wishing sportswriters would give him a day or two*: John Stallworth interview.

153 *a domestic in Tuscaloosa*: Ibid.

153 *he suffered chills, became feverish*: Ralph Wiley, "You Have to Be a Fool at Times," *Sports Illustrated*, August 25, 1986, p. 36.

153 *He made a silent vow to achieve in his life*: John Stallworth interview.

154 *But no offer came from coach Bear Bryant*: Wiley, "You Have to Be a Fool at Times," p. 44.

154 *"You won't be able to do that once Mel gets here"*: Lionel Taylor and John Stallworth interviews.

154 *"He couldn't say anything that would scare me more"*: John Stallworth interview.

155 *"Maybe it was, sorry to say, a black-white"*: Ibid.

155 *"Why are you dressing up like that"*: Donnie Shell interview.

155 *"Joe Greene cut the cord"*: John Stallworth interview.

156 *"Mike was fulfilled on the football field"*: *Pittsburgh Post-Gazette*, September 25, 2002.

156 *family dysfunction, divorce, a frightening house fire*: Pam Webster interview.

156 *a drunken Native American broke into their house*: Ibid.

156 *"Mike overcame a lot of stuff"*: Ibid.

156 *a prankster who threw a firecracker into the school auditorium*: Bill Makris interview.

156 *"To become All-Big-10 Conference at defensive"*: Ibid.

157 *"I think I should drop this class, eh, Greg?"*: Greg Apkarian interview.

157 *"Greg! Greg! Pull it out!"*: Ibid.

157 *"Oh, by the way, my dad gave you"*: Pam Webster interview.

157 *spent that night at the Aloha Inn in Madison*: Ibid.

158 *"What do you want the boxes for?"*: John Stallworth interview.

Chapter 12: 1974 AFC Title Game

PAGE

159 *"let's make Sunday Fun Day"*: Lynn Swann interview with Chris Barlow of NFL Films on July 27, 1995.

159 *"The best team in the NFL"*: Joe Greene interview with NFL Films on July 21, 1994.

160 *Franco Harris saying, "Yep!"*: Franco Harris interview with Bob Angelo of NFL Films on June 6, 2000.

160 *"I looked at the way he carried himself"*: John Vella interview.

160 *Madden showed the Raiders films of Greene and Lambert acting*: Ibid.

160   *"Joe was a beast"*: Mike Siani interview.

160   *"Joe Greene was the greatest defensive lineman"*: Dan Radakovich interview.

160   *"Whatcha watching, L.C.?"*: L. C. Greenwood interview.

161   *his wife sometimes rearranged it in the stadium parking lot*: Jim Otto with Dave New-house, *Jim Otto: The Pain of Glory* (Champaign, Ill.: Sports Publishing, 2000), p. 4.

161   *"How's your wife and children, Joe?"*: Jim Otto interview.

161   *"It was like war out there"*: Ibid.

161   *"Get away from me!"*: Mike Siani interview.

162   *"I mean, you hit him in the head"*: Joe Greene interview.

162   *He'd grown nearly dependent on the painkiller Darvon and muscle relaxers*: Otto with Newhouse, *Jim Otto*, p. 156.

162   *"His leg and knee didn't look like a leg and knee"*: John Vella interview.

162   *"You couldn't believe what he put his body through"*: Ibid.

162   *"only playoff team without a quarterback"*: Dan Jenkins, "For Openers, Super Bowl Viii½," *Sports Illustrated*, December 23, 1974, pp. 24–25.

162   *"All of them ran on Oakland"*: *Oakland Tribune*, December 30, 1974.

163   *"I'M GONNA KICK YOUR ASS!"*: Joe Greene and L. C. Greenwood interviews.

163   *"Far out, Ernie!"*: Joe Greene interview.

163   *"Let me take a few shots over on your side"*: Ron Jaworski with Greg Cosell and David Plaut, *The Games That Changed the Game: The Evolution of the NFL in Seven Sundays* (New York: Ballantine Books, 2010), p. 63.

163   *"You dirty . . ."*: Jim Otto interview.

163   *"The only person I hold is my wife!"*: Ibid.

164   *"I didn't hear anything anybody was saying"*: George Buehler interview.

164   *"I knew I had to get to Joe quickly"*: Ibid.

164   *"I don't mind another player shaking my hand"*: *Pittsburgh Post-Gazette*, December 30, 1974.

164   *He lifted his right leg, and tried to balance himself*: Otto with Newhouse, *Jim Otto*, p. 173.

164   *"They stopped Oakland's running"*: *Oakland Tribune*, December 30, 1974.

165   *The Chief watched the replay of that one*: *Pittsburgh Post-Gazette*, December 30, 1974.

165   *He benched Blount for the remainder*: Jaworski with Cosell and Plaut, *The Games That Changed the Game*, pp. 71–72.

165   *Gravelle saw Madden, in midtirade, look at him*: Gordon Gravelle interview.

166   *"Don't let the officials intimidate you"*: Ron Reid, "This Defense Never Rested," *Sports Illustrated*, January 6, 1975, p. 15.

166   *Noll likened him to "a third guard"*: Pete Axthelm, "Hail to the Chief," *Newsweek*, January 13, 1975, p. 47.

167   *"The zone is a place that you rarely visit"*: Joe Greene interview.

167   God, we're just one half from the Super Bowl!: Franco Harris interview with Jonathan Hock of NFL Films on June 8, 1994.

167   *"I just remember having butterflies in my stomach"*: Franco Harris interview with Bob Angelo of NFL Films on June 6, 2000. NFL-82847.

167   *"Defeat is a bitch"*: *Oakland Tribune*, December 30, 1974.

167   *"The Raider offensive line got so frustrated"*: Ibid.

167   *"one more chance"*: *Pittsburgh Post-Gazette*, December 30, 1974.

168   *"In the old days we'd have a great celebration"*: Reid, "This Defense Never Rested," p. 15.

168   *"This has been my life"*: *Pittsburgh Press*, December 30, 1974.

168   *"They just don't make 'em like Art Rooney"*: Ibid.

168   *"You know what I really want tonight?"*: Karen (Farmer) White interview.

168   *"Karen, would you go to the store"*: Ibid.

168   *"Mr. Rooney has something to say"*: Roy Blount Jr., *About Three Bricks Shy . . . and the Load Filled Up* (Pittsburgh: University of Pittsburgh Press, 2002), p. 268.

168   *Spotting the Chief, a band struck up "When Irish Eyes"*: *McKeesport (Pa.) Daily News*, December 30, 1974.

168   *Sixty Allegheny County sheriffs escorted the team*: Ibid.

168   *"I got more beat up by them"*: Blount, *About Three Bricks Shy*, p. 268.

169   *"Dwight, I cooked that chicken for you"*: Karen (Farmer) White interview.

169   *He crashed Dwight White's car right through it*: Ibid.

169   *Mad Dog returned home and ate fried chicken*: Ibid.

170   *"Going to the Super Bowl feels"*: *Oakland Tribune*, December 30, 1974.

170   *"Today the congratulations go to you"*: Axthelm, "Hail to the Chief," p. 47.

Chapter 13: Super Bowl IX

PAGE

171   *forty million Americans listening on radio*: Laura Hillenbrand, *Seabiscuit: An American Legend* (New York: Random House, 2001), p. xix.

172   *he preferred to watch NFL games, including Super Bowl IX, from the press box*: Joe Gordon interview.

172   *"I believe if we can hold this club together"*: *Pittsburgh Press*, January 13, 1975.

172   *and a chartered jet for 192 stadium*: *New York Post*, January 10, 1975. Also John Rooney interview.

173   *He peeked inside empty closets, poked his head*: Art Rooney Jr. interview.

173   *"But you can get these nuts hiding"*: Ibid.

173   *There, amid great fanfare, the foursome drank rows of Heineken*: Joe Greene interview.

174   *Mad Dog announced that he felt ill*: Ibid.

174   *An army of more than 1,500 media members*: Jerry Green, *Super Bowl Chronicles: A Sportswriter Reflects on the First 30 Years of America's Game* (Indianapolis: Masters Press, 1995), p. 96.

174   *Lamar Hunt, who noticed his young daughter playing*: Ibid., p. 4.

175   *"What kind of grades did you make?"*: *Pittsburgh Post-Gazette*, January 8, 1975.

175   *"I've been labeled 'Ozark Ike' and 'Dummy' "*: *New York Daily News*, January 9, 1975.

175   *Bud Carson's reasons for benching him in the AFC title game "stupid"*: *Pittsburgh Press*, January 10, 1975.

175   *"We had two toilets in the clubhouse"*: *Los Angeles Times*, January 13, 1975.

175   *"I remember one time the new coach"*: Ibid.

175   *"I've been in this league twelve years"*: Ray Mansfield interview with Jonathan Hock of NFL Films on June 6, 1994.

175   *"Nobody wants to talk to a muffucker like me"*: Roy Blount Jr., *About Three Bricks Shy . . . and the Load Filled Up* (Pittsburgh: University of Pittsburgh Press, 2002), p. 270.

176   *"While I was with them, [Steeler players] had tended"*: Ibid., p. 267.

176   *"with the mind of a child and the brains"*: Ibid.

176   *"Hello, Archenemy"*: Ibid., p. 269.

176   *"Get down, Texas!"*: Ibid., p. 270.

176   *"You're kidding"*: Karen (Farmer) White interview.

177   *"What I wouldn't do for a shot of Canadian Club"*: Art Rooney Jr. interview.

177   Don't you lose this game!: Terry Bradshaw with David Fisher, *It's Only a Game* (New York: Pocket Books, 2001), p. 77.

177   *Just then Bradshaw saw a fan, bare-chested*: Ibid.

177   *"Hey, bub: you know me!"*: Joe Greene interview.

178   *"You okay? How's your breathing?"*: Dwight White interview with Keith Cossrow of NFL Films, October 6, 2006. NFL-161516.

178   *"He's playing his heart out"*: *Los Angeles Times*, September 1, 1988.

179   *"We're whipping their asses off and still ain't"*: *Los Angeles Times*, January 13, 1975.

179   *"Shoot me up!"*: Ralph Berlin interview.

180   *"Hell, Clack, I'm all through"*: *Pittsburgh Press*, January 13, 1975.

180   *"I'll bet the 'Burgh looks like Hiroshima"*: Ibid.

180   *"We made it"*: Andy Russell interview.

180   *"watched the game with a kind of bemused detachment"*: *Los Angeles Times*, September 1, 1988.

180   *with his old friend Jake Mintz, posting flyers on barroom*: Frank Deford, "The Boxer and the Blonde," *Sports Illustrated*, June 17, 1985, p. 75.

180   *"What are you going to do when"*: *Los Angeles Times*, September 1, 1988.

181   *"I had never seen Noll's mouth so wide open"*: Blount, *About Three Bricks Shy*, p. 262.

181   *"All you want is for somebody to take"*: Bill Nunn Jr. interview.

181   *"You win, you feel good about it"*: Ibid.

181   *"I'll tell you, Joe Greene is . . . the best"*: *Pittsburgh Press*, January 13, 1975.

182   *"Wowie!"*: Ibid.

182   *"It was like one of those hokey"*: *Los Angeles Times*, January 13, 1975.

182   *"Everything but Lassie, right?"*: Ibid.

182   *"It looked kind of sad"*: Blount, *About Three Bricks Shy*, p. 262.

182   *He called to Art Rooney Sr., "Chief, c'mon up here!"*: Andy Russell interview.

183   *"A great part of me would've died if we had lost"*: *Pittsburgh Press*, January 13, 1975.

184   *He sat up in bed, his head throbbing*: Maury Z. Levy and Samantha Stevenson, "*Playboy* Interview: Terry Bradshaw, a candid conversation with the Steelers' country-boy Christian quarterback," *Playboy*, March 1980.

184   *Harris, Swann, and Greene played with, and wore, plastic Viking*: *Pittsburgh Press*, January 13, 1975.

184   *Greene pulled out his Nikomat camera*: Joe Greene interview.

184   *with a placard as "Bradshaw's Brains"*: Blount, *About Three Bricks Shy*, p. 272.

184   *local hospital, where he spent the next two and a half weeks*: Karen (Farmer) White interview.

184   *He couldn't find the chauffeured limousine*: *Pittsburgh Press*, January 13, 1975.

184   *"I never feel comfortable in those limousines"*: Ibid.

184   *"Hey, Dad, this is a collector's piece"*: Art Rooney Jr. interview.

184   *the Chief sat at a desk in his hotel suite and dashed off*: John Rooney interview.

184   *"We're in the big time!"*: Ibid.

Chapter 14: Days of Empire: 1975–1981

PAGE

187   *Perry walked directly to him after the ceremony*: Maxine Perry interview.

187   *Ford told Rooney that he'd always wanted to meet*: Ed Kiely interview.

187   *"Look, Mr. President, there are a lot"*: Ibid.

188   *"We'd say, 'After we beat the Cowboys'"*: Dwight White interview with Dave Petrelius of NFL Films on January 23, 2002. NFL-99803.

188   *Kicker Matt Bahr sometimes put on a glove*: Matt Bahr interview.

188   *Twenty-one of them made national commercials*: Peter King, "The Steel Age," *Sports Illustrated*, January 22, 1990, p. 75.

188   *Samsonite luggage, Ford's Fairlane, Uniroyal's*: Stan Isaacs, "Mean Joe: Goliath Plays Othello," *Sports Illustrated*, December 17, 1979.

189   *"The Steelers have, in fact, become football's"*: "Athletes in Adland," *Advertising Age*, December 31, 1979.

189   *"As a soldier, the thing you were most scared"*: Sebastian Junger, *War* (New York: Twelve, 2010), p. 210.

189   *"Webster's already in the fuckin' weight"*: Dan Radakovich interview.

189   *"If you don't put that projector away"*: Donnie Shell interview.

190   *an oversized plastic trash can that Parisi*: Tony Parisi interview.

190   *a group of Steelers usually met at Franco Harris's*: Franco Harris, Gerry (Moon) Mullins, and Ralph Berlin interviews.

191   *The old veterans Russell and Mansfield, preferring vodka*: Andy Russell interview.

191   *"Oh, man, I fanned on that blitz"*: Tunch Ilkin interview.

192   *"It wasn't fabricated"*: Rocky Bleier interview.

192   *"Whoever drank"*: Tony Parisi interview.

192   *"Webby, how in the world"*: Gary Dunn interview.

192   *"It was Jack Lambert's haven"*: Gerry (Moon) Mullins interview.

192   *"T, you guys can lose with me"*: J. T. Thomas interview.

193   *"You were on the outside looking in"*: Ibid.

193   *"Oh, shit, here come the Chobees"*: Ibid.

193   *Lambert showed up on the porch, shotgun in hand*: Ibid.

193   *"Jack didn't like the music"*: Ibid.

193   *"When he got to playing with those guns"*: Dennis (Dirt) Winston interview.

193   *"Jack would hold court"*: Rocky Bleier interview.

194   *"I don't even know why you showed up"*: Ibid.

194   *"We couldn't have won this game"*: Ibid.

194   *"That was a big part of Jack's life"*: Ibid.

194   *"God, you guys are awesome"*: King, "The Steel Age," p. 72.

194   *Lambert and Rudnay exchanged several violent smacks*: Jack Rudnay interview.

194   *"Holy shit! Is that the way"*: Ibid.

194   *"How's Disco Lady?"*: Ibid.

195   *in his bag he discovered several gifts*: Ibid.

195   *"Well, then can I come in there"*: Gary Dunn interview.

195   *"Bring her in, buddy!"*: Ibid.

195   *"Can you turn on some lights?"*: Ibid.

195   *"It was our escape"*: Terry Bradshaw interview.

196   Me play golf with Terry Bradshaw?: John Banaszak interview.

196   *"Yeah, Rock, well, if you were a marine"*: Ibid.

196   *"You want to go to dinner?"*: Ibid.

197   *"Is Bradshaw 'Too Dumb' to Be Super?"*: *New York Times*, January 7, 1975.

197   *"Li'l Abner Finally Makes It Big"*: *Sports Illustrated*, December 18, 1978.

197   *"When he did win them over"*: Joe Greene interview with Gerry Reimel of NFL Films on June 13, 2003. NFL-114630.

197   *"This guy's like buying Xerox"*: Roy McHugh, "The Making of the No. 1 Draft Choice," *Sport*, May 1970, p. 80.

197   *"I've always seen myself as put to music"*: Frank Deford, "Champagne, Roses, and Donuts," *Sports Illustrated*, December 10, 1979, p. 112.

198   *"seems to collect concussions and championship"*: Dan Jenkins, "Dallas Feels the Steeler Crunch," *Sports Illustrated*, January 26, 1976, p. 15.

198   *They were escorted into a red 1973 Cadillac El Dorado*: Gerry (Moon) Mullins interview.

198   *"Oh, yeah, I used to always sing"*: Ibid.

199   *"Bradshaw stood alone on stage for 40 minutes"*: News story from unspecified newspaper published in late February 1976. Terry Bradshaw Files at Ralph Wilson, Jr. Pro Football Research and Preservation Center, Pro Football Hall of Fame, Canton, Ohio. See also Associated Press story on Bradshaw's appearance at the Palomino Club in *Tuscaloosa (Ala.) News*, February 28, 1976.

199 *Shore invited Bradshaw to meet Reynolds*: Terry Bradshaw interview.

199 *"Dressed like a real maid"*: Gerry (Moon) Mullins interviews.

199 *"So classy, a southern gal"*: Terry Bradshaw interview.

199 *"You don't think Elizabeth Taylor"*: Ibid.

199 *"Terry, we've got to get up"*: Gerry (Moon) Mullins interview.

200 *"I love New Mexico!"*: Ibid.

200 *"He blew up about five thousand"*: Ibid.

200 *"DiMaggio-Monroe union"*: Cable Neuhaus, "Terry Bradshaw Is a Hero, but When Wife JoJo Skates Off, He's So Lonesome He Could Cry," *People*, January 22, 1979.

200 *Together the couple read from the Bible*: Maury Z. Levy and Samantha Stevenson, "*Playboy* Interview: Terry Bradshaw, a candid conversation with the Steelers' country-boy Christian quarterback," *Playboy*, March 1980.

200 *"JoJo was a city girl just sitting"*: Mel Blount interview.

200 *"Why would a woman want to go to graduate school?"*: Karen (Farmer) White interview.

201 *"I don't have anybody to hug"*: Ibid.

201 *Doctors strapped Bradshaw to a spine board*: Ralph Berlin interview.

201 *Holmes spoke not a word*: Ibid.

201 *"I don't know who we've got for this role"*: Terry Bradshaw interview.

202 *"That's as good acting"*: Ibid.

202 *She knew the Chief's vision and hearing were beginning to fail*: Art Rooney Jr. interview.

202 *He began joining Dan at NFL meetings once again*: Ibid.

203 *the men gathered with the Chief in the den, and the women*: Karen White and Agnes Greene interviews.

203 *"May I have my steak a little more well done?"*: Agnes Greene interview.

203 *"I hate those steaks rare, too!"*: Ibid.

203 Now, this is real interesting: Karen (Farmer) White interview.

203 *The Chief hadn't consumed a spot of alcohol*: Dan Rooney and Art Rooney Jr. interviews.

204 *"You know, I kind of like this"*: Joe Greene interview.

204 *"knocked the hair out of your nose"*: Dwight White interview with Angela Torma of NFL Films on October 12, 2004. NFL-132257.

204 *"I didn't have much training in formal dining"*: Franco Harris interview.

204 *"In the name of the Father, the Son"*: *Pittsburgh Press*, January 13, 1975.

204 *"Good people"*: Franco Harris interview.

204 *"He tosses nickels around like manhole"*: "They Said It," *Sports Illustrated*, February 13, 1967, p. 16.

204 *"Joe, my boy"*: Joe Greene interview.

205 *And now, as they all sat at the dining room table*: *Pittsburgh Press*, January 13, 1975.

205 *They began praying, without telling her why*: Karen (Farmer) White interview.

205 *"I thought there was something"*: Ibid.

205 *"Hey, Mr. Rooney!"*: Rob Ruck, Maggie Jones Patterson, and Michael P. Weber, *Rooney: A Sporting Life* (Lincoln: University of Nebraska Press, 2010), p. 391.

205   *"I don't think it was a swinging door"*: Dwight White interview with Rob Ruck, coauthor of *Rooney: A Sporting Life*, on July 5, 2002. A transcript of this interview was provided to the author.

205   *"I've been in Pittsburgh thirty years"*: Ruck, Patterson, and Weber, *Rooney: A Sporting Life*, p. 389.

206   *In addition to covering thirteen World Series*: Clark Booth interview.

206   *"seeking the darkest secrets of life"*: Clark Booth, "Death & Football," *Real Paper*, January 28, 1976, p. 13.

206   *Carrying his tape recorder, Booth posed*: Clark Booth interview.

206   *"Look, football players approach injuries"*: Booth, "Death & Football," p. 16.

206   *"Did the doctor say you could play?"*: Ibid., p. 13.

206   *"How is it possible to ignore the fact"*: Ibid.

207   *Russell saw Reger's body suddenly convulse*: Andy Russell interview.

207   *"I'm more scared of Buddy Parker"*: Booth, "Death & Football," p. 18.

207   *"The experiences and the reactions"*: Ibid., p. 16.

208   *he'd only done it to keep the Steelers from having to waste a time-out*: Chad Millman and Shawn Coyne, *The Ones Who Hit Hardest: The Steelers, the Cowboys, the '70s, and the Fight for America's Soul* (New York: Gotham Books, 2010), p. 224.

208   *"Getting hit again while he's on a pass"*: *New York Times*, February 3, 2005.

208   *"I'll say this about it"*: Booth, "Death & Football," p. 13.

209   *The heroin did its mysterious work*: Reggie Harrison (known today as Kamal Ali Salaam-El) interview. The scene of Joe Gilliam's heroin use in a hotel room is drawn from this interview.

209   *He called it Boy and he called it Girl*: Ibid.

209   *"Man, let me try some of that"*: Ibid.

209   *Bradshaw noticed Gilliam, in his cubicle, snorting powder*: Terry Bradshaw interview.

209   *used the money Gilliam paid in fines to buy him a reel-to-reel*: Joe Greene interview.

210   *"I got up and asked the maid what time it was"*: John (Frenchy) Fuqua and Reggie Harrison (known today as Kamal Ali Salaam-El) interviews.

210   *"You need to call Joey and talk with him"*: Coach Joe Gilliam Sr. interview.

210   *"Joey had his story ready: 'It's hard, Daddy' "*: Ibid.

210   *"Bradshaw, when he had his tough times"*: Art Rooney Jr. interview.

210   *"Let him play"*: Terry Hanratty interview.

211   *"He's fucked up, man. He's been snorting"*: Reggie Harrison (known today as Kamal Ali Salaam-El) interview.

211   *"Whatever Joe told Chuck"*: Ibid.

211   *"I used to talk to him about being a man"*: Joe Greene interview.

211   *and the following June, after missing several more team meetings*: *Pittsburgh Post-Gazette*, June 4, 1976.

211   *"This isn't just you"*: John (Frenchy) Fuqua and Reggie Harrison (known today as Kamal Ali Salaam-El) interviews.

211 *"Our distraction year"*: King, "The Steel Age," p. 74.

212 *on poster boards eight feet high*: William Oscar Johnson, "A Walk on the Sordid Side," *Sports Illustrated*, August 1, 1977, p. 13.

212 *one of Noll's attorneys cynically called his "sincere suit"*: Ibid., p. 14.

212 *That Davis often passed notes to Atkinson's attorneys*: Vito Stellino interview. Stellino covered the trial in San Francisco for the *Pittsburgh Post-Gazette*.

213 *"You have a criminal element in every society"*: *San Francisco Examiner*, July 12, 1977.

213 *"One of the morals in this case"*: Johnson, "A Walk on the Sordid Side," p. 13.

213 *"the leading cheap-shot artists in pro football"*: Ibid.

213 *"a team trying their best to destroy Mr. Atkinson's career"*: Ibid.

213 *"I'm labeled for the rest of my life"*: *San Francisco Chronicle*, July 15, 1977.

214 *"suffered every possible illegal blow"*: *Oakland Tribune*, July 12, 1977.

214 *"The hit by Atkinson was not that unusual"*: *San Francisco Chronicle*, July 13, 1977.

214 *"deliberately clobbered"*: *San Francisco Examiner*, July 20, 1977.

214 *"He completely, unwarrantedly, violently, maliciously"*: *Cleveland Plain Dealer*, July 20, 1977.

214 *"In sixteen years in this office"*: Johnson, "A Walk on the Sordid Side," p. 12.

214 *he called Atkinson's hit "a cowardly act"*: Ibid., p. 13.

214 *"I also believe, because of the number of Oakland Raider"*: Ibid.

214 *wrote on the clean board, "NOLL'S NFL CRIMINALS"*: *Oakland Tribune*, July 14, 1977.

215 *"If I had meant that I probably would have"*: Johnson, "A Walk on the Sordid Side," p. 14.

215 *"it wasn't an act I approved of"*: *Oakland Tribune*, July 14, 1977.

215 *"You didn't tell the press that there was a criminal"*: Ibid.

215 *"You're trying to drive a wedge"*: Ibid.

215 *announced that he would file a $5 million slander*: *San Francisco Chronicle* and *Oakland Tribune*, July 16, 1977. Also Robert Lane, "Atkinson vs. Noll: The NFL on Trial," *Black Sports*, September 1977, p. 34.

216 *"rag-tag kid brawling with the Establishment"*: Johnson, "A Walk on the Sordid Side," p. 15.

216 *"second only to the US government"*: Ibid.

216 *"since injury to reputation is the gist of slander"*: Ibid.

216 *"This trial has been the most depressing"*: Ibid.

217 *Fuqua told players he would arrange for two women to pop out*: John (Frenchy) Fuqua interview.

217 *"He did scare me that one night"*: Franco Harris interview.

217 *"Oh, my!"*: John Stallworth interview.

217 *"But short of an elephant rifle"*: Randy Grossman interview.

217 *Fats ate the entire roast and the entire pie*: Joe Greene interview.

217 *saw Holmes eat twelve plates of spaghetti*: Reggie Harrison (known today as Kamal Ali Salaam-El) interview.

218 *He dug his fingers deep inside, scooped out*: George Perles interview.

218   *"Where I come from"*: John Banaszak interview.

218   *"Fats sucked those eyeballs out"*: George Perles interview.

218   *"Ernie was a real piece of work"*: L. C. Greenwood interview.

218   *"He's just the opposite of the publicity"*: "Christ, Wife Change Life for Troubled Ernie Holmes," *Jet*, November 25, 1976, p. 44.

218   *"She helps keep my shoulders straight"*: Ibid.

218   *At the bachelor party, the Steelers sat at poker*: The description of Ernie Holmes's bachelor party is drawn from interviews with Steeler teammates in attendance.

218   *"You ain't got me no ladies?"*: John (Frenchy) Fuqua interview.

218   *Banaszak heard Fats in the suite's bedroom, on the phone*: John Banaszak interview.

218   *"When he took the top off"*: Reggie Harrison (known today as Kamal Ali Salaam-El) interview.

219   *"Don't do that. There's broken glass inside!"*: John (Frenchy) Fuqua interview.

219   *"I saw how narrow Ernie's eyes were getting"*: Franco Harris interview.

220   *together they dragged him into the suite's bedroom*: John (Frenchy) Fuqua interview.

220   *"I had a good time last night!"*: John (Frenchy) Fuqua interview.

220   *"The reason I came early for you"*: Ibid.

220   *several Pittsburgh linemen dominated the NFL's Strongest Man*: Shaun Assael, "Big Night," *ESPN the Magazine*, January 21, 2003.

220   *"Man, I'd look across the line at those Steelers"*: Skip Bayless, *God's Coach: The Hymns, Hype, and Hypocrisy of Tom Landry's Cowboys* (New York: Simon & Schuster, 1990), p. 212.

221   *"It started, really, in Pittsburgh"*: *Pittsburgh Post-Gazette*, March 24, 2005.

221   *"maybe it affected his mind"*: Ibid.

221   *"It made a difference"*: *Beaver County (Pa.) Times*, June 7, 2009.

221   *He wrote that Steeler offensive linemen often talked confidentially*: Steve Courson and Lee R. Schreiber, *False Glory: Steelers and Steroids* (Stamford, Conn.: Longmeadow Press, 1991), p. 49.

221   *created problems with acne, water retention*: Ibid., p. 55.

221   *a twenty-two-inch neck, twenty-inch biceps*: Jill Lieber, "Getting Physical—and Chemical," *Sports Illustrated*, May 13, 1985, p. 54.

221   *At a Halloween party in 1979 he slathered himself*: *Miami News*, January 3, 1980.

221   *he had just finished a six-week cycle on the anabolic*: Courson and Schreiber, *False Glory*, p. 25.

222   *He studied German on Berlitz tapes*: Lieber, "Getting Physical—and Chemical," p. 50.

222   *they tilted their heads back as a bartender*: Courson and Schreiber, *False Glory*, pp. 39–40.

222   *the bartender salted their lips*: Gary Dunn interview.

222   *Courson turned his Chevy Blazer into a battering ram*: Courson and Schreiber, *False Glory*, pp. 41–42.

222   *a shopping bag full of steroids (Winstrol, Dianabol*: Matt Chaney, *Spiral of Denial: Muscle Doping in American Football* (Warrensburg, Mo.: Four Walls Publishing, 2009), p. 106.

222 *"He was banging himself in the legs"*: John Banaszak interview.

222 *"All you want to do is body-build"*: Courson and Schreiber, *False Glory*, p. 57.

223 *"I learned a secret from those Rooskies"*: T. J. Quinn, "Pumped-up Pioneers: The '63 Chargers," www.espn.com, February 1, 2009.

223 *after taking Dianabol at a doctor's suggestion*: Lou Riecke interview.

223 *"steroid use has grown in direct proportion"*: *Pittsburgh Post-Gazette*, May 10, 1989.

223 *"Seventy-five percent of the linemen in the NFL"*: Lieber, "Getting Physical—and Chemical," p. 50.

223 *"It's very easy for people on the outside"*: Ibid., p. 54.

223 *"We're gonna go hunting some Jets today!"*: Gary Dunn interview.

223 *Courson blasted a tape of Wagner's "Ride of the Valkyries"*: Ibid.

223 *Courson, ever a showman, climbed atop the hood*: Ibid.

224 *"I never saw my mother and dad"*: John Rooney interview.

224 *the Chief ordering ham freshly sliced off the bone on Jewish rye*: Art Rooney Jr. interview.

225 *"He was some guy. Kind of a wild man"*: Ibid.

225 *"Now here's one! You didn't want to be left in the room"*: Ibid.

226 *"The wives like being Mrs. NFL probably more"*: Joe Greene interview.

226 *"Everyone else had a crush"*: Pam Webster interview.

226 *"I felt a little on the outside looking in"*: Debbie Furness Saletin interview.

226 *made enough food each night for six people*: Ibid.

227 *Knowing that his children were safe at home*: Pam Webster interview.

227 *"everybody to let their hair down, relax"*: Debbie Furness Saletin interview.

227 *The Websters memorized lines from these movies*: Pam Webster interview.

228 *"He was recognizable there"*: Debbie Furness Saletin interview.

228 *"I'm unhappy about it"*: *Washington (Pa.) Observer-Reporter*, August 19, 1981.

228 *"It was a very tough decision"*: Ibid.

228 *"If there's anything I can do"*: Ibid.

228 *She saw tears behind Debbie Furness's*: Pam Webster interview.

Chapter 15: Bar Scene at Pro Bowl, 1982

PAGE

231 *"Lynn would go anywhere on the field"*: Ronnie Lott interview.

231 *"Man, I don't know if you guys would've wanted"*: Ibid.

232 *"the old man with the cigar hugging those guys"*: Ibid.

233 *"My first encounter with true greatness"*: Ibid.

Chapter 16: Mean Joe

PAGE

234 *For thirty-five thousand dollars*: Joe Greene interview with Steve Sabol of NFL Films on November 29, 2004. NFL-135139.

234 *the Coca-Cola Company suggested using Terry Bradshaw*: Mark Pendergrast, *God, Coun-*

try, and Coca-Cola: The Definitive History of the Great American Soft Drink and the Company That Makes It (New York: Basic Books, 2000), pp. 319, 545. Author Pendergrast, in an endnote on page 545, writes that when Roger Mosconi, McCann Erickson's creative director for the Greene ad, first presented the storybook, the Coca-Cola Company wanted to use Bradshaw in the commercial, but Mosconi said he pressed for Greene.

234 *"we realized there would be more empathy"*: Penny Hawkey interview.

235 *"well, heck, I'm a ballplayer"*: Joe Greene interview with Steve Sabol of NFL Films on November 29, 2004. NFL-135139.

235 *For each take, Greene downed a bottle of Coke, more than twenty*: Joe Greene interview.

235 *Because of lighting problems and the boy's botched lines*: Pendergrast, *God, Country, and Coca-Cola*, p. 545.

235 *"You fumbled!"*: Joe Greene interview.

235 *"I'm endorsing this product"*: Ibid.

235 *"Mean Joe had this amazing aura about him"*: Penny Hawkey interview.

235 *"that little tiny transformation that had been at the heart"*: Ibid.

235 *"And it wasn't Dom Pérignon"*: Joe Greene interview.

236 *African Americans cheered, too, for the integration*: Penny Hawkey interview.

236 *"the glamour guys, the guys who score touchdowns"*: Joe Greene interview with Steve Sabol of NFL Films on November 29, 2004. NFL-135139.

236 *"He's just the ultimate because he brings"*: Franco Harris interview with Keith Cossrow of NFL Films on July 20, 2005. NFL-143735.

236 *"Gods do not answer letters"*: John Updike, "Hub Fans Bid Kid Adieu," *New Yorker*, October 22, 1960, p. 131.

237 *"I think that I missed my three kids [growing up]"*: Joe Greene interview.

237 *"I don't think* anybody *was better than Jim Brown"*: Ibid.

237 *"I probably said it the way I meant it"*: Ibid.

238 *"You're right, Dad. Joe plays team defense"*: Art Rooney Jr. interview.

238 *"I had no respect for anyone's ability"*: Ron Cook, "Yesterday's Heroes," *Football Digest*, July/August 1987, p. 86.

238 *"Hey, Gary, we don't hit Joe that way"*: Gary Dunn interview.

238 *"You don't talk that way to those people!"*: Ralph Berlin interview.

239 *The rookie offered his apologies*: Ibid.

239 *"If I get half a chance"*: *Cleveland Plain Dealer*, November 4, 1977.

239 *"my most embarrassing moment"*: Ibid., February 22, 1982.

239 *"If you come into this end zone"*: Dan Pastorini interview.

239 *"Man, don't ever do that to me again"*: Ibid.

239 *"It's up to you, Joe"*: Joe Gordon interview.

239 Can you imagine playing games like this: Cook, "Yesterday's Heroes," p. 86.

239 *"I'm a non-combatant now"*: *Canton (Ohio) Repository*, February 11, 1982.

239 *"There will never be another Joe Greene"*: *Cleveland Plain Dealer*, February 11, 1982.

239 *"What is this, a wake?"*: *Canton (Ohio) Repository*, February 11, 1982.

240 *"I tried, but my heart wasn't in it"*: Joe Greene interview.

240 *he became a member of the school's board of regents*: *USA Today*, October 18, 1983.

240 *"[Joe] used to absolutely terrify us"*: *Miami Herald*, February 16, 1992.

240 *"Over the years, I began to understand"*: *Chicago Tribune*, September 15, 1991.

240 *he'd explode more often than Chicago Bears coach Mike Ditka*: Joe Greene interview.

240 *As a coach, Greene tried to emulate Chuck Noll*: Ibid.

240 *"Joe still has that effect of grounding people"*: Art Rooney Jr. interview.

241 *"This is an* oooold *town"*: Joe Greene interview.

241 *each man sometimes earning $10,000 or more*: L. C. Greenwood interview.

241 *"a steak, two steaks, and then everything on the table"*: Ibid.

241 *"I'm gonna pray for you, Greene"*: Joe Greene interview.

242 *"Ernie was just* different *people"*: L. C. Greenwood interview.

242 *he and his wife, Karen, helped raise more than $36 million*: Karen (Farmer) White interview.

242 *"I happen to think that the ultimate test"*: Roy Blount Jr., *About Three Bricks Shy . . . and the Load Filled Up* (Pittsburgh: University of Pittsburgh Press, 2002), p. 324.

242 *"Ernie is very much like Pittsburgh"*: *Pittsburgh Press*, May 4, 1978.

242 *He worked as a bodyguard*: Roderick (Byron) Holmes interview.

242 *when the Reverend Jesse Jackson came to Jasper, Texas*: Ibid.

242 *In that film a vampire grabs Holmes by the neck*: Ibid.

243 *"That's what he told me on the phone"*: L. C. Greenwood interview.

243 *"It's like Biggie [Smalls] said in the movie"*: Roderick (Byron) Holmes interview.

243 *"He had his crazy moments"*: Ibid.

243 *"So I went out and set up camp"*: Rev. Ernie Holmes, a Sunday sermon, n.d. Personal files of his son, Roderick (Byron) Holmes.

244 *"He loved those guys"*: Roderick (Byron) Holmes interview.

244 *"Joe, I've got bad news for you"*: Joe Greene interview.

244 *On a dark night near Beaumont, Texas, Holmes's SUV*: "Peace Officer's Crash Report, Texas Department of Transportation, Austin, Texas. The crash that killed Ernie Holmes occurred on October 17, 2008, in Hardin County, Texas, near Lumberton, Texas.

244 *Holmes had complained to family members recently about chest pains*: Roderick (Byron) Holmes interview.

245 *sixteen—more than one in five—were Steelers*: *Los Angeles Times*, July 18, 2006.

245 *"I like us to have records"*: Franco Harris interview.

245 *"Fate"*: John Stallworth interview.

245 *"If you saw Ranger's body, you knew"*: Ibid.

245 *local police officers removed their hats, and placed*: Roderick (Byron) Holmes interview.

245 *"You can see a person grow up"*: L. C. Greenwood interview.

246 *"I don't do funerals real well"*: Joe Greene interview.

246 *"I get it now"*: Karen (Farmer) White interview.

246 *Together they grilled steaks, smoked Excalibur*: Joe Greene interview.

246   *White broached the idea of leaving a vacant chair*: Karen (Farmer) White and Joe Greene interviews.

246   *"Man, I've got to apologize"*: Joe Greene interview.

246   *"Hooomes"*: L. C. Greenwood interview.

246   *"Can't you give him something"*: Ibid.

247   *"He didn't make it"*: Joe Greene interview.

247   *Stunned, Greene phoned Karen White, and wept*: Karen (Farmer) White interview.

247   *"Joe, you can be angry, but the Lord's will"*: Joe Greene interview.

247   *"Do you think Dwight got in?"*: J. T. Thomas interview.

247   *"I guess there is a Texas way"*: L. C. Greenwood interview.

247   *"Dwight got in"*: J. T. Thomas interview.

247   *"We were the first to come"*: L. C. Greenwood interview.

247   *"Dwight's death is really tough on Joe"*: Karen (Farmer) White interview.

248   *"Hey, guys, what's up?"*: A video of the Steelers' White House visit can be found online at http://www.whitehouse.gov/video/President-Obama-and-the-Pittsburgh-Steelers.

248   *Greene told Obama that he was proud of him*: Joe Greene interview.

248   *"I watched him during the [2008] campaign"*: Ibid.

248   *"Pittsburgh Steelers fans are all over the place"*: Ibid.

249   *"Joe would never do that!"*: Agnes Greene interview.

249   *"I told her, the problem with a lot of people"*: Joe Greene interview.

249   *"That's one of the joys"*: Ibid.

250   *"If I can't say that— That's what I feel"*: Ibid.

250   *"No one on the team EVER felt"*: Ibid.

251   *"Who is THAT young man?"*: Agnes Greene interview.

251   *"Why did I put that stocking cap on?"*: Joe Greene interview.

Chapter 17: Brad

PAGE

252   *"you are the last one I am going to talk"*: Terry Bradshaw interview.

252   *"It's like I told you on the phone"*: Ibid.

252   *"That's why the writers always used to say"*: Ibid.

253   *"I mean I don't have any rapport"*: Ibid.

254   *"and there's not a dry eye in the place"*: Howie Long interview.

254   *"Would you like to meet the president?"*: Terry Bradshaw interview.

254   *"If you had been giving those kinds of speeches"*: Ibid.

254   *"Not everybody can say they had the president"*: Ibid.

254   *which starts at $40,000 per speech and moves upward*: Bradshaw's speaking fees are specified on the Washington Speakers Bureau website at http://www.washingtonspeakers.com/speakers/speaker.cfm?SpeakerID=428#.

254   *Once he was a registered Republican, he says, but now*: Terry Bradshaw interview.

254   *"Are you big-dogging me now?"*: Ibid.

254 *"Are you shittin' me?"*: Ibid.

254 *"Roo-die Giu-li-ah-nee!"*: Ibid.

255 *"Bradshaw couldn't spell 'cat' "*: Thomas Hollywood Henderson and Peter Knobler, *Out of Control: Confessions of an NFL Casualty* (New York: Pocket Books, 1988), pp. 1–5, 242–43.

255 *snorted it through his Vicks inhaler on the sideline*: Ibid., pp. 4–5.

255 *"Terry wore that like the 'A' in* The Scarlet Letter*"*: Verne Lundquist interview.

255 *"As much as I hate people saying that I'm dumb"*: Terry Bradshaw interview.

256 *"Why was Red Skelton popular?"*: Roy McHugh interview.

256 *"I just got a German shepherd"*: Terry Bradshaw interview.

257 *He sat on Leno's couch for the forty-ninth time in June 2012*: *New York Times*, June 20, 2012.

257 *"I'm sixty-three years old and I don't need"*: Terry Bradshaw interview.

258 *"Don't worry about what they say"*: Ibid.

258 *"It's just a friggin' game, folks"*: Ibid.

258 *"I wished away all my dignity"*: Verne Lundquist interview.

258 *"That tackle was made by Willie Anderson, free agent"*: Ibid.

259 *"I knew that's where he would make his mark"*: Ibid.

259 *"I don't have Fox. I don't have ranches"*: Terry Bradshaw interview.

259 *"It didn't take* anything *from me"*: Ibid.

259 *"I get this horrible nerve pain [from the neck]"*: Ibid.

260 *He couldn't remember players' names or statistics he'd studied*: Terry Bradshaw, "Bradshaw shares battle with concussions," www.foxsports.com, April 14, 2011. This column by Bradshaw can be read at http://msn.foxsports.com/nfl/story/Terry-Bradshaw-explains-concussions-short-term-memory-concerns-041211.

260 *he'd been reduced to sweats and crying jags*: L. Jon Wertheim, "Prisoners of Depression," *Sports Illustrated*, September 8, 2003. See also *USA Today*, January 30, 2004.

260 *"Not as bad as they thought [but] memory loss"*: Terry Bradshaw interview.

260 *"But you don't think about that"*: Ibid.

261 *"Bubba, it might be you"*: Verne Lundquist interview.

261 *"I didn't think we were that close"*: Ibid.

261 *Noll suggested maybe it was time for the thirty-five-year-old Bradshaw*: Jill Lieber, "Bradshaw Gets New Hope from the 'Scope," *Sports Illustrated*, December 1983, p. 19.

261 *But he left the field after the second scoring pass holding his arm*: *Pittsburgh Press* and *Pittsburgh Post-Gazette*, December 11, 1983.

261 *"I just shook his hand"*: Terry Bradshaw interview.

261 *"I'm not talking to him. You talk to him"*: Dan Radakovich interview.

262 *"You were great for us"*: Ibid.

262 *"Chuck was really good at it"*: Ibid.

262 *Bradshaw later admitted he'd made a mistake, and regretted it*: *Pittsburgh Post-Gazette*, October 20, 2003.

262 *it was seen in Pittsburgh as another example of his embitterment*: Ibid., August 3, 1989.

Chapter 18: Franco

PAGE

270   *Over the Feast of the Seven Fishes, they hugged*: Al Vento interview.

270   *Vento watched him slip twenty-dollar bills into the hands*: Ibid.

270   *flew several times to Nashville to participate in Gilliam's football*: Coach Joe Gilliam Sr.
      interview.

271   *Harris once discreetly handed an envelope with a $5,000*: Greg Garber, "Wandering
      Through the Fog," www.espn.com, January 27, 2005. This story, the fourth in Garber's
      excellent five-part series on Webster, can be read at http://sports.espn.go.com/nfl/news/
      story?id=1972288.

271   *"He's a guy I don't think I've ever, ever seen mad"*: J. T. Thomas interview.

271   *When Dana Harris spotted Vento sitting with his wife*: Al Vento interview.

272   *He intended to spend the night, and had brought*: Franco Harris interview.

272   KEEP AMERICA AMERICAN. NO NAZIS: *Pittsburgh Courier*, April 9, 1997.

272   *Three hundred officers—in riot gear, on horseback*: *Philadelphia Inquirer*, April 6, 1997.

272   *"This could be a bad scene"*: Dan Rooney interview.

273   *"My mother shouldn't have suffered"*: Ibid.

273   *"We can't let hate or evil take over"*: Franco Harris interview.

273   *"I have a hard time letting Nazis take over"*: *Pittsburgh Courier*, April 9, 1997.

273   *"Franco, I'm one hundred percent with you"*: Dan Rooney interview.

273   *Dan said he would go to that rally with Harris*: Ibid.

273   *Only thirty-nine Klansmen participated*: Dan Rooney as told to Andrew E. Masich and
      David F. Halaas, *My 75 Years with the Pittsburgh Steelers and the NFL* (New York: Da
      Capo Press, 2007), pp. 244–45.

273   *"I came here for one reason"*: *Philadelphia Inquirer*, April 6, 1997.

273   *Using megaphones, the Klan was heard to vilify the Reverend Jesse Jackson*: Ibid.

273   *"Just how sincere he is"*: Dan Rooney interview.

274   *"Tape doesn't lie"*: Jack Ham interview.

274   *At a family dinner at the St. Clair Country Club, he rose*: Art Rooney Jr. interview.

274   *"I just felt so sorry for him because he loved Franco"*: Ibid.

275   *"Before the Battle of Midway"*: Ibid.

275   *"What Joe Greene meant for the defense"*: Jack Ham interview.

275   *He was due to earn $385,000*: *Pittsburgh Post-Gazette*, January 20, 1985.

275   *"It's unfair"*: *Pittsburgh Post-Gazette*, August 24, 1984.

275   *"pivot point"*: Ibid.

275   *privately began calling Noll "Closet Nice Guy"*: Vito Stellino interview.

275   *"Chuck thought [NFL] records took care of themselves"*: Art Rooney Jr. interview.

275   *Mel Blount called Dan and offered to intervene*: Dan Rooney interview.

275   *"I talked to Franco and it's going to be okay"*: Ibid.

275   *"Just make sure that Franco is there"*: Ibid.

275   *"Chuck was a stubborn German, which he is"*: Joe Gordon interview.

262   *"I'm not going to question it"*: Ibid.

262   *"What is it with you people?"*: Bob Labriola, "Bradshaw Divorce from Steelers
       Steelers Digest, August 14, 1989, p. 3.

262   *"Thank you, number eighty-eight, Lynn Swann"*: Audio of Terry Bradshaw ind
       speech at Pro Football Hall of Fame, August 5, 1989. Ralph Wilson, Jr. Pro F
       Research and Preservation Center, Pro Football Hall of Fame, Canton, Ohio.

262   *"What I wouldn't give right now to put my hands"*: Ibid.

263   *"He's an antsy guy"*: Blair Buswell interview.

263   *"My hands were red and throbbing"*: Ibid.

263   *"I wish I'd a hell got out after the last one"*: Terry Bradshaw interview.

263   *"Here you have one of the great sports"*: Mike Wagner interview.

263   *"He was a playoff player"*: Art Rooney Jr. interview.

264   *"Hell, I'm on TV"*: Terry Bradshaw interview.

264   *"I do have Franco"*: Ibid.

264   *"Let me tell you something about the Steelers"*: Ibid.

264   *"So that's the way [Bradshaw] saw it"*: Donnie Shell interview.

265   *"I call him occasionally"*: Joe Greene interview.

265   *"I'm reaching out to Terry now a lot more frequently"*: Franco Harris interview.

265   *"So now that we're gone, what have they done lately?"*: *Cleveland Plain Dealer*, Ja
       ary 26, 1986.

265   *"There is nothing to patch up from my standpoint"*: *Cleveland Plain Dealer*, January 26, 19

265   *"I hated him—and I mean, HATED him"*: Terry Bradshaw interview.

265   *"for every unkind word and thought"*: *Pittsburgh Post-Gazette*, February 10, 2003.

265   *"my wrong, my childness [sic], my selfishness"*: Ibid.

265   *he privately told Noll that night that maybe they'd get together.*: Joe Gordon interview.

265   *"[Noll] makes you uncomfortable"*: Terry Bradshaw interview.

266   *"I've seen Terry once in the last twenty years"*: Verne Lundquist interview.

266   *Gordon had just toured Bradshaw's parents through the Steelers'*: Joe Gordon interview.

266   *"They're going to boo me"*: Ibid.

266   *"Terry shouldn't say some things"*: Dan Rooney interview.

267   *"Believe me when I say this"*: *Pittsburgh Post-Gazette*, October 22, 2002.

267   *"It's good to be home"*: Ibid.

268   *"Hey, how did* The X Factor *do this week?"*: This scene, including the comments made
       on air and off, was drawn from the author's visit to the set of *Fox NFL Sunday* on
       October 9, 2011.

268   *"a yin-and-yang, that kind of Martin-and-Lewis deal"*: Howie Long interview.

268   *"Terry just does it"*: Ibid.

276   *"What happened?"*: Ibid.

276   *"that was pretty stupid to make a statement"*: Franco Harris interview.

276   *"Franco told us what it would take"*: Dan Rooney interview.

276   *"Franco is forgiving, just turn the other cheek"*: Karen (Farmer) White interview.

276   *"We had someone who really didn't connect"*: Franco Harris interview.

277   *"I really shouldn't say that"*: Ibid.

277   *Franco sitting beside the Chief on a bench*: Art Rooney Jr. interview.

277   *"Hey, I had twelve great years with the Steelers"*: Franco Harris interview.

277   *"Franco's a tremendous guy"*: Art Rooney Jr. interview.

278   *"That's for the brain"*: Franco Harris interview.

278   *"I do think that all of us have brain damage"*: Ibid.

278   *"But I've always had a bad memory"*: Ibid.

278   *"The only reason to run out of bounds"*: *Palm Beach Post*, February 7, 1984. See also Jeff Pearlman, *Sweetness: The Enigmatic Life of Walter Payton* (New York: Gotham Books, 2011), pp. 269–71. Payton joined Harris and Brown on the *Phil Donahue Show*.

278   *"The smart guys who stay around know when to take a hit"*: Phil Villapiano interview.

278   *"Franco played thirteen years and I played nine"*: John (Frenchy) Fuqua interview.

278   *"I was the one that wanted to run over people"*: Reggie Harrison (known today as Kamal Ali Salaam-El) interview.

279   *"As the Persian general said"*: Franco Harris interview.

279   *"I mean, I'm fine with Jim"*: Ibid.

279   *SilverSport, a company that makes antimicrobial exercise products*: Ibid.

279   *"I swear, I think he's cloned"*: Jack Ham interview.

279   *Dan said no Steeler had ever been as actively committed*: Dan Rooney interview.

280   *Democratic kingmakers in Pittsburgh and across the state*: Franco Harris interview.

280   *"He's the best PR man we have"*: Al Vento interview.

280   *bused to different neighborhoods, handed out campaign leaflets*: Gerry (Moon) Mullins, J. T. Thomas, and Mike Wagner interviews.

281   *"I knew that politics would be a little sticky"*: Franco Harris interview.

281   *"He went to introduce his son"*: Mike Wagner interview.

281   *"I think you both know what happens"*: "Dok Harris Gets Rocky and Franco on His Team," Dok Harris for Mayor of Pittsburgh campaign video, www.Youtube.com. This ad can be seen at http://www.youtube.com/watch?v=VSRdDp1NK9g.

281   *"We need that type of leadership"*: Ibid.

281   *"And that's what you're doing here"*: Ibid.

281   *Despite an energetic campaign, Dok Harris got only 25*: *Pittsburgh Post-Gazette* and *Pittsburgh Business Times*, November 4, 2009.

281   *"I mean, not a lot of guys [former Steelers] supported"*: Franco Harris interview.

281   *Rendell defeated Swann easily*: *Pittsburgh Post-Gazette*, November 8, 2006.

281   *"Since the election me and Swann really aren't . . ."*: Franco Harris interview.

282   *he criticized the investigative report issued by former FBI director*: Frank Schwab, "Franco

Harris Continues to Debate Joe Paterno's Legacy, This Time at Town Hall Meeting," www.yahoo.com, November 7, 2012. This story can be read at http://sports.yahoo.com/blogs/ncaaf-dr-saturday/franco-harris-continues-debate-joe-paterno-legacy-time-225612248—ncaaf.html.

282   DUE PROCESS FOR PSU JVP: *Pittsburgh Post-Gazette*, September 4, 2012.

282   *"No way would Joe ever cover up"*: Kristian Dyer, "Former Penn Stater Franco Harris Defends Joe Paterno," www.yahoo.com, July 21, 2012. This story can be read at http://sports.yahoo.com/blogs/ncaaf-dr-saturday/former-penn-stater-franco-harris-defends-joe-paterno-133649026—ncaaf.html.

282   *They cost Harris his job as a spokesman for the Meadows Race*: *USA Today*, November 16, 2011.

282   *prompted Mayor Ravenstahl to call for Harris's resignation*: Ibid., November 17, 2011.

282   *"my heart aches for those young people"*: *Pittsburgh Post-Gazette*, November 18, 2011.

282   *later was reinstated by supportive board members*: Ibid., December 8, 2011.

282   *"Franco looks at friends and life"*: J. T. Thomas interview.

282   *"Loyalty has to be a two-way street"*: Joe Gordon interview.

283   *"These are Franco's shoes"*: Mike Wagner interview.

283   *For the thirty-fifth, he and Dana gave a pearl necklace*: Rocky Bleier and Al Vento interviews.

283   *"You are a part of the family, Al"*: Al Vento interview.

284   *Cope's eyes opened and grew wide with disbelief*: Joe Gordon interview. Gordon escorted Harris into Cope's room and witnessed their interaction.

284   *Harris leaned over the bed and hugged Cope*: Ibid.

284   *Harris stepped inside that room, held the man*: Ibid.

284   *"Franco is big about getting together"*: Rocky Bleier interview.

284   *"I want to reconnect Brad"*: Franco Harris interview.

285   *"Franco is one of my friends"*: Terry Bradshaw interview.

285   *Harris handed out small bronze statuettes*: Gerry (Moon) Mullins interview.

285   *"And we all talked about how good it was"*: Joe Greene interview.

286   *"Franco got pissed off at me last year for busting Roethlisberger"*: Ibid.

Chapter 19: Stall

PAGE

287   *He loved coaching for Noll and the Rooneys*: Lionel Taylor interview.

287   *"I had to find out if I could coach"*: Ibid.

288   *"How many did you catch yesterday?"*: Frank Deford, "Champagne, Roses, and Donuts," *Sports Illustrated*, December 10, 1979, p. 106.

288   *"Hey, Cheryl, how you doing, sweetheart?"*: Lynn Swann interview with Ray Didinger of NFL Films on September 17, 2001. NFL-94665.

288   *"Greatest catch I ever saw"*: Lionel Taylor interview.

288   *"I really don't have anything that hurts"*: John Stallworth interview.

288   *"It was a part of who they were"*: Ibid.

289 *"I just liked the sound of 'Grandfather' "*: Ibid.

289 *"My first impression when I look back"*: Ibid.

290 *"You can't beat talent"*: Paul Zimmerman, "They Were Just Too Much," *Sports Illustrated*, January 28, 1980, p. 12.

290 *"This game was an invitation engraved in gold"*: Ibid., p. 25.

290 *high school pep rallies crackled with the battle song "Dixie"*: Patrick J. Sauer, "How I Did It: John Stallworth, CEO, Madison Research," *Inc.*, August 1, 2006. See online at http://www.inc.com/magazine/20060801/hidi-stallworth.html.

290 *"And the world is watching"*: John Stallworth interview.

290 *sold it in 2006 reportedly for $69 million*: *Huntsville (Ala.) Times*, August 10, 2006.

291 *"I'm not going out there in my bare feet"*: Art Rooney Jr. interview.

291 *"There was something intrinsic about him"*: Ibid.

291 *"That's a side of John I've never seen"*: Chuck Noll interview with Ken Rodgers of NFL Films on September 10, 2001. NFL-94670.

291 *"I never saw John as an entrepreneur"*: Terry Bradshaw interview.

291 *"We've had players who have gone into business"*: Dan Rooney interview.

292 *"that's not what we do here"*: John Stallworth interview.

292 *"He was one of the guys who invited me to Bible study"*: Tunch Ilkin interview.

292 *"Sometimes it doesn't hit you"*: John Stallworth interview.

292 *"I looked around and Joe [Greene] wasn't there"*: Ibid.

293 *each man first phoning Ilkin, the team's union representative, to apologize*: Tunch Ilkin interview.

293 *"Stall came in one game at halftime"*: Greg Lloyd interview.

293 I guess Donnie got his last wish, too!: John Stallworth speech at Mel Blount Youth Home Celebrity Roast of Donnie Shell, April 4, 2008, KDKA television, Pittsburgh.

293 *"That wouldn't be right, would it, John?"*: *Pittsburgh Press*, December 27, 1991.

293 *"No, coach, it wouldn't"*: Ibid.

293 *"We had some guys who were around longer maybe"*: Ibid.

294 *At his son's soccer game, he met a retired army engineer*: Sauer, "How I Did It."

294 *"There were times"*: John Stallworth interview.

294 *For $271,000, Madison built*: Sauer, "How I Did It."

294 *"We didn't make a cent on it"*: John Stallworth interview.

294 *it won a $50 million contract to run a computer simulation center*: Sauer, "How I Did It."

294 *Madison gained advantage from the government's minority set-aside*: Ibid.

294 *"another opportunity to do something to be remembered"*: John Stallworth interview.

294 *"Athletes are not supposed to be the most cerebral"*: Ibid.

295 *"I'd go to a meeting and all they would"*: Ibid.

295 *"I had to prove that I was intelligent"*: Sauer, "How I Did It."

295 *"I modeled the way I wanted our employees to feel about me"*: John Stallworth interview.

295 *In 2008, Stallworth walked across midfield at Heinz*: Ibid.

295 *"We're looking to bring some partners"*: Ibid.

295   *"We wanted to bring in a minority"*: Dan Rooney interview.

295   *"It's still in the family"*: *Pittsburgh Tribune-Review*, March 24, 2009.

296   *"He's a class guy, that's for sure"*: Ibid.

296   *"just a small percent"*: John Stallworth interview.

296   *"Are you out of your mind?"*: Reggie Harrison (known today as Kamal Ali Salaam-El) interview.

296   *"No, man, call yo' boy"*: Ibid.

296   *"[It's] not like having one guy who is your big-time"*: Lynn Swann interview with Ray Didinger of NFL Films on September 17, 2001. NFL-94665.

296   *"2 and 4! 2 and 4!"*: Ibid.

296   *"Watch this: I'm gonna go over"*: John Stallworth interview.

296   *seeing a Steelers pass finally completed on the projector screen*: John Stallworth interview with Ray Didinger of NFL Films on September 17, 2001. NFL-94665. Stallworth and Swann conducted a joint interview with Didinger.

297   *"Here we are and it is something"*: Ibid.

297   *"I think the barrier was that we wanted"*: Ibid.

297   *"It was just a conscious acknowledgment"*: John Stallworth interview.

297   *"I'd become very callous about the whole thing"*: Lynn Swann interview with Ray Didinger of NFL Films on September 17, 2001. NFL-94665.

297   *"I think that's a great idea"*: Ibid.

297   *"I wanted to go in, too"*: John Stallworth interview.

298   *From his long wait, Swann said he had developed a deep appreciation*: Lynn Swann interview with Ray Didinger of NFL Films on September 17, 2001. NFL-94665.

298   *"He's been humbled a little bit"*: John Stallworth interview with Ray Didinger of NFL Films on September 17, 2001. NFL-94665.

298   *"I don't know if John could sense it but I was crying"*: Lynn Swann interview with Ray Didinger of NFL Films on September 17, 2001. NFL-94665.

298   *"renewed my spirit and confidence that one day I might be here"*: Ibid.

298   *"Please help me to bring forward one of the greatest"*: Audio of Lynn Swann induction speech at Pro Football Hall of Fame, August 4, 2001. Ralph Wilson, Jr. Pro Football Research and Preservation Center, Pro Football Hall of Fame, Canton, Ohio.

299   *"He hit me up for money for the campaign"*: John Stallworth interview.

299   *He became in 2009 one of relatively few black members of Augusta*: Sam Weinman, "Lynn Swann Among Augusta's New Members," *Golf Digest*, April 7, 2010.

299   *"Lynn can't do a whole lot of that"*: John Stallworth interview.

299   *"The man who introduced me today"*: Audio of Lynn Swann induction speech at Pro Football Hall of Fame, August 4, 2001.

299   *"And I say to Lynn here today"*: Audio of John Stallworth induction speech at Pro Football Hall of Fame, August 3, 2002. Ralph Wilson, Jr. Pro Football Research and Preservation Center, Pro Football Hall of Fame, Canton, Ohio.

Chapter 20: Webby

PAGE

300   *where life was lived on Lombardi Time*: David Maraniss, *When Pride Still Mattered: A Life of Vince Lombardi* (New York: Simon & Schuster, 1999), pp. 217, 272. Maraniss writes that Lombardi expected his players to be on time and that "Lombardi time" meant arriving ten minutes early.

300   *she saw him punch cabinets*: Pam Webster interview.

300   *He said it was her fault, all of it*: Ibid.

300   *Entering the house, she looked at her photo*: Ibid.

300   *Once, in anger, he told her that he'd thrown his four*: Ibid.

301   *"You have no medical insurance"*: Ibid.

301   Mike Webster's on cocaine! Steroids did this to him!: Garrett Webster and Pam Webster interviews.

301   Why did the kids' college fund disappear?: Pam Webster interview.

301   *though Courson finally asked him to leave*: Denise Masciola interview.

301   *It took days for Webster to find out that he'd been named*: Joe Gordon interview.

302   *The NFL pension board later would put a private investigator*: Bob Fitzsimmons interview.

302   *She replaced air fresheners in the men's room urinals*: Pam Webster interview.

302   *"God, why?"*: Ibid.

302   *"You can't do that, Brad!"*: Tunch Ilkin interview.

303   *Bradshaw called a time-out and in the huddle laughed*: Ibid.

303   *Parisi's mother-in-law, a seamstress, restitched their jerseys*: Tony Parisi interview.

303   *"His muscles were like trees"*: George Perles interview.

303   *"Here is this guy with arms like legs"*: Tunch Ilkin interview.

304   *His kids watched him drive the blocking sled*: Colin Webster, "Reflections in Iron: Mike Webster's Training Methods," www.startingstrength.com. In this article Mike Webster's oldest son, Colin, reflects on his father and his weight training methods. He also describes the scene of meeting his father in the woods. It can be read at http://starting strength.com/index.php/site/reflections_in_iron_mike_websters_training_methods.

304   *They saw him walk up and down their backyard incline*: Ibid.

304   *In the off-season, he ran with his father-in-law's Weimaraner*: Pam Webster interview.

304   *Webster admitted to brief experimentation with steroids*: Garrett Webster interview.

304   *"He saw it [steroid use] affecting his moods with the family"*: Ibid.

304   *"C'mon, rook, and run with me"*: Greg Lloyd interview.

304   *"Mike was in incredible shape"*: Ibid.

304   *"a high-end diesel tractor"*: Randy Grossman interview.

304   *"We'd be running plays against air"*: *Pittsburgh Tribune-Review*, July 20, 1997.

305   *"I only have to run five yards"*: Ralph Berlin interview.

305   *"The Webby Doom-and-Gloom Report"*: Tunch Ilkin interview.

305   *"Pilgrim, if you say it's a fine day"*: Ibid.

305   *"There's no way in hell we can do it!":* Ibid.

305   *"All right, cut the fuck out of him!":* Ibid.

305   *"Hey, Webby, how about taking it easy":* Gary Dunn interview.

306   *Webster lifted his trunk, took out a few beers:* Ibid.

306   *"Naaw, you're going to be a good player":* Ibid.

306   *He lifted Dunn and threw him into a nearby guardrail:* Ibid.

306   *Teammates held a retirement dinner for Webster, roasted him:* Los Angeles Times, September 16, 1989.

306   *He earned $350,000 during his last:* Pam Webster interview.

307   *"It was like a death":* Ibid.

307   *"He wanted to prove it to the Steelers":* Carl Peterson interview.

307   *wrote lengthy letters to Peterson about that, emphasizing commitment:* Ibid.

307   *NFL's oldest battery-mates since the Raiders' George Blanda and Jim Otto:* Rick Dean, "He Doesn't Just Lift . . . HE TRAINS!" *NFL GameDay* (Chiefs/Jets), September 1, 1989, p. 11.

307   *"You are running to the sideline for five seconds":* Tunch Ilkin interview.

308   *He would endure fifty-three surgeries on his knees:* Jim Otto interview.

308   *"I have so much metal in me":* Jim Otto with Dave Newhouse, *Jim Otto: The Pain of Glory* (Champaign, Ill.: Sports Publishing, 2000), p. 4.

308   *"Football took it":* Jim Otto interview.

308   *"What are you going to do, Mike?":* Ibid.

308   *"The thing about Webster and Otto":* Michael Oriard interview.

308   *"Webster didn't protect himself":* Ibid.

308   *"One thing you learn in this game":* Kansas City Star, March 12, 1991.

308   *"almost like an adolescent wrote them":* Carl Peterson interview.

309   *He made less than $6,000 in wages:* "Memorandum in Support of Plaintiff's Motion for Summary Judgment," filed December 20, 2004, p. 6. *Sunny Jani (as administrator of the Estate of Mike Webster, deceased), Plaintiff, v. The Bert Bell/Pete Rozelle NFL Player Retirement Plan and The NFL Player Supplemental Disability Plan, Defendants;* United States District Court for the District of Maryland (Northern Division), Civil Action No. WDQ-04-cv-1606.

309   *"But there was always something":* Rocky Bleier interview.

309   *"He came to see if we could raise some money":* Andy Russell interview.

309   *"He acted strange even during the early period":* Dan Rooney interview.

309   *"What do you do with worms?":* Ibid.

309   *"He was hard to engage":* Mike Wagner interview.

310   *"My relationship with him wasn't that good":* Ibid.

310   *He wrote copious notes on legal pads:* Bob Fitzsimmons and Garrett Webster interviews.

310   *Darvocet, Vicodin, Prozac, Ritalin, Dexedrine:* Greg Garber, "A Tormented Soul," www .espn.com, January 24, 2005. This story, the first in Garber's five-part series on Webster, can be read at http://sports.espn.go.com/nfl/news/story?id=1972285.

310 *Saying he wanted his players to see the look of a winner*: Carl Peterson interview.

310 *Webster was living at the Chiefs' facility, upstairs in a storage room*: Carl Peterson and Bob Moore interviews.

310 *"Don't say anything—he's living up there"*: Bob Moore interview.

310 *"Mike had such pride, he just refused"*: Carl Peterson interview.

311 *"I could tell there was the heart of a champion"*: Ronnie Lott interview.

311 *"Both of those guys exemplified something"*: Ibid.

311 *"He just didn't want to do any"*: Tunch Ilkin interview.

311 *But first they bought a plane ticket for him*: Ibid.

311 *"He got really suspicious of me"*: Ibid.

311 *"A few of us would write checks"*: Mike Wagner interview.

312 *"We were kind of going, 'Well, who is going to donate money to old football players?'"*: Ibid.

312 *"What can I do for you?"*: Terry Bradshaw interview.

312 *"The problem with men is pride"*: Ibid.

312 *Webster said he had obtained permission to market*: Joe Gordon interview.

312 *Webster would spend the next two months*: Ibid.

312 *Bradshaw wanted to get Webster's teeth fixed*: Terry Bradshaw interview.

312 *"I got him a haircut"*: Ibid.

313 *"What will happen after Bradshaw introduces"*: *Pittsburgh Post-Gazette*, July 24, 1997.

313 *Sunny Jani convinced him to go to Canton*: Pam Webster and Garrett Webster interviews.

313 *Married with a young family, Jani ran a grocery store*: Greg Garber, "Wandering Through the Fog," www.espn.com, January 27, 2005. This story, the fourth in Garber's five-part series on Webster, can be read at http://sports.espn.go.com/nfl/news/story?id=1972288.

313 *If he earned $1,500 at a signing, Webster sent $1,000*: Ibid.

313 *Jani drove nine hours, nearly to Milwaukee, to get him*: Ibid.

313 *Jani began to duct-tape money in hidden places*: Ibid.

313 *"if you don't pay our way there"*: Pam Webster interview.

313 *"He ranged between timid and quiet"*: Joe Horrigan interview.

313 *"We didn't want him to embarrass himself"*: Pam Webster interview.

314 *"He was the backbone upon which we were built"*: Transcript of Terry Bradshaw's introduction of Mike Webster at Pro Football Hall of Fame, July 26, 1997. Ralph Wilson, Jr. Pro Football Research and Preservation Center, Pro Football Hall of Fame, Canton, Ohio.

314 *"We were all afraid what he was going to say"*: Pam Webster interview.

314 *"Giving Bradshaw a forum and a microphone"*: Audio of Mike Webster's induction speech at Pro Football Hall of Fame, July 26, 1997. Ralph Wilson, Jr. Pro Football Research and Preservation Center, Pro Football Hall of Fame, Canton, Ohio.

314 *"the most important people in my life"*: Ibid.

314 *"It was like this man up there"*: Pam Webster interview.

314 *"If he would've just stopped at ten"*: Tunch Ilkin interview.

314   *"You only fail if you don't finish the game"*: Audio of Webster's induction speech at Pro Football Hall of Fame.

314   *"He would say things that were Old Webby"*: Tunch Ilkin interview.

315   *"He was not right"*: Terry Bradshaw interview.

315   *"I knew nobody would have the balls to go up"*: Pam Webster interview.

315   *"This is probably our last family photo"*: Ibid.

315   *"My heart is breaking that he doesn't want"*: Ibid.

315   *"I know I caused him some pain"*: Ibid.

315   *she sent out a plate with turkey, biscuits, and gravy*: Ibid.

316   *In February 1999, police arrested and handcuffed him*: Garber, "Wandering Through the Fog."

316   *Bleier, Blount, and Grossman came to lend*: *Chicago Tribune*, March 11, 1999.

316   *Two doctors treating Webster told reporters that Webster's frontal lobe*: *Pittsburgh Post-Gazette*, March 11, 1999.

316   *"All you do is control symptoms"*: Ibid.

316   *Dan had called Fitzsimmons before the press conference*: Bob Fitzsimmons interview.

316   *He sent Webster to four doctors and they all agreed*: Ibid.

317   *"They don't mean anything to me"*: Ibid.

317   *He pulled aside Webster and convinced him not to sell*: Ibid.

317   *"It's a wonder we didn't get shot"*: Ibid.

317   *"fighting the big evil giant"*: Ibid.

317   *"It's like having ginger ale in my skull"*: Garrett Webster interview.

318   *Several times during winter, he had wrapped himself in an Indian*: Colin Webster, "Reflections in Iron."

318   *He found a bare human footprint*: Ibid.

318   *"If there is meaning in life at all"*: Viktor E. Frankl, *Man's Search for Meaning* (New York: Washington Square Press, 1984), p. 88.

318   *"Abnormal reaction to an abnormal situation"*: Ibid., p. 38.

318   *He dropped the log and it crashed to earth with a thud*: Colin Webster, "Reflections in Iron."

318   *his father resembled a caveman*: Ibid.

318   *He saw no sign of a campfire, no kindling*: Ibid.

318   *It reaffirmed his lifelong love for the outdoors*: Ibid.

319   *still furious about those rude small-town whisperers who had mocked*: Garrett Webster interview.

319   *The IRS garnishments kept them virtually penniless*: Bob Fitzsimmons interview.

319   *Garrett put a small flag in the apartment's front window*: Garber, "Wandering Through the Fog."

319   *He played high school football, though without his father's dedication*: Garrett Webster interview.

319   *"Stay low on your blocks and have fun"*: Ibid.

319 *Garrett, Fitzsimmons, and Jani referred to themselves as the Team*: Ibid.

319 *A fitful sleeper, Webby often sat through long nights in a chair*: Ibid.

320 *"Having him in my corner meant everything"*: Ibid.

320 *"Don't tell him anything"*: Ibid.

320 *"There are seven deadly sins"*: Ibid.

320 *"Dad, you goin' to bed?"*: Ibid.

320 *"I'll tell you about this JFK stuff"*: Ibid.

320 *His father asked Garrett to use his stun gun on him*: Ibid.

320 *"It was supposed to paralyze [him]"*: Ibid.

321 *her husband of twenty-eight years didn't show up*: Pam Webster interview.

321 *"One of the emptiest feelings I've ever had"*: Ibid.

321 *Fitzsimmons sped toward Pittsburgh and called*: Bob Fitzsimmons interview.

321 *Jani called Pam in Wisconsin*: Pam Webster interview.

321 *"Daddy's gone"*: Ibid.

322 *Days later, at the small funeral home in Robinson Township*: *Pittsburgh Post-Gazette*, September 28, 2002.

322 *Harris heard former teammates saying privately*: Meryl Gordon, "Game Over," *Reader's Digest*, March 2003.

322 *Dan sent a check to pay for the funeral*: Pam Webster interview.

322 *Noll told Garrett that there was no player that he had loved*: Garrett Webster interview.

322 *"If Dad had been alive he would've laughed his ass off"*: Ibid.

322 *"Steve Courson looked like a Chippendale dancer"*: Pam Webster interview.

322 *Lambert, ever the soloist, did not attend the funeral, but arranged*: Garrett Webster interview.

322 *"We should never allow the passing of a loved one"*: *Pittsburgh Post-Gazette*, September 28, 2002.

322 *"When we are all together we realize how much we love"*: Terry Bradshaw interview.

323 *"Because he fucked up"*: Dan Radakovich interview.

323 *"He couldn't run across the field"*: Ibid.

323 *"He was a hell of a player and you are pissed"*: Ibid.

323 *"In the beginning, I wasn't sure what it was"*: Franco Harris interview.

323 *The weekend after the funeral, Harris made sure to attend*: Gordon, "Game Over."

323 *one of her former in-laws told her to rot in hell*: Pam Webster interview.

324 *"I don't think any of them blamed me"*: Ibid.

324 *"My God, you look good, your family is intact"*: Ibid.

324 *She put a letter in Webby's casket*: Ibid.

Chapter 21: The Rooneys

PAGE

326 *"They always said the right things"*: Bum Phillips interview.

326 *"You guys aren't taking care of me"*: Art Rooney Jr. interview.

326 *you must keep the Steelers viable,* and in Pittsburgh: Dan Rooney interview.

326 *"Gentlemen, let's discuss and think about":* Carl Peterson interview.

327 *Dan privately reassured him that a job in the Steelers' front office:* J. T. Thomas interview.

327 *"Tunch, keep them together":* Tunch Ilkin interview.

327 *"you didn't get it from me":* Ibid.

327 *But deep down he still was trying to prove value to his father:* Art Rooney Jr. interview.

327 *Once, in a pique, his wife, Kay, told him the draft was more important:* Ibid.

327 *Art Jr. rushed to the men's room at Three Rivers Stadium and threw up, blood:* Ibid.

327 *She began to take them away for a little vacation a day:* Ibid.

328 *"I know he never forgave me for Danny Marino":* Ibid.

328 *Only five Steelers picked in the dozen drafts between:* Rob Ruck, Maggie Jones Patterson, and Michael P. Weber, *Rooney: A Sporting Life* (Lincoln: University of Nebraska Press, 2010), p. 515. The five players were linebackers Robin Cole, Mike Merriweather, and David Little; receiver Louis Lipps; and offensive lineman Tunch Ilkin.

328 *To Dan, it was as if his younger brother had sealed off his department:* Dan Rooney interview.

328 *leather-upholstered with ultramodern cast-iron silver frames:* Art Rooney Jr. with Roy McHugh, *Ruanaidh: The Story of Art Rooney and His Clan* (Pittsburgh: Geyer Printing Company, 2010), pp. 470–71.

329 *"I want you out of the day-to-day business":* Ibid.

329 *"I can't make things happen anymore":* Ibid.

329 *"I didn't need you":* Art Rooney Jr. interview.

329 *"My dad asked me and young Art [II]":* John Rooney interview.

330 *"You cannot have palace revolts":* Art Rooney Jr. interview.

330 *"Our object is to establish direct lines of communication":* *New York Times,* January 7, 1987.

330 *"That was not an easy thing":* Dan Rooney interview.

330 *"But let me say this to you: in all honesty":* Ibid.

330 *"The 1980s was like the second-best decade":* Art Rooney Jr. interview.

331 *"you'll never have to worry about money":* Ibid.

331 *"Are you Dan Rooney's brother?":* Ibid.

331 *He waved away sportswriters, too emotional:* *Pittsburgh Post-Gazette,* August 26, 1988.

331 *"He was the Steelers":* Ibid.

331 *"He was the father figure of an entire region":* *Pittsburgh Press,* August 26, 1988.

331 *"The Chief has been to only a few thousand wakes":* *Pittsburgh Post-Gazette,* August 26, 1988.

331 *About five thousand people paid their respects:* *Pittsburgh Post-Gazette,* August 30, 1998.

331 *As the funeral procession made its way to the cemetery, Dan saw:* Ibid.

331 *"I don't know if there will ever be another":* Roy McHugh interview.

332 *"Up here at Sainte-Anne-de-Beaupré":* Art Rooney Jr. interview.

332 *he reached into a crack in the old man's recliner:* Ibid.

332 *"Don't sell the house":* Ibid.

332   *John chose a small stool his mother had crocheted*: John Rooney interview.

332   *"That belongs here!"*: Ibid.

333   *"I felt we were tearing our history apart"*: Dan Rooney interview.

333   *Dan didn't select any of his parents' possessions*: Ibid.

333   *"just didn't go well with me"*: Ibid.

333   *He also chose the Chief's black Buick automobile*: Art Rooney Jr. interview.

334   *"It was like—my father's life!"*: Ibid.

334   *"Don't Get Emotional"*: "Q&A with Dan Rooney About Noll," *Steelers Digest*, January 4, 1992, p. 10.

334   *During Noll's tenure in Pittsburgh, 170 head*: New York Times, January 5, 1992.

334   *That very morning he had told Noll that he wanted him to return*: Pittsburgh Post-Gazette, December 27, 1991.

335   *"Ready? Because I don't think I can do this twice"*: Bob Labriola, "An Era Comes to an End," *Steelers Digest*, January 4, 1992, p. 6.

335   *"You know, it's much easier coming in"*: Pittsburgh Post-Gazette, December 27, 1991.

335   *"I'll have to step back and see"*: Ibid.

336   *"It was like it happened to a relative"*: Art Rooney Jr. interview.

336   *In 2002, the NFL had just two African American head coaches and one*: Tampa Bay Times, January 19, 2012.

336   *"I felt [the rule] was the important thing"*: Dan Rooney interview.

337   *"To me the legacy of the family is really outstanding"*: Bill Nunn Jr. interview.

337   *"It wasn't like he was some true-blue"*: Art Rooney II interview.

337   *At a rally in Mellon Arena in Pittsburgh he presented Obama*: Pittsburgh Post-Gazette, October 27, 2008.

337   *From Ireland he would watch Steeler games on specially ordered*: Dan Rooney interview.

337   *He had a young family and said the timing simply wasn't right*: Art Rooney II interview.

337   *Art II in the backseat ready to dodge if either flew in*: Ibid.

338   *"Don't worry about filling anybody's shoes"*: Ibid.

339   *In 2006 NFL commissioner Roger Goodell approached Dan and asked*: New York Times, July 9, 2008.

339   *Dan finally offered his four brothers a debt-laden buyout deal*: Wall Street Journal, July 8, 2008.

339   *"Look, you are going to end up with a lot of money"*: Dan Rooney interview.

339   *His brothers retained Goldman Sachs, which, in a secret valuation*: Wall Street Journal, July 8, 2008.

339   *Steelers franchise value at between $800 million and $1.2 billion*: Ibid.

339   *"Once you go out and hire an investment"*: Art Rooney II interview.

339   *"Do you know who you are dealing with"*: Art Rooney Jr. interview.

339   *"He was trying to keep all of us away"*: Ibid.

340   *Art Jr. suffered anxiety and heart palpitations*: Ibid.

340   *"I wanted to divest myself"*: John Rooney interview.

340   *"It's Dan's baby"*: Ibid.

340   *Dan and Art II borrowed about $250 million*: Shira Ovide, "WSJ Blogs: Deal Journal—'Steelers Super Bowl Without the Rooneys? It Almost Happened,' " www.wsj.com, February 4, 2011. This *Wall Street Journal* article can be read at http://blogs.wsj.com/deals/2011/02/04/steelers-super-bowl-without-the-rooneys-it-almost-happened/.

340   *"At the end of the day"*: Art Rooney II interview.

340   *"I learned that he has an emotional attachment"*: Ibid.

340   *"I think our legacy here"*: Dan Rooney interview.

Chapter 22: It's Still Their Town

PAGE

343   *"This raincoat belongs to Art Rooney"*: Art Rooney Jr. interview.

344   *"The Chief wears nice shoes"*: Scene observed at Heinz Field on November 6, 2011, before the Sunday-night game between the Steelers and the Baltimore Ravens.

344   *"Contact sports is the best form"*: J. T. Thomas interview.

344   *Coach Bud Carson gave a big hello to Chuck Noll, except*: Bobby Walden interview.

345   *the two having hiked mountains in the Far West together*: Andy Russell interview.

345   *Lambert huffed that they were Pirates jackets*: Dan Radakovich and Dan Rooney interviews.

345   *"And he didn't say one word to me"*: Greg Lloyd interview.

345   *"What do you think of my ride?"*: Mike Wagner interview.

346   *"Some people are still afraid of Ernie"*: Ibid.

346   *"Joey, you behaving yourself now?"*: Ralph Berlin interview.

346   *"married to a fine lady"*: John Stallworth interview.

346   *"He was always short"*: Rocky Bleier interview.

346   *"Joey, are you using?"*: Reggie Harrison (known today as Kamal Ali Salaam-El) interview.

347   *"I remember seeing you all when you were kids"*: Art Rooney Jr. interview.

347   *President George H. W. Bush in 1989 named Blount his 524th*: Mel Blount with Cynthia Sterling, *The Cross Burns Brightly: A Hall-of-Famer Tackles Racism and Adversity to Help Troubled Boys* (Grand Rapids, Mich.: Zondervan, 1993), p. 18.

347   *"Rocky had deceptive speed"*: Mel Blount Youth Home Celebrity Roast of Rocky Bleier, April 21, 2006, KDKA television, Pittsburgh.

347   *"Rocky's hair loss is not natural"*: Ibid.

348   *"Brad's just a good ol' boy"*: Mel Blount Youth Home Celebrity Roast of Terry Bradshaw, April 16, 2004, KDKA television, Pittsburgh.

348   *"Can I sum up Tony Dungy?"*: Ibid.

348   *"Since we moved from Tampa to Indianapolis"*: Mel Blount Youth Home Celebrity Roast of Lynn Swann, April 20, 2007, KDKA television, Pittsburgh.

348   *"Lynn ran for governor"*: Ibid.

348   *"Our friendship will never die"*: Reggie Harrison (known today as Kamal Ali Salaam-El) interview.

348 *Fuqua underwent six surgeries on his wrists*: John (Frenchy) Fuqua interview.

349 *"What is out there is cold, tragedies"*: Ibid.

349 *"Joe, you should've made that tackle!"*: Ibid.

349 *"Fuck-wuh, you touched that ball!"*: Ibid.

350 *"I made a promise years and years ago"*: Ibid.

Chapter 23: The Legacy Haunted

PAGE

353 *He was born in the Biafran jungle in 1968*: Bennet Omalu interview. Also see Jeanne Marie Laskas, "Game Brain," *GQ*, October 2009.

354 *"Mike, we need to prove them wrong"*: Bennet Omalu interview.

354 *First he cut a V shape to open Webster's chest*: Ibid.

355 *He brought Webster's brain in a plastic tub back to his condo*: Ibid.

355 *He did the bread-loafing of Webster's brain*: Ibid.

355 *"Chronic Traumatic Encephalopathy in a National Football"*: Bennet I. Omalu, M.D., and Steven T. DeKosky, M.D., et al., "Chronic Traumatic Encephalopathy in a National Football League Player," *Journal of Neurosurgery* 57, no. 1 (July 2005): 128–34.

355 *They questioned his work and his interpretations*: Ira R. Casson, Elliot J. Pellman, and David C. Viano, letter to the editor, *Journal of Neurosurgery* 58, no. 5 (May 2006).

355 *"I was like the lone voice in the wilderness"*: Bennet Omalu interview.

356 *Waters had suffered at least fifteen concussions*: *Palm Beach (Fla.) Post*, September 14, 2010.

356 *For a time, in a coat closet at his condominium, Omalu stored*: Bennet Omalu interview.

356 *"You see, in science, when you report one case"*: Ibid.

356 *"I call families to talk to them"*: Garrett Webster interview.

356 *That same month a study under the auspices of the Centers*: *New York Times*, November 16, 2002.

357 *The threat of brain injuries has trickled down to Pop Warner*: *New York Times*, June 14, 2012.

357 *Among the names on the master list are twenty-five*: Two websites maintain updated master lists of concussion-based lawsuits against the NFL and the helmet manufacturer Riddell, Inc.: http://www.washingtontimes.com/footballinjuries/ and http://nflconcussionlitigation.com. The *Washington Times* site groups players by teams.

358 *"I believe every professional [football] player"*: Bennet Omalu interview.

358 *the accumulation of subconcussive hits—estimated at between 1,000*: Jane Leavy, "The Woman Who Would Save Football," Grantland, August 17, 2012. Grantland is a sports-based website at www.grantland.com.

358 *Omalu coined a new name for CTE—Mike Webster's Syndrome*: Bennet Omalu interview.

358 *The US Court of Appeals for the Fourth Circuit*: *New York Times*, December 14, 2006.

358 *"When you put that piece in there"*: Pam Webster interview.

359 *"When you have worked that hard"*: Debbie Furness Saletin interview.

359 *Debbie wondered if her Steeler husband might have suffered any brain*: Ibid.

359 *"So we're cut out of their lives"*: Pam Webster interview.

359 *they wear their Mike Webster jerseys*: Garrett Webster and Pam Webster interviews.

360 *Gilliam said he was writing a book*: Franco Harris interview.

360 *cocaine was found in his system*: *Pittsburgh Post-Gazette*, January 13, 2001.

360 *"wasn't a very strong person as far as character"*: Franco Harris interview.

360 *"I wish I had tried to be a little more mature myself"*: Ibid.

360 *Late on Christmas Eve, Bleier's cell phone rang*: Rocky Bleier interview.

360 *"And you were the last call he made"*: Ibid.

361 *the Reverend Jesse Jackson calling, friends, and former players*: Kim Gilliam Grant interview.

361 *Coach Gilliam launched more than eighty Tennessee State University*: Coach Joe Gilliam Sr. interview.

361 *"He's like the black Paul Brown"*: Bobby Mitchell interview.

361 *"There are no secrets about me and my family"*: Coach Joe Gilliam Sr. interview.

361 *his nineteen-year-old daughter Sonia, struggling with depression, fell*: Ibid.

361 *"I had given my damn life to this place"*: Ibid.

361 *She stripped off his clothes, put him in the bathtub*: Ibid.

361 *The old coach took him to drug rehabilitation centers*: Ibid.

362 *"He was eating Daddy alive"*: Kim Gilliam Grant interview.

362 *"We all recognized that Joey was our jewel"*: Ibid.

363 *"one of the greatest quarterbacks that will never be known"*: Reggie Harrison (known today as Kamal Ali Salaam-El) interview.

363 *"If you live long enough"*: Coach Joe Gilliam Sr. interview.

363 *Gilliam reached in with his butter knife and grabbed*: *Baltimore Sun*, July 20, 1991.

364 *had spoken to the judge as a character witness*: Coach Joe Gilliam Sr. interview.

364 *"I just made sure that things were right"*: Terry Bradshaw interview.

364 *"I lost my job to a cool dude"*: Ibid.

364 *Steve Courson picked up the* Washington Post *while sitting*: Unpublished letter written in 2005 by Steve Courson to a former Steeler teammate. This letter, a rambling, five-thousand-word telling of his post-NFL life odyssey, was retrieved from Courson's computer after his death in November 2005. A copy of this letter was given to the author with the understanding that the name of the teammate to whom it was written would not be used in this book.

364 A lonely way to die: Ibid.

364 *He had beaten alcohol addiction, reaffirmed his faith*: Ibid.

364 *diagnosed, at thirty-three, with dilated cardiomyopathy*: Steve Courson and Lee R. Schreiber, *False Glory: Steelers and Steroids* (Stamford, Conn.: Longmeadow Press, 1991), p. 4.

364 *A treadmill stress test on his forty-ninth birthday produced*: Denise Masciola interview. She was Courson's girlfriend at the time of his death in 2005.

365 *75 percent of the team's offensive linemen used steroids*: Courson and Schreiber, *False Glory*, pp. 48–49.

365 *"When it comes to your quote, 'If you're competitive'"*: *Pittsburgh Press*, July 31, 1988.

365 *"That would be a lie"*: Ibid.

365 *"Steve just wanted badly for [Steelers teammates] to come out"*: Denise Masciola interview.

365 *he admired and loved them still*: Ibid.

365 *"I'm just trying to clean up the league"*: Gary Dunn interview.

365 *"They weren't avoiding us like the plague"*: Denise Masciola interview.

366 *"Football with drugs or without drugs is society's drug"*: Unpublished letter written in 2005 by Steve Courson to a former Steeler teammate.

366 *"The part that is upsetting to me"*: Ibid.

366 *"We all are accountable for, and face"*: Ibid.

366 *But the tree struck Courson in the back, crushed his chest*: *USA Today*, November 11, 2005.

366 *No one mentioned steroids*: Gary Dunn interview.

366 *Kamal Ali Salaam-El takes OxyContin and other medications*: Reggie Harrison (known today as Kamal Ali Salaam-El) interview.

367 *Russell gets occasional massages, whereupon deep pains*: Andy Russell interview.

367 *"I feel like I've been rode hard"*: L. C. Greenwood interview.

367 *"I'm quite sure it's football"*: Donnie Shell interview.

367 *Dunn underwent ten knee surgeries*: Gary Dunn interview.

367 *"No, I don't regret it"*: Ibid.

367 *enroll in the University of North Carolina's memory recovery program*: Reggie Harrison (known today as Kamal Ali Salaam-El) interview.

367 *embrace Moorish American citizenship at a time*: Ibid.

368 *"You can buy yourself a new tongue"*: Ibid.

368 *"You go thirty-five or forty yards"*: Ibid.

368 *"That's what I miss right there!"*: John Banaszak interview.

369 *"I mean, you can't not get your head banged"*: John Stallworth interview.

369 *"It's what separates you from the faceless crowd"*: Randy Grossman interview.

Chapter 24: Noll & the Ambassador

PAGE

370 *Whispering among themselves*: This scene is drawn from Noll's appearance at the Collectors Showcase of America (CSA) sports collectibles show in Chantilly, Virginia, on July 10, 2011.

370 *"I'm like their daddy"*: Bum Phillips interview.

370 *"But Chuck is a private man"*: Jack Ham interview.

371 *"Chuck had that way about him"*: Tunch Ilkin interview.

371 *said he couldn't make a conversation with Noll*: Roy McHugh interview.

371 *"Work hard, keep your mouth shut"*: George Perles interview.

371 *"Marianne wouldn't let us have another bottle"*: Lionel Taylor interview.

371   *Collectors pay $75 for Noll's signature*: Catalog for Collectors Showcase of America (CSA) sports collectibles show in Chantilly, Virginia, on July 10, 2011.

372   *"Mr. Noll will include 1 inscription"*: Ibid.

372   *"I didn't know Chuck did these shows"*: Mike Wagner interview.

372   *"I understand you're bringing up the property values"*: Ibid.

372   *"He let us live our lives"*: Ibid.

372   *"Football is what you are doing now"*: Tony Dungy with Nathan Whitaker, *Quiet Strength: The Principles, Practices, & Priorities of a Winning Life* (Carol Stream, Ill.: Tyndale House, 2007), pp. 57–58.

372   *"It occurred to us that he had been in football"*: Ibid.

373   *"Chuck told me once when I was late"*: Joe Greene interview.

373   *"Some of that roughness that I brought"*: Ibid.

373   *"Probably the thing I appreciate most about football"*: *Steelers Digest*, January 4, 1992, p. 5. This quote is drawn from a transcript of Noll's final press conference.

373   *"Termination is not easy"*: Ibid.

373   *Noll doesn't recognize him at first*: Greg Lloyd interview.

373   *"Dan has my seat!"*: Dan Rooney interview.

373   *The helicopter set down on a rain-soaked field*: *Guardian (U.K.)*, May 23, 2011.

374   *nineteen-year-old shoemaker named Falmouth Kearney*: Ibid.

374   *James Rooney, Dan's great-great-grandfather, left for the New World*: Art Rooney Jr. with Roy McHugh, *Ruanaidh: The Story of Art Rooney and His Clan* (Pittsburgh: Geyer Printing Company, 2010), p. 2.

374   *Dan visited Newry but found no Rooneys*: Dan Rooney interview.

374   *connection made by a genealogist in 2007, and verified*: *Guardian (U.K.)*, May 23, 2011.

374   *"My name is Barack Obama, of the Moneygall O'bamas"*: Ibid.

374   *"We did so much preparation"*: Dan Rooney interview.

374   *Obama noticed how Dan seemed to walk nearly everywhere*: Transcript of President Barack Obama interview with Mark Fainaru-Wada of ESPN's *Outside the Lines*, aired September 10, 2010.

374   *"[He] just writes on the postcard saying, 'How are you doing?'"*: Ibid.

374   *"[Obama] knows everything that's happening"*: Dan Rooney interview.

374   *"We have to get a Guinness for the ambassador"*: Ibid.

375   *"What I like about this is that Lincoln"*: Ibid.

375   *"We'd raised our family for the most part"*: Patricia Rooney interview.

375   *For years Dan walked to Steelers home games*: *New York Times*, January 27, 2009.

375   *"We are in a bit of a discussion"*: Patricia Rooney interview.

376   *"We get everybody to guess what this is"*: Dan Rooney interview.

376   *"We did more things to that bush"*: Ibid.

Chapter 25: The Sauna, Once More

PAGE

377   *"It just was"*: Rocky Bleier interview.

378   *"What's going on in your life?"*: John Stallworth interview.

378   *"We ought to take this in because we may not"*: Ibid.

379   *They need to cherish each other*: Ibid.

Postscript: Mortal Immortals

PAGE

382   *In 1970 one NFL player exceeded three hundred pounds*: *New York Times*, January 28, 2011. This statistic was drawn from a study conducted by the Associated Press.

382   *Franco owns the trademark*: Kim Gamble, "Immaculate Interception," Grantland, December 19, 2012.

382   *be cut out and saved for him, and it was*: Ibid.

382   *Shell challenged him to put God before football*: Donnie Shell interview.

382   *"And what do you benefit if you gain"*: Tony Dungy with Nathan Whitaker, *Quiet Strength: The Principles, Practices, & Priorities of a Winning Life* (Carol Stream, Ill.: Tyndale House, 2007), pp. 50–51. Also *Pittsburgh Post-Gazette*, January 13, 2006.

383   *"I would rather be ashes than dust!"*: *San Francisco Bulletin*, December 2, 1916. This quote also is cited in the introduction (p. vii) of *Jack London's Tales of Adventure*, edited by Irving Shepard, London's literary executor, and published in Garden City, New York, by Doubleday in 1956.

BIBLIOGRAPHY

BOOKS

Anderson, Dave, ed. *The Red Smith Reader.* New York: Random House, 1971.

Bayless, Skip. *God's Coach: The Hymns, Hype, and Hypocrisy of Tom Landry's Cowboys.* New York: Simon & Schuster, 1990.

Bissinger, H. G. *Friday Night Lights: A Town, a Team, and a Dream.* New York: Harper Perennial, 1991.

Bleier, Rocky, with Terry O'Neil. *Fighting Back.* Pittsburgh: Rocky Bleier, Inc., 1975.

Blount, Mel, with Cynthia Sterling. *The Cross Burns Brightly: A Hall-of-Famer Tackles Racism and Adversity to Help Troubled Boys.* Grand Rapids, Mich.: Zondervan, 1993.

Blount, Roy Jr. *About Three Bricks Shy . . . and the Load Filled Up.* Pittsburgh: University of Pittsburgh Press, 2002.

Bradshaw, Terry, with David Fisher. *It's Only a Game.* New York: Pocket Books, 2001.

Bradshaw, Terry, with Buddy Martin. *Looking Deep.* Chicago: Contemporary Books, 1989.

Brown, Paul, with Jack Clary. *PB: The Paul Brown Story.* New York: Signet, 1979.

Callahan, Tom. *Johnny U: The Life & Times of John Unitas.* New York: Three Rivers Press, 2006.

Carroll, Bob. *When the Grass Was Real: Unitas, Brown, Lombardi, Sayers, Butkus, Namath, and All the Rest: The Ten Best Years of Pro Football.* New York: Simon & Schuster, 1993.

Chaney, Matt. *Spiral of Denial: Muscle Doping in American Football.* Warrensburg, Mo.: Four Walls Publishing, 2009.

Cope, Myron. *Double Yoi!* Champaign, Ill.: Sports Publishing, 2002.

Courson, Steve, and Lee R. Schreiber. *False Glory: Steelers and Steroids.* Stamford, Conn.: Longmeadow Press, 1991.

Danyluk, Tom. *The Super '70s: Memories from Pro Football's Greatest Era.* Chicago: Mad Uke Publishing, 2005.

Dubner, Stephen J. *Confessions of a Hero-Worshipper.* New York: Harper Perennial, 2007.

Dungy, Tony, with Nathan Whitaker. *Quiet Strength: The Principles, Practices, & Priorities of a Winning Life.* Carol Stream, Ill.: Tyndale House, 2007.

Finder, Chuck. *The Steelers Encyclopedia.* Philadelphia: Temple University Press, 2012.

Frankl, Viktor E. *Man's Search for Meaning.* New York: Washington Square Press, 1984.

Green, Jerry. *Super Bowl Chronicles: A Sportswriter Reflects on the First 30 Years of America's Game.* Indianapolis: Masters Press, 1995.

Hays, Samuel P., ed. *City at the Point: Essays on the Social History of Pittsburgh.* Pittsburgh: University of Pittsburgh Press, 1989.

Henderson, Thomas "Hollywood," with Peter Knobler. *Out of Control: Confessions of an NFL Casualty.* New York: Pocket Books, 1988.

Henderson, Thomas Hollywood, with Frank Luksa. *In Control: The Rebirth of an NFL Legend.* Austin, Tex.: Thomas Henderson Publishing, 2004.

Hendrickson, Paul. *Hemingway's Boat: Everything He Loved in Life, and Lost, 1934–1961.* New York: Alfred A. Knopf, 2011.

Hillenbrand, Laura. *Seabiscuit: An American Legend.* New York: Random House, 2001.

Holtzman, Jerome. *No Cheering in the Press Box.* New York: Holt, Rinehart, & Winston, 1973.

Jaworski, Ron, with Greg Cosell and David Plaut. *The Games That Changed the Game: The Evolution of the NFL in Seven Sundays.* New York: Ballantine Books, 2010.

Jenkins, Dan. *Semi-Tough.* New York: Scribner, 1984.

Junger, Sebastian. *War.* New York: Twelve, 2010.

Kahn, Roger. *The Boys of Summer.* New York: Harper & Row, 1972.

Kindred, Dave. *Heroes, Fools & Other Dreamers: A Sportswriter's Gallery of Extraordinary People.* Marietta, Ga.: Longstreet Press, 1988.

Lardner, John. *It Beats Working.* Philadelphia: J. B. Lippincott, 1947.

Lott, Ronnie, with Jill Lieber. *Total Impact: Straight Talk from Football's Hardest Hitter.* New York: Doubleday, 1991.

MacCambridge, Michael. *America's Game: The Epic Story of How Pro Football Captured a Nation.* New York: Random House, 2004.

Maraniss, David. *Clemente: The Passion and Grace of Baseball's Last Hero.* New York: Simon & Schuster, 2007.

———. *When Pride Still Mattered: A Life of Vince Lombardi.* New York: Simon & Schuster, 1999.

Meggyesy, Dave. *Out of Their League.* New York: Paperback Library, 1971.

Miller, John J. *The Big Scrum: How Teddy Roosevelt Saved Football.* New York: HarperCollins, 2011.

Millman, Chad, and Shawn Coyne. *The Ones Who Hit Hardest: The Steelers, the Cowboys, the '70's, and the Fight for America's Soul.* New York: Gotham Books, 2010.

O'Brien, Jim. *Lambert: The Man in the Middle . . . and Other Outstanding Linebackers.* Pittsburgh: James P. O'Brien Publishing, 2004.

Omalu, Dr. Bennet. *Play Hard, Die Young: Football, Dementia, Depression, and Death.* Lodi, Calif.: Neo-Forenxis Books, 2008.

Otto, Jim, with Dave Newhouse. *Jim Otto: The Pain of Glory.* Champaign, Ill.: Sports Publishing, 2000.

Pearlman, Jeff. *Sweetness: The Enigmatic Life of Walter Payton.* New York: Gotham Books, 2011.

Pendergrast, Mark. *For God, Country, and Coca-Cola: The Definitive History of the Great American Soft Drink and the Company That Makes It.* New York: Basic Books, 2000.

Pomerantz, Gary M. *Where Peachtree Meets Sweet Auburn: The Saga of Two Families and the Making of Atlanta.* New York: Scribner, 1996.

Povich, Shirley. *All Those Mornings . . . at the* Post. Edited by Lynn, Maury, and David Povich and George Solomon. New York: Public Affairs, 2005.

Rice, Grantland. *The Tumult and the Shouting: My Life in Sport.* New York: A. S. Barnes, 1954.

Richmond, Peter. *Badasses: The Legend of Snake, Foo, Dr. Death, and John Madden's Oakland Raiders.* New York: HarperCollins, 2010.

Roberts, Randy, and James S. Olson. *John Wayne: American.* Lincoln: University of Nebraska Press, 1995.

Roberts, Randy, and David Welky, eds. *One for the Thumb: The New Steelers Reader.* Pittsburgh: University of Pittsburgh Press, 2006.

Rooney, Art, Jr., with Roy McHugh. *Ruanaidh: The Story of Art Rooney and His Clan.* Pittsburgh: Geyer Printing Company, 2010.

Rooney, Dan, as told to Andrew E. Masich and David F. Halaas. *My 75 Years with the Pittsburgh Steelers and the NFL.* New York: Da Capo Press, 2007.

Ruck, Rob, Maggie Jones Patterson, and Michael P. Weber. *Rooney: A Sporting Life.* Lincoln: University of Nebraska Press, 2010.

Russell, Andy. *Beyond the Goalpost.* Pittsburgh: Self-published, 2009.

Trollope, Anthony. *North America*, vol. 1. Philadelphia: J. B. Lippincott, 1863.

Wenner, Jann S., ed. *Fear and Loathing at* Rolling Stone: *The Essential Writing of Hunter S. Thompson.* New York: Simon & Schuster, 2011.

Wexell, Jim. *Tales from Behind the Steel Curtain: The Best Stories of the '79 Steelers.* Champaign, Ill.: Sports Publishing, 2004.

Whitman, Walt. *Specimen Days & Collect.* New York.: Dover, 1995.

Zellers, Rob, and Gene Collier. *The Chief.* Pittsburgh: University of Pittsburgh Press, 2008.

INTERVIEWS

The author conducted more than 200 interviews for this book between January 2010 and February 2013. Many subjects graciously agreed to multiple interviews; Joe Greene, for instance, participated in a three-hour interview one evening at the William Penn Hotel in Pittsburgh, a four-hour interview in the living room of his home near Dallas, and in a lengthy phone interview. Dan Rooney shared two separate interviews at his office and a third at his home. In addition, NFL Films provided the author transcripts of its interviews with the following Steelers: Ray Mansfield, Franco Harris, Dwight White, Chuck Noll, Joe Greene, John Stallworth, Jack Lambert, and Lynn Swann, and with the Oakland Raiders' Jim Otto.

Interviews Conducted by the Author

1970s Steelers (Players, Coaches, Officials, Family Members)
Bahr, Matt; Banaszak, John; Beatty, Chuck; Berlin, Ralph; Bleier, Ellen; Bleier, Pamela; Bleier, Rocky; Blount, Mel; Bradshaw, Terry; Butler, Jack; Dunn, Gary; Fuqua, John (Frenchy); Gilliam, Craig; Gilliam, Joe Sr.; Gordon, Joe; Grant, Kimberly Gilliam; Gravelle, Gordon; Greene, Agnes; Greene, Joe (Mean); Greenwood, L. C.; Grossman, Randy; Haley, Dick; Ham, Jack; Hanratty, Terry; Harris, Franco; Harrison, Reggie (Kamal Ali Salaam-El); Hoak, Dick; Holmes, Roderick (Byron); Kiely, Ed; Lewis, Frank; Mullins, Gerry (Moon); Nunn, Bill, Jr.; Nunn, Bill, III; Parisi, Tony; Perles, George; Radakovich, Dan; Riecke, Lou; Rooney, Art, Jr.; Rooney, Art, II; Rooney, Dan; Rooney, John; Rooney, Patricia; Rooney, V. Tim; Russell, Andy; Saletin, Debbie Furness; Shell, Donnie; Stallworth, John; Taylor, Lionel; Thomas, J. T.; Wagner, Mike; Walden, Bobby; Webster, Garrett; Webster, Pam; White, Karen; Wiedenhofer, Bob (Woody); Winston, Dennis (Dirt).

NFL
Accorsi, Ernie; Brandt, Gil; Browne, Joe; Buehler, George; Casserly, Charley; Cronan, Pete; Fleener, Coby; Ilkin, Tunch; Kovach, Jim; Lloyd, Greg; Long, Howie; Lott, Ronnie; Mansperger, Dick; Meggyesy, David; Michaels, Walt; Mitchell, Bobby; Moore, Bob; Murphy, Mark; Otto, Jim; Pastorini, Dan; Peterson, Carl; Phillips, Bum; Rudnay, Jack; Siani, Mike; Spadia, Lou; Tomlin, Mike; Vella, John; Villapiano, Phil; Walls, Everson.

Others
Apkarian, Greg; Atkins, Tom; Blount, Roy, Jr.; Booth, Clark; Buswell, Blair; Callahan, Tom; Chaney, Matt; Fitzsimmons, Bob; Garner, Phil; Hawkey, Penny; Horrigan, Joe; Levosky, Sharon; Leyland, Jim; Litwack, Leon; Lundquist, Verne; Makris, Bill; Masciola, Denise; Mathieson, Andy; Mazeroski, Bill; McHugh, Roy; Omalu, Dr. Bennet; Ord, Michael; Perry, Maxine; Ruck, Rob; Stellino, Vito; Tekulve, Kent; Turley, Shannon; Vento, Al; Zellers, Rob.

Magazines

Advertising Age; Black Sports; Dolphins Digest; Ebony; ESPN the Magazine; Esquire; Family Weekly; Golf Digest; GQ; Inc.; Jet; Newsweek; New Yorker; NFL GameDay; People; Playboy; Pro!; Pro Football Weekly; Reader's Digest; Sport; Sports Illustrated; Steelers Digest; Time.

Newspapers

Akron Beacon-Journal; Baltimore News-American; Baltimore Sun; Beaumont (Tex.) Enterprise; Beaver County (Pa.) Times; Boston Globe; Canton (Ohio) Repository; Chicago Sun-Times; Chicago Tribune; Christian Science Monitor; Cleveland Plain Dealer; Dallas Morning News; Dallas Times-Herald; Detroit News; Evening Journal (N.Y.); Fort Lauderdale News and Sun-Sentinel;

Huntsville (Ala.) Times; Kansas City Star; Los Angeles Herald Examiner; Los Angeles Times; McKeesport (Pa.) Daily News; Miami Herald; Newark Star-Ledger; Newsday; New York American; New York Daily News; New York Post; New York Times; New York World-Telegram; Oakland Tribune; Palm Beach (Fla.) Post; Philadelphia Daily News; Philadelphia Evening Bulletin; Philadelphia Inquirer; Pittsburgh Business Times; Pittsburgh Courier; Pittsburgh Post-Gazette; Pittsburgh Press; Pittsburgh Tribune-Review; Provo (Ut.) Daily Herald; Real Paper (Mass.); *Rome (Ga.) News-Tribune; San Diego Union-Tribune; San Francisco Bulletin; San Francisco Chronicle; San Francisco Examiner; St. Louis Post-Dispatch; Temple (Tex.) Daily Telegram; Tuscaloosa News; USA Today; Valley News (Pa.) Dispatch; Wall Street Journal; Washington (Pa.) Observer-Reporter; Washington Post; Washington Star; Wisconsin State Journal.*

Medical and Academic Journals

American Journal of Forensic Medicine and Pathology; Journal of Forensic Nursing; Journal of Neurosurgery; Journal of Sport History; Journal of Sports Economics.

Dissertation

Deardorff, Donald L., II. "American Masculinity and the Gridiron: The Development of the Football Narrative." PhD diss., University of Rhode Island, 1994.

Court Documents

Sunny Jani (as administrator of the Estate of Mike Webster, deceased), Plaintiff, v. The Bert Bell/Pete Rozelle NFL Player Retirement Plan and The NFL Player Supplemental Disability Plan, Defendants; United States District Court for the District of Maryland (Northern Division), Civil Action No. WDQ-04-cv-1606.

Websites Monitoring NFL Concussion Litigation

http://nflconcussionlitigation.com
http://www.washingtontimes.com/footballinjuries/

Family Booklets and Correspondence

Bleier, Rocky. Letters from Vietnam to his parents, Bob and Ellen Bleier, in Appleton, Wis., June 1969 to September 1969. Personal papers of Ellen Bleier.

Hall, Clyde W., and Maud L. Blount Hall. *The Life and Times of Charlie and Mary Ann Sharpe of Montgomery County Georgia: An African-American Family.* Savannah, Ga.: Self-published, n.d.

Football Catalogs and Guides

Pittsburgh Steelers annual media guides, 1967–1991.

Audiotapes

Holmes, Ernie, Rev. A Sunday sermon, n.d. Personal files of his son, Roderick (Byron) Holmes.

Induction speeches at the Pro Football Hall of Fame by the following Steelers: Mel Blount, Terry Bradshaw, Joe Greene, Jack Ham, Franco Harris, Jack Lambert, Chuck Noll, Art Rooney Sr., Dan Rooney, John Stallworth, Lynn Swann, Mike Webster. Audio files at the Ralph Wilson, Jr. Pro Football Research and Preservation Center, Pro Football Hall of Fame, Canton, Ohio.

Documentary, Videotape, and Compact Disc

America's Game: The Super Bowl Champions, a series produced by NFL Films, on Super Bowls IX (Steelers v. Vikings), X (Steelers v. Cowboys), XIII (Steelers v. Cowboys), and XIV (Steelers v. Rams).

Joe Gilliam: What Could Have Been but Never Was, an eleven-minute independent documentary film by Dexter Rogers, producer, 2011. http://www.youtube.com/watch?v =oTZ0idRGDjc.

Mel Blount Youth Home Celebrity Roast, 2004–2011, DVD created annually by KDKA television, Pittsburgh.

Libraries and Archives Consulted

The Coca-Cola Company archives, Atlanta, Ga.; Doe Library, University of California, Berkeley; Green Library, Stanford University; Heinz History Center, Pittsburgh; Hillman Library, University of Pittsburgh; NFL Films, Mount Laurel, N.J.; Pittsburgh Steelers archives, Pittsburgh; Ralph Wilson, Jr. Pro Football Research and Preservation Center, Pro Football Hall of Fame, Canton, Ohio.

INDEX

ABC, 258, 298
ABC Sports, 297
About Three Bricks Shy of a Load (Blount), 175
Accorsi, Ernie, 42
Advertising Age, 189
AFC title games, 148, 211
  of 1972, 101
  of 1974, 148–49, 150, 152, 158, 159–61,
    162–70, 174, 175, 182, 249
  of 1975, 207–8, 213
  of 1984, 328
Afghanistan war, 253–54, 294
African American athletes, 48, 49, 155
  in baseball, 26–27, 49–50, 51, 56, 336
  drafting of, 47, 53, 56, 66–67, 73
  NFL's reluctant use of, as quarterbacks, 49, 121,
    123, 125
  Nunn's All-America football teams of, 46, 47,
    50, 52, 54
  Nunn's closeness with, 49–50
  racist mail received by, 8–9
  scouting of, 45–46, 54, 55, 56, 63, 71, 112,
    113, 125
  segregated living arrangements and facilities for,
    50, 60, 123
  team racial divisions and, 80–81
  see also specific black athletes
African American colleges, 8, 45–46, 47, 50, 54,
    55, 56, 113, 121, 123, 124, 155, 362
African Americans, 123, 124
  in NFL coaching positions, 53, 122, 336
  see also race relations
Alabama, University of, 154
Alabama A&M University, 56, 113, 154, 155,
    291, 293
Alcoa, 41
Ali, Muhammad, 48, 50, 54, 73, 312
Allen, Jimmy, 115, 116, 165, 219

Alzheimer's disease, 355, 356, 371
Amen Clinic, 260
American Football League (AFL), 43, 62, 65, 68
American Ireland Funds, 337
American Sportsman, The (TV show), 200
Americus Republican Club, 26
Anderson, Donny, 76, 226
Anderson, Ken, 135, 194
Apkarian, Greg, 157
Appleton, Wis., 76, 77, 78
Aqueduct Racetrack, 30, 38
Arizona Cardinals, 240, 248
Arkansas Agricultural Mechanical & Normal
    College (AM&N), 8, 56, 71, 144
Armstrong, Otis, 140
Army, US, 293, 294
Army football, 141
Astrodome, 133, 239
A-Team, The (TV show), 242
Atkinson, George, 151, 208
  slander lawsuit filed by, 211–16
Atlanta Falcons, 67, 85, 134–35, 140
Atlantic, 37
Augusta National Country Club, 299
August Wilson Center for African American
    Culture, 242, 280
Austin, Bill, 45, 61, 117

Bahr, Matt, 188, 322
Bailes, Julian, 356
Baltimore Colts, 61, 62, 63, 65, 66, 84, 110, 111,
    127, 131, 139, 148, 177, 362
Banaszak, John, 196, 198, 218, 219, 227, 357,
    368
Banaszak, Mary, 227
Banaszak, Pete, 167
Banks, Earl "Papa Bear," 50
Barney, Lem, 50

baseball, 5, 25, 26, 27, 36, 47, 51, 53, 99, 257, 326
    black players in, 26–27, 49–50, 51, 56, 336
Basketball Association of America, 52
Baugh, Sammy, 44
Bayless, Skip, 220
Beatty, Chuck, 68, 69, 71, 79, 81, 82
Beaver County Times, 118
Bechtel, Sam, 118
Bednarik, Chuck, 64
Bee, Clair, 51
Bell, Bert, 27, 38
Bell, Cool Papa, 27
Bell, Theo, 245, 288
Belmont Stakes, 27
Bengtson, Phil, 370
Berlin, Ralph "the Plumber," 72, 81, 94, 110, 116–17, 128, 144, 179, 190, 201, 210, 238–39, 283, 305, 346
Bidwell, Charles, 27, 224
Biederman, Les, 65
Black Brother on Black in Black, 91
Black Colleges All-America teams, 46, 47, 50, 52, 54
Black Nationalists, 91
Black Sox scandal, 5
Black Sunday, 208
Blair, Matt, 179
Blair, Tony, 254
Blanda, George, 164, 165, 307
Bleier, Bob, 76
Bleier, Ellen, 76, 77
Bleier, Jan, 285
Bleier, Pamela, 76, 78
Bleier, Rocky, 15, 75–79, 82, 94, 127, 132, 134, 135, 162, 167, 181, 192, 193–94, 196, 198, 207, 227, 262, 274, 281, 283, 284, 285, 292, 309, 316, 346–48, 360, 365, 377
    as butt of team jokes, 75, 80
    combat injuries suffered by, 75, 76–78
    military service of, 75–77, 80, 181, 182, 196
    1972 season of, 80
    in 1974 playoffs, 165, 166
    playing injuries of, 188
    in Super Bowl IX, 178, 179, 183
    TV movie on, 189, 348
BLESTO (Bears, Lions, Eagles, Steelers Talent Organization), 44, 45, 54, 66, 73, 84, 109, 110, 115
Blood (McNally), Johnny, 225, 279
Blount, Mel, 6, 7, 12, 14, 16, 56, 73, 80, 139, 175, 188, 193, 200, 211, 215, 232, 237, 245, 262, 264, 274, 275, 288, 292, 298, 316, 322, 372
    home for wayward boys founded by, 265, 280, 291, 347–48
    in 1974 playoffs, 164, 165
    1974 season of, 141
    Noll's brief falling out with, 212, 215, 216

    in Super Bowl IX, 179, 250
    in training camps, 154
Blount, Roy, 175–76, 181
Blount, Tianda, 347
Board, Dwaine, 275
Booth, Clark, 206–8
Borkowski, Iggy, 119
Boston Celtics, 5, 232
Boston University School of Medicine, 356
boxing, 4, 25, 26, 28, 30, 38, 50, 120, 180, 271, 354
Bradley, Ed, 179, 357
Bradshaw, Rachel and Erin, 266, 267
Bradshaw, Terry, 3, 4, 11, 13–14, 16, 80, 81, 121, 122, 123, 127–31, 162, 178–79, 188, 190, 192, 196–202, 209, 210, 212, 214, 234, 237, 248, 252–69, 271, 284, 288, 291, 292, 302–3, 320, 322, 323, 328, 333, 347, 348, 363, 364, 376, 377
    acting career of, 189, 201–2, 256
    broadcasting career of, 252, 255–56, 257–59, 260, 264, 267–69, 285, 286, 348
    celebrity of, 13, 189, 196, 198–99, 200, 253, 255–57, 259, 264
    Chief's unwavering support of, 127–28, 130, 188, 197, 253, 262
    concussions of, 198, 201, 259, 260
    controversial comments of, 256–57, 258, 266, 286
    country music career of, 189, 198–200
    endorsements of, 189, 256
    estrangement from former teammates of, 14, 261, 262, 263, 264–65, 266, 284–86, 322, 379
    failed marriages of, 128
    final seasons of, 261, 265
    "good-ol'-boy" persona of, 254–55, 256, 258, 263, 348, 379
    Hall of Fame induction of, 261, 262–63, 266, 298
    inconsistent play of, 121, 135, 166, 167
    injuries of, 16, 126, 128, 197, 201, 254, 259–60, 261, 296
    intelligence ridiculed in, 128, 129, 175, 183, 184, 197, 199, 200, 250, 255
    loneliness and isolation of, 127, 131, 196, 197, 198, 201, 264, 266
    media relations with, 175, 183, 184, 252–53
    NFL stats of, 121, 259
    in 1972 playoffs, 92, 93, 94, 95, 96, 99, 129, 267, 351, 382, 383
    in 1974 playoffs, 148, 164, 165, 166
    1974 season of, 134–35, 137, 155, 167
    Noll's complicated relationship with, 128, 129–30, 252, 261–62, 265–66, 277, 373, 379
    post-football life and career of, 252, 253–59, 264, 267–69
    postgame saunas of, 192, 193, 195, 253

quarterback controversy and, 121, 126, 127–28, 129–31, 134–35, 136, 137, 167, 364
religious faith of, 131, 200, 210
retirement of, 261–62, 274
in return to Heinz Field, 266–67
scouting and drafting of, 73, 197
on speaking circuit, 254–55, 257, 259
Starbuck's relationship with, 199, 200, 201
in Super Bowl IX, 177, 179–80, 183
in Super Bowl X, 197–98
in Super Bowl XIV, 289, 290
television appearances of, 198, 199, 200, 256, 257
in training camps, 126, 129, 252, 261, 296
uneasy fan relationship with, 128, 129, 197, 262, 264, 266–67, 378
on USO tour in Afghanistan, 253–54
at Webster's Hall of Fame induction, 312–14, 315
brain damage, 16, 17, 30, 278, 316, 323, 354, 355–59, 366, 367, 381–82
in lawsuits against NFL, 17, 357–58
research on, 355–57
Brain Injury Research Institute (BIRI), 356
Branch, Cliff, 92, 164, 165, 166, 215
Brandt, Gil, 44, 113–14
Brooklyn Dodgers, 51
Brookshier, Tom, 116, 288
Brown, Dave, 245
Brown, Jim, 42, 60, 63–64, 89, 237, 257, 263, 274, 278, 279
Brown, Larry, 73, 180, 227, 285
Brown, Paul, 14, 42, 58, 59–60, 64, 65, 105, 122, 135, 136, 159, 361
Brown, Roosevelt, 50
Brown, Vanessa, 227
Brown, Willie, 213, 216
Brown v. Board of Education, 51
Bryant, Bear, 154, 290
Buchanan, Buck, 50, 161
Buchanon, Willie, 83
Buehler, George, 163–64
Buffalo Bills, 65, 67, 89, 125, 148, 149
Burk, Adrian, 97
Bush, George H. W., 347
Bush, George W., 254, 281, 298, 320
Buswell, Blair, 263
Butkus, Dick, 73, 140
Butler, Jack, 40–41, 45, 177
Byrd, James, 242
Byrne, Ray, 41, 43

Callahan, Tom, 65
Campbell, Earl, 12, 192, 236, 274, 279
Campbell, Jim, 334
Canada, 123, 125
Candlestick Park, 9
Canton, Miss., 143–44

Carlos, John, 55
Carnegie, Andrew, 24, 37, 325
Carney, Art, 189
Carr, Roger, 115
Carson, Bud, 14, 96, 109, 165, 175, 181, 287, 344
Carter, Jimmy, 188, 248
Casper, Dave, 111
Casserly, Charley, 112
CBS, 239, 255, 258, 348
CBS Evening News, 127
Centers for Disease Control and Prevention, 356
Charles, Ezzard, 49, 181, 271
Charleston, Oscar, 26
Chester, Raymond, 98
Chicago Bears, 43, 72, 73, 126, 204, 240, 274, 361
Chicago Cardinals, 37
Chomyszak, Steve, 128
Christine, Bill, 129
Chronic Traumatic Encephalopathy (CTE), 353, 355–58
Churchill, Winston, 6, 319
Cincinnati Bengals, 89, 122, 128, 135, 136, 155, 215, 367
civil rights movement, 9, 48, 55, 60, 105, 290
Civil War, U.S., 12, 36, 317
Clack, Jim, 82, 118, 166, 180, 245, 365
Clark, Boobie, 209
Clark, Dwight, 10, 232
Clay, Cassius, *see* Ali, Muhammad
Clemente, Roberto, 5, 48, 49–50, 93, 181, 276
Cleveland Browns, 9, 63, 75, 89, 90, 125, 134, 135, 140, 141, 190, 196, 201, 215, 239, 259, 349
   Noll as player on, 14, 58, 59–60, 63–65, 105, 135, 191
Cleveland Stadium, 201
Cline, Tony, 94
Clinton, Hillary, 337
CNN, 348, 354, 364
Cobb, Ty, 25, 41
Coca-Cola, 189, 234–36, 238
cocaine, 218, 255, 301, 360
Cole, Larry, 197, 198
Collier, Blanton, 63
Collier, Gene, 331
Collier, Mike, 4
Collins, Rip, 25
concussions, 12, 16, 198, 201, 208, 212–13, 250, 259, 260, 278, 356, 358, 382
Conn, Billy, 4, 24, 38, 120, 173, 270
Connors, Chuck, 257
Conti, Samuel, 211–12
Cope, Myron, 78, 79–80, 90–91, 92, 100, 283–84
   "dress-off" competitions of, 79, 80, 81, 82
Corum, Bill, 29, 171
Cosell, Howard, 79

Courson, Steve, 221–22, 301, 304, 319, 322,
 364–66, 377
 death of, 366
 massive build of, 221, 322
 steroid use of, 221–22, 223, 364, 365
Cowher, Bill, 240, 335–36
Crawford Grill, 27, 49, 53, 280
Crimson Tide, 154, 290
Cronan, Debbie, 10
Cronan, Peter, 10
Cronin, Joe, 25
Crouse, Buck, 28, 30
Csonka, Larry, 180

Dalby, Dave, 93
Dallas Cowboys, 5–6, 10, 44, 66, 122, 127, 141,
 162, 206, 220, 305
 drafting of players by, 43–44, 54, 111,
 113–14
 in Super Bowl X, 197–98, 208, 368
 in Super Bowl XIII, 187, 188, 250, 255
Daugherty, Duffy, 126
Davis, Al, 212, 268, 285
Davis, Clarence, 163
Davis, Sam, 71, 190
Davis, Steve, 134
Davis, Willie, 50
Dawson, Dermontti, 306
Dawson, Len, 42
Dean, Dizzy, 257
DeBartolo, Eddie, 232
dementia, 354, 357
dementia pugilistica, 30, 354
Democratic National Convention (2008), 280
Dent, Richard, 361
Denver Broncos, 125, 131–32, 139, 140, 162,
 188, 362
Depression, Great, 17, 25, 29, 338
DeRogatis, Al, 249
Detroit, Mich., 79, 92, 348
Detroit Lions, 305
Dianabol, 221, 222, 223
Dickey, Eldridge, 49
dilated cardiomyopathy, 364
Dinah Shore Show, The, 198
DiNardo, Dirt, 195
Ditka, Mike, 204, 240
Diven, Joey, 119, 172–73, 183
Domres, Marty, 139
Duerson, Dave, 357
Dungy, James, 382
Dungy, Tony, 189, 264, 336, 348, 372, 382–83
Dunn, Gary, 12, 192, 195, 222, 223, 238, 305–6,
 322, 357, 365, 366, 367, 382
Duquesne University, 37, 41, 53, 335
Durocher, Leo, 90

Easterling, Ray, 357
Easton, Richie, 119

Edwards, Glen "Chobee Kid," 7, 8, 12, 140, 165,
 175, 177, 193, 357
 1974 season of, 141, 179, 215
 in Super Bowl IX, 12, 177, 179, 250
elections, US, of 2008, 248, 280, 336–37, 338,
 374
Eller, Carl, 177
Empire City Racetrack, 28, 30
Equal Opportunity Commission, 187
ESPN, 312, 354
Esquire, 81

Failure to Launch, 256
False Glory: Steelers and Steroids (Courson), 365
Farley, Jim, 23–24, 101
Favre, Brett, 258
Fawcett, Farrah, 236
Fenway Park, 236
Fighting Back: The Rocky Bleier Story, 189, 348
Finley, Charles, 101, 204
Fitzsimmons, Bob, 316–17, 319, 321, 355, 356
Flaherty, Peter, 168
Flood, Curt, 49
Florida State University, 105, 106–7, 115
Fontainebleau Hotel, 172–73, 174, 176, 184
football, 51, 67, 106, 126, 144, 232, 234, 249,
 295, 302, 353, 359, 366, 368, 371, 373,
 381–82
 Bradshaw's controversial comments on,
 256–57, 258, 266
 rise in popularity of, 5, 10, 171, 174, 180, 223,
 326
 violence in, 10–11, 12–13, 17, 64, 67, 95, 138,
 139, 161, 207, 212–13, 214, 215, 249, 250,
 288, 368, 369, 381–82
 see also National Football League
football players, 68, 294
 brain damage in, 16, 17, 278, 316, 323, 354,
 355–59, 366, 367, 381
 commercials and endorsements of, 177,
 188–89, 234–36, 256
 concussions and head trauma of, 10–11,
 12–13, 16, 17, 64, 73, 162, 198, 201,
 207–8, 212–13, 250, 259, 260, 278, 279,
 316, 323, 354, 356, 358, 367, 368, 369, 382
 depression suffered by, 260, 264, 300, 310,
 354, 355, 357
 injury-related lawsuits filed against NFL by, 17,
 250, 357–58
 long-term/permanent ailments suffered by,
 10–11, 16, 17, 95, 206–7, 237, 259–60,
 278–79, 288, 301, 308, 310, 316, 317,
 348–49, 355, 358, 366–67, 368–69, 381
 military service of, 64, 75–77, 105, 111, 181,
 182, 191
 off-season jobs held by, 15, 41, 117
 post-career transitional trauma of, 16, 306–7,
 355, 359, 378
 shorter life expectancy of, 245, 260, 278

spouses' lifestyle with, 225–28
steroid use of, 10, 11, 220–21, 222–23, 245, 304
suicides of, 355, 356, 357
Forbes Field, 40–41, 43, 49, 88, 91, 93, 99, 271
Ford, Gerald, 187
Foreman, Chuck, 178, 182
Foundation for the National Institutes of Health (NIH), 356
Fourth Circuit Court of Appeals, US, 358
Fox network, 258, 259, 260, 348
Fox NFL Sunday, 256, 267–69
Franco's Italian Army (fan club), 89–91, 92, 94, 95–96, 97, 101, 270, 271, 285
Frankl, Viktor, 318
Franklin, Aretha, 79
Franklin Field, 74
free agency, free agents, 9, 109–10, 111–12, 116–17, 196
Freeh, Louis J., 282
Freyvogel, Rodgers, 193
Frick, Henry Clay, 24, 325
Fright Night, 242–43
Fugett, Jean, 206
Fuqua, John "Frenchy," 13, 15, 75, 78–79, 80, 87–88, 92, 122, 131, 134, 190, 210, 211, 296, 343, 348–52, 357
    Holmes's bachelor party and, 216–17, 218, 219–20
    in Immaculate Reception play, 94, 95, 97, 99, 129, 231, 267, 348, 349–51
    injuries and surgeries of, 16, 278, 348–49, 367
    NFL stats of, 78, 349
    outrageous clothes of, 78, 79, 81–82, 343, 349
    showmanship and storytelling of, 78, 82, 285, 349, 350, 351
Furness, Debbie, 225–28, 358–59
Furness, Steve, 122, 174, 218, 226, 377
    post-football life of, 359
    in trade to Tampa, 228

Galimore, Willie, 50
Garagiola, Joe, 177
Gatski, Frank, 64, 191
Gehrig, Lou, 152, 358
Gerela, Roy, 14, 93, 98, 209, 348
Germany, Nazi, 86–87, 92, 272, 273
Gibson, Bob, 81
Gibson, Josh, 5, 27, 336
Gilliam, Barbara, 346, 360
Gilliam, Craig, 127, 132, 133
Gilliam, Joe, Jr., 14, 16, 80–81, 121–26, 154–55, 180, 345, 346, 359–64
    death of, 360–61
    drug addiction of, 133, 208–11, 270, 346, 360, 361–62, 363
    fun-loving personality of, 122, 123
    hate mail received by, 8–9, 132–33
    media attention on, 127, 131, 132, 133

nicknames of, 121, 124, 126, 209
1974 season of, 125–26, 131–32, 133–34, 136, 137
onfield struggles of, 133, 134, 136, 210
quarterback controversy and, 121–22, 126, 127, 129, 133–34, 135, 136, 137
as racial pioneer, 125, 131, 132
scouting and drafting of, 56, 125
slim physique of, 121, 122, 125
as student athlete, 121, 124–25, 362
in training camps, 81, 122–23, 126
Gilliam, Joe, Sr., 81, 123–25, 132–33, 360–63, 364
    coaching career of, 124, 361
    son's drug use and, 210, 361–62
Gilliam, John, 12, 179, 250
Gilliam, Joi, 132
Gilliam, Pa Henry, 123
Gilliam, Ruth, 124–25, 132–33, 361, 362, 363
Gilliam, Sonia, 361, 363
Gillman, Sid, 65, 222
Giuliani, Rudy, 254–55
Glick, Gary, 42
Goodell, Roger, 17, 339, 351–52
Gordon, Joe, 110, 175, 191, 266, 275–76, 282–83, 312, 360
Gowdy, Curt, 97, 177, 200
Gradishar, Randy, 131
Graham, Billy, 257
Graham, Otto, 135
Grambling State University, 50, 56, 113, 124, 362
Grant, Kim Gilliam, 362
Gravelle, Gordon, 9, 162, 165, 261–62
Great Depression, 17, 25, 29, 338
Greb, Harry, 24, 28
Green Bay Packers, 5, 9, 44, 63, 76, 130, 174, 188, 226, 232, 300, 370
Greene, Agnes, 4, 68–69, 176, 203, 205, 237, 239, 248, 249, 250, 251
Greene, "Mean" Joe, 3–4, 5, 6, 8, 11, 12, 16, 58–59, 66–69, 78, 80, 85, 87, 92, 94, 96, 107, 112, 128, 130–31, 138–39, 141, 142, 147, 148–49, 155, 161, 162, 167, 168, 172, 173–74, 176, 184, 190, 197, 200, 202, 203, 206, 208, 217, 219, 226, 232, 236–42, 244, 246, 247, 248–51, 264, 265, 271, 275, 284, 285, 288, 289, 290, 295–96, 311, 328, 343, 344, 346, 348, 349, 372–73, 376, 377, 381
    anger and combativeness of, 3, 4, 8, 59, 60–61, 66, 67–68, 72–73, 188, 239
    on card show/memorabilia circuit, 241–42, 246
    Chief's special relationship with, 4, 170, 204–5, 238, 331, 333
    Coke commercial of, 189, 234–36, 238
    contract holdout of, 70–71
    final seasons of, 227–28
    first training camp of, 71–72
    at funerals for teammates, 244, 245–46, 247
    Hall of Fame induction of, 236, 298

Greene, "Mean" Joe (*cont.*)
  injuries and ailments of, 16, 206–7, 228, 237, 238, 367
  leadership of, 144–45, 158, 160, 169, 211, 238–39, 292, 382
  long-term physical effects of football on, 237
  NFL coaching and scouting career of, 240, 241, 246
  nicknames of, 66, 72
  in 1974 playoffs, 160, 161, 163–64, 249
  1974 season of, 136, 139, 140–41
  Noll's methods questioned by, 74, 160
  Obama's meeting of, 248
  onfield aggressiveness and violence of, 71–72, 73, 139, 160, 163, 188, 215, 239, 249
  physical build of, 59, 67, 68, 236, 237
  post-football life and career of, 239–42
  retirement of, 239, 274
  scouting and drafting of, 58, 66–67
  as student athlete, 60–61, 66, 67, 68, 71
  in Super Bowl IX, 177, 178, 180, 181, 182, 183, 249, 251
  in Super Bowl XIII, 250
  as team spokesman, 145, 238
Greenlee, Gus, 27, 53
Greenwood, L. C., 8, 15, 16, 72, 79, 80, 81, 82, 92, 96, 138–39, 141, 143–44, 145, 146, 147, 148, 149, 160, 168–69, 173, 188, 218, 219, 242, 243, 274, 377
  on card show/memorabilia circuit, 241–42, 246
  final seasons of, 227–28
  at funerals for teammates, 245, 247
  gold-painted shoes of, 144, 166, 178
  head trauma of, 73
  nickname of, 144
  in 1974 playoffs, 163, 166
  1974 season of, 139, 140, 141
  physical build of, 143, 191
  post-football life and career of, 241–42
  in Super Bowl IX, 178, 182
  at training camps, 71, 72
  White's declining health and, 246–47
Greenwood, Moses, 144
Greenwood Cemetery, 363
Grier, Roosevelt, 53
Grossman, Randy, 5, 112, 116–17, 142, 217, 304, 316, 369
Groza, Lou, 64, 191

Hackett, Walt, 144
Halas, George, 27, 38, 204, 224, 335
Haley, Dick, 84, 87, 96, 109, 113, 114–15, 137, 328, 330
Ham, Jack, 6, 7, 8, 16, 73, 85, 92, 94, 141, 194, 233, 264, 275, 279, 298, 311, 370
  in 1974 playoffs, 163, 165, 167
  retirement of, 274
Hanneman, Craig, 92

Hanratty, Terry "Rat," 14, 67, 71, 80, 81, 87, 121, 122, 126–27, 128, 131, 135–36, 142–43, 144, 209, 253, 357
  injuries of, 210
  physical appearance of, 121
  quarterback controversy and, 121, 126, 135–37
  sense of humor of, 121, 126, 127, 131, 136, 137, 170
Harder, Pat, 97
Harlem Globetrotters, 52
Harris, Cadillac, 86
Harris, Cliff, 12, 208
Harris, Dana Dokmanovich, 204, 247, 270, 271, 277, 280, 283, 285
Harris, Franco, 3, 4–5, 11, 82, 83–91, 131, 134, 135, 160, 162, 169, 172, 183, 184, 190, 191, 197, 202, 204, 212, 214, 217, 219, 232, 236, 237, 245, 247, 248, 250, 262, 264, 265, 270–86, 289, 297, 311, 322, 323, 337, 343, 347, 348, 349, 359–60, 377, 382
  background of, 86–87, 92, 272–73
  biracial heritage of, 9, 85, 86, 92, 272
  bold, principled stands taken by, 117, 272–73, 276, 281–82
  charitable work and philanthropy of, 279–80
  evasive running style of, 83, 272, 278–79
  fan club devoted to, 89–91, 92, 94, 95–96, 97, 101, 270, 271, 285
  final season with Seahawks of, 273–74
  Hall of Fame induction of, 281, 298
  Immaculate Reception anniversary dinners hosted by, 283–84, 285–86
  Immaculate Reception of, 5, 92, 95–98, 99, 100–101, 129, 231, 267, 280, 283, 285, 351, 382, 383
  injuries of, 133, 188, 278
  NFL stats and records of, 89, 166, 180, 274–75, 278
  1972 season of, 87, 89
  in 1974 playoffs, 165, 166, 167
  1984 contract holdout of, 272, 275–76, 277, 282–83
  Noll's falling out with, 276–77, 282–83, 373
  post-football life and career of, 279–80, 282
  preventive measures against brain damage taken by, 277–78, 366
  scouting and drafting of, 83–85, 96, 328
  son's political career and, 280–81
  statues of, 4–5, 280, 285, 383
  strong personal loyalties of, 270–71, 281–82, 283, 284
  in Super Bowl IX, 178, 179, 180, 181
  thoughtful and deliberate playing style of, 83, 85, 95, 282
Harris, Franco Dokmanovich "Dok," 270, 277, 280–81, 285
Harris, Gina Parenti, 86–87, 92
Harris, James, 125, 134

Harrison, Reggie, 12, 125–26, 208–9, 217–19, 278–79, 296, 357, 363, 368–69
  Gilliam's drug use and, 208–9, 210–11, 346
  name change of, 367–68
  see also Salaam-El, Kamal Ali
Hart, Jack, 193, 343
Harvard University, 17
Haslett, Jim, 221
Hawkey, Penny, 234, 235, 236
Hayes, Abner, 68
Hayes, Bob, 111
Hayes, Ollie, 374
Hayes, Woody, 126
head trauma, 10–11, 12–13, 16, 17, 30, 64, 73, 162, 198, 201, 207–8, 212–13, 250, 257, 259, 260, 278, 279, 316, 323, 356, 358, 367, 368, 369, 382
  see also brain damage
Heidi, 289
Heinz, 27
Heinz, H. J., 38
Heinz, John, 337
Heinz Endowments, 280
Heinz Field, 5, 266–67, 285, 295, 343–44, 375
Heinz History Center, 271, 285
Henderson, Thomas "Hollywood," 255
Hepburn, Katharine, 227
heroin, 133, 208–9, 346
Hilgenberg, Wally, 179
Hitler, Adolf, 92
Hoak, Dick, 14, 71, 85, 96, 109, 275
Holland, John, 115
Holmes, Ernie "Fats," 8, 12, 14, 56, 73, 80, 122, 138–39, 140, 141–42, 144–45, 146–48, 155, 160, 176, 178, 201, 211, 227, 368, 377
  "arrowhead" haircut of, 147–48, 178, 242
  bachelor party of, 189, 216–17, 218–20
  on card show/memorabilia circuit, 241–42, 246
  Courvoisier consumption by, 143, 217, 218–20
  death and funeral of, 244–46, 247
  excessive eating of, 142, 173, 217–18, 241
  fame and recognition craved by, 142, 147, 216, 219
  massive size of, 14, 142, 243, 345, 378
  moody and unpredictable behavior of, 142, 217, 218, 219, 243
  nicknames of, 142, 147
  in 1974 playoffs, 149, 163
  1974 season of, 147
  paranoid psychotic episode of, 146–47, 243–44
  post-football life and career of, 241, 242–44
  religious faith of, 218, 241, 243–44, 346, 378
  in Super Bowl IX, 178, 249
  in trade to Tampa, 242
  in training camps, 142, 147
Holmes, Roderick "Byron," 243, 244
Homestead Grays, 27, 336
Homestead strike (1892), 24, 325
Hooper, 201–2

Hoopes, Mitch, 368
Hope-Harvey Football Club, 26
Horrigan, Joe, 313
horse racing, 3, 4, 6, 17, 21, 23, 24–26, 27, 28–31, 35, 36, 37, 38, 99, 120, 171, 172, 325, 337, 338, 340
Houston Oilers, 12, 87, 116, 119, 133, 134, 140, 167, 173, 190, 239, 370, 378
Hubbard, Marv, 164
Hunt, Lamar, 174, 314
Huntsville, Ala., 288, 290, 291, 293, 299
Hutson, Don, 113

Ilkin, Tunch, 292, 293, 303, 304, 305, 307, 311, 314–15, 319, 322, 327, 371
Immaculate Reception, 5, 92, 95–98, 99, 100–101, 129, 211, 231, 267, 283–84, 348, 349–51, 382, 383
  anniversary dinners held for, 283–84, 285–86
  coining of name for, 100, 284
  Fuqua's speech on, 350–52
  statues commemorating of, 4–5, 280, 285, 383
Indianapolis Colts, 266, 336, 382
Internal Revenue Service (IRS), 27, 317, 319
Ireland, 24, 325, 376
  Dan Rooney as US ambassador to, 337, 338, 373–75
Italy, 86–87, 272

Jackson, Jesse, 242, 273, 361
Jani, Sunny, 313, 319, 321
Jaworski, Ron, 307
Jenkins, Dan, 162, 198
Johnson, Billy "White Shoes," 116
Johnson, Charley, 139
Johnson, Jimmy, 267, 268
Johnson, Walter, 349
John Stallworth Foundation, 291
Jones, Bert, 139
Jones, Charlie, 183, 250, 251
Jones, Horace, 94
Jones, Joe "Turkey," 201, 259
Junger, Sebastian, 189
Jurgensen, Sonny, 126, 371

Kansas City Chiefs, 7, 13, 54, 68, 89, 134, 140, 141, 147, 148, 174, 181, 190, 194, 195, 311, 314, 362
  Webster's coaching jobs with, 310–11
  Webster's final seasons with, 307–8
Kearney, Falmouth, 374
Kennedy, John F., 43, 320, 338
Kerner Commission, 45
Keyes, Leroy, 67
Keys, Brady, 96–97
Kiely, Ed, 41, 86, 110
Kiesling, Walt, 36, 42, 225
King, Martin Luther, Jr., 55, 60, 88, 105
Kolb, Jon, 162, 285, 292, 319, 322

Korean War, 64
Ku Klux Klan, 272–73
Kunz, George, 67

Ladd, Cheryl, 288
Lambert, Jack, 3, 12, 16, 112, 139–40, 145, 148,
    155, 211, 217, 232, 233, 237, 264, 288,
    292, 298, 311, 333, 343, 344, 345, 365
  aggressive and reckless playing style of, 115,
    160
  boorish and prickly personality of, 7, 131, 140,
    193–94, 345
  independent spirit of, 7, 14, 15, 118, 193, 322,
    345
  injuries of, 16, 179, 274
  in 1974 playoffs, 164, 165, 166–67
  1974 season of, 131, 140
  post-football life and career of, 345
  postgame saunas of, 192, 193–94, 195, 253,
    377, 382
  scouting and drafting of, 111, 114–15, 116
  in Super Bowl IX, 179
  in Super Bowl X, 12, 197–98
  toughness of, 8, 114–15, 118
Lamonica, Daryle, 91
Landry, Tom, 306
Latrobe, Pa., 11, 17, 69, 70, 71, 75, 78, 85, 117,
    122, 123, 129, 189, 221, 228, 252, 271,
    305, 331
Lavelli, Dante, 64, 191
Lawless, Burton, 250
Lawrence, David L., 38, 120, 334
Lee, Bob, 140
Left Guard (supper club), 76
Leno, Jay, 256, 257
Leone, "Dago" Sam, 38, 40
Levosky, Sharon, 94, 99–100
Levy, Marv, 195
Lewis, Frank, 56, 73, 80, 131, 150, 296, 357
Lewis, Wallace "Boots," 47–48, 52, 81
Liberty Bell Park, 172
Lincoln, Abraham, 366, 375
Lloyd, Greg, 293, 304, 345, 373
Lodi, Wis., 301, 304, 309, 319
Lombardi, Marie, 63, 101
Lombardi, Vince, 5, 44, 45, 61, 63, 67, 76, 130,
    159, 183, 226, 300, 334, 335, 370
London, Jack, 383
Long, Howie, 253–54, 267–68
Long, Terry, 355, 356, 357
Los Angeles Rams, 6, 43, 134, 141, 144, 160,
    209, 210, 211, 274
  in Super Bowl XIV, 188, 287–88, 289–90,
    327, 365
Los Angeles Times, 245
Lott, Ronnie, 231–33, 311
Loudermilk, Kirk, 258
Lou Gehrig's disease, 356, 358
Louis, Joe, 67, 120

Louisiana Tech University, 73, 115, 265
Lundquist, Verne, 255, 258–59, 261, 262, 266

McCann Erickson, 234, 235
McDowell, Freeda, 291
McGinley, Barney, 271
McGinley family, 339
McHugh, Roy, 120, 145, 184, 255–56, 331
MacInnis, James, 213
McKay, Bob, 239
McKay, John, 112–13
McNally, Art, 97–98
McNulty, Alice, 35, 203, 224
Madden, Joe, 28, 29
Madden, John, 91, 92, 93, 97, 98, 159, 160, 212,
    214, 258
  in 1974 AFC title game, 164, 165, 166, 167
Madison Research Corporation, 294–95, 296
Magarac, Joe, 58–59
Makris, Bill, 156
Malavasi, Ray, 287
Malone, Mark, 304–5, 328
Mansfield, Ray "Old Ranger," 62, 69, 70, 73,
    118, 126, 149, 166, 175, 179, 180, 182,
    191, 298, 306, 345
  death of, 245
  at training camps, 69, 71, 151
Mansperger, Dick, 54, 113
Man's Search for Meaning (Frankl), 318
Mara, Tim, 27, 29, 30–31, 225, 338
Mara, Wellington, 338
Marino, Dan, 328
Marshall, George Preston, 27, 41
Marshall, Thurgood, 51
Maryland State College, 50, 55
Masciola, Denise, 365–66
Mason, Daniel, 214–15
Mazeroski, Bill, 5, 93, 99
Mel Blount Youth Home, 265, 280, 291, 347–48
Mellon, Richard K., 120, 325
Memorial Coliseum, 174, 209
Menefee, Curt, 267, 268, 269
Meredith, Don, 178–79, 258
Merritt, John, 45–46, 124
Metropolitan Stadium, 72
Miami Dolphins, 56, 101, 148, 159, 162, 240,
    328
Michaels, Walt, 63, 64
Michigan, University of, 53, 123, 187
Middle Atlantic League, 25
Mile High Stadium, 188
Minnesota Vikings, 5, 12, 72–73, 89, 141, 160,
    166, 168, 175, 184, 258
  in Super Bowl IX, 171, 174, 176–80, 182,
    249–50, 344
Mintz, Jake, 180
Mitchell, Bobby, 63–64, 125, 361
Mitchell, Lydell, 83
Mix, Ron, 222–23

Modell, Art, 63
Monday Night Football, 130, 258, 333, 351
Montana, Joe, 9–10, 232, 371
Montler, Mike, 188
Moore, Lenny, 42
Moore, Nat, 115
Morgan State, 50, 79
Morris, Jeannie, 172
Mosberg, Sammy, 25
Mullins, Gerry "Moon," 73, 98, 143, 179, 190,
    192, 198, 262, 280, 283, 285, 322
    as Bradshaw's road manager, 198–200
Mumford, Ace, 50
Municipal Stadium, 90, 135
Murray, Jim, 171, 177, 178, 180, 182
Musick, Phil, 116, 136
Myron Cope on Sports (radio show), 80

Namath, Joe, 62, 75, 121, 124, 128, 154, 177,
    236, 238, 274, 317, 382
Nashville, Tenn., 124, 198, 361, 363
National Association for the Advancement of
    Colored People (NAACP), 51, 105
National Basketball Association (NBA), 52
National Football League (NFL), 6, 9, 10, 16, 17,
    27, 43, 50, 73, 79, 97, 98, 131, 135, 141,
    152, 154, 166, 203, 206, 212, 215, 216,
    232, 237, 239, 258, 260, 275, 300, 301,
    313, 334, 340, 348, 359, 360, 361, 369,
    382, 383
    AFC title games in, *see* AFC title games
    AFL's merger with, 62
    average salaries in, 15
    black quarterbacks as rarity in, 49, 121, 123,
        125
    drafting of players in, 41–42, 44, 47, 54, 65,
        66–67, 68, 69, 73, 83, 84, 85, 105, 109–17,
        125, 144, 153, 221, 226, 327–28, 331
    growth of, 171, 174, 180, 216, 223, 326, 338
    hiring of blacks for coaching and senior
        positions in, 53, 122, 336
    lawsuits filed against, 17, 250, 357–58
    Mild Traumatic Brain Injury committee of, 355
    NFC title games in, 9–10, 44, 160
    1974 players' strike in, 117–18, 122, 154
    1987 players' strike in, 293, 327
    owners' meetings in, 27, 35, 43, 202, 326, 338
    pension board of, 302, 317, 320, 364
    players' union in, 43, 117, 293, 311, 326, 327
    Rooney Rule in, 336
    rule changes in, 139, 164, 188, 250, 357
    scouting of players in, *see* scouting, scouts
    steroid use in, 10, 11, 220–21, 222–23, 245,
        304, 364, 365
    Webster's disability claim with, 316, 317, 320,
        358, 364
    see also football; football players; *specific coaches,*
        players, and teams
NBC, 77, 97

NBC Sports, 172, 309
Negro League baseball, 5, 26–27, 51, 336
Neurosurgery, 355
New England Patriots, 65, 95, 140
Newhouse, Robert, 83, 84
New Orleans Saints, 126, 221, 357
New York Giants, 10, 29, 42, 44, 53, 72, 78, 107,
    126, 128, 225, 261, 268, 329
New York Jets, 62, 148, 177, 223, 261
New York Post, 29
New York Times, 197
New York Yankees, 5, 93, 189, 232, 358
NFC title games:
    of 1966, 44
    of 1974, 160
    of 1981, 9–10
NFL drafts, 41–42, 44, 47, 54, 69, 83, 84, 85,
    221, 327–28, 331
    of 1964, 111
    of 1969, 65, 66–67, 68, 144
    of 1970, 73
    of 1971, 73
    of 1972, 125, 226, 279
    of 1973, 105
    of 1974, 109–17, 153, 327
    of 1983, 328
NFL Films, 5, 237
Nitschke, Ray, 140, 226
Nittany Lions, 61, 99
Nixon, Richard, 117
Noll, Chuck, 6, 11, 14, 78, 80, 90, 91, 107,
    117, 120, 125, 126, 129, 132, 150, 151,
    156, 166, 167, 173, 176, 187, 190, 191,
    209, 211, 213, 217, 218, 220, 238, 239,
    240, 242, 287, 291, 293, 296, 306, 322,
    327, 330, 344–45, 347, 348, 370–73, 376,
    383
    Blount's brief falling out with, 212, 215, 216
    Bradshaw's complicated relationship with, 128,
        129–30, 252, 261–62, 265–66, 277, 373,
        379
    as Browns player, 14, 58, 59–60, 63–65, 105,
        135, 191
    catchphrases of, 14–15, 70, 120–21, 122, 136,
        372–73
    contract holdouts and, 275, 282–83
    defensive coach positions held by, 61, 65, 111,
        222–23
    in drafting process, 66, 73, 83, 84, 109, 110,
        111, 112, 113, 114, 115–16, 125, 328
    emotional distance from players kept by, 15,
        105, 107, 159, 160, 203, 215, 261–62,
        265–66, 274, 276, 370, 371
    epilepsy suffered by, 62, 64–65
    in first season as head coach, 72
    Gilliam's drug use and, 209–10
    Harris's falling out with, 276–77, 282–83, 373
    hiring of, 58, 62–63, 65–66
    intimidating presence of, 111, 122, 130, 371

Noll, Chuck (*cont.*)
    leadership style of, 15, 69–70, 74, 105, 107,
        122, 159, 190, 215, 371, 372–73
    loyalty to team veterans shown by, 275,
        293
    media disliked by, 133–34, 136–37, 175
    in 1972 playoffs, 93
    1974 season of, 120–21, 131–32, 133–37, 140,
        141, 167
    post-retirement years of, 370–72
    practice drills of, 71, 118
    pregame and halftime talks of, 149, 159–60,
        174
    quarterback controversy and, 120–22, 126,
        127, 129–30, 133–37, 167
    retirement of, 15, 240, 334–35
    seriousness and single-mindedness of, 64,
        69–70, 159, 307, 371
    slander lawsuit filed against, 211–16
    at sports collectors' shows, 370, 371–72, 373
    in Super Bowl IX, 177–78, 181
    team steroid use and, 222–23
    in training camps, 69–70, 71, 72, 75, 118,
        142, 275
    unapproachable demeanor of, 15, 107, 111,
        371
Noll, Marianne, 65, 322, 335, 370, 371
Northern Ireland, 337, 374
North Texas State University, 66, 68, 71
Notorious, 243
Notre Dame, 62, 67, 76, 121, 126–27, 141
Nunn, Bill, III, 55, 93
Nunn, Bill, Jr., 47–53, 55–57, 93, 96, 114, 115,
        142, 144, 181, 336, 337
    background of, 51–52, 123
    Black Colleges All-America football teams of,
        46, 47, 50, 52, 54
    in close rapport with black athletes, 49–50,
        113
    as NFL scout, 55, 56–57, 71, 73, 112, 113,
        125, 181, 328
    racial slights experienced by, 47–48, 53, 57
    sports journalism career of, 46, 48–49, 50, 52,
        55, 56, 181
    Steelers' hiring of, 52, 53, 54
Nunn, Bill, Sr., 48, 51, 53, 55, 336

Oakland Athletics, 204
Oakland Coliseum, 160
Oakland Raiders, 111, 133, 148–49, 150–51,
        152, 158, 162, 169, 173, 188, 190, 211,
        212, 215, 268, 278, 307, 308, 378
    aggressive and reckless playing style of, 94–95
    in 1972 playoffs, 5, 91–92, 129, 211, 267,
        350–51, 383
    in 1973 playoffs, 112, 149, 211
    in 1974 playoffs, 149, 150, 159, 160–61,
        162–67, 174, 211, 249
    in 1975 playoffs, 207–8, 211, 213

Steelers' blood rivalry with, 6, 163, 211, 214,
        350
Oakland Tribune, 164
Obama, Barack, 248, 280, 336–37, 338, 373–74,
        376
Obama, Michelle, 337, 374
Okon, Tommy, 235
Olsen, Merlin, 161, 257
Olympic Games, 222, 257
    of 1920 (Antwerp), 4, 25
    of 1964 (Tokyo), 223
    of 1968 (Mexico City), 55
    of 1984 (Los Angeles), 275
Omalu, Bennet, 353–56, 358
O'Neill, Eugene, 40
Orange Bowl, 61, 99, 208
Ord, Barney, 94, 95, 96, 97
Ord, Michael, 94, 96, 97, 99–100
Oriard, Michael, 308
Osborn, Dave, 178
Oswald, Lee Harvey, 43
Otto, Jim, 97, 112, 152, 156, 161–62, 166, 169,
        212, 214, 249, 307, 308, 311
    injuries of, 161, 162, 163, 164, 311

Page, Alan, 177, 180
Paige, Satchel, 5, 27, 271
Palin, Sarah, 248
Parcells, Bill, 106, 107
Parenti, Alvaro, 87, 272–73
Parilli, Babe, 96, 122
Parisi, Tony, 77, 94, 128, 158, 190, 192, 193,
        195, 283, 303
Parker, Buddy, 42, 43, 45, 47–48, 81, 207
Parker, Dorothy, 224
Parseghian, Ara, 126–27
Pastorini, Dan, 140–41, 239
Paterno, Joe, 61, 83, 95, 99, 126, 281–82, 283
Patterson, Floyd, 50
Payton, Walter, 274
Pearson, Barry, 93, 351
Pearson, Preston, 87, 134, 357
Penn State University, 8, 42, 61, 83, 84, 85, 86,
        87, 95, 99, 279
    sexual abuse scandal at, 281–82, 283
Pennsylvania, 24, 26, 299, 337
Penzo, Joseph, *see* Madden, Joe
Perles, George, 12, 109, 115, 142, 144–45, 147,
        158, 188, 218, 228, 371
Perry, Lowell, 53, 187, 327, 336
Perry, Rod, 289
Peterson, Cal, 114, 115
Peterson, Carl, 307, 308–9, 310–11, 314, 319
Peterson, Ted, 311, 357
Philadelphia Eagles, 37, 64, 67, 69, 74, 79, 126,
        135, 140, 141, 207, 355
Phillips, Bum, 119, 173, 326, 370
Phil-Pitt Steagles, 37
Pinkertons, 24, 30, 325

Pittsburgh, Pa., 3, 24, 26–27, 31, 63, 69, 88, 91, 92, 128, 132, 146, 180, 188, 198, 218, 226, 241, 242, 246, 247, 261, 270, 274, 276, 279, 301, 304, 309, 311, 313, 347, 355, 372, 374
    Bradshaw's estranged relationship with, 253, 262, 263–64, 266, 322
    Chief as beloved in, 4, 120, 205, 325, 331, 344
    Dok Harris's mayoral bid in, 280–81
    East Liberty neighborhood in, 88, 270
    fan celebrations in, 99–100, 168–69, 184
    Hill District in, 24, 27, 48, 49, 55, 56, 280, 336
    immigrant population in, 24, 26, 27, 88
    industrial life in, 24, 26, 27, 37–38, 59, 90, 128, 188
    KKK demonstration held in, 272–73
    North Side of, 3, 24, 36, 38, 205, 325
    race riots and tensions in, 55, 88, 143
    Rooneys as defining family in, 325–26, 337
Pittsburgh, University of, 41, 355
Pittsburgh Courier, 46, 47, 48, 50, 51, 52, 54, 55, 56, 181, 336
Pittsburgh Crawfords, 27, 271
Pittsburgh Hilton, 73, 126, 216–17, 312
Pittsburgh International Airport, 4–5, 168, 280, 285, 302, 319
Pittsburgh Pirates (MLB), 25, 38, 47, 49–50, 97, 188, 248, 271, 345
Pittsburgh Pirates (NFL), 27, 224
Pittsburgh Post-Gazette, 15, 79, 129, 133, 134, 136, 137, 313, 331
Pittsburgh Press, 65, 90, 116, 136, 331, 365
Pittsburgh Promise, 280, 282
Pittsburgh Steelers, 28, 35, 39, 46, 74, 75, 76, 77, 78, 80, 86, 90, 100, 119–20, 158, 206, 207, 213, 225, 231, 232, 235, 239, 240, 252, 260, 290–91, 294, 295, 300, 301, 313, 316, 321, 334, 335–36, 346, 359, 360, 374, 375
    alarming death rate of, 245, 247
    anniversary celebrations and reunions of, 14, 265, 266, 283–84, 285–86, 344–48, 359–60, 365–66, 378
    Bradshaw's estrangement from, 14, 261, 262, 263, 264–65, 266, 284–86, 379
    brotherhood and camaraderie on, 7, 16–17, 75, 78, 80, 82, 87, 123, 126, 170, 173, 189–94, 195, 211, 216, 217, 220, 232, 244, 245, 264–65, 292, 322, 347, 360, 377, 381, 382
    celebrity and fame of, 138–39, 173, 187, 188–89
    Chief's hosting of dinners for, 172, 189, 202–4
    Chief's purchasing of, 27, 328–29
    contract holdouts on, 70–71, 211, 275–76, 277, 282–83
    decline of dynasty and, 11, 16, 17, 227–28, 263, 274, 292–93, 306

    drafting of players by, 41–42, 53, 56, 58, 66–67, 68, 69, 73, 83, 84, 105, 109–17, 125, 153, 221, 226, 327–28, 331
    Dress-Off competitions of, 79, 80, 81, 82, 351
    era of ineptitude and mediocrity endured by, 36–37, 39, 40–42, 45, 52, 58, 61, 62, 72, 88, 175, 180, 181, 182, 298
    as family-run organization, 6, 42–43, 224, 295, 325–26, 329, 330, 335, 337–40
    franchise value of, 339
    free-agent signings by, 109–10, 111–12, 116–17, 196
    huddle interactions of, 7–8, 14, 140, 144–45, 163, 303, 305, 344
    Immaculate Reception of, *see* Immaculate Reception
    naming of, 27
    1969 season of, 72–73
    1970s empire of, 3, 5–6, 9, 16–17, 39, 101, 111, 187–89, 191, 225–26, 228, 241, 245, 248, 253, 262, 263, 264, 275, 300, 307, 330, 347, 348, 353, 377, 381, 382, 383
    in 1972 playoffs, 5, 91–99, 101, 129, 211, 231, 267, 285, 350–51, 382, 383; *see also* Immaculate Reception
    1972 season of, 80, 87, 89, 90, 91, 110, 283, 285
    in 1973 playoffs, 112, 149, 211
    1973 season of, 110, 112, 128, 149
    in 1974 playoffs, 6, 148–49, 150, 159–61, 162–70, 174, 175, 182, 211, 249
    1974 season of, 120–21, 125–26, 131–32, 133–37, 138, 139, 140–41, 147, 150–51, 152, 155, 167
    in 1975 playoffs, 207–8, 211, 213
    1975 season of, 209, 210–11
    1976 season of, 6–7, 212
    1980 season of, 227, 228, 239
    1980s struggles of, 227, 228, 239, 265, 306, 327, 328
    opposing players respected by, 194–95, 238, 382
    postgame saunas of, 16, 190–95, 253, 377, 382
    quarterback controversy of, 120–22, 126, 127–28, 129–31, 133–37, 167, 364
    race relations on, 47–48, 52, 80–81, 122, 130, 145, 155, 190, 193, 336–37
    racial diversity on, 8–9, 80–81, 138, 190
    Raiders' blood rivalry with, 6, 163, 211, 214, 350
    Rooney family buyout deal for, 338–40
    scouting of players by, 43, 44–46, 52, 53–55, 56–57, 66, 71, 73, 83–84, 109, 110, 112–13, 114–15, 125, 181, 197, 240, 246, 327, 328, 330, 346–47
    sellout games of, 188, 335
    Stallworth as minority owner of, 290, 295–96, 340, 378

Pittsburgh Steelers (*cont.*)
  Steel Curtain defensive unit of, *see* Pittsburgh
    Steelers, defensive unit of
  steroid use on, 220–22, 223, 245, 304, 364,
    365
  in Super Bowl IX, 9, 12, 171, 176–81, 182,
    183, 187, 188, 189, 206, 249–51, 344,
    367
  in Super Bowl X, 12, 187, 188, 197–98, 208,
    211, 228, 368
  in Super Bowl XIII, 187, 188, 228, 250, 255
  in Super Bowl XIV, 187, 188, 287–88, 289–90,
    327, 365
  in Super Bowl XLIII, 248, 336
  training camps of, 11, 69–70, 71–72, 75, 78,
    81, 85, 87, 117–18, 122–23, 126, 129, 142,
    147, 151, 154, 189, 212, 221, 226, 227–28,
    252, 261, 275, 296, 305–6, 382
  victory celebrations of, 168–70, 181–84, 217,
    222, 227
  White House visits of, 187, 188, 248
  see also specific coaches and players
Pittsburgh Steelers, defensive unit of, 6–8, 12,
    138–49, 216, 226, 227, 241, 247, 248, 296,
    304, 343
  aggressive and violent playing style of, 138,
    139, 148, 160, 163, 166, 215, 239, 249,
    250
  front four of, 72, 138–39, 140–41, 143,
    144–46, 147–48, 166–67, 169, 173–74,
    176, 178, 179, 182, 219, 244, 245, 246,
    264
  interceptions by, 134, 141, 165, 166, 167,
    178, 179
  in 1974 playoffs, 148–49, 163–65, 166–67,
    182, 249
  in 1974 season, 121, 134, 136, 138, 139,
    140–41, 147
  1974 season stats of, 138, 140
  sacks by, 138, 139, 140–41, 147, 163, 166,
    226, 228
  Steel Curtain nickname for, 6, 141, 164–65
  "Stunt 4-3" alignment of, 148, 163, 164
  in Super Bowl IX, 178, 179, 182, 249–50
  see also specific defensive players
Pitt Stadium, 75, 77
Plum, Milt, 59
Plunkett, Jim, 141
PNC Park, 5
Pollard, Red, 28
Polo Grounds, 120, 141
Pop Warner youth football, 357
Portman, Eric, 40
Posey, Cum, 53, 336
Prairie View A&M University, 56, 124, 362
Princeton University, 17, 280
Pro Bowls, 6, 112, 140, 188, 194, 232, 236, 238,
    274, 297, 305, 328
  of 1982, 232–33

Pro Football Hall of Fame, 6, 224–25, 232, 236,
    281, 297–98, 299, 338, 353, 361, 383
  Bradshaw's induction into, 261, 262–63, 266,
    298
  Webster's induction into, 298, 312–15
Prohibition, 26, 76

race relations, 45, 46, 49, 53, 55, 57, 85, 91, 105,
    107, 121, 143–44, 205, 336–37
  integration and, 51, 52, 105
  in Pittsburgh, 55, 88, 143
  in sports organizations, 47, 49, 50, 52, 123, 336
  Steelers and, 47–48, 80–81, 122, 130, 155,
    190, 193, 336–37
  see also civil rights movement; segregation, racial
race riots, 45, 55, 88
racism, 49, 55, 57, 125, 143, 272, 273
  in hate mail, 8–9, 132–33
Radakovich, Dan, 84, 109, 134, 145, 151–52,
    160, 189, 261–62, 287, 322–23
Ralston, John, 131
Ramsey, Steve, 139
Randall Park Race Track, 25–26
Rather, Dan, 127
Ravenstahl, Luke, 280, 281, 282
Real Paper, 206
Red Bull Inn, 304, 319, 359
Red Door (Pittsburgh bar), 143
Red Roof Inn, 312
Reese, Pee Wee, 257
Regan, Mary, 343
Reger, John, 207
reminiscence bump, 16
Rendell, Ed, 247, 281
Reynolds, Burt, 197, 199, 201–2
RFK Stadium, 10
Rhoads, Harry, Jr., 254
Rice, Grantland, 21, 141, 171
Rice, Jerry, 237
Richman, Milton, 168
Rickey, Branch, 56
Riecke, Lou, 223
Riggins, John, 274
Ritalin, 314, 315–16
Rivera, Gabe, 328
Riverfront Stadium, 135
Roberts, Ric, 48, 52
Robinson, Eddie, 50, 113
Robinson, Jackie, 49, 50, 51
Robinson, John, 231
Robinson, Sugar Ray, 48, 181
Roethlisberger, Ben, 258–59, 266, 269, 286
Rooney, Art, II (grandson), 96–97, 245, 267, 329,
    333, 337–38, 339, 340
Rooney, Art, Jr., 30, 31, 35, 36, 39–40, 56, 65, 67,
    70, 73, 80, 87, 88–89, 93, 96, 129, 147, 173,
    177, 183, 184, 210, 224–25, 238, 240–41,
    263–64, 274, 275, 277, 291, 322, 326, 336
  childhood and adolescence of, 39, 69

in divvying up parents' possessions, 332, 333–34

on draft days, 110, 111, 327–28

father's death and, 331–32

firing of, 328–31, 334, 335, 340

Harris as draft pick of, 83–84, 328

insecurities of, 54, 111, 327, 329

in 1974 draft, 109, 110–11, 112, 113, 114, 115, 116

Nunn Jr.'s hiring and, 53, 54

scouting career of, 43, 44–46, 53–54, 55, 63, 66, 84, 110, 112, 327, 328, 329, 330, 346–47

in Steeler buyout negotiations, 339–40

at Steeler reunions, 346–47

Rooney, Art, Sr. "the Chief," 3–4, 6, 23–31, 35–37, 38–40, 42, 48, 53, 54, 55, 61, 63, 65, 74, 80, 101, 111, 113, 138, 156, 189, 190, 238, 239, 262, 267, 314, 327, 328, 335, 337–39, 350, 371, 376

amateur and semipro athletic career of, 3–4, 25, 26

Art Jr.'s firing and, 329, 330, 331

casual management style of, 36–37, 42–43

Catholicism of, 6, 23, 29, 30, 61, 76, 205, 332, 334, 337

childhood and adolescence of, 25–26, 325

colorful characters in inner circle of, 27, 28, 38, 119–20, 172–73

common touch and unassuming nature of, 6, 23, 24–25, 29, 172, 184, 204–5, 295, 325, 331, 374

contract holdouts and, 70–71, 275

Dan groomed as heir apparent by, 42–43, 337

death and funeral of, 262, 266, 322, 331–32

declining health of, 202, 261, 274

dinners for players hosted by, 172, 189, 202–4, 205

faith in Bradshaw's talent of, 127–28, 130, 188, 197, 253, 262

as father, 35, 36, 37, 39–40, 325, 326, 332, 376

football legacy of, 331, 338, 340

friendly race relations of, 27, 53, 205, 336

generosity of, 26, 27, 30, 35, 120, 182

horse gambling of, 3, 4, 6, 17, 23, 24–26, 27, 28–31, 35, 38, 120, 171, 337, 338

house of, 3, 36, 39, 172, 203, 325, 326, 331–33, 375–76

Irish ancestry of, 23, 24, 171, 203, 325

Kass's relationship with, 27, 31, 35–36, 39, 224

local adoration of, 4, 120, 205, 325, 331, 344

1972 playoffs and, 91, 93, 98–99

in 1974 NFL draft, 109, 110

1974 players' strike and, 118

1974 playoffs and, 165, 168, 169, 170

physical appearance of, 3, 23, 171, 172, 325

players' close relationships and respect for, 4, 53, 76, 99, 118, 130, 147, 170, 182–83, 184, 202–5, 232, 238, 274, 277, 295, 331, 333

postcards sent by, 4, 6, 23–24, 61, 76, 77, 99, 171, 184, 332

in Pro Football Hall of Fame, 224–25, 338

quarterback controversy and, 128, 130

as sports promoter, 26–27, 35, 38, 180, 271, 336

sportswriters' good relations with, 168, 171–72, 177, 182

statue of, 5, 343–44

in Steelers' era of struggles and mediocrity, 36–37, 39, 40–41, 45, 62, 181, 182, 298

Steelers purchased by, 27, 328–29

Super Bowl IX and, 171, 172–73, 177, 178, 180–81, 182–83, 184, 250

trademark cigars of, 3, 4, 23, 24, 28, 29, 38, 71, 91, 117, 130, 165, 171, 177, 182–83, 203, 204, 232, 333, 337, 376

Rooney, Art (Chief's grandfather), 24

Rooney, Dan (Chief's brother), 25, 26, 30, 61
see also Silas, Father

Rooney, Dan (Chief's father), 24, 25–26, 232, 334

Rooney, Dan (Chief's son), 6, 45, 46, 48, 61, 72, 74, 84, 89, 96, 109, 110, 120, 129, 132, 137, 146, 177, 183, 202, 239, 240, 244, 245, 266, 267, 271, 273, 276, 279, 291, 295, 325–27, 331, 334–37, 360, 375–76

on alleged team steroid use, 221

Art Jr. fired by, 328–30, 334

Atkinson-Noll lawsuit and, 212, 214, 216

childhood and adolescence of, 31, 36–37, 39, 335, 376

in contract negotiations with players, 70, 117, 125, 204, 272, 275

controlling interest of Steelers granted to, 338–40

football legacy of, 335–36, 337, 338, 340

grooming of, as heir apparent, 42–43, 335, 337

Hall of Fame induction of, 338

NFL's Rooney Rule spearheaded by, 336

Noll's job interviews with, 62–63, 65

Noll's retirement and, 334–35

Nunn Jr.'s hiring and, 52, 53, 54, 56

in Obama's 2008 presidential campaign, 336–37, 338, 374

Steeler players looked after by, 129, 218, 272, 273, 309, 312, 316, 317, 322, 326–27

at Steeler reunions, 345–46

as US ambassador to Ireland, 337, 338, 373–75

Webster's post-football troubles and, 309, 312, 316, 317, 322

Rooney, James (Chief's great-grandfather), 374

Rooney, Jim (Chief's brother), 40

Rooney, John, 4, 35, 36, 39, 43, 172, 224, 329, 332, 340

Rooney, Kathleen McNulty "Kass," 27, 29,
30–31, 35–36, 37, 39, 43, 53, 130, 172,
173, 176–77, 183, 184, 202, 203, 204, 205,
224–25
death of, 326, 332, 334
at Pro Football Hall of Fame, 224–25
Rooney, Kay, 55, 110, 173, 177, 183, 224,
327–28, 333
Rooney, Pat, 4, 35, 43, 172, 329, 332, 333, 340
Rooney, Patricia, 335, 337, 375–76
Rooney, Tim (Chief's nephew), 96, 109
Rooney, Tim (Chief's son), 30–31, 36, 42, 172,
182, 225, 329, 332, 333, 340
Rooney family, 61, 176, 212, 216, 271, 276, 287,
295, 325–26, 337, 374, 375–76
in Steeler buyout deal negotiations, 338–40
Rooney Prize for Irish Literature, 337
Roosevelt, Franklin, 23
Roosevelt, Teddy, 17
Roosevelt Hotel, 38, 52, 54, 70
Roseboro, Mary, 203, 204, 205
Rose Bowl, 288
Rothstein, Arnold, 30
Roy, Alvin, 222
Rozelle, Pete, 43, 73, 174, 183, 212, 214, 250
Ruby, Jack, 43
Ruck, Rob, 205
Rudnay, Jack, 7, 194–95
Runyon, Damon, 28, 30
Russell, Andy, 7, 15, 62, 69, 70, 81, 112, 135,
175, 180, 182–83, 191, 207, 212, 218, 238,
291, 298, 309, 311, 343, 345, 347, 348
injuries of, 179, 367
in 1974 playoffs, 163, 165, 166

St. Clair Country Club, 274, 330
Saint Vincent College, 39, 69, 118
Salaam-El, Kamal Ali (formerly Reggie Harrison),
348, 357, 363, 367–68
permanent ailments suffered by, 366–67
Sample, Johnny, 50
San Diego Chargers, 65, 90, 91, 222–23, 274
Sandusky, Jerry, 281, 282
San Francisco 49ers, 9–10, 41, 129, 231, 232,
275, 334
Sant'Anna di Stazzema, Italy, 86–87
Saratoga racetrack, 28–30
Sayers, Gayle, 48, 73
Schottenheimer, Marty, 307
Schwarzenegger, Arnold, 257
scouting, scouts, 41, 43–45, 46, 52, 73, 83–84,
109, 110, 112–13, 114–15, 197, 240, 246,
327
Art Jr. and, 43, 44–46, 53–54, 55, 66, 84, 327,
328, 329, 330, 346–47
of black athletes, 45–46, 54, 55, 56, 63, 71, 73,
113, 125
BLESTO in, 44, 45, 54, 66, 73, 84, 109, 110,
115

computer analysis in, 44, 114, 327
Nunn Jr. and, 55, 56–57, 71, 73, 112, 113,
181, 328
Seabiscuit, 28, 171
Seattle Seahawks, 273–74
segregation, racial, 50, 52, 57, 60, 105, 123, 139,
143, 205
Seminoles, 106–7
Senate, US, 223
Sengstacke, John, 55, 56
Senior Bowl, 113, 181
Shakur, Tupac, 243
Shamrock Farm, 38
Shanklin, Ron, 150, 178, 245, 296
Shell, Art, 112, 152, 160, 163, 233
Shell, Donnie, 12, 16, 56, 112, 155, 189,
192–93, 211, 232, 264, 288, 292, 293, 357,
367, 382–83
Shore, Dinah, 199
Shula, Don, 58, 63, 65, 159, 240, 306, 334
Siani, Mike, 93, 160, 161
Sidney Lanier High School, 105
Silas, Father, 30, 99, 205, 333
    see also Rooney, Dan (Chief's brother)
SilverSport, 279
Simpson, O. J., 67, 148
Sinatra, Frank, 90–91, 270
Skorich, Nick, 63
slavery, 123
Smalls, Biggie, 243
Smith, Charlie, 165
Smith, Jim, 288
Smith, Tommie, 55
Smith, Wendell, 51, 52
Smizek, Bob, 136
Southern California, University of (USC), 8, 67,
112, 153, 155, 231
Southern University, 8, 50, 56, 73, 124, 362
Spadia, Lou, 41
Spigno Saturnia Italo-American Beneficial Society
of Pittsburgh, 88
Sports Illustrated, 131, 162, 175, 197, 198, 221,
223, 287, 365
Stabler, Ken, 92, 93, 98, 154, 163, 164, 165–66,
167, 350
Stagno, Tony, 88, 89–91, 92, 94, 96
Stallworth, Flo, 294
Stallworth, John, 3, 14, 16, 112, 152–55, 172,
190, 217, 219, 245, 253, 262, 264, 287–99,
311, 333, 343, 346, 347–48, 369, 372,
377–79
final seasons of, 292–93, 294
Hall of Fame induction and, 297–98, 299
injuries of, 155, 288, 292
insecurities of, 152–53, 155
intellect of, 291, 294
introverted personality of, 153, 291, 292
NFL stats of, 154, 155, 188, 287, 292, 297
in 1974 playoffs, 164, 166, 167

1984 season of, 292
physical build of, 153, 288
post-football life and career of, 289, 290, 291–92, 293–96, 299
religious faith of, 289, 291, 292
retirement of, 293
rookie year struggles of, 150–51, 154
scouting and drafting of, 56, 111, 113–14, 115, 116, 153
as Steelers' minority owner, 290, 295–96, 340, 378
as student athlete, 154, 290
in Super Bowl IX, 178–79
in Super Bowl XIV, 278–88, 289–90
Swann's friendly rivalry with, 152–53, 287–88, 296–98, 299
work ethic of, 155, 290–91, 292, 296
Stallworth, Mary and David, 153
Starbuck, JoJo, 199, 200, 201
Stargell, Willie, 188, 270
Starr, Bart, 130, 259
Staubach, Roger, 111, 122, 197
Stautner, Ernie, 279
Steeler Nation, 11, 223, 248, 266, 271, 378
    Bradshaw's uneasy relationship with, 128, 129, 197, 262, 264, 266–67, 378
Stellino, Vito, 275
steroids, 10, 11, 220–21, 222–23, 245, 301, 304, 364, 365, 366
Stingley, Darryl, 95
Stoudt, Cliff, 305, 328
Strahan, Michael, 268–69
suicide, 355, 356, 357, 361, 382
Summerall, Pat, 258
Super Bakery, Inc., 279
Super Bowl, 5, 7, 9, 14, 70, 76, 101, 107, 109, 110, 120, 129, 149, 159, 160, 163, 169, 170, 187, 189, 222, 226, 228, 232, 241, 252, 253, 259, 261, 262, 263, 266, 268, 274, 298, 300, 306, 316, 330, 336, 349, 377
    commercial spots in, 177
    creation of, 174
    media frenzy in lead-up to, 171, 172, 174
    television ratings for, 62, 171, 188, 198, 338
Super Bowl III, 62, 63, 75, 177
Super Bowl IX, 9, 12, 166, 168, 171, 174, 176–81, 182, 183, 187, 188, 189, 206, 249–51, 277, 336, 344, 367
    days in lead-up to, 171–76
    postgame celebrations at, 181–84
    pregame media press conference for, 174–76
Super Bowl X, 12, 187, 188, 197–98, 206, 208, 211, 217, 228, 368
Super Bowl XIII, 187, 188, 228, 250, 255
Super Bowl XIV, 187, 188, 287–88, 289–90, 327, 365
Super Bowl XL, 335
Super Bowl XLIII, 248, 336
Supreme Court, US, 51

Swann, Lynn, 11, 16, 131, 132, 152–53, 155, 170, 184, 190, 191, 212–13, 214, 215, 231–32, 262, 264, 283, 287–88, 291, 292, 297, 311, 322, 333, 343, 372, 377
    Atkinson's illegal hit against, 212–13, 214
    concussions of, 16, 208, 212–13
    gubernatorial bid of, 281, 299, 348
    Hall of Fame induction of, 297–98, 299
    injuries of, 207–8, 214, 231
    NFL stats of, 188
    in 1974 playoffs, 165, 166
    in 1975 playoffs, 207–8, 213
    post-football life and career of, 281, 297, 298–99
    scouting and drafting of, 111, 112–14, 116, 153
    Stallworth's friendly rivalry with, 152–53, 287–88, 296–98, 299
    in Super Bowl IX, 178
    in Super Bowl X, 197–98, 208
Swearingen, Fred, 97–98

Tagliabue, Paul, 339
Tampa Bay Buccaneers, 223, 228, 242, 373
Tarkenton, Fran, 72, 175, 177, 178, 180, 221
Tatum, Jack, 94–95, 97, 129, 150–51, 167, 207, 215, 231, 267, 348, 349–50, 351
Taylor, Lionel, 85, 109, 113, 122, 123, 150–51, 154, 287, 288, 371
television, 5, 75, 172, 180, 338
    Bradshaw's broadcasting career on, 252, 255–56, 257–59, 260, 264, 267–69, 285, 286, 348
    Bradshaw's guest appearances on, 198, 199, 200, 256, 257
    celebrity endorsements on, 177, 188–89, 234–36, 256
    Super Bowl ratings on, 62, 171, 188, 198, 338
Temple University, 112, 116
Tennessee State University, 8, 45–46, 56, 80, 113, 115, 123, 124–25, 361
Texas, 145, 237, 240, 242, 244, 247, 254
Texas Southern University, 56, 73, 142, 243, 246
Theismann, Joe, 10
Thomas, J. T., 8, 11, 105–8, 142, 166, 193, 271, 277, 280, 282, 344
    inflammatory disease of, 193, 326–27
    1974 season of, 136, 140
    spirituality of, 106, 108, 285
    at teammate funerals, 245, 247, 322
Thompson, Jess, 66, 73
Thorpe, Jim, 3
Three Rivers Stadium, 3, 5, 88, 89, 91–92, 101, 109, 119, 129, 130, 131, 132, 138, 149, 152, 173, 188, 195, 200, 202, 208, 220, 222, 223, 227, 231, 232, 242, 262, 285, 327, 343–44, 350, 360, 378, 382
    Allegheny Club at, 91, 191

Three Rivers Stadium (*cont.*)
  1972 playoff game vs. Raiders at, 91–99
  postgame saunas at, 16, 190–95, 377
  Webster's grueling workouts at, 156, 189,
    304
Thurston, Fuzzy, 76
Time, 127, 138
Tingelhoff, Mick, 178
Tinker, Gerald, 115
Toews, Loren, 179, 227
Tomlin, Mike, 336
Tonight Show, 256, 257
Touch of the Poet, A, 40
Traynor, Pie, 38
Trollope, Anthony, 37
Tulane Stadium, 166, 171, 184
  Super Bowl IX at, 176–81
Tuscaloosa (Ala.) News, 47–48
Tuscany, Italy, 86
TV Guide, 255
20th Century-Fox studios, 267

unions, 24, 26, 28, 43, 117, 293, 326, 327
Unitas, Johnny, 37, 41–42, 121, 274
United Press International, 77, 168
Updike, John, 236
Upshaw, Gene, 112, 149, 152, 160, 163, 212
Urich, Robert, 189
US Football League, 10
US News & World Report, 347
US Steel, 41

Valle, Bob, 164–65
Vance, Leonard "Speedy," 67–68
Van Dyke, Bruce, 62, 71, 149, 285
Veeck, Bill, 101
Vella, John, 93, 160, 162
Vento, Al, 88, 89–91, 92, 94, 95–96, 270, 271,
  280, 281, 283, 285
Vento's Pizza, 270
Venturi, Ken, 90
Viet Cong, 76, 77
Vietnam War, 75, 76–77, 80, 181, 182, 196
Villapiano, Phil, 212, 214, 278
  in Immaculate Reception play, 5, 95, 285
Vince Lombardi Trophy, 6, 183, 188, 250, 353

Wagner, Honus, 5, 24, 25, 41, 271
Wagner, Mike, 8, 73, 92, 98, 99, 123, 132, 140,
  194, 198, 263, 264, 280–81, 283, 296,
  309–10, 311–12, 345, 346, 372
Walcott, Jersey Joe, 271
Walden, Bobby, 14, 80, 99, 128–29, 179, 196,
  264, 344–45
Walls, Will, 44–45
Wall Street Journal, 339
Walsh, Bill, 9, 112, 135
War Admiral, 171
Warren, Jimmy, 95, 96

Washington, Mark, 197
Washington Post, 10, 364
Washington Redskins, 10, 41, 63, 125, 274, 370
Washington Speakers Bureau, 254
Waters, Andre, 355–56, 357
Wayne, John, 227, 305, 320
Webster, Brooke, 321
Webster, Colin, 317–19, 323
Webster, Garrett, 301, 304, 315, 319–20, 321,
  322, 323, 356, 359
Webster, Hillary, 321
Webster, Mike, 6, 112, 151–52, 156–57, 166,
  172, 181, 227, 228, 233, 237, 258, 262,
  270–71, 292, 293, 300–324, 331, 333, 343,
  357, 364, 369, 382
  aging and physical decline of, 301, 309, 310,
    312, 318, 320
  angry outbursts of, 300, 306, 313, 359
  autopsy performed on, 353–55, 356
  blocking technique of, 303, 305, 323
  brain damage of, 316, 323, 358, 359
  cognitive issues of, 271, 300, 308–9, 310, 311,
    312, 313, 314–15, 316, 317–18, 319, 320,
    322, 359
  death and funeral of, 321–24, 354
  depression of, 300, 310, 354
  divorce of, 321, 323, 358
  final seasons of, 307–8
  financial problems of, 271, 301, 302, 309–10,
    311–13, 316–17, 319, 322
  growing suspicion and paranoia of, 311, 317,
    320
  grueling workout regimens of, 156, 157, 189,
    226, 303–4, 310, 318–19
  Hall of Fame induction of, 298, 312–15
  injuries and surgeries of, 151, 157, 189, 303,
    305, 311
  intense approach to game of, 303, 304–5
  Kansas City Chiefs coaching jobs of, 310–11
  marital issues of, 300, 301, 302, 309, 310, 315,
    321, 322
  NFL disability claim filed by, 316, 317, 320,
    358, 364
  permanent physical ailments of, 301, 310
  physical appearance and build of, 303, 321
  post-football troubles of, 300–302, 308–22,
    323, 354, 359, 378
  prescription drug use of, 310, 314, 315–16
  retirements of, 306–7, 308
  rookie year struggles of, 151
  scouting and drafting of, 111, 115, 116
  steroid use of, 304, 365
  as student athlete, 156, 157
  toughness of, 157, 308
  in training camps, 117, 118, 151, 226, 305–6
Webster, Pam, 151, 156, 225–27, 300–302, 306,
  307, 311, 316, 317, 322, 358–59, 364
  Debbie Furness's friendship with, 226–27, 228,
    358–59

divorce of, 321, 358
marital troubles of, 300, 301, 302, 309, 315, 321, 322
Mike's death and, 321, 323–24
at Mike's Hall of Fame induction, 313, 314, 315
Mike's wedding to, 157
Weismuller, Johnny, 257
Wells, Lloyd, 54, 181
"West Coast offense," 135, 263
Western Pennsylvania Sports Museum, 271, 280, 283, 285
Westinghouse, George, 37–38
Westinghouse High School, 48, 51
West Virginia State University, 51–52, 123
Wheeler, Wayne, 115
Wheeling (WV) Stogies, 25, 26
White, Dwight "Mad Dog," 7–8, 9, 12, 73, 80, 107, 138–39, 142, 143, 144, 145, 147, 148, 149, 160, 163, 168, 169, 172, 173, 187–89, 200, 202, 204, 205, 209, 217, 218, 219, 235, 245, 246, 271, 274, 283, 336, 343, 377, 378
  on card show/memorabilia circuit, 241–42, 246
  death and funeral of, 14, 247, 378
  declining health of, 246–47
  Greene's friendship with, 145, 247
  1974 season of, 139, 140–41
  post-football life and career of, 242
  postseason hospitalization of, 174, 176, 181, 182, 184, 206
  spirituality of, 246, 247
  in Super Bowl IX, 178, 182, 206

White, Ed, 178
White, Karen Farmer, 143, 168, 169, 176, 200, 203, 205, 242, 246, 247, 248, 276
White, Randy, 220–21, 305
White House, 187, 188, 248
Whitman, Walt, 12
Widenhofer, Woody, 109, 115, 371
Williams, Edward Bennett, 63
Williams, Gerald, 240
Williams, Smokey Joe, 26
Williams, Ted, 236
Wilson, Nemiah, 164
Winston, Dennis, 193, 357
Wisconsin, University of, 152, 156–57
W. J. Hale Stadium, 124, 362
Wolfley, Craig, 304, 311, 314, 319, 322
Woodruff, Dwayne, 322
World Series, 91, 204, 206
  of 1909, 41
  of 1919, 30
  of 1960, 49–50, 93, 99
  of 1979, 188
World War I, 25
World War II, 64, 86–87, 191, 275
Woy, Bucky, 70, 71
WrestleMania 2, 242
Wrigley Field, 72, 73

Yale University, 17
Yankee Stadium, 72, 128
Yellow Banana (nightclub), 243
Yonkers Raceway, 172, 333, 339
Young, George, 84, 110, 329–30
Youngblood, Jack, 210